Modeling Contextual Effects in Longitudinal Studies

Modeling Contextual Effects in Longitudinal Studies

Edited by

Todd D. Little
University of Kansas

James A. Bovaird
University of Nebraska at Lincoln

Noel A. Card
University of Arizona

Psychology Press
Taylor & Francis Group

New York   London

Copyright ©2007, by Lawrence Erlbaum Associates, Inc.

First Published by Lawrence Erlbaum Associates, Inc., Publishers
10 Industrial Avenue
Mahwah, New Jersey 07430

Reprinted 2009 by Psychology Press

Cover design by Kathryn Houghtaling

Cover graphics by Elizabeth K. McConnell and Todd D. Little

Library of Congress Cataloging-in-Publication Data

Modeling Contextual Effects in Longitudinal studies

ISBN 978-0-8058-5019-2–ISBN 0-8058-5019-8 (cloth)
ISBN 978-0-8058-6207-2–ISBN 0-8058-6207-2 (pbk)
ISBN 978-1-4106-1587-9–ISBN 1-4106-1587-1 (e book)

Copyright information for this volume can be obtained by contacting the Library of Congress.

Printed in the United States of America
10   9   8   7   6   5   4   3   2

Contents

Preface

Modeling the impact and influence of contextual factors on human development is something that many talk about but few actually do. The goal of this book is to provide researchers with an accessible guide to understanding the many different ways that contextual factors can be including in longitudinal studies of human development. In fact, many of the chapters will provide concrete and clear examples of how contextual factors can be included in most research studies across the behavioral and social sciences. This book is intended for researchers in the behavioral social sciences who desire a didactic yet sophisticated treatment of the various ways that contextual factors can be represented in research studies. As such the content is both accessible and useful for both graduate students and seasoned investigators.

The introductory chapter of this volume provides a detailed rationale for the ways in which contextual factors can be represent (e.g., as covariates, predictors, outcomes, moderators, mediators, and mediate effects). The introductory chapter also serves as the guide to the book so that readers can identify the needed chapters that will most directly facilitate their needs. The book itself also covers general issues that are part and parcel of doing best-practice research including such topics as how best to treat missing data in the context of longitudinal designs (chapter 2), making appropriate model comparisons (chapter 3), and scaling across developmental age ranges (chapter 4). The middle chapters focus on the use of various statistical techniques from Multilevel modeling (chapter 5 and 8), multiple-group SEM (chapter 6), and multi-level SEM (chapter 7) as well as how to incorporate complex tests of mediation, moderation and moderated mediation (chapters 9 and 10). The book also covers person-centered approaches (chapter 11), dyadic and interdependent data designs (chapters 12 and 13), dynamic intra-individual analyses (chapter 14), and social contagion models (chapter 15). In the later part of the book, critical measurement theoretical issues are discussed including the various ways that age can be represented (chapter 16) and the ways that context can be conceptualized (chapter 17). Finally, the capstone chapter (chapter 18) provides a succinct and poignant discussion of how all the topics discussed in this book provide an integrated and compelling call to take context seriously and include contextual factors in both ones theorizing and ones research.

We wish to thank the ever-present support of Larry Erlbaum, Debra Riegert, Rebecca Laursen and the many other wonderful folks at LEA who have assisted us in the process of putting this volume together. Of course, a project such as this would not be possible without the financial support of key organizations. Three funding sources provided the financial backing for the conference from which this volume emerged. Namely, we wish to express our gratitude to the support of the National Science Foundation (BCS-0345677), the Merrill Advanced Study Center at the University of Kansas (Mabel Rice, director), and the Trustees of the Society of Multivariate Experimental Psychology (SMEP). The editors of this volume would also like to acknowledge key support of other grants that contributed to the conduct of the work contained herein. Namely, this work was supported in part by grants from the NIH to the University of Kansas through the Mental Retardation and Developmental Disabilities Research Center (5 P30 HD002528; Steve Warren, PI), the Center for Biobehavioral Neurosciences in Communication Disorders (5 P30 DC005803; Mabel Rice, PI), an Individual National Research Service Award (F32 MH072005; Noel Card, PI) and a NFGRF grant (2301779; Todd Little, PI) from the University of Kansas.

—*Todd D. Little*
Lawrence, Kansas

—*James A Bovaird*
Lincoln, Nevada

—*Noel A Card*
Tucson, Arizona

CHAPTER ONE

Modeling Ecological and Contextual Effects in Longitudinal Studies of Human Development

Noel A. Card
University of Arizona

Todd D. Little
University of Kansas

James A. Bovaird
University of Nebraska at Lincoln

The quality of scientific knowledge is highly dependent on the quality of the scientific methods used to obtain it. Although it is true that some research questions are easier to address than others, the steady increases in computational capabilities over the past decades have spurred a parallel surge in the complexity of research methodologies and the corresponding data analyses. At the same time, methodological and analytic techniques do not—and should not—arise independent of theoretical conceptualization. The coordinated development of theory, research methodology, and data analysis is important for advancing our understanding of human development.

For human development researchers, modeling processes of change, growth, and transformation represent one of the most difficult, yet necessary, classes of methodological challenges (see Collins & Sayer, 2001; Little, Schnabel, & Baumert, 2000). Not only are longitudinal studies our best alternative in many situations for attempting to infer directions of causal influence, but the study of change over time is of itself a central consideration in studying human development. Various analytic approaches have been used to study this change. Basic regression analyses, and better yet, latent structural models, have been effectively used to examine relations of interindividual (between-person) differences across time. Modeling of average intraindividual (within-person) change over time is also an important endeavor that has been approached through simple growth curve analyses, for example. Combining these two approaches, interindividual differences in intraindividual change (see Nesselroade & Baltes, 1979) have been effectively modeled within both random-effects multilevel models as well as structural equation models. However, although the techniques we have just mentioned have been effectively used in a variety of circumstances, we do not wish to portray longitudinal data analysis as a field in which all problems are resolved. Indeed, there is an ongoing need to consider alternative approaches to modeling longitudinal data in light of emerging developmental theories and unique situations. Moreover, there are fundamental issues, such as those of measurement and missing data, that are central concerns in longitudinal research which have not been completely resolved.

Although the modeling of change is difficult in itself, modeling the contexts in which developmental processes unfold adds an additional level of complexity to the task of the developmental researcher. The goal of this book is to discuss the challenges of modeling these types of data, to consider alternative approaches to modeling contextual influences, and ultimately to provide concrete suggestions of methodologies and data analytic strategies for developmental researchers to use in their work.

WHAT IS CONTEXT?

Bronfenbrenner and Morris (1983) defined environment as "any event or condition outside the organism that is presumed to influence, or be influenced by, the person's development" (pp. 359). This definition is broad, and necessarily so. In the study of human development, then, we will define context (a term that we use synonymously with "environment") as features outside of the growing, changing person that potentially affect or are affected by the individual and his/her growth. As mentioned, studying an individual's change within an environment that itself may be changing adds additional complexity and challenges (as well as opportunity) to developmental research.

Given this operational definition of context, development clearly occurs within numerous contexts–for example, within families, peer groups, schools, neighborhoods, communities, nations, and historic periods–all of which might be expected to influence, and be influenced by, the individual and his or her growth. Bronfenbrenner (e.g., Bronfenbrenner, 1977; Bronfenbrenner & Morris, 1998; see also Widaman, Chap. 17, this volume) classified ecological contexts into four nested levels: the microsystem level consisting of the individual's immediate social settings that directly affect the individual's life (e.g., family, peer group, classroom), the mesosystem level that connects the various microsystems together (e.g., parents' relations with school personnel), the exosystem made up of larger formal or informal structures (e.g., neighborhood, community) that affect the functioning of micro- and meso- systems, and the overarching macrosystem of cultural, political, and economic patterns that influence the lower levels (e.g., the system by which the elderly are cared for within a culture or nation). Although the lines between levels can be fuzzy, this hierarchical organization allows us to consider factors ranging from those that directly influence or are influenced by one or a few individuals to those that have more distal influences on a larger number of people.

Time can also be considered an important component of context (chronosystem; Bronfenbrenner, 1986), although one that has received less attention than it likely warrants. One aspect of time that has been shown to be an important consideration is that of the historic period (e.g., the Great Depression, World War II; see Elder, 1998; Grimm & McArdle, Chap.16, this volume). However, time as context might be more flexibly considered as a temporal ecology that cuts across all levels of the ecological context described above (i.e., main effect of time) and might also be expected to influence the magnitude of the interconnections among different ecological levels (i.e., moderating effect of time). Therefore, in addition to considering time only as the lag across which development occurs, one can consider time as a context in itself. Research using the ecological perspective assumes that such aspects of context are a major source of developmental influence, yet those potential sources are too often overlooked or ignored in developmental research. It is also the case that ecological theorists generally do not try to study the effects of environmental influences in the lab, maintaining that true understanding must be obtained in a natural setting. Therefore, researchers often can not rely on experimental methods to draw firm conclusions about causality (although exceptions do exist). Instead, as previously mentioned, longitudinal studies remain the method by which many developmental researchers attempt to draw conclusions about directions of influence under various ecological contexts. The complexity of the nested-levels theoretical perspective combined with the intricacies of longitudinal research necessarily pose unique difficulties in terms of theoretic conceptualizations, data collection methods, and analytic approaches.

PATTERNS OF INFLUENCE BETWEEN INDIVIDUALS AND THEIR CONTEXTS

To borrow from Bronfenbrenner (1977) again, "the ecology of human development is the scientific study of the progressive, mutual accommodation, throughout the life span, between a growing human organism and the changing immediate environments in which it lives, as this process is affected by the relations obtaining within and between these immediate settings, as well as the larger social contexts, both formal and informal, in which the settings are embedded" (Bronfenbrenner, p. 514). In other words, Bronfenbrenner conceptualized mutual, direct influence between the developing person and the immediate context. The influence of context on the individual seems intuitive enough, though this influence is too often not directly studied in developmental research. On the other hand, the influence that individuals may have on their environment is frequently forgotten—individuals may directly change the environment in which they develop (e.g., children influencing parents' behavior; Bell, 1968) as well as select into different environments (e.g., adolescents affiliating with deviant peers; Kandell, 1978).

At the same time, influences between individuals and their environments is not always direct. Some influences may be indirect or mediated, as when a more distal environmental feature (e.g., exosystemic neighborhood characteristics) impacts a more proximal environmental feature (e.g., microsystemic family processes), which in turn impacts the child. We may also have reason to conceptualize context as a moderator; for example, there is evidence to suggest that personal risk factors are related to children being victimized by peers primarily when they have (i.e., in the context of) poor peer relations (Hodges, Malone, & Perry, 1997). In short, realistic theories of development typically posit complex relations among various aspects of the individual and environment; therefore, the statistical models used to evaluate hypotheses stemming from such theories typically must be more complex than simple 'X predicts Y' relations. These considerations were the primary motivation behind this volume. Supported by grants from the Merrill Advanced Studies Center, National Science Foundation, and Society of Multivariate Experimental Psychology, the various authors and other interested colleagues met to discuss to discuss these challenges and offer potential solutions.

AN OVERVIEW OF THE BOOK

Following this introductory chapter, this book contains 17 chapters arranged to cover general issues in modeling context in longitudinal studies (e.g., missing data, measurement), chapters describing specific applications or techniques (multilevel models, structural equation models, EMOSA models, and dynamic factor analyses), and finally chapters that are more theoretically oriented. However, because each of these issues must be considered whenever modeling context in development, these rough groupings should in no way be taken to imply that chapters describing data analytic techniques are devoid of theory, or vice versa. The authors of these chapters have worked hard to ensure that each chapter can be understood independently; therefore, readers who may prefer closer consideration of theoretical issues before considering analytic issues can do so simply be reading the later chapters first. In the following, we provide a brief synopsis of the remaining chapters of this volume.

Great advances have been made in missing data techniques over the past decade or so, making it difficult for most researchers to stay current on the state of the art. Falling behind on these advances is especially problematic for developmental researchers conducting longitudinal studies, since missing data, often in the form of nonrandom attrition, is especially prevalent in this sort of research. Fortunately, Scott Hofer and Lesa Hoffman (Chap. 2) have provided a clear, practical guide to the most recent techniques for managing missing data. Specifically, they provide a taxonomy of the types of missingness, describe several sources of missingness and their implications, offer a clear description of the most recent techniques of missing data management, and discuss the merits and limitations of these techniques in longitudinal research. It is important to note that these techniques are relevant when data regarding either the individual or the context are missing, situations that are all-too-common in developmental research.

In Chapter 3, Kristopher Preacher, Li Cai, and Robert MacCallum describe methods of comparing alternative models with one another and with observed data. Although Preacher and colleagues do so using examples of covariance structure models, also called latent variable or structural equation models, the principles they outline are flexible. In their chapter, the authors describe modeling versus null hypothesis testing (and 'small difference' versus 'no difference' null hypotheses), and the rationales and merits of each. Extending this line of reasoning, the authors describe approaches to power analysis for complex models from each of these perspectives. Perhaps most importantly, Preacher and colleagues describe and discuss an alternative criterion for model comparison based on the principle of minimum description length, which maximizes generalizability yet avoids some undesirable qualities of traditional information-based criteria such as AIC and BIC.

The chapter by Susan Embretson (Chap. 4) provides a sobering demonstration of errors that can arise when using inappropriately scaled measures in longitudinal, cross-contextual research. Specifically, her simulations convincingly illustrate that estimates of change over time, as well as between-group (e.g., groups in different contexts) differences in change, can be severely biased when measures are inappropriate for the level of a trait 'difficulty' characteristic of a given group and/or time period. Here, difficulty refers not only to its classic use in educational measurement, but to the threshold on any construct above which a participant is likely to answer affirmatively. Fortunately, Embretson describes ways in which these errors can be avoided, or at least minimized: using item response theory (rather than classical test theory) scaling, multilevel tests, and adaptive testing. Equally important, Embretson's clear demonstration of the problems of inappropriate scaling can serve as a clear warning to researchers to carefully plan a measurement strategy that includes ranges appropriate for both the multiple contexts and the varying time points investigated in their study.

As mentioned earlier, multilevel models have been widely used in longitudinal research. Patrick Curran, Michael Edwards, R. J. Wirth, Andrea Hussong, and Laurie Chassin (Chap. 5) describe the value of multilevel growth curve models in many circumstances but note that these models are problematic when researchers use categorical variables and/or wish to incorporate multiple indicators of a construct. The authors discuss the merits and limits of several one-stage techniques that may be used in these situations. Improving on these models, however, they then describe a new two-stage approach to estimating growth curves involving multiple categorical indicators of a construct. This two-stage approach is then demonstrated within a longitudinal study of growth in externalizing problems among adolescents of parents with histories versus no histories of alcoholism (see also Chap. 10).

In chapter 6, Todd Little, Noel Card, David Slegers, and Emily Ledford describe the use of multiple-group Means and Covariance Structures (MACS) models in comparing individuals in discrete contexts. Specifically, they describe techniques of ensuring that latent variables capture the same constructs across contexts (i.e., measurement invariance), which is generally only assumed, rather than tested, in manifest variable analyses. They then describe methods of comparing latent means and variances across groups (which can be considered main-effect contextual effects) and of comparing latent correlations across groups (which can be considered moderating effects). This illustration of evaluating across-group differences in means, variances, and covariances should alert researchers to the possibilities that exist beyond simple main-effect differences (i.e., mean differences) across contexts.

In Chapter 7, James Bovaird promotes the consideration of multilevel structural equation models for ecological investigations. He discusses the principles of multilevel modeling, especially as they apply to the modeling of complex multivariate hypotheses as typically done in structural equation modeling. A historical overview and synthesis with the current state of the art is provided as well. To illustrate the usefulness of multilevel structural equation modeling, Bovaird presents two empirical examples: a multilevel multivariate latent growth curve model of the development of locus of control throughout adolescence, and a multilevel MIMIC (multiple indicators and multiple causes) model of kindergarten readiness as predicted by county-level contextual characteristics when investigating contextual factors at multiple levels of the ecological hierarchy. The empirical examples provide a clear demonstration of the utility of multilevel structural equation modeling when investigating contextual factors at multiple levels of the ecological hierarchy.

Donald Hedeker and Robin Mermelstein (Chap. 8) provide a straightforward introduction to multilevel models (which they refer to by the alternative name of mixed-effects regression models). Their focus, however, is on modeling differences across groups and time in variance components—both within-person variance as well as between-person variance. Hedeker and Mermelstein's emphasis on conceptualizing and testing between-group differences in variance components is important because too few researchers consider and test these differences (more often the focus is on differences in means). The authors present data on adolescent smoking to (a) illustrate the conceptual importance of differences in within- and between-person variance and (b) clearly show how to proceed with testing these potential differences. An interesting detail that readers may find useful is that the authors demonstrate how to compare models of variance differences in which groups are considered nominal (i.e., the variances differ in an unspecified way across groups) versus ordinal (i.e., the variances differ in a specified way, such as in a linear manner, across successive groups).

In Chapter 9, Todd Little, Noel Card, James Bovaird, Kristopher Preacher, and Christian Crandall provide an introduction to testing mediation and moderation within latent variable structural equation models. For each process, they outline conceptual, methodological, and analytic considerations the researcher should take into account when evaluating hypotheses involving mediation, moderation, mediated moderation, or moderated mediation. In other words, this chapter describes current practices for analyzing not only mediation and moderation, but also provides suggestions for evaluating more complex—and perhaps more realistic—models involving mediated moderation and moderated mediation.

David Flora, Siek Toon Khoo, and Laurie Chassin (Chap. 10) describe methods of evaluating longitudinal mediational hypotheses when the predictor, mediator, and outcomes are growth in a variable rather than static levels of it. Specifically, they describe how structural equation representations of longitudinal growth curves can be used to evaluate mediational processes among the growth parameters themselves. They further extend this idea by considering potential moderating influences on the mediational processes, or moderated mediation (see also Chap. 9). To illustrate their approach, the authors use data on the change in externalizing behaviors and alcohol use among adolescents with parents with or without histories of alcoholism (see also Chap. 5).

There have been several calls in recent years for developmental research to adapt a "person-centered" approach (see e.g., Cairns, Bergman, & Kagan, 1998). In Chapter 11, Daniel Bauer and Michael Shanahan compare this approach with the more traditional variable-oriented analytic strategy using simulated data on adolescent school dropout. Not only do Bauer and Shanahan compare person-centered (latent profile analysis) and variable-centered (logistic regression, including interaction terms) approaches, but they also demonstrate the comparability of results from each approach. Therefore, this chapter does much to reconcile two often distant approaches to developmental research.

Much of development occurs within a dyadic social context, in which an individual's thoughts, emotions, and behaviors are interdependent with a partner's (e.g., a mother–child relationship). However, our inferential data analytic techniques typically assume independence of observations, leaving us faced with the choice of either ignoring these interdependencies (and violating assumptions of our analyses) or attempting to avoid this interdependency, which may in itself be of substantive interest. Niall Bolger and Patrick Shrout (Chap. 12) describe a method of analyzing longitudinal dyadic data that makes these interdependencies the focus of attention, rather than a nuisance to be avoided (see also Chaps. 13 and 14). Specifically, they present data on the anger experienced by law students and their romantic partners over a seven day period, and the authors analyze the concurrent and longitudinal interdependencies between partners from both multilevel and structural equation modeling frameworks.

In Chapter 13, Steven Boker and Jean-Philippe Laurenceau conceptualize individuals and their environments as dynamic systems with potential mutual regulation. Such a conceptualization has several merits, including the introduction of systemic concepts (e.g., of an equilibrium point) into developmental research and the ability to model complex change processes. Boker and Laurenceau demonstrate this modeling approach using data of self-disclosure among married couples (i.e., context of marital dyad; see also Chapters 12 and 14).

In Chapter 14, Nilam Ram and John Nesselroade describe Cattell's data cube, distinguishing individual versus contextual variables by 'splitting' the cube along the 'variables' axis. From this conceptualization, they go on to describe how P-data analyses (i.e., variables by occasions), including dynamic factor models, can similarly be split to model across-time change in the individual, the individual's context, and the relations between individual and context. Ram and Nesselroade discuss this approach in the context of studying marital relations (in which each partner can be considered the other's context) and more traditionally (in which there is a clear individual and context).

There is both intuitive and empirical support for the role of peer context in adolescents' decisions to smoke or drink alcohol. In Chapter 15, Joseph Rodgers provides a clear description of two processes, general diffusion and social contagion, by which the peer context can foster the emergence of these behaviors. Rodgers then describes the Epidemic Model of the Onset of Social Activities (EMOSA) as a tool for evaluating the relative contribution of each process to the onset of these problem behaviors. After demonstrating the use of this model with data on adolescents' first use of cigarettes and alcohol, he discusses several limitations to this model. Despite these limitations, however, we suspect that this model will serve as a valuable tool for studying the role of social influence in the emergence of a variety of behaviors.

In Chapter 16, Kevin Grimm and John McArdle accomplish two goals. First, they succinctly describe the complexities of separating 'time' in terms of chronological age, birth cohort, and historic period. Such distinctions are important if we are to understand the specific ecologies associated with each. Second, they present analyses of growth in verbal ability and memory across the lifespan of two cohorts who experienced macrosystemic influences (i.e., Great Depression, World War II) at different ages. These analyses go beyond standard growth curve models, however, by modeling cognitive growth using separate slope functions for childhood and adulthood, evaluating potential cohort differences, and considering the important contextual predictor of military service. Thus, the authors apply a sophisticated data-analytic model to effectively test the impact of several ecological factors on cognitive development.

Keith Widaman, in Chapter 17, provides a clear outline of Bronfenbrenner's ecological model, pointing out that this model focuses primarily on social ecology. Widaman then proposes a parallel model of physical ecology and argues that both physical and social ecologies, in combination with personal qualities, are important foci of developmental research. Widaman also discusses various considerations for modeling the effects of context, including the timing and patterning of the contextual influence; the functional form and resulting numeric representations of the association between influence and effect; and the degree of specificity, timing, and directness of this association. These points are illustrated using data from a sample of mothers and their children with phenylketonuria (PKU), in which the associations between prenatal phenylalanine (PHE) exposure and children's intellectual development (individuals with PKU cannot metabolize PHE, resulting in brain damage) are examined.

In the final chapter Helena Jelicic, Christina Theokas, Erin Phelps, and Richard Lerner offer a theoretical synthesis of the other works in this volume. As they persuasively argue, developmental theory and methodology go hand-in-hand, with theory guiding models to be empirically evaluated and methodology offering a framework of conceptualizing developmental processes. Jelicic and colleagues describe the advantages, challenges, and central features of modern developmental systems theories, and then comment upon the other works in this volume from this framework. This fusion of modern theoretical and methodological approaches is a critical key to the advancement of developmental science.

CONCLUSIONS

As we hope you agree, this collection goes far in extending our conceptualization and methods of analyzing the interplay between individual development and the context in which this development occurs. As we have described earlier, longitudinal data are critical for understanding how individuals change across time, and consideration of the ecologies in which this change occur are crucial to a complete understanding of development. Modeling these contextual influences within longitudinal research is difficult, yet critical for testing complex, ecologically grounded hypotheses. Although new challenges will inevitably arise in readers' own research, we believe that the authors of the chapters in this volume have offered clear, concrete advice to allow the researcher to face these challenges.

ACKNOWLEDGMENTS

This work was supported by an Individual National Research Service Award (F32 MH072005) to the first author while at the University of Kansas, a new faculty grant to the second author from the University of Kansas (NFGRF 2301779), and grants from the NIH to the University of Kansas through the Mental Retardation and Developmental Disabilities Research Center (5 P30 HD002528) and the Center for Bio-behavioral Neurosciences in Communication Disorders (5 P30 DC005803). Its contents are solely the responsibility of the authors and do not necessarily represent the official views of these funding agencies. This work was also partly supported by grants to the first author from NSF (BCS-0345677), the Merrill Advanced Study Center at the University of Kansas (Mabel Rice, director), and the Society of Multivariate Experimental Psychology (SMEP).

REFERENCES

Bell, R. Q. (1968). A reinterpretation of the direction of effect in studies of socialization. *Psychological Review, 75*, 81-95.

Bronfenbrenner, U. (1977). Toward an experimental ecology of human development. *American Psychologist, 32*, 513-531.

Bronfenbrenner, U. (1986). Ecology of the family as a context for human development: Research perspectives. *Developmental Psychology, 22*, 723-742.

Bronfenbrenner, U., & Morris, P. A. (1983). The evolution of environmental models in developmental research. In P. H. Mussen (Series Ed.) & W. Kessen (Vol Ed.) (Eds.), *Handbook of child psychology: Vol. 1. History, theory, and methods* (pp. 357-414). New York: Wiley.

Bronfenbrenner, U., & Morris, P. A. (1998). The ecology of developmental processes. In W. Damon (Series Ed.) & R. M. Lerner (Vol Ed.) (Eds.), *Handbook of child psychology: Vol. 1. Theoretical models of human development* (5th ed., 993-1028). New York: Wiley.

Cairns, R. B., Bergman, L. R., & Kagan, J. (1998). *Methods and models for studying the individual.* Thousand Oaks, CA: Sage.

Collins, L. M., & Sayer, A. G. (Eds.). (2001). *New methods for the analysis of change.* Washington, D.C.: American Psychological Association.

Elder, G. H., Jr. (1998). The life course and human development. In W. Damon (Series Ed.) & R. M. Lerner (Vol Ed.) (Eds.), *Handbook of child psychology: Vol. 1. Theoretical models of human development* (pp. 939-991). New York: Wiley.

Hodges, E. V. E., Malone, M. J., & Perry, D. G. (1997). Individual risk and social risk as interacting determinants of victimization in the peer group. *Developmental Psychology, 33,* 1032-1039.

Kandell, D. B. (1978). Homophily, selection, and socialization in adolescent friendships. *American Journal of Sociology, 84,* 427-436.

Little, T. D., Schnabel, K. U., & Baumert, J. E. (Eds.). (2000). *Modeling longitudinal and multilevel data: Practical issues, applied approaches, and specific examples.* Mahwah, NJ: Lawrence Erlbaum Associates.

Nesselroade, J. R., & Baltes, P. B. E. (Eds.). (1979). *Longitudinal research in the study of behavior and development.* Mahwah, NJ: Lawrence Erlbaum Associates.

CHAPTER TWO

Statistical Analysis With Incomplete Data: A Developmental Perspective

Scott M. Hofer

Oregon State University

Lesa Hoffman

University of Nebraska

One of the thorniest problems that developmental researchers must face is that of *missing* or *incomplete data*. Incomplete data can take many forms, such as item or scale nonresponse, participant attrition (i.e., study drop-out), and mortality within the population of interest (i.e., lack of initial inclusion or incomplete follow-up due to death). Statistical analysis in general is aimed at providing inferences regarding level or state, subgroup differences, variability, and construct relations within a population, and incomplete data complicate this process. In order to make appropriate population inferences about development and change, it is important not only to consider thoroughly the processes leading to incomplete data, but also to obtain measurements of these selection and attrition processes to the greatest extent possible. A developmental, ecological perspective is useful in this regard by providing a framework in which to consider the impact of many static and dynamic individual and contextual factors on selection and attrition processes in addition to the impact these factors have on developmental processes of interest.

In this chapter, we outline some of the general issues for making statistical inferences to populations when data are incomplete. We begin by briefly reviewing statistical theory as to the different types of incomplete data, as well as their likely sources within a developmental context. An overview of common approaches for analysis with incomplete data is then provided,   including two-

stage multiple imputation and single-stage likelihood-based estimation procedures. Current approaches for the analysis with incomplete data rely on the
statistical assumption that the data are at least *Missing at Random* (where the
probability of missing information is related to covariates and previously measured outcomes), and in the latter parts of this chapter we emphasize what this
means in terms of measurements and modeling approaches for developmental
studies. We describe several statistical methods through which the impact of
contextual variables on selection and attrition processes can be incorporated
properly. In the final section, we discuss complications that can result from
heterogeneity in the timing and sources of incomplete data when the goal is to
make inferences about developmental processes.

Methods for addressing incomplete data and their statistical complexities
remain a very active area of research. Thus, we aim to provide a conceptual
understanding of these methods, directing readers to current resources for analysis with incomplete data, rather than to provide a complete tutorial. Excellent overviews of current methods for addressing incomplete data can be found,
among others, in Allison (2002), Diggle, Liang, and Zeger (1994), Graham,
Cumsille, and Elek-Fisk (2003), and Schafer and Graham (2002), as well as the
larger works of Little and Rubin (1987, 2002) and Schafer (1997). Our emphasis
in this chapter is on the importance of considering multiple types of processes
that may lead to incomplete data in order to achieve appropriate population
inferences about developmental processes.

STATISTICAL THEORY FOR THE ANALYSIS
OF INCOMPLETE DATA

We have seen large strides in recent decades in the development of methods with
which to address incomplete data in statistical analyses. However, while these
methods may offer a ray of hope to the analyst faced with copious amounts
of missing data, in exchange one must be willing to make certain assumptions
regarding the missing data mechanisms, or reasons why certain values are missing. If these assumptions are not plausible, one could end up making inferences
that are at best underpowered, and at worst, wrong. In this section we provide
a brief overview of the types of mechanisms that can lead to incomplete data,
as was first explicated by Rubin (1976) (see also Allison, 2002; Little & Rubin,
1987, 2002). Despite the somewhat nonintuitive nature of these terms, they are
standard among methodologists and users of missing data treatments, and as
such will be used here as well.

Missing Completely at Random (MCAR)

The most restrictive assumption that can be made regarding the nature of the missingness in one's data is known as *Missing Completely at Random* (MCAR), in which the probability of data being observed does not depend on the value of the missing information or that of any other variables in the dataset. Despite the use of the term random, systematic patterns of missing data can still qualify as MCAR if the mechanism generating the missing data is unrelated to the outcomes of interest. For example, items skipped accidentally on a questionnaire or data lost to equipment, computer, or experimenter error could likely be considered MCAR. Similarly, missingness could also be considered MCAR if it results from participants being absent from data collection for reasons unrelated to the variables of interest.

In contrast to unintentional missingness, incomplete data may be intentionally introduced by design in order to minimize response burden or fatigue effects yet maximize statistical power and breadth of measurement. In this approach, often referred to as *planned missingness* (e.g., Graham, Hofer, & MacKinnon, 1996; Graham, Hofer, & Piccinin, 1994; Graham, Taylor, & Cumsille, 2001; McArdle, 1994), different items or variables are collected purposively across separate subsets of the same sample, and missing data methods are used to analyze data across the subsets as if it were complete in the full sample. Planned missingness is a superior alternative to unintentional missingness, in that the causes of missingness are known and unrelated to participant characteristics in the former case, but may be due to unmeasured characteristics of the participant in the latter. Any data that are missing due to planned non-administration (e.g., random assignment of different forms) would be considered Missing Completely at Random, provided that data were indeed collected from everyone as intended.

Missing at Random (MAR)

A less-restrictive assumption is that of *Missing at Random* (MAR), also known as *Ignorable, Accessible,* or *Non-Informative Missingness*. Simply put, in this scenario the probability of having missing information on a given variable is unrelated to the missing values themselves *after* controlling for other variables that are related to the missingness on that variable. The assumption of MAR is often realistic provided that individual or contextual covariates are collected that predict the probability of missingness. For example, consider nonresponse to a survey question about annual income. It is possible that the question was skipped accidentally, but it is also possible that persons with lower or higher incomes would be less likely to answer questions regarding their annual incomes.

If the researchers have collected other variables from the participants that are likely to be related to annual income, such as educational attainment or type of employment, they could make use of those "proxy" variables in order to continue to make appropriate inferences regarding the distribution of the annual income variable or the relationship of annual income with other variables in the sample. Within a longitudinal context, missingness at a given occasion of measurement could be considered MAR if the values of the missing variable could be predicted from those obtained on previous occasions.

Not Missing at Random (NMAR)

Finally, the least restrictive assumption regarding possible mechanisms of missingness is that of *Not Missing at Random* (NMAR; also referred to as *Missing Not at Random*), also known as *Non-Ignorable*, *Non-Accessible*, or *Informative Missingness*. NMAR represents the worst-case scenario for a data analyst, in that the probability of missingness on a given variable is related to the missing values themselves after controlling for other relevant variables. Let us reconsider the earlier examples, If the probability of skipping a given item on a questionnaire was related to the response of that item (e.g., persons with lower incomes were less likely to report their incomes) and no other information was available that was related to this nonresponse, the missingness would be considered NMAR. Similarly, in computer-administered timed tasks, if computer error was more likely on trials with longer response times, and no other data was available that was related to response time for that task, the missingness would be considered NMAR. Finally, if the probability of missing a measurement occasion is related to the values that would have been obtained at that occasion or in the future (i.e., unobserved variables), but was not predictable from previous observations, the missingness would again be considered NMAR. When incomplete data arise from NMAR processes, the estimation of parameters will be biased in unknown ways when analyzed using methods that assume the data are at least MAR.

SOURCES OF INCOMPLETE DATA: TYPES OF ATTRITION PROCESSES

In evaluating which mechanism or mechanisms might be responsible for incomplete data within a given study, one must consider the substantive processes that could be involved. An important first step is to distinguish developmental processes of substantive interest (i.e., as measured in study outcomes) from other developmental processes that may be related to item nonresponse (e.g., fatigue, lack of motivation, embarrassment) and unit nonresponse (e.g., study attrition, mortality). We next consider the case of unit nonresponse or study attrition from a developmental orientation and the extent to which such incomplete data can be considered as mere nuisance, as a natural process, or as a problem of threshold or censoring.

Attrition as a Nuisance

In many cases, the processes leading to nonresponse or attrition may not be of direct interest. For example, the moving away of participants from a longitudinal data collection project is an unfortunate event, but may not be substantively noteworthy, assuming the move was due to reasons unrelated to the areas under investigation. Similarly, computer or equipment malfunction is a process one typically wishes to minimize, not explore further. Incomplete data is assumed to arise from nuisance processes such as these in many substantive analyses. In these cases, the emphasis is on the best use of all available data in order to achieve appropriate population inferences in the presence of missing data. Covariates for missingness (i.e., variables related to the probability of missingness) may not be available or relevant, and as a result may not be incorporated into the method of addressing the missingness. The statistical analysis procedures reviewed in the next section are well-suited for this scenario, and permit estimation of unbiased and efficient population parameters when data are Missing Completely at Random (i.e., when the probability of missingness is unrelated to the process under study) or Missing at Random (i.e., unrelated after accounting for covariates related that can predict the probability of missingness).

Attrition as a Natural Process

In contrast to the previous examples in which missing data are largely seen as a hurdle to overcome, incomplete data can also be the natural result of developmental and population aging processes. For example, attrition in studies of aging is often nonrandom, or *selective*, in that it is likely to result from mortality or declining physical and mental functioning of the participants over the period of observation (Cooney, Schaie, & Willis, 1988; Rabbitt, Watson, Donlan, Bent, & McInnes, 1994; Riegel, Riegel, & Meyer, 1967; Siegler & Botwinick, 1979; Streib, 1966). In diary studies of daily experiences, participants may vary in compliance as a function of individual characteristics as well as the types of experiences they are recording (Bolger, Davis, & Rafaeli, 2003). In studies of adolescent substance abuse, high levels of alcohol or drug use at the previous time point may be related to attrition at the next time point (Graham, Hofer, Donaldson, MacKinnon, & Schafer, 1997). In long-term intervention studies, participants who do not feel they are benefiting from the treatment (i.e., those in the placebo group) as well as those who feel they have already improved 'enough' may opt to discontinue participation (Hedeker & Gibbons, 1997). In these examples the fact that the values are missing is likely to be informative of the value that would have been obtained (Diggle & Kenward, 1994).

These scenarios can present an important inferential problem for the analysis of longitudinal studies, in that at each new wave of assessment the sample becomes less and less representative of the population from which it originated. As such, generalizations from the sample of continuing participants to the initial population may become difficult to justify (e.g., Nesselroade, 1988; Vaupel & Yashin, 1985). It is important to note, however, that the problem of nonrandom attrition is not unique to longitudinal studies. In cross-sectional studies, nonrandom population attrition (i.e., mortality; morbidity) manifests itself as nonrandom initial sample selection. Particularly pertinent to research on aging, cross-sectional samples of individuals of different ages are necessarily comprised of individuals who are the surviving members of the population, making inferences to a single population of "aging" individuals difficult to justify. Such differential population selection (mortality, morbidity) is often related to the processes of interest and cannot be evaluated in cross-sectional studies, given that data are typically not collected on nonparticipants. In longitudinal studies, however, information about the nonreturning participants prior to their departure may be available and the relationship with the probability of missingness can be carefully considered (e.g., Graham, Hofer, Donaldson, MacKinnon, & Schafer, 1997). Inferences to population subgroups or parameters conditional on both age and survival are possible in such cases.

In scenarios of selective nonresponse or attrition such as these, it is critically important to consider possible sources of missing data during the early design stages of a study in order to obtain measurements on individual and contextual covariates that are likely to be related to the probability of missingness. It is only through the appropriate inclusion of such covariates in the subsequent models that the assumption on which most statistical methods of addressing missing data are based, that of Missing at Random (MAR), can possibly be satisfied.

Problems of Threshold or Censoring

In addition to missing data arising from nuisance or substantive processes, incomplete data can also be the result of problems of range restriction within a measurement instrument. Sometimes measurement instruments may not be appropriate for all individuals within a defined population, or the phenomenon of interest may not apply to all individuals. For example, the Mini-Mental Status Exam (Folstein, Folstein, & McHugh, 1975) is often given as a measure of general cognitive status in older adults, but most healthy adults will score at ceiling (i.e., will be right-censored), with deficits observed only for those with severely declining abilities, such as in advancing dementia. Thus, the measure may only be useful within certain subsets of the sample. Similarly, in studies of substance abuse, adolescents who do not smoke or drink will necessarily score at the floor of a measure of amount or intensity of use (i.e., will be left-censored), resulting in a zero-inflated distribution of substance use, given that only those who engage in the activity can logically vary in amount or intensity (Brown, Catalano, Fleming, Haggerty, & Abbot, 2005).

In these instances, although the censored data are not truly missing, they are also often not informative about individual characteristics for portions of the sample or for certain time points (i.e., for which measurements away from ceiling or floor could not be obtained). Under such conditions, analyses may be performed for the subsample of individuals with noncensored responses, an approach that is less than optimal. An alternative approach has been recently developed by Olsen and Schafer (2001); (see also Brown, Catalano, Fleming, Haggerty, & Abbot, 2005), that of two-part latent growth curve models. In this approach, responses on a single censored outcome are modeled as two distinct variables: A dichotomous indicator for whether or not each case is censored (e.g., whether or not the participant smokes), and a continuous indicator of the value if not censored (e.g., number of cigarettes smoked per day). Predictors of each outcome can then be evaluated simultaneously. Although use of the two-part latent growth curve models thus far has largely been limited to substance use research, they are likely to have many other applications as well.

STATISTICAL APPROACHES FOR ANALYSIS WITH INCOMPLETE DATA

The options for addressing incomplete data within a statistical analysis depend largely on the hypothetical reasons for missingness. If the source of the missingness for a given variable can be considered Missing Completely at Random (MCAR), then many options exist for addressing this missingness. These include *listwise deletion* (i.e., complete cases analysis), the old standby and default in many statistical analysis packages, as well as newer methods based on maximizing likelihoods or multiple imputation, as presented in the next section. In the case of MCAR, regardless of which method is used, model parameters (e.g., means, variances, correlations, or regression weights) from analyses including the variable with missingness are likely to be *unbiased*, which means that the obtained parameter estimate will be a close match to the value that would have been obtained had the data been complete. Parameter estimates may vary across missing data methods in their *efficiency*, the extent to which the standard error around the parameter estimate is as small as it would have been if the data were complete (Graham, Hofer, & MacKinnon, 1996; Schafer & Graham, 2002). This lack of efficiency translates directly into a loss of statistical power and a greater likelihood of a Type II error (i.e., failing to reject the null hypothesis when it should be rejected). Thus, in the case of MCAR, maximum likelihood and multiple imputation methods can offer considerable improvements over listwise deletion.

If the missingness on a given variable is not Missing Completely at Random (MCAR), then the use of listwise deletion will likely lead to biased as well as inefficient estimates, and is generally not recommended. It is important to note that single imputation methods, such as mean-based or regression-based imputation, are *not* recommended. These procedures are known to result in biased estimates if the data are not MCAR although with very low proportions of missing values the bias may be negligible (but the magnitude of bias remains unknown unless more appropriate procedures are used for comparison). A major problem with these approaches is that there is no appropriate statistical basis with which to obtain standard errors of the parameter estimates (Graham, Hofer, Donaldson, MacKinnon, & Schafer, 1997; Graham, 2003).

When it appears that either Missing at Random (MAR) or Not Missing at Random (NMAR) is applicable, then the analyst must carefully consider the various mechanisms behind the probability of missingness and incorporate all individual or contextual covariates that could be related to the probability of missingness for each variable within the missingness model (as discussed in the next section). Maximum likelihood and multiple imputation methods for treating missing data carry with them the assumption that the missingness is at least Missing at Random (MAR). Unfortunately, unlike other statistical assumptions such as multivariate normality, one cannot empirically evaluate the extent to which the missingness in the to-be-analyzed data can be considered ignorable (MAR) or nonignorable (NMAR). Thus, the appropriateness of missing data treatments with regard to the inferences that can be made to the target population depends largely on principled argument and the availability of measured covariates at the individual and contextual levels that can presumably capture the missingness processes. We return to this point later in the chapter.

In the next section, we describe briefly the available statistical approaches for the analysis of incomplete data, assuming data are Missing at Random. These include two-stage approaches, the *expectation-maximization (EM) algorithm* and *multiple imputation*, in which the missing data model is generated separately from the substantive model, such that a complete analysis requires both steps. In contrast, in single-stage models that make use of *full information maximum likelihood* (FIML) procedures, the missing data model and the substantive model can be estimated simultaneously (i.e., in one step). We also briefly describe alternative approaches that do not assume Missing at Random.

Expectation-Maximization (EM) Algorithm

Dempster, Laird, and Rubin (1977)(see also Little & Rubin, 1987, 2002) described the utility of the *expectation-maximization* (EM) algorithm for analysis with incomplete data. A general form of the EM algorithm is used to obtain sufficient statistics, such as covariances and means, on which other forms of statistical analysis can be performed. In a typical EM algorithm, one begins with user-specified starting values for the variances, covariances, and means of the variables in the dataset or rely on listwise deletion to provide starting values. In the *expectation* step, the "best guess" is filled in for any missing value based on regression equations in which each variable with missing values serves as an outcome and all other variables serve as predictors. In the *maximization* step, means for the newly completed data are calculated in the typical manner, but the variances and covariances are calculated with additional components of variance added to them in order to correct for underestimation. The variances, covariances, and means are then compared to those given as starting values. The new estimates of these parameters are then used to update the regression equations for use in a second expectation step, followed by a second maximization step, and the updated estimates are again compared to those from the previous run. The EM algorithm continues to repeat until the estimates change a negligible amount between iterations.

The most typical implementation of the EM algorithm is the generation of maximum likelihood estimates of variances, covariances, and means for continuous variables that may then be analyzed with other statistical analysis programs (e.g., general linear models, structural equation models). The estimates produced using the EM algorithm are unbiased and efficient under the assumption of MAR (Graham et al., 1994; Graham et al., 1997). However, standard errors for the estimates must be generated separately, such as with a bootstrap procedure (Efron & Tibshirani, 1998), given the different sample sizes on which each of the parameters (e.g., covariances) are based. Nevertheless, this approach is useful for providing maximum likelihood estimates of variances, covariances, and means for reporting summary descriptive statistics even when single-stage methods of model estimation are used (as described shortly). Several software programs are available that use this method, including EMCOV (Graham & Hofer, 1993), NORM (Schafer, 1997), S-PLUS, SAS Proc MI, and SPSS Missing Value Analysis.

Multiple Imputation (MI)

Multiple imputation (MI; Rubin, 1987) permits the analysis of "complete" data
sets within standard statistical models (e.g., general linear models), with the
additional strength that standard errors for model parameters can be obtained
that properly account for both between-imputation and within-model variabiliity. The MI procedure accounts for missing data in an initial step, referred
to as the *missing data model*. The missing data model need not be the same
as the substantive model of interest, and should contain all covariates believed
to relate to the probability of missingness across variables. Missing values are
"filled in" or *imputed* based on regression-predicted values (in which all other
variables in the missing data model serve as predictors) along with a random
error term. A series of data imputations is performed, in which multiple "complete" data sets are generated from the missing data model. Usually between 5
and 10 imputations are sufficient, but up to 20 imputations may be necessary
when large proportions of data are missing (see Schafer, 1997). These MI models can be performed on mixtures of continuous and categorical outcomes and
covariates.

The next step is to estimate the statistical model of interest within each
imputed or "complete" data set. Because the issue of informativeness (i.e.,
nonrandom missingness) has already been addressed by the covariates within
the missing data model, only covariates of substantive interest need to be included in the substantive model. Finally, the parameter estimates and their
standard errors from each of the substantive models need to be combined appropriately. Although the parameter estimates can simply be averaged across
models, the aggregation of their standard errors requires the application of Rubin's (1987) rules, which include both between-imputation and within-model
variability in arriving at the final standard errors. Several software programs
make data imputation and the combining of results with Rubin's rules quite
easy, including NORM (Schafer, 1997), the SAS programs of Proc MI and Proc
MI Analyze, SPLUS, and LISREL. Detailed examples for multiple imputation
with NORM are provided by Graham and Hofer (2000) and Graham, Cumsille,
and Elek-Fisk (2003). Allison (2002) provides detailed examples using the SAS
MI procedures.

Full Information Maximum Likelihood (FIML)

In contrast to the two-stage approaches in which missing data and substantive
statistical models are considered in separate stages, in *full information maximum likelihood* (FIML; also known as *Direct ML*) methods, substantive model
parameters can be estimated from incomplete data in a single step without any

additional iterations or calculations (Little & Rubin, 1987, 2002). Maximum likelihood estimates of the variances, covariances, and means can be generated for reporting purposes as well. Although much more convenient than multiple imputation, the use of FIML carries with it the assumption of Missing at Random (MAR), or that the probability of missingness is unrelated to what the missing values would have been. Thus, all covariates related to the probability of missingness (e.g., previous observations, individual or contextual characteristics) need to be included in the substantive model, which can be difficult to accomplish in practice. In particular, cases with any missing covariates will not be included in the substantive model within certain types of multilevel modeling programs (e.g., HLM, SAS Proc Mixed, MLwin), although this requirement can be relaxed to include cases with partially observed covariates in other general programs for multilevel and/or structural modeling that also use FIML (e.g., Mplus, Mx, AMOS, LISREL, EQS).

Within the context of general structural equation modeling, Graham (2003) discussed the issue of how to properly include covariates for missingness that are not of substantive interest. He presented two FIML-based structural models, the extra dependent variable model and the saturated correlates model, through which one can include covariates for missingness in such a way so as not to distort the substantive model. In the *extra dependent variable model*, covariates for missingness are specified as dependent variables (i.e., as endogenous variables predicted by the exogenous variables), and their residual variances are correlated with those of other endogenous variables. In the *saturated correlates model*, covariates for missingness are specified as independent variables that are correlated directly with other exogenous variables, and correlated with the residual variances of endogenous variables. Covariates for missingness are allowed to correlate with each other in both models. Simulation results revealed that both models performed as well as two-stage approaches (e.g., multiple imputation, EM algorithm) in terms of recovering parameter estimates and standard errors. With regard to assessing model fit, however, the saturated correlates model resulted in model fit statistics equivalent to the substantive model (i.e., without covariates for missingness), and was to be preferred over the extra dependent variable model, for which discrepancies were found.

An older, related method is that of multiple group structural equation modeling (see Allison, 1987; Graham, Hofer, & Piccinin, 1994; Muthèn, Kaplan, & Hollis, 1987). Essentially, each missing data pattern represents a different group in the model, and equality constraints on the model parameters are placed across groups for variables that are present. The main limitation of the multiple group approach is that each pattern of missingness must be defined as a separate group, which quickly becomes unwieldy in complex models and can result in a loss of information because sample sizes for particular patterns may be insufficient.

Extensions of the multiple group structural equation modeling approach for incomplete data have been used for cohort sequential analyses (e.g., Duncan, Duncan, & Hops, 1996, McArdle & Hamagami, 1992, Miyazaki & Raudenbush, 2000), in which longitudinal trajectories of participants who began the study at different ages are pieced together to form a single aggregate trajectory under the assumption of Missing at Random (i.e., that observations for the ages before and after the time of study are simply Missing at Random). This approach, however, requires the assumption of *age convergence*, or that estimates of between-person differences will converge onto estimates of within-person changes. In other words, age convergence models assume that the only characteristics that separate individuals are chronological age, with no additional processes operating that create differences across birth cohorts that would lead to lack of age convergence, such as nonrandom selection, attrition, or mortality. As such, age convergence models may not be tenable in many longitudinal applications, particular with samples from the latter parts of the lifespan.

Alternatives to Missing at Random

Despite our best efforts to predict probability of missingness with observed covariates, the pattern of missingness may still be informative about the outcomes of interest, a scenario that falls within the category of nonignorable missingness (i.e., Not Missing at Random or NMAR; Little, 1995). Two approaches may be used within this scenario: Pattern-mixture models and selection models. In *pattern-mixture models* (Hedeker & Gibbons, 1997; Little, 1993, 1995), subgroups are identified based on patterns of missing data, and the analysis includes indicators of the subgroup membership. Thus, results are conditional on missing data patterns, although the mechanisms thought to be responsible for the different patterns are not considered explicitly. *Selection models* (Diggle & Kenward, 1994; Verbeke & Molenberghs, 2000) require one to first specify a distribution for the outcomes (e.g., multivariate normal), and then to specify the manner in which the probability of missingness is related to the outcomes. Details about these statistically complex models go beyond the scope of this chapter, but they are an important area of continuing development.

INFERENTIAL ISSUES FOR THE ANALYSIS
OF INCOMPLETE DATA

Single Versus Conditional Populations

As reviewed in the last section, great strides have been made in the options for addressing incomplete data in terms of the quality of the parameters that can be obtained from statistical models. Yet the resulting population inferences from those parameters remain problematic conceptually within developmental studies. Most notably, these methods and their corresponding assumptions are based on the notion of a single, accessible population of individuals. That is, they assume that model parameters from the aggregate sample can be used to infer about an "average" individual across time. Some forms of nonparticipation do logically permit inference to a single population, such as with substance abuse in adolescence (i.e., in most cases, drop-outs are still members of the general population of adolescents even if they are not in school or available for measurement).

Yet in other forms of nonparticipation, such as that of mortality in aged populations, inference to individuals within a single, stationary population over time is logically impossible because deceased individuals have left the population of interest, and thus the population is continually being redefined. In cross-sectional studies, sample-level means across age are comprised of distinct groups of individuals (i.e., those who were available to be measured when the study was conducted out of everyone who was originally could have lived to that age), and as such, initial sample selection is already confounded with population mortality. Thus, aggregate-level model parameters cannot be used to make inferences to individual-level change processes in cross-sectional studies. In longitudinal studies, however, individual-level change processes can be evaluated directly. As discussed in the following sections, however, aggregate-level model parameters in longitudinal studies with selective morality must be defined as conditional on the probability of surviving or remaining in the study at a given time point, and not in reference to an immortal population (e.g., "all older adults") that has no real-world counterpart (DuFouil, Brayne, & Clayton, 2004; Harel, 2003; Kurland & Heagerty, 2004, 2005; Ribaudo, Thompson, & Allen-Mersh, 2000).

Temporal Spacing of Observations in Measuring
Sources of Missingness

As discussed previously, multiple imputation (MI) and full information maximum likelihood (FIML) approaches require the assumption of Missing at Random (MAR). The extent to which MAR is satisfied depends largely on the availability of covariates that adequately capture the missingness process. It is important to note that results obtained from using either MI or FIML will be asymptotically equivalent provided that the missing data model is the same in each, or if the same covariates of missingness used in the imputation model are also included in the analysis model estimated with FIML (i.e., as saturated correlates in a structural model or as predictors in a multilevel model). Thus, the choice of one method over another may be based on practical considerations. It is generally easier to include covariates for missingness within an imputation model than as extra variables in a substantive model, but this advantage may be offset by the additional effort needed to conduct substantive analyses on each imputed dataset and then combine the results appropriately within MI, a process unnecessary within FIML.

Simulation research has repeatedly shown that the inclusion of covariates related to missingness within MI and FIML will result in parameter estimates and standard errors comparable to what would have been observed with complete data (e.g., Graham, 2003; Graham, Hofer, & Piccinin, 1994; Graham, Hofer, & MacKinnon, 1996; Graham & Schafer, 1999). Further, it appears there is no downside to also including covariates not related to missingness in the hope of satisfying MAR (Collins, Schafer, & Kam, 2001). Although the assumption of MAR is not testable, many scholars have expressed optimism about the utility of MAR-based methods in real-world data, noting that, "...In many psychological research settings the departures from MAR are probably not serious" (Schafer & Graham, 2002, p. 154), and that, "...With MAR missingness, although there is bias when the causes of missingness are not included in the model, the bias is much less of a problem than previously thought (Graham, Cumsille, & Elek-Fisk, 2003), even preferring MAR-based methods to alternatives for non-ignorable missingness: "...The MAR assumption has been found to yield more accurate predictions of the missing values than methods based on the more natural NMAR mechanism" (Little & Rubin, 2002, p. 19).

Within longitudinal research, however, one must consider not only which events or processes related may be related to nonresponse but more specifically, the timing and spacing of the measurements of those processes. Although it is often stated that the inclusion of covariates in the missingness model can render the assumption of MAR tenable, the measurement time frame of dynamic covariates is not often explicitly considered. Probabilities, general patterns, and sources of missingness may change over time as a result of other changes occurring during the observation period. At issue, then, is how best to obtain measures of the dynamic and heterogeneous nature of these missing data processes.

Cohen (1991) and Gollob and Reichardt (1987, 1991) consider the issue of temporal spacing within the context of the measurement of time-varying covariates. Essentially, causal mechanisms need time for their influences to be exerted, and the size of the effect will vary with the time interval between the causal influence and the outcome. Thus, if one statistically controls for a covariate measured at a time before it exerts it causal influence, resultant model parameters may still be biased by the covariate. Time-varying covariates must be measured within the time frame in which they are exerting their influence in order to provide adequate representations of the causal, time-dependent processes that result in participant nonresponse in a viable missing data model. However, deciding on what an appropriate time frame might be is not an easy task, and may not be informed by previous longitudinal studies, given that the data collection intervals from many studies are determined by logistical and financial factors, rather than theoretical expectations about the timing of developmental processes (Cohen, 1991).

The model for missing data must be at least as rich as the substantive model of interest. For group comparison and interaction, effects can be maintained in the imputation model by imputing within group or modeling the group by outcome interaction effect within the imputation model. When researchers are interested in nonlinear influences of context and the moderated effects at different levels of contextual variables, such interaction and higher order effects must be included in the imputation model as well.

Heterogeneity in the Timing and Causes of Nonresponse

Given the importance of covariates that relate to the probability of missingness in satisfying the assumption of Missing at Random (MAR) that is implicit in most of the current approaches to analysis with incomplete data, how might covariates be included that capture changing probabilities of missingness over time as a function of different mechanisms? One way in which attrition can be considered as a dynamic process is in the context of an important event that may lead to or increase the likelihood of nonresponse over time. When time to or from a significant event is an important predictor of an attrition process, a covariate of time-to-event may also be included within the statistical model. For example, in studies in which differential mortality is an issue, a covariate of time-to-death could be included, such that population inference would then be conditional on not only chronological age but also on remaining age, permitting further examination of the observed selection process over time (e.g., Johansson et al., 2004). Similarly, when selective attrition is thought to be related to a disease process, a covariate of time-since-diagnosis could be included (e.g., Sliwinski, Hofer, Hall, Buschke, & Lipton, 2003). In separating aging-related changes from other mechanisms of change (e.g., mortality, disease-related change), inferences can then be defined as conditional on the probability of surviving or remaining in the study.

Although time-to-event covariates can easily be included when complete data for the event are available (e.g., age at death or diagnosis), other methods may be required when time to event information is not known for all participants. One such method was used by Harel and colleagues (Harel, 2003; Harel, Hofer, & Schafer, 2003, March; see also Rubin, 2003), that of *two-stage multiple imputation*, in which imputation for missing age at death values was performed first, followed by imputation for the other missing values using the just-imputed age at death values. Additional alternatives have been presented by Guo and Carlin (2004), who estimated joint survival and growth curve models using Bayesian methods, and by DuFouil, Brayne, and Clayton (2004), who proposed a conditional model that incorporates both study attrition and death. Although evaluation of these approaches is still ongoing, the results thus far have been encouraging with regard to the treatment of distinct processes leading to non-response.

CONCLUSIONS

The last decade has seen considerable theoretical and computational advances in conducting statistical analyses in the presence of incomplete data. Methods such as multiple imputation and full information maximum likelihood are widely available in custom and commercial software, and have shown great promise in their ability to provide model parameters that are unbiased and efficient (or at the very least, less biased and less inefficient compared with older approaches such as listwise deletion and mean-based or regression-based imputation). However, the utility of these newer methods is contingent upon the extent to which individual and contextual covariates and scores obtained at the current and previous occasions can predict the probability of missingness, an untestable assumption known as *Missing at Random*.

Within developmental studies, study attrition may not simply be a nuisance that complicates examination of developmental processes, but rather may be an indicator of or a natural result of a developmental process in and of itself. One must consider that the forces leading to incomplete data are likely to differ in their origin and timing across persons, and include temporally-relevant covariates for those processes within the analysis framework to the greatest extent possible. With regard to the inferences that can be made from analyses of incomplete data, one must also consider the extent to which the impact of incomplete data on the results can safely be "ignored" if appropriate analyses are performed, or whether the results must instead be considered conditional (i.e., nonignorable) on the processes leading to incomplete data. This is primarily a problem of whether one can make inferences to a single, accessible population of developing individuals, or whether the population itself is undergoing dynamic changes (i.e., mortality), such that individuals comprising the population are different across age strata or different developmental periods. In the latter case, population inference may instead need to refer to multiple or conditional populations (e.g., of individuals who remain in the population at a given developmental period) rather than to a single, stationary, and nonexistent population.

REFERENCES

Allison, P. D. (1987). Estimation of linear models with incomplete data. In C. Clogg (Ed.), *Sociological methodology 1987* (pp. 71-103). San Francisco: Jossey Bass.

Allison, P. D. (2002). *Missing data (Sage university papers series on quantitative applications in the social sciences, series no. 07-136).* Thousand Oaks, CA: Sage.

Bolger, N., Davis, A., & Rafaeli, E. (2003). Diary methods: Capturing life as it is lived. *Annual Review of Psychology, 54*, 579-616.

Brown, E. C., Catalano, C. B., Fleming, C. B., Haggerty, K. P., & Abbot, R. D. (2005). Adolescent substance use outcomes in the raising healthy children project: A two-part latent growth curve analysis. *Journal of Consulting and Clinical Psychology.*

Cohen, P. (1991). A source of bias in longitudinal investigations of change. In L. M. Collins & J. L. Horn (Eds.), *Best methods for the analysis of change: Recent advances, unanswered questions, future directions* (pp. 18-25). Washington, DC: American Psychological Association.

Collins, L. M., Schafer, J. L., & Kam, C. M. (2001). A comparison of inclu-sive and restrictive strategies in modern missing data procedures. *Psychological Methods, 6 (4)*, 330-351.

Cooney, T. M., Schaie, K. W., & Willis, S. L. (1988). The relationship between prior functioning of cognitive and personality dimensions and subject attrition in longitudinal research. *Journal of Gerontology: Psychological Sciences, 43*, 12-17.

Dempster, A. P., Laird, N. M., & Rubin, D. B. (1977). Maximum likelihood from incomplete data via the EM algorithm (with discussion). *Journal of the Royal Statistical Society, B39*, 1-38.

Diggle, P. J., & Kenward, M. G. (1994). Informative drop-out in longitudinal data analysis. *Applied Statistics, 43*, 49-93.

Diggle, P. J., Liang, K., & Zeger, S. L. (1994). *Analysis of longitudinal data.* Oxford, England: Clarendon Press.

DuFouil, C., Brayne, C., & Clayton, D. (2004). Analysis of longitudinal studies with death and dropout: A case study. *Statistics in Medicine, 23*, 2215-2226.

Duncan, S. C., Duncan, T. E., & Hops, H. (1996). Analysis of longitudinal data within accelerated longitudinal designs. *Psychological Methods, 1*, 236-248.

Efron, B., & Tibshirani, R. J. (1998). *An introduction to the bootstrap.* New York, NY: Chapman and Hall.

Folstein, M. F., Folstein, S. E., & McHugh, P. R. (1975). Mini-mental state: A practical method for grading the cognitive state of patients for the clinician. *Journal of Psychiatric Research, 12*, 189-198.

Gollob, H. F., & Reichardt, C. S. (1987). Taking account of time lags in causal models. *Child Development, 58*, 80-92.

Gollob, H. F., & Reichardt, C. S. (1991). Interpreting and estimating in-direct eects assuming time lags really matter. In L. M. Collins & J. L. Horn (Eds.), *Best methods for the analysis of change: Recent advances, unanswered questions, future directions.* (pp. 243-259). Washington, DC: American Psychological Association.

Graham, J. W. (2003). Adding missing-data-relevant variables to FIML-based structural equation models. *Structural Equation Modeling, 10*, 80-100.

Graham, J. W., Cumsille, P. E., & Elek-Fisk, E. (2003). Methods for handling missing data. In J. A. Schinka & W. F. Velicer (Eds.), *Research methods in psychology* (pp. 87-114). New York: Wiley.

Graham, J. W., & Hofer, S. M. (1993). EMCOV.EXE user's guide. textupUnpublished manuscript.

Graham, J. W., & Hofer, S. M. (2000). Multiple imputation in multivariate research. In T. D. Little, K. U. Schnabel, & J. Baumert (Eds.), *Modeling longitudinal and multilevel data: Practical issues, applied approaches, and specific examples* (pp. 201-218). Mahwah, NJ: Lawrence Erlbaum Associates.

Graham, J. W., Hofer, S. M., Donaldson, S. I., MacKinnon, D. P., & Schafer, J. L. (1997). Analysis with missing data in prevention research. In K. Bryant, M. Windle, & S. West (Eds.), *The science of prevention: Methodological advances from alcohol and substance abuse research* (pp. 325-366). Washington, DC: American Psychological Association.

Graham, J. W., Hofer, S. M., & MacKinnon, D. P. (1996). Maximizing the usefulness of data obtained with planned missing value patterns: An application of maximum likelihood procedures. *Multivariate Behavioral Research, 31*, 197-218.

Graham, J. W., Hofer, S. M., & Piccinin, A. M. (1994). Analysis with missing data in drug prevention research. In L. M. Collins & L. Seitz (Eds.), *Advances in data analysis for prevention intervention research.* National Institute on Drug Abuse Research Monograph Series (#142). Washington, D.C.: National Institute on Drug Abuse.

Graham, J. W., & Schafer, J. L. (1999). On the performance of multiple imputation for multivariate data with small sample size. In R. Hoyle (Ed.), *Statistical strategies for small sample research* (pp. 1-29). Thousand Oaks, CA.: Sage.

Graham, J. W., Taylor, B. J., & Cumsille, P. E. (2001). Planned missing-data designs in analysis of change. In L. M. Collins & A. G. Sayer (Eds.), *New methods for the analysis of change* (pp. 335-353). Washington, DC: American Psychological Association.

Guo, X., & Carlin, B. P. (2004). Separate and joint modeling of longitudinal and event time data using standard computer packages. *The American Statistician, 58,* 16-24.

Harel, O. (2003). *An introduction to the bootstrap.* Unpublished doctoral dissertation. Unpublished doctoral dissertation, Department of Statistics, University Park, PA.

Harel, O., Hofer, S. M., & Schafer, J. L. (2003, March). *Analysis of longitudinal data with missing values of two qualitatively different types.* Paper presented at the annual meeting of the International Biometric Society (Eastern North American Region). Tampa, Florida.

Hedeker, D., & Gibbons, R. D. (1997). Application of the random-effects pattern-mixture models for missing data in longitudinal studies. *Psychological Methods, 2(1),* 64-78.

Johansson, B., Hofer, S. M., Allaire, J. C., Piccinin, A. M., Berg, S., & Pedersen, N. L. (2004). Change in cognitive capabilities in the oldest old: The effects of proximity to death in genetically related individuals over a 6-year period. *Psychology and Aging, 19,* 145-156.

Kurland, B. F., & Heagerty, P. J. (2004). Marginalized transition models for longitudinal binary data with ignorable and non-ignorable drop-out. *Statistics in Medicine, 23,* 2673-2695.

Kurland, B. F., & Heagerty, P. J. (2005). Directly parameterized regression conditioning on being alive: Analysis of longitudinal data truncated by deaths. *Biostatistics, 6,* 241-258.

Little, R. J. A. (1993). Pattern-mixture models for multivariate incomplete data. *Journal of the American Statistical Association, 88,* 125-134.

Little, R. J. A. (1995). Modeling the drop-out mechanism in repeated-measures studies. *Journal of the American Statistical Association, 90,* 1112-1121.

Little, R. J. A., & Rubin, D. B. (1987). *Statistical analysis with missing data* (1st ed.). New York: Wiley.

Little, R. J. A., & Rubin, D. B. (2002). *Statistical analysis with missing data* (2nd ed.). Hoboken, NJ: Wiley.

McArdle, J. J. (1994). Structural factor analysis experiments with incomplete data. *Multivariate Behavioral Research, 29,* 409-454.

McArdle, J. J., & Hamagami, F. (1992). Modeling incomplete longitudinal and cross-sectional data using latent growth structural models. *Experimental Aging Research, 18,* 145-166.

Miyazaki, Y., & Raudenbush, S. W. (2000). Tests for linkage of multiple cohorts in an accelerated longitudinal design. *Psychological Methods, 5,* 44-63.

Muthèn, B., Kaplan, D., & Hollis, M. (1987). On structural equation modeling with data that are not missing completely at random. *Psychometrika, 52,* 431-462.

Nesselroade, J. R. (1988). Sampling and generalizability: Adult development and aging research issues examined within the general methodological framework of selection. In K. Schaie & R. Campbell (Eds.), *Methodological issues in aging research* (pp. 13-42). New York, NY: Springer.

Olsen, M. K., & Schafer, J. L. (2001). A two-part random-effects model for semicontinuous longitudinal data. *Journal of the American Statistical Association, 96,* 730-745.

Rabbitt, P., Watson, P., Donlan, C., Bent, N., & McInnes, L. (1994). Subject attrition in a longitudinal study of cognitive performance in community-based elderly people. *Facts and Research in Gerontology,* 29-34.

Ribaudo, H. J., Thompson, S. G., & Allen-Mersh, T. G. (2000). A joint analysis of quality of life and survival using a random effects selection model. *Statistics in Medicine, 19,* 3237-3250.

Riegel, K. F., Riegel, R. M., & Meyer, G. (1967). A study of the drop-out rates in longitudinal research on aging and the prediction of death. *Journal of Personality and Social Psychology, 4,* 342-348.

Rubin, D. B. (1976). Inference and missing data. *Biometrika, 63,* 581-592.

Rubin, D. B. (1987). *Multiple imputation for nonresponse in surveys.* New York: Wiley.

Rubin, D. B. (2003). Nested multiple imputation of NMES via partially incompatible MCMC. *Statistica Neerlandica, 57,* 3-18.

Schafer, J. L. (1997). *Analysis of incomplete multivariate data.* New York: Chapman and Hall.

Schafer, J. L., & Graham, J. W. (2002). Missing data: Our view of the state of the art. *Psychological Methods, 7,* 147-177.

Siegler, I. C., & Botwinick, J. (1979). A long-term longitudinal study of intellectual ability of older adults: The matter of selective subject attrition. *Journal of Gerontology, 34,* 242-245.

Sliwinski, M. J., Hofer, S. M., Hall, C. B., Buschke, H., & Lipton, R. B. (2003). Modeling memory decline in older adults: The importance of preclinical dementia, attrition, and chronological age. *Psychology and Aging, 18,* 658-671.

Streib, G. (1966). Participants and drop-outs in a longitudinal study. *Journal of Gerontology, 21,* 200-209.

Vaupel, J., & Yashin, A. (1985). Heterogeneity's ruses: Some surprising effects of selection on population dynamics. *American Statistician, 39,* 176-185.

Verbeke, G., & Molenberghs, G. (2000). *Linear mixed models for longitudinal data.* New York: Springer-Verlag.

CHAPTER THREE

Alternatives to Traditional Model Comparison Strategies for Covariance Structure Models

Kristopher J. Preacher
University of Kansas

Li Cai
Robert C. MacCallum
University of North Carolina at Chapel Hill

In this chapter we discuss two related issues relevant to traditional methods of comparing alternative covariance structure models (CSM) in the context of ecological research. Use of the traditional test of parametrically nested models in applications of CSM (the χ^2 difference or likelihood ratio [LR] test) suffers from several limitations, as discussed by numerous methodologists (MacCallum, Browne, & Cai, 2005). Our primary objection is that the traditional approach to comparing models is predicated on the assumption that it is possible for two models to have identical fit in the population. We argue instead that any method of model comparison which assumes that a point hypothesis of equal fit can hold exactly in the population (e.g., the LR test) is fundamentally flawed. We discuss two alternative approaches to the LR test which avoid the necessity of hypothesizing that two models share identical fit in the population. One approach concerns framing the hypothesis of interest differently, which naturally leads to questions of how to assess statistical power and appropriate sample size. The other approach concerns a radical realignment of how researchers approach model evaluation, avoiding traditional null hypothesis testing altogether in favor of identifying the model that maximizes generalizability.

Power presents a recurrent problem to those familiar with null hypothesis significance testing (NHST). How large should a sample be in order to have adequate probability of rejecting a false null hypothesis? What is the probability of rejecting a false null if our sample is of size N? These questions present special challenges in the context of CSM because the relative status of null and alternative hypotheses are interchanged from their familiar positions — the null hypothesis in CSM represents the theory under scrutiny, and power is framed in terms of the sample size necessary to reject a false model. Traditional goodness-of-fit tests deal with the null hypothesis under which the model fits exactly in the population (exact fit test). Point hypotheses tested by the exact fit test are likely never true in practice, so how should power be conceptualized? We present an alternative strategy extending earlier work on power for tests of close fit (rather than exact fit) of single models to tests of *small difference* (rather than no difference) in comparisons of nested models. The null hypothesis in a test of small difference states that the model fits nearly as well, but not the same, as a less constrained model.

Another alternative to traditional methods of model assessment is to avoid the hypothesis-testing framework altogether, instead adopting a model selection approach that uses comparative replicability as the criterion for selecting a model as superior to its rivals (Weakliem, 2004). Specifically, we argue that the evaluation of models against arbitrary benchmarks of fit gets the researcher nowhere — only in the context of model comparison can science advance meaningfully (Burnham & Anderson, 2004). Maximizing generalizability involves ranking competing models against one another in terms of their ability to fit present and future data. Adopting this model selection strategy, however, necessitates proper quantification of *model complexity* — the average ability of a model to fit any given data. Most model fit indices include an adjustment for complexity that is a simple function of the number of free model parameters. We argue that this adjustment is insufficient; the average ability of a model to fit data is not completely governed by the number of parameters. Consequently, we present and illustrate the use of a new information-theoretic selection criterion that quantifies complexity in a more appropriate manner. This, in turn, permits the adoption of an appropriate model selection strategy that avoids pitfalls associated with LR tests.

We begin by providing a review of the traditional representation of the covariance structure model (with mean structure), with an emphasis on its application to multiple groups. We then describe advantages granted by adopting a model comparison perspective in CSM. One way around the problems with traditional approaches is to change the hypothesis under scrutiny to a more realistic one. In describing this alternative approach, we describe an approach to power analysis in CSM involving an extension of recently introduced methods to nested model scenarios. Following our discussion of power, we further explore the potential value of adopting a model selection approach that avoids hypothesis testing — and thus most problems associated with LR tests—altogether. In the process, we introduce the topic of model complexity, suggesting and illustrating the use of a new selection criterion that permits appropriate model comparison even for nonnested models.

COVARIANCE STRUCTURE MODELING

Covariance structure modeling (CSM) is an application of the general linear model combining aspects of factor analysis and path analysis. In CSM, the model expresses a pattern of relationships among a collection of observed (manifest) and unobserved (latent) variables. These relationships are expressed as free parameters representing path coefficients, variances, and covariances, as well as other parameters constrained to specific, theory-implied values or to functions of other parameters. For simplicity, we restrict attention to the *all-y* model (LISREL Submodel 3B; Jöreskog & Sörbom, 1996), which involves only four parameter matrices, although the points we discuss later apply more broadly.

Model Specification

Model specification in CSM involves a data model, representing the relationship between manifest indicators and latent variables, as well as mean and covariance structures implied by the data model. The data model can be specified as:

$$\mathbf{y} = \Lambda_y \eta + \varepsilon \tag{1}$$

where $\mathbf{y}$ denotes a vector of response scores, Λ_y denotes a matrix of factor loadings regressing the p items on the m latent variables in the vector η, and ε denotes a vector of unique factors. The covariance structure obtained by taking the expectation of the square of (1) is:

$$\Sigma_{yy}(\theta) = \Lambda_y \Psi \Lambda_y' + \Theta_{\varepsilon\varepsilon}, \tag{2}$$

where $\Sigma_{yy}(\theta)$ denotes the population covariance matrix of $\mathbf{y}$, with parameters (θ) in Λ_y, Ψ, and $\Theta_{\varepsilon\varepsilon}$, The covariance matrix of the latent variables is denoted Ψ, and $\Theta_{\varepsilon\varepsilon}$ denotes the (usually diagonal) covariance matrix of the unique factors.

A mean structure may also be derived by taking the expectation of (1):

$$\mu_y = \Lambda_y \alpha \tag{3}$$

where μ_y is a vector of population means of measured variables and α is a vector of latent means.

Ecological modeling often involves comparison of key model parameters across two or more groups hypothesized to differ in some important way. Extending these models to the multiple group case is straightforward. For example, Equations 2 and 3 may be extended for multiple groups as:

$$\Sigma_{yy}^{(g)}(\theta) = \Lambda_y^{(g)} \Psi^{(g)} \Lambda_y^{(g)} + \Theta_{\varepsilon\varepsilon}^{(g)}, \tag{4}$$

$$\mu_y^{(g)} = \Lambda_y^{(g)} \alpha^{(g)}, \tag{5}$$

where the addition of a superscripted "g" denotes group membership. Equality constraints may be placed on corresponding parameters across groups.

Free parameters are estimated by employing one of a number of discrepancy minimization techniques, most often maximum likelihood (ML) or weighted least squares (WLS). The value assumed by the discrepancy function at convergence can be used to gauge the model's degree of fit to data. For example, the ML discrepancy function is:

$$F_{ML}(\mathbf{S}, \mathbf{\Sigma}) = \ln|\mathbf{\Sigma}| - \ln|\mathbf{S}| + tr[\mathbf{S}\mathbf{\Sigma}^{-1}] - p \tag{6}$$

When the model is "correct" and if N is large enough, $(N-1)\hat{F}_{ML}$ is distributed as χ^2 with $df = p(p+1)/2 - q$, where q is the effective number of free parameters. The χ^2 statistic can be used to determine if the degree of model misfit is within chance levels, and serves as the basis for a variety of model fit indices and selection criteria.

The Importance of CSM to Ecological Research

There are several advantages associated with CSM that make it especially appropriate for addressing hypotheses in the context of ecological models. First, CSM permits the specification and testing of complex causal and correlational hypotheses. Sets of hypotheses can be tested simultaneously by constraining model parameters to particular values, or equal to one another within or across multiple groups or occasions of measurement, in ways consistent with theoretical predictions. Second, by permitting several measured variables to serve as indicators of unobserved latent variables, CSM separates meaningful variance from variance specific to items, allowing researchers to test structural hypotheses relating constructs that are not directly observed. Third, CSM is appropriate for testing correlational or causal hypotheses using either (or both) experimental or observational data. One of the central ideas behind ecological modeling is that there is much knowledge to be gained by collecting data observed in context that would be difficult or impossible to learn under artificial conditions. Finally, CSM is a flexible modeling approach that can easily accommodate many novel modeling problems.

The Importance of Adopting a Model Comparison Perspective

In practice, CSMs are typically evaluated against benchmark criteria of good fit. Based on how well a model fits data relative to these criteria, the model is usually said to fit well or poorly in an absolute sense. The reasoning underlying this strategy of gauging a model's potential usefulness is predicated on an approach to science termed *falsificationism* (e.g., Popper, 1959), which holds that evidence accumulates for theories when their predictions are subjected to, and pass, realistic "risky" tests. If a model passes such a test under conditions where it would be expected to fail if false (i.e., if it shows good fit), evidence accumulates in favor of the theory whose predictions the model represents. If it fails, the model is either rejected or modified, with implications for the revision or abandonment of the theory. Ideally, a model is subjected to repeated risky tests to give a better idea of its long-term performance, but replication is unfortunately rare in the social sciences.

An alternative philosophical perspective maintains that the evaluation of models in isolation tells us very little, and that the fit of a model to a particular data set is nearly uninformative. Rather, science progresses more rapidly if competing theories are compared to one another in terms of their abilities to fit existing data and, as we will discuss, their abilities to fit *future* data arising from the same latent process (Lakatos, 1970; MacCallum, 2003). This approach is sometimes termed *strong inference* (Platt, 1964), and involves model comparison as a signature feature. We know from the outset that no model can be literally true in all of its particulars, unless one is extraordinarily lucky or possesses divinely inspired theory-designing skills. But it stands to reason that, given a set of alternative models, one of those models probably represents the objectively true data-generating process better than other models do. It is the researcher's task to identify this model and use it as the best working hypothesis until an even more appropriate model is identified (which, by design, inevitably happens). Every time a model is selected as the optimal one from a pool of rivals, evidence accumulates in its favor. This process of rejecting alternative explanations and modifying and re-testing models against new data continues *ad infinitum*, permitting scientists to constantly update their best working hypotheses about the unobserved processes underlying human behavior.

Because no model is literally true, there is an obvious logical problem in testing the null hypothesis that a model fits data perfectly in the population. Yet, this is precisely the hypothesis tested by the popular LR test of model fit. Moreover, most fit indices require the researcher to choose arbitrary values to represent benchmarks of good fit. A model comparison approach goes far in avoiding these problems, although it cannot avoid them altogether. Most damning, it is possible to assert *apriori* that the hypothesis tested with the χ^2 statistic — that a model fits exactly in the population or that two models share exactly the same fit — is false in virtually every setting (Bentler & Bonett, 1980; Tucker & Lewis, 1973). A model selection approach avoids the pitfalls inherent in hypothesis testing by avoiding such tests altogether.

In addition to adhering more closely to scientific ideals and circumventing logical problems inherent in testing isolated models, the practice of model comparison avoids some problems associated with confirmation bias. Confirmation bias reflects the tendency for scientists unconsciously to increase the odds of supporting a preferred hypothesis (Greenwald, Pratkanis, Leippe, & Baumgardner, 1986). Regardless of why or how much the deck is stacked in favor of the researcher's preferred model in terms of absolute fit, one model is virtually guaranteed to outperform its rivals. Model comparison does not entirely eliminate confirmation bias, but it certainly has the potential to improve the researcher's objectivity.

In the foregoing we have explained that the popular LR test is fundamentally flawed in that the hypothesis it tests is rarely or never true in practice; thus, persistent and frequent use of the LR test is of questionable utility. We have also explained that adopting a model selection approach, in which at least two theory-inspired models are compared, has potentially greater scientific potential. In the following two broad sections, we outline some practical solutions to logical problems imposed by use of the traditional LR tests of model fit in ecological research. The first suggested approach emphasizes the utility of avoiding the hypothesis that two models have identical fit in favor of a hypothesis that the difference is within tolerable limits. This approach recognizes that no model can realistically fit perfectly in the population, and points out that shifting the focus to a less stringent hypothesis is more logical, yet has consequences for statistical power and identifying the necessary sample size. We describe and discuss methods that can be used to address these problems. The second section focuses more closely on the model selection perspective just outlined, emphasizing that model fit is overrated as a criterion for the success or usefulness of a theory. Rather, more attention should be paid to a model's ability to cross-validate, or generalize, relative to competing models. Special attention is devoted to a new model selection criterion that considers aspects of model complexity beyond simply the number of free parameters.

POWER ANALYSES FOR TESTS OF DIFFERENCE
BETWEEN MODELS

Researchers often conduct tests of the difference between competing models. Such difference tests are commonly performed, for example, when one is interested in determining the level of factorial invariance characterizing a scale administered to two samples from different populations (Steenkamp & Baumgartner, 1998; Vandenberg & Lance, 2000). In principle, this strategy involves specifying at least two models, with one model nested within the other, and the test of difference draws upon the general theory of LR tests to construct decision rules. To formalize, suppose that we are given two models, Model A nested in Model B, with degrees of freedom d_A and d_B for A and B, respectively. We assume $d_A > d_B$, and we denote the *population* ML discrepancy function values for the two models as F_A and F_B. When the two models are fitted to the sample covariance matrix, the sample discrepancy function values are minimized, and we denote them as $\hat{F}_A$ and $\hat{F}_B$. The difference between the two sample discrepancy function values, when scaled by a factor of $(N - 1)$, is commonly referred to as the *chi-square difference*, or $\Delta\chi^2$. In this chapter, we denote this well-known likelihood ratio (LR) test statistic for the difference between models as:

$$T = (N - 1)(\hat{F}_A - \hat{F}_B). \tag{7}$$

The No-Difference Hypothesis

In applications, the most frequently encountered test of difference involves the specification of the null hypothesis $H_0 : (F_A - F_B) = 0$, i.e., the two models yield the same population discrepancy function values, against the general alternative of no restrictions, using T as the test statistic. We refer to this test as the test of *no-difference*. Under the null hypothesis, the asymptotic distribution of T is that of a central χ^2 variable with $d = (d_A - d_B)$ degrees of freedom. By fixing an α-level, a critical value c can be obtained from a table of the reference chi-square distribution such that

$$\alpha = 1 - G(c; d), \tag{8}$$

where $G(c; d)$ is the cumulative distribution function (CDF) of a central χ^2 random variable with d degrees of freedom, and $1 - G(c; d)$ gives the tail-area probability of this χ^2 variable to the right of c. If T exceeds c, the null hypothesis is rejected. In practice, rejecting the null hypothesis leads to the conclusion that there is a statistically significant difference in the fit of the two models, with B fitting better than A.

Contemplation of the null hypothesis tested in the no-difference test reveals that it is actually rather uninteresting from a substantive perspective, for the very same reason why the null hypothesis in the χ^2 test of goodness of fit for a single model is like a "straw man." We do not expect that two nested models would ever yield exactly the same discrepancy function values in the population, and whether or not the null hypothesis is rejected is primarily a function of the sample size (Bentler & Bonett, 1980; Tucker & Lewis, 1973). Therefore, the usual no-difference test, if applied blindly, can have serious consequences for model selection. That being said, a pressing issue in applications of the no-difference test is the lack of a simple procedure to perform power analysis, so that researchers can have at least some sense of the power of the test given the size of the existing sample, or can plan ahead in study designs to ensure that N is large enough to achieve an adequate level of power to detect the difference.

Power Analysis for the No-Difference Test

Conducting power analysis requires knowledge of the distribution of the test statistic under the alternative hypothesis. The power analysis procedure outlined here is an extension of the results in MacCallum, Browne, and Sugawara (1996), and hence follows their general principle. To begin, we state a well-known distributional result given in Steiger, Shapiro, and Browne (1985). When H_0 is false, an alternative hypothesis of the form $H_1 : (F_A - F_B) = \delta$ must be true, where $\delta > 0$. Under the assumption of *population drift*, the distribution of T under H_1 is approximately noncentral χ^2 with d degrees of freedom and noncentrality parameter

$$\lambda = (N - 1)(F_A - F_B) = (N - 1)\delta. \tag{9}$$

The *population drift* assumption basically stipulates that neither Model A nor B be badly misspecified (for details, see Steiger et al., 1985, p. 256).

Given both the null and alternative distributions of the test statistic T, computation of power of the no-difference test requires specification of the noncentrality parameter, δ, but this proves difficult if one attempts to somehow compute it directly using the ML discrepancy function defined in Equation 6, because the scale of the maximum Wishart likelihood is not directly interpretable. We need a sensible way to establish δ, preferably in terms of a measure of effect size that is easily interpretable and on a more standardized scale. We note that the specification of the noncentrality parameter is a common theme in all power analysis procedures, and once it is specified, computation of power becomes straightforward.

One viable option is to establish δ by using a measure of goodness of fit that is a function of the population discrepancy function value. More specifically, we propose using the RMSEA measure (Browne & Cudeck, 1993; Steiger & Lind, 1980) because the scale of this measure is somewhat better understood in comparison with alternative measures such as the GFI and AGFI (Jöreskog & Sörbom, 1996), especially when it is applied in the context of power analysis for covariance structure models (see, e.g., MacCallum & Hong, 1997). There already exist guidelines for interpreting this measure (Browne & Cudeck, 1993) and it has been studied in large-scale simulations (e.g., Curran, Bollen, Paxton, Kirby, & Chen, 2002; Hu & Bentler, 1999). Although there are no rigid decision rules regarding the interpretation of RMSEA values, it is relatively common in applications to view RMSEA values in the range of .05 or lower as indicating close fit, values in the range of .07 – .08 as fair fit, and values greater than .10 as poor fit. Note that there is also simulation evidence that these cutoff values may change as model characteristics change (Curran et al., 2002). It has also been shown that the magnitude of error variances may impact RMSEA values (Browne, MacCallum, Kim, Andersen, & Glaser, 2002). Although not infallible, we feel that in general RMSEA serves the purpose of specifying the noncentrality parameter reasonably well.

We designate the two population RMSEA values as $\varepsilon_A = \sqrt{F_A/d_A}$ and $\varepsilon_B = \sqrt{F_B/d_B}$, for Model A and Model B, respectively. By simple algebra, we find that δ can be expressed in terms of the pair of RMSEA values as

$$\delta = (F_A - F_B) = (d_A \varepsilon_A^2 - d_B \varepsilon_B^2). \tag{10}$$

Therefore, the researcher may simply choose RMSEA values for each model in such a way as to represent the smallest difference in model fit that would be desirable to detect. Then δ and λ can be computed immediately from Equations 9 and 10. Note that one would normally choose $\varepsilon_A > \varepsilon_B$ because Model A is more constrained than model B and would tend to have poorer fit. Once this pair of RMSEA values is chosen, and λ determined, the distribution of T under the alternative hypothesis is completely specified, and computation of power becomes routine. Let π be the power of the test under consideration, then

$$\pi = 1 - G(c; d, \lambda), \tag{11}$$

where $G(c;d,\lambda)$ is the cumulative distribution function of a noncentral χ^2 variable with d degrees of freedom and noncentrality parameter λ, and $1 - G(c;d,\lambda)$ gives the tail-area probability of this noncentral χ^2 variable to the right of the critical value c. Distributions and relevant areas for a typical case are illustrated in Figure 3.1. A SAS program for the computation of power is provided in MacCallum et al. (2005).

As an illustration, we apply the foregoing procedure to an empirical study. Shorey, Snyder, Yang, and Lewin (2003) compared a series of structural equation models using the no-difference test (pp. 700-701, esp. Table 2), and we demonstrate how power can be computed for the test of the difference between what they called Model 1 and Model 5, where Model 5 is nested in Model 1.

FIGURE 3.1
Null and alternative distributions of the test statistic for determining statistical Power.

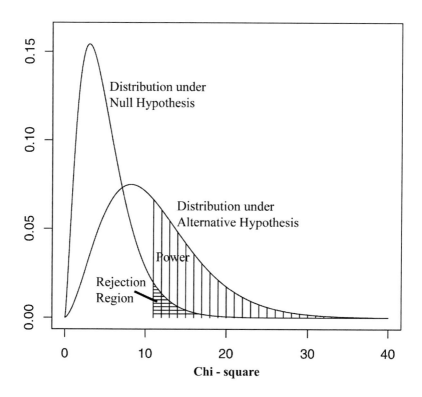

Adapting their numbering system, their Model 1 corresponds to Model B in our notation, and their Model 5 is our Model A. Their sample size was $N = 196$. To compute power, we need to specify a pair of RMSEA values. Some general guidelines for choosing the RMSEA values can be found in MacCallum et al. (2006). There is no doubt that a better choice can be made by incorporating substantive knowledge, but here we simply choose $\varepsilon_A = .06$ and $\varepsilon_B = .04$ for illustrative purposes. Using these values, we obtain $\delta = .2144$ from Equation 10, so the noncentrality parameter is $\lambda = (N - 1)d = 41.808$ using Equation 9.

From Equation 11, we compute the tail-area probability to the right of c under the noncentral χ^2 distribution with 4 degrees of freedom and noncentrality λ, and this probability is equal to .99. Thus, for Models A and B as described earlier, if the true difference in fit is represented by $\varepsilon_A = .06$ and $\varepsilon_B = .04$, and if we conduct a test of the null hypothesis of no difference in fit using $N = 196$ and $\alpha = .05$, the probability of rejecting that null hypothesis is approximately .99.

The result of the test conducted by Shorey et al. (2003) can be summarized as follows. With a sample size of $N = 196$, Model A yielded a minimum discrepancy function χ^2 of 191.64 with $d = 104$ degrees of freedom, and for Model B, $\chi^2 = 190.11$ with $d = 100$ degrees of freedom. Consequently, $T = 1.53$. Referring T to the CDF of a central χ^2 distribution with $d = 4$ degrees of freedom, we find the p-value for the null hypothesis, $H_0 : (F_A - F_B) = 0$, to be 0.82, so there is not enough evidence to reject the null. Because the probability of rejecting the null hypothesis of no difference was about .99, the authors' finding of a nonsignificant difference between the two models in question cannot be attributed to low statistical power (at least under the conditions of the power analysis just presented).

A related question is the determination of the sample size N necessary to achieve a desired level of power given Models A and B and a specified effect size. The capability to address questions of this form would be valuable in research design. A simple procedure has been developed and is described along with corresponding SAS code in MacCallum et al. (2005).

It is also of interest to see whether the method we described can be adapted to the case of multisample models. Extension of the developments in this article to the multisample case requires consideration of whether or how to modify the definition of RMSEA for that case. Steiger (1998) proposes a modification of this definition wherein RMSEA is expressed as $\varepsilon = \sqrt{G}\sqrt{F/df}$, where G is the number of groups, but this new definition alters the original interpretation of RMSEA as the square root of discrepancy per degrees of freedom. We choose to retain the original definition of RMSEA, i.e., $\varepsilon = \sqrt{F/df}$, and thus the developments in Equations (10) and (11) are left unaltered even in the multisample case. Researchers wishing to adopt Steiger's (1998) definition may simply divide the right-hand side of Equation (10) by $\sqrt{G}$, and from there everything else remains the same.

Alternative Power Analysis Procedures for the No-Difference Test

The critical feature of the method for power analysis described earlier is the use of the RMSEA fit measure as the basis for establishing an effect size, and in turn a value of the noncentrality parameter of the distribution of T under the alternative hypothesis. This RMSEA-based approach follows directly from previous work by MacCallum et al. (1996), but it is not the only possible method for establishing the noncentrality parameter. A more complete account of alternative procedures is given in MacCallum et al. (2006), so here we mention only one method that is quite different from our procedure.

This alternative procedure is essentially an extension of Satorra and Saris' (1985) power analysis procedure for testing the fit of a single model. Adapting their method to the case of two competing models, with A nested in B, the first step is to establish numerical values for all parameters in Model B. Given such a set of parameter values for Model B, the implied covariance matrix $\mathbf{\Sigma}_B$ can be easily computed, for instance, by simply fixing all parameter values in a structural equation modeling software application and taking the implied covariance matrix from the output as $\mathbf{\Sigma}_B$. Model A is then fit to $\mathbf{\Sigma}_B$, yielding a discrepancy function value designated F_A. The noncentrality parameter for the distribution of T under the alternative hypothesis is $\lambda = (N-1)F_A$. (Note that in general $\lambda = (N-1)(F_A - F_B)$, but that $F_B \equiv 0$ in the Satorra-Saris formulation.) From this point on, the computation of power proceeds exactly as defined earlier in Equation 11. Therefore, the alternative procedure due to Satorra and Saris simply uses a different approach for specifying λ. However, there are important conceptual differences between the two power analysis procedures. The method based on the work of Satorra and Saris treats Model B as correctly specified in the population, hence $F_B \equiv 0$, and Model A as misspecified in a way defined by the difference in specification of the two models. The parameters that differentiate the models are assigned numerical values that are treated as if they were true population values. By contrast, the RMSEA-based procedure that we proposed earlier does not treat either model as if it were correct in the population. Rather, both models can be viewed as being incorrect in the population (via specification of nonzero RMSEA values), a feature that is undoubtedly more consistent with the nature of models in the real world. In addition, in the procedure we propose, there is no need to assign numerical values to parameters that the models have in common, and the outcome of the power computation will not depend on which parameters differentiate the models.

A Null Hypothesis of Small-Difference

As we have argued earlier, the null hypothesis of no difference between two competing models is of limited practical value, and we also mentioned that the same issue is present in the context of testing the fit of a single model. The null hypothesis in a conventional LR test is that the model under scrutiny is exactly correct in the population, which is always false in practice for any parsimonious model. To deal with this problem, Browne and Cudeck (1993) proposed a test of the null hypothesis of close fit rather than exact fit. Using RMSEA as a basis for their approach, they suggested testing $H_0 : \varepsilon \leq .05$, meaning that the model fits closely in the population. This null hypothesis may well be true and is certainly of more empirical interest, and a test of this hypothesis is not compromised by having a very large N. Browne and Cudeck's (1993) approach can be viewed as a direct application of The Good-Enough Principle (Serlin & Lapsley, 1985), which, when applied to the present context, basically holds that a range hypothesis of acceptable fit is preferable to a point hypothesis of perfect fit.

We suggest that in the context of model comparisons, the Good-Enough Principle can be applied constructively again, by considering a null hypothesis of small difference in population discrepancy function values. Given Models A and B, we propose to test a null hypothesis of the form $H_0 : (F_A - F_B) \leq \delta^*$, where δ^* is some specified small number. Building on Browne and Cudeck's (1993) work, we make use of the RMSEA as a basis for establishing δ^*. By the Good-Enough Principle, one could specify values of ε_A^* and ε_B^* so as to represent a small difference in fit between the models (e.g., $\varepsilon_A^* = .06$ and $\varepsilon_B^* = .05$). Once this pair of RMSEA values is determined, δ^* can be computed from the relationship between fit function values and the RMSEA laid out in Equation (10), i.e., $\delta^* = (d_A \varepsilon_A^{*2} - d_B \varepsilon_B^{*2})$. We still use T as the test statistic, but under this null hypothesis, T has a noncentral χ^2 distribution with $d = (d_A - d_B)$ degrees of freedom, and noncentrality parameter $\lambda^* = (N - 1)d^*$. Then the decision as to whether H_0 is rejected at level α becomes a matter of finding a critical value c^* from the aforementioned noncentral χ^2 distribution, such that

$$\alpha = 1 - G(c^*; d, \lambda^*), \tag{12}$$

where $G(c^*; d, \lambda^*)$ is the CDF of a noncentral χ^2 variable with d degrees of freedom, and noncentrality parameter λ^*. Rejection of the null hypothesis of small difference implies that the observed difference between the models is too large for us to believe that the true difference is small. Failure to reject will imply that the observed difference is small enough for us to believe that the true difference is small. Such an approach will also alleviate the sample size problem associated with the no-difference hypothesis test. SAS code for carrying out the necessary computations is provided in MacCallum et al. (2006).

To illustrate the potential utility of this approach in evaluating differences between models, we test a null hypothesis of a small difference in fit in an empirical example that utilizes multi-sample CSM analysis in a cross-cultural context. Kang, Shaver, Sue, Min, and Jing's (2003) study involved respondents from four countries, and total $N = 639$. On page 1603 the authors tested a series of nested models to determine whether a particular coefficient should be constrained to be equal across groups. The χ^2 difference is $T = 9.05$ with $d = d_A$ $- d_B = 761 - 758 = 3$. For the test of no difference, the critical value from a central χ^2 distribution is $c^* = 7.81$, so the decision is to reject the constraints imposed in Model A, meaning that the groups differ significantly with respect to this particular path coefficient. It would be interesting to look at the result of a test of small difference, say, $\varepsilon_A^* = .06$ and $\varepsilon_B^* = .05$, so $\delta^* = [(761)(.06)^2$ $- (758)(.05)^2] = .8446$ by Equation 10. We can then define the null hypothesis as $H_0 : (F_A^* - F_B^*) \leq .8446$. The reference distribution for T under this null hypothesis is noncentral χ^2 with $d = 3$ degrees of freedom and noncentrality parameter $\lambda^* = (639 - 1)(.8446) = 538.85$. At $\alpha = .05$, the critical value is $c^* = 619.99$, indicating clear failure to reject the null hypothesis of the small difference as represented by $\varepsilon_A^* = .06$ and $\varepsilon_B^* = .05$. Therefore the constraint in question may well be plausible (according to the Good-Enough Principle) and perhaps should not have been rejected based on the result of the test of no-difference alone.

Power Analysis for the Small-Difference Test

Given the preceding developments, it is straightforward to combine our power analysis procedure with the specification of the null hypothesis of small difference into a more general power analysis procedure in which the null hypothesis specifies a small difference in fit and the alternative hypothesis specifies a larger difference, with those differences defined in terms of specified RMSEA values for the models.

We give a brief account of this procedure here; a more complete discussion can be found in MacCallum et al. (2006). The null hypothesis is that of a small difference in fit, that is, $H_0 : (F_A^* - F_B^*) \leq \delta_0^*$. The alternative hypothesis specifies that the difference $(F_A^* - F_B^*)$ be greater than δ_0^*, i.e., $H_1 : (F_A^* - F_B^*) = \delta_1^*$, where $\delta_1^* > \delta_0^*$. As before, we suggest establishing useful values of δ_0^* and δ_1^* by selecting two pairs of RMSEA values and obtaining δ_0^* and δ_1^* using Equation 10. To establish a value for δ_0^* one would select a pair of RMSEA values, denoted now as ε_{0A} and ε_{0B}, to represent the small difference in fit that defines H_0. To establish a value for δ_1^*, one chooses RMSEA values ε_{1A} and ε_{1B} to represent a larger difference in fit under H_1. From then on, the procedure follows the same general template as the method described earlier, with the simple modification that now both the null and the alternative distributions (as shown in Figure 3.1) are noncentral χ^2. Specifically, the distribution of the test statistic T under H_0 will be noncentral χ^2, with $d = (d_A - d_B)$ degrees of freedom and noncentrality parameter $\lambda_0 = (N - 1)\delta_0^*$. The distribution under H_1 will be noncentral χ^2 with the same degrees of freedom and noncentrality parameter $\lambda_1 = (N - 1)\delta_1^*$. Given a specified level of α, a critical value can be determined from the null distribution, and power is computed as the area under the alternative distribution to the right of that critical value, just as shown in Figure 3.1 earlier. Again, SAS code for carrying out the necessary computations is provided in MacCallum et al. (2006).

Concluding Remarks

There are two broad issues that we wish to emphasize to close this section on power analysis and specification of the null hypothesis when performing comparisons of nested models. The first issue is the choice of pairs of RMSEA values. Essentially the results of any application of any of the methods we described are contingent on the particular RMSEA values that the user selects. Here we can offer only some general principles. For a more thorough discussion of this issue we refer the reader to MacCallum et al. (2006). For specifying RMSEA values for testing a null hypothesis of a small difference in fit, the user should regard the Good-Enough Principle (Serlin & Lapsley, 1985) as the objective, and pick RMSEA values for Models A and B that represent a difference so small that the user is willing to ignore it. In the context of power analysis, the relevant general principle would be to choose values that represent a difference that the investigator would wish to have a high probability of detecting. In practice, users will need to rely on guidelines for the use of RMSEA as mentioned earlier (Browne & Cudeck, 1993; Steiger, 1994), as well as the characteristics of the models under comparison.

The second issue has to do with the assumptions involved in our developments. All of the methodological developments presented thus far rely on well known distribution theory and its assumptions. Specifically, we make extensive use of the assumptions that ensure the chi-squaredness of the LR test statistic T, for both the central and noncentral cases. These include multivariate normality, the standard set of regularity conditions on the likelihood to carry out asymptotic expansions, and the population drift assumption (Steiger et al., 1985). As always, however, such assumptions never hold exactly in the real world, so the user should always be cautious in the application of these methods in data analysis and should watch for potential pitfalls due to assumption violations. MacCallum et al. (2006) discuss the consequences of such violations.

MODEL SELECTION AND MODEL COMPLEXITY

Model Selection and Generalizability

In the preceding section we provide and illustrate methods for comparing rival models in terms of a noncentrality-based fit index, RMSEA. We suggest that this strategy is appropriate for statistically comparing the fit of rival, parametrically nested models, but the procedure depends in part on the researcher's judgment of appropriate choices for ε_A^* and ε_B^*, or what, in the researcher's judgment, constitutes the smallest difference in fit that it would be interesting to detect. In practice, a model can demonstrate good fit for any number of reasons, including a theory's proximity to the objective truth (or *verisimilitude*; Meehl, 1990), random chance, simply having many free parameters, or by possessing a structure allowing parameters to assume values which lead to good model fit for many different data patterns—even those generated by other processes not considered by the researcher. In other words, models can demonstrate close fit to data for reasons other than being "correct," even if one grants that true models are possible to specify (we do not), so good fit should represent only one criterion by which we judge a model's usefulness or quality.

Another criterion of model success that has found much support in mathematical psychology and the cognitive modeling literature is *generalizability* (or replicability). The idea here is that it is not sufficient for a model to show good fit to the data in hand. If a model is to be useful, it should *predict* other data generated by the same latent process, or capture the regularities underlying data consisting of signal and noise. If a model is highly complex, refitting the model to new data from scratch will not advance our knowledge by much; if a model's structure is complex enough to show good fit to one data set, it may be complex enough to show good fit to many other data sets simply by adjusting its parameters. In other words, pure goodness of fit represents fit to signal *plus* fit to noise. However, if model parameters are fixed to values estimated in one setting, and the model still demonstrates good fit in a second sample (i.e., if the model *cross-validates* well), the model has gained considerable support. A model's potential to cross-validate well is its generalizability, and it is possible to quantify generalizability based only on knowledge of the model's form and of its fit to a given data set. By quantifying a model's potential to cross-validate, generalizability avoids problems associated with good fit arising from fitting error or from a model's flexibility. It also does not rely on unsupportable assumptions regarding a model's absolute truth or falsity. Therefore, generalizability is arguably a better criterion for model retention than is goodness of fit per se (Pitt & Myung, 2002).

Earlier we stated that adopting a model selection perspective requires a fundamental shift in how researchers approach model evaluation. Traditional hypothesis testing based on LR tests results in a dichotomous accept–reject decision without quantifying how much confidence one should place in a model, or how much relative confidence one should place in each member of a set of rival models. In model comparison, on the other hand, no null hypothesis is tested (Burnham & Anderson, 2004). The appropriate sample size is not selected based on power to reject hypotheses of exact or close fit (obviously, since no such hypotheses are tested), but rather to attain acceptable levels of precision of parameter estimates. Rather than retaining or discarding models on a strict accept–reject basis, models are ranked in terms of their generalizability, a notion that combines fit with parsimony, both of which are hallmark characteristics of a good model.

The model selection approach does not require that any of the rival models be correct, or even (counterintuitively) that any of the models fit well in an absolute sense. The process is designed in such a way that researchers will gravitate toward successively better models after repeated model comparisons. The more such comparisons a particular model survives, the better its track record becomes, and the more support it accrues. Therefore, it is incumbent upon scientists to devise models that are not only superior to competing models, but also perform well in an absolute sense. Such models will, in the long run, possess higher probabilities of surviving risky tests, facilitate substantive explanation, predict future data, and lead to the formulation of novel hypotheses. But, again, the model selection strategy we advocate does not require that any of the competing models be correct or even close to correct in the absolute sense.

Adjusting Fit for Complexity

With rare exceptions, traditional fit indices in CSM are based on the LR test statistic described earlier in Equation (7). In recognition of the limitations of the raw χ^2, most indices employ some correction for model complexity. For example, the Δ_2 index proposed by Bollen (1989) subtracts df from the denominator as an adjustment for complexity:

$$\Delta_2 = \frac{\chi_b^2 - \chi_m^2}{\chi_b^2 - df_m} \tag{13}$$

where χ_b^2 is the fit associated with a baseline model and χ_m^2 and df_m are associated with the hypothesized model. The adjustment has the effect of penalizing fit for the number of free parameters. Many fit indices contain similar adjustments. For example, RMSEA divides by df as a way of distributing lack of fit across all parameter constraints. In this way, RMSEA penalizes fit due to unnecessary free parameters.

However, complexity is not governed completely by the number of free parameters (MacCallum, 2003; Pitt, Myung, & Zhang, 2002; Preacher, 2003, in press). The corrections employed in most indices carry the implicit assumption that all free parameters contribute equally to a model's ability to fit data (or, that all model constraints contribute equally to *lack* of fit). Yet it is easy to see how, in a loose sense, some parameters may be more important than others in a given model. For example, constraining a covariance parameter linking otherwise disparate sections of a model to zero would probably limit a model's potential to fit data more than would constraining, say, a factor loading to zero. More generally, parameters that appear in many equations for implied covariances likely influence complexity more so than do parameters that appear in fewer equations. Fortunately, information theory offers some alternatives to traditional fit indices that avoid quantifying complexity as if it were a strict linear function of the number of parameters.

Information-Theoretic Criteria

In contrast to model selection methods rooted in Bayesian or frequentist traditions, much research points to information theory as a likely source for the optimal model selection criterion. Selection criteria based on information theory seek to locate the one model, out of a pool of rival models, which shows the optimal fidelity, or signal-to-noise ratio; this is the model that demonstrates the best balance between fit and parsimony. This balance was termed *generalizability* earlier. Several popular model selection criteria were either derived from, or are closely related to, information theory. The most popular such criteria are the Akaike information criterion (AIC; Akaike, 1973) and the Bayesian information criterion (BIC; Schwartz, 1978). Excellent treatments of AIC and BIC can be found elsewhere (e.g., Burnham & Anderson, 2002, 2004; Kuha, 2004).

Many information-based criteria may be construed as attempts to estimate the Kullback–Leibler (K–L) distance. The K-L distance is the (unknown) information lost by representing the true latent process with an approximating model (Burnham & Anderson, 2004). Even though we cannot compute the K–L distance directly because there is one term in the K–L distance definition that is not possible to estimate, we can approximate *relative* K–L distance in various ways by combining knowledge of the data with knowledge of the models under scrutiny. Of great importance for model comparison, the ability to approximate relative K–L distance permits the ranking of models in terms of their estimated verisimilitude, tempered by our uncertainty about the degree of approximation. In other words, using information-based criteria, models can be ranked in terms of estimated generalizability.

Minimum Description Length and the Normalized Maximum Likelihood

Information-based criteria such as AIC and BIC are used with great frequency in model comparisons and with increasing frequency in applications of CSM. However, they suffer from at least two major drawbacks. First, they employ complexity adjustments that are functions only of the number of free model parameters. Second, they implicitly require the strong assumption that a correct model exists. We focus instead on a newer criterion that remains relatively unknown in the social sciences, yet we feel has great promise for application in model selection. This is the principle of *minimum description length* (MDL: Grünwald, 2000; Myung, Navarro, & Pitt, 2005; Rissanen, 1996, 2001; Stine, 2004). The MDL principle involves construing data as compressible strings, and conceiving of models as compression codes. If models are viewed as data compression codes, the optimal code would be one that compresses (or simply represents) the data with the greatest fidelity. With relevance to the limitations of criteria such as AIC and BIC, the MDL principle involves no assumption that a true model exists. If one accepts that a model's proximity to the truth is either undefined (i.e., that the notion of a true model is merely a convenience and bears no direct relation to reality) or is at any rate impossible to determine, then the MDL principle offers a viable alternative to traditional methods of model selection. Excellent discussions of the MDL principle can be found in Grünwald (2000), Grünwald, Myung, and Pitt (2005), Hansen and Yu (2001), and Markon and Krueger (2004). Three quantifications of the MDL principle are *normalized maximum likelihood* (NML), *Fisher information approximation* (FIA), and *stochastic information complexity* (SIC). NML is quantified as:

$$\text{NML} = \frac{L(y|\hat{\theta})}{\int\limits_{S} L(z|\hat{\theta}(z))dz}, \tag{14}$$

or the likelihood of the data given the model divided by the sum of all such likelihoods. FIA is quantified as:

$$\text{FIA} = -\ln L\left(y|\hat{\theta}\right) + \frac{q}{2}\ln\left(\frac{N}{2\pi}\right) + \ln\int\limits_{\Theta} \sqrt{|I(\theta)|}d\theta, \tag{15}$$

an approximation to the negative logarithm of NML that makes use of the number of free parameters (q) and the determinant of the Fisher information matrix, $I(\theta)$. SIC, an approximation to FIA that is typically more tractable in practice, is quantified as:

$$\text{SIC} = -\ln L\left(y|\hat{\theta}\right) + \frac{1}{2}\ln|nI(\theta)|. \tag{16}$$

The Appendix (see Quant.KU.edu) contains more detailed discussion of these criteria. NML, FIA, and SIC all represent model fit penalized by the model's average ability to fit any given data.

NML is similar in spirit to selection criteria such as AIC and BIC in several respects, save that preferable models are associated with higher values of NML but with lower values of AIC or BIC.[1] All of these criteria can be framed as functions of the likelihood value adjusted for model complexity, although the complexity correction assumes different forms for different criteria. NML differs from criteria like AIC and BIC mainly in that not every parameter is penalized to the same extent. NML imposes an adjustment commensurate with the degree to which each free parameter increases complexity, as reflected in the model's general data-fitting capacity. Consequently, NML does not assume (as do AIC and BIC) that each parameter contributes equally to goodness of fit. Therefore, both parametric and structural components of complexity are considered. A major additional advantage of NML (which it shares with AIC and BIC) is that it does not require rival models to be nested. Thus, if two competing theories posit different patterns of constraints, such models can be directly compared using criteria derived from information theory.

Applying MDL in Practice

To illustrate how the MDL principle may be employed in practice, we present two brief examples from the applied literature. In both examples we compute NML; in the second, we supplement NML with computation of SIC because original data were available with which to compute the $|nI(\theta)|$ term. Neither the denominator term in NML (see Equation [A1]) nor the structural complexity term in FIA (see Equation [A2]) can be computed directly in the context of CSM. Numerical integration techniques are typically applied instead. To facilitate computation of NML, we simulated the data space by generating large numbers of random uniform correlation matrices (R) using Markov chain Monte Carlo (MCMC) methods.[2] These matrices were uniform in the sense that all possible R matrices had equal *apriori* probabilities of being generated. All models were fit to all simulated matrices, and the likelihoods were averaged to form the denominator of the NML formula.[3] The numerators were supplied by simply noting the likelihood value associated with the converged solution for each model applied to real data.

Example 1. Our first demonstration makes use of models provided by In-

---

[1]In fact, BIC may be obtained as a special case of MDL if structural complexity is neglected (Myung et al., 2005).

[2]Fortran 90 code is available from the first author upon request. See Preacher (2003) for details.

[3]An average was used rather than a sum because (a) computation of NML is more manageable and intuitive using the mean likelihood rather than a sum of likelihoods and (b) the rank ordering of models is not affected. Solutions with estimation errors were omitted from this averaging.

gram, Betz, Mindes, Schmitt, and Smith (2001) in a study of the effects and correlates of unsupportive social interactions.

Part of their study involved comparison of five rival confirmatory factor models, depicted in Figure 3.2, which we denote Models $I1 - I5$. The four primary factors in each model represent dimensions of the Unsupportive Social Interactions Inventory (USII). Each factor was measured by three 2-item parcels, for a total of $p = 12$ variables. After removing one outlier, the five models were fit to data from $N = 221$ introductory psychology students. Based on LR tests, the authors selected Model $I5$ as superior to its rivals.

NML was computed for each model. The empirical likelihoods were obtained by employing the following formula using the χ^2 statistics reported in Ingram et al. (2001, Table 4):

$$L(y|\hat{\theta}) = e^{\frac{\chi^2}{-2(N-1)}} \tag{17}$$

The complexity estimates were obtained by fitting each model to 10,000 random $\mathbf{R}$ matrices and computing the mean obtained likelihood. Computation of complexity was based only on proper solutions with no convergence errors. The resulting NML, along with the number of solutions on which computation was based, can be found in Table 3.1.

Whereas the authors chose Model $I5$ as the preferred model based on LR tests ($I5$ showed significantly better fit in terms of χ^2 than did the next-worst fitting model), application of NML indicates a preference for Model $I2$. The higher order factor model was characterized by the highest NML in the set of models compared, implying that $I2$ has greater potential for replicating in future samples than its rivals. Although Model $I5$ demonstrated the best absolute fit, it did so at the price of having a more complex structure and more free parameters.

TABLE 3.1
NML Estimates for the Five Factor Models Compared by Ingram et al. (2001)

Model	Empirical χ^2	df	NML	Solutions without Estimation Errors
I1 One Factor	325.34	54	2.867	9,999
I2 Higher Order	155.38	50	3.528	9,870
I3 Four Factor	152.45	48	3.223	9,848
I4 Higher Order with One Cross-Loading	145.83	49	3.003	9,699
I5 Four Factor with One Cross-Loading	131.42	47	3.188	9,716

TABLE 3.2

NML and SIC Estimates for the Three Models Compared by Larose et al. (2002)

Model	Empirical χ^2	df	NML	SIC	Solutions without estimation Errors
L1 Cognitive Bias	17.07	8	1.759	66.294	9,319
L2 Social Networks	24.57	7	1.520	71.088	9,221
L3 Cognitive-Network	4.94	6	1.404	76.448	9,225

Note. Because the x^2 values obtained through reanalysis differed slightly from those reported by Larose et al. (2002), we report the values we obtained. These differences are likely to due rounding error in Larose et al.'s reported correlations.

This finding has implications for the conclusions drawn by Ingram et al. (2001). Because the authors used a model selection approach that does not consider the relaive complexities of rival models, the model that showed the best absolute fit was also the one with the highest complexity, or the best *apriori* expected fit. In essence, the chosen model capitalized on an unfair advantage. In contrast, a selection criterion that appropriately adjusts fit for complexity selected a model with a better balance of fit and parsimony.

Example 2. Our second example draws on three covariance structure models compared by Larose, Guay, and Boivin (2002). The authors were primarily interested in comparing the Cognitive Bias Model and Social Network Model, two models proposed to explain variability in a Loneliness latent variable using Attachment Security, Emotional Support, and Social Support. These two models (which we denote $L1$ and $L2$) are presented in the first two panels of Figure 3.3. Based on results indicating that both models fit the data well and were thus viable explanations for the observed pattern of effects, the authors devised a third model combining features of the first two, dubbed the Cognitive-Network Model ($L3$ in Figure 3.3).

All three models were found to fit the data well using self-report measures ($N = 125$), and to fit even better using friend-report measures. In both cases, the Cognitive-Network Model was found to fit the data significantly better than either the Cognitive Bias Model or the Social Network Model. Following procedures already described, we reevaluated Larose et al.'s models (fit to self-report data) using NML. Results are reported in Table 3.2. Because raw data were available in their article, we are also able to provide estimates of SIC.

Contrary to the authors' findings, both NML and SIC indicate that the Cognitive Bias Model performs better than either the Social Networks Model or the proposed Cognitive-Network Model in terms of generalizability. Combining features of two already well-fitting models does not necessarily grant a scientific advantage when the resulting model is more complex than either of its

FIGURE 3.2
Rival models investigated by Ingram et al. (2001).

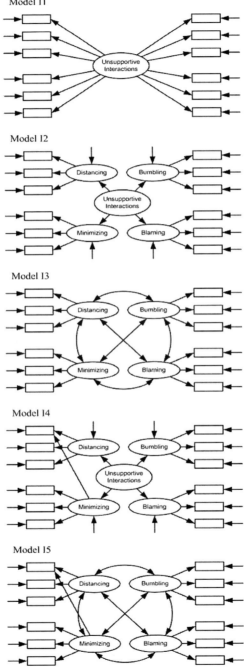

FIGURE 3.3
Rival models investigated by Larose et al. (2002).

Model L1

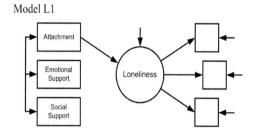

Model L2

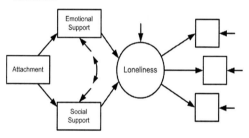

Model L3

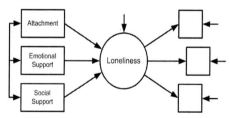

competitors. In this instance, as in the previous example, the chosen model was
selected primarily because it showed better absolute fit; this better fit was due
in part to the fact that the Cognitive-Network Model was more complex than
its competitors. An implication of this finding is that, whereas the Cognitive-
Network Model may fit the given data set better than the Cognitive Bias Model
and the Social Networks Model in absolute terms, it has a lower likelihood of
generalizing well to future data.

Summary

Like other information-theoretic selection criteria, MDL does not require rival
models to be parametrically nested. Nor does its use require the assumption
that a true model exists. Furthermore, MDL considers more sources of complexity than simply a model's number of parameters. In sum, we feel that the
MDL principle has great potential for use in model comparisons in CSM.

Limitations

Of course, NML is not a panacea. Three limitations of NML are that it is
difficult to compute, it relies on the assumptions of maximum likelihood, and
it involves often arbitrary bounds on the data space. The first limitation will
be overcome as processor speeds increase and as NML becomes included in
standard model estimation packages. In the meantime, the more tractable MDL
approximation, SIC (Rissanen, 1989), can be used if the numerical integration
necessary for NML proves too time-intensive. As for the second limitation, it is
unknown how robust MDL methods are to violations of ML assumptions. This
would be a fruitful avenue for future research.

The third limitation is more challenging because it requires the researcher
to make a subjective decision regarding boundaries on the data space. We
restricted attention to correlation matrices for simplicity. We recognize that
many modeling applications require covariance matrices rather than correlation matrices (and sometimes also mean vectors). For example, virtually any
application in which models are fit to multiple groups simultaneously, such as
in factorial invariance studies, requires the use of covariance matrices. Growth
curve modeling requires covariance matrices and mean vectors. Lower and upper boundaries must be imposed on generated means and variances if such data
are required, and these choices constitute even more subjective input. It is
generally agreed that data generated for the purpose of quantifying model complexity should be uniformly representative of the data space (Dunn, 2000), yet
choices regarding the range of data generation may exert great influence on the
ranking of competing models. It is thus important that reasonable bounds be

investigated to ensure reasonable and stable model rankings. A discussion of the implications for arbitrary integration ranges can be found in Lanterman (2005).

DISCUSSION

We have proposed two alternatives to traditional methods of comparing co-variance structure models. Both alternatives were suggested in response to limitations of the popular LR test; the most severe limitation is that the hypothesis tested by the LR test (that two models have identical fit) is never true in practice, so investigating its truth or falsity would seem to be a questionable undertaking (MacCallum et al., 2006). The first alternative procedure posits a modified null hypothesis such that the difference in fit between two nested models is within tolerable limits. The second alternative we discuss is to compare rival (not necessarily nested) models in terms of relative generalizability using selection indices based on the MDL principle. Both methods encourage a model comparison approach to science that is likely to move the field in the direction of successively better models.

There are interesting parallels between the strategies proposed here and a framework for model assessment proposed by Linhart and Zucchini (1986) and elaborated upon by Cudeck and Henly (1991) in the context of CSM. Because it relies on RMSEA to specify null and alternative hypotheses, the first approach (using RMSEA to specify hypotheses of close fit) can be seen as way to compare nested models in terms of their *approximation discrepancy*, or lack of fit in the population. In other words, this method is a way to gauge models' relative nearness to the objectively true data-generating process, or their relative verisimilitudes. The second method of model comparison makes use of the MDL principle to facilitate comparison of models in terms of their relative generalizabilities, or abilities to predict future data arising from the same generating process. This strategy can be seen as a way to compare models (nested or non-nested) in terms of their *overall discrepancy*, tempering information about lack of fit with lack of confidence due to sampling error. When N is large, enough information is available to support highly complex models if such models are appropriate. When N is small, uncertainty obliges us to conservatively select less complex models until more information becomes available (Cudeck & Henly, 1991). Thus, NML and similar criteria are direct applications of the parsimony principle, or Occam's razor.

The parallels between the measures of verisimilitude and generalizability on one hand, and the Linhart–Zucchini and Cudeck–Henly frameworks on the other, perhaps deserve more attention in future research. High verisimilitude and high generalizability are both desirable characteristics for models to possess, but selecting the most generalizable model does not necessarily imply that the selected model is also closest to the objective truth. Therefore we do not advocate choosing one approach or the other, or even limiting attention to these two strategies. Rather, we suggest combining these strategies with existing model evaluation and selection techniques so that judgments may be based on as much information as possible. Regardless of what strategy the researcher chooses, the strongest recommendation we can make is that researchers should, whenever circumstances permit it, adopt a model selection strategy rather than to evaluate single models in isolation. The methods illustrated here are viable alternatives to the standard approach, and can be applied easily in many modeling settings involving longitudinal and/or ecological data.

ACKNOWLEDGMENTS

This work was funded in part by National Institute on Drug Abuse Grant DA16883 awarded to the first author while at the University of North Carolina at Chapel Hill. We thank Daniel J. Navarro for providing helpful comments.

REFERENCES

Akaike, H. (1973). Information theory and an extension of the maximum likelihood principle. In B. N. Petrov & F. Csaki (Eds.), *Second international symposium on information theory* (p. 267). Budapest, Hungary: Akademiai Kiado.

Bentler, P. M., & Bonett, D. G. (1980). Significance tests and goodness of fit in the analysis of covariance structures. *Psychological Bulletin, 88*, 588–606.

Bollen, K. A. (1989). *Structural equations with latent variables.* New York: Wiley.

Browne, M. W., & Cudeck, R. (1993). Alternative ways of assessing model fit. In K. A. Bollen & J. S. Long (Eds.), *Testing structural equation models* (pp. 136-162). Newbury Park, CA: Sage.

Browne, M. W., MacCallum, R. C., Kim, C., Andersen, B. L., & Glaser, R. (2002). When fit indices and residuals are incompatible. *Psychological Methods, 7,* 403-421.

Burnham, K. P., & Anderson, D. R. (2002). *Model selection and multimodel inference: A practical information-theoretic approach* (2nd ed.). New York: Springer.

Burnham, K. P., & Anderson, D. R. (2004). Multimodel inference: Understanding AIC and BIC in model selection. *Sociological Methods & Research, 33*, 261-304.

Cudeck, R., & Henly, S. J. (1991). Model selection in covariance structures analysis and the "problem" of sample size: A clarification. *Psychological Bulletin, 109*, 512-519.

Curran, P. J., Bollen, K. A., Paxton, P., Kirby, J., & Chen, F. (2002). The noncentral chi-square distribution in misspecified structural equation models: Finite sample results from a Monte Carlo simulation. *Multivariate Behavioral Research, 37,* 1-36.

Dunn, J. C. (2000). Model complexity: The fit to random data reconsidered. *Psychological Research*, *63*, 174-182.

Greenwald, A. G., Pratkanis, A. R., Leippe, M. R., & Baumgardner, M. H. (1986). Under what conditions does theory obstruct research progress? *Psychological Review*, *93*, 216-229.

Grünwald, P. (2000). Model selection based on minimum description length. *Journal of Mathematical Psychology*, *44*, 133-152.

Grünwald, P., Myung, I. J., & Pitt, M. A. (2005). *Advances in minimum description length: Theory and applications*. Cambridge, MA: The MIT Press.

Hu, L., & Bentler, P. M. (1999). Cutoff criteria for fit indexes in covariance structure analysis: Conventional criteria versus new alternatives. *Structural Equation Modeling*, *6*, 1-55.

Ingram, K. M., Betz, N. E., Mindes, E. J., Schmitt, M. M., & Smith, N. G. (2001). Unsupportive responses from others concerning a stressful life event: Development of the Unsupportive Social Interactions Inventory. *Journal of Social and Clinical Psychology*, *20*, 173-207.

Jöreskog, K. G., & Sörbom, D. (1996). *LISREL 8 user's reference guide*. Uppsala: Scientific Software International.

Kang, S., Shaver, P. R., Sue, S., Min, K., & Jing, H. (2003). Culture-specific patterns in the prediction of life satisfaction: Roles of emotion, relationship quality, and self-esteem. *Personality and Social Psychology Bulletin*, *29*, 1596-1608.

Kuha, J. (2004). AIC and BIC: Comparisons of assumptions and performance. *Sociological Methods & Research*, *33*, 188-229.

Lakatos, I. (1970). Falsification and the methodology of scientific research programmes. In I. Lakatos & A. Musgrave (Eds.), *Criticism and the growth of knowledge* (pp. 91-196). Cambridge, England: Cambridge University Press.

Lanterman, A. D. (2001). Schwarz, Wallace and Rissanen: Intertwining themes in theories of model selection. *International Statistical Review*, *69*, 185-212.

Lanterman, A. D. (2005). Hypothesis testing for Poisson vs. geometric distributions using stochastic complexity. In P. D. Grünwald, I. J. Myung, & M. A. Pitt (Eds.), *Advances in minimum description length: Theory and applications* (pp. 99-123). Cambridge, MA: The MIT Press.

Larose, S., Guay, F., & Boivin, M. (2002). Attachment, social support, and loneliness in young adulthood: A test of two models. *Personality and Social Psychology Bulletin*, *28*, 684-693.

Linhart, H., & Zucchini, W. (1986). *Model selection*. New York: Wiley.

MacCallum, R. C. (2003). Working with imperfect models. *Multivariate Behavioral Research*, *38*, 113-139.

MacCallum, R. C., Browne, M. W., & Cai, L. (2006). Testing differences between nested covariance structure models: Power analysis and null hypotheses. *Psychological Methods*, *11*, 19-35.

MacCallum, R. C., Browne, M. W., & Sugawara, H. M. (1996). Power analysis and determination of sample size for covariance structure modeling. *Psychological Methods*, *1*, 130-149.

MacCallum, R. C., & Hong, S. (1997). Power analysis in covariance structure modeling using GFI and AGFI. *Multivariate Behavioral Research, 32*, 193-210.

Markon, K. E., & Krueger, R. F. (2004). An empirical comparison of information-theoretic selection criteria for multivariate behavior genetic models. *Behavior Genetics, 34*, 593-610.

Meehl, P. E. (1990). Appraising and amending theories: The strategy of Lakatosian defense and two principles that warrant it. *Psychological Inquiry, 1*, 108-141.

Myung, J. I., Navarro, D. J., & Pitt, M. A. (2005). Model selection by normalized maximum likelihood. *Journal of Mathematical Psychology, 50*, 167-179.

Pitt, M. A., & Myung, I. J. (2002). When a good fit can be bad. *TRENDS in Cognitive Sciences, 6*, 421-425.

Pitt, M. A., Myung, I. J., & Zhang, S. (2002). Toward a method of selecting among computational models of cognition. *Psychological Review, 109*, 472-491.

Platt, J. R. (1964, October 16). Strong inference. *Science, 146(3642)*, 347-353.

Popper, K. R. (1959). *The logic of scientific discovery.* London: Hutchinson.

Preacher, K. J. (2003). *The role of model complexity in the evaluation of structural equation models.* Unpublished doctoral dissertation. Ohio State University, Columbus, OH.

Preacher, K. J. (in press). Quantifying parsimony in structural equation modeling. *Multivariate Behavioral Research.*

Rissanen, J. (1989). *Stochastic complexity in statistical inquiry.* Singapore: World Scientific.

Rissanen, J. (1996). Fisher information and stochastic complexity. *IEEE Transactions on Information Theory, 42*, 40-47.

Rissanen, J. (2001). Strong optimality of the normalized ML models as universal codes and information in data. *IEEE Transactions on Information Theory, 47*, 1712-1717.

Satorra, A., & Saris, W. E. (1985). The power of the likelihood ratio test in covariance structure analysis. *Psychometrika, 50*, 83-90.

Schwarz, G. (1978). Estimating the dimension of a model. *The Annals of Statistics, 6*, 461-464.

Serlin, R. C., & Lapsley, D. K. (1985). Rationality in psychological research: The good-enough principle. *American Psychologist, 40*, 73-83.

Shorey, H. S., Snyder, C. R., Yang, X., & Lewin, M. R. (2003). The role of hope as a mediator in recollected parenting, adult attachment, and mental health. *Journal of Social and Clinical Psychology, 22*, 685-715.

Steenkamp, J.-B. E. M., & Baumgartner, H. (1998). Assessing measurement invariance in cross-national consumer research. *Journal of Consumer Research, 25*, 78-90.

Steiger, J. H. (1994). *Structural equation modeling (computer program).* In Statistica/w, version 4.5. Tulsa, OK: Statsoft.

Steiger, J. H. (1998). A note on multiple sample extensions of the RMSEA fit index. *Structural Equation Modeling, 5*, 411-419.

Steiger, J. H., & Lind, J. C. (1980). Statistically based tests for the number of factors.

Paper presented at the annual meeting of the Psychometric Society, Iowa City, IA.

Steiger, J. H., Shapiro, A., & Browne, M. W. (1985). On the multivariate asymptotic distribution of sequential chi-square tests. *Psychometrika*, *50*, 253-264.

Stine, R. A. (2004). Model selection using information theory and the MDL principle. *Sociological Methods & Research*, *33*, 230-260.

Tucker, L. R., & Lewis, C. (1973). A reliability coefficient for maximum likelihood factor analysis. *Psychometrika*, *38*, 1-10.

Vandenberg, R. J., & Lance, C. E. (2000). A review and synthesis of the measurement invariance literature: Suggestions, practices, and recommendations for organizational research. *Organizational Research Methods*, *3*, 4-70.

Weakliem, D. L. (2004). Introduction to the special issue on model selection. *Sociological Methods & Research*, *33*, 167-187.

Zhang, S. (1999). *Applications of geometric complexity and the minimum description length principle in mathematical modeling of cognition*. Unpublished doctoral dissertation. Ohio State University, Columbus, OH.

CHAPTER FOUR

Impact of Measurement Scale in Modeling Development Processes and Ecological Factors

Susan E. Embretson
Georgia Institute of Technology

Developmental and lifespan studies typically involve multiple age groups or multiple occasions of measurement or both. Studies of ecological factors in development can further complicate the analyses by adding yet another grouping factor. That is, grouping may occur on variables that may impact the development of traits, such as interventions, exposure to environmental factors or demographic variables. Such variables may take considerable time to impact the trait. So, measurement is often needed over a broad range of ages and groups.

In these studies, trend or change over time is a primary dependent variable. Such data presents special problems for analysis. Periodically, conferences have been devoted to understanding the issues and resolving the problems in developmental data (Collins & Horn, 1991; Collins & Sayer, 2001; Little, Schnabel & Baumert, 2000). Powerful modeling techniques, including both longitudinal models and multilevel models, have been applied to resolve many complexities in analyzing these data. For example, trend can be related to demographic and grouping variables by applying special formulations of structural equation modeling (e.g., McArdle & Bell, 2000). Furthermore, issues about sample selectivity can be examined by combining structural equation modeling and multilevel modeling (Little, Lindenberger & Maier, 2000).

Although advances in methods for longitudinal data analysis can increase the validity of inferences from developmental and lifespan data, all analyses depend on the quality of the measurements that are used. Most statistical models are applied to measurements that are based on classical test theory.

That is, the measurements have fixed item content and are scaled by reference to group norms. Although problems in using classical test scores for measuring change have been discussed for decades (e.g., Bereiter, 1963; Cronbach & Furby, 1970), their limitations for analyzing trend are less well known.

Consider the growth data in Figure 4.1 which shows the means on three measures at five time periods. All three measures are scaled as classical T-scores, with the mean of 50 and the standard deviation of 10 using the middle time point, Time 3, as the norm group. Considerable growth is observed on all three measures; however, the trend is different. For Measure 2, growth appears linear across time, so that approximately equal changes are observed between each time periods. However, for Measure 1, a decelerating rate of growth is observed. Thus, the greatest change is observed early. For Measure 3, an accelerating rate is observed. Growth is slow initially but then increases with time. If these measures represented three different constructs, a seemingly appropriate conclusion would be that the constructs have different patterns of development. However, this would not be an appropriate inference for the data presented in Figure 4.1. The *same* construct is assessed for all three measures. Thus, the apparent differences in trend result from another factor; namely, the three measures differ in item difficulty level.

FIGURE 4.1

Mean scores of three measures across time.

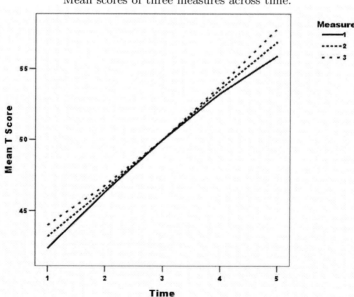

The data shown on Figure 4.1 are simulation data in which the scores for all three measures were generated from the same true trait levels within each time period. The only difference between the three measures was item difficulty level. The easiest measure was Measure 1, which showed a decelerating rate of change over time. The most difficult measure was Measure 3, which showed an accelerating rate of change. The apparent differences in the growth patterns are due merely to scaling artifacts.

Scaling effects also have statistical importance. In a series of studies, Embretson (1994; 1996) showed that statistical inferences are impacted by scaling artifacts such as shown in Figure 4.1. Thus, significant differences will be found in observed scores when the latent true scores do not differ. Contemporary methods for analyzing change, such as latent growth curve analysis (Raykov, 1994; McArdle & Bell, 2000), are also vulnerable to these effects because, although change is measured as a latent variable, the estimation of the effects relies on the metric of the observed scores.

The goal of this chapter is to further elaborate the scale interval problem and to explore solutions. The results are relevant to studies that compare groups that differ in initial levels of the dependent variable. Included in the chapter are simulations of both group differences in trend and group differences in change. Methods for resolving scaling issues are described and applied to the simulation data.

SIMULATION DATA

The methods employed to generate the simulation data in the examples reported below are described in this section. The methods are developed formally to accurately describe the data. However, the reader need not follow each development to generally understand the methods.

Model. Data for three groups were generated from a latent variable model of relationships over time. The true trait scores for the five time periods were specified to have increasing means, strong relationships between adjacent time periods and constant variances. Figure 4.2 presents the design with five time periods. Within each time period, the true trait level is represented in the circles, with the labels t_1 to t_5. For each true trait level, the variance is specified as 1.0. True trait means are not constant over time, however. The initial mean is represented by the intercept, α_1. The changes in mean trait level are represented by the intercepts α_2 to α_5. Individual differences in trait level vary between time periods. The relationship between successive trait levels is represented by a constant regression coefficient of .90, which is equal to a simple correlation in this model. Thus, the proportion of variance in trait level predicted from the preceding time period is .81 (i.e., $.9^2$). At each successive time period, relative changes to individuals are represented by the impact of a time-specific factor with a variance of .19 so that the total trait variance at each time is 1.0.

FIGURE 4.2
True trait model for simulation study.

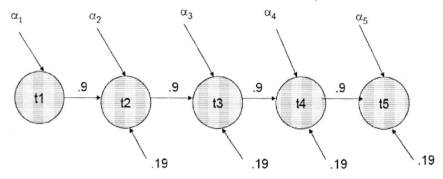

Formally, the model for (true) factor scores over time may be expressed as follows:

$$\eta = \alpha + \eta B + \zeta \tag{1}$$

where η is the vector of true trait scores, ζ is vector of time-specific influences on true trait scores, B is a matrix for the relationship between the true trait scores and α is a vector of intercepts that determine trait score means. Assuming that the expected value of the time-specific influences is zero, $[\mathrm{E}(\zeta) = \mathbf{0}]$, then the expected value of true trait scores may be given as follows:

$$E(\eta) = [I - B]^{-1}\alpha \tag{2}$$

If the influence of true trait levels extends only to the preceding time period, as in Figure 4.2, then **B** is a Markov simplex matrix as follows:

$$
\begin{vmatrix}
0 & 0 & 0 & 0 & 0 \\
\beta_{21} & 0 & 0 & 0 & 0 \\
0 & \beta_{32} & 0 & 0 & 0 \\
0 & 0 & \beta_{43} & 0 & 0 \\
0 & 0 & 0 & \beta_{54} & 0
\end{vmatrix}
$$

Thus, for example, Equation 2 would give the expected values of trait level at Time 3 as depending on the trait levels at the preceding time, weighted by B$_{32}$, and the intercept at Time 3, α_3.

For simplicity, a quasi-Markov simplex design (i.e., a Markov design with error variance) was used to generate all the examples in this paper. It should be noted that more complex designs may be relevant in developmental research. For example, non-linear growth, correlated changes over time, lagged impact of trait levels and non-constant variances may characterize some developmental research. However, the current design was selected for its simplicity. Designs with other features would require examining variation in these features for generality. For non-linearity, for example, the form and degree of non-linearity should be varied to understand impact. More complex models should be studied for scaling effects; however, there is no reason to believe that these features would remove the basic patterns of effects found from the simple quasi-Markov model of development.

Simulation design. Scores for three groups with 1,000 cases each were generated. The groups differed in mean trait levels at each time. The individual scores were generated as a random sample from a standard normal distribution with specified means and variances. For simplicity, a constant trait variance of 1.0 was specified for each group at each time. However, mean trait levels were specified to vary over the five time periods as follows:

$$\text{Low Group E}(\eta_1) = [\text{-}1.0, \text{-}.5, .0, .5, 1.0]$$

$$\text{Moderate Group E}(\eta_2) = [.0, .5, 1.0, 1.5, 2.0]$$

$$\text{High Group E}(\eta_3) = [1.0, 1.5, 2.0, 2.5, 3.0] \tag{3}$$

In Equation 4, successive group means differed by 1.0 at Time 1. Since the standard deviation was specified at 1.0, the effect size between successive groups was one standard deviation unit. Further, growth was linear and equal between groups since a constant increase of .5 was specified for the means at successive time periods.

Individual differences were specified by a constant regression of trait level at time t on time $t - 1$ of .9 and a constant variance of 1.0. The impact of the time-specific influences ζ was specified as random disturbances which were uncorrelated with each other or with true trait level. Thus, the covariance matrix of time-specific influences, Ψ, was a diagonal matrix as follows:

$$Diag\Psi = [1, (1 - \beta_{21}), (1 - \beta_{32}), (1 - \beta_{43}), (1 - \beta_{54})](5). \tag{4}$$

Generating test scores. Observed scores were generated for three tests with different difficulty levels. In many studies with traditional fixed content tests, a test is selected to be most appropriate for the whole series of time points. This leads to selecting a test that is most appropriate at the middle time period. Thus, in the simulation design, the item difficulties for the three tests were specified so that each test would be most appropriate for one of the three groups at the middle time period, Time 3.

Each simulated test had 30 items. Item difficulties were scaled to be appropriate for the one parameter logistic (1PL) item response model, which gives the probability that person s solves item i, $P(X_{is} = 1)$, as follows:

$$P(X_{is} = 1) = exp(\theta_s - \beta_i)/(1 + exp(\theta_s - \beta_i)), \qquad (5)$$

where θ_s is the ability of person s and β_i is the difficulty of item i. Notice that what drives the probability is the difference between the person's ability and the item's difficulty. In IRT models, item difficulties may be directly compared to trait levels because they are measured on the same scale. For further details on the 1PL and more complex IRT models, see Embretson and Reise (2000).

Item difficulties for each test were determined by randomly sampling 30 item difficulties from normal distributions of item difficulty specified as follows:

Easy Test Mean Difficulty = 0 (SD=1)

Moderate Test Mean Difficulty = 1 (SD=1)

Hard Test Mean Difficulty = 2 (SD=1). $\qquad (6)$

These test difficulties are most appropriate for one group each at the middle time period, Time 3, as noted above. That is, the Easy Test mean and standard deviation matches the Low Group trait level at Time 3. Similarly, the Moderate Test is most appropriate for the Moderate Group at Time 3, while the Hard Test is most appropriate for the High Group at Time 3.

To generate item response data, the 1PL model was first applied to calculate the probability of a correct response for each item, i, and person, j, at each time, k. The probability from the 1PL model, $P(X_{ijk}=1)$ is given as follows:

$$P(X_{ijk} = 1) = 1/[1 + exp(-1.7(\eta_{jk} - \beta_i))] \qquad (7)$$

where η_{jk} is the ability of person j at time k, and β_i is the difficulty of item i on a test. Thus, since three tests of 30 items each were generated, a total of 90 probabilities were calculated for each person. Then, to determine if each of the 90 items was passed or failed by a person, the computed probability was compared to a random number drawn from a uniform distribution of probabilities ranging from 0 to 1.0. If the probability exceeded the random number, then the item was passed; otherwise, the item was failed. This method works because, for example, if the probability was calculated at .90, then 90 percent of the time it would be expected to exceed the random number.

Once the item responses were generated for each person, total scores could be computed by summing the number of passed items. For each test, five total scores were computed for each person to represent the five time periods.

GROWTH CURVES: THE ANALYSIS OF TREND

To examine possible group differences in trend, group means across time are compared. Group means at each time period were computed, for each of the three measures. Thus, for a given person, 15 scores were available; five scores (across time) for each of the three tests. Thus, 15 means on the generated test scores were computed for each person.

Also available, of course, are the true trait values for each person at each time. For the design described above, growth for the generated true trait scores will be linear and have the same slope for each group. The intercepts, however, should differ by 1.0.

Results. The upper left of Figure 4.3 is a plot of mean true trait level at the five time periods for each group. It can be seen that the trend is linear with apparently the same slopes for each group. Furthermore, the intercept difference of 1.0 between groups at Time 1 is maintained over time periods. Thus, the generated data match the specifications well, as expected.

Trend effects can be globally evaluated by a Group (3) by Time (5) repeated measures analysis of variance. Table 4.1 shows the results for the true trait level and for the three CTT measures. Effect size indices (η^2) are presented rather than significance tests since the large sample size renders even trivial effects significant. For the within-subjects effects, Time and Time by Group, the effect size indices shown on Table 4.1 are associated with Wilk's Lambda. The true trait effect sizes provide a baseline for interpreting the results from the three CTT measures. For the Group effect, the true trait effect size is .453. The maximum difference observed from the true trait baseline is .023 (for the Easy Test). Thus, the group effect is well defined by all measures. However, the within-subjects effect sizes are impacted more substantially as compared to the true trait baseline. The Time effect is underestimated by all three CTT measures, with the effect size differences from the true trait baseline ranging from. .064 to .098. The Group by Time effect, for which the true trait effect is zero ($\eta^2 = .001$), is overestimated from all three CTT measures, particularly from the Easy Test and the Hard Test. Thus, for all three generated CTT measures, the effect sizes seemingly warrant some interpretation of differences in group trends. Figure 4.3 shows the trends observed from the three generated

FIGURE 4.3

Plots of test scores across time for three groups for four different measures.

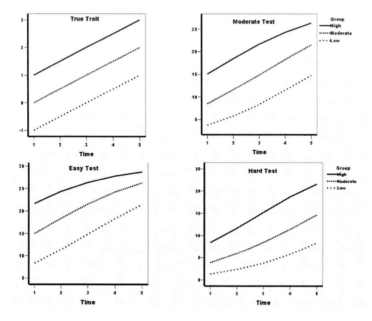

CTT measures. Although the three groups increase over time on all three tests, the trend differs between groups, depending on the particular test. On the Easy Test, in the lower left panel of Figure 4.3, the High Group has a decelerating rate over time; thus, the greatest gain occurs early. The Moderate Group also has a decelerating positive trend, but not nearly as great as for the High Group. Finally, the Low Group has a positive trend with a somewhat accelerating rate: thus, gain is increasing over time. Differing group trends implies that the relative differences between the groups varies over time. The results from the Easy Test indicate that the differences are decreasing over time.

For the Moderate Test, a different pattern is observed. The upper right panel of Figure 4.3 shows that the High Group shows a positive trend with a decelerating rate, as observed from the Easy Test. However, the Moderate Group has a nearly linear trend while the Low Group has a trend with an accelerating rate. Interestingly, with these patterns of trend over time, the differences between the groups is greatest in the middle of the time periods, Time 3. Differences between the groups are smaller at the extreme time periods. Last, for the Hard Test, yet a different pattern of results is observed. The lower right panel of Figure 4.3 shows that the High Group has a nearly linear trend, while both the Moderate Group and the Low Group have positive trends

TABLE 4.1

Effect Sizes for Group by the Time Analysis of Trend From Different Measures.

	CTT Group	CTT Time	CTT-Time by Group	IRT Group	IRT Time	IRT-Time by Group
True Trait	.453	.850	.001	.453	.850	.001
Easy Test	.430	.754	.104	.433	.780	.015
Moderate-Test	.453	.786	.031	.448	.797	.003
Hard Test	.439	.752	.099	.446	.789	.011

with decelerating rates. On this test, the largest difference between groups is observed at the last time period, Time 5.

Discussion. Even though the groups did not differ in trend over time on true scores, the observed trends from the three tests do show group differences. One might speculate about the types of interpretations that could be given to results from each of the three different tests. Consider the following hypothetical example from an educational context. Suppose that the three groups are as follows: 1) the Low Group consists of learning disabled children, 2) the Moderate Group consists of mainstream children and 3) the High Group consists of Gifted Children. Suppose further that the tests are achievement tests, administered every six months during the course of a special intervention, such as an extended school day.

From the Easy Test results, one might say that the achievement differences between groups, although large initially, tend to dissipate over exposure to the extended school day. Thus, the extended school day may be interpreted as not only leading to increased achievement, but additionally it allows the initially less able children to catch up. From the Moderate Test, although performance is generally increasing as well, the groups differ most at the middle time. Perhaps there is a critical stage for development, which differs by group. The learning disabled children, for example improve more slowly at first, but then increase achievement more rapidly with the extended school day. The gifted children, in contrast, improve more rapidly at first but then their scores rise less rapidly with increasing intervention. From the Hard Test results, one might interpret the results as showing that the extended school day actually increases group differences. That is, the higher ability children profit more than the lower ability children.

Obviously, none of the interpretations from the observed test scores, which are classical test scores as typical in many studies, would be valid. True growth on the latent trait is linear over time and the group differences are maintained. The cause of the differences that are observed from the test comparisons results from the differing difficulty levels of the tests.

GAIN SCORES AT DIFFERENT TIME INTERVALS

Assessing trend requires observations at multiple time periods. Often studies have limited resources so that only two observations are available. In this case, gain scores can be computed. Although simple gain scores are seemingly basic for measuring change, they have well known problems. Bereiter (1963) noted three serious problems. First, gain scores have paradoxical reliability. As the correlations between the two measures increases, as characteristic of a reliable test, the reliability of the gain score decreases. Second, gain scores have a spurious correlation with initial status. The initial score, X_1 has an implicit source of negative correlation with gain, which is $X_2 - X_1$. Third, the scale intervals of gain may be unequal from different initial levels. A one point gain from a high level score may have greater implications than the same change from a moderate score.

In this section, only the scaling problem will be considered. Simple gain scores will be compared between groups using tests of different difficulty levels. Using the same data as for the trend analysis above, the three groups are compared for gain over several time intervals. Although only simple gain is computed here, similar scaling problems can be expected for other gain measures, such as residualized gain. In the most basic residualized gain score, gain is the residual score in the later time period that is not predicted from the preceding time.

Simple gain was also calculated for each interval using total score on the three tests. Each test included 30 items, so the simple gain is the difference in the number of items solved from specified time periods. Simple gain was also computed for the true trait scores. Since the three groups were generated to have equal changes across time on the true trait scale, the mean true gain should be equal.

Results. The upper plot in Figure 4.4 shows the mean true gains by group when calculated at three different intervals; Time 1 to Time 3, Time 2 to Time 4 and Time 3 to Time 5. It can be seen that across each interval, the mean true gains for all groups is approximately 1.0 on the IRT latent trait scale. Thus, the generating procedures led to true scores with the expected pattern of gains.

The lower panel of Figure 4.4 shows the raw gain for each test and each group from Time 2 to Time 4. Although the true trait gain was equal between groups, raw scores on the three tests do not show equal gain between groups.

FIGURE 4.4
Gain scores for true trait and tests at middle time interval.

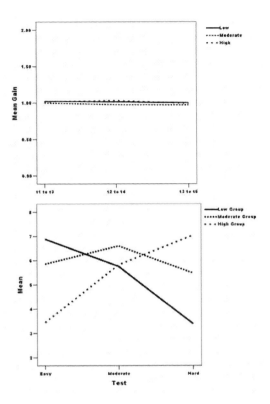

Further, the pattern of relative gain depends on the difficulty level of the test. If only one test could be selected to observe the three groups over the middle time period, the Moderate Test would be most appropriate for the sample as a whole. On the Moderate Test, however, the groups do not show equal gains. The Moderate Group has a somewhat larger gain (about 1 point) than either the Low Group or the High Group. If the Hard Test is selected, the High Group has a very large gain, while the other two groups show much smaller gains. If the Easy Test is selected, the opposite pattern is observed; the Low Group has a much larger gain than the other groups. To understand more fully the impact of test difficulty level on gain score comparisons between groups, a standardized effect size, d, was computed. For the possible pairwise comparisons between the groups, (i.e., High Group versus Moderate Group, High Group versus Low Group and Moderate Group versus Low Group), d compares the mean difference in gain to the standard deviation for gain as follows:

$$d = (Mean_1 - -Mean_2)/SD_{total} \tag{8}$$

Table 4.2 shows the mean and maximum values for the standardized effect sizes for comparing the groups. To provide a baseline, the effect sizes for the generated true trait scores were also computed. The maximum effect size for the true trait was .09. For the Moderate Test, larger effect sizes were observed, with the maximum effect size of .17. For the Easy Test and Hard Test, however, the mean and the maximum observed effect sizes are quite substantial. The maximum observed effect of .70 on the Easy Test (i.e., High Group versus Low Group).

FIGURE 4.5

GGain scores for tests at extreme time intervals.

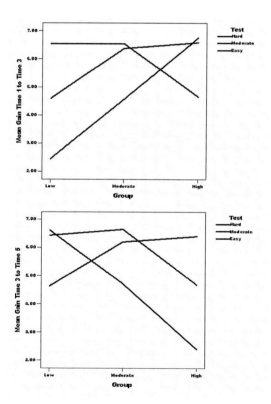

Figure 4.5 shows the simple gains at two other time periods. The upper panel of Figure 4.5 shows the mean gains for the Time 1 to Time 3 interval. Compared to the Time 2 to Time 4 interval, the true trait scores are lower for all groups. Thus, the impact of test difficulty level is somewhat different. For the Time 1 to Time 3 interval, the most dramatic differences between groups is shown by the Hard Test. The High Group shows a very large gain while the Moderate Group shows a more moderate gain. The Low Group shows a small gain. For the Easy Test, large gains are observed for both the Low Group and the Moderate Group, while a much smaller gain is observed for the High Group. For the Moderate Test, large gains are observed for the Moderate Group and the High Group, while a more modest gain is observed for the Low Group.

TABLE 4.2

Mean and Maximum Standardized Effect Sizes for Group Comparisions From Test Scores

		Mean Effect Size	Maximun Effect Size
Time 2 to Time 4	True	.06	.09
	Easy Test Score	.46	.70
	Moderate Test Score	.11	.17
	Hard Test Score	.46	.69
Time 1 to Time 3	True	.02	.03
	Easy Test Score	.25	.37
	Moderate Test Score	.26	.39
	Hard Test Score	.58	.87
Time 3 to Time 5	True	.03	.05
	Easy Test Score	.59	.88
	Moderate Test Score	.26	.39
	Hard Test Score	.25	.37

Table 4.2 also shows the effect sizes for Time 1 to Time 3. Effect sizes for the true trait scores are included as a baseline, which shows a maximum effect size of .03. However, the group means differ substantially when the comparisons are based on test scores, with the maximum effect sizes over tests ranging from .37 to .87.

The lower panel of Figure 4.5 shows the mean gains for the Time 3 to Time 5 interval, where true trait scores are relatively higher for all groups. For this time interval, the Easy Test shows the most dramatic differences in gain between the three groups. The Low Group has a large mean gain, the Moderate Group has a more modest gain and the High Group has a smaller gain. For the Moderate Test, very large gains are observed for both the Low Group and the Moderate

Group. A more modest gain is observed for the High Group. Finally, for the Hard Test, large gains are observed for both the High Group and the Moderate Group, while a more modest gain is observed for the Low Group. Table 4.2 also shows large mean and maximum effect sizes for group differences in gain computed over this time interval. The effect sizes for the three tests range from .37 to .88, while the maximum effect size for the true trait is .05.

Discussion. Although the three groups have equal true gains over all three time intervals, the generated raw scores on the three tests showed large group differences at all three time periods. Obviously, valid inferences about gain cannot be made from raw scores on any of these tests. Perhaps worse, the results did not show a single pattern of bias. Which group gained the most depended on *both* the test difficulty level and the time period.

Consider the implications for the hypothetical educational example. In the middle time period, T2 to T4, selecting the moderately difficult test would have lead to diagnosing the mainstream students as gaining the most from the extended school day. If the easy test were selected instead for the comparisons, the learning disability students would gain the most. And finally, if hard test were selected for the comparisons, then the gifted students would be observed as gaining the most from the extended school day.

In the other two time periods, T1 to T3 and T3 to T5, the impact of test difficulty is also observed, but the patterns are different than in the T2 to T4 period. Any of the three groups could be found as gaining the most from the extended school day, depending on the choice of time period and test difficulty level. But, in these simulation data, the groups gain equally.

This perplexing pattern of results can be explained by the relative appropriateness of the test difficulty level for the groups. Since the true trait levels of the groups change over the time periods, the relative appropriateness of the three tests for a particular group will change as well. Precise calculations of test appropriateness (i.e., test information) is possible with IRT. Although elaborating the test information concept is beyond the scope of this paper, an intuitive understanding of test appropriateness can be gleaned from the plot in Figure 4.6. Figure 4.6 shows the mean trait level for each group, averaged over the time interval. For example, the mean trait level for the Low Group in the Time 2 to Time 4 interval, all scores considered, is .0. Similarly, the Moderate Group has a mean trait level of 1.0 while the High Group has a mean trait level of 2.0 in the Time 2 to Time 4 interval. Also shown on Figure 6 are straight lines to represent the mean item difficulty level of the three tests.

Test appropriateness for a group may be indicated by the distance of the group trait mean from the mean test difficulty level. For the Time 2 to Time 4 interval, test appropriateness is clear for each group. The true trait mean is equal to the difficulty level of one of the three tests. For example, the true trait

FIGURE 4.6

Comparison of test and trait levels by time and group

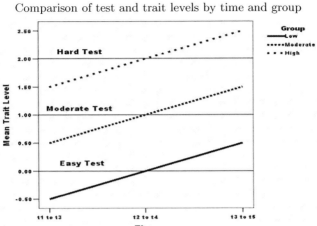

mean of .0 for the Low Group equals the mean item difficulty of .0 for the Easy Test. Similarly, the Moderate Group is matched to the Moderate Test while the High Group is matched to the Hard Test. For the Time 1 to Time 3 interval, the match of the group mean trait level to the tests is not unique. While the trait mean for the Low Group is closest to the Easy Test, the Moderate Group trait mean is equally close to both the Easy Test and the Moderate Test. Finally, the High Group trait mean is closest to the Hard Test.

In general, larger gains are observed as test appropriateness increases. For example, consider the pattern of group differences on the Moderate Test in the Time 2 to Time 4 interval. A large gain was observed for the Moderate Group. An inspection of Figure 4.6 shows that the Moderate Test difficulty level is maximally matched to the trait level of the Moderate Group in this time interval. The Low Group and the High Group showed somewhat smaller gains than the Moderate Group on the Moderate Test. Figure 4.6 shows that both groups differed by .5 from the Moderate Test. Now consider the pattern of differences on the Hard Test in the Time 2 to Time 4 interval. A very large gain was observed for the High Group, for which test difficulty level is equal to the true trait mean. A more moderate gain was observed for the Moderate Group, for which the true trait mean differed by 1.0 from test item difficulty. Finally, for the Low Group, a much smaller gain was observed. The true trait level for this group differed by 1.0 from the mean item difficulty level of the Hard Test. Similar explanations can be given for the pattern of results shown for the other two time intervals. The distance of the true trait level from mean item difficulty mirrors the relative differences in simple gain between the groups.

Thus, it can be concluded that groups differing in initial true trait level cannot be meaningfully compared for gain by using raw scores on a single test. Relative differences between groups in gains can be merely a function of the appropriateness of the test difficulty level for the various group. Unfortunately, transforming scores into standard scores will not produce better results. Standard scores are typically linear transformations of raw scores, such that the same pattern of differences will be preserved.

Scaling problems, then, can provide a challenge to drawing meaningfully inferences about group differences in change. Item difficulty levels on a test can confound any real differences between groups in change. In fact, and perversely, measures can be selected to show the largest change for a favored group when it differs in initial levels from the comparison groups.

This is obviously a very unsatisfactory situation. The next section explores some solutions to the scaling problem.

SOLUTIONS: RESCALING BY IRT

The results described above were based on CTT scaling in which item responses are summed into a total score. CTT applications typically involve rescaling the total scores into a standard score, such as a T-score, which is based on a norm group. However, properties of the total score will be inherited by the standard score when it is a linear transformation of raw scores. Thus, the results here will also apply to common standard scores.

IRT provides an alternative scaling of persons that may counteract the impact of varying test difficulty levels on group comparisons of trend and change. IRT scaling can be applied to the response patterns from each test to provide a more optimal scaling of scores. Whether or not the IRT scaling is sufficient to counteract the confounding effect of item difficulty levels in a particular test is an issue.

To apply IRT scaling to persons, the item parameters for each measure must be available. In the simulated data sets above, the item parameters (i.e., item difficulty) are available since they were used to generate the data. For real data, item parameters should be estimated from a group with a sufficient range of trait levels so as to have reasonably precise estimates for all items. It is possible to estimate item parameters simultaneously with the study of trend or change, using standard IRT models. However, often the groups in such studies do not have a sufficient representation of more extreme trait levels so that some item difficulties are not precisely estimated. As shown in standard textbooks on IRT, the trait level distribution has a direct impact on the standard error for estimating item parameters (e.g., Embretson & Reise, 2000; Hambleton & Swaminathan, 1995). Poorly estimated item parameters could mitigate improvement in scaling that is afforded by IRT.

It should be noted that item response theory is a qualitatively different type of scaling than classical test scores. It is model-based scaling obtained by finding the most likely trait level of the examinee, given the observed responses, parameters (e.g., difficulty) of the items administered and, for some methods, a prior distribution of trait level. Typically, IRT scaling stretches out the extremes of the distribution. That is, small score changes at the extremes entail large changes in trait level.

Trend Analysis. To demonstrate the impact of IRT scaling on the analysis of trend, trait levels were estimated for each person from their generated item responses. The (known) true item difficulties were used in the Rasch IRT model to obtain maximum likelihood estimates of trait level for each person. The expected a posterior method (EAP) was used to obtain the estimates. EAP is a Bayesian estimation method which requires that a prior distribution of trait levels is specified. In the current study, a normal distribution with a mean of 0 and standard deviation of 1 was specified.

Results. Table 4.1 presents results that are relevant to impact of IRT scaling on assessing trend. The Time by Group effect in a repeated measures ANOVA indicates the extent to which differential trend is observed between groups. The true trait data was generated to have a .00 effect. However, as shown above, the Time by Group effect was not zero for the generated classical test scores. Table 4.1 presents the corresponding effect sizes (i.e., η^2) from the IRT scaling of the generated item responses. It can be seen that the Time by Group effect sizes were all quite small, averaging about .01. For the Moderate Test, the effect was very close to the true trait level.

Thus, for group comparisons of trend, the IRT parameters have clearly improved the results. However, it should be noticed that although the effect size estimates for Time were somewhat closer to the true trait estimates, it is still substantially underestimated, particularly for the Easy Test and the Hard Test.

Discussion. The IRT scaling of the tests improved the assessment of trend from all three generated tests. It was most successful for Moderate Test, which is most appropriate for the sample as a whole. The IRT scaling was also effective for the tests that are somewhat out of range. That is, the Easy Test and the Hard Test were much improved as well. Last, the Time effect was somewhat underestimated from all measures.

These results seem encouraging. With minimal effort, rescaling the test scores by IRT adjusted the scores such that spurious group differences in trend virtually disappeared. However, it should be noted that the rescaling in the current study was optimal in several ways: the true item parameters were used in estimating IRT scores, a known prior distribution of scores could be specified and the only item parameter in the model was item difficulty. In real studies, of course both the true item parameters and the prior distribution are unknown. However, when item difficulty is the only unknown item parameter, reasonably precise estimates can be obtained from the data at hand. But, if a more complex IRT model is required, obtaining estimates from the data may be less effective. Item differences in discrimination, for example, which is quite often required to fit real test data, are less well estimated from samples that are not broadly representative of all trait levels.

Gain Scores

To examine the impact on gain scores, gains at three time periods were calculated from the IRT estimates of trait level used in the trend analysis above. Change scores were computed from the IRT trait level estimates that were used in the trend analysis above. Change scores were computed in the following intervals: Time 1 to Time 3, Time 2 to Time 4 and Time 3 to Time 5.

Results. Table 4.3 shows the standardized effect sizes for the group comparisons from the IRT scaling for three tests as well as the effect sizes from the true generated trait values. To provide a baseline, the effect sizes for the group comparisons of gain from the true trait scores were computed. These effect sizes were generally small and in no case yielded a d larger than .09.

For the IRT scaling of the test scores, it can be seen that the effect sizes were all much smaller as compared to the effect size estimates from raw scores on Table 4.2. However, some non-ignorable effect sizes were still observed. For example, on the Easy Test, an effect size of .20 was observed for the Time 2 to Time 4 interval and an effect size of .33 was observed for the Time 3 to Time 5 interval.

To further examine the effects, plots of mean gains by group and test were prepared for each time period. The upper panel of Figure 4.7 shows the mean gain from Time 2 to Time 4 for the three groups on the three tests. Although the impact is not as dramatic as for the CTT scores, the same pattern of group differences in mean gains by item difficulty level was observed. For example, on the Easy Test, the greatest mean gain is shown by the Low Group. The lower left panel of Figure 4.7 shows the group means by test for the Time 1 to Time 3 interval. Again, the pattern of gains varies somewhat by test difficulty level, in a manner similar as to the plots of raw gains in Figure 4.5. Last, the lower right panel of Figure 4.7 shows the corresponding plot for the Time 3 to Time 5 interval, again with the pattern of gains depending somewhat on the test.

Thus, although the effect sizes were much reduced, as shown on Table 4.3, the magnitude of gain is still related to test difficulty level. In the current

TABLE 4.3

Mean and Maximum Standardized Effect Sizes for Group Comparisions From Test Scores

		Mean Standardized Effect	Maximun Standardized Size
Time 2 to Time 4	True	.06	.09
	Easy Test-IRT	.13	.20
	Moderate Test-IRT	.01	.02
	Hard Test-IRT	.12	.18
	Multilevel Test	.05	.07
	Partially Adaptive Test	.05	.07
Time 1 to Time 3	True	.02	.03
	Easy Test-IRT	.06	.09
	Moderate Test-IRT	.08	.11
	Hard Test-IRT	.18	.26
	Multilevel Test	.04	.07
	Partially Adaptive Test	.02	.03
Time 3 to Time 5	True	.03	.05
	Easy Test-IRT	.22	.33
	Moderate Test-IRT	.09	.14
	Hard Test-IRT	.06	.09
	Multilevel Test	.01	.01
	Partially Adaptive Test	.02	.04

study, with the large sample size of 1,000 per group, the interaction effects are significant.

Discussion. In summary, although the IRT scaling substantially reduced the confounding impact of test difficulty level on gain scores, it did not entirely remove it. The remaining problem, although still a scaling problem, rests in the nature of the test item responses. That is, tests with fixed item content are more appropriate for persons at some trait levels than for others. In a situation with large initial group differences, coupled with substantial change over time, a single test cannot provide optimal measurement for all groups at all times.

Thus, the remaining difficulty rests with the range of item difficulties on a particular test. Further, again it should be noted that the IRT rescaling was optimal in the current data because the true item difficulties were known and did not need to be estimated from the data. Practically, when the item difficulties must be estimated from the data at hand, the IRT rescaling will be less effective.

FIGURE 4.7

IRT Estimates of gain for three tests by group for various time intervals.

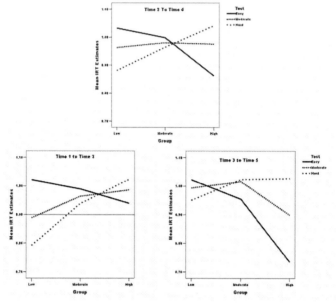

MULTILEVEL TESTS WITH IRT SCALING

Another way to correct for the impact of item difficulty is to optimally select the measures for each group. That is, different groups will be given different test forms, depending on their initial level. For some constructs, particularly for ability measurement, multilevel tests are available. Under certain conditions, multilevel tests can correct for the impact of item difficulty when comparing groups at initially different levels. Those conditions are the following: 1) the tests at the different levels are equally discriminating measures of the same construct, 2) the tests can be optimally selected for a particular group, and 3) comparable scores can be estimated from each test. The latter condition is optimally implemented by IRT scaling so that scores may be placed on the same continuum through vertical or non-equivalent group equating techniques (e.g., Bock & Zimowski, 1997). In contrast, normatively-scaled test scores allow interpretation within the same test, but not between tests.

To show the potential improvement from a multilevel test, each group in the simulation test was represented by scores from the single test that best represented their trait level over all the time intervals. Thus, the groups were given the IRT trait estimates obtained from a single test as follows: 1) the Low Group from the Easy Test, 2) the Moderate Group from the Moderate Test and 3) the High Group from the Hard Test. Thus, at any one time, the IRT estimates are based on different tests for different groups.

Since the IRT rescaling alone provided reasonably unbiased indices of trend for the groups, only the gain scores will be reanalyzed with the multilevel tests.

Results. Table 4.3 shows the mean and maximum effect sizes for group comparisons from the multilevel trait estimates. It can be seen that for all time intervals the estimates are quite small and close to the true trait level. Since Table 4.3 also presents the IRT estimates from the three tests when not optimally selected, comparisons can be made directly. Obviously, the occasionally large effect sizes remaining by using a single test for all groups is diminished.

Discussion. Multilevel tests, with IRT scaling, provided estimates of trait changes that were not confounded with item difficulty in the current study. The trick, however, was to optimally select the measure prior to actual testing. For some well established multilevel tests, such as ability tests that can be administered to school age children, this may be feasible since item difficulties are carefully developed for each level. However, for other traits and for other groups, optimal selection may not be possible and thus mitigate any increased improvement in scaling.

A remaining advantage that may be obtained from the multilevel tests is more reliable measurement of individual scores. This feature is important for research in which explanations for individual differences in trait level are sought. Figure 4.8 shows the regression of two different IRT estimates of trait gain for Time 3 to Time 5, the multilevel test and the Moderate Test. The sample mean for the two time periods combined is 1.5, so that either the Moderate Test or the Hard Test are equally appropriate. The correlation of the IRT estimates with true gain is somewhat higher for the multilevel test ($r^2 = .4948$) than for the Moderate Test ($r^2 = .4680$). However, neither of these reliabilities is high.

ADAPTIVE TESTS

While the improvements from multilevel testing may be sufficient for many applications, the researcher must appropriately select the test for the groups. Thus, prior knowledge of trait levels in the various groups is required. Often such knowledge is not available. In fact, a purpose of the study may be to determine the level of initial group differences, in addition to measuring trend or change. Thus, multilevel testing may not be practical for many studies.

Another approach is adaptive testing. In adaptive test, item difficulties are optimally selected for each examinee during the course of testing. The difficulty of each selected item depends on the responses to the previously administered items. If items are failed, then easier items are administered; if items are passed, harder items are administered. Thus, no prior knowledge is required.

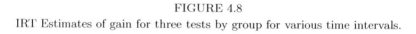

FIGURE 4.8

IRT Estimates of gain for three tests by group for various time intervals.

An overview of the various issues in contemporary adaptive testing is presented by Wainer (1990). For the present purposes, however, the basic requirements for an adaptive testing are the following: 1) an item bank with sufficient range and representation of difficulty levels for the study design, 2) calibrated item parameters from an IRT model that is appropriate for the trait, 3) computer test administration to estimate abilities continuously, and 4) a stopping criterion, such as a minimum standard error or number of items. In a developmental and ecological context, the range and representation of item difficulties is a particularly crucial requirement. If items are not available at the extremes, then measurement will not be much improved by adaptive testing.

With adaptive testing, trait level estimates with small measurement errors can be obtained efficiently if the above criteria are adequately met. That is, the optimal items for measuring trait level can be administered to each person, regardless of group membership or time period. Although a simulation of adaptive testing is beyond the scope of this paper, it is expected to give the best adjustment for scaling issues in assessing trend and change. Research has shown how adaptive testing can lead to accurate estimates of true trait change. For example, Embretson (1994) compared IRT estimates for assessing gain between a fixed content test and an adaptive test. The study had a smaller range of trait levels than in the current study. IRT estimates from a fixed content test (i.e., like the Moderate Test in the current study) had a correlation of .864

($r^2 = .746$) with true gain. However, IRT estimates from an adaptive test had a correlation of .947 ($r^2 = .897$) with true gain. With the broader range of trait levels in the current study, even greater improvement could be expected.

Since adaptive testing leads to the most appropriate test difficulty for each examinee, scaling issues for measuring trend and change can be expected to disappear. As computerized testing becomes increasingly commonplace, particularly with the increasing availability of internet testing (see Naglieri et al, 2005), adaptive testing will become not only the best alternative, but also the most practical alternative.

SUMMARY AND CONCLUSIONS

This paper explored the implications of measurement scaling for inferences about trend and change. In a developmental and ecological context, measurement is often needed over a broad range of trait levels. Studies may involve both multiple time periods and multiple groups that differ initially in trait level. Typically, classical tests are administered repeatedly over time to each group. Although the repeated tests (or equivalent test forms) have the same item difficulty, the individuals change over time. Hence, the relative difficulty of the test depends on the time period. Thus, a potential scaling problem is created.

The impact of test difficulty level on observed group differences in trend and change was examined in a simulation study. Three groups with different mean trait levels initially were observed at five time intervals. True trait level was specified to have a linear growth at an equal rate across groups. Total scores for three tests, varying in difficulty, were generated from the simulation parameters.

The simulation results showed that group differences in trend depended on the difficulty of the test. For example, if the groups were compared on an easy test over time, then the initially high level group grew at a decelerating rate, while the lowest group had a more constant rate of change. If the groups were compared on a hard test, however, the high group had an accelerating rate of change. The time interval at which the greatest differences between the groups also depended on test difficulty. That is, the easy test diagnosed a different time period for the maximum group differences than the hard test. Similarly, gain scores computed over three different intervals also showed differential changes between the groups, but again, the pattern of changes depended on the difficulty level of the test.

These results were consistent with a single interpretation. Group differences in trend or change depend on the appropriateness of the test difficulty level for the group. When the item difficulty level is well matched to the trait level of the group, the greatest amount of gain is observed. If item difficulty is poorly matched to the group (e.g., a low group receives a hard test), little change is observed even though the group has the same change on the true trait as another group. This confounding of change with item difficulty level creates a problem for any comparison of the groups.

Several solutions to this scaling problem were considered which involved the application of IRT models to scale and equate the observed test scores. The solutions considered included obtaining IRT estimates from fixed content tests, multilevel tests and adaptive tests. Simply rescaling scores from fixed content tests by applying IRT models led to substantial improvements for the assessment of trend. However, bias remained in comparing groups for change. Multilevel testing, where test difficulty level is optimally selected for each group, provided substantial correction of the remaining bias in comparing change across groups. However, since multilevel testing requires prior knowledge to select the most appropriate test for each group, it may not be practical.

Finally, adaptive testing was discussed as the best alternative to the scaling problem. Tests are optimally selected for each person at each time by their pattern of item responses. Thus, given a sufficient item bank, optimal measurement can be obtained for all individuals and the scaling problem will no longer confound group comparisons. The adaptive testing solution is becoming increasingly feasible for many measures. Although adaptive testing requires prior calibration of the item bank and computer administration, increasingly these conditions are being met for many psychological tests. As adaptive testing becomes feasible for research applications, it will be interesting to reconsider findings from older studies that may have had scaling problems contribute to the assessment of group differences in trend or change.

REFERENCES

Bereiter, C. (1963). Some persisting dilemmas in the measurement of change. In C. W. Harris (Ed.), *Problems in measuring change* (pp. 3-20). Madison: University of Wisconsin Press.

Bock, R. D., & Zimowski, M. F. (1997). Multiple group IRT. In W. J. van der Linden & R. Hambleton (Eds.), *Handbook of modern item response theory* (pp. 433-488). New York: Springer-Verlag.

Collins, L., & Horn, J. (1991). *Best methods for analyzing change*. Washington, DC: American Psychological Association Books.

Collins, L., & Sayer, A. G. (2001). *New methods in the analysis of change*. Washington, DC: American Psychological Association Books.

Cronbach, L., & Furby, L. (1970). How should we measure change – or should we? *Psychological Bulletin, 74*, 68-80.

Embretson, S. (1995). A measurement model for linking individual change to processes and knowledge: Application to mathematical learning. *Journal of Educational Measurement, 32*, 277-294.

Embretson, S. E. (1994). Comparing changes between groups: Some perplexities arising from psychometrics. In D. Laveault, B. D. Zumbo, M. E. Gessaroli, & M. W. Boss (Eds.), *Modern theories of measurement: Problems and issues.* Ottawa: Edumetric Research Group, University of Ottawa.

Embretson, S. E. (1996). Item response theory models and inferential bias in multiple group comparisons. *Applied Psychological Measurement, 20*, 201-212.

Little, T. D., Lindenberger, U., & Maier, H. (n.d.). Selectivity and generalizability in longitudinal research: On the effects of continuers and dropouts. In T. D. Little, K. U. Schnabel, & J. Baumert (Eds.), *Modeling longitudinal and multilevel data* (pp. 187-200). Mahwah, NJ: Lawrence Erlbaum Associates.

Little, T. D., Schnabel, K. U., & Baumert, J. (2000). *Modeling longitudinal and multilevel data.* Mahwah, NJ: Lawrence Erlbaum Associates.

McArdle, J. J., & Bell, R. Q. (2000). An introduction to latent growth curve models for developmental data analysis. In T. D. Little, K. U. Schnabel, & J. Baumert (Eds.), *Modeling longitudinal and multilevel data* (pp. 69-107). Mahwah, NJ: Lawrence Erlbaum Associates.

Naglieri, J. A., Drasgow, F., Schmit, M., Handler, L., Prifitera, A., Margolis, A., et al. (2004). Psychological testing on the internet: New problems, old issues. *American Psychologist, 59*, 150-162.

Wainer, H. (1990). *Computerized adaptive testing: A primer.* Mahwah, NJ: Lawrence Erlbaum Associates.

CHAPTER FIVE

The Incorporation of Categorical Measurement Models in the Analysis of Individual Growth

Patrick J. Curran
Michael C. Edwards
R. J. Wirth
Andrea M. Hussong
University of North Carolina at Chapel Hill

Laurie Chassin
Arizona State University

The empirical study of human development is a daunting task, particularly when focusing on the first few decades of life when change is both rapid and variable. The fields of child development and developmental psychopathology are supported by rich and dynamic theoretical models that strive to capture the complex and subtle processes of individual growth over time. For example, developmental theory is built upon core tenets such as homotypic continuity (Kagan, 1971), developmental coactions and transactions (e.g., Gottlieb & Halpern, 2002; Sameroff, 1995), and dynamic processes of multifinality and equifinality (e.g., Cicchetti & Rogosch, 1996; Gottlieb, Wahlsten, & Lickliter, 1998), to name a few. However, it is often challenging, if not impossible, to fully test these complex theories from an empirical perspective (e.g., Curran & Willoughby, 2003; Wohlwill, 1970, 1973). A core issue is the need to select a statistical model that optimally corresponds to the theoretical model that gave rise to the proposed research hypotheses.

The degree to which the theoretical model diverges from the statistical model directly impacts the validity of our empirically based conclusions (Curran & Willoughby, 2003; Curran & Wirth, 2004; Wohlwill, 1970). We must take great care in selecting a statistical model that optimally corresponds to the theoretical model under study. This issue is particularly salient when considering developmental processes both within and across different contexts. Although there are a large number of components that must be considered when selecting an appropriate statistical model to test a given theory of interest, we focus on three specific issues here: The need to explicitly incorporate repeated measures that are discretely scaled (e.g., dichotomous or ordinal); to differentially weight individual items when forming a scale as a function of item reliability and severity; and to incorporate optimally-derived scale scores in growth curve models of developmental stability and change over time.

Our motivating goal is to describe and empirically demonstrate a two-stage procedure of scale construction and growth curve analysis that addresses challenges encountered when studying individual and contextual influences on development. The first stage involves the calculation of individual and time specific scale scores based on a set of dichotomous repeated measures. We consider three scoring methods: proportion scores, item response theory, and categorical confirmatory factor analysis. The second stage involves incorporating these scale scores into a general multilevel modeling framework for the analysis of developmental trajectories over time. Although we focus our attention on the multilevel (or hierarchical linear) model, all of our arguments extend directly to the structural equation based latent curve model as well (e.g., Bollen & Curran, 2006). Our expectation is that the development and application of a proper measurement model in the first stage will improve the validity and reliability of the growth curve models fitted in the second stage.

We begin with a brief review of the standard linear multilevel growth curve model and highlight the assumptions of continuous outcomes and the modeling of a single score over time. We then summarize existing methods for the simultaneous estimation of a growth curve model with a multiple item measurement model. Next we present three existing measurement models for categorical repeated measures data: the proportion score, the 2-parameter logistic (2PL) item response theory model, and the categorical confirmatory factor analysis model. We then demonstrate the comparative utility of these models by examining multiple repeated assessments of externalizing symptomatology in a sample of 444 adolescents ranging in age from 10 to 21. We conclude with potential expansions of these models and recommendations for the use of these techniques in practice.

MULTILEVEL GROWTH CURVE MODELS

The estimation of longitudinal growth curves has been an interest in the social sciences for nearly two centuries (see Bollen & Curran, 2006, for a historical review). There are several powerful methodological frameworks that can be applied to the estimation of growth curves based on repeated measures data. Two widely used approaches are the structural equation modeling based latent curve analysis (LCA; Bollen & Curran, 2006; McArdle, 1988, 1989; Meredith & Tisak, 1984, 1990), and the multilevel (or mixed) modeling framework (e.g., Bryk & Raudenbush, 1987; Raudenbush & Bryk, 2002; Willett & Sayer, 1994). There are many important elements shared between these two modeling approaches, but several key differences remain (Bauer, 2003; Curran, 2003; Raudenbush, 2001; Willett & Sayer, 1994).

Multilevel modeling is a general analytic framework that allows for the explicit modeling of nested (or nonindependent) data structures (e.g., Goldstein, 1986; Mason, Wong, & Entwisle, 1983; Raudenbush & Bryk, 2002). Classic examples include children nested within families, classrooms nested within schools, and households nested within neighborhoods. However, repeated assessments over time can be conceptualized as nested within individuals, and thus the multilevel model can be directly applied to the analysis of growth curves (Bryk & Raudenbush, 1987).

For the standard linear multilevel growth curve model, we can define a level-1 or within-person equation, and a level-2 or between-person equation. We define the level-1 equation as:

$$y_{ti} = \beta_{0i} + \beta_{1i}x_{ti} + e_{ti} \;, \tag{1}$$

where the outcome variable y assessed at time t for individual i can be expressed as an additive function of an intercept (β_{0i}), a linear slope (β_{1i}) multiplied by the value of time at assessment t for individual i (x_{ti}), and a time- and individual-specific residual (e_{ti}). Because the individually varying intercepts and slopes are treated as random variables, these can be expressed as:

$$\beta_{0i} = \gamma_{00} + u_{0i} \tag{2}$$
$$\beta_{1i} = \gamma_{10} + u_{1i} \;, \tag{3}$$

where γ_{00} and γ_{10} represent the mean intercept and slope, respectively, and u_{0i} and u_{1i} represent individual deviations from these means.

The level-1 and level-2 distinction is for heuristic value only. Equations 2 and 3 can thus be substituted into Equation 1 to result in the reduced form expression

$$y_{ti} = (\gamma_{00} + \gamma_{10}x_{ti}) + (u_{0i} + u_{1i}x_{ti} + e_{ti}) \;. \tag{4}$$

The parameters of interest are the fixed and random effects associated with Equation 4. Specifically, the fixed effects (γ_{00} and γ_{10}) represent the mean intercept and mean slope pooling over all individuals. The random effects include the variance of the residuals at level-1 (denoted $var(e_{ti}) = \sigma^2$), and the variance of the individual deviations around the mean intercept and slope (denoted $var(u_{0i}) = \tau_{00}$ and $var(u_{1i}) = \tau_{11}$, respectively). It is common to assume that the level-1 residual variance is homoscedastic and independent over time (e.g., $\sigma^2 \mathbf{I}$), although this restriction can be tested and relaxed if needed. It is also common to estimate the covariance between the intercepts and slopes (denoted $cov(u_{0i}, u_{1i}) = \tau_{01}$), which can in turn be rescaled as a correlation coefficient (but see Biesanz, Deeb-Sossa, Aubrecht, Bollen, & Curran, 2004, for details of the scale-dependence of this covariance).

There are a variety of interesting ways in which this model can be expanded. For example, Equation 1 can include powered terms of time (e.g., x_{ti}^2) to estimate more complex members of the polynomial trajectory family (e.g., quadratic, cubic). Similarly, two measures of time could be defined that allow for the estimation of linear splines connected at a knot point (Raudenbush & Bryk, 2002). Time varying covariates (TVCs) can be incorporated in Equation 1 to include time-specific predictors of the repeated measures net the influence of the underlying random trajectories (e.g., days of school missed per year, onset of a new medical diagnosis, recent alcohol consumption). Time invariant covariates (TICs) can be incorporated in Equations 2 and 3 to predict individual variability in intercepts and slopes (e.g., gender, ethnicity, country of origin). The multilevel model is characterized by a multitude of significant strengths and has been widely used in the analysis of repeated measures data.

Despite these strengths, there are several issues of which we must be aware when considering the application of these techniques to developmental data. First, the standard multilevel model described earlier assumes that the residuals are continuously and normally distributed; however, many outcomes in developmental research are dichotomous, ordinal, or count variables which directly violate this distributional assumption. Second, the standard two-level model assumes that the outcome is a single individual and time specific score (i.e., y_{ti}). However, as developmental researchers, we are often not interested in a single score, but instead would like to incorporate a psychometric scale consisting of multiple items (e.g., scales assessing internalizing symptomatology or delinquent behavior), and to then fit growth models to these measurement models. The inclusion of multiple item psychometric models not only increases the content validity of the assessment of our construct, but also increases reliability and power (e.g., Bollen, 1989).

The purpose of our chapter is to present alternative methods that can be used to create individual and time specific scale scores from a set of dichotomous measures for use in multilevel models. From a statistical standpoint, the ideal approach would estimate the measurement model and the growth model simultaneously. However, as we discuss in greater detail next, these single-stage methods are often not easily applied within developmental research settings. Prior to presenting our two-stage analytic strategy, we briefly review existing single-stage approaches to this problem.

Single-Stage Categorical Growth Curve Models

As noted earlier, the standard multilevel model typically assumes that the repeated measures are continuously (and often normally) distributed. However, for many areas within developmental research, the repeated measures of interest are often discretely scaled (e.g., dichotomous or polytomous). This is particularly evident in studies of developmental psychopathology in which child outcomes are measured in terms of specific symptoms, discrete behaviors, or diagnostic status. It is well established that the application of our standard measurement and growth curve models to measures that are discretely scaled introduces potentially significant bias in the analysis and subsequent inferences (Mehta, Neale, & Flay, 2004; Muthén & Kaplan, 1985). Therefore, we must carefully consider the scaling of the outcome measure when selecting the optimal analytic method to test our research hypotheses. Fortunately, there are well developed modeling strategies that allow for the explicit incorporation of categorical repeated measures data in both measurement and growth curve models. There are two important approaches currently available.

The first method for the simultaneous estimation of categorical repeated measures in growth curve analysis is nonlinear multilevel models (e.g., Davidian & Giltinan, 1995; Diggle, Heagerty, Liang, & Zeger, 2002; Gibbons & Hedeker, 1997; Zeger, Liang, & Albert, 1988). Whereas the linear multilevel model imposes an identity link function for the analysis of continuous dependent measures, the nonlinear multilevel model incorporates a variety of alternative link functions for the analysis of dichotomous, ordinal, and count data (e.g., McCullagh & Nelder, 1989). Although well developed for single item outcomes, these models become quite complex when fitting measurement models to a set of items hypothesized to define an underlying construct (e.g., multiple dichotomous items assessing childhood aggression). Furthermore, it is often quite difficult to achieve numerical convergence of nonlinear multilevel models when fitted to empirical data of the type commonly encountered in developmental research (e.g., small sample sizes, scales consisting of multiple dichotomous items, many repeated assessments, attrition over time). An important related alternative is the three-level nonlinear multilevel Rasch model proposed by Raudenbush, Johnson, and Sampson (2003). This method is both creative and powerful, but also imposes certain restrictions to achieve identification, restrictions that might not hold in many areas of developmental research. In sum, these nonlinear approaches are both analytically elegant and highly promising but are currently infeasible for testing many developmental questions of interest.

The second available method for fitting growth curve models is the non-linear structural equation model (SEM; e.g., Jöreskog, 1994; Muthén, 1983; 1984). This approach is conceptually similar to the nonlinear multilevel model, although the estimation procedures differ in important ways (Wirth & Edwards, 2005). As we describe in greater detail later, the nonlinear SEM is based on the premise that the observed dichotomous measures are discrete realizations of a truly continuous unobserved response distribution. The goal is to simultaneously estimate the correlation structure among the underlying distributions and to fit the growth curve model of interest (e.g., Mehta et al., 2004). As with the nonlinear multilevel model, the nonlinear SEM is both powerful and flexible. However, this approach can be characterized by significant convergence and estimation problems when fitted to empirical data of the type commonly encountered in developmental research. Finally, as with the three-level Rasch model of Raudenbush et al. (2003), restrictive constraints are similarly needed to identify a growth model fitted to dichotomous scales (Muthén, 1996). Taken together, although the nonlinear SEM is a highly promising analytic strategy, this too is currently limited when simultaneously fitting measurement and growth curve models to developmental data.

In sum, there are a number of existing methodologies for the simultaneous analysis of psychometric measurement models fitted to dichotomous repeated measures combined with a random coefficient growth curve model. We have briefly reviewed the nonlinear multilevel model and the nonlinear SEM, although there are several other approaches we do not detail here (e.g., the random coefficient 2PL item response model; Fox, 2003, 2005). Despite both great flexibility and promise, these simultaneous estimation techniques are often empirically intractable given the many complexities encountered in developmental research settings. For this reason, we instead approach the problem from a two-stage perspective in which we separate the fitting of the psychometric model from the fitting of the growth curve model. This two-stage approach is not ideal from a statistical efficiency perspective given that not all model parameters are estimated simultaneously and there is thus some loss of statistical information. However, we view this strategy as a pragmatic alternative to the more elegant, yet analytically less tractable, single-stage methods.

THREE CATEGORICAL MEASUREMENT MODELS

Proportion Scoring

Arguably the most widely used method for imposing a measurement model on a set of categorical (and typically dichotomous) repeated measures is the proportion score.[1] Here, the manifest (or observed) individual and time specific variable p_{ti} is calculated as the proportion of items endorsed positively relative to the total number of available items. More formally,

$$p_{ti} = \frac{\sum_{j=1}^{J_{ti}} y_{jti}}{J_{ti}} \tag{5}$$

where y_{jti} is the observed score on dichotomous item $j = 1, 2, ..., J_{ti}$ at time $t = 1, 2, ...T$ for individual $i = 1, 2, ..., N$ with possible outcome 0 or 1. The values p_{ti} are computed from Equation 5 and the outcome is the unit of analysis for subsequent modeling.[2] For example, each individual subject i might have endorsed $J_t = 10$ items at time t indicating the presence or absence of ten specific antisocial acts having occurred in the prior 30 days. The individual and time specific measure p_{ti} would thus range from 0 to 1 by increments of .1 and reflect the proportion of items endorsed at each time period. Depending upon the age range under study, we might expect these proportion scores to systematically increase or decrease as a function of time (e.g., Moffitt, 1993).

Potential advantages of this approach include intuitive appeal, ease of implementation, and direct interpretation of the associated metric (e.g., .4 unambiguously reflects that 4 of 10 items were endorsed). However, there are two significant limitations that may well outweigh the potential advantages. First, there is no accounting for variation in the *severity* of items within individual or across time. This is because the endorsement of any given item is weighted equally across all available items (e.g., *lying to adults* and *using a weapon in a fight* are equally weighted in the computation of p_{ti}). Second, this approach assumes that the equal weighting of the set of $J-$items validly and reliably captures the underlying construct across time and development (e.g., *pinching and biting* is assumed to be equally indicative of antisocial behavior for all ages between 5 and 15). It is important to realize that the proportion score is a psychometric measurement model, but one that imposes a number of strict conditions. Violation of these conditions may introduce significant bias in the resulting inferences made from models fitted to measures scored in this way.

---

[1] Note that the proportion score is simply the mean of a set of dichotomous items. If the number of items is constant over time, the proportion score is a simple linear transformation of the sum of a set of dichotomous items. Thus all of our developments here apply to both proportion scores and sum scores when the item set is constant over time.

[2] We use the triple subscripts of j, t, and i to provide a maximally general framework that allows for the possibility of variations in the number of items over both time and individual.

Item Response Theory

The second categorical measurement model we consider is the item response theory (IRT) model. IRT is a collection of statistical models that formally link individuals and discretely scaled test items. In general, IRT models attempt to explain an observed item response in terms of item parameters and the unobserved examinee level on the underlying trait being measured. Importantly, IRT models are intrinsically nonlinear and thus specifically designed for categorical data.

The two parameter logistic model (2PL) is one of the most widely used IRT models and is conventionally written as

$$P(y_{jti} = 1|\theta_{ti}) = \frac{1}{1 + e^{-1.7a_{jt}(\theta_{ti} - b_{jt})}} \ , \tag{6}$$

where P indicates probability, y_{jti} is the observed response for item j at time t for individual i, θ_{ti} is the latent construct hypothesized to underlie the observed item response patterns, a_{jt} is the discrimination (or slope) parameter and b_{jt} is the threshold (or severity) parameter for item j at time t, and the constant value 1.7 scales the logistic approximation to the normal ogive model.

Discrimination (i.e., a_{jt}) reflects the degree to which responses to the item distinguish between different levels of the latent variable. Alternately, discrimination can be considered a measure of the degree of relation between a particular item and the underlying construct being measured (with higher values indicating a stronger relationship). *Severity* (i.e., b_{jt}), which is also considered *difficulty* in the context of educational testing, is the location on the underlying dimension at which an individual has a 50% chance of endorsing item j at time t. Readers familiar with IRT will note that the standard 2PL model is typically subscripted for item and not time. However, the inclusion of a subscript for time allows for the potential inclusion of longitudinally varying item parameters.

An alternative to the 2PL IRT model for dichotomous data is the 1-parameter logistic (1PL) model, often referred to as the Rasch model (Bond & Fox, 2001; Rasch, 1960). The equation for this model is identical to Equation 6, with the important exception that the slope parameter does not vary over items (i.e., a_{jt} is constant over all items j and times t). This model implies that all items are equally related to the latent construct. In other words, all items are restricted to be equally discriminating. When this model holds the parameter estimation and interpretation of the resulting parameters are greatly simplified. However, in practice, scales not specifically built to Rasch specifications rarely display Rasch-like properties. For this and other reasons, we focus on the 2PL model for the remainder of the chapter.

Our primary goal here is to use the 2PL IRT model as a first stage analysis to obtain individual and time specific estimates of the underlying latent score, and then to take these scores to our second stage analysis consisting of the multilevel growth model. To accomplish this, we first fitted IRT models for item calibration; this step provides the item-specific a and b parameters linking each item to the underlying latent distributions. We then used these calibration parameters to compute individual- and time-specific scores (denoted $\hat{\theta}$). The calibration stage provides the item parameters necessary for creating scores. No currently implemented estimation procedure allows for the simultaneous estimation of all item and person parameters.

Several methods for scoring are available, and Thissen and Wainer (2001) provide an excellent discussion of the technical details of these calculations. Briefly, each unique response pattern (e.g., each pattern of endorsed and nonendorsed items) is characterized by a posterior distribution which is the product of the population distribution and the trace lines corresponding to the pattern of endorsed/not endorsed items. While an entire posterior is available for each response pattern, it is often more convenient to have point estimates for each individual along with a corresponding measure of precision. Two popular estimates of $\hat{\theta}$ are the *modal a posteriori* (MAP) and the *expected a posteriori* (EAP). For the empirical results we present here, we estimate $\hat{\theta}$ via the MAP procedure.[3]

Categorical Confirmatory Factor Analysis

The third and final measurement model we consider is the categorical confirmatory factor analysis (CCFA) model. Key strengths of the CCFA include the ability to differentially weight items as a function of item discrimination, the explicit modeling of measurement error within and across time, and the provision of formal tests of measurement invariance. There is a close correspondence between the CCFA and the 2PL IRT approaches (e.g., Takane & de Leeuw, 1987), although we do not detail this here. We begin with a brief review of the standard linear confirmatory factor analysis (CFA) model fitted to continuously distributed indicators, and then extend this to the more complicated CCFA model.

The data model for the standard linear CFA is defined as:

$$y_{jti} = v_{y_{jt}} + \lambda_{y_{jt}}\eta_{ti} + \varepsilon_{jti} , \qquad (7)$$

---

[3]It is also possible to compute standard errors for the $\hat{\theta}$ scores, although the formal inclusion of these in the second stage analysis significantly complicates estimation and inference. Future research is needed regarding how to use these standard errors in two-stage analysis.

where y_{jti} is the observed continuously distributed score on item j at time t for individual i. This observed score is expressed as a linear combination of an item and time specific intercept $(v_{y_{jt}})$, a time and individual specific latent score on the hypothesized theoretical construct (η_{ti}), an item and time specific factor loading linking the observed item to the underlying latent factor $(\lambda_{y_{jt}})$, and an item, time and individual specific error (ε_{jti}). Importantly, a variety of equality constraints can be imposed over item and across time to simplify these expressions considerably, and we make use of these constraints later.

Equation 7 defines the data model for our observed repeated measures. The covariance and mean structure implied by Equation 7 as a function of the parameters contained in vector $\boldsymbol{\theta}$ is

$$\boldsymbol{\Sigma}(\boldsymbol{\theta}) = \boldsymbol{\Lambda}_y \boldsymbol{\Psi}_{\eta\eta} \boldsymbol{\Lambda}_y' + \boldsymbol{\Theta}_{\varepsilon\varepsilon} \ , \tag{8}$$

with corresponding mean structure

$$\boldsymbol{\eta} = \boldsymbol{\mu_\eta} + \boldsymbol{\zeta}. \tag{9}$$

Here, $\boldsymbol{\Sigma}(\boldsymbol{\theta})$ represents the the model-implied covariance matrix for N individuals measured on p variables y. $\boldsymbol{\Lambda}_y$ denotes a $p \times m$ matrix of factor loadings (i.e., regression coefficients), $\boldsymbol{\Psi}_{\eta\eta}$ denotes a $m \times m$ variance/covariance or correlation matrix of latent factors, and $\boldsymbol{\Theta}_{\varepsilon\varepsilon}$ denotes a $p \times p$ matrix of unique variances (and potentially covariances). The m-vector of latent factors, $\boldsymbol{\eta}$, is equal to a m-vector of latent means, $\boldsymbol{\mu_\eta}$, plus a m-vector of latent deviations, $\boldsymbol{\zeta}$.

Assumptions imposed for the estimation of these model parameters include the mean of the residuals equal to zero $(E(\varepsilon) = 0)$, the residuals are uncorrelated with one another $(cov(\varepsilon_i, \varepsilon_j) = 0, i \neq j)$, the residuals are uncorrelated with the latent factors $(cov(\varepsilon_i, \eta) = 0)$, and that the model is linear in the parameters (e.g., all model parameters enter the model linearly; Bollen, 1989). Although the validity of these assumptions can be evaluated to varying degrees, the assumption of linearity is almost always violated in the presence of categorical data. In fact, the presence of categorical indicators implicitly introduces a nonlinear relationship into the system of equations. Two key assumptions are violated when treating an ordinal measure as if it were continuous.

First, we can think of each observed repeated ordinal measure in vector $\mathbf{y}$ linked to a corresponding continuous underlying measure $\mathbf{y}^*$. The standard linear model assumes that $\mathbf{y} = \mathbf{y}^*$; that is, that the repeated measures are continuous (or at least rough approximations). However, when we have observed a dichotomous or ordinal $\mathbf{y}$, this equality will not hold. In this situation, our fitted growth models will hold for $\mathbf{y}^*$ but *not* for $\mathbf{y}$. Second, we can write the moment structure hypotheses as $\boldsymbol{\Sigma}^* = \boldsymbol{\Sigma}(\boldsymbol{\theta})$ and $\boldsymbol{\mu}^* = \boldsymbol{\mu}(\boldsymbol{\theta})$, where $\boldsymbol{\Sigma}^*$ is the population covariance matrix of $\mathbf{y}^*$, $\boldsymbol{\mu}^*$ is the vector of means of $\mathbf{y}^*$, $\boldsymbol{\Sigma}(\boldsymbol{\theta})$ is the implied covariance matrix, $\boldsymbol{\mu}(\boldsymbol{\theta})$ is the implied mean vector, and θ is the vector of model parameters. Given that the observed variables $\mathbf{y}$ are collapsed versions of $\mathbf{y}^*$, in nearly all cases $\boldsymbol{\Sigma} \neq \boldsymbol{\Sigma}^*$ and $\boldsymbol{\mu} \neq \boldsymbol{\mu}^*$ so that $\boldsymbol{\Sigma} \neq \boldsymbol{\Sigma}(\theta)$ and $\boldsymbol{\mu} \neq \boldsymbol{\mu}(\boldsymbol{\theta})$. Thus, the moment structure hypotheses will typically not hold for the observed repeated ordinal measures.

Part of the corrective procedure to overcome these violations is to explicitly link $\mathbf{y}$ to $\mathbf{y}^*$ (Jöreskog, 1994; Muthén, 1983, 1984; Muthén & Satorra, 1995). An auxiliary threshold model is a natural way to show the nonlinear relation between these categorical and continuous variables in which $y_{it} = c_t$ when $\tau_{c_t-1} < y_{it}^* \leq \tau_{c_t}$ where $c_t = 1, 2, 3, ..., C_t$ the total number of ordered categories, τ_{c_t-1}, τ_{c_t} are the lower and upper thresholds for category c_t with $\tau_{0_t} = -\infty$ and $\tau_{C_t} = +\infty$, and the thresholds are ordered from lowest to highest. This model connects the ordinal variable to its underlying continuous counterpart such that when the continuous variable lies between two thresholds, the ordinal variable will register in the category those thresholds determine. The mean $(\mu_{y_t^*})$ and variance $(\sigma_{y_t^* y_t^*})$ of y_{it}^* are unknown as are the thresholds from τ_{1t} to τ_{C_t-1}, but a subset of these can be estimated from the observed multivariate frequency distribution (Mehta et al., 2004). Finally, the correlation structure among the unobserved response distributions can be estimated, and these are often referred to as tetrachoric (for dichotomously scaled items) or polychoric (for polytomously scaled items) correlations.

The classic estimator in SEM for fitting polychoric correlation matrices is Weighted Least Squares (WLS) which is given as

$$F_{WLS} = [\widehat{\boldsymbol{\rho}}^* - \boldsymbol{\rho}^*(\boldsymbol{\theta})]' \mathbf{W}^{-1} [\widehat{\boldsymbol{\rho}}^* - \boldsymbol{\rho}^*(\boldsymbol{\theta})], \tag{10}$$

where $\widehat{\boldsymbol{\rho}}^*$ is a vector that contains all the estimated polychoric correlations and the means of the $\mathbf{y}^*$ variables, $\boldsymbol{\rho}^*(\boldsymbol{\theta})$ is the model-implied values of the polychoric correlations and the means, $\boldsymbol{\theta}$ contains all of the model parameters, and $\mathbf{W}$ is an optimal weight matrix (Browne, 1984). However, limitations of WLS include the need for very large sample sizes for the preceding asymptotic properties to hold, which has led researchers to seek alternative estimators including diagonal WLS (Jöreskog & Sörbom, 1979), corrected ML (Jöreskog, Sörbom, Du Toit, & Du Toit, 1999), robust WLS (Muthén, Du Toit, & Spisic, 1997), and 2SLS (Bollen, 1996), among others.

Recall that one of our goals is to use a two-stage process in which we first fit a measurement model to our observed categorical repeated measures, and then fit a growth model to the resulting individual specific scale scores. Equations 8 and 9 provide insight into a method for obtaining individual latent scores, also known as factor scores (e.g., Grice, 2001). Specifically, if we can estimate the relationship between the items and obtain an estimate of the individual variability around the latent factor, we can work backwards to obtain the individual factor scores. Given that these factor scores take both the differentially weighted items as well as measurement error into account, they provide a more accurate estimate of individual scores and variability than the standard proportion score methodology.

The estimation of the CCFA model just described above provides estimates of the covariance among the latent factors, $\hat{\boldsymbol{\Psi}}$, the factor loadings, $\hat{\boldsymbol{\Lambda}}_y$, and the model-implied covariance matrix, $\hat{\boldsymbol{\Sigma}}_{yy}$. These estimates can then be used to obtain the ordinary least squares regression coefficients used to premultiply $\mathbf{y}$ resulting in individual factor score estimates, $\hat{\eta}_i$.

Formally,

$$\widehat{\boldsymbol{\eta}} = \hat{\boldsymbol{\Psi}}\hat{\boldsymbol{\Lambda}}_y'\hat{\boldsymbol{\Sigma}}_{yy}^{-1}\mathbf{y} \ , \tag{11}$$

where all parameters are as defined earlier. Once factor scores have been obtained via Equation 11, these can then be used within a second stage of analysis such as the standard multilevel framework.

SUMMARY

In sum, we have described three possible approaches for obtaining individual and time specific measures of an underlying construct based on a set of observed discretely scaled items: the proportion score methodology, the 2PL IRT, and the categorical CFA. Each approach is characterized by certain advantages and disadvantages. Of key importance to our goals here, despite rather widespread use in practice, the proportion score appears to be the most limited given the imposition of equal item weighting and the untestable assumption of measurement invariance. In contrast, both the IRT and CCFA models allow for differential item weighting as a function of severity and the strength of the relation between the item and the underlying construct. Furthermore, the IRT model provides formal tests of differential item functioning (e.g., Thissen, Steinberg, & Wainer, 1988) and the CCFA models offer the possibility of formal tests of measurement invariance (e.g., Meredith, 1964; 1993). This is particularly useful for evaluating the equivalence of measurement structures across different contexts. To better understand the applicability of these three approaches in developmental research, we now turn to an empirical examination of the relative behavior of these three methods when fitted to a single empirical sample of children followed from ages 10 to 21.

TRAJECTORIES OF EXTERNALIZING SYMPTOMATOLOGY IN ADOLESCENTS

The Adolescent and Family Development Project

To compare the three methods of scoring categorical measurement scales, we examined data drawn from the Adolescent and Family Development Project (AFDP: Chassin, Rogosch, & Barrera, 1991). The total sample consisted of 454 adolescents and their parents who completed repeated computerized, in-home interviews. Of these, 246 included a biological and custodial alcoholic parent whereas 208 were matched controls. COA families were recruited by means of court records (n = 103), wellness questionnaires from a health maintenance organization (n = 22), and community telephone surveys (n = 120). Inclusion criteria for COA families were Hispanic or non-Hispanic Caucasian ethnicity, Arizona residency, having a 10 − 15 year old adolescent, English-speaking, and lack of cognitive limitations precluding an interview.

Lifetime presence of parent alcoholism was determined through diagnostic interviews with parents using the Diagnostic Interview Schedule or through spousal report using the Family History Research Diagnostic Criteria (if the alcoholic parent was not interviewed). Matched control families were recruited by phone screens of families identified through reverse directory searches based on identified COAs. Control families matched COA families on the basis of ethnicity, family composition, target child's age (within 1 year), and socioeconomic status (using the property value code from the reverse directory). Direct interview data confirmed that neither biological nor custodial parents met criteria for a lifetime alcoholism diagnosis.

These families were initially interviewed when the adolescents were aged 10 − 15 (wave 1) and re-interviewed on an annual basis when the adolescents were aged 12 − 16 (wave 2) and 13 − 17 (wave 3), and again after a 5 year lag when the target adolescents were aged 18 − 21 (Wave 4). Sample retention has been high, with 444 (97.8%) interviewed at all of the first three waves and 407 (90%) were interviewed again at the fourth wave. For the current analysis, 444 adolescents were considered with a complete age range of 10 to 21.[4]

The theoretical construct of interest here is adolescent externalizing symptomatology. For our demonstration, we considered a subset of eight items drawn from the Child Behavior Check List (CBCL; Achenbach & Edelbrock, 1983).

---

[4]There were 29 children who are 10 years of age at the first assessment. These subjects were included in the calibration and scoring steps, but were omitted from the multilevel growth models given the small sample size at the first observed age. All substantive findings were similar for all analyses when including these 29 cases.

TABLE 5.1

Item Parameters From Proportion Scores (p), 2PL IRT (a and b), CCFA (λ and τ), From Calibration Sample of 435 10 − 15 Year Old Children for the Eight CBCL Items at First Wave of Assessment

Item	Item Wording	p	a	b	λ	τ
1	Argues a lot	0.81	2.27	−1.13	0.79	−0.89
2	Cruelty, bullying, or meanness to others	0.24	2.12	0.92	0.76	0.70
3	Destroys things	0.06	1.42	2.52	0.56	1.61
4	Gets in many fights	0.17	2.66	1.14	0.81	0.94
5	Lying or cheating	0.29	1.29	0.89	0.64	0.54
6	Physically attacks people	0.07	1.81	2.04	0.64	1.45
7	Threatens people	0.15	2.73	1.26	0.83	1.04
8	Steals	0.07	1.53	2.20	0.64	1.45

Note. p = proportion of sample endorsing item, a = IRT discrimination, b = IRT severity, λ = CCFA factor loading, and τ = CCFA threshold.

These items were mother's report of the extent to which the adolescent argues, is cruel, destroys things, fights, lies, attacks others, threatens, or steals (see Table 5.1 for details). The data were originally collected using a three-response format (not true, somewhat or sometimes true, very true or often true), but there were sparse responses within and across time in the highest category denoted "very true or often true". Such sparseness introduces instability in the estimation of parameters in the subsequent measurement models (Thissen, Chen, & Bock, 2003). Because of this, the trichotomous response was collapsed to a binary response of "not true" and "sometimes or very true".

Calculation of Scale Scores

We used the three scoring methods described earlier to compute individual and time specific scale scores of externalizing symptomatology based on the eight CBCL items assessed on the 444 adolescents from the AFDP. For the IRT and CCFA approaches, we needed to use a calibration sample from which to estimate the parameters necessary for the scoring step. The sample used for the item calibration consisted of all children between age 10 and 15 at wave 1 of the mother's report of the eight CBCL items. This resulted in 435 cases (nine cases from the total sample did not meet the selection criteria).

Proportion Scores

Unlike the IRT and CCFA approaches, there is no calibration step necessary in the calculation of the proportion scores. Instead, the proportion scores were calculated using Equation 5 for adolescents within each individual age. For comparison purposes only, we present the proportion scores based on the calibration sample that was used for the IRT and CCFA models in Table 5.1. Thus, the column denoted p represents the proportion of the eight CBCL items endorsed by all subjects in the calibration sample between the ages of 10 and 15 at first wave of assessment. We present the mean proportion scores across all ages next.

IRT Scores

The IRT analysis consisted of two steps: the calibration step and the scoring step. The calibration step provided the discrimination and severity parameters for each item (e.g., a and b from above), and the scoring step used these parameters to calculate the individual and time specific $\hat{\theta}$ values. We first fitted a standard 2PL IRT model to the eight dichotomously scored items on the 435 subjects in the calibration sample using maximum marginal likelihood estimation available in Multilog (Thissen, Chen, & Bock, 2003). This strategy allowed us to estimate the difficulty and discrimination parameters for each of the eight items that were then used in the creation of the individual scale scores.

The resulting IRT parameters are presented in Table 5.1, and the trace lines for eight items are presented in Figure 5.1 with four items specifically labeled ("argues a lot", "cruelty, bullying, or meanness", "lying or cheating", and "destroys things"). The discrimination parameter (i.e., a) reflects the steepness of the trace line for any given item. Comparing the "cruelty" item with the "lying" item shows the difference between slopes of 2.12 and 1.29, respectively. These numbers suggest that the "cruelty" item better discriminates at higher levels of externalizing symptomatology than does the "lying" item. Another useful analogy can be made between IRT discrimination parameters and factor loadings from the factor analysis literature. Discrimination parameters, much like factor loadings, can also be thought of as indexes of the extent to which an indicator is related to the latent construct (Takane & De Leeuw, 1987). Higher slopes indicate a stronger relationship between an item and the underlying construct. In the current example, we would say that the "cruelty" item is more strongly related to externalizing symptomatology than the "lying" item.

Comparing "argues" and "destroys things" shows the difference between items with severity values of -1.13 and 2.52, respectively. Following convention for setting the scale metric in IRT models, the b parameters are in a standard normal metric. This allows us to conclude that an individual would need to be approximately 1.1 standard deviations below the mean level of externalizing symptomatology to have a 50% chance of endorsing the "argues" item. On the

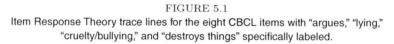

FIGURE 5.1
Item Response Theory trace lines for the eight CBCL items with "argues," "lying,"
"cruelty/bullying," and "destroys things" specifically labeled.

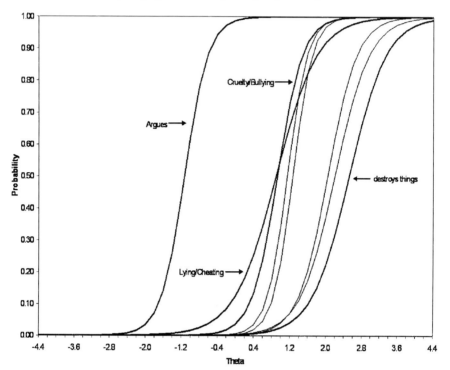

other hand, an individual would have to be approximately 2.5 standard deviations above the mean level of externalizing symptomatology to have a 50% chance of endorsing "destroys things". These values make intuitive sense: Individuals who destroys things are (generally) demonstrating greater externalizing symptomatology than individuals who argue. So, although arguing is still reflective of underlying externalizing symptomatology, endorsement of this item reflects a lower level of externalizing symptomatology than do other behaviors such as destroying things.

Finally, we used the item parameters from the calibration step to calculate individual- and time-specific scale scores for externalizing symptomatology for each of the 444 subjects. Multilog (Thissen et al., 2003) was used to produce modal a posteriori (MAP) scores for each subject at each time of assessment. The individual and time specific MAP is the mode of the posterior distribution of θ_{ti}, and we refer to these scores as $\hat{\theta}_{ti}$.

CCFA scores

As with the IRT approach, we again used a two step procedure to calculate the CCFA scores: a calibration step and a scoring step. For the calibration step, we used the same calibration sample from the IRT analysis. We estimated an eight item, one factor, CCFA model using robust weighted least squares (RWLS) fitted to tetrachoric correlations available in Mplus (version 2.14; Muthén & Muthén, 2001). The model was identified by constraining the latent mean to zero and latent variance to unity (see Figure 5.2 for a path diagram of this calibration model). The model fit the observed data well ($\chi^2(14) = 27.8$, $p = .015$, $CFI = .99$, $TLI = .98$, $RMSEA = .048$), and the final factor loadings (λ) and item thresholds (τ) are presented in Table 5.1.

For the scoring step, these calibration parameter estimates were then used to calculate ordinary least squares factor-score regression coefficients (see Bollen, 1989, pp. 305 – 306)[5]. As part of the scoring, the observed binary data was recoded in order to take advantage of all available information. Specifically, endorsing an item was coded .5, failing to endorse an item was coded −.5, and missing responses were coded zero. This rescaling allowed all available information to be used in factor score estimation. The choice of −.5 and .5 retains the 1−unit interval width between responses that was present in the 0/1 coding, yet allows us to incorporate the small number of cases with some subset of CBCL items missing within a given time period. Our motivation was thus to treat "missing" differently from "not endorsed" in the scoring step. This had the further advantage of maximizing the correspondence between the CCFA and IRT scoring methods. Using this approach, we calculated the individual and time specific factor scores based on the relevant model matrices in Equation 11. We refer to these estimated factor scores as $\hat{\eta}_{ti}$.

Calibration Invariance

When considering the study of development within and across context, it is critical that measurement models be evaluated for invariance across known contextual influences. For example, recall that our calibration sample consisted of children aged 10 to 15 at first assessment. This resulted in a mean age of 12.7, with 43% of the sample 12 years of age or younger. Given the importance of the IRT and CCFA parameters to the subsequent scoring steps that are based on this calibration sample, it is important to evaluate measurement invariance

---

[5]Although the methods described in Bollen (1989) were developed for continuously distributed indicators, we modified these calculations slightly to allow for the incorporation of dichotomous indicators.

FIGURE 5.2

Path diagram for categorical CFA model fitted to the 8 CBCL items.

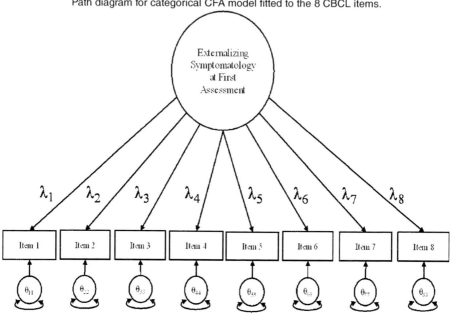

in terms of young (10, 11, or 12 years of age) versus old (13, 14, or 15 years of age) children. [6]

Unfortunately, the very nature of the psychometric model used for the calculation of the proportion scores does not allow for any testing of the invariance of this model as a function of child age. We can thus bring no empirical information to bear on this question for our estimates of p_{ti}.

To empirically evaluate the degree to which the item parameters from the 2PL IRT were invariant over age within the calibration sample, we performed differential item function (DIF) analyses using the freely available program IRTLRDIF (www.unc.edu/~dthissen/dl.html). Briefly, this approach allows for a series of one degree-of-freedom chi-square tests to ascertain the equality of the pair of parameters associated with each individual item (i.e., discrimination and severity) as a function of group membership. The results indicated that there was no significant DIF associated with any item parameter in comparing the "young" and "old" groups of children. This is strong evidence that the item

---

[6]It is important to remember that here we are evaluating the degree of measurement invariance as a function of young versus old children within the calibration sample only. This is thus testing invariance across children and over age, and is not a test of measurement invariance within child over age. This is an equally important issue to consider, a full treatment of which is beyond the scope of the current chapter.

parameters calculated on the full calibration sample and used in subsequent scoring do not vary for children aged 10 to 12 compared to children aged 13 to 15.

We were similarly able to empirically evaluate the invariance of the CCFA parameter estimates as a function of young versus old children using the multiple group approach as estimated in Mplus (Muthén & Muthén, 2001). The CCFA allows for an omnibus chi-square test of the equality of all parameter estimates across group membership. Two models were fitted to the two subsamples of young versus old children in the calibration sample. The first allowed all model parameters to be freely estimated over the two groups ($\chi^2(40) = 64.9$, $p = .008$, $CFI = .99$, $TLI = .98$, $RMSEA = .05$), and the second imposed equality constraints on all model parameters ($\chi^2(54) = 74.9$, $p = .02$, $CFI = .99$, $TLI = .99$, $RMSEA = .045$). Although the constrained model is nested within the unconstrained model, we can not calculate a formal chi-square difference test given our use of RWLS (Muthén et al., 1997). However, the constrained model reflects equal or superior fit on all indices compared to the unconstrained model thus suggesting that the equality constraints were appropriate relative to the characteristics of the sample data. These results converged with those of the IRT DIF analysis indicating that the measurement model of externalizing symptomatology was invariant with respect to age within the calibration sample.

Comparison of Three Scoring Methods

Following the methods described earlier, we calculated three different individual and time specific scale scores for the eight CBCL items: p_{ti}, $\hat{\theta}_{ti}$, and $\hat{\eta}_{ti}$. We compare these scores in three ways: in terms of means, correlations, and fixed and random effects from fitted multilevel growth models.[7]

Mean comparisons

The first comparison of interest relates to the pattern of change in age-specific means of externalizing in the three different score types over time. We present the age specific means of the externalizing symptomatology scale scores at each age for all three scoring methods in Table 5.2. Direct comparison of both the means and standard deviations are difficult given that all three scale scores are on different metrics (e.g., the proportion is bounded between 0 and 1, and the

---

[7]It is possible to draw more specific analytic relations between p_{ti}, $\hat{\theta}_{ti}$, and $\hat{\eta}_{ti}$, although a detailed treatment of this is beyond the scope of our chapter. See chapters 15 and 16 of Lord and Novick (1968) and Takane and de Leeuw (1987) for further details.

IRT and CCFA are theoretically bounded between negative and positive infinity). Furthermore, even within the IRT and CCFA, the underlying metrics are not comparable in absolute terms but only in relative terms. Thus, it is evident that the highest level of externalizing symptomatology across all three scale scores occurs at the youngest age of 11. Additionally, the externalizing symptomatology scores systematically decrease with increasing age. (Again, recall that through our use of the accelerated longitudinal design, we are able to track these scores over 11 distinct ages although no single child provided more than four waves of data.)

We can also compare these age-specific means graphically through the use of multiple $y-$axes to denote the scale of each score. In Figure 5.3 we present the pattern of means of the IRT and proportion scores from age 11 to 21.[8] The IRT scores are scaled on the left-hand y-axis, and the proportion scores are scaled on the right-hand y-axis. It is graphically clear that the age specific mean externalizing scores are both decreasing in a nonlinear trend for both the proportion and IRT scores. Note that these trends are quite similar from age 11 through 17, but begin to diverge slightly up to age 21. Although the trend lines are slightly offset, both scores appear to be approximately following the same trend over time.

Despite the similarity in age specific mean scores over time, this comparison does not allow us to consider characteristics of the individual scores within each age. To explore this, we next turn to an examination of the within time correlations among the three scores.

Correlation Comparisons

An important initial comparison is to simply assess the degree to which the three types of scores correlate with one another within each distinct age. We thus computed standard Pearson correlations among the three types of scores. Overall, the correlations among the three scores within a given age were extremely high. For example, across all ages the range of correlations between the proportion and IRT scores was $.96 - .97$, between the proportion and CCFA scores was $.97 - .99$, and between the IRT and CCFA scores was $.97 - .98$. Given that a squared correlation represents the proportion of overlapping variance between the two variables, the overall shared variability was $92\% - 98\%$. Clearly, there is a large amount of shared information among these three scoring methods.

---

[8]We do not present the CCFA scores here given that we can only use two different scales on the y-axis. However, the pattern of the CCFA scores nearly identically track that of the IRT scores.

TABLE 5.2

Age Specific Means (and Standard Deviations) for the Proportion (p), IRT ($\hat{\theta}$), and CCFA ($\hat{\eta}$) Scale Scores of Externalizing Symptomatology

Age	Sample Size	p	$\hat{\theta}$	$\hat{\eta}$
11	103	.25(.21)	.13(.82)	−.26(.27)
12	181	.24(.20)	.08(.81)	−.28(.27)
13	256	.23(.20)	.06(.84)	−.28(.28)
14	281	.22(.19)	.02(.79)	−.30(.26)
15	236	.21(.20)	−.04(.82)	−.31(.27)
16	143	.21(.21)	−.07(.85)	−.31(.28)
17	55	.20(.21)	−.13(.88)	−.34(.28)
18	76	.16(.25)	−.36(.97)	−.38(.31)
19	78	.13(.18)	−.51(.82)	−.44(.24)
20	95	.12(.18)	−.54(.88)	−.44(.25)
21	91	.09(.14)	−.71(.72)	−.49(.20)

However, these high correlations do not yet allow us to conclude that these these three scoring methods offer an equivalent representation of the underlying construct. The reason is that the correlations reflect a high degree of overlap in the rank ordering of scores relative to the score mean; yet these do not reflect potentially important differences in other aspects of the score characteristics.

Most importantly, the correlations do not reflect potential differences in the variability among the individual scores within and across time. Given that the IRT and CCFA scores incorporate differential item severity, but the proportion scores do not, we predicted that there would be potentially important differences with respect to individual variability among the scores. This is particularly salient given our desire to fit random coefficients growth models to these scores, a type of analysis in which variability plays a key role.

To better understand this issue, consider the values presented in Table 5.3. The first eight columns reflect different patterns of endorsement of the eight items just within age 14. Consistent with how the proportion scores are calculated, the seven unique combinations of endorsement of any two items observed in the sample resulted in a proportion score of .25. There is thus no variability within the proportions scores for the endorsement of 2 of 8 items at age 14. However, recall that the IRT and CCFA scoring approach explicitly incorporate information about differential item properties. This means that the associated IRT or CCFA score for the endorsement of 2 of 8 items depends on *which* two items were endorsed. This in turn introduces greater variability among the individual and time specific scores, variability that might play a critical role when fitting random coefficient growth curve models.

FIGURE 5.3

Age-specific means of proportion and IRT scores for 8 CBCL items with IRT scores scaled on the left y-axis, and proportion scores scaled on the right.

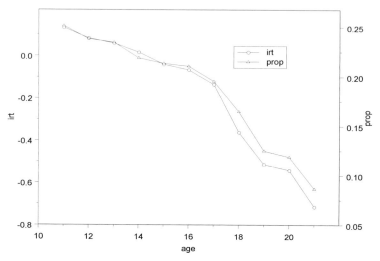

Note. IRT represents item response theory score and "prop" represents proportion score.

Multilevel Growth Curve Models

As a final comparison of the three methods of scoring the eight dichotomous items, we fitted a random coefficients multilevel growth model using SAS PROC MIXED (SAS Institute, 1999). Importantly, we used chronological age and not wave of assessment as the time metric of interest. There were thus 11 distinct ages ranging from 11 to 21, although no single child was assessed more than four times (see, e.g., Mehta & West, 2000). We began by fitting fixed and random effects for a linear trajectory as a function of chronological age. Age was scaled such that 0 represented age 11; this allowed for the intercept term to be interpreted as the model-implied mean externalizing at the youngest age in the sample. This model was fit to all three scores separately, and significant fixed and random effects were found for the intercept and linear slope term in all three models.

However, as is evidenced from the mean trends presented in Figure 5.3, it seemed likely that a curvilinear trajectory might better capture the observed pattern of change over time. Thus a quadratic term was added to each of the three models, and the addition of the squared term of age significantly improved model fit as tested by the likelihood ratio test (e.g., testing the difference in deviance statistics between the more and the less restricted models; Raudenbush

TABLE 5.3

Proportion Scores (p), IRT Scores ($\hat{\theta}$), CCFA Scores ($\hat{\eta}$), and Frequency of Endorsement ($freq$) of any 2 of the 8 CBCL Items Observed in the Sample at Age 14

1	2	3	4	5	6	7	8	$freq$	p	$\hat{\theta}$	$\hat{\eta}$
1	0	0	0	1	0	0	0	19	.25	.175	−.312
1	0	1	0	0	0	0	0	1	.25	.214	−.336
1	0	0	0	0	1	0	0	4	.25	.322	−.308
1	1	0	0	0	0	0	0	18	.25	.401	−.241
0	1	0	0	0	0	1	0	1	.25	.507	−.185
1	0	0	1	0	0	0	0	7	.25	.524	−.194
1	0	0	0	0	0	1	0	6	.25	.539	−.159

Note. The integers 1 through 8 represent the CBCL item presented in Table 5.1, and $freq$ is frequency of endorsement of those two items at age 14.

& Bryk, 2002). We selected the quadratic trajectory model for interpretation here.

The point estimates and standard errors for the fixed and random effects of the quadratic model fitted to the three different scores are presented in Table 5.4. The fixed effects for all three scores are rather similar. That is, although the point estimates differ depending on scoring method (as would be expected given the differences in scaling described earlier), the pattern of significance is quite similar. Specifically, there is a significant fixed effect for the intercept, a nonsignificant fixed effect for the linear slope, and a significant fixed effect for the quadratic slope. This reflects the general trend seen in the mean trends in Figure 5.3 and in the model-implied mean trajectory for the IRT scores presented in Figure 5.4. There is a decreasing trend in the means over time, but the rate of decrease is larger as time progresses. Thus, in terms of the fixed effects, the substantive conclusions are quite similar across the three scoring methods.

However, these results do not reflect potential differences introduced into the multilevel model due to increased variability in the IRT and CCFA scores. Consistent with this prediction, there are important differences among these scoring methods in terms of the random effects of the trajectories that define the quadratic trajectory. Although there is a significant random effect for the intercept term for all three score types, differences across these models were evident for the random slope effects. For the proportion score, the random effect for the linear term is only marginally significant ($p = .074$) and the random effect for the quadratic term is nonsignificant ($p = .143$). However, the random effect for the linear term is significant for both the CCFA ($p = .030$) and IRT ($p = .013$) models. Moreover, the quadratic term is marginally signi-

TABLE 5.4
Fixed and Random Effects for Quadratic Growth Curve Model Fitted to all Three Scale Scores

Parameter	p	$\hat{\theta}$	$\hat{\eta}$
$\hat{\gamma}_{00}$	$.246\ (.014)^*$	$.117\ (.057)^*$	$-.268(.018)^*$
$\hat{\gamma}_{10}$	$-.003\ (.006)^{ns}$	$-.008\ (.024)^{ns}$	$-.002(.008)^{ns}$
$\hat{\gamma}_{20}$	$-.001\ (.0005)^*$	$-.008\ (.002)^*$	$-.002(.0007)^*$
$\hat{\tau}_{00}$	$.025\ (.004)^*$	$.447\ (.078)^*$	$.046(.008)^*$
$\hat{\tau}_{11}$	$.001\ (.001)^{ns}$	$.040\ (.018)^*$	$.003(.001)^*$
$\hat{\tau}_{22}$	$.0001\ (.0001)^{ns}$	$-.003\ (.0001)^*$	$.00002(.00001)^{\S}$
$\hat{\sigma}^2$	$.014\ (.001)^*$	$.238\ (.013)^*$	$.026(.001)^*$

Note. $\hat{\gamma}_{00}$ = fixed intercept; $\hat{\gamma}_{10}$ = fixed linear; $\hat{\gamma}_{20}$ = fixed quadratic; $\hat{\tau}_{00}$ = random intercept; $\hat{\tau}_{11}$ = random linear; $\hat{\tau}_{22}$ = random quadratic; $\hat{\sigma}^2$ = level-1 residual; $ns = p > .05$; $* = p < .05$; $\S = p < .10$.

ficant for the CCFA scores ($p = .072$), and is significant for the IRT scores ($p = .031$). As predicted, the added variability associated with CCFA and IRT scoring procedures is reflected in greater individual variability in the growth curve models.

These differences could be quite salient from a substantive point of view. Fitting the growth model to the proportion scores would suggest that although the group curve of externalizing is decreasing nonlinearly over time, there is no evidence of individual variability in rates of change around this mean curve. In comparison, the CCFA and, even more clearly, the IRT results suggest that there is meaningful individual variability among the externalizing trajectories over time. This supports a very different substantive conclusion than that derived from the analysis of the proportion scores and demonstrates the impact that differing scoring procedures can have on evaluating change over time.

CONCLUSIONS

A major part of what makes empirical research in developmental psychology both fun and rewarding is the very thing that makes it an equally vexing task. Namely, it is hard; and it is even harder to do well. Consider just a random sampling of issues that commonly arise in the study of developmental processes over time: missing data, categorical and non-normally distributed repeated measures, nonlinear trajectories, nesting of children within families or schools, changes in the manifestation or even meaning of a construct over development. Furthermore, consistent with the theme of this book, all of these issues are even more salient when attempting to study the development of individuals

FIGURE 5.4

Observed means (dashed line) and model-implied quadratic trajectory (solid line) for IRT scores from the multilevel growth model fitted to the sample of 439 adolescents.

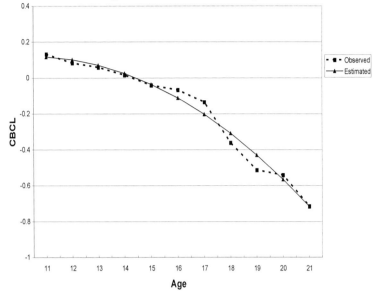

embedded within one or more contexts. Finally, these issues all assume that the data has already been collected; equally challenging issues arise in the design and execution of a developmental study.

Among these many challenges, we have focused our attention on the incorporation of psychometric scales made up of multiple dichotomous items in the analysis of individual growth curves over time. We described a two-stage procedure in which scale scores are first calculated, and growth curve models are then fitted to these scores. In contrast to this approach, there exist several advanced analytic methods that allow for the simultaneous estimation of a formal measurement model of a set of dichotomous items with a growth curve model. Although unquestionably the ideal strategy, these techniques impose certain restrictions that may not be appropriate in many areas of developmental research and, more importantly, these methods are also currently difficult (if not impossible) to implement in practice. Given our desire to consider methods that can be applied in developmental research settings, we have approached this problem using the two-stage strategy.

For the first analytic stage we considered three methods for calculating the scale scores based on a set of dichotomous items: the proportion score, the 2PL IRT model, and the CCFA model. Not surprisingly, the resulting scores from all three of these methods were highly correlated with each other. Indeed, within age correlations ranged from .96 − .99 with most in the .98 range. This prompts one to wonder if all of the added complexity of the IRT and CCFA approaches are worthwhile given these high linear relations. However, we strongly believe that these alternative approaches are important to consider because these high correlations only tell part of the story.

More specifically, the proportion score simply reflects the number of dichotomous items that were endorsed by an individual within an assessment period. Thus a score of .25 unambiguously reflects that two of the eight items were endorsed. However, what is critical to understand is that this same score of .25 results from the endorsement of *any* two of the eight items. So endorsing "lying" and "arguing" is assigned the same numerical value as endorsing "cruelty" and "physically attacks people". It may be (and our findings suggest that it is) very important to use a measurement model that allows for differential contributions of these items depending upon severity and the strength of the relation of the item to the underlying construct of externalizing symptomatology. For this, we turned to the IRT and CCFA models.

In contrast to the proportion score, the IRT and CCFA methods explicitly allow for differential item weighting in the creation of a scale score. Importantly, it is not just that two of eight items were endorsed, but *which* two of the items were endorsed. Because different scores are assigned based on the specific set of items that were endorsed, this allows for greater variability among the individual and time specific scores. This increased variability was clearly evident when comparing the different IRT and CCFA scores resulting from different patterns of item endorsement (see Table 5.3). This in turn increases the variability available for modeling in the subsequent growth curve analysis. Whereas the results of the growth model fitted to the proportion scores indicated no individual variability in developmental trajectories over time, the very same model fitted to the IRT and CCFA scores indicated significant individual variability. This would have been missed had we relied solely on the proportion scores alone.

Potential Model Extensions

We have only touched on a few of the potential applications of these methods for testing a variety of research hypotheses derived from developmental theory. Specifically, we considered a rather simple situation in which there was a single set of eight dichotomous items assessed at each time period. However, the IRT and CCFA methods naturally extend to more complex and more interesting conditions.

For example, the full AFDP study incorporated 25 items to assess externalizing symptomatology in the first three waves of study, but only 8 of the 25 items in the fourth wave. We used the common 8 items here, but these models could be expanded to include all available items within any given wave of assessment. This would not only allow for greater precision in measuring the underlying construct, but would also allow for changing item sets over time that were calibrated on the same metric to allow for subsequent growth modeling. A particular advantage of this approach is the possibility for addressing heterotypic continuity; that is, developmental theory often predicts that the very manifestation of a theoretical construct changes across context and development. The explicit modeling of changing item sets across development is one method for addressing this challenge.

A related extension is to consider not only changing item sets over time within a study, but also changing item sets in data drawn from multiple studies. For example, we are currently applying these techniques to combine data from one study that spans ages 3 to 15 with a second study that spans ages 10 to 21. Using methods of item equating in IRT and multiple group equality constraints in CCFA, it is possible to combine data drawn from two or more independent data sets and to calculate scale scores that are on a comparable metric across study and over time. This allows for the study of trajectories from age 3 to 21, and is also a highly efficient use of existing data.

Additionally, although we focused on dichotomously scored items here, both the IRT and CCFA naturally extend to consider three or more response scales (e.g., trichotomous, ordinal, Likert, and so forth). These more complicated models do of course require more parameters to be estimated relative to the dichotomous outcome. However, given sufficient sample size, all of our IRT and CCFA developments presented here extend naturally to items with more than two response categories.

Finally, a particularly exciting future direction involves the implementation of new studies that are explicitly designed to include these methodological techniques. For example, a single study could be designed to include a set of shared "anchor" items over time, and subsets of items could rotate in and out depending on developmental relevance. Further more, the inclusion of a set of anchor items across multiple studies would expand the possibilities for item equating across study and over time. Combined with advances in accelerated longitudinal designs (Duncan, Duncan, & Hops, 1994) and planned missingness (e.g., Schafer & Graham, 2002), the inclusion of more comprehensive psychometric models can result in powerful and efficient experimental designs for the study of individual development across the lifespan.

Conclusions and Recommendations for Applied Researchers

As quantitative psychologists, we strive to strike a balance between what is ideal from a statistical perspective and what is feasible from a pragmatic perspective. Clearly the single-stage analytic strategy is the gold standard to which we aspire, but these methods are not currently applicable in many settings commonly encountered in developmental research. In comparison, we believe the two-stage procedures we used here allow for the inclusion of a more general psychometric model of our theoretical construct while retaining our ability to fit these models to actual data. We conclude with a few recommendations for the use of these techniques in developmental research.

Regarding the use of proportion scores, we see only a small number of situations where this is the optimal scoring strategy. As we have demonstrated both analytically and empirically, the proportion score is the least psychometrically sound approach of all three methods considered here. All items are unit-weighted in which information about item severity, discrimination, and reliability is disregarded. The situation in which the use of a proportion score might be beneficial is when the available sample size is too small to support the estimation of the more complex IRT or CCFA approaches. If nothing else, it would be beneficial to compare the proportion score analysis with those of the IRT or CCFA to determine if potentially valuable information is being lost using the former technique.

We see a number of significant advantages in the use of the IRT and CCFA scale scores. First, both approaches not only consider how many items were endorsed, but which items were endorsed; this allows for greater psychometric rigor and increased variability among the individual and time specific scores. Second, these methods allow for the inclusion of changing item sets over time and within study, or even across multiple studies. Third, both the IRT and CCFA approaches can provide formal tests of measurement invariance both in terms of the calibration step (as we demonstrated above), but also of longitudinal measurement invariance across development (which we did not pursue here). As we noted earlier, tests of invariance allow for powerful insights into measurement properties both within and across developmental contexts. Finally, the use of the IRT and CCFA methods naturally allow for access to all of the strengths of each of these approaches in isolation (e.g., DIF analysis with the IRT; multiple group analysis with the CCFA). Taken together, we believe these methods have much to offer the analysis of individual differences in developmental stability and change.

REFERENCES

Achenbach, T., & Edelbrock, C. (1983). *Manual for the child behavior checklist and revised child behavior profile.* Burlington, VT: University Associates in Psychiatry.

Bauer, D. J. (2003). Estimating multilevel linear models as structural equation models. *Journal of Educational and Behavioral Statistics, 28,* 134-167.

Biesanz, J. C., Deeb-Sossa, N. P., Aubrecht, A. M., Bollen, K. A., & Curran, P. J. (2004). The role of coding time in estimating and interpreting growth curve models. *Psychological Methods, 9,* 30-52.

Bollen, K. A. (1989). *Structural equations with latent variables.* Wiley Series in Probability and Mathematical Statistics. New York: Wiley.

Bollen, K. A. (1996). An alternative 2SLS estimator for latent variable models. *Psychometrika, 61,* 109-21.

Bollen, K. A., & Curran, P. J. (2006). *Structural equations with latent variables. wiley series in probability and mathematical statistics.* New York: Wiley.

Bond, T. G., & Fox, C. M. (2001). *Applying the rasch model: Fundamental measurement in the human sciences.* Mahwah, NJ: Lawrence Erlbaum Associates.

Browne, M. W. (1984). Asymptotic distribution free methods in the analysis of covariance structures. *British Journal of Mathematical and Statistical Psychology, 37,* 127-141.

Bryk, A. S., & Raudenbush, S. W. (1987). Application of hierarchical linear models to assessing change. *Psychological Bulletin, 101,* 147-158.

Chassin, L., Rogosch, F. A., & Barrera, M. (1991). Substance use and symptomatology among adolescent children of alcoholics. *Journal of Abnormal Psychology, 100,* 449-463.

Cicchetti, D., & Rogosch, F. A. (1996). Equifinality and multinality in developmental psychopathology. *Development and Psychopathology, 8,* 597-600.

Curran, P. J. (2003). Have multilevel models been structural equation models all along? *Multivariate Behavioral Research, 38,* 529-569.

Curran, P. J., & Willoughby, M. J. (2003). Implications of latent trajectory models for the study of developmental psychopathology. *Development and Psychopathology, 15,* 581-612.

Curran, P. J., & Wirth, R. J. (2004). Inter-individual differences in intraindividual variation: Balancing internal and external validity. *Measurement: Interdisciplinary Research and Perspectives, 2,* 219-227.

Davidian, M., & Giltinan, D. M. (1995). *Nonlinear models for repeated measurement data.* Boca Raton, FL: CRC Press.

Diggle, P., Heagerty, P., Liang, K.-Y., & Zeger, S. (2002). *Analysis of longitudinal data* (2nd ed.). Oxford, England: Oxford University Press.

Duncan, T. E., Duncan, S. C., & Hops, H. (1994). The effect of family cohesiveness and peer encouragement on the development of adolescent alcohol use: A cohort-sequential approach to the analysis of longitudinal data. *Journal of Studies on Alcohol, 55,* 588-599.

Fox, J.-P. (2003). Stochastic em for estimating the parameters of a multilevel IRT model. *British Journal of Mathematical and Statistical Psychology, 56*, 65-81.

Fox, J.-P. (2005). Multilevel IRT using dichotomous and polytomous response data. *British Journal of Mathematical Psychology*, 145-172.

Gibbons, R. D., & Hedeker, D. (1997). Random-effects probit and logistic regression models for three-level data. *Biometrics, 53*, 1527-1537.

Goldstein, H. (1986). Multilevel mixed linear model analysis using iterative generalized least squares. *Biometrika, 73*, 43-56.

Gottlieb, G., & Halpern, C. T. (2002). A relational view of causality in normal and abnormal development. *Development and Psychopathology, 14*, 421-435.

Gottlieb, G., Wahlsten, D., & Lickliter, R. (1998). The significance of biology for human development: A developmental psychobiological systems view. In R. M. Lerner & D. William (Eds.), *Handbook of child psychology: Volume 1: Theoretical models of human development* (5th ed., pp. 233-273). New York: Wiley.

Grice, J. W. (2001). Computing and evaluating factor scores. *Psychological Methods, 6*, 430-450.

Jöreskog, K. G. (1994). On the estimation of polychoric correlations and their asymptotic covariance matrix. *Psychometrika, 59*, 381-389.

Jöreskog, K. G., & Sorbom, D. (1979). *Advances in factor analysis and structural equation models*. Cambridge, MA: Abt Books.

Jöreskog, K. G., Sorbom, D., Du Toit, S., & Du Toit, M. (1999). *Lisrel 8: New statistical features*. Chicago, IL: Scientific Software.

Kagan, J. (1971). *Change and continuity in infancy*. Oxford, England: Wiley.

Lord, F., & Novick, M. (1968). *Statistical theory of mental test scores*. Reading, MA: Addison-Wesley.

Mason, W. M., Wong, G. Y., & Entwisle, B. (1983). Contextual analysis through the multilevel linear model. In S. Leinhardt (Ed.), *Sociological methodology 1983* (pp. 72-103). San Francisco: Jossey-Bass.

McArdle, J. J. (1988). Dynamic but structural equation modeling of repeated measures data. In J. R. Nesselroade & R. B. Cattell (Eds.), *Handbook of multivariate experimental psychology* (2nd ed.). New York: Plenum Press.

McArdle, J. J. (1989). Structural modeling experiments using multiple growth functions. In P. Ackerman, R. Kanfer, & R. Cudeck (Eds.), *Learning and individual differences : Abilities, motivation and methodology* (pp. 71-117). Hillsdale, NJ: Lawrence Erlbaum Associates.

McCullagh, P., & Nelder., J. A. (1989). *Generalized linear models*. London, England: Chapman and Hall.

Mehta, P. D., Neale, M. C., & Flay, B. R. (2004). Squeezing interval change from ordinal panel data: Latent growth curves with ordinal outcomes. *Psychological Methods, 9*, 301-333.

Meredith, W. (1964). Notes on factorial invariance. *Psychometrika, 29*, 177-186.

Meredith, W. (1993). Measurement invariance, factor analysis and factorial invariance. *Psychometrika, 58*, 525-543.

Meredith, W., & Tisak, J. (1984). "Tuckerizing" *curves*. Santa Barbara, CA: Paper presented at the annual meeting of the Psychometric Society.

Meredith, W., & Tisak, J. (1990). Latent curve analysis. *Psychometrika, 55*, 107-122.

Moffitt, T. E. (1993). Adolescence-limited and life-course-persistent antisocial behavior: A developmental taxonomy. *Psychological Review, 100*, 674-701.

Muthèn, B. O. (1983). Latent variable structural equation modeling with categorical data. *Journal of Econometrics, 22*, 48-65.

Muthèn, B. O. (1984). A general structural equation model with dichotomous, ordered categorical, and continuous latent variable indicators. *Psychometrika, 49*, 115-132.

Muthèn, B. O. (1996). Growth modeling with binary responses. In A. V. Eye & C. Clogg (Eds.), *Categorical variables in developmental research: Methods of analysis* (pp. 37-54). San Diego, CA: Academic Press.

Muthèn, B. O., Du Toit, S., & Spisic, D. (1997). Robust inference using weighted least squares and quadratic estimating equations in latent variable modeling with categorical and continuous outcomes. *Unpublished manuscript,* University of California, Los Angles.

Muthèn, B. O., & Kaplan, D. (1985). A comparison of some methodologies for the factor-analysis of non-normal likert variables. *British Journal of Mathematical and Statistical Psychology, 38*, 171-180.

Muthèn, B. O., & Satorra, A. (1995). Technical aspects of muthèn's liscomp approach to estimation of latent variable relations with a comprehensive measurement model. *Psychometrika, 60*, 489-503.

Muthèn, L. K., & Muthèn, B. O. (2001). *Mplus user's guide.* Los Angeles: Muthèn & Muthèn.

Rasch, G. (1960). *Probabilistic models for some intelligence and attainment tests.* Copenhagen, Denmark: Danish Institute for Educational Research.

Raudenbush, S. W. (2001). Toward a coherent framework for comparing trajectories of individual change. In L. M. Collins & A. G. Sayer (Eds.), *New methods for the analysis of change* (pp. 35-64). Washington, D.C: American Psychological Association.

Raudenbush, S. W., & Bryk, A. S. (2002). *Hierarchical linear models. applications and data analysis methods* (2nd ed.). Thousand Oaks: Sage Inc.

Raudenbush, S. W., Johnson, C., & Sampson, R. J. (2003). A multivariate multilevel rasch model with application to self-reported criminal behavior. *Sociological Methodology, 33*, 169-212.

Sameroff, A. J. (1995). General systems theories and developmental psychopathology. In D. J. Cohen & D. cicchetti (Eds.), *Developmental psychopathology, vol. 1: Theory and methods* (pp. 659-695). Oxford, England: Wiley.

SAS Institute, I. (1999). *Sas documentation, version 8.* Cary, NC: SAS Publications.

Schafer, J. L., & Graham, J. W. (2002). Missing data: our view of the state of the art. *Psychological Methods, 7*, 147-177.

Thissen, D., Chen, W.-H., & Bock, R. (2003). *Multilog (version 7) [computer sotware].* Lincolnwood, IL: Scientific Software International.

Thissen, D., Steinberg, L., & Wainer, H. (1988). Use of item response theory in the study of group differences in trace lines. In H. Wainer & H. Braun (Eds.), *Test validity* (pp. 659-695). Hillsdale, NJ: Lawrence Erlbaum Associates.

Thissen, D., & Wainer, H. (2001). *Test scoring*. Mahwah, NJ: Lawrence Earlbaum Associates.

Willett, J. B., & Sayer, A. G. (1994). Using covariance structure analysis to detect correlates and predictors of individual change over time. *Psychological Bulletin, 116*, 363-381.

Wirth, R. J., & Edwards, M. C. (2005). *Recent advances in item factor analysis. under review.*

Wohlwill, J. F. (1970). The age variable in psychological research. *Psychological Review, 77*, 49-64.

Wohlwill, J. F. (1973). *The study of behavioral development*. New York: Academic Press.

Y., T., & Leeuw J. de. (1987). On the relationship between item response theory and factor analysis of discretized variables. *Psychometrika, 52*, 393-408.

Zeger, S. L., Liang, K.-Y., & Albert, P. S. (1988). Models for longitudinal data: A generalized estimating equation approach. *Biometrics, 44*, 1049-1060.

CHAPTER SIX

Representing Contextual Effects in Multiple-Group MACS Models

Todd D. Little
University of Kansas

Noel A. Card
University of Arizona

David W. Slegers
Emily C. Ledford
University of Kansas

In keeping with the goals of this volume, we explore the various uses and advantages of mean and covariance structures (MACS) models for examining the effects of ecological/contextual influences in developmental research. After addressing critical measurement and estimation issues in MACS modeling, we discuss their uses in two general ways. First, we focus primarily on discrete ecological factors as grouping factors for examining main-effect as well as moderating or interactive influences. Second, we briefly discuss the simplest case — including ecological factors as within-group direct and mediated effects — because these types of effects are covered in more detail elsewhere in this volume (see Little, Card, Bovaird, Preacher, & Crandell, chap. 9, this volume; see also McKinnon, in press). Our focus in this chapter will be on how such effects might be moderated by the discrete contextual factor(s) used to define groups.

Discrete ecological factors can be conceptualized at various levels, from macrosystems such as sociocultural contexts to exosystem structures such as neighborhoods and communities. Other discrete ecological factors such as developmental level, ethnicity, and gender are particularly amenable to study using multiple-group MACS modeling procedures. Although these factors can often be conceptualized at many levels of abstraction, a key characteristic of discrete ecological factors is that the categories define meaningful, mutually exclusive, subgroups or subpopulations. As we discuss in detail, including mean-level information is particularly important when one wishes to compare across discrete ecological contexts (or subgroups).

In this chapter, we will utilize the hypothetical running example relating the effects of parental monitoring to adolescents' engagement in delinquency in two discrete contexts: An inner-city context marked by low social-economic status (SES) and high risk versus an affluent suburban context marked by relatively low risk. As shown in later figures, we depict two core developmental concepts, parental monitoring and adolescent delinquency, as latent constructs, each measured with three indicators: Child disclosure, parental solicitation, and parental control for *Monitoring* and substance use, theft, and starts fights for *Deliquency*.[1] In this hypothetical example, we consider context as a discrete variable representing two subpopulations (inner-city vs suburban communities), although more groups could easily be added.

CONSTRUCT COMPARABILITY ACROSS DISCRETE SUB-GROUPS

In situations when one has discrete sub-populations of individuals, fundamental questions arise that must be addressed in order to proceed with testing hypotheses about the influence of the ecological factors on human development. The most basic question that arises is "are the constructs comparably measured across the sub-populations?" This question addresses the factorial or measurement invariance of the constructs across the apriori defined sub-groups.

Including mean-level information is required in order to determine the degree of factorial invariance across groups. Because of this requirement, a multiple-group MACS model is the procedure of choice to make these determinations (Little, 1997). With multiple-group MACS models, the hypothesized factorial structure can be estimated simultaneously in two or more groups, and the cross-group equivalence of the key measurement parameters (i.e., intercepts and loadings) can be established. In addition, estimates of the latent constructs' means and covariances are estimated as true and reliable values (i.e., disatten-

---

[1] Readers familiar with these substantive areas will realize that both of these constructs are actually multifactorial (see Frick et al., 1993; Stattin & Kerr, 2000) and that directions of effects are not straightforward. We nevertheless use this hypothetical model for simplicity and because of its intuitive nature.

uated). As a result of these desirable qualities, substantive hypotheses about possible cross-group differences on the constructs can be tested rigorously.

Identifying the degree of factorial invariance of constructs across groups is a crucial first step in analyzing multiple groups within the MACS modeling framework. Factorial invariance addresses the comparability of constructs across two or more subgroups; that is, are the constructs' measurement properties the same? There are several levels or degrees of factorial invariance: Configural invariance, weak invariance, strong invariance, and strict invariance (Meredith, 1993; Widaman & Riese, 1997). Using our hypothetical example, these different levels of invariance are summarized in Figure 6.1, which shows the parameters that are involved in establishing the equivalency of measurement for *Monitoring* and *Delinquency* across low- vs. high-SES communities.[2]

Configural invariance is demonstrated when the same factor structure is maintained across groups. With configural invariance, the same corresponding indicators and constructs must be present in all groups and the same pattern of fixed and freed parameters must be preserved across groups (e.g., the same paths are present in both groups in our diagrammatic representation in Figure 6.1). If one group requires parameters such as dual-loadings or correlated residuals whereas the other does not, this weakest level of invariance is, to a degree, violated. Even if achieved, however, configural invariance is the least meaningful of the degrees of invariance because it only provides a qualitative basis to make cross-group comparisons. As a general rule of thumb, the requirements of configural invariance should be viewed as a minimal requirement from which more rigorous and meaningful degrees of invariance can be examined.[3]

Weak factorial invariance is a more constrained and, therefore, more rigorous level of invariance than is configural invariance. At this level of invariance, the respective loadings (λ's) of the indicators are equated across groups. Here, the intercepts and residual variances of the indicators are still free to vary across groups. The construct variances also vary across groups, which, technically

---

[2]Although we are specifying a directional relation between parental monitoring and adolescent delinquency in our hypothetical example, Figure 6.1 displays nondirectional paths between these two constructs. The reason for this is because measurement invariance is generally established within a confirmatory factor analysis framework (i.e., all latent nondirectional covariances are estimated). Only after measurement invariance is evaluated and the researcher has conducted any comparisons of latent means desired, should hypothesized structural relationships be modeled.

[3]This black and white rule-bound requirement can be relaxed if the reasons for not satisfying invariance requirements are theoretically meaningful. For example, the concept of partial invariance can be invoked in situations in which one group requires a dual-loading that is not invariant but the remaining loadings are found to be invariant.

speaking, makes the loadings proportionally, rather than absolutely, equivalent (i.e., they are weighted by the differences in latent variances).

Strong factorial invariance is established when both the loadings (λ's) *and* the intercepts (τ's) of the indicators are constrained to be equal across groups. With strong invariance, the residual variances of the indicators (θ's) are still allowed to vary freely across groups. As with weak invariance, the variances (e.g., $\Psi_{rr's}$ where $r = r$) of the constructs and their latent means (α's) are also allowed to vary across all groups. With strong factorial invariance, measurement equivalence is established. If strong invariance is supported by the data,

FIGURE 6.1
Steps in establishing invariance across groups.

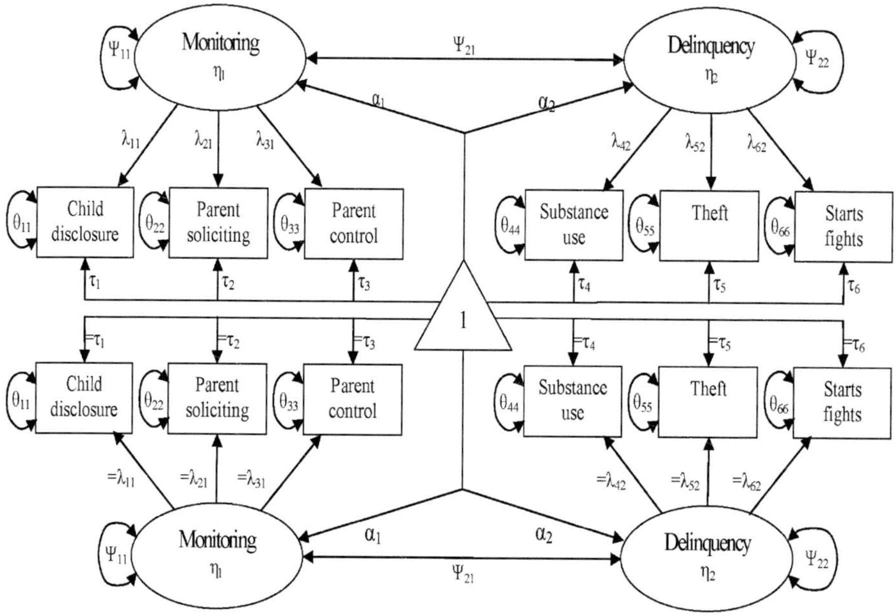

Note. Figures on top and bottom halves represents hypothetical relation between parental monitoring and adolescents' delinquency in inner-city versus suburban contexts. Configural invariance is established if the same patterns of paths are evident in both groups. Weak factorial invariance is established if the factor loadings (λ's) can be equated across groups. Strong factorial invariance is established if indicator intercepts (τ's) can be equated across groups. Although generally not recommended, strict factorial invariance would be established by equating the indicator residual variances (θ's) across groups.

constructs can be meaningfully compared across groups because their reliable measurement properties have been defined in the same operational manner. This degree of invariance allows comparisons across groups to be made in a meaningful and truly comparable manner because it demonstrates that individuals in separate groups with the same level of the latent construct will have the same expected score on the measured indicators (see Little & Slegers, 2005; Little, Slegers, & Card, 2006).

Strict factorial invariance goes a step further than strong factorial invariance, by including constraints on the residual variances (θ's) of the indicators across groups. In all latent variable modeling approaches, residuals contain two sources of variance: A reliable but indicator-specific source and a random (unreliable) source. Strict invariance, therefore, tests whether the sum of these sources of residual variability are equal in magnitude across the subgroups. In most cases, this form of invariance will be overly restrictive and can be biasing if the two sources of indicator-specific error are only approximately equal across groups. More specifically, if the specific error of the indicators is not precisely the same across groups, equality constraints placed on the residuals will spread the error across all model parameters and, thereby, introduce some degree of bias in all the estimates. Because the residuals contain both the random sources of error, for which there is no theoretical reason to expect equality across contexts (or occasions), and the item-specific component, which can vary as a function of various measurement factors (e.g., sampling variability, assessment conditions), forcing these sources of error to be equal is generally an untenable proposition. Moreover, strict invariance does not provide any additional evidence of the comparability of the constructs because the important (i.e., reliable and construct common) measurement parameters (i.e., loadings and intercepts) are contained under the strong invariance condition. Therefore, strong (not strict) invariance is the recommended condition to be met prior to making cross-group (or cross-time) comparisons among latent parameter estimates.

IDENTIFICATION ISSUES IN TESTING FOR INVARIANCE

In conducting these various tests of invariance (indeed, whenever one is performing latent variable analysis), a number of issues related to identification and scale setting emerge. In order to understand these scaling and identification issues, we utilize the full equation for the general factor model: Let Y be a p x 1 vector of p observed variables with mean vector, μ, and a variance-covariance matrix, Σ. Let Y^g represent the vector of observed responses for the

g^{th} population (g = 1, 2, ..., G).

$$Y^g = \tau^g + \Lambda^g \eta^g + \varepsilon^g \tag{1}$$

where τ^g is a $(p \times 1)$ vector of indicator means, or intercepts for the gth group, Λ^g is the $(p \times r)$ pattern matrix defining the relations between (p) indicators and (r) constructs in the gth group, η^g is a $(r \times 1)$ vector of latent constructs, and ε^g is a $(p \times 1)$ vector of unique factors (i.e., specific variance and error terms). The mean structure for any given subgroup can be represented as:

$$\mu^g = \tau^g + \Lambda^g \alpha^g, \tag{2}$$

where τ^g is the $(p \times 1)$ vector of indicator means for the gth group and α^g is a $(r \times 1)$ vector of latent construct means for the gth group. The covariance structure for any given subgroup can be represented as:

$$\Sigma^g = \Lambda^g \Psi^g \Lambda^{g'} + \Theta^g, \tag{3}$$

where Ψ^g is a $(r \times r)$ latent construct covariance matrix and Θ^g is a $(p \times p)$ diagonal matrix of the variances of the residual or error terms, ε.

There are several assumptions of this common factor model: (a) the means of the unique factors (the ε's in equation 1) are zero, (b) the unique factors do not correlate with the common factors, and (c) the unique factors are uncorrelated with each other. As we will see, this last assumption can be relaxed in SEM applications of this model, either because of a prior theory or post hoc empirical necessity.

At least three methods can be used to identify and set the scale of the variance and the mean-level information for a given latent variable (Little & Slegers, 2005; Little et al., 2006). As we will see, each method has implications for the interpretation of the variances, covariances, and means of the latent variables. We also note here that the term *group*, which we will consider primarily in terms of discrete subgroups defined by differing contexts (e.g., low- vs. high-SES communities in our example), can also refer to measurement occasion. That is, the same identification constraints and their interpretability apply when fitting longitudinal models with means. One key difference between multiple-group models verses multiple-occasion models is that with multiple-occasion data, the analysis is conducted as a single group model where the indicators of the constructs at all occasions of measurement are included in one big covariance matrix. Because multiple-occasion data is represented in such a manner, the assumption that the residual variances of the indicators are independent is no longer applicable. Instead, the residuals of the repeatedly measured indicators are assumed to co-vary over time because the indicators' unique factors are expected to correlate with each other over time. Despite these two differences, the logic and implications of what follows is fundamentally the same for multiple-group and multiple-occasion data.

Latent Standardization Method (Method 1)

One method is to define the scale and provide the identification restrictions by fixing the variances of the latent constructs to 1.0 and the means of the latent constructs to be 0. This method, which is how estimates are identified and scaled in exploratory factor analysis, is quite common for single-group analyses. A consequence of this method, however, is that it essentially removes the mean level information from active consideration at the latent level. In multiple-group and multiple-occasion situations, on the other hand, the mean-level information is brought back into consideration at the latent level when invariance of the intercepts is specified.

With this method of identification, when invariance of the loadings is placed across groups or occasions, the variances of the constructs in all subsequent groups and occasions can now be estimated because their scale is based on the fixed 1.0 in the first group. Here, the identification restriction that allows these variances to be estimated is the cross-group (or cross-time) equality constraint on the corresponding loadings (see Figure 6.2 for a cross-group example). Similarly, when invariance of the intercepts is placed across groups, the means of the constructs in all subsequent groups can now be estimated. Like the variances, the scale of the latent means estimates is determined by the fixed 0s of the latent means (i.e., α's) in the first group (or first measurement occasion). Returning to our hypothetical example shown in Figure 6.2, the latent means and variances of *Monitoring* and *Delinquency* would be fixed in the first group (thereby identifying the constructs), but would be freely estimated in the second group. Referring to Equations 2 and 3, this method imposes $\alpha_r^1 = 0$ and $\Psi_r^1 = 1$ in the first group, while both Ψ_r^g and α_r^g are estimated (where r is a given construct and g is not equal to 1; see Little & Slegers, 2005; Little et al., 2006).

Interpreting the parameters from this method has the advantage of estimating the latent means in each subsequent group and occasion as relative mean-level differences from the mean of the first group/occasion. More specifically, these mean-level differences reflect the weighted average of the differences between the observed means of the respective indicators in the first group and each subsequent group. In this respect, the first group is referred to as the reference group. With this method of identification, the significance of the difference from zero for the mean-level estimates in each subsequent group (or occasion) is also the significance of the difference between the first group's (occasion's) latent means and the corresponding latent variable's means in the comparison

FIGURE 6.2

Identification by fixing latent means and variances in one group (Method 1).

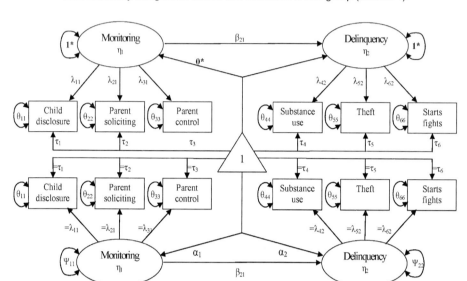

Note. This method of identification involves fixing the latent variances to 1 and the latent means to 0 in one group. The variances and means of subsequent groups (which are identified due to strong factorial invariance constraints) are interpreted in relation to this reference group.

subgroups. To compare differences between the means of any two subsequent groups, one would need to conduct a nested-model chi-squared difference test by equating across groups any two respective means and evaluating the loss in fit from the model in which the respective means were allowed to vary freely across groups.

This method also has the advantage of estimating the associations among the latent constructs in the first group in correlational metric, which is a readily interpretable metric to gauge the strength of the associations among the constructs. On the other hand, the associations among the constructs in the subsequent groups are less readily interpretable because these associations are estimated in covariance metric. Because of these differences in the metrics, one cannot make a direct comparison of cross-group differences in the strengths of the associations.

As shown in Figure 6.3, however, this interpretation problem can be remedied by including higher order 'phantom' constructs in the modeling such that the variances of the constructs are estimated as the regression of the lower order construct on to the higher order construct (this is accomplished by fixing the variance of the lower order constructs to 0; see Card & Little, 2006; Little, 1997;

FIGURE 6.3

Using phantom variables to test differences in associations across groups.

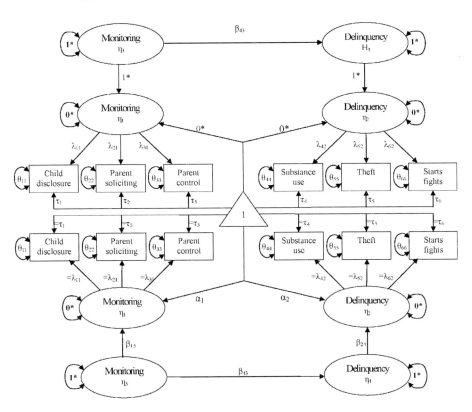

Note. When latent variances differ across groups (regardless of method of identification), it is necessary to create phantom variables in order to compare associations across groups. To create phantom variables, a set of higher order constructs paralleling the original lower order constructs are introduced, with the variances of the lower and higher order constructs being fixed at 0 and 1, respectively. The latent variances are indexed by the squared loadings between these lower and higher order constructs (β_{13} & β_{24}). Paths between the higher-order phantom variables are in a standardized metric and are thus comparable across groups.

Rindskopf, 1984). In the first group or first measurement occasion, the regression linking the lower and higher order constructs is fixed at 1 to identify and set the scale for the lower order loadings and intercepts. Setting the scale of the higher order phantom constructs is determined by fixing their variances to 1.0 in all groups or measurement occasions. This scale setting constraint also provides the necessary identification constraint for the higher order constructs. Using phantom constructs in this manner allows the estimates of association among the higher order latent constructs to be estimated in correlational metric in each group or measurement occasion. Tests of any cross-group differences in the strength of the association can thus be meaningfully conducted using nested-model chi-squared difference tests because the associations are estimated using a common metric across the groups (or measurement occasions).

Marker Variable Method (Method 2)

A second method of identification and scale setting is known as the marker variable method. In this case, the loading and the intercept of one of the indicators of each construct is fixed to be one and zero, respectively. In other words, $\lambda_{ir}^{g} = 1$ and $\tau_{ir}^{g} = 0$, where i is one of the possible (unique) indicators of a given latent factor, r, in each of the g groups. As shown in Figure 6.4, fixing the loadings and intercepts of the indicators 'child disclosure' and 'substance use' would identify and set the scale for the constructs of *Monitoring* and *Delinquency*.

This method is similar to the ANOVA dummy-coded model. As with dummy coding, the choice of which indicator to fix is somewhat arbitrary, although rationales based on construct representativeness, degree of communality, or magnitude of variability can be applied (Little et al., 2006; see also Little, Lindenberger, & Nesselroade, 1999, on selecting indicators in general). No matter which indicator is chosen, however, the interpretation of the latent variable parameters is relative to the chosen maker variable. More specifically, both the mean and the variance of the latent construct reflect the mean and the reliable common variance of the chosen maker variable.

When invariance constraints are specified across groups or measurement occasions, this method has the advantage of not needing to subsequently free the latent mean and variance of the constructs in the subsequent groups or occasions (i.e., the latent means and variances are freely estimated for *all* groups and, if phantom variables are employed, all regressions linking lower and higher order constructs are freely estimated). On the other hand, this method has the undesirable property that the estimated means and variances of the latent constructs vary depending on which indicator is chosen as the marker variable. Under some circumstances, the arbitrary nature of the metric of the latent parameters can lead to substantive differences in the interpretations of cross-group or cross-time differences (see also Gonzalez & Griffin, 2001).

Effects Coding Method (Method 3)

A third method that can be used is analogous to effects-coding in the ANOVA model. Here, we simply constrain all of the factor loadings to average 1 and all

FIGURE 6.4
Marker variable method of identification (Method 2).

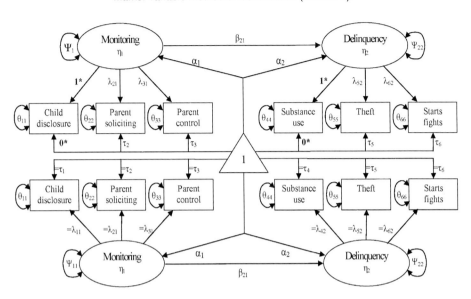

Note. This method of identification involves fixing the factor loading to 1 and the indicator intercept to 0 for one indicator of each construct. The metric of the latent constructs is set in reference to this marker variable, though the selection of which indicator is considered the marker variable is often arbitrary.

of the indicator intercepts to sum to zero (see Figure 6.5). More formally:

$$\sum_{i=1}^{p} \lambda_{ir}^{g} = p \ \ and \ \ \sum_{i=1}^{p} \tau_{ir}^{g} = 0 \tag{4}$$

where $i = 1$ to p refers to summation across the set of p unique indicators for a given latent construct, r, in each of g groups.

For example, with two indicators of a construct, placing the constraint $\lambda_{1r}^{g} = 2 - \lambda_{2r}^{g}$ and $\tau_{1r}^{g} = 0 - \tau_{2r}^{g}$, would satisfy the identification and location conditions needed to estimate the latent mean of a construct. Similarly, the identification and location conditions can be met for three indicators with the constraints, $\lambda_{1r}^{g} = 3 - \lambda_{2r}^{g} - \lambda_{3r}^{g}$ and $\tau_{1r}^{g} = 0 - \tau_{2r}^{g} - \tau_{3r}^{g}$, and so on (see Little et al., 2006). It is the case that when one has a very large number of indicators per construct, the system of constraints can get unwieldy and possibly unstable. In such situations, it may be prudent to create item parcels to measure the constructs of interest with a just-identified three-indicator representation (see Little, Cunningham, Shahar, & Widaman, 2002, for a discussion of parceling).

FIGURE 6.5
Identification by effects-coded constraints (Method 3).

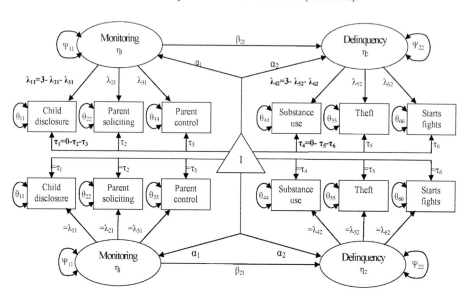

Note. This method of identification constrains the factor loadings to average 1 and the intercepts to sum to zero for the indicators of each construct, resulting in the construct being in the metric of the (weighted average) of all indicators.

This method of identification is shown in Figure 6.5 for the example of three indicators per construct.

Unlike the marker variable method, this method has the distinct advantage of estimating the latent variable parameters in the original metric of the observed indicators. Although the marker variable method does allow estimates of the latent variable parameters in a metric that is close to that of the observed variables, the metric is, in fact, only approximate, because the metric is determined by the specific marker variable that is chosen (for details, see Little et al., 2006). With the effects constraints of Method 3, the metric of the latent variables is the weighted average of the set of indicators. In line with the basic principles of aggregation, the average of a set of indicators would be a more accurate estimate of the population value than any one indicator arbitrarily chosen from the set.

Moreover, this method of identification can be used for single-group SEM models such that the inherent mean-level information does not need to be ignored. This advantage has implications for substantive researchers who might desire the ability to test whether the mean of one latent variable is different from the mean of another latent variable. So long as the observed variables are measured using a comparable scale and the question is of reasonable substantive interest, this method would allow researchers to scale the latent variable in a meaningful and non-arbitrary manner (e.g., in our hypothetical example, we might have measured the parental monitoring from the perspective of the adolescent and the parent using similar scales; this method would allow us to compare the means of the two reporters' perspectives). Only this method of scaling would allow such a comparison to be done with reasonable verisimilitude. In this case, the comparison would be done by equating the latent means of the two focal constructs and evaluating the loss in fit by way of the nested-model chi-squared test.

Finally, another advantage of this method that is similar to that of Method 2 (i.e., fixed indicator method) is that when invariance constraints are placed on the loadings and intercepts, no other fixed parameters need to be subsequently freed in the other groups. In this regard, none of the groups is considered the reference group because the latent variable parameters are defined by the metric of the observed indicators within each group or measurement occasion.

The effects coding method of identification is not without limitations, however. Specifically, using this method can prove frustrating in terms of getting the software program to converge on the appropriate solution, especially in complex models. In our own experiences, we have found that (a) estimating a preliminary model using the marker variable approach, (b) outputting the obtained parameter estimates, and (c) using these estimates as start values for the model using effects coding often alleviates this problem. In other words, the marker-variable approach (Method 2) generally converges with minimal need to provide start values and the parameter estimates of this preliminary model can be used as the start values for the model in which the method 3 constraints are placed.

It is also the case that the default convergence criteria may sometimes need to be slightly relaxed (e.g., the default convergence criterion in LISREL is more stringent than in Mplus). The effect of relaxing the convergence criterion can be evaluated by comparing all the model fit parameters between the preliminary model that was estimated using the marker variable approach and the converged model fit estimates of the effects-coded constraints model (i.e., the Method 3 approach). If the model fit estimates are not identical across the two solutions then relaxing the convergence criterion would not be warranted, and one would need to check the model for possible misspecifications or check the data for problem signs.

Comparisons of Methods of Identification and Scale Setting

A few points of comparison can be offered regarding the differences in the three methods of identification. First, for all methods, the model fit information will be identical. That is, each method of identification is simply an alternative but equivalent parameterization of the different models.

Second, all three methods will ultimately yield identical effect size estimates of standardized mean differences across groups (e.g., Cohen's d or Hedges' g, computed by the difference between group means divided by the pooled standard deviation of the two groups; for a summary of these effect size indices see Rosenthal, 1994). Method 1 has the additional feature of providing latent means in subsequent groups in terms of Glass' Δ (the difference between means of a subsequent group and the comparison group in terms of the standard deviation of the comparison group), an effect size that may be of interest if there is reason to believe that the comparison group yields the most accurate estimate of the relevant population variance (though this could also be computed using Methods 2 or 3). If the metric of the variable is meaningful (e.g., if adolescent delinquency in our example was assessed using indicators on a norm-referenced scale), then an important effect size might simply be the differences in means in raw score units, an index only interpretable when using Method 3.

A third point of comparison is that only Method 3 would allow researchers to make comparisons between constructs when measurement invariance is assumed to not exist. Nesselroade (in press), for example, has argued in the context of p-technique comparisons that the idiographic nature of potential indicators of a construct across two or more individuals would not be obliged to meet the nomothetic expectation of measurement invariance. From this perspective, the measured indicators would still reflect a veridical construct that characterizes the individual and one would have a substantive basis to want to compare the resulting constructs' latent space across individuals. Here, using effects-coded constraints to identify and scale the latent construct parameters would allow one to estimate these parameters in a metric that reflects the idiographic behavior of the indicators within each individual, yet retain meaningful latent variable estimates that could then be compared. In fact, the degree of idiographic variability in the behavior of a set of indicators could be quite large. For example, one individual could have a construct that is reflected by numerous indicators of varying validity while another is more limited in the number of indicators and their relative loadings. Effects-coded constraints could be tailored to the configuration of variables that load on a construct for each individual.

Regardless of which method of identification a researcher chooses to use, the method should be consistent for both the loadings and the intercepts. Particularly for Method 3, if one uses effects coded constraints to identify and scale the location parameters but chooses to model the variance–covariance information by fixing the latent factor variance to 1, the estimates for the location parameters would not be properly scaled and would thereby bias the estimated latent variable mean. This bias would undermine the meaningfulness of the estimated value of the latent variable means.

Extensions to longitudinal models

As mentioned, the three methods of identification and scale setting are readily extended to the longitudinal case (Little & Slegers, 2005). In the context of a single-group longitudinal model, Method 1 would use the data from the first measurement occasion as the reference 'group' or time period and would evaluate invariance of the intercepts and loadings over time. Method 2 would use the same marker variable at each time point to identify and establish the scale of the latent variable parameters. In terms of measuring multiple constructs over multiple occasions, Method 3 would have the same advantages as it would for cross-group comparisons (e.g., meaningful latent metric, the ability to make cross-construct comparisons).

Many applications of the MACS modeling approach would combine both multiple-occasion and multiple-group assessments (where all of the issues related to identification, scale setting, and invariance testing across occasion and group would apply). In fact, we see the ability to model longitudinal relations in conjunction with meaningful grouping variables as a particular strength of this general class of SEM procedure. Some combinations of the longitudinal and multigroup approach, for example, can be used to test more dynamic models of change where contextual influences might shift overtime and could be included as time-varying covariates to evaluate their impacts.

ISSUES RELATED TO INVARIANCE TESTING

In conducting cross-group or cross-occasion tests of the various parameters in the context of multiple-group and multiple-occasion models, at least six different sets of parameters can be tested for equality (i.e., invariance). As we have mentioned already, three sets of parameters that can be compared at the measurement level: (a) the reliable variance of the indicators that is associated with the constructs (i.e., λ's, or loadings), (b) the intercepts of the regressions of the indicators on their respective constructs (i.e., τ's, or the mean-level information of the indicators), and (c) the unique factors of the indicators (i.e., θ's, or residual variances). Again, as mentioned previously, finding evidence of invariance for the loadings and the intercepts provides the necessary foundation to establish measurement invariance to make comparisons of latent parameters across groups or time (i.e., strong factorial invariance; Meredith, 1993). If this level of invariance is achieved, then one can proceed to examine similarities and differences in the construct information. At the latent variable (or structural) level, therefore, at least three sets of parameters can be compared (see Card & Little, 2006; Little, 1997): (a) the variances of the latent variables (ψ_{rr}, where $r = r$), (b) the means of the latent variables (α's), and (c) the covariances (or correlations) among the latent variables ($\psi_{rr'}$, where $r \neq r'$).

Regarding tests of the variances and covariances among a set of latent variables across two or more groups, a number of issues arises. First, one can conduct an omnibus test of the complete set of variances and covariances across two or more groups. This test would be a true test of the homogeneity of the variance–covariance matrix among the latent variables (if invariance of the loadings is enforced). Some might argue that a test of the homogeneity of the variance-covariance matrix should be conducted at the level of the observed variance–covariance matrix. Although this idea has some intuitive appeal, there is a problem in that the observed variance–covariance matrix for a given group also contains the unique indicator variances, making this test a more difficult hypothesis to reject. In our view, conducting such tests at the level of the latent variance–covariance matrix is more defensible than at the observed variable level. The main argument for this view point is that the latent variable associations are considered unbiased estimates of the (sub-) population parameter estimates because they are estimated free of measurement error.

At times, omnibus tests are not substantively informative, because a researcher may have specific hypotheses about which subset of construct parameters would differ across subgroups. In this case, an omnibus test could possibly mask important a priori expectations regarding a subset of parameters. One remedy to this problem would be to conduct the cross-group comparisons in a set-wise manner, grouping constructs according to some a priori rationale. Generally speaking, the more a researcher has specific theoretical expectations about similarities or differences among constructs, the more specific the tests of the expectations can be.

A second issue in testing variances and covariances across groups is that the metric of these estimates is based on the group-specific estimates of a given construct's latent variances. If these variance estimates are not equal across groups or occasions, the covariances would not be comparably scaled to allow a direct comparison of any differences in the latent associations across the group. As mentioned earlier and shown in Figures 6.3, this problem can be alleviated if one incorporates higher order phantom constructs for each lower order construct because using phantom constructs provides estimates of the latent associations on a rescaled common metric (i.e., it separates latent variance and correlation information).

EVALUATING THE ADEQUACY OF MODEL FIT

Keep in mind that all models at best can be considered a judiciously chosen set of half-truths or approximations (MacCallum & Austin, 2000). In this regard, the χ^2 statistic computed for evaluating model fit represents a test of exact fit, which, as McCallum and Austin point out, is virtually always false. Similarly, the use of the χ^2 statistic in nested model comparisons provides a test of an exact point hypothesis of zero differences in population discrepancy function values, which may not be tenable, depending on the parameters that are being compared. Because of these characteristics of the χ^2 statistic, using it to evaluate both overall model fit and cross-group equality constraints has led to the development of a number of alternative measures of fit. Some of the more popular and commonly used measures include: The Root Mean Squared Error of Approximation (RMSEA), the Non-Normed Fit Index (also known as the Tucker–Lewis Index, TLI/NNFI), the Comparative Fit Index (CFI), and the Incremental Fit Index (IFI), among others (see Bentler & Bonett, 1980; Browne & Cudek, 1993; Hu & Bentler, 1995; Steiger, 1990).

In terms of evaluating overall model fit, however, a number of other issues also arise in the context of multiple-group and multiple-occasion MACS models. First, all major software programs calculate model fit indices under assumptions that are generally only appropriate for single-group analysis of variance–covariance matrices, with the exception of the RMSEA measure of model fit, which has a correction factor for the number of groups (for details on why this correction factor is now included in the calculation of the RMSEA, see Steiger, 1998, and see Dudgeon, 2004, for extensions to other fit measures based on the noncentrality parameter).

Regarding the RMSEA and its use with longitudinal models, if one were to extend the logic of 'groups' to measurement occasions, a similar correction factor may need to be incorporated. As seen in Table 6.1, the formula for the RMSEA contains k which represents the number of groups. By extension, k could also represent the number of measurement occasions. To the best of our knowledge, this latter extension has not been articulated in the literature. We bring it up here, however, to make the point that a number of issues for these kinds of models have not been fully resolved. As another example of an unresolved issue, we know of no Monte Carlo work that has examined the behavior and cutoff criteria for the RMSEA when the mean-structures information is included in the modeling process. At this point, we recommend that one proceeds with the general rules of thumb for evaluating good (RMSEA < .05), acceptable (.05 < RMSEA < .08), and poor (< .08 RMSEA < .10) model fit.[4]

---

[4]Hu and Bentler (1999) evaluated the RMSEA in the context of single-group covariance structures models and suggested an RMSEA of about .06 as the lower cutoff of acceptable

TABLE 6.1

Some Commonly Used Fit Indices and Their Definitional Formulas

Fit index	Definitional formula
Absolute fit indices	
(McDonald's) Centrality Index (CI or Mc)	$\exp\left[-\frac{1}{2}\left(\frac{\chi_t^2 - df_t}{N-1}\right)\right]$
Root Mean Square Error of Approximation (RMSEA)	$\sqrt{\frac{\max\left[\frac{\chi_t^2 - df_t}{N-1}, 0\right]}{df_t/k}}$
Relative fit indices	
Comparative Fit Index (CFI)	$1 - \frac{\max[(\chi_t^2 - df_t), 0]}{\max[(\chi_t^2 - df_t), (\chi_0^2 - df_0), 0]}$
Incremental Fit Index (IFI)	$\frac{\chi_0^2 - \chi_t^2}{\chi_0^2 - df_0}$
Tucker-Lewis Index (TLI) or Non-Normed Fit Index (NNFI)	$\frac{(\chi_0^2/df_0) - (\chi_t^2/df_t)}{(\chi_0^2/df_0) - 1}$

Note. Fit indices for Model t of k groups, with null model 0 (for the relative fit indices). Adapted from Hu and Bentler (1998) and Widaman and Thompson (2003).

Turning to the relative fit measures (e.g., TLI, IFI, CFI), the null model (also called the independence model) that is estimated for use in their calculations is one in which only the variances of the indicators are reproduced and no covariances are estimated. This model attempts to index the amount of meaningful covariance information that is contained in the data to be analyzed. The goal of the null model is to yield a model chi-squared value that reflects the maximum amount of model mis-fit possible given the data to be analyzed, provided that the null model is nested within the tested model (Widaman & Thompson, 2003). The relative fit statistics then provide an index of how much of this information the tested model accounts for. If the goal of an analysis

model fit and that .95 and better should be used for most relative fit statistics (cf. Marsh, Hau, & Wen, 2004, for a critique of Hu & Bentler's recommendations). However, we do not know the behavior of these fit statistics in the context of multiple-group and/or multiple-occasion data when the mean-structures information is included in the model. Therefore, we recommend that one sticks with the traditional cutoffs of about .90 and higher for the relative measures of model fit and about .08 or less for the RMSEA.

is to simply model the covariance structure information (and nothing about the variances or means), then this standard null model probably is appropriate. However, as Widaman and Thompson (2003) argued, many applications of SEM models will require one to specify and estimate an appropriate, nested null model and then calculate the fit statistics oneself, instead of relying on the default null model of the various SEM software packages.

In the context of multiple-group and multiple-occasion models, a more appropriate null model would also place restrictions on the estimated variances because potential changes in variances across groups and across occasions is a feature of the observed data that is modeled as part of the tested model. Here, an appropriate null model would assume that the variance of a given indicator is equal across groups and/or across time (e.g., the variance of indicator i in group 1 would be constrained to be equal each of the g groups). In addition, because one models the mean-structure information in MACS models, the null model needs to account for the amount of misfit information represented in the intercepts of the indicators. Here, an appropriate null model would assume that the mean of a given indicator is equal across groups and/or across time (the intercept of indicator i in group 1 would be constrained to be equal across each of the g groups; see Quant.KU.edu) for examples of null models and other support materials, .

EVALUATING THE TENABILITY OF INVARIANCE CONSTRAINTS

Numerous authors have discussed the optimal evaluation criteria for testing invariance. At least two rationales can be used for making such tests (Little, 1997). The first rationale is based on strict statistical considerations. Here, any test of cross-group or cross-occasion equality (i.e., invariance) of any parameter or set of parameters should be based on the nested-model chi-squared difference test. For this test, the difference in the chi-squared values ($\Delta\chi^2$) between any two nested models is itself distributed as a χ^2 with degrees of freedom equal to the differences in the respective model's degrees of freedom (Δdf). From this perspective, if this $\Delta\chi^2$ value on Δdf is significant then the equality constraints are not warranted and the hypothesis of invariance is not supported. As is well known, the fidelity of the χ^2 test is sensitive to sample size. Given the basic asymptotic assumptions of SEM models, researchers are required to use sufficiently large sample sizes to adequately satisfy this assumption. This need for large sample sizes has the unintended effect of often making the χ^2 test too sensitive, rendering even trivial differences significant. This sensitivity is particularly compounded when multiple constraints are placed across groups —

that is, the sensitivity to trivial differences is compounded and almost always leads to a significant χ^2 value, particularly with real-world data.

Cheung and Rensvold (1999) have argued that a change in the CFI of less than .01 amounts to a trivial difference in model fit. They further argue that the .01 criterion can be used to evaluate cross-group equality constraints. If the change in CFI is less than .01 then the set of cross-group constraints is tenable and one can proceed with making further comparisons. Relatedly, Little (1997) argued that a .05 difference in the TLI/NNFI amounts to a trivial difference in model fit. His reasoning was based on the arguments of Tucker and Lewis who suggested the .05 rule in the context of exploratory factor analyses. In hindsight, because of the greater precision and theoretical guidance with confirmatory approaches such as multiple-group MACS modeling, the .05 criterion would most likely be overly insensitive to violations of invariance. Perhaps using a similar .01 criteria for the TLI/NNFI as Cheung and Rensvold (1999) argued for the CFI would improve the fidelity of this approach.

Another approach that has intuitive appeal but, to the best of our knowledge has not been evaluated, is to use the RMSEA and the estimates of its 90% confidence interval. Here, if the RMSEA value for the model with cross-group equality constraints were to fall within the bounds of the 90% confidence interval of the model without these constraints, then one would have evidence that the invariance constraints still provide a reasonable approximation of the data given the degree of approximation of the original model. For a more detailed description of using the RMSEA in the context of model comparisons, see Preacher, Cai and McCallum (chap. 3, this volume).

Both the statistical approach and the relative-fit approach can be used to evaluate cross-group (or cross-time) invariance constraints. Cheung and Rensvold (1999) and Little (1997) have argued that a modeling rationale using relative-fit measures is appropriate for testing invariance of intercepts and loadings. At least two arguments can be made for using relative model-fit information for testing the measurement invariance hypothesis.

First, because measurement invariance is a matter of degree, presuming an exact statistical approximation is overly conservative, particularly given the sensitivity of the χ^2 statistic to both large numbers of constraints and large sample sizes. Therefore, establishing a less sensitive criterion to evaluate the tenability of the invariance hypotheses is needed. In this regard, refining the use of relative-fit statistics for making this determination is clearly a key topic for future work and discussion.

A second, related argument is that the measurement space is rife with fallibility. This fallibility includes the random measurement error, sampling variability, and the imprecision of the indicator-specific components of a construct's indicators. From this view point, the measurement invariance hypothesis is seen as an a priori expectation about the model to approximate the observed data. In fact, from this perspective, one could argue that testing for invariance could be based solely on the adequacy of the measurement-invariant model to approximate the data (e.g., RMSEA $<$ .08, TLI/NNFI $>$ .90, CFI $>$ .90, etc.). In other words, if the measurement-invariant model fits the data at acceptable levels, questions of how well the non-invariant model fits in relation to the invariant model is, in many ways, rendered irrelevant.

At the latent variable level, on the other hand, significance testing takes on a different character. Because the estimates of the latent variable parameters are now error free and, therefore, unbiased estimates of a given (sub-)population at a given point in time, their meaning and interpretation should be evaluated in a more rigorous statistical manner. In this regard, Little (1997) argued that any tests of specific hypotheses concerning latent variable parameters (i.e., means, variances, and correlations/covariances) should be conducted using standard nested-model χ^2 difference test. As described in the next section, these tests can be conducted in one of two approaches, a traditional hypothesis testing approach or a model building approach.

HYPOTHESIS TESTING OF LATENT PARAMETERS VERSUS A MODEL BUILDING APPROACH

Generally speaking, the traditional hypothesis testing approach to comparing means, variances, and covariances across groups or occasions involves testing (a) whether a given parameter estimate deviates significantly from zero, (b) whether a given parameter estimate deviates significantly from a known or hypothesized non-zero value, and (b) whether a given parameter estimate deviates significantly from a corresponding parameter that is estimated across two or more groups or across two or more occasions. Of course, more sophisticated hypotheses can also be entertained such as inequality constraints, proportional constraints, and nonlinear constraints, but these are not typically offered in the context of traditional hypothesis testing.

As with any hypothesis testing endeavor, researchers still need to be cognizant of issues such as Type I and Type II error, family-wise error, and effect size. With the typical power of SEM models for testing specific hypotheses, the most common error would be Type I error — rejecting the null hypothesis when the null is, in fact, correct. Therefore, if one does not have a strong a priori hypothesis regarding an anticipated difference, one could adopt a more stringent rejection p-value such as .01, .005, or even .001, depending on the power of a particular comparison. With this approach, parameters are not necessarily removed or equated if they are found to be nonsignificantly different from zero or different from another parameter estimate. Instead, the effects are simply tested and the p-values of the tests are noted.

Too often, questions of effect size are not explicitly addressed. For example, cross-group or cross-time estimates of latent mean differences are typically expressed as the observed differences, but they are not rescaled in terms of standard deviation units (i.e., scaled in terms of Cohen's d, Hedges' g, or Glass's Δ; see e.g., Rosenthal, 1994). Similarly, measures of association are only expressed in standardized r metric (an index of effect size) unless one explicitly requests that the parameters be rescaled into a standardized metric. Otherwise, the association parameters are expressed in terms of the unstandardized metric of the chosen scaling constraints (unless phantom constructs are employed; see Figure 6.2).

In contrast to a traditional hypothesis testing approach, a model building approach attempts to derive a best fitting model by eliminating nonsignificant estimates and equating parameters that do not differ from one another. Although power generally is not an issue, the most common potential error from this approach is a Type II error — failing to reject the null when the null is, in fact, false. The goal of a modeling approach is to derive a more parsimonious expression of the latent variable relationships that adequately captures the estimated relationships among the latent constructs. To achieve this goal, the task is to impose constraints on a model (e.g., equating or setting parameters to zero) until any further constraint would yield a significant drop in the overall χ^2 of the model. In other words, constraints are systematically added so long as the model fit is at about the same level of fit as the super-ordinate model in which no constraints on the latent variable parameters are placed.

To guard against the problem of Type II error, some authors have used a p-value of .10 or greater as the criterion for determining whether the set of constraints on a particular model deviate significantly from the fit of the model in which the parameters are unconstrained (for an example of this approach see Little and Lopez, 1997). Depending upon the degree to which constraints are based on theoretical versus empirical considerations, using a cross-validation approach may be warranted. Here, the data would be divided in to two random samples, A and B. The modeling building would be conducted on Sample A and then cross-validated on Sample B. A good practice would be to also build the model on Sample B, perhaps by an analyst who is blind to the outcome of the model built on Sample A, and cross-validate it on sample A. If none or a few discrepancies occur, then one can have confidence that the derived model is a reasonable approximation of the estimated latent parameters. If many discrepancies occur, one could raise the p-value to guard even more against type II error or abandon the model building approach and resort to a more traditional hypothesis testing approach.

REPRESENTING CONTEXTUAL/ECOLOGICAL FACTORS

As mentioned in the introduction to this chapter, we now turn our attention to the various ways that contextual effects can be represented in multiple-group, multiple-occasion MACS models. The first approach, which we have already alluded to in our discussion of multiple-group comparisons and in our running hypothetical example, is representing contextual/ecological factors as discrete variables. Here, each discrete level of a contextual variable is treated as a grouping variable and, further, persons are mutually exclusively represented within each subgroup. If nesting is involved, then one would need to represent the nested layers as either multi-level regression models or multi-level SEM models–models that are discussed elsewhere in this volume.

Discrete grouping factors are quite common. Examples include, gender, age-cohorts, socioeconomic class, ethnicity, schools, neighborhoods, regions (rural vs. urban, east vs. west), cultures, and so on. One advantage of the multiple-group MACS framework is that the effects of such discrete grouping variables can be evaluated in terms of both their main-effect influences and their interaction effects. Moreover, the various effects can be evaluated for their influences on the mean-level information, the variability information, and the degrees of association among the latent constructs.

Testing for moderation and main effects

Main effect differences in multiple-group models are revealed when the mean-levels of the latent constructs differ across one or more of the discrete subgroups represented in the MACS model. Main effect differences are also revealed in multi-occasion data when the mean-levels of the latent constructs differ across one or more occasions of measurement. Main-effect differences in means are both commonly hypothesized and readily interpretable. Above, we have elaborated extensively on the ways in which such tests can be conducted.

Main effect differences in multiple-group models are also revealed when the variances of the latent constructs differ across one or more of the groups (or occasions). Although variances are less commonly examined as potential outcomes of a contextual factor, any observed difference in variances is, in fact, a substantive outcome that can either be predicted a priori or interpreted post hoc. For example, it might be of substantive interest in our hypothetical example whether there are different degrees of variability in either *Monitoring* or *Delinquency* in low- vs. high-SES communities. For longitudinal research, Hedeker and colleagues (chap. 8, this volume) describe ways in which the multi-level analysis system can be used to test changes in variances over time. In the context of multiple-group, multiple-occasion MACS modeling, it is relatively easy to test or model differences and simple changes in variances as a function of time or ecological context. Modeling a complex monotonic function of change in variances (or means) is also possible in these models, but is a more complex matter of placing carefully constructed inequality constraints on the estimated parameters.

The moderating influence of discrete contextual factors can also be tested quite easily in the multiple-group framework. Here, any association between two constructs that differs significantly across levels of the discrete contextual factor is a moderated influence. That is, the strength of association between the two constructs depends upon the level of the discrete contextual grouping variable. Returning once more to our hypothetical example, differences in the relation between *Monitoring* and *Delinquency* in low- vs. high-SES communities would be an example of contextual moderation (for a more detailed discussion of moderation as well as mediation with continuous variables see Little, Card, Bovaird, Preacher, & Crandall, chap. 9, this volume).

Adding covariates that represent context effects

Often times, researchers will have a number of contextual/ecological variables that are assessed, only some of which are discrete factors that could be used to define subgroups. The general MACS model framework that we have outlined here, because it is a simple extension of the general SEM framework, allows one to include other contextual/ecological factors in these models as either direct effects on the modeled constructs or as mediating or mediated effects. When these types of variables are also measured across discrete contextual subgroups, one can further test whether these direct or mediational effects are further moderated by the discrete contextual factor. For example, our hypothetical study relating parental monitoring with adolescent delinquency in different economic contexts might also assess various continuous contextual variables associated with the outcomes of interested, such as family cohesion, parental support, and media influence as variables (or constructs, if multiple indicators are measured) within each group. Their direct influence within each group could be evaluated by treating these factors as exogenous predictors of the endogenous constructs of interest. Or, these factors could be included as potential mediators of some expected associations.

As with simple associations, if one tests the significance of the differences in the direct influences of the within-group contextual factors, then one has evidence that these contextual variables interact in their influence on the outcome of interest. That is, when the direct effects are moderated across the levels of the grouping factor, then the continuous and discrete contextual factors interact with one another. One interesting feature of the multiple-group framework is that one can test whether a complex series of relationships, such as a mediating pathway, is moderated by the discrete contextual variable (see Flore, Khoo, & Chassin, chap. 10, this volume). Specifically, the strength of a mediated relationship across the discrete subgroups can be tested for equality across groups. If these associations differ, then one has evidence of a moderated mediational relationship.

CONCLUSIONS

In this chapter, we have discussed various issues using multiple-group and multi-occasion MACS models to examine the effects of discrete contextual/ecological factors. We did not elaborate extensively on the longitudinal application of MACS models because the extension to multiple-occasion data is straightforward. Moreover, other chapters in this volume elaborate more fully on the issues associated with modeling the variance-covariance relationships across time, including testing for mediation and moderation with continuous variables and making such tests across time. In the end, we see a great deal of merit in analyzing the mean-structures information in addition to the variance and co-variance information. In this regard, our focus in this chapter was to discuss in detail the issues associated with incorporating mean-level information and providing meaningful identification and scaling constraints, particularly as these issues apply to multiple-group, multiple-occasion designs.

ACKNOWLEDGMENTS

This work was supported in part by grants from the NIH to the University of Kansas through the Mental Retardation and Developmental Disabilities Research Center (5 P30 HD002528), the Center for Biobehavioral Neurosciences in Communication Disorders (5 P30 DC005803), an Individual National Research Service Award (F32 MH072005) to the second author and a new faculty grant to the first author from the University of Kansas (NFGRF 2301779). Its contents are solely the responsibility of the authors and do not necessarily represent the official views of these funding agencies. This work was also partly supported by grants to the first author from NSF (BCS-0345677), the Merrill Advanced Study Center at the University of Kansas (Mabel Rice, director), and the Society of Multivariate Experimental Psychology (SMEP).

REFERENCES

Bentler, P. M., & Bonett, D. G. (1980). Significance tests and goodness of fit in the analysis of covariance structures. *Psychological Bulletin, 88*, 588-606.

Browne, M. W., & Cudek, R. (1993). Alternative ways of assessing model fit. In K. A. Bollen & J. S. Long (Eds.), *Testing structural equation models* (pp.136-162). Newbury Park, CA: Sage.

Card, N. A., & Little, T. D. (2006). Analytic considerations in cross-cultural research on peer relations. In X. Chen, D. C. French, & B. Schneider (Eds.), *Peer relations in cultural context* (pp. 75-95). New York: Cambridge University Press.

Cheung, G. W., & Rensvold, R. B. (1999). Testing factorial invariance across groups: A reconceptualization and proposed new method. *Journal of Management, 25*, 1-27.

Dudgeon, P. (1999). A note on extending steiger's (1998) multiple group RMSEA adjustment to other noncentrality parameter-based statistics. *Structural Equation Modeling, 11*, 305-319.

Frick, P. J., Lahey, B. B., Loeber, R., Tannenbaum, L., Van Horn, Y., Christ, M. A. G., et al. (1993). Oppositional defiant disorder and conduct disorder: A meta-analytic review of factor analyses and cross-validation in a clinic sample. *Clinical Psychology Review, 13*, 319-340.

Gonzalez, R., & Griffin, D. (2001). Testing parameters in structural equation modeling: Every "one" matters. *Psychological Methods, 6*, 258-269.

Hu, L. T., & Bentler, P. M. (1998). Fit indices in covariance structure modeling: Sensitivity to underparameterized model misspecification. *Psychological Methods, 3*, 424-453.

Hu, L. T., & Bentler, P. M. (1999). Cutoff criteria for fit indexes in covariance structure analysis: Conventional criteria versus new alternatives. *Structural Equation Modeling, 6*, 1-55.

Little, T. D. (1997). Mean and covariance structures (macs) analyses of cross-cultural data: Practical and theoretical issues. *Multivariate Behavioral Research, 32*, 53-76.

Little, T. D., Cunningham, W. A., Shahar, G., & Widaman, K. F. (2002). To parcel or not to parcel: Exploring the question, weighing the merits. *Structural Equation Modeling, 9*, 151-173.

Little, T. D., Lindenberger, U., & Nesselroade, J. R. (1999). On selecting indicators for multivariate measurement and modeling with latent variables: When "good" indicators are bad and "bad" indicators are good. *Psychological Methods, 4*, 192-211.

Little, T. D., & Lopez, D. F. (1997). Regularities in the development of children's causality beliefs about school performance across six sociocultural contexts. *Developmental Psychology, 33*, 165-175.

Little, T. D., & Slegers, D. W. (2005). Factor analysis: Multiple groups with means. In B. Everitt, D. Howell, & D. Rindskopf (Section Ed.) (Eds.), *Encyclopedia of statistics in behavioral science* (Vol. 2, pp 617-623). Chichester, UK: Wiley.

Little, T. D., Slegers, D. W., & Card, N. A. (2006). A non-arbitrary method of identifying and scaling latent variables in SEM and MACS models. *Structural Equation Modeling, 13*, 59-72.

MacCallum, R. C., & Austin, J. T. (2000). Applications of structural equation modeling in psychological research. *Annual Review of Psychology, 51*, 201-226.

Marsh, H. W., Hau, K. T., & Wen, Z. (2004). In search of golden rules: Comment on hypothesis-testing approaches to setting cutoff values for fit indexes and dangers in overgeneralizing Hu and Bentler's (1999) findings. *Structural Equation Modeling, 11*, 320-341.

Meredith, W. (1993). Measurement invariance, factor analysis and factorial invariance. *Psychometrika, 58*, 525-543.

Nesselroade, J. R. (in press). Factoring at the individual level: Some matters for the second century of factor analysis. In R. Cudeck & R. C. MacCallum (Eds.), *Factor analysis at 100: Historical developments and future directions.* Mahwah, NJ: Lawrence Erlbaum Associates.

Rindskopf, D. (1984). Using phantom and imaginary latent variables to parameterize constraints in linear structural models. *Psychometrika, 49*, 37-47.

Rosenthal, R. (1994). Parametric measures of effect size. In H. Cooper & L. V. Hedges (Eds.), *The handbook of research synthesis* (pp. 231-244). New York: Russell Sage Foundation.

Stattin, H., & Kerr, M. (2000). Parental monitoring: A reinterpretation. *Child Development, 71*, 1072-1085.

Steiger, J. H. (1990). Structural model evaluation and modification: An interval estimation approach. *Multivariate Behavioral Research, 25*, 173-180.

Steiger, J. H. (1998). A note on multiple sample extensions of the RMSEA fit index. *Structural Equation Modeling, 5*, 411-419.

Widaman, K. F., & Riese, S. P. (1997). Exploring the measurement invariance of psychological instruments: Applications in the substance use domain. In K. J. Bryant, M. Windle, & S. G. West (Eds.), *The science of prevention: Methodological advances from alcohol and substance abuse research* (pp. 281-324). Washington, DC: APA.

Widaman, K. F., & Thompson, J. S. (2003). On specifying the null model for incremental fit indices in structural equation modeling. *Psychological Methods, 8*, 16-37.

CHAPTER SEVEN

Multilevel Structural Equation Models for Contextual Factors

James A. Bovaird
University of Nebraska-Lincoln

To borrow a term from biology, a growing number of developmental psychologists are choosing to look at the *ecosystem* in which a human being seeks to strive. That is, it is not sufficient to observe behavior and development in isolation, but rather one must also consider the impact of the child's environmental context. Children in the same environmental context tend to be more similar than children in other contexts, and both the children and their contexts have distinguishing characteristics that may be of substantive interest. Such an ecological system can be conceptualized as containing multiple levels, nested within one another. The complexity of the nested-levels theoretical perspective and the additional intricacies that result from such complex sampling necessarily pose unique difficulties in terms of data analysis, thus the need to consider multilevel modeling (MLM) as a means of data analysis. Not coincidentally, multilevel modeling is sometimes referred to as contextual modeling (Kreft & de Leeuw, 1998).

This chapter demonstrates how principles of traditional multilevel models, whether they be contextual (i.e., children in classrooms) or longitudinal (i.e., observations within persons) in nature, can be combined with traditional structural equation modeling (SEM), resulting in the multilevel structural equation model (MSEM). As this volume deals primarily with longitudinal contextual modeling, the language used in most discussions in this chapter reflects longitudinal multilevel modeling. However, in many cases, any reference to "time" as the predictor can be replaced by another continuous predictor variable in a cross-sectional contextual model. Multilevel structural modeling allows the researcher to simultaneously model behavior within a context and between contexts. First, MLM and SEM are briefly discussed as general analysis paradigms, followed by the standard formulation of a longitudinal MLM, often referred to as a latent growth model (LGM), as a 1-level SEM. The interested reader will be directed to additional resources for more in-depth coverage and for topics beyond the scope of this chapter. This will be followed by a discussion of the history, principles, and current issues related to multilevel structural equation modeling. Finally, two empirical examples — a four-level multilevel multivariate growth model and a two-level multilevel multiple indicators and multiple causes (MIMIC; see Kline, 2005) model — are presented to illustrate how MSEM can be used to model contextual effects both within and between multiple contextual layers.

MULTILEVEL MODELING

Broadly defined, a multilevel model simply contains variables measured at different levels of a sampling hierarchy. Data sets can be called *multilevel* if they have some clearly identified levels of aggregation or if they arose through complex or stratified sampling procedures. It is important to not confuse a statistical model of such hierarchically *nested* data with a statistical model containing a hierarchically *ordered* set of regression equations. For instance, when studying children in a school context, students may be described as nested within classroom and classrooms may be further nested within schools. A corresponding multilevel analysis model might include a combination of variables measured at the child, classroom, and school levels. Although a multilevel model need only involve variables measured at multiple levels of a hierarchical structure, the term *multilevel modeling* has become synonymous with the terms *hierarchical linear modeling* (HLM) and *random coefficient modeling* (RCM).   Muthén (1994) distinguished two data analysis perspectives leading to the need for multilevel modeling procedures — complex sampling versus random parameters. Both perspectives lead to the need to decompose the variability in outcome measures into between-group (contextual) and within-group (individual) sources. That is, there can be a general effect of a variable on an outcome within each contextual group, but that effect can vary randomly to a degree across groups. When a multilevel data structure occurs, researchers have three options for data analysis. *Disaggregation* ignores the complex sampling nature of the data and uses the individual level data, resulting in the potential for underestimated standard errors and inflated Type I error rate. *Aggregation* involves obtaining aggregated group level data by summarizing the individual level data, a process often referred to as an *ecological analysis*. However, aggregation may suffer from reduced statistical power, inaccurate representations of group level relations, and an increased risk of committing an *ecological fallacy* (Robinson, 1950) by incorrectly making causal inferences concerning individual level behavior from group level data. This leaves the third approach, *multilevel modeling*, as the recommended procedure when data is obtained through a complex sampling process as it accounts for the nonindependence due to complex sampling, incorporates sample sizes at all levels, and allows the researcher to make *simultaneous* inferences at all levels of the hierarchy.

Although a simplistic approach to modeling multilevel data would be to pose a separate model at each level of the hierarchy, as is done in 'slopes-as-outcomes' analyses (Burstein, Linn, & Cappel, 1978), it is essential that the model employ a statistical integration of all levels of the hierarchy. This can be accomplished by extending the general linear model to include random sources of variance in addition to fixed sources. Goldstein (1986), Laird and Ware (1982), and Longford (1987), among others, can be credited with providing some of the seminal work in extending the general linear model to allow for complex nested data structures.

In a multilevel model, a population of micro-level experimental units are considered nested within a macro-level population of groups of experimental units, where micro-level units are nonindependent due to a shared macro-level influence. Like in most forms of modeling, there is a fundamental assumption of independence of residuals and that any existing dependency between observations is modeled. Thus, in most standard single-level procedures, there is an assumption that there is independence over micro-level units, whereas in multilevel modeling, there is an implicit assumption of independence over macro-level units (Muthén, 1994). For instance, if observations are nested within individuals, it is assumed there is no context for individuals to be nested in, or if students are nested within classrooms, there is no higher level context (such as schools) for classrooms to be nested within. The consequences for ignoring complex sampling involve underestimating the true variance of estimators (i.e., standard errors) depending upon the homogeneity of micro-level units within a macro-level unit and an overestimation of the magnitude of the effect and a potential Type I error.

Multilevel models attempt to represent the dynamic nature of change as a "mixed" combination of fixed and random coefficients or effects, hence the term *mixed model* that is sometimes used to describe this type of analysis. In the mixed model, the basic components of change for a sample of individuals are (a) the *fixed* average intercept, level, or starting point; (b) the *fixed* average slope, or degree of change over time; (c) the *random* individual variability around the average starting point; and (d) the *random* individual variability around the average shape of change. If we make the key assumption that the sample is homogeneous with regard to the change process that is being modeled, then we assume that the data follows a two-level hierarchy (observations within individuals) and there is not a higher level of sampling present in the data (i.e., a "level 3"). As a two-level MLM, the analysis framework can be specified by two sets of equations. The micro-level regression equation is

$$y_{ti} = \pi_{0i} + \pi_{1i}T_{ti} + e_{ti} \tag{1}$$

where y_{ti} is the outcome variable score (e.g., language score) at time t for child i, T_{ti} is the representation of time that varies within child i, π_{0i} represents the overall average performance when time equals zero (intercept), π_{1i} represents the average change or gain in performance from the intercept, and e_{ti} is a within-person observation-level residual. This equation models the change in performance within an individual.

Conceptually, the micro-level model above defines a separate regression equation for each of the i individuals, such that across individuals, there is a typical intercept and typical slope, but individuals are allowed to deviate. These individual differences in trajectory are modeled by the macro-level regression equations:

$$\pi_{0i} = \beta_{00} + r_{0i}$$
$$\pi_{1i} = \beta_{10} + r_{1i} \tag{2}$$

where β_{00} is the mean intercept, β_{10} is the mean slope, and the r's are individual-level residuals. By substituting the macro-level equations into the micro-level equation, β_{00} and β_{10} become the traditional fixed effects as would be seen in a GLM approach, but the single GLM random effect (i.e., the error term) has been divided into three seperate random sources of variance.

$$y_{ti} = \beta_{00} + T_{ti}\beta_{10} + r_{0i} + T_{ti}r_{1i} + e_{ti} \tag{3}$$

Equations 2 and 3 could easily be expanded to include additional predictors or covariates by adding additional π or β parameters respectively. Assuming all participants are observed at the same time periods, in matrix notation, the two-level model would be presented as:

$$\boldsymbol{y}_i = \boldsymbol{X}_i\boldsymbol{\beta}_i + \boldsymbol{r}_i$$
$$\boldsymbol{\beta}_i = \boldsymbol{W}_i\boldsymbol{\Gamma} + \boldsymbol{u}_i \tag{4}$$

which upon substituting the macro-level model into the micro-level model via β_i, results in the reduced form

$$\boldsymbol{y}_i = \boldsymbol{X}_i\boldsymbol{W}_i\boldsymbol{\Gamma} + \boldsymbol{X}_i\boldsymbol{u}_i + \boldsymbol{r}_i \tag{5}$$

where $\boldsymbol{y}_i$ is an N_i x 1 response vector containing outcome measures y_{ti} for participant i at time t, $\boldsymbol{X}_i$ is a N x p level-1 design matrix holding N scores for the p level-1 predictors, $\boldsymbol{W}_i$ is a N x q level-2 design matrix, Γ is the vector of fixed level-2 parameters to be estimated, r_i is a vector of level-1 residuals, and u_i is the vector of level-2 residuals. In this example, X_i is an N x 2 matrix with a column vector of 1s for the intercept and a column vector of time-scores T, W_i is a N x 1 matrix containing only a column vector of 1s and thus drops out, and Γ is a vector containing β_{00} and β_{10}. Assuming all participants are observed at the same time periods, X becomes unscripted and the simplified equation is

$$y_i = X\Gamma + Xu_i + r_i \tag{6}$$

The multilevel model assumes that the micro-level residual and macro-level random effects are independent and multivariate normally distributed as

$$r_i \sim N\left(0, \Sigma_{r_i} = \sigma^2 I_{N_i}\right) \tag{7}$$

and

$$u_i \sim N\left[\begin{pmatrix} 0 \\ 0 \end{pmatrix}, T = \begin{pmatrix} \tau_{00} & \\ \tau_{10} & \tau_{11} \end{pmatrix}\right] \tag{8}$$

where T is the symmetric covariance matrix of the random effects containing individual differences in intercept τ_{00}, individual differences in slope τ_{11}, and a covariance between intercept and slope τ_{10}. The random effects matrix is commonly unstructured and the residuals are homoscedastic and independent (i.e. a common residual σ^2), although these particular structures are common convention and may be modified.

STRUCTURAL EQUATION MODELING

The general and mixed linear models are extremely flexible analytic tools (see Cohen, Cohen West, & Aiken, 2003, for example). However, they are not flexible enough to allow for latent variables and factor analysis or simultaneous equations and path analysis. As an alternative procedure, structural equation modeling (SEM), not only allows for latent variables and path analysis, but it includes all univariate and multivariate procedures based on the general linear model, including all variants of the analysis of variance, multiple regression, discriminant function analysis, and canonical correlation as special cases. For a general introduction to the paradigm, consult one of the numerous texts, including Bollen (1989) and Kline (2005), among others.

In SEM, also sometimes referred to as covariance structure analysis, there are two fundamental sets of simultaneous equations — those that define the latent measurement portion of the model and those that define the structural relations. The measurement model establishes the relationship between observed variables and latent constructs. Assuming an endogenous, or "y-side," parameterization (Jöreskog & Sorbom, 1993), the measurement model can be expressed as:

$$y = v + \Lambda\eta + \varepsilon \tag{9}$$

where y is a p x 1 vector of p observed variables, v is a p x 1 matrix of measurement intercepts, Λ is a p x k matrix of factor loadings relating the p observed variables to the k latent factors, η is a k x 1 matrix of latent factor scores, and ε is a p x 1 vector of residuals with a covariance matrix Θ_ε similar to Σ_r in Equation 7.

The structural portion of the model relates the latent elements of the measurement model to one another:

$$\eta = \mu + \beta\eta + \zeta, \tag{10}$$

where η is defined previously, μ is a k x 1 vector of latent factor means and intercepts, β is a k x k matrix of regression coefficients among the latent factors and ζ is a k x 1 vector of latent disturbances with a covariance matrix Ψ similar to the covariance matrix T in Equation 8. The structural model can be substituted into the measurement model via η and rearranged to group the mean structure (means and intercepts), the structural coefficients (factor loadings and factor regressions), and the error terms (latent disturbances and observed residuals) together:

$$y = (v + \Lambda\mu) + (\Lambda\beta\eta) + (\Lambda\zeta + \varepsilon). \tag{11}$$

The model-implied covariance and mean structures are

$$\begin{aligned} \Sigma(\theta) &= \Lambda (I - \beta)^{-1} \Psi (I - \beta)^{-1'} \Lambda' + \Theta_\varepsilon \\ \mu(\theta) &= v + \Lambda\mu + \Lambda\beta\eta \end{aligned} \tag{12}$$

where $\Sigma(\theta)$ is the p x p covariance matrix y expressed as a function of model parameters in θ; θ is the vector of model parameters from Λ, Ψ, Θ_ε, v, β, and μ; Λ_y, v, β, and μ are previously defined; Ψ is the k x k covariance matrix among latent factors, Θ_ε is the p x p covariance matrix of residuals, and $\mu(\theta)$ is the p x 1 vector of means of y as a function of the parameters in θ that were previously defined.

MULTILEVEL MODELS AS STRUCTURAL EQUATION MODELS

Great strides have been made over the last two decades in developing multilevel models for the types of data that developmental researchers employing the ecological model may reasonably acquire. Several authors have demonstrated that both the standard latent growth model for repeated measures or longitudinal data (observations nested within individuals) and the traditional contextual MLM example (students within classrooms) can be parameterized as a structural equation model, most recently by Bauer (2003), Curran (2003), and Mehta and Neale (2005). Conversely, Bauer (2003); Li, Duncan, Harmer, Acock, and Stoolmiller (1998); and Raudenbush, Rowan, and Kang (1991) demonstrated how a measurement model can be implemented in a multilevel model. Implementation of multilevel models as structural models additionally allows for even more complex modeling by allowing latent constructs as both predictor and outcome variables, flexible multiple group

comparisons, and simultaneous modeling of multiple parallel outcomes all while considering nested sources of influence. In addition, conducting multilevel modeling in the SEM context also allows for testing mediation (indirect effects), formal model fit testing, and extension to latent class analysis and finite mixture models.

A distinction can be made between two forms of multilevel modeling in the SEM framework: The LGM parameterized as a 1-level SEM and 2-level SEM, or multilevel structural equation modeling (MSEM), consisting of multiple levels of interrelated variables. SEM utilizes a *multivariate* approach to implementing a LGM where the unit of analysis is the individual and the accompanying data is a t-variate outcome vector, where t is the number of repeated observations. Comparatively, the MLM approach to implementing a LGM is considered a *univariate* approach where the individual outcome is the unit of analysis and the accompanying data has a hierarchical structure with the repeated outcomes nested within individuals. Although the LGM would be considered a two-level model in the MLM context, the LGM is considered a single-level model in the SEM context because of the parameterization of the random effects (between-groups variability in the MLM) as latent variables. See Mehta and Neale (2005) for a more detailed discussion of why this is the case.

Figure 7.1a presents a path diagram of a basic linear LGM, parameterized as a structural equation model. The model parameters are labeled to correspond with the model parameters in Equations 3, 7, and 8. Latent growth curve models are more elegantly described in a variety of sources, including Duncan, Duncan, Strycker, Li, and Alpert (1999); Ferrer, Hamagami, and McArdle (2004); Little, Bovaird, and Slegers (2006); and Willett and Sayer (1994). Upon initial inspection, the path diagram appears to reflect four measured variables (the equally spaced repeated measurements) all loading on two correlated constructs. Both constructs have a mean, a variance, and a specific and fixed pattern of factor loadings that have very specific roles. The factor loadings for the first construct, a vector of 1's, define the construct as an intercept, and the pattern of loadings for the second construct, values that represent the relative

FIGURE 7.1

A: Univariate latent growth curve depicted as a multivariate structural equation model. Loadings for the intercept factor (I) are fixed to 1.0 and slope factor (S) loadings are fixed to the values of the time variable T from Equation 1. Group membership contrast variables (g_1 and g_2) are included as predictors. B: Univariate latent growth curve with individually-varying time points depicted as a multivariate structural equation model with slope factor (S) loadings represented as values of an individually-varying definition variable, *age*. Loadings for the intercept factor (I) are fixed to 1.0. C: Representation of the same univariate latent growth model as a random-slope model popularized by the program Mplus.

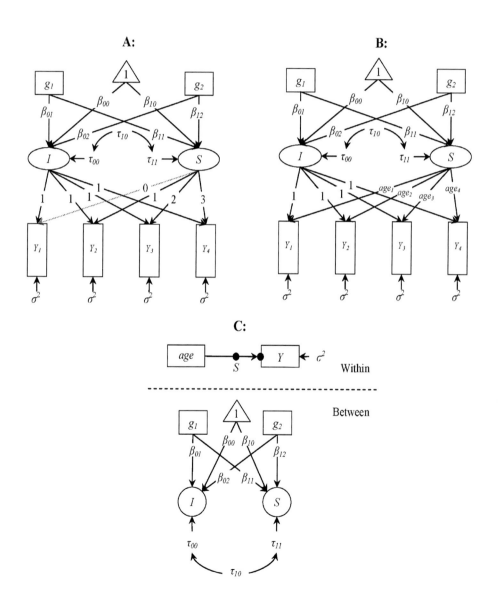

passage of time across the repeated observations, define the linear slope. Note that the initial loading for the slope is 0, thus defining the intercept as the first occasion of measurement. See Kreft, de Leeuw, and Aiken (1995); McArdle and Nesselroade (2002); or Rovine and Molenaar (1998) for additional discussions of defining the intercept.

In the SEM matrix notation presented previously, the measurement and structural models for the linear growth curve are:

$$\begin{aligned} \boldsymbol{y}_i &= \boldsymbol{\Lambda}\boldsymbol{\eta}_i + \boldsymbol{\varepsilon}_i \\ \boldsymbol{\eta}_i &= \boldsymbol{\mu} + \boldsymbol{\zeta}_i \end{aligned} \quad , \tag{13}$$

where $\boldsymbol{\Lambda}$ contains a column vector of 1's and a column vector for the time effect. Once again, these equations can be further reduced to

$$\boldsymbol{y}_i = \boldsymbol{\Lambda}\boldsymbol{\mu} + \boldsymbol{\Lambda}\boldsymbol{\zeta}_i + \boldsymbol{\varepsilon}_i \quad , \tag{14}$$

which implies a covariance structure

$$\boldsymbol{\Sigma}(\boldsymbol{\theta}) = \boldsymbol{\Lambda}\boldsymbol{\Psi}\boldsymbol{\Lambda}' + \boldsymbol{\Theta}_\varepsilon \tag{15}$$

and a mean structure

$$\boldsymbol{\mu}(\boldsymbol{\theta}) = \boldsymbol{\Lambda}\boldsymbol{\mu}. \tag{16}$$

The description and SEM parameterization of the LGM should remind the reader of the previous description and parameterization of the longitudinal multilevel model in Equations 1 to 8. It follows that the two sets of parameterizations are indeed identical differing only in the notations used out of convention. Due to this isomorphism in parallel parameterizations of the same model, parameter estimates obtained from either a MLM program or an SEM program with the same estimator (usually ML) should be equivalent. Any minor variations in parameter estimates or standard errors can be attributed to proprietary differences in programming algorithms. The notational differences indicated here reflect differences in the respective modeling traditions more so than practical differences between the paradigms. A primary practical difference between the paradigms involves the use of the restricted maximum likelihood (REML) estimator in the MLM paradigm for exploring the variance structure, but REML is not available in the SEM paradigm.

Curran (2003), Bauer (2003), and Mehta and Neale (2005) give very thorough discussions of the isomorphism between the univariate MLM approach and the multivariate SEM approach as well as demonstrate how the clustered or traditional classroom MLM example can be formulated as a SEM. In addition, these three sources also demonstrate how SEM can be used to model the effect of time when individuals vary in both the number of observations and the time point at which they were observed (individually varying time points) as well as extend the multivariate SEM approach to LGM to situations where a variable other than time has a random effect on an outcome.

MULTILEVEL STRUCTURAL EQUATION MODELS

Any model that can be defined as a single-level SEM may be nested within a higher hierarchical level. For instance, one might be interested in establishing the factor structure for a measure of kindergarten readiness, but the sample arose from complex sampling where a sample of kindergarten students was obtained from each of several schools. Ignoring the between-school variability in readiness may lead to an underestimation of parameter variance (standard errors) and an incorrect inference. Consequently, a multilevel confirmatory factor analysis (MCFA) would be necessary to accurately model the variance attributable to within-school sources and the between-school source. This hypothetical example would result in a two-level MCFA or a three-level model in the MLM context (see Li et al., 1998; and Raudenbush, 1991). However, a limitation of implementing this model in a MLM context is that the factor loadings must be known and fixed *a priori*, where these parameters are regularly estimated in the SEM paradigm.

Similarly, the parameterization of the LGM as a single-level SEM can be extended to consider variance attributable to a higher level of nesting. For instance, development of math skills may be tracked over the course of the school year, but the sample contains students sampled from several classrooms. This example could be parameterized as a three-level MLM with observations nested within students and students nested within classrooms. It could alternatively be parameterized as a two-level MSEM with the repeated observations nested within students parameterized as a LGM as in Figure 7.1, and the LGM would then be nested within classrooms.

Both of these hypothetical examples indicate sources of variance to be modeled *within* classrooms as well as variance to be modeled *between* classrooms. In the previous MLM parameterizations, the micro-level equation was described as a within-groups model and the macro-level model was described as a between-groups model. Similarly, in the SEM context, we can specify both a within-groups model and a between-groups model. Several approaches have been suggested as to how to model the between-groups variance. Schmidt (1969) demonstrated an early approach using a ML estimator for general multilevel covariance structure modeling. However, Schmidt's demonstration did not include group level variables. The first efforts at implementing a full-information maximum likelihood (FIML) estimator for MSEM were by Goldstein and McDonald (1988), McDonald (1993, 1994), and McDonald and Goldstein (1989), but these approaches were very limited in their application. However, McDonald and Goldstein (1989) provided the mathematical proof for FIML estimation of a two-level SEM with latent variables, and McDonald (1994) presented a new computer program (BIRAM) for a general two-level SEM. Muthén and Satorra (1989) were the first to show a variety of possible special cases of multilevel covariance structure modeling. Longford and Muthén (1992) introduced the multilevel factor analysis model, and Muthén (1989, 1994) showed how it could be implemented with existing SEM software, notably LISREL, using a limited-information maximum likelihood estimator, MUML (Muthén's Maximum Likelihood), for unbalanced data. McArdle and Hamagami (1996) compared multiple group SEM with MSEM. Chou, Bentler, and Pentz (2000) based a two-stage approach on the two-stage slopes-as-outcomes approach to MLM introduced by Burstein (1980). Newer efforts at implementing FIML estimation in MSEM have been contributed by Bentler and Liang (2003), du Tiot and du Toit (2003), Liang and Bentler (2004), and Mehta and Neale (2005).

For more didactic treatments of MSEM, see articles by Kaplan and Elliott (1997) for a didactic example appropriate for studying organizations; Li et al. (1998) for a tutorial on implementing a measurement model in MLM using SEM software; and Cheung and Au (2005) for an application of MSEM appropriate to cross-culture research. Duncan, Duncan, Okut, Strycker, and Li (2002) provided an example for extending the MSEM to four levels of hierarchical data. Excellent chapters on multilevel covariance analysis are also available in Heck and Thomas (2000), Kaplan (2000), and Hox (2002).

Partitioning Variance Approach: Approximate Maximum Likelihood

Muthén (1989, 1991, 1994) proposed an approximate maximum likelihood estimator (MUML) that is analogous to the random-coefficients regression or multilevel model previously presented. For a more thorough introduction than what is provided here, see Hox (2002), Kaplan and Elliott (1997), Li et al. (1998), or Muthén (1994).

According to Muthén, it is possible to formulate a MSEM by dividing the total variance-covariance matrix into separate within-groups and between-groups covariance matrices. The MSEM is then implemented as a multiple-groups problem in any standard SEM program (i.e., LISREL, EQS, Mplus, AMOS, etc.) where one "group" is the within-groups model and the other "group" is the between-groups model. The primary hurdle in a partitioning variance approach to MSEM is the proper estimation of the within and between-group covariance matrices.

According to this approach, individual observations, y_{gi}, are decomposed into the aggregated mean of context g of which individual i is a member, y_g, and the individual deviation from the context mean, y_w. Accordingly, since y_g and y_b are uncorrelated, decomposition of variables into within- and between-groups sources leads to a decomposition of the covariance matrix,

$$V(y_{gi}) = \Sigma_T = \Sigma_B + \Sigma_W, \tag{17}$$

where a portion of the total variance is attributed between individuals and a portion is attributed between groups. However, the sample covariance matrix S is not simply partitioned into between and within sources. Muthén (1989, 1994) demonstrated that the unbiased estimate of the population within-groups covariance matrix (Σ_W) is indeed the pooled within-group sample covariance matrix S_{PW} but S_B is the unbiased estimate of the composite matrix $(\Sigma_W + c\Sigma_B)$ rather than the population between-groups covariance matrix (Σ_B). The parameter c is an ad hoc estimator for the scaling parameter, roughly equivalent to the average sample size within groups. Since S_B is a weighted sum of Σ_W and Σ_B, it necessary to model the between- and within-groups models simultaneously in order to model S_B properly.

Although the actual formulas for estimating S_T, S_{PW}, and S_B may appear daunting (see Hox, 2002; Muthén, 1994), obtaining the necessary covariance matrices is rather straightforward. Hox (2002) suggests an approach for hand-calculating the necessary matrices using standard statistical packages such as SPSS or SAS. There are also special software programs available that can compute the matrices directly, like STREAMS (Gustaffson & Stahl, 1999). The resulting matrices can then be used as input for any standard SEM software that allows for multiple groups.

The same factor structure can be hypothesized at both levels. The population covariance matrices can then be described by separate models where

$$\begin{aligned} \Sigma_B &= \Lambda_B \Psi_B \Lambda_B' + \Theta_B \\ \Sigma_W &= \Lambda_W \Psi_W \Lambda_W' + \Theta_W \end{aligned} \tag{18}$$

For instance, in a MCFA, the individual-level relationship can be defined in a manner similar to Equation 9 with the added subscript designating that the parameters may vary across groups:

$$y_{gi} = v + \lambda \eta_{gi} + \varepsilon_{gi}, \tag{19}$$

where y_{gi} is a vector of items or indicators, v is a vector of means, λ is a vector of factor loadings, η_{gi} represents a factor, and ε_{gi} is a vector of residual variances. The between-group model is then

$$\eta_{gi} = \alpha + \eta_{Bg} + \eta_{Wg}, \tag{20}$$

where α is the overall grand mean for η_{gi}, η_{Bg} is a random factor component capturing organizational effects, and η_{Wg} is a random-factor component varying over individuals within organizations. Thus, for scores for student i in school g, a flexible formulation that allows the measurement model to contain multiple factors and differ at the between and within levels is

$$\boldsymbol{y}_{gi} = \boldsymbol{v} + \boldsymbol{\Lambda}_W \boldsymbol{\eta}_{Wgi} + \boldsymbol{\varepsilon}_{Wgi} + \boldsymbol{\Lambda}_B \boldsymbol{\eta}_{Bg} + \boldsymbol{\varepsilon}_{Bg}, \tag{21}$$

where $\boldsymbol{\Lambda}_W$ is a matrix of factor loadings for the within-group model, $\boldsymbol{\eta}_{Wgi}$ is a matrix of within-group latent factor scores, $\boldsymbol{\varepsilon}_{Wgi}$ is a vector of within-group residuals, $\boldsymbol{\Lambda}_B$ is a matrix of factor loadings for the between-group model, $\boldsymbol{\eta}_{Bg}$ is a matrix of between-group latent factor scores, and $\boldsymbol{\varepsilon}_{Bg}$ is a vector of between-group residuals.

Full Information Maximum Likelihood

In SEM, MLM, and numerous other analytical techniques, it is desirable to obtain maximum likelihood (ML) estimates of model parameters because they are the ones that maximize the likelihood that the observed data were drawn from a particular population. As a normal theory estimation method, under the assumption that the population distribution for endogenous variables is multivariate normal, the covariance matrix and mean vector provide sufficient information for ML parameter estimation. In the case of balanced within-group sample sizes in MSEM, MUML estimation is equivalent to ML estimation. In the case of unbalanced sample sizes, however, MUML is only an approximation to ML. In the presence of unbalanced sample sizes and/or missing data, full-information, or raw data, maximum likelihood (FIML) is necessary in order to achieve asymptotically optimal parameter estimates because its estimates have the smallest possible standard errors among other estimators. As a contrast to FIML, Muthén's MUML approach (Muthén, 1989, 1990, 1994) has been referred to as a limited-information (Hox, 2002; Hox & Maas, 2001) or pseudo-balanced (McDonald, 1994) approach largely due to its reliance on the ad hoc group sample size estimator c and its use of $\boldsymbol{\Sigma}_W$ and $\boldsymbol{\Sigma}_B$ as input rather than the raw data.

Although FIML is preferable, it has historically been demanding to use especially with unbalanced data as it effectively requires specifying a structure for every group or sample size, or in the case of longitudinal data, every individual or unique combination of time points. FIML was first introduced to SEM to handle missing data (Arbuckle, 1996) where the missing data created response vectors with unequal numbers of observations. With FIML estimation, the model-implied mean and covariance matrices are computed for each response pattern with individual data vectors, and the standard ML fit function is obtained by summing twice the negative log likelihood (-2LL) across all of the individual data vectors. Thus, FIML offers the possibility of fitting new types of models in which the model-implied means and covariances are different for each individual or group.

The traditional multivariate approach to LGM presented in Figure 7.1a is restrictive in that it requires that all individuals are observed at the same time points or that all possible time points are represented as an observed variable in the model. The introduction of FIML estimation in SEM software, particularly Mx (Neale, Boker, Xie, & Maes, 2004) and Mplus (Muthén & Muthén, 2006), has enabled the user to develop this model in a manner more comparable to the MLM approach. In the case of unbalanced designs (number of observations) and individually-varying time points, individual data vectors are modeled rather than the traditional covariance matrix and mean vector (see Mehta & West, 2000; Mehta & Neale, 2005). Mx and Mplus allow model parameters to be fixed to an individual's data values where the variable used to fix model parameters can be called a definition variable. This is especially illustrated in the case of a LGM with individually varying (both in location and number) time points as depicted in Figure 7.1b. The LGM in Figure 7.1a can be generalized in Figure 7.1b so that the factor loadings for the slope construct represent values of a definition variable rather than as fixed values, thus allowing individually varying time points (Mehta & Neale, 2005).

MUML Versus FIML

The robustness of the MUML estimator as compared with FIML estimation has been explored by Hox (1993), Hox and Maas (2001), McDonald (1994), Muthén (1990), and most recently by Yuan and Hayashi (2005). Hox and Maas (2001) in particular studied the robustness of MSEM using the MUML estimator to unequal sample sizes between groups, small sample sizes both within- and between-groups, and the presence of a low versus a high intraclass correlation (ICC). In general, they found that estimation of the within portion of the MSEM does not pose a problem. However, estimating the between portion of the model experiences an increased occurrence of inadmissible estimates, especially when there is a small number of groups (50 or less) and a low intraclass correlation (ICC). Hox and Maas found that the occurrence of inadmissible estimates could be partially compensated by increasing the number of groups. They also found that the standard errors for the between-groups portion of the model were negatively biased, leading to a tendency for overall tests of model fit to over-reject correct models. Yuan and Hayashi (2005) additionally found that the MUML standard error and test statistic biases come from two sources. A common finding, the first source is related to sample sizes and disappears as sample sizes increase. The other source of bias is due to the ratio of the variance in between-groups sample sizes to the average between-groups sample size.

When this ratio, known as the coefficient of variation, is small, standard errors and test of model fit with MUML tend to be unbiased, but when the coefficient of variation is large, bias occurs. Although the general recommendation in the MLM literature is to include as many groups as possible (increase the between-groups sample size), Yuan and Hayashi recommend that it is preferable to avoid collecting groups with small sample sizes because they not only contribute to a smaller average between-groups sample size, but they increase the variance in the between-groups sample size as well, thus increasing the coefficient of variation.

MUML has been found to have computational and convergence advantages over FIML due to easier calculations and faster convergence and has been found to be a reasonable approximation to FIML (Muthén, 1990; McDonald, 1994; Hox, 1993; Hox & Maas, 2001; Yuan & Hayashi, 2005). As a result, the MUML procedure for MSEM has been regularly implemented in recent versions of popular SEM software (EQS 6.0, Mplus 2.12 on, and LISREL 8.7). However, there have been several recent advances that have made FIML estimation in MSEM feasible. Bentler and Liang (2003) and Liang and Bentler (2004) generalized a procedure for exact ML estimation via an expectation maximization (EM) algorithm (Lee, 1990; Lee & Poon, 1998) from a two-level model without a mean structure to the case with both a mean and covariance structure. Raudenbush (1995) showed how ML estimation for a two-level SEM with an unbalanced design could be accomplished through an EM algorithm with available software. Bauer (2003) and Curran (2003) used a hierarchical factor model structure to conceptualize multilevel latent variable models with FIML estimation using standard covariance and mean SEM. However, their approach included several restrictive conditions including an assumption of invariant factor loadings across levels, an assumption of zero variances of observed indicators at the cluster level, and in the case of unbalanced sample sizes, a very burdensome data management situation.

Random Slopes. The MUML approach is limited to random intercepts only. When random slopes are of interest, the MUML approach limits the researcher to specifying random slopes as latent variables in a one-level model as demonstrated by Bauer (2003) and Curran (2003). In the event of large amounts of missing data and/or individually varying occasions of measurement, a very burdensome data management situation can result. The FIML implementations in LISREL and EQS are also limited to models with random intercepts only. However, there have been several recent advances that have made FIML estimation in MSEM feasible as well as introducing the capability of modeling random slopes in addition to random intercepts.

Random slopes in MLM imply that covariances are a function of some predictor, and since it is necessary to allow a different relationship between the outcome and the definition variable for each individual by definition of a random slope, it follows that FIML is central to MSEM, especially with random slopes (Mehta & Neale, 2005). In contrast to the LGM parameterization in Figure 7.1a, the LGM can be conceptualized as a random coefficient MSEM with a within-group model equivalent to the MLM Equation 1, and a between-group model equivalent to the MLM Equation 2. Figure 7.1c presents a LGM parameterized as a MSEM with dots at the within level representing the random effects. The dot on the within-regression labeled S indicates that the effect of time (T) on the outcome (Y) varies across individuals at the between level. The dot on the within-outcome indicates that the value of the intercept also varies across individuals. Both S and the random intercept (I) are then represented as random variables at the between level. The between and within levels are separated by a dashed line. The MSEM parameterization of the LGM in Figure 7.1c allows unbalanced designs and individually varying time points because of FIML estimation.

Software

Direct FIML estimation is available in the current versions of LISREL, EQS, Mx, GLLAMM, and Mplus. LISREL allows for general two-level SEM using FIML and including the chi-square test and RMSEA for testing goodness of model fit. The implementation of FIML in EQS is made possible via an EM algorithm (Bentler & Liang, 2003; Liang & Bentler, 2004). Mx has the necessary features to allow FIML estimation, but as it is designed for behavioral genetics, it is limited to only a small number of individuals per cluster, a small number of variables, and models must be specified in terms of matrices and model-implied means and covariances (Mehta & Neale, 2005). GLLAMM (Generalized Linear Latent and Mixed Models: Rabe-Hesketh, Skrondal, & Pickles, 2004) is a STATA macro that also permits link functions for different response scales such as binary, ordinal, or count data. Mplus has emerged as an exceptional package for all forms of latent variable modeling, including MSEM. In addition to MUML for random intercept models with continuous data and no missing data, Mplus offers FIML for models with random slopes for both continuous and categorical (binary or ordinal) outcomes and missing data. Mplus also allows individually varying values of definition variables (i.e., individually varying time points) and random slopes for time-varying covariates. For MUML and FIML estimation of random intercept models, chi-square tests and robust chi-square tests are available for test of model fit along with the CFI, TLI, and RMSEA approximate fit indices. No fit statistics are available in Mplus for models with random slopes. Mplus will be used in the empirical examples later in this chapter.

General Procedural Framework

Muthén (1994) initially outlined a four-step process for informing the full MSEM. This is the approach that has been most widely followed in didactic and substantive applications of MSEM (see Cheung & Au, 2005; Heck, 2001; and Kaplan, 2000). It involves a) conducting a conventional SEM analysis ignoring the multilevel structure to try out model ideas, b) determining the degree of between-groups variance by computing the estimated ICC for each observed variable, c) exploring the within groups structure, and d) exploring the between-groups structure. Hox (2002) outlined a slightly different step-wise procedure for developing a MSEM that includes testing a set of nested null, independence, and saturated models to determine whether there is any between-groups structure at all rather than investigate individual-variable ICC's. For each of these steps, Hox suggested that model fit can and should be evaluated at each step with some combination of available fit indices. Testing model fit in such a manner is also possible using Muthén's recommended steps, but it was not explicitly stated. Mehta and Neale (2005) followed the common MLM procedures for testing the empty model to determine degree of clustering, determining the fixed or structural component of the model, and then focusing on the random portion of the model when developing an empirical MCFA example.

The model development steps proposed by Muthén (1994) were presented in the context of the MUML approach for MSEM which is primarily a two-group SEM model. While the MUML approach has its advantages, the regular implementation of FIML estimation and the possibility of random slopes in MSEM make the Muthén steps less applicable as the model can be conceptualized as a random coefficient model as in the MLM context, rather than as a two-group model. Consequently, the procedural steps followed by Hox (2002) and Mehta and Neale (2005) which involve testing a series of model modifications and rejecting competing models is more intuitive and in parallel with procedures suggested in the MLM literature (Snijders & Bosker, 1999).

LOCUS OF CONTROL DEVELOPMENT THROUGH ADOLESCENCE

This empirical example illustrates the use of MSEM to extend the LGM to four hierarchical levels by modeling the development of locus of control (LOC) among nondisabled and disabled children age 8 through age 20 with children nested within schools across four states. The development of locus of control will be investigated as a four-level MSEM with 3 LOC measures nested within each observation period, observation period (Year 1 up to Year 3) nested within individual, and individual ($N = 1337$) nested within school ($k = 101$). Using a pseudo cohort-sequential design, 1,337 students between the ages of 8 and 18 from 101 schools were followed for up to 3 years. Students completed three measures of locus of control — the Nowicki–Strickland Internal External Scales (NS) and the Successes (Positive) and Failures (Negative) Subscales (IP and IN) of the Intellectual Achievement Responsibility Questionnaire during each year of assessment. The main analytic objective is to examine developmental differences in the locus of control construct, as measured by the NS, IP, and IN scales, across three disability groups — no disability (ND), learning disability (LD), and mental retardation (MR) — while considering the complex sampling nature of the data.

Substantive findings in this data set were reported in Shogren, Bovaird, Wehmeyer, and Palmer (2005). The data used here is for illustrative purposes only, and the reader is urged not to infer any substantive meaning from the reported results. While the general results are comparable, elements of the data used in this chapter were selected to illustrate MSEM principles rather than infer substantive findings on the development of locus of control. In the original analyses, a multiple-group framework was used to address hypotheses of heterogeneity of variances between disability groups and the school level was not initially considered. The use of multiple groups is not easily compatible with the concurrent use of random slopes and two-level modeling in SEM, so disability group will be investigated here using a contrast variable approach in a single-group model. In the original analysis, gender and ethnicity were also considered, but they have been excluded here in order to simplify the model and better illustrate the nested nature of the data.

Design

The three measures of locus of control — NS, IP, and IN — can be combined to form a measurement model of LOC measured on three occasions. As shown by Bauer (2003), Li et al. (1998), and Mehta and Neale (2005), this is in itself a two-level model. Thus, the three measures of locus of control (Level 1) are nested within each occasion of measurement (Level 2) and are represented as a measurement model for locus of control with three indicators in Figure 7.2. The factor loading for NS (λ_1) was fixed to 1.0 for identification of the measurement model at each occasion of measurement. Factor loadings and residual variances for each measure were constrained to be equal across the three measurement occasions and the latent disturbance for the LOC construct (Ψ) was constrained as well to achieve temporal measurement invariance.

FIGURE 7.2
Four-level multilevel curve of factors (MCOF) model with multiple outcomes nested within
observations, observations nested within individuals, and individuals nested within schools.
Parameters with identical labels are constrained to be equal.

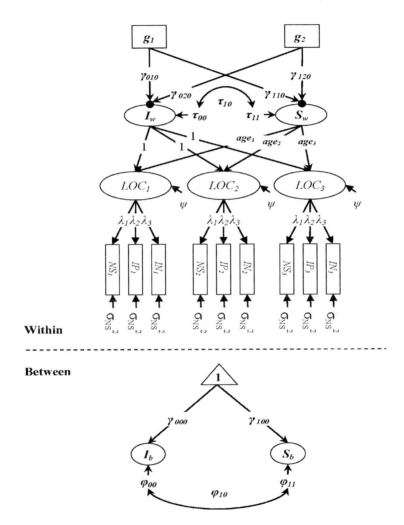

Individuals vary widely both in the age at each observation (individually varying
time points) and in the number of observations per individual (up to three). If
modeled with the traditional LGM depicted in Figure 7.1a, this example would
require that each individual has a 13-observation data vector (age $8 - 20$) that
would include anywhere from 10 to 12 missing data points and would experience
substantial estimation problems due to the enormous amount of missing data.

Alternatively, the single-level definition variable approach depicted in Figure 7.1b will be used to model the within-school development of locus of control as an individually varying time point LGM (IVT-LGM). Change in the latent construct can be modeled as a growth curve making this a three-level model, often referred to as a *curve-of-factors* (COF) model (Duncan et al., 1999).

In order to take into consideration that students (Level 3) were sampled within schools (Level 4), a second set of random effects are specified for inter-school variability in initial status and rate of change. The total random effects will now potentially include (dependent upon estimation feasibility and statistical significance) random intercepts, slopes, and covariances at both individual and school levels, as well as a within-individual residual. However, variance (or covariance) estimates found to contribute to estimation problems or estimated as a negative value (for variances only) were removed from the model.

Disability status was dummy coded (see Cohen et al., 2003) into two contrast variables (g_1 and g_2) with ND as the reference group and was included as a set of two individual-level predictor variables. Due to the use of dummy coding, the between-schools intercept (γ_{000}) and slope (γ_{100}) fixed effects are interpreted as the mean initial status and mean slope for all individuals in the ND group, the first within-school contrast effect and its interaction with the slope are the difference in initial status (γ_{010}) and slope (γ_{110}) between the ND and LD groups, and the second within-school contrast effect and its interaction with the slope are the difference in initial status (γ_{020}) and slope (γ_{120}) between the ND and MR groups. Age was centered at age 8, so initial status parameters are interpreted as level of locus of control at age 8, and slopes are the rate of change since age 8.

Results

Final parameter estimates for the multilevel COF model are reported in Table 7.1. Model fit indices are not available. Examination of the fixed effects suggests that the disability groups significantly differ in level of locus of control at age 8 (γ_{000}, γ_{010}, and γ_{020}). All three disability groups also showed significant growth in locus of control with no difference between the ND and LD groups (γ_{110}), and the MR group showing a slower rate of change than the ND and LD groups (γ_{120}). Overall, there were individual (student) differences in intercept only (τ_{00}), and schools varied in their average initial status (ϕ_{00}) but not in the average rate of change in locus of control among students within a school. This suggests that there are individual differences in initial status to be accounted for beyond just disability status. Schools vary in the average initial status of students within those schools, indicating that there may be additional school-level variables to consider in this model if they were available.

TABLE 7.1
Multilevel Curve of Factors Model (MCOF) Parameter Estimates

	Est.	SE	
Factor Loadings			
NS	1	0	
IP	0.50	0.003	*
IN	0.42	0.003	*
Residuals			
NS	16.50	0.79	*
IARP	5.45	0.25	*
IARN	5.49	0.23	*
Random Effects[+]			
S Intercept (ϕ_{00})	2.91	1.69	*
S Slope (ϕ_{11})	7.18	4.55	
S Cov (ϕ_{00})	-4.20	2.82	
I(S) Intercept (τ_{00})	9.14	2.06	*
I(S) Slope (τ_{11})	3.45	6.13	
I(S) Cov (τ_{00})	-2.33	3.56	
Residual (σ^2)	0.67	0.61	
Fixed Effects			
Intercept (γ_{000})	24.63	0.46	*
Slope (γ_{100})	4.35	0.78	*
g1 (γ_{010})	-1.17	0.57	*
g2 (γ_{020})	-2.67	0.82	*
slope*g1 (γ_{110})	-1.52	0.98	
slope*g2 (γ_{120})	-3.44	1.18	*
Deviance	-12493.47		
BIC	25115.82		

Note. *Statistically significant at the $p < .05$ level. [+] S indicates variability between schools, and I(S) indicates variability between individuals (I) within a school (S).

READINESS FOR KINDERGARTEN

The second empirical example illustrates a cross-sectional MSEM of readiness for kindergarten with students nested within county. Substantive findings were reported in Bovaird (2005) and Bovaird, Martinez, and Stuber (2006). The focus of the project and this example is to develop a multilevel MIMIC model to describe the relationship between county-level contextual characteristics and kindergarten preparedness, controlling for student-level characteristics.

FIGURE 7.3
Multilevel confirmatory factor analysis (MCFA) model of readiness for kindergarten. The within residual covariances are not included for clarity. A: Traditional representation. B: Representation popularized by the program Mplus.

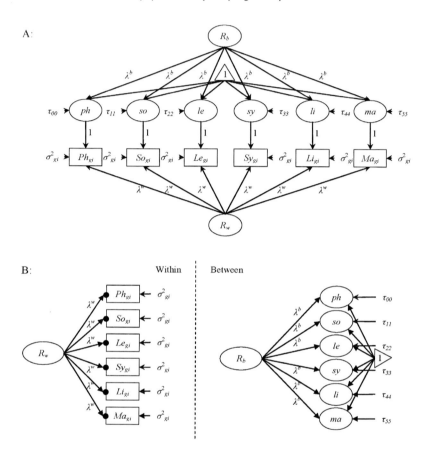

A statewide data collection effort resulted in data from 1997 kindergarten students from 95 (out of 105) counties in a Midwestern state. Teachers completed a measure of kindergarten preparedness for each student consisting of six aspects of readiness: symbolic development (Sy), literacy development (Li), mathematical knowledge (Ma), social skills development (So), learning to learn (Le), and physical development (Ph). Student-level measures of age (Age), body-mass index (BMI), gender (Sex), language status (ELL), eligibility for free or reduced lunch (FRL), and IEP status (IEP) were also available. The original study included 21 county-level contextual variables supplied by state agencies and grouped into three goal areas: the *Family Goal* (children live in safe and stable families that support learning), the *Community Goal* (children live in safe and stable communities that support learning, health, and family services), and the *School Goal* (children attend schools that support learning). However, for the purposes of this example, only a selected number of county characteristics are explored: percentage of mothers with at least a high school education (MHS), the number of children placed out of home (COH), the percentage of kindergarten students on free or reduced lunch (PFR), and the crime rate per capita (CRC) form a socioeconomic status construct (SES) representing the *family* goal; three measures of the typical classroom environments in a county — the physical environment rating (PER), the social context score (SCS), and the instructional environment rating (IER) — form a classroom quality construct (CLQ) representing the *school* goal; and the total child care capacity (CCC) and the total preschool capacity (PSC) form a child care construct (CAR) representing the *community* goal.

Univariate Random Intercepts Models

Univariate random-intercept models were fit to each of the six outcome variables and six student-level predictors with students nested within counties. Although all measures with the exception of gender were shown to have statistically significant variability between counties, most significant ICCs were small ranging from 0.02 to 0.14. A notable exception was ELL with a substantial ICC of 0.29. This suggests that the proportion of males (or females) is constant across counties, and there is variability between counties on all other student-level variables, especially the proportion of ELL students.

Developing the Measurement Model

A unidimensional measurement model of readiness was fit at each level. To determine if the meaning of the readiness factor is the same at both the within- and between-county levels, the factor loadings were constrained to be equal at both levels implying there is a random intercept for the latent variable. This equates the scales of the latent factor across levels, allowing the latent variances at both levels to be comparable. The factor loading for physical development was fixed at 1.0, allowing for a freely estimated factor variance at both levels and the computation of the latent ICC. The constrained MCFA model is graphically presented in Figure 7.3.

TABLE 7.2
Standardized Solution for the Multilevel MIMIC Model of Kindergarten Readiness

Measure	Unstand. Loading	Stand. Loading	Residual Variances	Intercept	R^2
		Within County			
Factor Loadings					
Ph	1.000^1	0.711	0.494		0.506
So	1.208	0.735	0.460		0.540
Le	1.382	0.883	0.221		0.779
Sy	1.232	0.748	0.440		0.560
Li	1.566	0.872	0.239		0.761
Ma	1.377	0.797	0.364		0.636
Latent Variances					
R_w			0.847		0.153
Structural Coefficients[3]					
Age	0.064	0.128			
BMI	-0.007	-0.070			
Sex	0.075	0.144			
ELL	0.160	0.153			
FRL	0.074	0.134			
IEP	0.198	0.262			
		Between County			
Factor Loadings					
ph	1.000^1	0.854	0.270	2.752	0.730
so	1.208	0.932	0.132^2	2.634	0.868
le	1.382	0.931	0.132	2.650	0.868
sy	1.232	0.592	0.650	2.617	0.350
li	1.566	0.934	0.129	2.614	0.871
ma	1.377	0.879	0.228	2.658	0.772
Latent Variances					
R_b			0.907		0.093
Structural Coefficients[3]					
SES	0.004	0.289			
CLQ	0.002^2	0.034			
CCC	0.002^2	0.106			
Age[4]	5.604	–			
ELL[4]	0.902	–			
FRL[4]	0.586	–			
IEP[4]	0.852	–			

Note. [1]The factor loading for Physical Development was fixed at 1.0 for model identification.
[2]Not statistically significant at the $p < .05$ level.
[3]All structural coefficients predict Readiness.
[4]Latent means.

Constraining the within-county and between-county factor loadings[1] for the readiness construct resulted in a model that did not fit the data well, $\chi^2(23)$ = 1114.71, $p < .01$, CFI = 0.89, RMSEA = 0.15. Exploration of the residual variance–covariance matrix and the modification indices[2] indicated a substantial unresolved residual covariance between math and literacy at the within-county level. Allowing the within-county math and literacy residual variances to covary resulted in a significant improvement in model fit, $\chi^2(22) = 278.42$, $p < .01$, CFI = 0.97, RMSEA = 0.08; $\Delta\chi^2(1) = 836.29$, $p < .01$. Modification indices also suggested a within-county residual correlation between social development and learning development, and this too resulted in a significant improvement in model fit, $\chi^2(21) = 132.8769$, $p < .01$, CFI = 0.989, RMSEA = 0.05; $\Delta\chi^2(1) = 145.46$, $p < .01$. The latent ICC was calculated to be 0.08. Table 7.2 summarizes the parameter estimates for the constrained MCFA model.

Within- and Between-County Covariates

Upon establishment of the readiness construct, the relationship between county-level contextual characteristics and kindergarten readiness, controlling for student-level characteristics, can be established. There are several intermediary steps that determined which model parameters are necessary and relevant to the phenomenon of kindergarten readiness, and the interested reader is directed to Bovaird, Martinez, and Stuber (2006) for details.

All six student-level variables were found to be significant within-county predictors of readiness. Univariate random intercept models also suggested that five of the six variables (the exception was gender) showed significant variability between counties. Although BMI was initially found to have a marginally significant random intercept ($p = .04$), it was found to have a nonsignificant random intercept in the multivariate model and was not included in the between-county model. Age is a continuous variable, but ELL (1 = native English speaker), FRL (1 = not eligible), Sex (1 = female), and IEP (1 = no IEP) are dummy coded categorical variables. Thus, between-county variance for Age reflects variability between counties in the mean age of their kindergarten population, while between-county variances for ELL, FRL, Sex, and IEP represent variability in

---

[1]Table 7.2 summarizes the parameter estimates for multilevel MIMIC model, but the parameter estimates are comparable to those obtained for the constrained MCFA model.

[2]It is important to note that in this case, use of the modification indices was not driven by theory and rather to illustrate that they are available and useful for model development when used to support theoretical implications.

FIGURE 7.4

Multilevel MIMIC model of kindergarten readiness. Parameter labels at both levels, within-level residual covariances, and between-level latent covariances are not included for diagrammatic clarity.

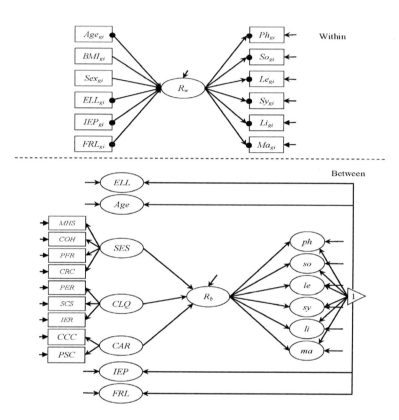

proportions between counties. The four random intercepts were entered in as predictors of the between-county readiness construct, but only Age was found to be a significant predictor of readiness. The other three variables were kept as random intercepts but with no predictive effects at the between-county level.

To explore the effects of the county-level predictors of kindergarten readiness, three county-level latent constructs were formed as described in the introductory paragraph for this section. The SES and CLQ constructs were identified by fixing the factor loadings for MHS and PER to 1.0, respectively. The CAR construct was identified by fixing both loadings to 1.0. SES, CLQ, and CAR were entered as between-county predictors of readiness along with the random intercept for Age. All exogenous between-county variables were allowed to covary. This resulted in the model presented in Figure 7.4. The standardized solution for the readiness construct and the structural coefficients at both levels are available in Table 7.2. This model fit the data well, $\chi^2(228) = 642.99$, $p < .01$, CFI = 0.95, RMSEA = 0.03; however, Mplus provided a warning that some standard errors may not be trustworthy, due most likely to having more parameters than the number of counties. To simplify the model, all nonsignificant between-county structural and covariance parameters between exogenous variables were dropped, resulting in a comparably well-fitting model with no technical warnings, $\chi^2(243) = 651.00$, $p < .01$, CFI = 0.95, RMSEA = 0.03.

As reported in Table 7.2, at the between-county level, SES was a marginal predictor of between-county readiness ($t = 1.880$), but CLQ ($t = 0.166$) and CAR ($t = 0.373$) were not found to be significant predictors. The predictive effect of the random intercept of age on readiness became nonsignificant, so age was left as a random intercept at the between level. There was a significant positive correlation between FRL and SES ($r = 0.698$), ELL and SES ($r = 0.294$), and CLQ with CAR ($r = 0.523$), and a negative correlation between IEP and CAR ($r = -0.502$). These results suggest that counties with higher levels of SES tend to also have children who are more ready for kindergarten. Counties with higher SES levels also tend to have a lower proportion of kindergarten students eligible for free or reduced lunch and a lower proportion of English-language learners. Counties with a higher child care capacity tend to also have higher SES levels and more kindergarten students with an IEP. Within counties, older female students with a lower body-mass index tended to be more ready for kindergarten, as were students who were native English speakers, not eligible for free or reduced lunch, and not in special education.

Random Slopes

The final model in this example investigates the potential random slopes for the six student-level covariates. The interpretation of such parameters, if statistically significant, would entail that the within-county predictive effect of a covariate on readiness varies across counties. Mplus allows for estimation of random slopes with MSEM models, but such estimation can be computationally intensive, often requiring numerical or Monte Carlo integration to obtain ML estimates (Muthén & Muthén, 2006). In order to simplify the example, especially because the between-county model is rather complex and the number of counties relative to the number of parameters has already been indicated to be problematic, student-level predictor random intercepts (and all associated covariances) were removed from the between portion of the model, resulting in an acceptable overall model fit, $\chi^2(218) = 566.86$, $p < .01$, CFI = 0.95, RMSEA = 0.03. Supplemental univariate analyses indicated that the effects of IEP and ELL may vary between counties. Estimation of the variability in slope for ELL

FIGURE 7.5

Multilevel MIMIC model of kindergarten readiness with random slopes. Formatting is consistent
with Figure 4. Parameter estimates involving the random slopes for IEP and ELL are included.
The asterisk indicates that the parameter is statistically different from zero at the $p < .05$ level.

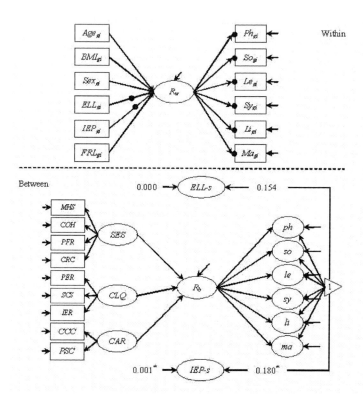

approached zero, and estimation of the random slope for IEP was achieved, and
significant. Thus, the effect of ELL status on readiness within a county does
not vary between counties, but the effect of IEP status does. The resulting
model is presented in Figure 7.5 with parameter estimates for the ELL and IEP
effects. Further fit information is not available in Mplus for multilevel models
with random slopes.

CONCLUSIONS

This chapter reviewed the use of structural equation modeling for multilevel
data and in the presence of contextual variables such as county characteristics

and disability status. Two empirical examples illustrated many of the principles discussed. Multilevel structural equation modeling is a relatively new methodological development that has progressed rapidly with the recent technological advances. Although the technique has been discussed for 15 years, primarily since Muthén's (1989, 1994) MUML procedure was first introduced, it was another 10 years before a series of didactic articles and chapters (Heck & Thomas, 2000; Kaplan, 2000; Kaplan & Elliott, 1997) were published that MSEM began to make its way into the substantive literature. However, the limitations of the MUML approach — initially the need to determine unbiased estimates of the within- and between-covariance matrices, only approximate ML estimation, and the capacity for random intercepts only — have left room for the improvements provided by FIML estimation. Now, with the implementation of FIML estimation in standard SEM packages, especially Mx and Mplus, individually varying occasions of measurement and random slopes are possible as illustrated in the chapter examples.

There are still numerous areas for active methodological research however, namely refining the efficiency of the estimation process especially when numerical or Monte Carlo integration is required and determining the appropriate means of standardizing the solution. Of particular concern to applied researchers is the lack of development of useful fit indices like what are available with standard SEM for all applications and the appropriate role of the multiple sample sizes involved in multilevel modeling.

The first difficulty caused by sample sizes is the potentially small sample sizes obtained at the upper hierarchical levels. Generally speaking, a "large" sample size is required for SEM primarily because of the use of ML estimation methods. In MSEM, obtaining a large sample size at the lower level is often not a problem, but obtaining a sufficiently large sample size in terms of the number of groups is. Many sources in the MLM literature (see Snijders & Bosker, 1999, for example) recommend a minimum of at least 50 to 100 groups. If a decision must be made regarding sampling more individuals versus more groups, preference is given toward sampling fewer subjects within a group and more groups. Simulation results reported in Hox and Maas (2001) led them to recommend a group-level sample size of at least $n = 100$ units. Cheung and Au (2005) additionally explored issues related to a finite level 2 population as occurs in cross-cultural research and geographical contexts.

Numerous fit indices have been developed for standard mean and covariance based SEM, but it is unclear whether any of these indices are applicable to MSEM. The presence of a nested data structure adds an additional level of complexity that has not yet been overcome. Most fit indices take the sample size into consideration to varying degrees depending on the particular index. In MSEM, there are at least three sample sizes to consider: The number of clusters, the number of participants, and possibly the number of participants within clusters. The question remains as to determining which sample size is most comparable to SEM. Mehta and Neale (2005) suggest that the most appropriate sample size is the number of clusters, but there is not a clear consensus.

Despite these limitations, the development of MSEM represents several advances that can be of use to the developmental researcher, merging the capacity to appropriately model increasingly common hierarchical data structures (multilevel modeling) with the capacity to model multiple latent variables in a simultaneous model (SEM). Although not illustrated in this chapter, the MSEM framework can be expanded to multiple-group modeling, latent class modeling, mixture modeling, and generalized modeling for noncontinuous variables. In many ways, the conceptual limitation is only the creativity of the researcher or analyst and not in the technical modeling itself.

REFERENCES

Arbuckle, J. L. (1996). Full information estimation in the presence of incomplete data. In G. A. Marcoulides & R. E. Schumacker (Eds.), *Advanced structural equation modeling: Issues and techniques* (pp. 243-277). Mahwah, NJ: Lawrence Erlbaum Associates.

Bauer, D. J. (2003). Estimating multilevel linear models as structural equation models. *Journal of Educational and Behavioral Statistics, 28*, 135-167.

Bentler, P. M., & Liang, J. (2003). Two-level mean and covariance structures: Maximum likelihood via an em algorithm. In S. P. Reise & N. Duan (Eds.), *Multilevel modeling: Methodological advances, issues, and applications* (pp. 53-70). Mahwah, NJ: Lawrence Erlbaum Associates.

Bollen, K. A. (1989). *Structural equations with latent variables.* New York: Wiley.

Bovaird, J. A. (2005). *A statistical exploration of the Kansas vision for school readiness.* Topeka: Kansas State Department of Education.

Bovaird, J. A., Martinez, S., & Stuber, G. (2006, August). Multilevel modeling of kindergarten readiness with finite sample sizes. Paper presented at the annual meeting of the American Psychological Association, New Orleans, LA.

Burstein, L. (1980). The analysis of multilevel data in educational research and evaluation. In D. Berliner (Ed.), *Review of research in education.* (Vol. 8, pp. 158-233). Washington, DC: American Educational Research Association.

Burstein, L., Linn, R. L., & Cappel, F. (1978). Analyzing multilevel data in the presence of heterogeneous within-class regression. *Journal of Educational Statistics, 3*, 347-383.

Cheung, M. W. L., & Au, K. (2005). Applications of multilevel structural equation modeling to cross-cultural research. *Structural Equation Modeling, 12*, 598-619.

Chou, C., Bentler, P. M., & Pentz, M. A. (2000). A two-stage approach to multilevel structural equation models: Application to longitudinal data. In T. D. Little,

K. U. Schnabel, & J. Baumert (Eds.), *Modeling longitudinal and multilevel data: Practical issues, applied approaches and specific examples* (pp. 33-50). Mahwah, NJ: Lawrence Erlbaum Associates.

Cohen, J., Cohen, P., West, S. G., & Aiken, L. S. (2003). *Applied multiple regression/correlation analysis for the behavioral sciences* (3rd ed.). Mahwah, NJ: Lawrence Erlbaum Associates.

Curran, P. J. (2003). Have multilevel models been structural equation models all along? *Multivariate Behavioral Research, 38*, 529-569.

Duncan, T. E., Duncan, S. C., Okut, H., Strycker, L. A., & Li, F. (2002). An extension of the general latent variable growth modeling framework to four levels of the hierarchy. *Structural Equation Modeling, 9*, 303-326.

Duncan, T. E., Duncan, S. C., Strycker, L. A., Li, F., & Alpert, A. (1999). *An introduction to latent variable growth curve modeling: Concepts, issues, and applications*. Mahwah, NJ: Lawrence Erlbaum Associates.

Ferrer, E., Hamagami, F., & McArdle, J. (2004). Modeling latent growth curves with incomplete data using different types of structural equation modeling and multilevel software. *Structural Equation Modeling, 11*, 452-483.

Goldstein, H. I. (1986). Multilevel mixed linear model analysis using iterative general least squares. *Biometrika, 73*, 43-56.

Goldstein, H. I., & McDonald, R. P. (1988). A general model for the analysis of multilevel data. *Psychometrika, 53*, 455-467.

Gustaffson, J. E., & Stahl, P. E. (1999). *Streams user's guide, vs. 2.0*. Mlndal, Sweden: MultivariateWare.

Heck, R. H. (2001). Multilevel modeling with SEM. In G. A. Marcoulides & R. E. Schumacker (Eds.), *New developments and techniques in structural equation modeling* (pp. 89-128). Mahwah, NJ: Lawrence Erlbaum Associates.

Heck, R. H., & Thomas, S. L. (2000). *An introduction to multilevel modeling techniques*. Mahwah, NJ: Lawrence Erlbaum Associates.

Hox, J. J. (1993). Factor analysis of multilevel data: Gauging the Muthén model. In J. H. L. Oud & R. A. W. van Blokland-Vogelesang (Eds.), *Advances in longitudinal and multivariate analysis in the behavioral sciences* (pp. 141-156). Nijmegen, NL: ITS.

Hox, J. J. (2002). *Multilevel analysis: Techniques and applications*. Mahwah, NJ: Lawrence Erlbaum Associates.

Hox, J. J., & Maas, C. J. M. (2001). The accuracy of multilevel structural equation modeling with pseudobalanced groups and small samples. *Structural Equation Modeling, 8*, 157-174.

Jöreskog, K. G., & Sörbom, D. (1993). *LISREL 8: User's reference guide*. Chicago, IL: Scientifc Software International.

Kaplan, D. (2000). *Structural equation modeling: Foundations and extensions*. Thousand Oaks, CA: Sage.

Kaplan, D., & Elliott, P. R. (1997). A didactic example of multilevel structural equation modeling applicable to the study of organizations. *Structural Equation Modeling, 4*, 1-24.

Kline, R. B. (2005). *Principles and practices of structural equation modeling* (2nd ed.). New York: Guilford Press.

Kreft, I. G. G., & de Leeuw, J. (1998). *Introduction to multilevel modeling.* London: Sage.

Kreft, I. G. G., de Leeuw, J., & Aiken, L. (1995). The effect of different forms of centering in hierarchical linear models. *Multivariate Behavioral Research, 30,* 1-22.

Laird, N. M., & Ware, J. H. (1982). Random effects models for longitudinal data. *Biometrics, 38,* 963-974.

Lee, S. Y. (1990). Multilevel analysis of structural equation models. *Biometrics, 77,* 763-772.

Lee, S. Y., & Poon, W. Y. (1998). Analysis of two-level structural equation models via EM type algorithms. *Statistica Sinica, 8,* 749-766.

Li, F., Duncan, T. E., Harmer, P., Acock, A., & Stoolmiller, M. (1998). Analyzing measurement models of latent variables through multilevel confirmatory factor analysis and hierarchical linear modeling approaches. *Structural Equation Modeling, 5,* 294-306.

Liang, J., & Bentler, P. M. (2004). An EM algorithm for fitting two-level structural equation models. *Psychometrika, 69,* 101-122.

Little, T. D., Bovaird, J. A., & Slegers, D. (2006). Methods for the analysis of change. In D. Mroczek & T. D. Little (Eds.), *Handbook of personality development* (pp. 181-211). Mahwah, NJ: Lawrence Erlbaum Associates.

Longford, N. T. (1987). A fast scoring algorithm for maximum likelihood estimation in unbalanced mixed models with nested effects. *Biometrika, 74,* 817-827.

Longford, N. T., & Muthén, B. O. (1992). Factor analysis for clustered observations. *Psychometrika, 57,* 581-597.

McArdle, J. J., & Hamagami, F. (1996). Multilevel models from a multiple group structural equation perspective. In G. A. Marcoulides & R. E. Schumacker (Eds.), *Advanced structural equation modeling: Issues and techniques.* Mahwah, NJ: Lawrence Erlbaum Associates.

McArdle, J. J., & Nesselroade, J. R. (2002). Growth curve analysis in contemporary psychological research. In J. Schinka & W. Velicer (Eds.), *Comprehensive handbook of psychology, volume two: Research methods in psychology* (pp. 447-480). New York: Wiley.

McDonald, R. P. (1993). A general model for two-level data with responses missing at random. *Psychometrika, 58,* 575-585.

McDonald, R. P. (1994). The bilevel reticular action model for path analysis with latent variables. *Sociological Methods & Research, 22,* 399-413.

McDonald, R. P., & Goldstein, H. (1989). Balanced versus unbalanced designs for linear structural relations in two-level data. *British Journal of Mathematical and Statistical Psychology, 42,* 215-232.

Mehta, P. D., & Neale, M. C. (2005). People are variables too: Multilevel structural equations modeling. *Psychological Methods, 10,* 259-284.

Mehta, P. D., & West, S. G. (2000). Putting the individual back into individual growth curves. *Psychological Methods*, *5*, 23-43.

Muthén, B. O. (1989). Latent variable modeling in heterogeneous populations. *Psychometrika*, *54*, 557-585.

Muthén, B. O. (1990). *Means and covariance structure analysis of hierarchical data*. Los Angeles, CA: UCLA Statistics series, No. 62.

Muthén, B. O. (1991). Multilevel factor analysis of class and student achievement components. *Journal of Educational Measurement*, *28*, 338-354.

Muthén, B. O. (1994). Multilevel covariance structure analysis. *Sociological Methods and Research*, *22*, 376-398.

Muthén, B. O., & Satorra, A. (1989). Multilevel aspects of varying parameters in structural models. In R. D. Bock (Ed.), *Multilevel analysis of educational data* (pp. 87-99). San Diego, CA: Academic Press.

Muthén, L. K., & Muthén, B. O. (2006). *Mplus user's guide* (4th ed.). Los Angeles, CA: Muthén & Muthén.

Neale, M. C., Boker, S. M., Xie, G., & Maes, H. H. (2004). *Mx: Statistical modeling* (5th ed.). Richmond: Virginia Commonwealth University, Department of Psychiatry.

Rabe-Hesketh, S., Skrondal, A., & Pickles, A. (2004). Generalized multilevel structural equation modeling. *Psychometrika*, *69*, 167-190.

Raudenbush, S. W. (1991). Hierarchical models for studying school effects and schooling: The next wave of innovation. In B. P. M. Creemers & G. Reezigt (Eds.), *Evaluation of educational effectiveness* (pp. 35-69). Enschedde, The Netherlands: Inter-University Consortium on Educational Evaluation and Educational Effectiveness.

Raudenbush, S. W. (1995). Maximum likelihood estimation for unbalanced multilevel covariance structure models via the EM algorithm. *British Journal of Mathematical and Statistical Psychology*, *20*, 210-220.

Raudenbush, S. W., Rowan, B., & Kang, S. J. (1991). A multilevel, multivariate model of studying school climate with estimation via the EM algorithm and application to U. S. high school data. *Journal of Educational Statistics*, *16*, 296-330.

Robinson, W. S. (1950). Ecological correlations and the behaviors of individuals. *American Sociological Review*, *15*, 351-357.

Rovine, M. J., & Molenaar, P. C. M. (1998). A nonstandard method for estimating a linear growth model in LISREL. *International Journal of Behavioral Development*, *22*, 453-473.

Schmidt, W. H. (1969). *Covariance structure analysis of the multivariate random effects model*. Unpublished doctoral dissertation, University of Chicago.

Shogren, K. A., Bovaird, J. A., Wehmeyer, M. L., & Palmer, S. B. (2005, August). *Development of perceptions of control in children and youth with mental retardation*. Paper presented at the American Psychological Association annual meeting. Washington, DC.

Snijders, T., & Bosker, R. (2005). *Multilevel analysis: An introduction to basic and advanced multilevel modeling*. Thousand Oaks, CA: Sage.

du Toit, S., & du Toit, M. (2003). Multilevel structural equation modeling. In J. D. Leeuw & I. G. G. Kreft (Eds.), *Handbook of quantitative multilevel analysis* (pp. 273-321). Boston: Kluwer.

Willett, J. B., & Sayer, A. G. (1994). Using covariance structure analysis to detect correlates and predictors of individual change over time. *Psychological Bulletin, 116*, 363-381.

Yuan, K. H., & Hayashi, K. (2005). On muthén's maximum likelihood for two-level covariance structure models. *Psychometrika, 70*, 147-167.

CHAPTER EIGHT

Mixed-Effects Regression Models With Heterogeneous Variance: Analyzing Ecological Momentary Assessment (EMA) Data of Smoking

Donald Hedeker
Robin J. Mermelstein
University of Illinois at Chicago

Longitudinal studies are increasingly common in psychological and social sciences research. In these studies, subjects are measured repeatedly across time and interest often focuses on characterizing their growth or development across time. Mixed-effects regression models (MRMs) have become the method of choice for modeling of longitudinal data; variants of MRMs have been developed under a variety of names: Random-effects models. Laird and Ware (1982),variance component models (Dempster, Rubin, & Tsutakawa, 1981) , multilevel models (Goldstein, 1995), hierarchical linear models (Bryk & Raudenbush, 1992), two-stage models. Bock (1989), random coefficient models (Leeuw & Kreft, 1986), mixed models (Longford, 1987; Wolfinger, 1993), empirical Bayes models (Hui & Berger, 1983; Strenio, Weisberg, & Bryk, 1983), and random regression models (Bock, 1983b, 1983a; Gibbons, Hedeker, Waternaux, & Davis, 1988). A basic characteristic of these models is the inclusion of random subject effects into regression models in order to account for the influence of subjects on their repeated observations. These random effects reflect each person's growth or development across time, and explain the correlational structure of the longitudinal data. Additionally, they indicate the degree of subject variation that exists in the population of subjects.

There are several features that make MRMs especially useful in longitudinal research. First, subjects are not assumed to be measured on the same number of timepoints, thus, subjects with incomplete data across time are included in the analysis. The ability to include subjects with incomplete data across time is an important advantage relative to procedures that require complete data across time because (a) by including all data, the analysis has increased statistical power, and (b) complete-case analysis may suffer from biases to the extent that subjects with complete data are not representative of the larger population of subjects. Because time is treated as a continuous variable in MRMs, subjects do not have to be measured at the same timepoints. This is useful for analysis of longitudinal studies where follow-up times are not uniform across all subjects. Both time-invariant and time-varying covariates can be included in the model. Thus, changes in the outcome variable may be due to both stable characteristics of the subject (e.g., their gender or race) as well as characteristics that change across time (e.g., life-events). Finally, whereas traditional approaches estimate average change (across time) in a population, MRMs can also estimate change for each subject. These estimates of individual change across time can be particularly useful in longitudinal studies where a proportion of subjects exhibit change across time that deviates from the average trend.

In developmental research, MRMs have been used to describe and statistically compare growth or development across groups of subjects. For example, Huttenlocher, Haight, Bryk, and Seltzer (1991) used MRMs in studying gender differences in early vocabulary development. Additionally, these models have been used to examine the effects of contextual variables on growth or changes over time. In this regard, Neff and Karney (2004) examined (time-varying) negative stressors and their effect on marital satisfaction during the first four years of marriage. Other applications of MRMs can be found in many fields including studies on alcohol (Curran, Stice, & Chassin, 1997), smoking (Niaura et al., 2002), HIV/AIDS (Gallagher, Cottler, Compton, & Spitznagel, 1997), drug abuse (Carroll et al., 1994; Halikas, Crosby, Pearson, & Graves, 1997), psychiatry (Elkin et al., 1995; Serretti, Lattuada, Zanardi, Franchini, & Smeraldi, 2000), and child development (Campbell & Hedeker, 2001) to name a few.

Typically, statistical tests of the regression coefficients (i.e., the fixed effects) of the model are of primary interest. For example, the effect of gender on growth, or the time-varying effect of stress on satisfaction. Here, one tests whether or not the regression coefficients, which indicate the influence of the independent variables on the dependent variable, equal zero in the population (i.e., have zero slope). Usually, the error variance, which characterizes the within-subjects variance, and the variance parameters of the random effects, which characterize the between-subjects variance, are treated as being homogeneous across subject groups. However, longitudinal designs can allow relaxation of these homogeneity of variance assumptions, and indeed allow researchers the

ability to model differences in variances, both between and within, across subject groups. The study of intraindividual variabiliity has received increasing
attention in psychology(Fleeson, 2004; Hertzog & Nesselroade, 2003; Martin
& Hofer, 2004; Nesselroade & Boker, 1994; Nesselroade & Schmidt McCollam,
2000; Nesselroade, 2001, 2004); these articles describe many of the conceptual
issues and some statistical approaches for examining such variation. MRMs can
be used to broaden this study by assessing the determinants of both intraindividual (within-subjects) and interindividual (between-subjects) variation.

For example, in smoking research a common theme is that physical and
subjective emotional reactions to smoking stabilize as one's experience with
smoking increases. Indeed, one aspect of the concept of dependence is that
responses to smoking become more internally stable or driven, and less dependent on external or situational contexts. To examine this issue, we present
analyses of data from a longitudinal study of adolescent smoking. This study
contains multilayered longitudinal data in that subjects are measured across
three measurement waves, and at each wave data from 7 days are collected
from each subject using hand-held computers ("ecological momentary assessments" or "real-time data capture"). This type of design follows the "bursts
of measurement" approach described by Nesselroade (1991), and allows us to
address several issues in terms of the stability of variance parameters, both
at a given wave as well as across time. For a given measurement wave, we
examine how the variances in these reactions to smoking vary across groups
of subjects characterized by their smoking history. We also explore this issue
longitudinally, across waves, to examine the degree to which variances change
as adolescents progress in their smoking career. Standard software (e.g., SAS
PROC MIXED) can be used to fit these models; several syntax examples are
available from the first author on request. However, before we describe these
heterogeneous variance models, which are the focus of this chapter, we begin
with a basic introduction to MRMs for longitudinal data analysis. A more
complete introduction can be found in Hedeker (2004).

MRMs FOR LONGITUDINAL DATA

To introduce MRMs, consider a simple linear regression model for the measurement y of individual i ($i = 1, 2, \ldots, N$ subjects) on occasion j ($j = 1, 2, \ldots, n_i$
occasions):

$$y_{ij} = \beta_0 + \beta_1 t_{ij} + \epsilon_{ij}. \tag{1}$$

This model represents the regression of the outcome variable y on the independent variable time (denoted t). The subscripts indicate whose observation it is

(subscript i) and the relative timing of the observation (the subscript j). The actual timing is represented by the independent variable t which may represent time in weeks, months, etc. Both y and t carry the i and j subscripts, and so they are allowed to vary both by individuals and occasions. In a linear regression model, like Equation 1, the errors ϵ_{ij} are assumed to be normally and *independently* distributed in the population with zero mean and common variance σ_ϵ^2. This assumption of independence is generally unreasonable for longitudinal data. Instead, it is much more likely to assume that errors within an individual are correlated. Thus, individual-specific effects are added to the model to account for this data dependency, as in

$$y_{ij} = \beta_0 + \beta_1 t_{ij} + \upsilon_{0i} + \varepsilon_{ij} , \qquad (2)$$

where the additional term υ_{0i} indicates the influence of individual i on his or her repeated observations. Specifically, β_0 is the overall population intercept, υ_{0i} is the intercept deviation for subject i, and β_1 is the overall population slope (i.e., the effect of time). Thus, individuals deviate from the regression of y on t in a parallel manner in this model.

Because individuals in a sample are usually thought to be representative of a larger population of individuals, the individual-specific effects υ_{0i} are treated as random effects. This population distribution is usually assumed to be a normal distribution with mean 0 and variance σ_υ^2. With the random effects υ_{0i} in Equation 2, the errors ϵ_{ij} are now assumed to be normally and *conditionally independently* distributed in the population with zero mean and common variance σ_ϵ^2. That is, the errors are independent conditional on the random individual-specific effects υ_{0i}. As the errors now have an influence due to individuals removed from them, this conditional independence assumption is much more reasonable than the ordinary independence assumption associated with (1).

This variance σ_υ^2 represents the between-subjects variance and indicates the degree of heterogeneity in the population of subjects. In contrast, the residual variance σ_ϵ^2 is the within-subjects variance. It is often of interest to express the between-subjects variance in terms of an intraclass correlation (ICC), namely,

$$ICC = \frac{\sigma_\upsilon^2}{\sigma_\upsilon^2 + \sigma_\epsilon^2}. \qquad (3)$$

This ratio of the between-subjects variance σ_υ^2 to the total variance $\sigma_\upsilon^2 + \sigma_\epsilon^2$ represents the degree of association of the longitudinal data within subjects. Specifically, it indicates the proportion of variance in the data, conditional on the model covariates, that is attributable to individuals. As the heterogeneity in the population of subjects increases, so does the ICC. Conversely, as subjects are more similar to each other, the ICC diminishes.

An extension of the random-intercepts model that is popular for longitudinal data, is the random trend model. In this model, subjects deviate in terms of the intercept and the trend across time:

$$y_{ij} = \beta_0 + \beta_1 t_{ij} + \upsilon_{0i} + \upsilon_{1i} t_{ij} + \epsilon_{ij} \tag{4}$$

where, β_0 is the overall population intercept, β_1 is the overall population slope, υ_{0i} is the intercept deviation for subject i, υ_{1i} is the slope deviation for subject i, and ϵ_{ij} is an independent error term distributed normally with mean 0 and variance σ_ϵ^2. The errors are independent conditional on both υ_{0i} and υ_{1i}. With two random individual-specific effects, the population distribution of intercept and slope deviations is assumed to be a bivariate normal $\mathcal{N}(0, \boldsymbol{\Sigma}_\upsilon)$, where $\boldsymbol{\Sigma}_\upsilon$ is a 2×2 variance–covariance matrix. This model can be thought of as a personal trend or development model because it represents the measurements of y as a function of time, both at the individual (υ_{0i} and υ_{1i}) and population (β_0 and β_1) levels. The intercept parameters indicate the starting point, and the slope parameters indicate the degree of change over timepoints. The population intercept and slope parameters represent the trend for the population, whereas the individual parameters express how the individual deviates from the population trend.

Whereas the random-intercept model posits that the between-subjects variance σ_υ^2 is constant across time, the random trend model allows this variance to change across time, since for a particular timepoint t the between-subjects variance equals:

$$\sigma_{\upsilon_0}^2 + 2t\sigma_{\upsilon_0 \upsilon_1} + t^2 \sigma_{\upsilon_1}^2. \tag{5}$$

Notice that if both $\sigma_{\upsilon_0 \upsilon_1}$ and $\sigma_{\upsilon_1}^2$ are positive, then the between-subjects variance increases across time. Diminishing variance across time is also possible if, for example, $-2\sigma_{\upsilon_0 \upsilon_1} > \sigma_{\upsilon_1}^2$.

Often a researcher is interested in assessing the influence of covariates, such as treatment group, on the responses across time. For this, covariates that either do not change over time (time invariant) or that vary across measured occasions (time varying) can be added to the model:

$$y_{ij} = \beta_0 + \beta_1 t_{ij} + \beta_2 x_i + \beta_3 x_{ij} + \upsilon_{0i} + \upsilon_{1i} t_{ij} + \epsilon_{ij} \ . \tag{6}$$

Here, β_2 is the coefficient for the time invariant covariate x_i, and β_3 is the coefficient for the time varying covariate x_{ij}. Interactions between the covariates can be included in the same way as interactions are included into an ordinary multiple regression model. For example, x_i might represent the treatment group that a subject is assigned to (for the course of the study), and x_{ij} might be the treatment by time interaction that is obtained as the product of x_i by t_{ij}. Similarly, contextual variables that are time invariant or time varying are easily added to the model.

Thus far, we have only allowed for a linear time effect, but one could also have higher order polynomials in the model (e.g., quadratic and cubic trends) to model nonlinear changes across time. Additionally, these trends can be treated as random effects to further allow nonlinearity in terms of both the population and individual trends. The complexity of the model for time clearly depends on the number of timepoints. With few timepoints (e.g, three or four) a linear effect for time might be reasonable, whereas if there are many timepoints (e.g., five or more), this would be less plausible. More general models of time are also possible (Wu & Zhang, 2002), as are models that allow for random effects for other time-varying predictors; an example of this type of random coefficients model for psychological data is presented in Hedeker, Flay, and Petraitis (1996). In the longitudinal example presented in this chapter there are only three timepoints, and so only a linear time effect is considered.

HETEROGENEOUS VARIANCE MODELS

Most applications of MRMs focus on estimation and testing of the regression coefficients. In this section, we focus on extensions of the basic random intercepts model that allows estimation and testing of variance parameters. Specifically, we show how the model can be extended to allow heterogeneous within- and between-subjects variance. We first consider the situation of two groups of subjects with heterogeneous variances, and then extend to situations of multiple groups. Additionally, these same models can be used to examine whether the variation in the dependent variable changes or is constant across groups of observations (e.g., different contexts).

Varying ICCs by Groups

Suppose that we are considering a random-intercept model, but there is interest in allowing the ICC to vary by groups of subjects, e.g., by gender. For this, let M_i and F_i represent indicator variables (i.e., variables coded either 0 or 1) for males and females, respectively. Then to allow the between-subjects variance to vary across gender groups, these two indicators would be treated as random effects. Additionally, because males and females are distinct groups of subjects, these two random effects need to be specified as independent, that is,

$$\boldsymbol{\Sigma}_v = \begin{bmatrix} \sigma_{v_M}^2 & 0 \\ 0 & \sigma_{v_F}^2 \end{bmatrix}. \tag{7}$$

The two between-subjects variance parameters $\sigma^2_{\upsilon_M}$ and $\sigma^2_{\upsilon_F}$ would indicate the degree of heterogeneity in the population of males and females, respectively. Similarly, one can also specify gender-varying within-subject variance using these same dummy-codes,

$$\sigma^2_\epsilon = M_i \sigma^2_{\epsilon_M} + F_i \sigma^2_{\epsilon_F} . \tag{8}$$

Now, there are two ICCs — one for each gender group:

$$\begin{aligned}
\text{ICC} &= \sigma^2_{\upsilon_M}/(\sigma^2_{\upsilon_M} + \sigma^2_{\epsilon_M}) \quad \text{for Males} \\
&= \sigma^2_{\upsilon_F}/(\sigma^2_{\upsilon_F} + \sigma^2_{\epsilon_F}) \quad \text{for Females.}
\end{aligned}$$

Comparing such a model that allows heterogeneous variances to a model that does not, allows one to test whether the within- and between-subjects variance varies by group or not. In other words, are the within- and between-subjects variances a function of group, or are they constant across groups. Additionally, this kind of heterogeneous ICC model can easily be generalized to more than two groups. In this situation, with k groups, there would be k between-subjects variance parameters and k within-subjects parameters.

Trends Across Groups

When there are more than two groups, it may be of interest and/or parsimonious to estimate a trend in the variances across the k groups. This makes sense if the grouping variable reflects some kind of ordering of subjects. For instance, suppose that a grouping variable g_i is ordered as $0 = $ low, $1 = $ med, and $2 = $ high in terms of some attribute. In our example, we consider three ordered groups based on their previous smoking history. To allow the between-subjects variance to increase across these three groups, one could specify an intercept and the variable g_i as two independent random effects. Here,

$$\boldsymbol{\Sigma}_\upsilon = \begin{bmatrix} \sigma^2_{\upsilon_0} & 0 \\ 0 & \sigma^2_{\upsilon_g} \end{bmatrix} \tag{9}$$

where $\sigma^2_{\upsilon_0}$ represents the intercept variance and $\sigma^2_{\upsilon_g}$ reflects how the between-subjects variance varies across groups. Note that the between-subjects (BS) variance is equal to a function of these two parameters,

$$\text{BS variance} = \sigma^2_{\upsilon_0} + g_i^2 \sigma^2_{\upsilon_g} \tag{10}$$

which shows why the coding of g_i is important. For example, with three groups

$$
\begin{aligned}
\text{BS variance} \ &= \ \sigma_{v_0}^2 \\
&= \ \sigma_{v_0}^2 + \sigma_{v_g}^2 \\
&= \ \sigma_{v_0}^2 + 4\sigma_{v_g}^2
\end{aligned}
$$

for the three groups coded as $g_i = 0, 1, 2$ respectively. This coding of g_i assumes that the variance increases across groups, because variances can never be negative. Reverse coding (i.e., 2, 1, 0) can be used if the variance decreases across groups. It is also possible to use non-integer coding for g, e.g., $\sqrt{g_i} = 0, 1, \sqrt{2}, \sqrt{3}, \ldots$, to permit a strict linear increase of the BS variance in variance units, namely, BS variance $= \sigma_{v_0}^2 + g_i \sigma_{v_g}^2$.

Incorporating varying between-subjects variance is easily accomplished within the mixed model. The primary feature is that the random effects (i.e., either the group dummy codes, or the intercept and the group variable g_i) need to be treated as independent, since subjects belong to only one of the subject groups. Most popular software programs for mixed model analysis (e.g., SAS PROC MIXED, SPSS MIXED, MLwiN, HLM) allow these specifications.

For estimating a trend in the within-subjects (WS) variance across subject groups, a log-linear representation is often used in ordinary multiple regression (Aitkin, 1987; Harvey, 1976), and implemented within a mixed model in SAS PROC MIXED. Here, in terms of the grouping variable g_i, this representation would be

$$
\text{WS variance} \ = \ \sigma_\epsilon^2 \exp(g_i \tau) \,. \tag{11}
$$

Notice that the WS variance would equal σ_ϵ^2 for the first group ($g_i = 0$), $\sigma_\epsilon^2 \exp \tau$ for $g_i = 1$, and $\sigma_\epsilon^2 \exp 2\tau$ for $g_i = 2$. This representation thus allows for both increasing and decreasing variance across groups. For example, if $\tau > 0$ then variance increases over groups, while if $\tau < 0$ then it decreases over the groups. Including trends in both the BS and WS variance across groups, the ICC for a particular group, coded g_i, would equal:

$$
\text{ICC} = \frac{\sigma_{v_0}^2 + g_i^2 \sigma_{v_g}^2}{\sigma_{v_0}^2 + g_i^2 \sigma_{v_g}^2 + \sigma_\epsilon^2 \exp(g_i \tau)} \,. \tag{12}
$$

The log-linear modeling of the WS variance allows it to depend on more than one variable, namely,

$$
\text{WS variance} \ = \ \sigma_\epsilon^2 \exp(\boldsymbol{w}_{ij}' \boldsymbol{\tau}) \,. \tag{13}
$$

where $\boldsymbol{w}_{ij}$ is a $s \times 1$ vector of variables influencing the within-subjects variance. This regression-like structure allows estimation of separate WS variance by group, as well as more complicated multiple regression-like forms for the WS variance. In this way, one can examine whether contextual variables are related to the WS variance. For example, it may be the case that the variation in responses to smoking is very different for adolescents depending on whether or not they are smoking alone or with friends.

By combining modeling of the WS variance with the inclusion of random effects in the mixed model (to model the BS variance), a wide variety of heterogeneous variance models can be estimated and compared. The illustrations that follow give a sense of some of these possibilities and their usefulness in psychological research.

ILLUSTRATION: ADOLESCENT SMOKING STUDY

Data for the analyses reported here come from a longitudinal, natural history study of adolescent smoking (Mermelstein, Hedeker, Flay, & Shiffman, 2002). Students included in the longitudinal study were either in grade 8 or 10 at baseline, and self-reported on a screening questionnaire 6 to 8 weeks prior to baseline that they either had never smoked, but indicated a probability of future smoking, or had smoked in the past 90 days, but had not smoked more than 100 cigarettes in their lifetime. Written parental consent and student assent were required for participation. A total of 562 students completed the baseline measurement wave. The longitudinal study utilized a multimethod approach to assess adolescents at three time points: Baseline, 6 months, and 12 months. The data collection modalities included self-report questionnaires, a week-long time/event sampling method via palmtop computers (Ecological Momentary Assessments), and in-depth interviews.

Data for the analyses presented here came from the ecological momentary assessments. Adolescents carried the hand held computers with them at all times during the 7 consecutive day data collection period at each wave and were trained to both respond to random prompts from the computers and to event record (initiate a data collection interview) smoking episodes. Immediately after smoking a cigarette, participants completed a series of questions on the hand held computers. Questions included ones about place, activity, companionship, mood, and other subjective items. The hand held computers date and time-stamped each entry. For inclusion in the analyses reported here, adolescents must have smoked at least two cigarettes during the 7-day baseline data collection period; 100 adolescents met this inclusion criterion. We used a cutpoint of two smoking reports because of our interest in modeling variation.

These 100 adolescents began the study with varying amounts of cigarette smoking experience. Adolescents were divided into three groups based on their lifetime smoking levels: Those who had smoked less than 6 cigarettes in their lifetimes (n = 18), representing very novice smokers; Those who had smoked between 6 and 99 cigarettes in their lifetimes ($n = 48$), representing a group of irregular or experimental smokers; and those who had smoked 100 or more cigarettes during their lifetimes ($n = 34$), representing more regular smokers. This (trichotomous) ordered smoking history variable is the grouping variable used in the first set of analyses. We chose not to treat smoking history as a continuous variable because the effect of this variable is not thought to be the same across its levels. That is, the effect of lifetime smoking history in adolescents is substantively not the same contrasting, say, individuals who have smoked 5 and 6 cigarettes versus those who have smoked 100 and 101 cigarettes. Of course, higher order polynomials could be used to model such a nonlinear effect, but the trichotomous treatment of this variable is simpler to interpret and is based on useful, though somewhat arbitrary, cutpoints of this smoking history variable for adolescents.

The dependent variable concerns the responses to questions asking about subjective physiological sensations immediately after and prior to smoking a cigarette. Specifically, the subjects rated their subjective physiological sensations in terms of two items, "*Sick*" and "*Buzzed*," on an analog ladder-type scale, by moving a stylus to the appropriate point on the ladder scale. Immediately after smoking the cigarette, subjects turned on their hand-held computer to complete a variety of questions. They were first asked about their moods and feelings "right now" (after smoking) and later about how they felt just before smoking. The definition of these items varied slightly for the before and after assessments. Specifically, for the after assessment, they were prompted as:

- Sick: Think about how you feel right now: Do you feel sick?

- Buzzed: Think about how you feel right now: Do you feel buzzed?

whereas, for the before assessment the prompts were:

- Sick: Now think about the time just before you smoked: I felt sick.

- Buzzed: Now think about the time just before you smoked: I felt buzzed.

For all four questions, subjects rated their feelings on the 1 (*not at all*) to 10 (*very*) ladder. Correlations of these two items were modest (.24 for sick and buzzed after responses, and .36 for sick and buzzed before responses), however separate analyses of these two items did not reveal any major substantive differences, and so here we only present analyses considering these two items together. Specifically, for each subject, an average of the "*Sick*" and "*Buzzed*" after responses and an average of the before responses were obtained, and a change score (after – before) was calculated. These represent the changes in the level of subjective physiological sensations attributable to smoking a cigarette.

Because participants could smoke more than two cigarettes during the assessment week, there were multiple observations per subject. In all, there was a total of 517 observations clustered within these 100 subjects. A question of interest is whether the change (after – before) in physiological sensations varies between smoking groups defined by level of smoking experience. We would expect, for example, that both means and variances diminish as smoking level increases. In particular, we address this in terms of differences in means and variances across these groups. Table 8.1 presents some descriptive statistics broken down by smoking history group.

The BS and WS variance estimates were obtained separately for each group using a random-intercepts MRM for each. These results suggest that there is not a great deal of difference in means. However, both BS and WS variances decrease with increasing smoking history. This supports notions from smoking research that physical reactions to smoking stabilize as one's experience with smoking increases.

We address these observations more formally using models with varying BS and WS variance parameters. Specifically, we consider models of separate variance across smoking groups, and also trend in variance across the smoking groups. These variance parameterizations are summarized in Table 8.2. Note that the separate variance parameterizations require three parameters, whereas the trend versions only require two parameters. Also, because the variance decreased across the groups, the specification of the group codes was reversed for the BS variance, as mentioned earlier. Results are presented in Table 8.3.

Nine models are estimated by considering three representations for both the BS and WS variance: Common variance, group trend in variance, and separate group variance. Model selection can be based on the model deviance, and two penalized versions of the deviance: The Akaike Information Criterion (AIC; Akaike (1973)) and the Bayesian Information Criterion (BIC; Schwarz (1978)). The penalties are for model complexity and the BIC penalty is greater than the AIC penalty. Thus, BIC tends to suggest simpler models relative to AIC. In the present case, AIC would select Model IIc as best, whereas BIC selects Model Ib. Because they are not nested, these two models cannot be compared to each other using a likelihood-ratio (LR) test. However, each of these models can be compared to the homogeneous BS and WS variance model (Model Ia). For Model Ib, the LR chi-square statistic equals 2037.4 - 1992.8 = 44.6, which is highly significant on 1 degree of freedom. Similarly for Model IIc, the LR χ^2 equals 48.7 on 3 degrees of freedom, which again is highly significant. Both models reject the notion of homogeneous WS variance, and Model IIC additionally rejects homogeneity of BS variance. Table 8.4 lists the

TABLE 8.1

Changes in Physiological Sensations by Smoking Group: Numbers of Subjects, Observations, Means, Variances, and ICCs

Smoking Group	Subjects N	Observations $\sum n_i$	Mean $\bar{y}_{ij}$	BS Variance $\hat{\sigma}_v^2$	WS Variance $\hat{\sigma}_\epsilon^2$	ICC
LO: < 6 cigs	18	50	.54	2.69	4.23	.39
MID: 6-99 cigs	48	183	.80	.89	3.55	.20
HI: 100+ cigs	34	284	.50	.66	1.54	.30

ICC = intraclass correlation

TABLE 8.2

Variance Parameterizations

Group	Separate Variance WS Variance	BS Variance	Code	Trend in Variance WS Variance	Code	BS Variance
< 6 cigs	$\sigma_{\epsilon_{LO}}^2$	$\sigma_{v_{LO}}^2$	0	σ_ϵ^2	2	$\sigma_{v_0}^2 + 4\sigma_{v_1}^2$
6-99 cigs	$\sigma_{\epsilon_{MID}}^2$	$\sigma_{v_{MID}}^2$	1	$\exp(\tau)\,\sigma_\epsilon^2$	1	$\sigma_{v_0}^2 + \sigma_{v_1}^2$
100+ cigs	$\sigma_{\epsilon_{HI}}^2$	$\sigma_{v_{HI}}^2$	2	$\exp(2\tau)\,\sigma_\epsilon^2$	0	$\sigma_{v_0}^2$

parameter estimates for three of the models: Homogeneous WS and BS variance, Model Ib (best BIC), and Model IIc (best AIC). The first model is for comparison only since, as shown earlier, this model is rejected in favor of either Model Ib or IIc. Statistical tests for specific parameters can be obtained by dividing the parameter estimate by its standard error (i.e., Wald statistic) and comparing to a standard normal distribution (at $\alpha = .05$, the two-tailed critical value is 1.96 or approximately 2). Although Wald tests are routinely used for fixed-effects parameters, for variance parameters their use is dubious (see Verbeke & Molenberghs, 2000, pages 64-65). In terms of the fixed effects there are no statistically significant results. Thus, the three smoking history groups are similar in terms of the average level of change in subjective physiological sensations.

Turning to the variance estimates, based on both Models Ib and IIc, it is clear that the WS variance decreases across smoking history groups. The latter model estimates separate variances across these groups, while the former estimates a decreasing trend across the groups. Based on this trend estimate of

TABLE 8.3
Change in Subjective Physical Sensation Before vs After Smoking: Model Comparisons

Model	Fixed	p	BS Variance	r	WS Variance	s	Deviance	AIC	BIC
Ia	I + G	3	I	1	I	1	2037.4	2041.4	2046.6
Ib	I + G	3	I	1	I + T	2	1992.8	1998.8	2006.6
Ic	I + G	3	I	1	I + G	3	1991.0	1999.0	2009.4
IIa	I + G	3	I + T	2	I	1	2027.0	2033.0	2040.8
IIb	I + G	3	I + T	2	I + T	2	1991.6	1999.6	2010.1
IIc	I + G	3	I + T	2	I + G	3	1988.7	1998.7	2011.7
IIIa	I + G	3	I + G	3	I	1	2027.0	2035.0	2045.4
IIIb	I + G	3	I + G	3	I + T	2	1991.6	2001.6	2014.6
IIIc	I + G	3	I + G	3	I + G	3	1988.5	2000.5	2016.2

Model Ib, the WS variance is estimated as 6.62, $6.62 \times \exp(-.72) = 3.22$, and $6.62 \times \exp(2 \times -.72) = 1.57$ for groups LO, MID, and HI, respectively. Thus, the WS estimates for Models Ib and IIc are in close agreement, except for the LO group which has the fewest numbers of subjects and observations. Additionally, Model IIc posits that the BS variance diminishes across smoking history groups, from .63 for HI, to $.63 + .42 = 1.05$ for MID, and $.63 + 2^2 \times .42 = 2.31$ for LO.

These estimates can be used to generate ICCs based on each model. For the naive Model Ia, we obtain:

$$\text{ICC} = \frac{1.23}{1.23 + 2.41} = .34$$

as the common ICC for all groups. For Model Ib, we get:

$$\text{LO ICC} = \frac{.80}{.80 + 6.62} = .11$$

$$\text{MID ICC} = \frac{.80}{.80 + [\exp(-.72) \times 6.62]} = .20$$

$$\text{HI ICC} = \frac{.80}{.80 + [\exp(2 \times -.72) \times 6.62]} = .34$$

for the three groups. Similarly, the ICCs based on model IIc are:

$$\text{LO ICC} = \frac{.63 + 4 \times .42}{(.63 + 4 \times .42) + 4.33} = .35$$

$$\text{MID ICC} = \frac{.63 + .42}{(.63 + .42) + 3.50} = .23$$

$$\text{HI ICC} = \frac{.63}{.63 + 1.54} = .29.$$

Based on these estimates, Model IIc is the best in terms of matching the stratified ICCs presented in Table 8.1. Also, Model Ib does badly in terms of the LO
group, suggesting that Model IIc can be chosen as the "best" model both in
terms of AIC and also in matching the stratified results. Thus, there is evidence
of decreasing variation in physical subjective sensation change across smoking
history groups in terms of both BS and WS variance.

Variation in Variation Across Time: Baseline to 12 months

The foregoing results suggest clear differences in physical subjective sensation
variation across smoking history groups, and it is tempting to attribute these
differences to smoking history. Although this conclusion is certainly logical,
it could be that another variable, and not smoking history, is responsible for
the group differences in physical subjective sensation variation. To address this
possibility, we examined a subset of subjects with longitudinal data across time.

TABLE 8.4
Change in Subjective Physical Sensation Before vs After Smoking:
REML Estimates & Standard Errors (se) for Select Models

Term	Model Ia Estimate	se	Model Ib Estimate	se	Model IIc Estimate	se
Fixed Effects						
Intercept	.71	.35	.63	.43	.71	.47
MID cigs	.12	.40	.18	.47	.11	.52
HI cigs	-.24	.41	-.16	.46	-.24	.50
BS Variance						
Intercept variance	1.23	.31	.80	.24	.63	.22
Group trend (LO=2, MID=1, HI=0)					.42	.32
WS Variance						
Intercept variance	2.41	.17	6.62	1.18		
Group trend (LO=0, MID=1, HI=2)			-.72	.11		
LO cigs					4.33	1.10
MID cigs					3.50	.42
HI cigs					1.54	.14
Deviance $(-2 \log L)$	2037.4		1992.8		1988.7	

Specifically, we are interested in seeing whether the cross-sectional variation patterns observed earlier are also evident longitudinally as subjects progress in their smoking careers.

Because of our focus on variance modeling (both between- and within-subjects), we included subjects who provided two or more smoking reports at two or more timpoints (baseline, 6-, and 12-month follow-ups). In all, there were 46 subjects meeting these criteria: 37 provided data at baseline (mean number of reports = 8.05), 40 at 6-months (mean number of reports = 7.93), and 37 at 12-months (mean number of reports = 11.92). In terms of the smoking history grouping variable used in the foregoing analyses , 2, 8, and 27 of these 46 subjects were in the LO, MID, and HI groups, respectively. Additionally, 9 of these 46 subjects were not included in the earlier analyses because they provided no smoking reports at baseline.

These 46 subjects were classified into two groups based on a separate latent growth analysis, which is briefly summarized here. This analysis was based on data obtained from a time-line follow-back interview at four questionnaire waves: Baseline, 6-, 12-, and 18-month follow-ups. At each wave interviewers guided adolescents through a structured calendar-based recall of their smoking, noting the amount (even a puff) smoked on specific days over the past months. These data represent counts of numbers of cigarettes per day, over time, anchored to specific real-time calendars. For each subject, and at each wave, we calculated the following summary variable: The number of cigarettes smoked per day for each of the two 90-day intervals within the six-month interval. Since this outcome was highly non-normal it was categorized into an ordinal variable as follows: 0 = 0 cigarettes (none); 1 = greater than 0 cigarettes but less than 1 cigarette per month (quarterly); 2 = greater than or equal to 1 cigarette per month but less than 1 cigarette per week (monthly); 3 = greater than or equal to 1 cigarette per week but less than 1 cigarette per day (weekly); 4 = greater than or equal to 1 cigarette per day (daily). Subjects who gave at least one non-zero ordinal response across time were then analyzed in the latent growth analysis. This analysis identified five latent smoking groups, which we labeled as triers, escalators, quitters, rapid escalators and regular smokers.

The analysis in this chapter uses only a fraction of the subjects that were used in the latent growth analysis (because of our criteria that a subject must have two or more smoking reports at two or more timepoints). Of the 46 subjects included here, 18 were classified as smoking escalators or rapid escalators and 28 as regular smokers in the latent growth analysis. We treat escalators and rapid escalators as a single group because of the small numbers. Figure 8.1 plots the means by these two groups for this ordinal cigarette rate variable across time.

FIGURE 8.1
Smoking group means across time.

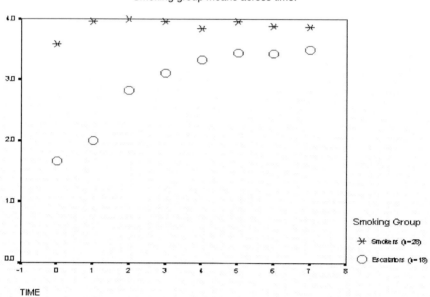

TIME

As can be seen, the groups have very different average trajectories across time. The means that the regular smokers are at or near daily smoking at all timepoints, whereas escalators are a bit under monthly smoking initially, but increase to between weekly and daily smoking by the end. In terms of the timing, timepoints 0 and 1 in the figure correspond to the two 90-day periods before baseline, timepoints 2 and 3 to the two 90-day periods before the 6-month follow-up, timepoints 4 and 5 to the two 90-day periods before the 12-month follow-up, and timepoints 6 and 7 to the two 90-day periods before the 18-month follow-up. Since the analysis in this chapter focuses on smoking reports at baseline, 6-, and 12- month follow-ups, the figure means from timepoints 0 to 5 are most useful in getting a sense of how the two groups here compare.

Table 8.5 lists descriptive information regarding the smoking reports from these two groups. It appears that the means diminish across time, but that there are no large group differences in terms of the means. The variances also diminish across time, and whereas the variances for the groups are very different at baseline, they are quite similar at 12 months.

To these data, we fit five models of WS variance: Common WS variance, group varying, time varying, group and time varying, and group by time varying. The latter model is the one of most interest because it would suggest that the pattern of WS variance across time was different for the two groups. Based

TABLE 8.5

Changes in Physiological Sensations by Time and Smoking Group:
Numbers of Subjects, Observations, Means, Variances, and ICCs

Time	Group	N	$\sum n_i$	$\bar{y}$	BS Variance	WS Variance	ICC
Baseline	Escalators*	12	43	.71	1.53	2.94	.34
	Smokers	25	255	.58	.48	1.69	.22
6 months	Escalators*	15	77	.49	.09	1.82	.05
	Smokers	25	239	.44	.30	1.38	.18
12 months	Escalators*	15	139	.17	.20	1.41	.13
	Smokers	22	302	.21	.21	1.45	.13

* escalators and rapid escalators combined

on smoking theory and our earlier cross-sectional results , we hypothesized that escalators would have a much greater decrease in variation in their physical sensations across time than smokers.

For BS variance, we fit four models: common variance, group varying, time varying, and group by time varying. The common variance model is simply a random-intercepts model, whereas the group-varying model includes separate random intercepts for the two groups. The time varying model includes a random subject intercept and a random time trend, which are correlated. This yields three parameters in the 2×2 variance–covariance matrix: Intercept variance, time variance, and the covariance between the intercept and slope. As noted earlier, for the random trend model, the BS variance is then a function of time. The final BS variance model specifies separate 2×2 variance–covariance matrices for each of the two smoking groups. This corresponds to a group by time modeling of the BS variance, because the BS variance is a function of time for each group separately. Table 8.6 lists results for these models.

Based on BIC values, the model with group by time WS variance and time BS variance is "best." Though not presented, the AIC criterion would also select this model. Likelihood ratio tests also support selection of this model, which we dub the WS(GT) and BS(T) model. For example, comparing the selected model to the WS(G+T) and BS(T) model (i.e., the Model 1 row directly above our selected model) yields $\chi_1^2 = 3568.0 - 3562.5 = 5.5, p < .05$, supporting the hypothesis that the WS variance varies across time differently for the two groups. In terms of the BS variance, the similar hypothesis of group by time influence is not supported. Comparing the selected model relative to the WS(GT) and BS(GT) model (i.e., the model 1 column directly to the right of our selected model) yields $\chi_3^2 = 3562.5 - 3562.1 = 0.4$, which is clearly non-significant. Thus, while the BS variance does vary across time, there is no evidence that it additionally varies across time by group. It should be noted, however, that the numbers of subjects in these two groups are relatively small and so our ability to detect group by time differences in BS variance is limited.

Table 8.7 lists the parameter estimates of our selected model, as well as estimates from the simplest model including only one WS variance and one BS variance parameter, the WS(I) and BS(I) model. Inspecting the fixed effects yields similar conclusions from both models. The group by time interaction is not significant, but the time effect approaches significance and is negative (i.e., $z = -.31/.16 = 1.94, p < .063$). Removing the non-significant interaction (not shown) yields a highly significant main effect of time (i.e., $z = -.235/.082 = -2.88, p < .006$)

Thus, the (change in) physical sensation means of both groups of subjects are decreasing across time.

Comparing the two models in Table 8.7 via a likelihood ratio test supports the BS(T) and WS(GT) model; $\chi_5^2 = 3599.9 - 3562.5 = 37.4, p < .001$. Examining the WS variance terms, all estimates exceed their standard errors by 1.96 and so are significant based on the Wald test. The estimates indicate that initially the smokers have significantly less WS variance (group $z = -.62/.21 = -2.89, p < .004$), that the WS variance decreases significantly

TABLE 8.6

Change in Subjective Physical Sensation Before vs After Smoking: Model Deviance and *BIC*

| WS Variance | Intercept | BS Variance | | Group × Time | s |
		Group	Time		
Intercept	3599.9	3598.8	3577.7	3575.9	1
	3607.6	*3610.2*	*3593.0*	*3602.7*	
Group	3597.8	3597.1	3574.8	3573.4	2
	3609.3	*3612.4*	*3593.9*	*3604.0*	
Time	3590.0	3589.4	3571.8	3570.3	2
	3601.5	*3604.7*	*3590.9*	*3601.0*	
Group + Time	3587.0	3586.7	3568.0	3566.9	3
	3602.3	*3605.9*	*3591.0*	*3601.4*	
Group × Time	3581.6	3581.6	3562.5	3562.1	4
	3600.8	*3604.6*	*3589.3*	*3600.4*	
r	1	2	3	6	

Note. $s =$ number of WS variance parameters and $r =$ number of BS variance parameters. For all models: fixed effects = Intercept + Group + Time + Group × Time across time for the escalators (time $z = -.40/.12 = 3.21, p < .002$), and that the time trend for smokers is significantly less than for escalators (group by time $z = .32/.14 = 2.32, p < .02$). Turning to the BS variance terms, it's clear that there is significant subject heterogeneity in their intercepts and slopes, and that these two are modestly negatively associated.

Table 8.8 presents estimated BS and WS variances across time for both groups based on the WS(GT) and BS(T) model. Comparing these to the stratified estimates obtained in Table 8.5 gives a sense of the degree of model fit. As can be seen, the model estimates agree well with the stratified results of the WS variances for both groups across time. These estimates clearly support our earlier interpretation that the two groups are quite dissimilar initially but converge across time. As our selected model did not include any group-related terms in terms of the BS variance, the estimated BS variances are the same for the two groups, but do vary across time. As Table 8.8 indicates, the estimated BS variance diminishes quite a bit following baseline, though it is relatively consistent at the two follow-ups. This pattern agrees reasonably well with the stratified results in Table 8.5 for the smokers, but not for the escalators. Again, though, this latter group only has a total of 18 subjects, and so precise estimation of BS variances is limited for this relatively small sample.

TABLE 8.7

Change in Subjective Physical Sensation Before vs After Smoking: REML Estimates & Standard Errors (se) for Two Models

Term	Model BS(I) WS(I) Estimate	se	Model BS(T) WS(GT) Estimate	se
Fixed Effects				
Intercept	.77	.22	.81	.28
Group (smokers = 1)	-.13	.25	-.15	.32
Time (0, 1, 2)	-.24	.12	-.31	.16
Group by time	.06	.13	.10	.19
BS Variance				
Intercept variance	.29	.09	.54	.20
Int, time covariance			-.22	.10
Time variance			.14	.06
WS Variance				
Intercept variance	1.65	.07	3.04	.60
Group			-.62	.21
Time			-.40	.12
Group by time			.32	.14
$-2 \log L$	3599.9		3562.5	

TABLE 8.8

Change in subjective physical sensation before vs after smoking: Estimated variances based on the BS(T) and WS(GT) model

Time	Group	BS variance	WS variance
Baseline	Escalators*	.54	3.04
	Smokers	.54	1.64
6 months	Escalators*	.24	2.04
	Smokers	.24	1.52
12 months	Escalators*	.22	1.37
	Smokers	.22	1.40

* escalators and rapid escalators combined.

CONCLUSIONS

This chapter has illustrated how mixed models for longitudinal data can be used to model differences in variances, and not just means, across subject groups and time. As such, these models can help to identify predictors of both within-subjects and between-subjects variation, and to test psychological hypotheses about these variances.

As an example, we used these models to examine important aspects of the development of dependency to cigarette smoking among adolescent smokers. One of the key concepts in dependence is the development of tolerance, or the diminishing of effects of a substance with its continued use. A common experience, reported by adolescents, during early trials of cigarette smoking is feeling "sick" or "buzzed" after smoking a cigarette, and the equally common notion is that these subjective feelings diminish over time as one's experience with smoking increases. However, to date, researchers have been able to examine changes in these subjective experiences primarily through paper and pencil, retrospective questionnaire reports. Thus, it has been difficult to document adequately exactly how symptoms of dependence develop or with what level of smoking experience. Our analyses indicated an increased consistency of subjective physiological responses as experience with smoking increased, both cross-sectionally and longitudinally. Our data thus provide one of the few ecologically valid examinations of the development of tolerance. Adolescents' self-reports, in real time, of their subjective responses to smoking changed over time as a function of experience with smoking. Importantly, too, these changes were relatively dramatic over a 1-year period. Thus, these analytic models provide a way to examine changes in subjective intrapersonal experiences that have not been readily feasible before.

More applications of this class of models clearly exist in psychology. For example, many questions of both normal development and the development of psychopathology address the issue of variability or stability in emotional responses to various situations and/or contexts. Often, a concern is with the range of responses an individual gives to a variety of stimuli or situations, and not just with the overall mean level of responsivity. These models also allow us to examine hypotheses about cross-situational consistency of responses as well.

In order to reliably estimate variances, one needs a fair amount of both WS and BS data. Modern data collection procedures, such as ecological momentary assessments (EMA) and/or real-time data captures, provide this opportunity. Such designs are in keeping with the "bursts of measurement" approach described by Nesselroade (1991), who called for such an approach in order to assess intraindividual variability. As noted by Nesselroade, such bursts of measurement increase the research burden in several ways, however they are necessary for studying intraindividual variation.

This chapter has focused on models for continuous normally-distributed outcomes, and has illustrated how such models can be estimated with standard software. Because ordinal data are often obtained in many research areas as well, we are currently extending these procedures for ordinal data. For example, many variables in psychology are measured using Likert scales or other similar types of ordinal categories. Admittedly, there is typically more information in continuous than ordinal responses, so the ability to model variances in ordinal data may not be as general as what is possible using the methods presented in this chapter. Thus, we hope to examine the degree to which these models of variation can be applied to ordinal outcomes.

ACKNOWLEDGMENTS

Thanks are due to Siu Chi Wong for statistical analysis, and to Todd Little for organizing the conference and for his helpful comments on a previous draft of this chapter. This work was supported by National Institutes of Mental Health grant MH56146, National Cancer Institute grant CA80266, and by a grant from the Tobacco Etiology Research Network, funded by the Robert Wood Johnson Foundation. Correspondence to Donald Hedeker, Division of Epidemiology & Biostatistics (M/C 923), School of Public Health, University of Illinois at Chicago, 1603 West Taylor Street, Room 955, Chicago, IL, 60612-4336. e-mail: hedeker@uic.edu

REFERENCES

Aitkin, M. (1987). Modelling variance heterogeneity in normal regression using GLIM. *Applied Statistics, 36,* 332-339.

Akaike, H. (1973). Information theory and an extension of the maximum likelihood principle . In B. N. Petrov & F. Csaki (Eds.), *Second international symposium on information theory* (pp. 267-281). Budapest: Academiai Kiado.

Bock, R. D. (1983a). The discrete Bayesian. In H. Wainer & S. Messick (Eds.), *Modern advances in psychometric research* (pp. 103-115). Hillsdale, NJ: Lawrence Erlbaum Associates.

Bock, R. D. (1983b). Within-subject experimentation in psychiatric research. In R. D. Gibbons & M. W. Dysken (Eds.), *Statistical and methodological advances in psychiatric research* (pp. 59-90). New York: Spectrum.

Bock, R. D. (1989). Measurement of human variation: A two stage model. In R. D. Bock (Ed.), *Multilevel analysis of educational data* (pp. 319-342). New York: Academic Press.

Bryk, A. S., & Raudenbush, S. W. (1992). *Hierarchical linear models: Applications and data analysis methods.* Newbury Park, CA: Sage.

Campbell, S. K., & Hedeker, D. (2001). Validity of the test of infant motor performance for discriminating among infants with varying risks for poor motor outcome. *The Journal of Pediatrics, 139,* 546-551.

Carroll, K. M., Rounsaville, B. J., Nich, C., Gordon, L., Wirtz, P., & Gawin, F. (1994). One-year follow-up of psychotherapy and pharmacotherapy for cocaine dependence. *Archives of General Psychiatry, 51,* 989-997.

Curran, P. J., Stice, E., & Chassin, L. (1997). The relation between adolescent and peer alcohol use: A longitudinal random coefficients model. *Journal of Consulting and Clinical Psychology, 65,* 130-140.

Dempster, A. P., Rubin, D. B., & Tsutakawa, R. K. (1981). Estimation in covariance component models. *Journal of the American Statistical Society, 76,* 341-353.

Elkin, I., Gibbons, R. D., Shea, M. T., Sotsky, S. M., Watkins, J. T., Pilkonis, P. A., et al. (1995). Initial severity and differential treatment outcome in the NIMH treatment of depression collaborative research program. *Journal of Consulting and Clinical Psychology, 63,* 841-847.

Fleeson, W. (2004). Moving personality beyond the person-situation debate. *Current Directions in Psychological Science, 13,* 83-87.

Gallagher, T. J., Cottler, L. B., Compton, W. M., & Spitznagel, E. (1997). Changes in HIV/AIDS risk behaviors in drug users in St. Louis: Applications of random regression models. *Journal of Drug Issues, 27,* 399-416.

Gibbons, R. D., Hedeker, D., Waternaux, C. M., & Davis, J. M. (1988). Random regression models: A comprehensive approach to the analysis of longitudinal psychiatric data. *Psychopharmacology Bulletin, 24,* 438-443.

Goldstein, H. (1995). *Multilevel statistical models, 2nd edition.* New York: Halstead Press.

Halikas, J. A., Crosby, R. D., Pearson, V. L., & Graves, N. M. (1997). A randomized double-blind study of carbamazepine in the treatment of cocaine abuse. *Clinical Pharmacology and Therapeutics, 62*, 89-105.

Harvey, A. C. (1976). Estimating regression models with multiplicative heteroscedasticity. *Econometrica, 44*, 461-465.

Hedeker, D. (2004). An introduction to growth modeling. In D. Kaplan (Ed.), *The SAGE handbook of quantitative methodology for the social sciences* (pp. 215-234). Thousand Oaks, CA: Sage.

Hedeker, D., Flay, B. R., & Petraitis, J. (1996). Estimating individual differences of behavioral intentions: An application of random-effects modeling to the theory of reasoned action. *Journal of Consulting and Clinical Psychology, 64*, 109-120.

Hertzog, C., & Nesselroade, J. R. (2003). Assessing psychological change in adulthood: An overview of methodological issues. *Psychology and Aging, 18*, 639-657.

Hui, S. L., & Berger, J. O. (1983). Empirical Bayes estimation of rates in longitudinal studies. *Journal of the American Statistical Association, 78*, 753-759.

Huttenlocher, J. E., Haight, W., Bryk, A. S., & Seltzer, M. (1991). Early vocabulary growth: Relation to language input and gender. *Developmental Psychology, 27*, 236-248.

Laird, N. M., & Ware, J. H. (1982). Random-effects models for longitudinal data. *Biometrics, 38*, 963-974.

Leeuw, J. de, & Kreft, I. (1986). Random coefficient models for multilevel analysis. *Journal of Educational Statistics, 11*, 57-85.

Longford, N. T. (1987). A fast scoring algorithm for maximum likelihood estimation in unbalanced mixed models with nested random effects. *Biometrika, 74*, 817-827.

Martin, M., & Hofer, S. M. (2004). Intraindividual variability, change, and aging: Conceptual and analytical issues. *Gerontology, 50*, 7-11.

Mermelstein, R., Hedeker, D., Flay, B., & Shiffman, S. (2002). *Situational versus intraindividual contributions to adolescents' subjective mood experience of smoking*. Savannah, GA: Annual Meeting for the Society for Research on Nicotine and Tobacco.

Neff, L. A., & Karney, B. R. (2004). How does context affect intimate relationships? linking external stress and cognitive processes within marriage. *Personality and Social Psychology Bulletin, 30*, 134-148.

Nesselroade, J. R. (1991). The warp and woof of the developmental fabric. In R. Downs, L. Liben, & D. Palarmo (Eds.), *Visions of development, the environment, and aesthetics: The legacy of Joachim F. Wohlwill.* (pp. 213-240). Hillside, NJ: Lawrence Earlbaum Associates.

Nesselroade, J. R. (2001). Intraindividual variability in development within and between individuals. *Eur Psychol, 6*, 187-193.

Nesselroade, J. R. (2004). Intraindividual variability and short-term change. *Gerontology, 50*, 44-47.

Nesselroade, J. R., & Boker, S. M. (1994). Assessing constancy and change. In T. Heatherton & J. Weinberger (Eds.), *Can personality change?* (pp. 503-541). Washington, DC: American Psychological Association.

Nesselroade, J. R., & Schmidt McCollam, K. M. (2000). Putting the process in developmental processes. *International Journal of Behavioral Development, 24,* 295-300.

Niaura, R., Spring, B., Borrelli, B., Hedeker, D., Goldstein, M., Keuthen, N., et al. (2002). Multicenter trial of fluoxetine as an adjunct to behavioral smoking cessation treatment. *Journal of Consulting and Clinical Psychology, 70,* 887-896.

Schwarz, G. (1978). Estimating the dimension of a model. *Annals of Statistics, 6,* 461-464.

Serretti, A., Lattuada, E., Zanardi, R., Franchini, L., & Smeraldi, E. (2000). Patterns of symptom improvement during antidepressant treatment of delusional depression. *Psychiatry Research, 94,* 185-190.

Strenio, J. F., Weisberg, H. I., & Bryk, A. S. (1983). Empirical Bayes estimation of individual growth curve parameters and their relationship to covariates. *Biometrics, 39,* 71-86.

Verbeke, G., & Molenberghs, G. (2000). *Linear mixed models for longitudinal data.* New York: Springer.

Wolfinger, R. D. (1993). Covariance structure selection in general mixed models. *Communications in Statistics, Simulation and Computation, 22,* 1079-1106.

Wu, H., & Zhang, J.-T. (2002). Local polynomial mixed-effects models for longitudinal data. *Journal of the American Statistical Association, 97,* 883-889.

CHAPTER NINE

Structural Equation Modeling of Mediation and Moderation With Contextual Factors

Todd D. Little
University of Kansas

Noel A. Card
University of Arizona

James A. Bovaird
University of Nebraska-Lincoln

Kristopher J. Preacher
Christian S. Crandall
University of Kansas

Researchers often grapple with the idea that an observed relationship may be part of a more complex chain of effects. These complex relationships are described in terms such as indirect influences, distal vs. proximal causes, intermediate outcomes, and ultimate causes; all of which share the concept of *mediation*. Similarly, researchers must often consider that an observed relationship may be part of a more complex, qualified system. These relationships are described using concepts such as interactions, subgroup differences, and shocks; all of which share the concept of *moderation*. Generally speaking, a mediator can be thought of as the carrier or transporter of information along the causal chain of effects. A moderator, on the other hand, is the changer of a relationship in a system.

In this chapter, we explore both empirical and theoretical considerations in modeling mediation and moderation using structural equation modeling. Our primary focus is on how to model contextual factors that are measured as continuous latent variables, highlighting the power of SEM to represent and test these types of influence (see Little, Card, Slegers, & Ledford, chap. 6, this volume, for a discussion of moderating contextual factors that are measured as categorical variables).

MEDIATION

Contextual factors can be conceptualized as mediated influences where the contextual information is deemed to be a distal causal influence. For example, early prenatal conditions can influence cortical development, which in turn can influence later intellective functioning (see Widaman, chap. 17, this volume). Contextual factors can also be conceptualized as the mediating influence where the contextual information is deemed to carry the distal causal associations. For example, children's temperament characteristics may influence the overall classroom environment, which in turn may influence the quality of learning or school well-being of the children.

Throughout our discussion of mediation, we use the standard convention of referring to the exogenous causal influence as X. The endogenous causal influence, or mediator, is referred to as M, and the dependent variable or outcome is referred to as Y.

Empirical Conditions for Mediation

Baron and Kenny's (1986) influential paper on mediation analyses stated three necessary but not sufficient conditions that must be met in order to claim that mediation is occurring (but see Kenny, Kashy, & Bolger, 1998; MacKinnon, Lockwood, Hoffman, West, & Sheets, 2002).

1. *X is significantly related to M.*

2. *M is significantly related to Y.*

3. *The relationship of X to Y diminishes when M is in the model.*

In other words, each of the three constructs must show evidence of a nonzero monotonic association with each other, and the relationship of X to Y must decrease substantially upon adding M as a predictor of Y (for a review and comparison of methods of testing mediation, see MacKinnon et al., 2002).[1] The

---

[1]Typically, these associations are adequately captured as linear relationships. Although it is beyond the scope of the current discussion, nonlinear modeling can also be employed for testing nonlinear mediation.

regression weight of Y regressed on X is sometimes denoted c. A key feature of a mediation analysis is the nature of the correlational structure among the set of three variables. For example, if the X-to-M link (denoted a) corresponds to a .8 correlation and the M-to-Y link (denoted b) also corresponds to a .8 correlation, the implied correlation between X and Y is .64 (i.e., in standardized metric: $.8 \times .8$), assuming the relationship of X to Y controlling for M is zero. When this correlational structure is observed in the data, a mediation analysis will provide support for mediation (in this case, full mediation, see the following). If the observed correlation is larger than that implied by the product of the two pathways (a and b) then a direct positive effect of X to Y (denoted c') may be needed, depending on the magnitude of the deviation from the model implied correlation. On the other hand, if the observed correlation is smaller than the correlation implied by the product of the two pathways (a and b) then a direct negative value of c' may be needed, depending on the magnitude of the deviation from the model implied correlation, and *suppression* is in evidence. In other words, the empirical need for a direct pathway from X to Y is driven by the magnitude and direction of the deviation of the observed from the implied correlation between X and Y when the c' path is not represented in the model. Table 1 depicts three idealized correlation patterns that would be consistent with full mediation, partial mediation, and partial suppression. Although these variations on the kinds of mediation that can emerge in a mediation analysis are intuitively appealing, they do not necessarily do justice to a more complete understanding of mediation effects. Briefly we describe the concepts as typically found in the current literature, but then turn to a discussion of why these distinctions are unsatisfying descriptors.

If the relationship between construct X and construct Y is *fully mediated*, then all of the significant variance of that relationship will be accounted for by the direct effect from construct M to construct Y (b). That is, the influence

TABLE 9.1

Idealized Correlational Structures That Would be Consistent With Full Mediation, Partial Mediation, and Suppression

	1. *Full Mediation*			2. *Partial Mediation*			3. *Suppression*		
	X	M	Y	X	M	Y	X	M	Y
X	1.0	.60	.30	1.0	.60	.50	1.0	.60	.20
M	.80	1.0	.50	.80	1.0	.50	.80	1.0	.50
Y	.64	.80	1.0	.80	.80	1.0	.46	.80	1.0

Note. High levels of intercorrelation are depicted below the diagonal and low levels of intercorrelation are depicted above the diagonal.

FIGURE 9.1
Types of mediation.

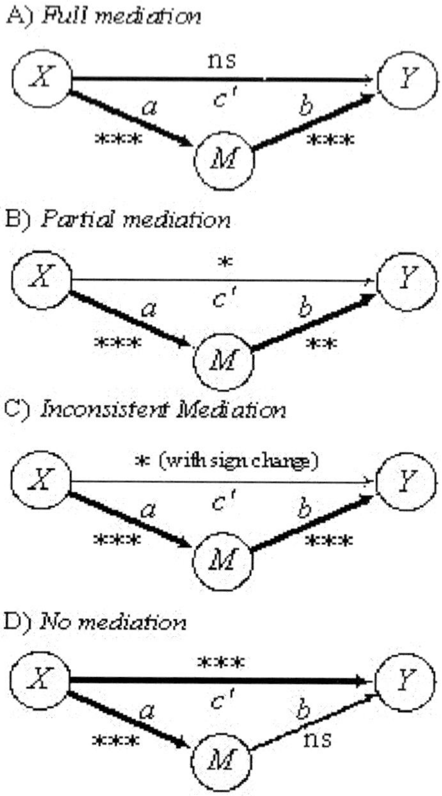

A) *Full mediation*

B) *Partial mediation*

C) *Inconsistent Mediation*

D) *No mediation*

Note. In these idealized models, the correlations among all three constituents are assumed to be positive in sign and significant. All paths are positive except where noted in Panel C. ∗ indicates relative strengths of associations.

of X on construct Y is adequately captured as an indirect influence through M (see Figure 9.1, Panel A) and the observed association between X and Y is accurately captured by tracing the pathways from Y back to M (b) and from M back to X (a). (See e.g., Loehlin, 1987, for a discussion of Wright's tracing rules; and see Table 9.1)

A *partially mediated* relationship is indicated if the direct effect of the mediator construct, M, accounts for a significant amount of variance in Y, but c' remains significant. If c' remains significant but differs in sign from the zero-order correlation between X and Y, then mediation with suppression is evident (see Figure 9.1, Panel C). In other words, if c' differs in sign from the product of a and b (e.g., one is a positive effect while the other is negative) one interpretation would be that X contains two sources of variance that reflect two opposing channels by which it influences Y. Specific interpretations would depend on the signs of the various pathways and the composition of the various constructs. More specifically, one channel would influence Y via the indirect pathway of the mediator, M, while the other channel would influence Y in the opposite direction once the influence of M is accounted for in Y. In this regard, both c' and b would need to remain significant when they are both in the model (see Figure 9.1, Panel C; and see Table 1). For more information on suppression and its relationship to mediation, consult MacKinnon, Krull, and Lockwood (2000).

Finally, if b is nonsignificant when c' is present in the model, then no mediation is evident (see Figure 9.1, Panel D). Other patterns of associations are also consistent with a lack of mediation. For example, if a is not significant and b is significant, the b pathway would be interpreted as a covariate and not a mediator. Similarly, if a, b, and c' are all nonsignificant then no mediation would be evident.

Some Notes of Caution. Despite the pervasiveness of terms like full and partial mediation, we caution against their use. *Full* and *partial* are essentially informal effect size descriptors. They are intended to capture and communicate the magnitude or importance of a mediation effect, yet they are traditionally defined in terms of statistical significance. In other words, an effect is termed *partial* or *complete* based not only on the strength of the effect, but also on the p-values associated with c and c', and hence on sample size. Traditionally, statistical significance and practical significance are separate concepts, and the latter should not invoke N.

One negative consequence of using p-values to define effect size is that some circumstances are likely to lead to conclusions of full mediation that should more intuitively be considered partial mediation. In other words, there exists the danger of unwittingly exaggerating the size or importance of an effect. For example, given that an indirect effect is statistically significant, the smaller the sample is, the more likely we are to conclude that the total effect of X on Y is fully mediated because the standard error of c' increases as N decreases. In other words, the researcher is rewarded with apparently more extensive mediation the smaller N becomes, but no one would seriously advocate using small samples to achieve large apparent effect sizes. A second negative consequence is that the smaller the total effect (c) is, the more likely one is to demonstrate full mediation; restated, the smaller an effect is, the easier it is to fully mediate it. A consequence of this is that the less reliable one's X and Y variables are, the more likely one is to achieve full mediation. It can be misleading to claim that an inconsequential but statistically significant effect is "fully mediated."

Finally, full mediation can never logically exist in the population because it requires a regression weight to be exactly equal to zero. The probability of this occurring in practice is zero. Finding $c' = 0$ and c' not significantly different from zero are two very different things; with the latter, all the researcher can claim is that there is not enough evidence to reject the hypothesis of full mediation (but given a larger N, we almost certainly would). We recommend instead investigating the statistical significance of the mediation effect and *separately* considering whether or not the effect is practically important or meaningful. What constitutes a practically meaningful effect will vary from context to context, and relies on the scientist's judgment and background knowledge. In what follows, we examine some methods that can be used to establish the statistical significance of a mediation effect.

Key Considerations in Testing for Mediation. One consideration for finding support for mediation is whether the indirect pathway from X to M to Y ($a \times b$) is statistically significant (Shrout & Bolger, 2002). All major SEM programs provide estimates of indirect effects and their associated standard errors which are used to determine the significance of the effect by way of the Wald statistic (i.e., an estimate divided by its standard error provides a large-sample Z-value to gauge the statistical significance of the effect). The standard error is given in a number of sources (e.g., Baron & Kenny, 1986; Sobel, 1982) as:

$$se_{a \times b} \sqrt{a^2 se_b^2 + b^2 se_a^2} \tag{1}$$

The test is conducted by dividing ($a \times b$) by its standard error and comparing the result to a standard normal distribution. This test is very simple to apply, directly tests the hypothesis of interest, and can be used to form confidence intervals for the population indirect effect. However, it should be used only in large samples because a central assumption underlying its use—that ($a \times b$) is normally distributed across repeated sampling—is typically violated in practice. However, as N grows larger, the distribution of ($a \times b$) tends to approximate normality and the normality assumption becomes more tenable.

Other methods for determining the significance of the indirect effect include the use of resampling (or bootstrapping) and the *distribution of the product* strategy (MacKinnon et al., 2002; MacKinnon, Lockwood, & Williams, 2004). Resampling is especially useful in small samples, and makes fewer distributional assumptions than the Wald test. Resampling involves repeatedly drawing N cases (with replacement) from the original N cases to form a sampling distribution of ($a \times b$). This sampling distribution, in turn, is used to form asymmetric confidence intervals without having to assume normality (for descriptions of this method, see Bollen & Stine, 1990; MacKinnon et al., 2004; Preacher & Hayes, 2004; and Shrout & Bolger, 2002). The distribution of the product strategy is a recently proposed method that is similar to the Wald test described earlier, but invokes a more complex sampling distribution than the standard normal distribution. Research on the subject is still in its infancy (MacKinnon, Fritz, Williams & Lockwood, in press), but the method has shown much promise.

Theoretical Considerations in Testing for Mediation

Although the empirical conditions for mediation are straightforward, a number of theoretical issues must also be considered when evaluating the validity of the tested mediation model. In many cases, even though the empirical data are consistent with a mediated relationship, the mediation model has not captured the true indirect pathway. An empirical finding of mediation may support a preferred model, but it does not rule out a wide range of possible alternatives (just a handful of them). These alternative models may be equally consistent with the data, yet may be quite different from the hypothesized mediation model. Because of these equally plausible alternative models, a number of threats to the validity of a mediation analysis must also be considered.

Threat 1: Plausible Equivalent Models: When one is testing for mediation using nonexperimental data with measurements made at the same occasion, any number of interpretive problems can arise (see, e.g., Cole & Maxwell, 2003). Figure 9.2 (Panel A), for example, shows a simple demonstration that a perfect mediated relationship has two statistically

FIGURE 9.2
Alternate mediation models.

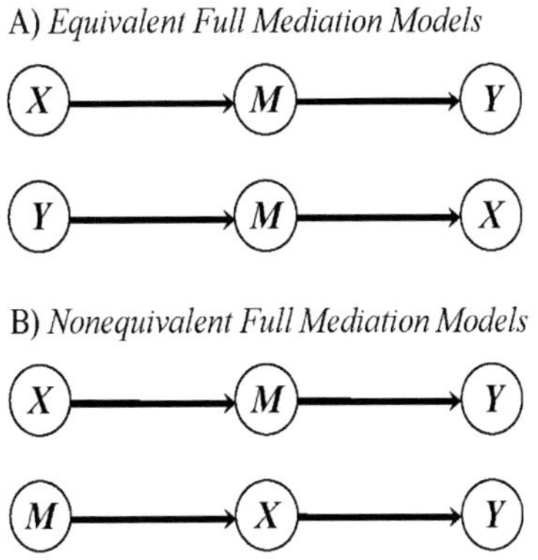

A) *Equivalent Full Mediation Models*

B) *Nonequivalent Full Mediation Models*

equivalent models that could fit the data with c' fixed to zero. In contrast, Panel B of Figure 9.2 shows a set of nonequivalent models that could also be fit to the data. Although the competing models of Panel B can be contrasted statistically, the order of the predictive chains in Panel A must be evaluated on the basis of theory. Without strong theory and good measurement, the order of the predictive chain can be in any combination—although a significant test of mediation may provide support for all of these models equally, it does not provide support for one model over the other.

Threat 2: Unmodeled Variables That Are Correlated With M and Y: In experimental work, one can have a situation in which X is manipulated and one then tests the significance of $a \times b$. If b is high prior to the manipulation because of some other source of shared variability (D) between M and Y, the manipulation of X may lead to a correlational structure that is consistent with mediation, but concluding that mediation has occurred could be invalid (i.e., the true indirect path might be from X to D to Y, or there may be no indirect path at all). To remedy this problem in experimental work, one might conduct experiments testing *each* of the putative components of the causal chain (i.e., the manipulation of X is found to cause change in M as well as change in Y that is accounted for by change in M; and the manipulation of M causes changes in Y) in order to test the relations among X, M, and Y (Spencer, Zanna, & Fong, 2005). However, in nonexperimental work, it may be difficult or impossible to determine whether a variable, M, is a true mediator of the relationship between X and Y or whether it is simply highly correlated with an unmeasured variable, D, that has causal influence over M and Y. In short, simple tests of mediation models are especially dependent on accurate model specification; when relevant and correlated variables go unmeasured, the results of mediation tests, no matter what level of statistical significance is achieved, may point in the wrong direction.

Threat 3: When Measured Variables Are Proxies for True Causal Variables: In both experimental and nonexperimental work, a key threat to the validity of the mediation analysis is related to the issue of whether the measured variable is the 'true' variable or a proxy of the intended variable. This issue can take a number of forms in that the proxy for the true variable can be located in any of the X, M, or Y constituents of the causal chain.

Proxy Causal Variables. Among exogenous variables, an unmeasured true cause may be highly correlated with the measured/manipulated variable. In this case, X' is a proxy for the true distal cause, X. In school-based studies, for example, free and reduced lunch status is used as a proxy for SES. If one tests a model of whether the effect of SES on academic outcomes is mediated by parental involvement, using a proxy measure may provide support for the hypothesized model. In this case, it may appear as if the effect of the 'false cause' is mediated by M when, in fact, the measured X' is not the true causal effect on M. Similarly, consider an experiment in which one manipulates X' but believes they have manipulated X. If X' has a substantial causal effect on M and Y, and its effect on Y is mediated by M, then one might incorrectly conclude that M mediates the X effect on Y.

A similar situation can occur when there are more links in the causal chain, such as when X_1 causes X_2 which in turn affects Y through mediator M, and the researcher measures only X_1. Ignoring more distal causes is not a specification error *per se*, but ignoring a more proximal cause would be a specification error. Another variation on the unmeasured variable problem occurs when X_1 and X_2 are highly correlated because both are caused by D, and the researcher measures X_1 or X_2, when D is the 'true' cause.

Proxy Mediator Variables. A second type of proxy problem occurs when the presumed mediator variable is a proxy variable, M', for the 'true' mediator, M. This scenario is important because the probability of measuring a proxy variable can be substantial, such as when a related concept is more appropriate (e.g., ethnicity vs. SES), when the true mediator cannot be easily measured (e.g., SES), or when a specific variable is measured when a more construct-level measure is more appropriate (e.g., free-reduced lunch status vs. SES). If the presumed mediator variable is a 'proxy' or even a mere strong correlate of the true mediator variable, which is unmeasured (or simply not specified in the model), then mediation analyses can 'work' when they should not. This kind of problem increases to the extent that the variables in the mediation analyses are conceptually close to one another. That is, proxy variables can be quite problematic when analyzing mediation models involving constructs with precise theoretical distinctions and where variables in the actual analysis have enough measurement and conceptual overlap to act as proxies for the true cause.

Proxy Dependent Variables. Finally, one may measure a proxy variable for Y (i.e., the measured dependent variable is only correlated with the true outcome variable). In many cases, dependent variables are not the conceptual variables themselves, but are conceptualized as proxy measures (e.g., choice behavior as a proxy for a preference, discrimination as a proxy for prejudice, grades as a proxy for school performance, test scores as a proxy for aptitudes, etc.). But in some cases highly correlated proxy variables (e.g., self-esteem for anxiety or depression) can lead to significant but misleading indirect effects. Similarly, if Y_1 causes Y_2, but only Y_2 is measured as the outcome variable, one would draw an invalid conclusion about the actual causal chain.

Threat 4: Differential Reliability of Measurement: This source of potential error is empirical in nature. If the constructs are measured with differential levels of reliability then the 'true' relationships will be differentially attenuated such that one would not be able to conduct a valid test of mediation (Judd & Kenny, 1981). When new measures that are not honed, focused, and validated are used, unreliability may bias the true mediation process. Lack of measurement development is especially a problem when a construct has a high level of meaning in one group, but not another, for example, racial identity for majority and minority groups (e.g., White identity is much weaker, less meaningful, and has a lower reliability and internal consistency than Latino and Black identity). In such cases, the low reliability of measures—for one group but not the other—may cause mediation to masquerade as between-group moderation. As mentioned above, the latent-variable SEM approach to testing mediation mitigates the problem of differential reliability and allows one to test, and thereby ensure, that the constructs are measured equivalently across the groups (see Little, Card, Slegers, & Ledford, chap.6, this volume).

MODERATION

Thus far we have focused on the technical and theoretical issues associated with mediation analyses. As mentioned in the introduction, however, researchers may also be interested in questions related to moderation, or the changing of a relationship as a function of some moderating influence. When the moderating influence is measured in a continuous manner, this influence is generally modeled by creating a new variable that is the product of the variable that is being moderated (X) and the variable that is moderating (W). This interaction term (XW) is then entered into the regression equation after the linear main effects on the outcome (Y) of the moderating (W) and moderated variables (X) are estimated. If the effect of XW is significant, then the effect of X on Y is dependent upon the levels of W. Aiken and West (1991) describe simple procedures for taking the estimated regression weights from the full equations and plotting a number of implied regressions in order to provide a visualization of the moderated effect. Such plots might look like the one depicted in Figure 9.3.

FIGURE 9.3
Hypothetical plot of a moderate relationship between X and Y as a function of a moderator (W).

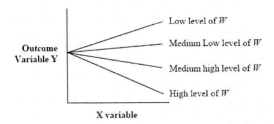

As with mediation analysis, a number of technical and theoretical issues arise when testing for moderation. A key theoretical issue is conceptualizing which variable is the moderator (W) and which is the focal predictor (X). Mathematically, the product term (XW) used to represent an interaction does not distinguish which variable is which—it simply provides empirical evidence that the nonlinear combination (product) of the two variables accounts for a unique amount of variability in the outcome variable (Y) above and beyond the linear main effects of the two variables (X and W). For example, in standard ordinary least squares regression, the product of two variables can be used to represent the interactive effect, as seen in Equation 2:

$$Y = b_0 + b_1 X + b_2 W + b_3 XW + e \qquad (2)$$

where Y is the outcome variable of interest, e is the assumed error term, X and W are the first-order predictor variables, and XW is the newly formed multiplicative term. Such a regression equation specifies that the slope of the line relating X to Y changes at different levels of W. In an equivalent way, however, this equation specifies that the slope of the line relating W to Y changes at different levels of X (see Saunders, 1956). Similar to product terms, powered variables (i.e., natural polynomials such as X^2, X^3, X^4, etc.) can be used to represent other nonlinear functions such as quadratic, cubic, or quartic relationships between X and Y.

Under typical conditions, the product and powered terms will be highly correlated with the first-order predictor variables from which they are derived. The resulting collinearity of the product or powered term compromises the stability and interpretation of some regression coefficients. A high degree of collinearity indicates that within the predictor set, one or more of the variables are highly linearly related to other predictors. Under these conditions, even minor fluctuations in the sample, such as those related to measurement and sampling error, can have major impacts on the regression weights and their standard errors. In other words, the collinearity of the powered and product terms with the first-order predictor variables is often problematic because it can create instability in the values for the estimated regression weights, leading to 'bouncing beta weights.'

Ideally, an interaction term will be uncorrelated with (orthogonal to) its first-order effect terms. For example, orthogonal contrast codes are commonly used when there are a small number of categories needed to represent the levels of the variables involved. However, with continuous variable interaction terms, the orthogonality property is harder to achieve. Several authors (i.e., Aiken & West, 1991; Cohen, 1978; Cronbach, 1987) have shown that if the first-order variables are mean centered (i.e., transformed from a raw-score scaling to a deviation-score scaling by subtracting the variable mean from all observations), the resulting product term will be minimally correlated or uncorrelated with the first-order variables if the variables are more or less bivariate normal.

Even though the significance of the partial regression coefficient of an interaction term does not differ depending on whether or not the constituent predictors are mean centered (see Kromrey & Foster-Johnson, 1998 for a convincing demonstration; see also Little, Bovaird, & Widaman, 2006), mean centering the predictor variables prior to creating interaction or product terms has two distinct advantages. First, mean centering alleviates problems of collinearity among the predictor variables that results from the 'nonessential' collinearity among the main effects and their interaction term when one simply forms the product of the variables (as well as powered terms such as X^2 or X^4; see Marquardt, 1980). This reduction in collinearity reduces or eliminates the associated instability of regression estimates and standard errors when collinearity is not removed (i.e., the 'bouncing beta weight' problem).

The second characteristic of mean centering concerns the interpretability of the estimates. The regression coefficient for a mean centered predictor may be more *practically* meaningful than the same coefficient for the same predictor with an arbitrary zero point (i.e., interpreting the relative size of change in Y for a one-unit change in X at a given level of W may be easier if the zero point of W is the average value of W rather than an arbitrary and nonmeaningful scale value). Plotting the predicted relationship between X and Y over a range of plausible W-values can then be done, which would also increase interpretability of the interaction (e.g., Aiken & West, 1991; Cohen, Cohen, West, & Aiken, 2003; Mossholder, Kemery, & Bedeian, 1990).

Under most circumstances, mean centering is an adequate solution to the collinearity problem using multiplicative terms. At times, however, the resulting product or powered term will still have some degree of correlation with its first-order constituent variables, resulting in partial regression coefficients that may still show some modest instability (e.g., when bivariate normality is substantially violated). To remedy this lack of complete orthogonality when performing mean centering, a simple two-step regression technique called *residual centering* is available that ensures full orthogonality between a product term and its first-order effects (Lance, 1988). As with mean centering, this technique is also generalizable to powered terms.

Residual centering is an alternative approach to mean centering that also serves to eliminate nonessential multicollinearity in regression analyses. Residual centering (see Lance, 1988) is a two-stage ordinary least squares (OLS) procedure in which a product term or powered term is regressed onto its respective first-order constituent terms. The residual of this regression is then saved and subsequently used to represent the interaction or powered effect. The reliable variance of this new orthogonalized interaction term contains the unique variance that fully represents the interaction effect, independent of the first-order effect variance. Similarly, the reliable variance of a residual-centered powered term contains the unique variance accounted for by the curvature component of a nonlinear relationship, independent of the linear components.

Residual centering has a number of inherent advantages for regression analyses. First, the regression coefficients for orthogonalized product or powered terms are stable. That is, the regression coefficients and standard errors of the first-order variables remain unchanged when the higher order term is entered. Second, the significance of the product or powered term is unbiased by the orthogonalizing process. Third, unlike mean centering, orthogonalizing via residual centering ensures full independence between the product or powered term and its constituent main effect terms (Lance, 1988; Little et al., 2006).

Both mean centering and residual centering are beneficial for testing interactions in regression models; however, estimating interaction effects within regression models is still problematic. A key concern is the effect of measurement error on the power to detect such effects. Because OLS regression assumes that variables are measured perfectly reliably (i.e., without error), violating this assumption will lead to bias in the parameter estimates (Busemeyer & Jones, 1983). Measurement error is problematic for all variables in a regression analysis, but it is particularly troublesome for an interactive or nonlinear term because the unreliabilities of the constituent variables are compounded in the interactive or higher order term. A related concern is the differentiation of multiplicative and nonlinear effects under such conditions of low power (for more complete discussions, see Cortina, 1993; Ganzach, 1997; Kromrey & Foster-Johnson, 1998; Lubinski & Humphreys, 1990; MacCallum & Mar, 1995).

Structural equation modeling (SEM) represents an important advance in the study of multiplicative or nonlinear effects because of its ability to properly address the presence of measurement error within a statistical model. In SEM, the proportion of variance common to multiple indicators of a given construct is estimated, and the structural relations among these latent constructs may then be modeled, disattenuated for measurement error. Numerous authors have described techniques to represent latent variable interactions within the context of SEM (see Algina & Moulder, 2001; Jaccard & Wan, 1995; Jöreskog & Yang, 1996; Ping, 1996a, 1996b; Schumacker & Marcoulides, 1998; Wall & Amemiya, 2001). Most of these approaches are based on the Kenny and Judd (1984) product-indicator model and require complex nonlinear constraints.

As described in Little et al. (in press), Bollen (1995, 1996, 1998), and Bollen and Paxton (1998) presented a two-stage least squares (2SLS) approach that does not require the nonlinear constraints but has been found to be less effective than other methods (Moulder & Algina, 2002; Schermelleh-Engel, Klein, & Moosbrugger, 1998). Klein and Moosbrugger (2000) proposed a latent moderated structural model approach (LMS) utilizing finite mixtures of normal distributions which was further refined by Klein and Muthén (2002) as a quasi-maximum likelihood (QML) approach. The LMS/QML approach was found to perform well under conditions where first-order indicators are normally distributed (Marsh, Wen, & Hau, 2004). Finally, Marsh et al. (2004) proposed an unconstrained product-indicator approach that also performed well, even when underlying distributional assumptions are not met.

Most SEM software programs can implement the nonlinear constraints that are necessary to model latent variable interactions based on the Kenny and Judd (1984) product-indicator method. The less-effective 2SLS approach is available through PRELIS, the pre-processor for LISREL (Jöreskog & Sörbom, 1996), while the LMS/QML approach was made available in Mplus starting with version 3 (Muthén & Asparouhov, 2003; Muthén & Muthén, 2006). Although these programs make latent variable interactions more accessible, researchers must either use these two software programs or implement complex nonlinear constraints.

Little et al. (2006) recently proposed a straightforward method that can be used across any SEM platform. Their method is also based in principle on the product-indicator approach but uses the orthogonalizing procedures described earlier to create product indicators that are uncorrelated with the indicators of the main-effect constructs. In our view, the orthogonalizing technique (a) is less technically demanding than alternative methods of including interactive and powered terms in latent variable models based on nonlinear constraints, (b) can be implemented in any SEM software platform, and (c) provides reasonable estimates that are comparable to other existing procedures including the LMS/QML approach of Mplus (see Little et al., 2006, for a comparison). Other advantages of the orthogonalizing technique include: (a) main effect parameter estimates are unaffected when the interaction latent construct is entered into the model, (b) model fit is not degraded once the interaction latent construct is entered into the model, and (c) the orthogonalizing technique is readily generalizable for creating powered latent variables to represent quadratic, cubic, or higher order nonlinear relationships.

Although the steps and procedures are detailed in Little et al. (2006), we briefly outline the steps and technical issues related to implementing the orthogonalized latent variable interaction construct. Like other procedures that utilize the product-indicator approach, the orthogonalizing technique begins with the formation of all possible products of the corresponding indicators of the two constructs involved in the interaction. Assuming the moderated construct has three indicators (X_1, X_2, X_3) and the moderating construct has three indicators (W_1, W_2, W_3), one would calculate nine total product variables ($X_1 W_1$, $X_1 W_2$, $X_1 W_3$, $X_2 W_1$, $X_2 W_2$, $X_2 W_3$, $X_3 W_1$, $X_3 W_2$, $X_3 W_3$. In the next step, each of the product indicators would be regressed onto the set of indicators representing the indicators of the main-effect constructs in order to remove any of the main-effect information contained in any of the indicators of the constructs:

$$X_1 W_1 = b_0 + b_1 X_1 + b_2 X_2 + b_3 X_3 + b_4 W_1 + b_5 W_2 + b_6 W_3 + e_{x1w1}. \quad (3)$$

For each regression, the residuals of the prediction (e.g., e_{x1w1} from equation 3) would be saved as a new variable in the dataset (e.g., $o\_X_1 W_1$, where $o\_$ denotes the fact that this variable has been orthogonalized with respect to the set of main-effect indicators). The nine new orthogonalized indicators would then be brought into the SEM model to serve as indicators for a latent interaction construct. Each of the nine indicators would be allowed to load on the latent interaction construct which, thereby, would be defined as the common variance among the nine orthogonalized indicators. For the interaction effect to be estimated in an unbiased manner, however, specific residuals are expected to correlate. For example, in the case of nine orthogonalized indicators, there are 18 combinations of residuals among the nine indicators that need to be allowed to correlate. Specifically, each pair of orthogonalized product indicators that share a common indicator in their composition should be allowed to correlate. For example, $o\_X_1 W_1$ should be allowed to correlate with each product indicator that shares X_1 and each product indicator that shares W_1. That is, because $o\_X_1 W_1$ contains unique variance associated with X_1, one would expect correlated residuals with $o\_X_1 W_2$ and $o\_X_1 W_3$. Similarly, because $o\_X_1 W_1$ contains unique variance associated with W_1, one would expect correlated residuals with $o\_X_2 W_1$ and $o\_X_3 W_1$). The product indicators would not be correlated with the corresponding main effect indicators because the linear information associated with these main effect indicators has been removed via the orthogonalizing steps.

When this latent interaction term is included in the model, the focus is solely on the significance of the estimated effect of this latent interaction construct onto the outcome construct. As mentioned, because the latent interaction construct is orthogonal to the main effect constructs, the estimates for the latent main effects would be unchanged between the model in which the interaction construct is present and when it is not included in the model (see Little et al., 2006; see also Marsh et al., 2004; Marsh, Wen, Hau, Little, Bovaird, Widaman, in press).

COMBINING MODERATION AND MEDIATION

It is not uncommon for hypotheses about moderation and mediation relationships to occur in the same context. Models in which interaction effects are hypothesized to be mediated or indirect effects are hypothesized to be moderated are appearing with increasing frequency. When an interaction effect is mediated by M, the effect is termed *mediated moderation* (Baron & Kenny, 1986). When an indirect effect is moderated by at least one moderator variable, the effect is termed *moderated mediation* (James & Brett, 1984; Lance, 1988; Muller, Judd, & Yzerbyt, 2005).

Mediated moderation

It is often of interest to ascertain how a moderation effect is transmitted to a dependent variable. A theoretical precedent for investigating such effects can be found in Hyman (1955), who termed moderation *specification* and mediation *interpretation*: "... specification may almost always be considered a prelude to interpretation, rather than an analytic operation which is sufficient in itself" (p. 311). Indeed, Kraemer, Wilson, Fairburn, and Agras (2002) recommend that moderation be automatically considered in any mediation analysis. Echoing Hyman (1955), Baron and Kenny (1986) described an intuitive method for assessing *mediated moderation* (a term they coined) that involves first showing an interaction effect of X and W on Y, then introducing a mediator of that interaction effect. Wegener and Fabrigar (2000) characterize mediated moderation as occurring "when a moderator interacts with an IV to affect a DV, but the moderator has its effect via some mediating variable" (p. 437). Morgan-Lopez and MacKinnon (2006) note that mediated moderation models "involve the interaction effect between two predictor variables on a mediator which, in turn, affects an outcome." Mediated moderation, according to Muller et al. (2005), "can happen only when moderation occurs: The magnitude of the overall treatment effect on the outcome depends on the moderator (p. 853)."

Under such circumstances, the same procedures used to assess simple mediation may be applied to key regression weights in the model (Lance, 1988; Morgan-Lopez, 2003; Morgan-Lopez, Castro, Chassin, & MacKinnon, 2003; Morgan-Lopez & MacKinnon, 2006). The hypothesis is simply that the product of the regression weights linking XW to M and M to Y is too large relative to its standard error to be considered due to chance. Morgan-Lopez and MacKinnon (2006) recommend probing significant effects, but doing so implies that the researcher has ceased thinking of the effect as mediated moderation and has instead adopted a moderated mediation hypothesis (see following). We suggest instead that, because the mediated moderation effect as defined above *is not* conditional on W, no probing is necessary (it is the interaction effect that is hypothesized to be mediated, and this effect is considered constant across all X and W unless higher order terms are added to the model), although it may be of interest to plot and probe the interactive effects of X and W on M and Y separately by computing simple slopes (Aiken & West, 1991) or by using the Johnson-Neyman technique (Bauer & Curran, 2005; Preacher, Curran, Bauer, in press).

Moderated Mediation

If the moderator is a discrete variable, one might combine the mediation analyses described here with multiple-group approaches (see Little et al., chap. 6, this volume). If the moderator is a continuous variable, one might create an interaction term to reflect how a is moderated by W (i.e., create an X by W latent interaction variable that would predict M) and/or a second interaction term to reflect how b is moderated by W or another moderator Z (Lance, 1988). Lance (1988) and Preacher, Rucker, and Hayes (in press) have outlined frameworks for assessing indirect effects that are conditional on the value of at least one moderator. We briefly describe their approaches.

Lance (1988) describes a strategy for assessing moderated mediation that involves using residual centering. In Lance's approach, the product of mediator M and moderator W is computed and regressed on its constituent terms, yielding residuals o_MW. These residuals in turn may be included in a standard mediation model: $X \rightarrow o\_MW \rightarrow Y$, and mediation may be assessed by any of a number of traditional methods described here and elsewhere. Lance's approach is limited to the situation in which b is moderated by some variable W, but it would be straightforward to extend the method to other models. Lance's approach may be applied in SEM with latent mediators by computing products of residual centered variables and using them as indicators of a latent mediator. However, it is unclear how the moderation effect can be further explored or clarified by means of simple slopes analysis.

Preacher et al. (in press) describe five archetypal models of moderated mediation to establish a framework for discussing *conditional indirect effects*, defined as the magnitude of an indirect effect conditional on (or at a hypothetical value of) at least one moderator. These models are illustrated in schematic form in Figure 9.4 (Lance's [1988] model corresponds to the model in Panel C). These models provide a starting point for discussing moderated mediation, and by no means do they exhaust the range of models that could describe moderated mediation processes. In each of the models depicted in Figure 9.4, a mediation effect is potentially being moderated by W and/or Z. If the conditional indirect effect varies significantly as a function of the moderator(s), then moderated mediation is said to occur.

For example, say a researcher hypothesizes that the number and severity of children's internalizing problems affect self-esteem indirectly through physical and verbal victimization by peers, but that this indirect effect depends on peer rejection (for similar hypotheses see Hodges, Malone, & Perry, 1997; Hodges & Perry, 1999). If this turns out to be the case, then the indirect effect of internalizing on self-esteem through victimization is moderated by peer rejection. This hypothesis resembles Preacher et al.'s (in press) Model 2. The relevant regression equations are:

$$\boldsymbol{Victimization} = a_0 + a_1(\boldsymbol{Internalizing}) + a_2(\boldsymbol{Rejection})$$
$$+a_3(\boldsymbol{Internalizing} \times \boldsymbol{Rejection}) + e_V. \qquad (4)$$

$$\boldsymbol{Self\text{-}Esteem} = b_0 + b_1(\boldsymbol{Victimization}) + c_1'(\boldsymbol{Internalizing})$$
$$+c_2'(\boldsymbol{Rejection}) + c_3'(\boldsymbol{Internalizing} \times \boldsymbol{Rejection}) + e_S. \qquad (5)$$

In this model, the conditional indirect effect of internalizing on self-esteem can be quantified as $(a_1 + a_3(\boldsymbol{R})) \times b_1$, where $\boldsymbol{R}$ represents a conditional value of peer rejection. Preacher et al. provide normal-theory standard errors and resampling approaches for testing the significance of such effects, as well as software to conduct these analyses.[2] Of potentially greater value and utility to the applied researcher, the method can be adapted to reveal the range of values of the moderator(s) for which the indirect effect of X on Y is statistically significant (the *region of significance*). Although their method was developed for the case in which all variables are measured rather than latent,

---

[2]An SPSS macro is available at http://www.quantpsy.org/ for use with measured variables.

the method can be straightforwardly extended for use in SEM with latent variables. Point estimates and standard errors for conditional indirect effects at any value of the moderator may be computed using parameter estimates and asymptotic variances and covariances available from most SEM software. Alternatively, resampling may be used in SEM if AMOS or Mplus is used to estimate model parameters. All of the issues we discussed earlier with respect to simple

FIGURE 9.4
Five types of moderated mediation.

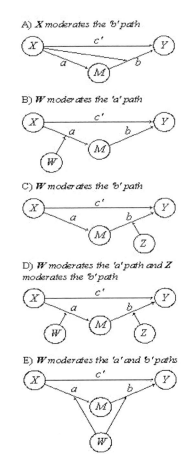

mediation—regarding proxy variables, unmodeled variables, equivalent models, and unreliab-ility—are at least as important in assessing moderated mediation as for assessing simple mediation. Also worth emphasizing is that the methods described by Preacher et al. are intended to address *statistical* significance rather than *practical* significance. In applied settings, both are important.

CONCLUSIONS

Hypotheses about mediation and moderation are commonly offered up by developmentalists, particularly those who are keenly interested in the influence of contextual variables on key developmental outcomes. In comparison to standard regression approaches, such complex extensions of these concepts of mediation and moderation are readily analyzable in the context of SEM analyses. Moreover, the basic tests of mediation and moderation in SEM are handled in a way that provides strong empirical evidence for or against a mediation or moderation hypothesis, particularly because effects are corrected for measurement error. With the added ability to directly estimate indirect relationships (as opposed to inferring them from a series of sequentially estimated regressions) and make direct statistical tests of the significance of any of the pathways modeled, SEM approaches to testing such complex hypotheses are very powerful. We hope that researchers will now find these approaches to be readily accessible. To aid in this accessibility, LISREL and Mplus scripts for testing mediation and moderation are available on the support Web page for this volume at Quant.KU.edu.

ACKNOWLEDGMENTS

This work was supported in part by grants from the NIH to the University of Kansas through the Mental Retardation and Developmental Disabilities Research Center (5 P30 HD002528), the Center for Biobehavioral Neurosciences in Communication Disorders (5 P30 DC005803), an Individual National Research Service Award (F32 MH072005) to the second author while at the University of Kansas, an Individual National Research Service Award (F32 DA016883-03) to the fourth author while at the University of North Carolina at Chapel Hill, and a NFGRF grant (2301779) from the University of Kansas to the first author. This work was also partly supported by grants to the first author from NSF (BCS-0345677), the Merrill Advanced Study Center at the University of Kansas (Mabel Rice, director), and the Society of Multivariate Experimental Psychology (SMEP). The views expressed herein are not necessarily those of the sponsoring agencies.

REFERENCES

Aiken, L. S., & West, S. G. (1991). *Multiple regression: Testing and interpreting interactions.* Newbury Park, CA: Sage.

Algina, J., & Moulder, B. C. (2001). A note on estimating the Jöreskog-Yang model for latent variable interaction using LISREL 8.3. *Structural Equation Modeling*, *8*, 40-52.

Baron, R. M., & Kenny, D. A. (1986). The moderator-mediator variable distinction in social psychological research: Conceptual, strategic, and statistical considerations. *Journal of Personality and Social Psychology*, *51*, 1173-1182.

Bauer, D. J., & Curran, P. J. (2005). Probing interactions in fixed and multilevel regression: Inferential and graphical techniques. *Multivariate Behavioral Research*, *40*, 373-400.

Bollen, K. A. (1995). Structural equation models that are nonlinear in latent variables: A least-squares estimator. *Sociological Methodology*, *25*, 223-251.

Bollen, K. A. (1996). An alternative two stage least squares (2SLS) estimator for latent variable equations. *Psychometrika*, *61*, 109-121.

Bollen, K. A., & Paxton, P. (1998). Interactions of latent variables in structural equation models. *Structural Equation Modeling*, *5*, 267-293.

Bollen, K. A., & Stine, R. (1990). Direct and indirect effects: Classical and bootstrap estimates of variability. *Sociological Methodology*, *20*, 115-140.

Busemeyer, J. R., & Jones, L. (1983). Analysis of multiplicative combination rules when the causal variables are measured with error. *Psychological Bulletin*, *93*, 549-562.

Cohen, J. (1978). Partialed products are interactions, partialed powers are curve components. *Psychological Bulletin*, *85*, 858-866.

Cohen, J., Cohen, P., West, S. G., & Aiken, L. S. (2003). *Applied multiple regression/correlation analysis for the behavioral sciences* (3rd ed.). Mahwah, NJ: Lawrence Erlbaum Associates.

Cole, D. A., & Maxwell, S. E. (2003). Testing mediational models with longitudinal data: Questions and tips in the use of structural equation modeling. *Journal of Abnormal Psychology*, *112*, 558-577.

Cortina, J. M. (1993). Interaction, nonlinearity, and multicollinearity: Implications for multiple regression. *Journal of Management*, *19*, 915-922.

Cronbach, L. J. (1987). Statistical tests for moderator variables: Flaws in analyses recently proposed. *Psychological Bulletin*, *102*, 414-417.

Ganzach, Y. (1997). Misleading interaction and curvilinear terms. *Psychological Methods*, *2*, 235-247.

Hyman, H. (1955). *Survey design and analysis: Principles, cases and procedures*. Glencoe, IL: The Free Press.

Jaccard, J., & Wan, C. K. (1995). Measurement error in the analysis of interaction effects between continuous predictors using multiple regression: Multiple indicator and structural equation approaches. *Psychological Bulletin*, *117*, 348-357.

James, L. R., & Brett, J. M. (1984). Mediators, moderators, and tests for mediation. *Journal of Applied Psychology*, *69*, 307-321.

Jöreskog, K. G., & Sörbom, D. (1996). *LISREL 8: Structural equation modeling*. Chicago: Scientific Software International.

Jöreskog, K. G., & Yang, F. (1996). Nonlinear structural equation models: The

Kenny-Judd model with interaction effects. In G. A. Marcoulides & R. E. Schumacker (Eds.), *Advanced structural equation modeling: Issues and techniques* (pp. 57-89). Mahwah, NJ: Lawrence Erlbaum Associates.

Judd, C. M., & Kenny, D. A. (1981). Process analysis: Estimating mediation in treatment evaluations. *Evaluation Review, 5,* 602-619.

Kenny, D. A., & Judd, C. M. (1984). Estimating the nonlinear and interactive effects of latent variables. *Psychological Bulletin, 96,* 201-210.

Kenny, D. A., Kashy, D. A., & Bolger, N. (1998). Data analysis in social psychology. In D. Gilbert, S. T. Fiske, & G. Lindzey (Eds.), *The handbook of social psychology* (4th ed., Vol. 1, pp. 223-265). New York: McGraw-Hill.

Klein, A., & Moosbrugger, H. (2000). Maximum likelihood estimation of latent interaction effects with the lms method. *Psychometrika, 65,* 457-474.

Klein, A., & Muthén, B. O. (2002). *Quasi maximum likelihood estimation of structural equation models with multiple interaction and quadratic effects.* Unpublished manuscript, Graduate School of Education, University of California, Los Angeles.

Kraemer, H. C., Wilson, G. T., Fairburn, C. G., & Agras, W. S. (2002). Mediators and moderators of treatment effects in randomized clinical trials. *Archives of General Psychiatry, 59,* 877-883.

Kromrey, J. D., & Foster-Johnson, L. (1998). Mean centering in moderated multiple regression: Much ado about nothing. *Educational and Psychological Measurement, 58,* 42-67.

Lance, C. E. (1998). Residual centering, exploratory and confirmatory moderator analysis, and decomposition of effects in path models containing interactions. *Applied Psychological Measurement, 12,* 163-175.

Little, T. D., Bovaird, J. A., & Widaman, K. F. (2006). On the merits of orthogonalizing powered and product terms: Implications for modeling latent variable interactions. *Structural Equation Modeling, 13,* 479-519.

Loehlin, J. C. (1987). *Latent variable models: An introduction to factor, path and structural analysis.* Mahwah, NJ: Lawrence Erlbaum Associates.

Lubinski, D., & Humphreys, L. G. (1990). Assessing spurious "moderator effects": Illustrated substantively with the hypothesized ("synergistic") relation between spatial and mathematical ability. *Psychological Bulletin, 107,* 385-393.

MacCallum, R. C., & Mar, C. M. (1995). Distinguishing between moderator and quadratic effects in multiple regression. *Psychological Bulletin, 118,* 405-421.

MacKinnon, D. P., Fritz, M. S., Williams, J., & Lockwood, C. M. (in press). Distribution of the product confidence units for the indirect effect: Program prodclin. *Behavior Research Methods, Instruments, and Computers.*

MacKinnon, D. P., Krull, J. L., & Lockwood, C. M. (2000). Equivalence of the mediation, confounding, and suppression effect. *Prevention Science, 1,* 173-181.

MacKinnon, D. P., Lockwood, C. M., Hoffman, J. M., West, S. G., & Sheets, V. (2002). A comparison of methods to test mediation and other intervening variable effects. *Psychological Methods, 7,* 83-104.

MacKinnon, D. P., Lockwood, C. M., & Williams, J. (2004). Confidence limits for the indirect effect: Distribution of the product and resampling methods. *Multivariate Behavioral Research, 39*, 99-128.

Marquardt, D. W. (1980). You should standardize the predictor variables in your regression models. *Journal of the American Statistical Association, 75*, 87-91.

Marsh, H. W., Wen, Z., & Hau, K. T. (2004). Structural equation models of latent interactions: Evaluation of alternative estimation strategies and indicator construction. *Psychological Methods, 9*, 275-300.

Marsh, H. W., Wen, Z., Hau, K. T., Little, T. D., Bovaird, J. A., & Widaman, K. F. (in press). Unconstrained structural equation models of latent interactions: Contrasting residual and mean-centered approaches. *Structural Equation Modeling*.

Morgan-Lopez, A. A. (2003). A simulation study of the mediated baseline by treatment interaction effect in preventive intervention trials. Unpublished Dissertation: Arizona State University.

Morgan-Lopez, A. A., Castro, F. G., Chassin, L., & MacKinnon, D. P. (2003). A mediated moderation model of cigarette use among mexican-american youth. *Addictive Behaviors, 28*, 583-589.

Morgan-Lopez, A. A., & MacKinnon, D. P. (in press). Demonstration and evaluation of a method to assess mediated moderation. *Behavior Research Methods*.

Mossholder, K. W., Kemery, E. R., & Bedeian, A. G. (1990). On using regression coefficients to interpret moderator effects. *Educational and Psychological Measurement, 50*, 255-263.

Moulder, B. C., & Algina, J. (2002). Comparison of methods for estimating and testing latent variable interactions. *Structural Equation Modeling, 9*, 1-19.

Muller, D., Judd, C. M., & Yzerbyt, V. Y. (2005). When moderation is mediated and mediation is moderated. *Journal of Personality and Social Psychology, 89*, 852-863.

Muthén, B. O., & Asparouhov, T. (2003). Modeling interactions between latent and observed continuous variables using maximum-likelihood estimation in mplus. Mplus Web Notes #6.

Muthén, L. K., & Muthén, B. O. (2006). *Mplus user's guide (4th ed.)*. Los Angeles, CA: Muthén and Muthén.

Ping, R. A., Jr. (1996a). Latent variable regression: A technique for estimating interaction and quadratic coefficients. *Multivariate Behavioral Research, 31*, 95-120.

Ping, R. A., Jr. (1996b). Latent variable interaction and quadratic effect estimation: A two-step technique using structural equation analysis. *Psychological Bulletin, 119*, 166-175.

Preacher, K. J., Curran, P. J., & Bauer, D. J. (in press). Computational tools for probing interaction effects in multiple linear regression, multilevel modeling, and latent curve analysis. *Journal of Educational and Behavioral Statistics.*.

Preacher, K. J., & Hayes, A. F. (2004). SPSS and SAS procedures for estimating indirect effects in simple mediation models. *Behavior Research Methods, Instruments, & Computers, 36*, 717-731.

Preacher, K. J., Rucker, D. D., & Hayes, A. F. (in press). Suggested procedures for addressing moderated mediation hypotheses. *Multivariate Behavioural.*

Saunders, D. R. (1956). Moderator variables in prediction. *Educational and Psychological Measurement, 16,* 209-222.

Schermelleh-Engel, K., Klein, A., & Moosbrugger, H. (1998). Estimating nonlinear effects using a latent moderated structural equations approach. In R. E. Schumacker & G. A. Marcoulides (Eds.), *Interaction and nonlinear effects in structural equation modeling* (pp. 203-238). Mahwah, NJ: Lawrence Erlbaum Associates.

Schumacker, R. E., & Marcoulides, G. A. (1998). *Interaction and nonlinear effects in structural equation modeling* (pp. 203-238). Mahwah, NJ: Lawrence Erlbaum Associates.

Shrout, P. E., & Bolger, N. (2002). Mediation in experimental and nonexperimental studies: New procedures and recommendations. *Psychological Methods, 7,* 422-445.

Sobel, M. E. (1982). Asymptotic confidence intervals for indirect effects in structural equation models. In S. Leinhart (Ed.), *Sociological methodology* 1982 (pp. 290-312). San Francisco: Jossey-Bass.

Spencer, S. J., Zanna, M. P., & Fong, G. T. (2005). Establishing a causal chain: Why experiments are often more effective than mediational analyses in examining psychological processes. *Journal of Personality and Social Psychology, 89,* 845-851.

Wall, M. M., & Amemiya, Y. (2001). Generalized appended product indicator procedure for nonlinear structural equation analysis. *Journal of Educational and Behavioral Statistics, 26,* 1-30.

Wegener, D. T., & Fabrigar, L. R. (2000). Analysis and design for nonexperimental data: Addressing causal and noncausal hypotheses. In H. T. Reis & C. M. Judd (Eds.), *Handbook of research methods in social and personality psychology* (pp. 412-450). New York: Cambridge University Press.

CHAPTER TEN

Moderating Effects of a Risk Factor: Modeling Longitudinal Moderated Mediation in the Development of Adolescent Heavy Drinking

David B. Flora
York University

Siek Toon Khoo
Australian Council for Educational Research

Laurie Chassin
Arizona State University

Mediation analysis is commonly used to examine hypotheses about causal mechanisms underlying the relationships between an independent variable and an outcome. For instance, in prevention research, researchers test mediational hypotheses to examine the theoretical mechanisms explaining how a prevention program influences the desired outcome (MacKinnon & Dwyer, 1993). Mediation analysis is also frequently used to assess the pathways by which risk factors such as parental alcoholism or unemployment lead to negative outcomes (e.g., Colder, Chassin, Stice, & Curran, 1997; Conger et al., 1990). Other applications can be found in studies of organizational behavior as well as basic cognitive and social psychology research.

Baron and Kenny (1986) did much for substantive researchers in psychology to clarify the distinction between statistical *mediation* and *moderation* (see also James & Brett, 1984). Nonetheless, some confusion about the difference between a mediating variable and a moderating variable has persisted in the psychological literature (Frazier, Tix, & Barron, 2004; Holmbeck, 1997). Simply put, a mediating variable explains "how" or "why" an independent variable predicts or causes an outcome variable, whereas a moderating variable addresses "when" or "for whom" an independent variable is most strongly related to an outcome variable. That is, a mediator is the mechanism through which a predictor influences an outcome, while moderation is nothing more than an interaction effect where the relationship between two variables depends on the level of the interacting, or moderating, variable. Given this distinction, Baron and Kenny then described *moderated mediation* as a situation where a moderator interacts with a mediational relationship.

Figure 10.1 presents the basic mediational process as described by Kenny

FIGURE 10.1
Basic three-variable mediation model.

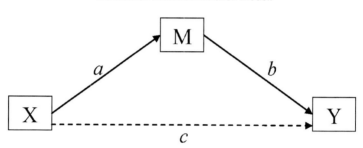

and colleagues (Baron & Kenny, 1986; Judd & Kenny, 1981; Kenny, Kashy, & Bolger, 1998). This model implies a causal order in which an independent variable influences an intervening variable, or mediator, which in turn influences an outcome. These relationships are commonly estimated using either hierarchical multiple regression (see Kenny et al., 1998) or covariance structure modeling. In the analysis steps outlined by Kenny et al. (1998), first the outcome variable is regressed on the independent variable to establish that there is an effect that may be mediated. Next, the mediator is regressed on the independent variable to estimate path a in Figure 10.1 and then the outcome variable is regressed on the mediator (path b) and independent variable (path c) simultaneously. The estimate of the *mediated effect* is given by the product of a and b and the residual direct effect is given by c. Numerous methods are available for calculating confidence intervals or establishing the statistical significance of the mediated effect. MacKinnon, Lockwood, Hoffman, West, and Sheets (2002) reviewed these methods and compared their finite sample properties with a simulation study.

The mediation model can also be estimated and tested in the covariance structure modeling framework (see Bollen, 1989, pp. 376-389). The three paths depicted in Figure 10.1 are estimated simultaneously, leading to tests of fit for the entire model. The simultaneous estimation of the effects of more than one mediating variable is also possible. Additionally, covariance structure modeling allows the researcher to estimate latent variable models, or structural equation models (SEMs). There are several advantages to specifying and estimating mediation models in the latent variable framework. Any or all of the independent, mediating, and outcome variables can be latent variables rather than observed variables. That means these variables can be latent constructs measured with multiple indicators to improve the validity and reliability of measures and to decrease the attenuation of relationships among the variables. More importantly, in this chapter, the mediator and outcome variables are latent variables which are growth factors specified in latent growth models. We perform the analyses in the SEM framework which facilitates the simultaneous estimation of two parallel growth models and the mediational relationships among the independent variable, the latent mediator factor and the latent outcome factor. Mediational analyses have been employed in both experimental studies, where the independent variable is a randomized factor identifying the treatment and control groups, and observational studies, where the independent variable is nonrandomized. In observational investigations studying the effects of contextual variables such as risk factors, a common type of independent variable is a grouping variable identifying the preexisting high-risk group and the normative group. In these settings, researchers may posit causal hypotheses about mediational processes, but definitive causal inferences cannot be made. However, the plausibility of causal relationships can be evaluated if certain assumptions are met (see e.g., Bollen, 1989, pp. 40-79; Pearl, 2000). One such assumption is that the variables are ordered in time, with the change in outcome occurring after the change in the mediator and the mediator is related to the preexisting independent variable (Cole & Maxwell, 2003). This assumption underscores the importance of explicating methods for examining mediation using longitudinal models. Additionally, as we discuss shortly, it is possible for a nonrandomized independent variable to moderate the relationship between a mediator and an outcome variable, thus resulting in *moderated mediation.*

In this chapter, we illustrate a method for assessing *longitudinal moderated mediation* when both the mediating construct and the outcome construct are measured repeatedly over time. This illustration examines whether growth trajectories in externalizing behavior mediate the relationship between parental alcoholism and trajectories of heavy drinking behavior during adolescence and whether parental alcoholism moderates the relationship between externalizing trajectories and heavy drinking trajectories. After describing the motivating substantive research questions and the data used for the analyses, we present separate univariate latent growth models (LGMs) for both externalizing behavior (the mediator process) and heavy drinking (the outcome process). Next, we describe and assess longitudinal mediation using a parallel-process LGM (Cheong, MacKinnon, & Khoo, 2003). Finally, we illustrate longitudinal moderated mediation through the use of a two-group parallel-process LGM.

DATA AND SUBSTANTIVE BACKGROUND

The analyses presented in this chapter use data drawn from a longitudinal study of parental alcoholism conducted by Chassin and colleagues (e.g., Chassin, Rogosch, & Barrera, 1991). Given this volume's focus on ecological and contextual effects, it is important to emphasize that the participants for this study were sampled directly from the community rather than from clinical treatment population, as the effects of risk factors such as parental alcoholism may differ in treated and untreated samples (Chassin, Carle, Nissim-Sabat, & Kumpfer, 2004). Indeed, parental alcoholism presents an adverse developmental context that is characterized by an unstable and disorganized family environment with elevated levels of parent–adolescent conflict, increased likelihood of parental divorce, and increased exposure to family violence as well as higher levels of more general negative uncontrollable life events such as poorer education and lower income (see Chassin et al., 2004, for a review).

Previous research, both with the current sample and other sources, has demonstrated conclusively that children of alcoholics are at increased risk for heavy alcohol consumption relative to the general population (see Sher, 1991, and Chassin, Barrera, & Montgomery, 1997, for reviews). Researchers have hypothesized that the higher levels of problematic drinking observed among COAs might operate as part of a broader pattern of "deviance proneness" (Jessor & Jessor, 1977; Sher, 1991). This theory postulates that adolescent COAs are likely to have poor self-regulation and self-control. These behaviorally undercontrolled individuals are more likely to display conduct problems (i.e., externalizing behaviors), which are then viewed as predictors of heavy drinking patterns (e.g., Chassin, Pitts, & Prost, 2002). Although this theory invokes multiple potential mediating variables, in this chapter we use LGM to examine whether externalizing behavior prospectively mediates the relationship between parental alcoholism and heavy drinking behavior.

Details about study design, recruitment strategies, and sample representativeness are given in Chassin et al. (1991) and Chassin, Barrera, Bech, and Kossak-Fuller (1992). Approximately 50% of the participants had at least one biological and custodial parent diagnosed with alcohol abuse or dependence at the first assessment (COAs) and the remaining participants were demographically matched controls (non-COAs). Here, we used longitudinal data for 355 participants (193 COAs and 162 non-COAs) observed from age 11 to 15 years old.[1] Each of the models was estimated with the Mplus software (Muthén & Muthén, 2004) using full-information maximum likelihood estimation (e.g., Arbuckle, 1996) to account for the presence of incomplete data.[2]

The mediating construct, externalizing behavior, was measured with 12 self-report items from the Child Behavior Checklist (Achenbach, 1978). These items had a 5-point Likert-type format, with responses coded to range from 0 to 4. We took the mean of the items to form a scale with higher scores representing higher levels of externalizing behavior. This scale had good internal consistency (coefficient $\alpha = .80$).[3] Descriptive statistics for this scale across ages 11 to 15 and COA status are in Table 10.1, while a plot of means by age and COA status is in Figure 10.2.

FIGURE 10.2
Externalizing observed means.

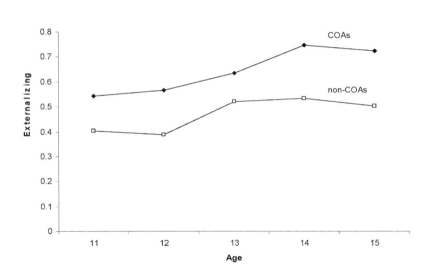

---

[1]The study actually followed a cohort-sequential design such that there were three annual measurement waves with participant age varying within a given wave. Because of the within-wave age heterogeneity, the time variable for the current analyses was age (rounded to the nearest year) instead of wave.

[2]Because of the cohort-sequential study design, not all participants were observed at each age from 11 to 15, thus necessitating the use of a data analytic method to account for this source of incomplete data.

[3]Psychometric analyses for both the externalizing and heavy drinking scales were conducted using data from the first measurement wave.

TABLE 10.1
Descriptive Statistics for Externalizing and Drinking Behavior Scales by Time and COA Status

	Full Sample			*Control*			*COA*		
	N	*M* (*SD*)	*RANGE*	*N*	*M* (*SD*)	*RANGE*	*N*	*M* (*SD*)	*RANGE*
Externalizing									
Age 11	70	0.48 (0.39)	0 - 1.42	32	0.40 (0.35)	0 - 1.42	38	0.54 (0.44)	0 - 1.33
12	150	0.48 (0.43)	0 - 2.08	69	0.38 (0.38)	0 - 1.75	81	0.57 (0.47)	0 - 2.08
13	246	0.58 (0.46)	0 - 3.17	112	0.52 (0.49)	0 - 3.17	134	0.64 (0.44)	0 - 1.92
14	271	0.65 (0.52)	0 - 2.83	125	0.53 (0.47)	0 - 2.83	146	0.75 (0.54)	0 - 2.42
15	185	0.62 (0.47)	0 - 2.25	83	0.50 (0.42)	0 - 2.00	102	0.73 (0.48)	0 - 2.25
Drinking									
Age 11	70	0.05 (0.15)	0 - 0.97	32	0.07 (0.20)	0 - 0.97	38	0.03 (0.08)	0 - 0.47
12	150	0.13 (0.37)	0 - 2.88	69	0.08 (0.21)	0 - 1.22	81	0.19 (0.46)	0 - 2.88
13	246	0.20 (0.46)	0 - 2.66	112	0.09 (0.24)	0 - 1.44	134	0.30 (0.56)	0 - 2.66
14	271	0.44 (0.87)	0 - 6.00	125	0.17 (0.34)	0 - 1.44	146	0.66 (1.10)	0 - 6.00
15	185	0.80 (1.21)	0 - 5.50	83	0.34 (0.55)	0 - 2.19	102	1.18 (1.45)	0 - 5.50

Note. Means and standard deviations are estimates using full information maximum likelihood method to adjust for incomplete data. MIN = minimum, MAX = maximum.

The dependent construct, heavy drinking behavior, was the mean of four self-report items related to alcohol consumption behavior over the past year. Items included the following: (1) "How often did you drink wine or beer?" with responses ranging from 0 = *never* to 7 = *everyday*; (2) "When you drink, about how many cans of beer or glasses of wine do you usually have?" with responses ranging from 0 to 7 = *7 to 8* and 8 = *9 or more*; (3) "How often have you had 5 or more drinks at one time?" with responses ranging from 0 = *never* to 7 = *everyday*; and (4) "How many times have you gotten drunk on alcohol?" with responses ranging from 0 = "never" to 7 = "everyday." By including items (3) and (4), this scale taps into more serious "binge" drinking behavior. The mean of items formed a scale with good internal consistency (coefficient α = .86).[4]

---

[4]Because item (2) had 9 possible responses while the other items ranged from 0 to 7, we rescaled item (2) to range from 0 to 7 before averaging responses across items.

Additionally, a confirmatory factor analysis supported the hypothesis that these four items formed a unidimensional "heavy drinking" factor. Table 10.1 gives descriptive statistics for this scale across ages 11 to 15 and COA status and Figure 10.3 contains a plot of means by age and COA status. Higher scores on the scale are indicative of greater alcohol consumption.

UNIVARIATE LATENT GROWTH MODELS

In the SEM framework for estimating LGMs (e.g., McArdle & Epstein, 1987; Meredith & Tisak, 1990; Muthén & Khoo, 1998), Willet & Sayer, 1994), a particular specification of the measurement model for the repeated measures of a given observed variable leads to the following growth model:

$$Y_i = \Lambda \eta_i + \varepsilon_i \tag{1}$$

where $\mathbf{Y}_i$ is a $T \times 1$ vector of repeated measures of the variable Y for individual i over the T time points ($t = 0,1,2,\ldots,T$), Λ is a $T \times J$ matrix of factor loadings on the growth factors, η_i is a $J \times 1$ vector of J latent factors representing the growth parameters, and ε_i is a $T \times 1$ vector of measurement errors. Factor means describe the average growth curve, and individual differences around the mean growth curve are captured in the factor variances. If the factor variances are substantial, the latent factors can be regressed on K individual background variables in a $K \times 1$ vector $\mathbf{X}_i$:

$$\eta_i = \mu_\eta + \Gamma X_i + \zeta_i \tag{2}$$

where μ_η is a $J \times 1$ vector of regression intercepts, Γ is a $J \times K$ matrix of regression coefficients, and ζ_i is a $J \times 1$ vector of residual terms.

For a basic linear LGM, there are two growth factors, namely an intercept factor, η_{1i}, and a linear slope factor, η_{2i}. In the current application, there are $T = 5$ equally spaced time-points (i.e., ages 11-15). Setting the loadings on η_{1i} as $\lambda' = (1, 1, 1, 1, 1)$ and on η_{2i} as $\lambda' = (0, 1, 2, 3, 4)$ leads to a model with η_1 representing the initial status of Y and η_2 representing the linear change over the repeated measures. Importantly, the model need not be parameterized such that η_1 represents *initial* status. For example, setting the loadings on η_{2i} as $\lambda' = (-1, 0, 1, 2, 3)$ leads to a model with η_1 representing the status of Y at the second, rather than first, time point; thus, the interpretation of η_1 depends on the centering of time. In the following examples , η_1 for externalizing represents status at age 12, while η_1 for heavy drinking represents status at age 13. These status factors are defined at different ages to allow for the prospective prediction of heavy drinking levels from externalizing levels. Additionally, this LGM framework is easily extended to include models for nonlinear growth.

FIGURE 10.3
Heavy drinking observed means.

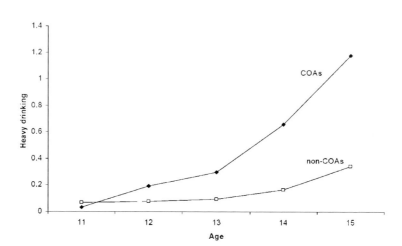

Next, we represent nonlinear growth in heavy drinking using a piecewise linear model. Figures 10.4 and 10.5 give path diagrams showing the parameterization for the externalizing and heavy drinking LGMs, respectively, conditioned on COA status.

Univariate Growth Model Results

Using the data described earlier, we fit separate unconditional LGMs to the repeated measures of externalizing (the mediator) and heavy drinking (the outcome). Table 10.2 summarizes the parameter estimates from these models. For externalizing, a linear growth model fit the data well. The mean of the latent intercept factor (parameterized to represent externalizing status at age 12) was significantly greater than zero, indicating that, on average, participants report some non-zero amount of externalizing at age 12. The variance of the intercept factor was also significant, suggesting that there is substantial variability in the amount of externalizing behavior at age 12 across participants. The mean of the latent slope factor (representing per-year change in externalizing behavior) was significantly greater than zero, meaning that, on average, participants engaged in increasing amounts of externalizing behavior as they grew older. Although the change was significant, it is noteworthy that the mean of the slope factor was only 0.05, which is a very small per-year increase given that the externalizing scale ranged from zero to a maximum possible score of four. An interesting result from this model estimation was that although there was significant vari-

FIGURE 10.4
Externalizing growth model conditioned on COA status.

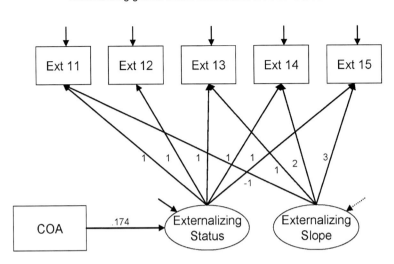

ability in the latent intercept factor, the variance of the latent slope factor was not significantly greater than zero. Thus, in all subsequent models, the externalizing slope factor neither served as a predictor nor an outcome. Consequently, we only assessed the latent intercept factor, and not the slope factor, of externalizing as a potential mediator of the relationship between COA status and growth trajectories of heavy drinking behavior.

Reflecting the nonlinear mean trend in Figure 10.2, an unconditional linear LGM would not adequately explain the functional form of the average heavy drinking growth trajectory.[5] Instead, we found that a two-piece linear model provided better fit to the data (see Table 10.2 for model fit statistics). The first linear piece captured the growth trajectory from ages 11 to 13, while the second linear piece described the growth trajectory from ages 13 to 15, with the intercept factor representing heavy drinking status at age 13. The mean intercept was small but significantly greater than zero, indicating that, on average, participants engaged in a low level of drinking behavior at age 13. Both linear slope factor means were significantly greater than zero, suggesting that participants increased their drinking across the entire age range from 11 to 15. However, reflecting the pattern in Figure 10.2, the mean of the second linear piece was much greater than that of the first piece (0.08 vs. 0.28), suggesting that, on average, participants increased their alcohol consumption at a much greater rate from ages 13 to 15 than from 11 to 13. Finally, there was significant

---

[5]Model fit for linear LGM: χ^2 (9) = 54.03, $p < .001$, RMSEA = .12 (90% CI: .09, .15)

TABLE 10.2
Unconditional Univariate Growth Models

Parameter	Mediator[a] (externalizing behavior)	Outcome[b] (drinking behavior)
Status at age 12		
M	0.517 (0.025)*	
Variance	0.104 (0.013)*	
Status at age 13		
M		0.197 (0.028)*
Variance		0.197 (0.029)*
Growth rate (age 11-15)		
M	0.045 (0.012)*	
Variance	0.005 (0.003)	
Growth rate (age 11-13)		
M		0.076 (0.016)*
Variance		0.052 (0.008)*
Growth rate (age 13-15)		
M		0.278 (0.037)*
Variance		0.197 (0.036)*

Note. $N = 355$. Standard errors in parentheses. [a]Linear growth model; $\chi^2 (9) = 14.38$, $p = .11$, RMSEA $= .04$ (90% CI: .00, .08). [b]Two-piece linear growth model; $\chi^2 (7) = 17.27$, $p = .02$, RMSEA $= .06$ (90% CI: .03, .10). $*p < .05$.

variability in the intercept and both slope factors, suggesting substantial heterogeneity across individual drinking trajectories.

Next, we fit univariate LGMs separately for both externalizing and heavy drinking conditioned on COA status. Table 10.3 summarizes the estimates from these models. For the externalizing LGM, the intercept factor was regressed on COA status, but the slope factor was not (because the variance of the slope factor was not significant in the unconditional model). Parent alcoholism was a significant predictor of externalizing status at age 12 such that the model-implied mean externalizing score for COAs was greater than that for non-COAs ($M = 0.60$ vs. $M = 0.42$). A path diagram for this model is in Figure 10.4.

For the heavy drinking LGM, the intercept factor and both slope factors in the two linear pieces were regressed on COA status. Parent alcoholism was a significant predictor of drinking status at age 13 such that COAs drank more

TABLE 10.3
Univariate Growth Models Conditioned on COA Status

Parameter estimate	Mediator[a] (externalizing)	Outcome[b] (heavy drinking)
Regression of mediator status (age 12)		
Intercept	0.421* (0.034)	
COA effect	0.174* (0.041)	
Residual variance	0.098* (0.012)	
Mediator slope (age 11-15)		
Mean	0.045* (0.011)	
Variance	0.004 (0.003)	
Regression of outcome status (age 13)		
Intercept		0.086* (0.040)
COA effect		0.205* (0.054)
Residual variance		0.172* (0.026)
Regression of outcome slope 1 (age 11-13)		
Intercept		0.008 (0.023)
COA effect		0.125* (0.031)
Residual variance		0.044* (0.008)
Regression of outcome slope 2 (age 13-15)		
Intercept		0.113* (0.052)
COA effect		0.305* (0.071)
Residual variance		0.168* (0.033)

Note. $N = 355$. Standard errors in parentheses. [a]Linear growth model; $\chi^2 (13) = 16.44$, $p = .23$, RMSEA $= .03$ (90% CI: .00, .06). [b]Two-piece linear growth model: $\chi^2 (9) = 15.82$, $p = .07$, RMSEA $= .05$ (90% CI: .00, .08). *$p < .05$.

than non-COAs ($M = 0.29$ vs. $M = 0.09$). Additionally, COAs increased their drinking from ages 11 to 13 significantly more than non-COAs (mean slope $= 0.12$ vs. $M = 0.01$) and COAs increased their drinking from ages 13 to 15 significantly more than non-COAs (mean slope $= 0.42$ vs. $M = 0.11$). This model is presented in Figure 10.5.

PARALLEL-PROCESS MODEL

The SEM framework for examining growth in a single variable can be extended to examine latent growth processes for two or more variables simultaneously in

FIGURE 10.5
Heavy drinking growth model conditioned on COA status.

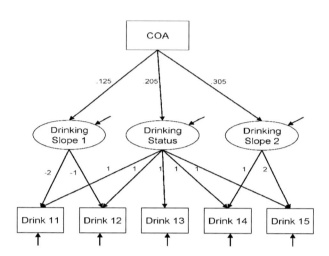

a multiple-process model, allowing estimation of the interrelationships among the growth parameters of these processes (e.g., MacCallum, Kim, Malarkey, & Kiecolt-Glaser, 1997; Willet & Sayer, 1996). Importantly, this type of model allows for the evaluation of longitudinal mediation where both the mediating process and the outcome process are modeled simultaneously. The mediator can potentially be either the status factor or the growth factor (or both) of one longitudinal process, while the outcome can be either the status factor or slope factor (or both) of a second longitudinal process. In the current analyses, the status factor of the externalizing process mediates the relationship between parent alcoholism and both the status factor and linear growth factor of the heavy drinking process.

Cheong, MacKinnon, and Khoo (2003) outlined a procedure for assessing mediation using parallel-process LGM. As we have done earlier for the externalizing and heavy drinking growth processes, initial unconditional LGMs are estimated for each process separately (i.e., one LGM for the mediating process and a second LGM for the outcome process) to establish their functional form and then these separate LGMs are conditioned on the independent variable. Next, the two conditional LGMs are specified as parallel processes in a single model. Mediation is evaluated in the structural part of this model by testing relationships among the independent variable, the growth factors of the mediating process, and the growth factors of the outcome process. See Cheong et al.(2003) for additional detail.

To examine whether externalizing at age 12 mediates the relationship between parent alcoholism and heavy drinking growth curves, we fit the parallel-process mediation model to the data. To assess the prospective prediction of heavy drinking from externalizing behavior, the intercept growth factor representing drinking status at age 13 was regressed on the intercept factor representing externalizing status at age 12, and the slope factor representing the linear change in drinking from ages 13 to 15 was also regressed on externalizing status at age 12. The relationship between the slope factor representing the linear change in drinking from ages 11 to 13 and the externalizing intercept factor was represented as a covariance because this relationship does not relate to the prospective prediction of drinking trajectories. Additionally, the heavy drinking growth factors and the externalizing intercept factor were each regressed on COA status. Mediation is then inferred from the relationship between COA status and the externalizing intercept, which in turn predicts the heavy drinking growth factors.

The estimates from this model are summarized in Table 10.4 and a path diagram is presented in Figure 10.6. First, as with the univariate model, COA status was a significant predictor of the externalizing intercept factor, such that COAs engaged in higher levels of externalizing at age 12 than non-COAs. The externalizing intercept factor was a significant predictor of the drinking intercept factor and the second linear slope factor, suggesting that higher levels of externalizing behavior at age 12 lead to both higher levels of heavy drinking behavior at age 13 and a greater increase in heavy drinking from ages 13 to 15. COA status remained a significant predictor of both drinking slope factors controlling for the externalizing intercept factor, but was not a significant predictor of the drinking intercept factor.

Because COA status predicts externalizing at age 12, which in turn predicts heavy drinking status at age 13 as well as the increase in heavy drinking from ages 13 to 15, we have preliminary evidence that externalizing mediates the relationship between parent alcoholism and heavy drinking growth trajectories. To test for the mediated effect formally, we used the first-order solution method (Sobel, 1982) to estimate the standard error of the product of the coefficient relating the risk factor (COA status) to the mediator (externalizing intercept) and the coefficients relating the mediator to the outcomes (drinking intercept and slope factors). We found that the externalizing intercept significantly mediated the relation between COA status and the drinking intercept factor, $z = 3.31$, $p < .01$, as well as the second drinking slope factor, $z = 3.10$, $p < .01$.

FIGURE 10.6
Parallel-process mediation model. Dashed lines represent non-significant paths.

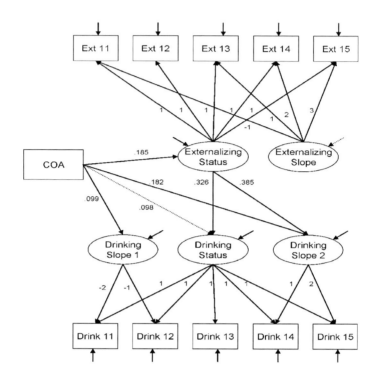

LONGITUDINAL MODERATED MEDIATION

Moderated mediation occurs when either the relationship between the independent variable and the mediator or the relationship between the mediator and outcome varies according to a moderator. In other words, the moderator interacts with the mediational process. For instance, the moderator may be a demographic variable such as gender, and moderated mediation would thus imply that the mediational process is different for male participants than for females. In longitudinal intervention studies, moderation often occurs in the context of a baseline-treatment interaction (Khoo, 2001). In this case, the baseline variable can be a potential moderator in a moderated mediation process. Next, we describe how a nonrandomized independent variable, rather than some other exogeneous variable, may itself serve as the variable moderating the relation between a hypothesized mediator and an outcome.

In experimental studies, there is random assignment of participants to the levels of the independent variable. As a consequence of this randomization, it is usually assumed that the relationship between a potential mediator and the outcome variable is equivalent across the levels of the independent variable. That is, the mediator is expected to be equally predictive of the outcome for both the treatment group and the control group. Thus, prediction of the outcome may be expressed using the following regression equation:

$$Y_i = b_0 + cX_i + b_1 M_i + \varepsilon_i \tag{3}$$

where X_i represents the independent variable and M_i represents the mediator. Here, as pictured in Figure 10.1, c is the residual direct relationship between X and Y when M is included in the model, while b_1 is equivalent to path b in Figure 10.1. In observational studies, however, the relationship between the mediator and outcome might not be constant across the levels of a non-randomized independent variable, implying that the independent variable itself may interact with, or moderate, the relationship between the mediator and the outcome. Equation 3 is then expanded to include the interaction term,

$$Y_i = b_0 + cX_i + b_1 M_i + b_2(X_i * M_i) + \varepsilon_i \tag{4}$$

where b_2 is the coefficient of the independent variable by mediator interaction representing the moderation of the relationship between the mediator and outcome as a function of the independent variable. If the independent variable X is coded as a dummy variable with values (0,1), the relationship between the mediator and outcome is equal to b_1 for $X = 0$, but equal to $(b_1 + b_2)$ for $X = 1$.

Although the methodological literature has addressed the application of mediational analysis in observational studies (e.g., Shrout & Bolger, 2002), to our knowledge, it has not yet been explicitly stated that the independent variable may moderate the relation between the proposed mediator and the outcome. We recommend that researchers conducting observational studies with mediational hypotheses test for this possible type of moderated mediation. Extending this idea to longitudinal mediation using parallel process growth models, the moderated effect is an interaction between an observed variable (i.e., the independent variable) and a latent variable (i.e., a growth factor for the mediator) in the prediction of the outcome growth process.

MULTIPLE-GROUP PARALLEL-PROCESS MODEL

When the independent variable is a discrete grouping variable, the moderated mediation already described, can be assessed using *multiple-group* SEM. In this approach, different model-implied covariance structures for each group are simultaneously estimated and nested model comparisons are used to test whet-

TABLE 10.4
Parallel-Process Growth Model

Parameter estimate	Mediator[a] (externalizing)	Outcome[b] (heavy drinking)
Regression of mediator status (age 12)		
Intercept	0.409* (0.034)	
COA effect	0.185* (0.041)	
Residual variance	0.110* (0.012)	
Mediator slope (age 11-15)		
Mean	0.049* (0.011)	
Variance	0.000[c]	
Regression of outcome status (age 13)		
Intercept		0.000[c]
COA effect		0.098 (0.052)
Mediator status effect		0.326* (0.067)
Residual variance		0.138* (0.024)
Regression of outcome slope 1 (age 11-13)		
Intercept		0.032 (0.018)
COA effect		0.099* (0.028)
Residual variance		0.039* (0.007)
Regression of outcome slope 2 (age 13-15)		
Intercept		0.000[c]
COA effect		0.182* (0.071)
Mediator status effect		0.385* (0.090)
Residual variance		0.143* (0.031)

Note. $N = 355$. Standard errors in parentheses. χ^2 (43) $= 97.07$, $p = .00$, RMSEA $= .06$ (90% CI: .04, .08). The drinking growth rate from ages 11-13 is significantly correlated with the externalizing intercept factor. [a]Linear growth model. [b]Two-piece linear growth model. Standard errors in parentheses. *$p < .05$. [c]Parameter is fixed without significant decrement to model fit.

her certain model parameters may be constrained to be equal across groups without significant decrement in model fit (see Bollen, 1989, pp. 360-361).

To evaluate longitudinal moderated mediation, we can fit a multiple-group parallel-process LGM. This model is identical to the parallel-process model described above, but with one crucial difference: Paths are not included that regress the growth factors on the independent variable; instead, the independent variable determines the groups for which separate parallel-process LGMs will be estimated. We assume that the functional forms of growth in the mediator process and the outcome process are the same across the groups defined by the independent variable (i.e., Λ is constrained to be equivalent across groups), but we allow model-implied factor means, variances, and covariances to vary across groups. In other words, the mean and variance of the mediating growth process are allowed to vary across groups, as is the regression of the outcome growth process on the mediator growth process. Thus, separate estimates of the relationship between the mediator and the outcome are obtained for the different groups defined by the independent variable; if these estimates differ across groups, there is evidence for moderated effects due to group membership.

To examine moderated mediation using the current data, we tested a two-group parallel-process LGM. The relationship between COA status and the externalizing status at age 12 was determined by testing whether the mean of

FIGURE 10.7
Two-group parallel-process mediation model.

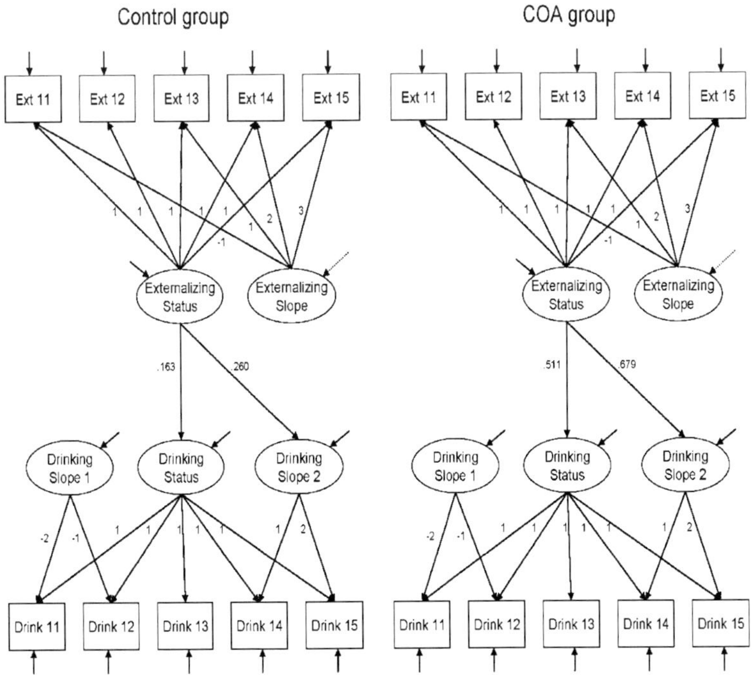

the externalizing intercept factor significantly differs for COAs compared to non-COAs. Next, we tested the regressions of the heavy drinking growth factors on the externalizing intercept factor to observe the relationship between the mediating process and outcome process across the two groups. If these regressions varied significantly across the two groups defined by COA status, there was evidence that parent alcoholism interacts with, or moderates, the relationship between the externalizing intercept factor and the heavy drinking growth factors.

Table 10.5 summarizes the results estimates from this model, and the corresponding path diagram is presented in Figure 10.7. Again, as was found in the one-group model, externalizing status at age 12 was a significant predictor of both drinking status at age 13 and the change in drinking from ages 13 to 15. However, both of these relationships were much stronger in the COA group than in the non-COA group, a finding that cannot be inferred from the one-group model described before. By imposing equality constraints on the regression coefficients across groups and testing the impact on model fit using nested χ^2tests, we tested whether COA status significantly moderates the relation between the externalizing intercept factor and drinking growth trajectories. First, we constrained the relation between the externalizing intercept factor and the drinking intercept factor to be equal across groups. Relative to our final model in Table 10.5, this constraint led to a significant decrement in overall model fit, χ^2 (1) $= 20.98$, $p < .01$, showing that the relationship between externalizing status at age 12 and drinking status at age 13 significantly differs across the COA and non-COA groups. Next, we constrained the relation between the externalizing intercept factor and the second drinking slope factor to be equal across groups. This constraint also led to a significant decrement in model fit relative to the final model, χ^2 (1) $= 4.42$, $p < .05$. Thus, the relationship between externalizing at age 12 and the change in heavy drinking from ages 13 to 15 also significantly differs across groups.

Additionally, we constrained the mean externalizing intercept factor to be equal across groups. This constraint led to a significant decrement in model fit, χ^2 (1) $= 18.11$, $p < .01$, showing that externalizing status at age 12 significantly differs across the COA and non-COA groups, an effect also found with the one-group model. Thus, with the two-group model formulation, we can infer that externalizing mediates the relation between parent alcoholism and drinking trajectories by noting that COA status predicts a significantly greater mean externalizing intercept factor, which in turn predicts a greater mean drinking status at age 13 as well as a greater mean increase in drinking from ages 13 to 15. However, unlike the one-group model, the two-group model reveals that the relationship between externalizing and heavy alcohol consumption is greater for COAs than for non-COAs.

DISCUSSIONS

The primary purpose of this chapter has been to illustrate the use of multiple-group parallel process LGM for assessing longitudinal moderated mediation. In the analyses presented earlier, we first presented evidence that externalizing behavior mediated the relationship between parental alcoholism and the longitudinal course of heavy drinking during early adolescence. This analysis applied the methods outlined by Cheong et al. (2003) using parallel-process LGM for examining longitudinal mediation. However, given that COA status is a preexisting risk factor rather than a randomized independent variable, we suggested that COA status itself could moderate the relationship between the mediating construct, the externalizing intercept factor, and the outcome, the heavy drinking status and slope factors. We then used a two-group parallel-process LGM to examine this possible type of longitudinal moderated mediation. Because the relationships between the externalizing intercept factor and the heavy drinking status and slope factors significantly varied as a function of COA status, we concluded that there was in
fact evidence for moderated mediation. This analysis differs from other analyses of moderated mediation in that COA status is both the independent variable and the moderator.

Substantively, the findings reported here also have implications for understanding the developmental context of COAs. First, consistent with previous research and the deviance proneness hypothesis, the results showed that COAs had elevated levels of externalizing symptoms during early adolescence relative to non-COAs. Additionally, the results echoed previous findings that adolescent COAs escalate heavy alcohol involvement at a much faster rate than do non-COAs, especially after age 13. Most importantly, the results from the moderated mediation analyses showed that this escalation into heavy drinking among COAs is at least partially predicted from their increased levels of externalizing and that externalizing is more strongly predictive of heavy drinking for COAs than for controls. As mentioned above, however, externalizing behavior is only one of a multitude of contextual variables that is hypothesized to contribute to heavy alcohol involvement. Here, we have presented data pertinent to only a small portion of the complex nature of parental alcoholism as an adverse developmental context. For example, given the large literature linking impaired parenting and elevated family conflict to children's externalizing behaviors, it is likely that the negative impact of parental alcoholism on parenting and on family harmony also contributes to these pathways (Chassin et al., 2004; Sher, 1991).

TABLE 10.5
Two-Group Parallel-Process Model

Parameter estimate	Mediator[a] (externalizing)		Outcome[b] (heavy drinking)	
	Control	COA	Control	COA
Mediator status (age 12)				
Mean	0.425*(0.033)	0.600*(0.032)		
Variance[d]	0.108*(0.011)	0.108*(0.011)		
Mediator slope (age 11-15)				
Mean[d]	0.042*(0.011)	0.042*(0.011)		
Variance	0.000[c]	0.000[c]		
Regression of outcome status (age 13)				
Intercept			0.000[c]	0.000[c]
Mediator status effect			0.163* (0.034)	0.511* (0.067)
Residual variance			0.037* (0.009)	0.140* (0.046)
Outcome slope 1 (age 11-13)				
Mean			0.000[c]	0.140* (0.020)
Variance			0.001 (0.006)	0.034* (0.013)
Regression of outcome slope 2 (age 13-15)				
Intercept			0.000[c]	0.000[c]
Externalizing effect			0.260* (0.053)	0.679* (0.091)
Residual variance			0.035* (0.009)	0.227* (0.069)

Note. $N = 355$. Standard errors in parentheses. χ^2 (76) = 151.74, $p = .00$, RMSEA = .08 (90% CI: .06, .09). The drinking growth rate from ages 11-13 is significantly correlated with the externalizing intercept factor in the COA group but not in the control group. [a]Linear growth model, [b]Two-piece linear growth model, [c]Parameter is fixed without significant decrement to model fit. [d]Parameter is constrained to equality across groups without significant decrement to model fit. *$p < .05$.

This multiple-group method for testing moderated mediation is of course limited to situations where the independent variable is a grouping variable with a small number of discrete categories, such as a variable representing membership in an at-risk group versus a normative control group. However, in other applications, the independent variable in a mediation analysis may not have a small number of discrete categories. For example, rather than using an independent variable comparing COAs to non-COAs as earlier, studies of the mediating mechanisms underlying the intergenerational transmission of alcoholism might instead investigate the effects of a "family history density of alcoholism" variable (e.g., Stoltenberg, Mudd, Blow, & Hill, 1998). This type of independent variable represents a weighted average of the number of first and second degree relatives with alcohol disorder diagnoses, and as such may be considered a continuous independent variable.

To test whether a continuous independent variable moderates the relationship between a mediating growth process and an outcome growth process in the context of parallel-process LGM, it is necessary to use alternative methods for estimating the effects of an observed by latent variable interaction (because the continuous independent variable is observed but the mediator is a latent growth factor). One possibility is to use the "latent moderated structural equations" (LMS) approach by Klein and Moosbrugger (2000). Another possibility is to estimate a discrete latent class variable from the continuous independent variable, and then test whether the relationships among the outcome growth process and the mediating growth process differ as a function of latent class membership (e.g., Muthén, 2002). Additional research is needed to examine the practical feasibility of these techniques.

As mentioned earlier, research hypotheses often imply that mediational processes unfold over time, and longitudinal data enhances the ability to present evidence toward the plausibility of the causal nature of relationships within a mediational chain. In fact, Cole and Maxwell (2003) showed that when mediational relationships hold longitudinally, analyses only using cross-sectional data are likely to produce inaccurate estimates of true, longitudinal mediated effects. Furthermore, even when the independent variable, mediator, and outcome are measured in proper longitudinal sequence, the power to detect the true mediating effect is directly affected by the amount of time that elapses between these measurements, contingent on the amount of time needed for the true causal process to occur (Cole & Maxwell, 2003; Shrout & Bolger, 2002). If multiple repeated measures of the mediator and outcome are collected, the researcher can enhance the likelihood of observing them within the optimal time-frame for detecting the true mediational effect. The use of LGM on multiple repeated measures of the mediator and outcome could potentially overcome this difficulty, although a thorough demonstration of this possibility is beyond the scope of this chapter. Specifically, growth curve models use observed, discrete repeated measures to infer a continuous, latent growth process that can span the points in time during which mediational effects occur, even if these points are not directly observed. However, it is crucial to specify the proper functional form (e.g., linear vs. nonlinear) of the latent growth process for this benefit to be present.

CONCLUSIONS

In sum, we have shown that the SEM framework for latent growth modeling is a highly flexible method for examining mediational hypotheses when both the mediating construct and the outcome are measured longitudinally. With this type of analysis, mediational hypotheses are examined by testing relationships among latent growth factors, thus allowing inferences about rates of *change* in addition to inferences about static mean levels at a given point in time. Furthermore, we described how a nonrandomized, discrete independent variable could potentially moderate the relationship between a mediator and an outcome. We then demonstrated how this potential source of moderated mediation can be examined using multiple-group parallel-process latent growth modeling. We concluded with a discussion of potential directions for future methodological research.

ACKNOWLEDGMENTS

This work was partly supported by a grant from the National Institute of Drug Abuse (DA05227 to Laurie Chassin).

REFERENCES

Achenbach, T. M. (1978). The child behavior profile: I. boys 6-11. *Journal of Consulting and Clinical Psychology, 47*, 223-233.

Arbuckle, J. (1996). Full information estimation in the presence of incomplete data. In G. Marcoulides & R. Schumacker (Eds.), *Advanced structural equation modeling: Issues and techniques* (pp. 243-277). Hillsdale, NJ: Lawrence Erlbaum Associates.

Baron, R. M., & Kenny, D. A. (1986). The moderator-mediator variable distinction in social psychological research: Conceptual, strategic, and statistical considerations. *Journal of Personality and Social Psychology, 51*, 1173-1182.

Bollen, K. A. (1989). *Structural equations with latent variables.* New York: Wiley.

Chassin, L., Barrera, M., Bech, K., & Kossak-Fuller, J. (1986). Recruiting a community sample of adolescent children of alcoholics: A comparison of three subject sources. *Journal of Studies on Alcohol, 53*, 316-320.

Chassin, L., Barrera, M., & Montgomery, H. (1997). Parent alcoholism as a risk factor. In S. Wolchik & I. Sandler (Eds.), *Handbook of children's coping* (pp. 101-130). New York: Plenum.

Chassin, L., Carle, A., Nissim-Sabat, D., & Kumpfer, K. L. (2004). Fostering resilience for children of alcoholic parents. In K. Maton, C. Schellenbach, B. Leadbeater, & A. Solarz (Eds.), *Investing in children, youth, families, and communities: Strengths-based research and policy* (pp. 137-156). Washington, DC: American Psychological Association.

Chassin, L., Pitts, S. C., & Prost, J. (2002). Binge drinking trajectories from adolescence to emerging adulthood in a high-risk sample: Predictors and substance use outcomes. *Journal of Consulting and Clinical Psychology, 70*, 67-78.

Chassin, L., Rogosch, F., & Barrera, M. (1991). Substance use and symptomatology among adolescent children of alcoholics. *Journal of Abnormal Psychology, 100*, 449-463.

Cheong, J., MacKinnon, D. P., & Khoo, S. T. (2003). Investigation of mediation processes using parallel process latent growth curve modeling. *Structural Equation Modeling, 10*, 238-262.

Colder, C. R., Chassin, L., Stice, E. M., & Curran, P. J. (1997). Alcohol expectancies as potential mediators of parent alcoholism eects on the development of adolescent heavy drinking. *Journal of Research on Adolescence, 7*, 349-374.

Cole, D. A., & Maxwell, S. E. (2003). Testing mediational models with longitudinal data: Questions and tips in the use of structural equation modeling. *Journal of Abnormal Psychology, 112*, 558-577.

Conger, R. D., Elder, G. H., Jr, Lorenz, F. O., Conger, K. J., Simons, R. L., & Whitbeck, L. B., et al. (1990). Linking economic hardship to marital quality and instability. *Journal of Marriage and the Family, 52*, 643-656.

Frazier, P. A., Tix, A. P., & Barron, K. E. (2004). Testing moderator and mediator effects in counseling psychology research. *Journal of Counseling Psychology, 51*, 115-134.

Holmbeck, G. N. (1997). Toward terminological, conceptual, and statistical clarity in the study of mediators and moderators: Examples from the child-clinical and pediatric psychology literatures. *Journal of Consulting and Clinical Psychology, 65*, 599-610.

James, L. R., & Brett, J. M. (1984). Mediators, moderators, and tests for mediation. *Journal of Applied Psychology, 69*, 307-321.

Jessor, R., & Jessor, S. K. (1977). *Problem behavior and psychosocial development: A longitudinal study of youth.* New York: Plenum Press.

Judd, C. M., & Kenny, D. A. (1981). Process analysis: Estimating mediation in treatment evaluations. *Evaluation Review, 5*, 602-619.

Kenny, D. A., Kashy, D. A., & Bolger, N. (1998). Data analysis in social psychology. In D. Gilbert, S. T. Fiske, & G. Lindzey (Eds.), *Handbook of social psychology* (4th ed., Vol. 1, pp. 233-265). New York: McGraw-Hill.

Khoo, S. T. (2001). Assessing program effects in the presence of treatment baseline interactions: A latent curve approach. *Psychological Methods, 6*, 234-257.

Klein, A., & Moosbrugger, H. (2000). Maximum likelihood estimation of latent interaction effects with the lms method. *Psychometrika, 65*, 457-474.

MacCallum, R. C., Kim, C., Malarkey, W. B., & Kiecolt-Glaser, J. K. (1997). Studying multivariate change using multilevel models and latent curve models. *Multivariate Behavioral Research, 32*, 215-253.

MacKinnon, D. P., & Dwyer, J. H. (1993). Estimating mediated effects in prevention studies. *Evaluation Review, 17*, 144-158.

MacKinnon, D. P., Lockwood, C. M., Hoffman, J. M., West, S. G., & Sheets, V. (2002). A comparison of methods to test mediation and other intervening variable effects. *Psychological Methods, 7*, 83-104.

McArdle, J. J., & Epstein, D. B. (1987). Latent growth curves within developmental structural equation models. *Child Development, 58*, 110-133.

Meredith, W., & Tisak, J. (1990). Latent curve analysis. *Psychometrika, 55*, 107-122.

Muthén, B. (2002). Beyond sem: General latent variable modeling. *Behaviormetrika, 29*, 81-117.

Muthén, B., & Khoo, S. T. (1998). Longitudinal studies of achievement growth using latent variable modeling. *Learning and Individual Differences, 10*, 73-101.

Muthén, L. K., & Muthén, B. O. (2004). *Mplus user's guide* (3rd ed.). Los Angeles: Muthén & Muthén.

Pearl, J. (2000). *Causality: Models, reasoning, and inference.* Cambridge, England: Cambridge University Press.

Sher, K. J. (1991). *Children of alcoholics: A critical appraisal of theory and research.* Chicago: University of Chicago Press.

Shrout, P. E., & Bolger, N. B. (2002). Mediation in experimental and non-experimental studies: New procedures and recommendations. *Psychological Methods, 7*, 422-445.

Stoltenberg, S., Mudd, S., Blow, F., & Hill, E. (1998). Evaluating measures of family history of alcoholism: Density versus dichotomy. *Addiction, 8*, 1511-1520.

Willet, J. B., & Sayer, A. G. (1994). Using covariance structure analysis to detect correlates and predictors of individual change over time. *Psychological Bulletin, 116*, 363-381.

Willet, J. B., & Sayer, A. G. (1996). Cross-domain analyses of change over time: Combining growth modeling and covariance structure analysis. In G. Marcoulides & R. Schumacker (Eds.), *Advanced structural equation modeling techniques.* Hillsdale, NJ: Lawrence Erlbaum Associates.

CHAPTER ELEVEN

Modeling Complex Interactions: Person-Centered and Variable-Centered Approaches

Daniel J. Bauer

University of North Carolina at Chapel Hill

Michael J. Shanahan

University of North Carolina at Chapel Hill

In recent decades the developmental systems perspective has grown increasingly influential in the behavioral sciences. Richard Lerner (1998) observed that this perspective is actually a metatheory because it emphasizes several themes that are common to many conceptual models of human development, including the ecological theory (Bronfenbrenner & Morris, 1998), probabilistic epigenesis (Gottlieb, Wahlsten, & Lickliter, 1998), life course sociology (Elder, 1998), and the holistic-interactionist paradigm (Magnusson & Stattin, 1998). One such theme is that a developmental system is comprised of multiple levels (e.g., biological, psychological, sociological, and cultural) that are "inextricably fused" to create a functioning holism. Furthermore, this fusion reflects high levels of interactions both within and between levels of the system (see Gariépy, 1995; Sameroff, 1983; Shanahan, Valsiner, & Gottlieb, 1997). The methodological challenge this perspective presents is the need to capture potentially nonlinear interactions among many variables. It is this challenge that motivates the present work.

In a developmental systems framework, the problem takes several forms, including person–person, context–context, and person–context interactions. Person–person interactions occur among and between, for example, psychological and biological levels of analysis (e.g., Bergman, Magnusson, & El-Khouri, 2003). Person–context interactions refer to the contingent effects of characteristics of the person and contextual factors, and are especially prominent in models of person–environment fit (e.g., Eccles & Midgley, 1989). Far less frequently considered are context–context interactions, whereby two or more contextual factors have nonadditive effects on behavior (Shanahan & Hofer, 2005). In theory, such interactions are pervasive and detecting and understanding them is central to empirical research on behavioral development.

Many proponents of the systems perspective have relied on traditional linear models to test hypotheses concerning interaction. However, other scholars, notably David Magnusson and Robert Cairns, have asserted that there is a fundamental mismatch between the holism emphasized by contemporary developmental theory and linear models (e.g., Bergman & Magnusson, 1997; Cairns & Rodkin, 1998; Magnusson & Cairns, 1996; Magnusson, 1998; see also Richters, 1997). Specifically, general and generalized linear models (e.g., multiple regression, logistic regression, or structural equation modeling) typically involve the estimation of a main effect for each variable in the model controlling for (or holding constant) the other variables. This atomistic focus on individual variables is inconsistent with the interactionist principle that no variables have "unique" effects divorced from other relevant operating factors. Put simply, such models are "variable-centered," potentially failing to capture the configurations of factors that jointly explain behavioral processes.

As an alternative, Bergman and Magnusson (1997) advocated the use of "person-centered analyses" that identify key patterns of values across variables, where the person, viewed holistically, is the unit of analysis.[1] Implicit in their argument is that only methods that identify configurations of variables — quite typically, cluster analyses, but also latent class analysis, mixture models and similar techniques — are capable of appreciating the high level of interaction and nonlinear relationships that are likely to characterize developmental systems. These techniques result in the identification of a small set of clusters or classes that then supplant the individual variables as predictors or outcomes in subsequent data analysis. The assumption is that the complex dynamics of the system of variables, including possible nonlinear effects and interactions, have been preserved in the configurations.

Methodologists have countered that the practice of rendering continuous variables into a few discrete categories may actually hinder the identification of true nonlinear and or interactive effects. In a recent review of the methodological literature on this topic, MacCallum, Zhang, Preacher, and Rucker (2002) admonished that the categorization of continuous variables often obscures or attenuates true effects and can even sometimes produce spurious effects. Method-

---

[1]The term *person-centered* emanates from a focus on intraindividual functioning and is perhaps ill chosen, as the operating factors of interest may lie both within the person and their context.

ological studies of categorization have generally focused on relatively simple cases, such as bivariate linear and nonlinear relationships, and the treatment of two-way interactions in regression/ANOVA models (e.g., Cohen, 1983; Humphreys, 1978; Maxwell & Delaney, 1990). Even for complex models involving many variables with potentially nonlinear interactions, however, MacCallum, Zhang, Preacher, and Rucker (2002) state

> We have repeatedly encountered the argument that dichotomization is useful so as to allow the testing of interactions . . . In fact, it is straightforward to incorporate and test interactions in regression models, and such an approach would avoid . . . biased measures of effects size and spurious significant effects. Furthermore, regression models can easily incorporate higher way interactions as well as interactions of a form other than linear × linear . . . (p. 32)

Later, commenting specifically on the use of cluster analysis and related methods to capture complex relationships, MacCallum, Zhang, Preacher, and Rucker (2002) summarize the views of many methodologists, stating that the classifications obtained by such methods "do not provide any insight about variables of interest nor about relationships of those variables to others. Basing analyses and interpretation on such arbitrary groups is probably an oversimplification and potentially misleading (p. 34)." Thus, the methodological literature appears to stand in opposition to the assertions of person-centered theoreticians.[2]

The current chapter aims to bring some additional clarity and insight to this dialogue between theoreticians and methodologists. Namely, we provide a direct comparison between person-centered and variable-centered approaches to capturing interactive effects in realistically complex data. To our knowledge, this comparison is the first of its kind. Whereas advocates of the person-centered approach have often asserted that configurations and clusters capture nonlinear effects and interactions in a more optimal and interpretable way than traditional linear models, they have neither demonstrated how person-centered methods capture these effects nor have they compared these methods with linear models containing higher order terms. Likewise, advocates of variable-centered approaches for studying nonlinear and/or interactive effects have generally re-

---

[2]In contrast, MacCallum, Zhang, Preacher, and Rucker (2002) suggest that clustering may be justified if the aim is to recover qualitatively distinct groups of individuals, but they also note that the existence of such groups can be difficult to establish empirically, a view we share (Bauer & Curran, 2003a, 2004). Here, however, we are concerned only with the use of clusters to recover interactions, leaving aside for the moment the issue of whether the clusters really represent 'true groups.'

stricted their analyses to patterns of effects among a few variables that can readily be modeled and interpreted with polynomial and product terms. Furthermore, they have primarily considered relatively poor classification methods when studying the detrimental effects of categorization (e.g., median/mean splits or the creation of extreme groups). In this chapter, we use a realistically complex case study to compare person-centered and variable-centered approaches to recovering interactions that involve many variables.

We first introduce the empirical example that will serve as the basis for our case study. We then analyze these data using a traditional variable-centered model, first modeling only main effects, and then modeling the possible interactions that may be present. We follow with an analysis of the same data using a person-centered approach, namely a probabilistic clustering model known as latent profile analysis (LPA). Next, we draw on and extend recent analytical work by Bauer (2005) to provide a direct comparison of the results of the two fitted models. Our conclusions focus on the advantages and disadvantages of each approach as well as important directions for future research.

EMPIRICAL EXAMPLE

The data for the empirical example are artificial, but are loosely based on results presented by Cairns, Cairns, and Neckerman (1989). The focus of the original study was to identify configurations of variables representing social competencies, age and maturation, and socioeconomic status among students in Grade 7 that might differentially predict school dropout by Grade 11. We have simplified matters by basing our example on the results presented for male participants for the four dimensions of the Interpersonal Competence Scale (ICS): aggression, popularity, academic competence, and 'all-American' (reflecting sports, looks, dominance).

Data for the four ICS variables and the dichotomous dropout variable were generated with as much fidelity as possible to the actual characteristics of the data reported by Cairns, Cairns, and Neckerman (1989).[3] There were, however, two aspects of the simulated data that differed from the original data. First, we generated data for 2000 cases, whereas only 213 male subjects were originally studied. We chose this sample size to ensure the stability of our results and because we were not interested in studying sampling variability with replicate samples of smaller size. This does not preclude the application of similar mod-

---

[3]Details on the data generation are available from the first author upon request. We do not provide this information here for two reasons. First, we wish to keep the level of technical detail to a minimum. Second, we wish to retain a high degree of verisimilitude to real empirical research where the population-generating model is not known.

els with smaller samples. Second, the ICS variables were simulated to be on a standardized scale, whereas the original metric was 1 to 7. Standardization facilitates both variable-centered and person-centered analyses. (In the former case, variables are commonly standardized prior to forming product terms to improve the interpretation of main effects and reduce multicollinearity; see Aiken & West, 1991, and Jaccard, Turrisi, & Wan, 1990. In the latter case, standardization facilitates interpretation of cluster profiles — zero is the grand mean against which cluster means on specific variables can be judged as high or low.)

Throughout the remainder of the chapter we reference the artificially generated ICS data by the same variable labels that were used by Cairns, Cairns, and Neckerman (1989) to enhance the realism and intuitiveness of the results. Consistent with the original study, our analyses focus on the prediction of dropout by the four ICS variables using both variable- and person centered approaches. We caution, however, that the results we report are from the simulated data only and have the sole purpose of providing a realistically complex example for comparing between person-centered and variable-centered approaches. No substantive implications should be drawn from the results presented here, as it is unclear whether the same results would be obtained from the actual data of Cairns and his colleagues.

A VARIABLE-CENTERED APPROACH

We first fit a logistic regression model to predict dropout (1 = dropped out of school by Grade 11; 0 = otherwise) as a function of the four continuous ICS variables. We begin by describing the logistic regression model in general terms, and then proceed to describe the results obtained by fitting logistic regressions with and without interaction terms to the ICS data.

The Logistic Regression Model

In general, if the probability of occurrence of the outcome (e.g., dropout) for individual i is designated τ_i, then the logistic regression model can be written as

$$\ln\left(\frac{\tau_i}{1-\tau_i}\right) = \alpha + \boldsymbol{\beta}' \boldsymbol{x}_i. \tag{1}$$

where the log of the odds (ratio of the probability of the outcome to its complement), or logit, is assumed to be a linear function of the predictors within the vector $\mathbf{x}_i$. The intercept of the regression of the logit on $\mathbf{x}_i$ is designated

α and the regression coefficients are contained in the vector $\boldsymbol{\beta}$. Exponentiation of these coefficients gives the odds-ratios for the predictors. The predicted probability of the event is then given by

$$\tau_i = \frac{1}{1 + e^{-(\alpha + \boldsymbol{\beta}' \boldsymbol{x}_i)}}. \tag{2}$$

Thus the model assumes that the predictors relate linearly to the logit, but that they are nonlinearly related to the actual probability of the outcome occurring.

Following conventional practice for linear models, interactions are estimated in the logistic regression model through the formation of product terms. For instance, to asses an interaction between x_1 and x_2, the product term $x_1 \times x_2$ would be added to the model. The significance of a two-variable product term, net the main effects, is taken as evidence of a bilinear interaction between two variables (Cohen, 1978), indicating that the effect of one variable on the log-odds changes linearly with the value of the other. Similar interpretations obtain for still higher order interactions involving three or more variables (e.g., for a three-way interaction, the magnitude of the bilinear interaction between two variables is a linear function of a third variable). Interactions that are not linear in form can potentially be modeled through the creation of linear $\times$ quadratic product terms (e.g., $x_1 \times x_2^2$, although this is rarely done in practice. Given the partialling of lower and higher order terms (e.g., main effects and interactions) that takes place in the estimation of interactions, it is sometimes difficult to interpret the individual coefficients. Plotting the relations implied by the model can aid in this endeavor. The most frequently used approach is to compute and graph 'simple slopes' indicating the effect of one predictor on the criterion at certain selected levels of the moderating variables (see Aiken & West, 1991; Jaccard, Turrisi, & Wan, 1990).

Logistic Regression Modeling Results

The results of the initial logistic regression model, including only the main effects of the four ICS variables, are presented in Panel A of Table 11.1. The estimated odds-ratio for aggression indicated that with each standard deviation increase in aggression the odds of an individual dropping out of school increased by a factor of 1.75. In addition, with each standard deviation increase in academic competence the odds of dropping out decreased 1.72 times.(the reciprocal of .58). The effects of the popularity and all-American variables were nonsignificant. Note that the focus of these interpretations is on the unique effect of each variable, not on configurations of values across variables. For this reason, advocates of the person-centered approach have roundly criticized

TABLE 11.1
Results of Logistic Regression Models Excluding and Including Product Interaction Terms (effects
that are statistically significant at the .05 level are listed in bold)

Variable	Coefficient(β)	se$_\beta$	Odds-Ratio[a]
Panel A. Main Effects Model (-2*Log-Likelihood = 1631)			
Intercept	**-1.86**	.074	
Agg	**.56**	.067	**1.75**
Pop	.05	.070	1.06
Acad	**-.54**	.068	**.58**
	-.13	.070	.88
Panel B. Interaction Model (-2*Log-Likelihood = 1604)			
Intercept	**-1.83**	.078	
Agg	**-.58**	.077	
Pop	-.12	.096	
Acad	**-.54**	.080	
Amer	**-.26**	.088	
Agg × Pop	.06	.092	
Agg × Acad	-.03	.07	
Agg × Amer	.11	.088	
Pop × Acad	.20	.102	
Pop × Amer	**-.20**	.074	
Acad × Amer	.09	.086	
Agg × Pop × Acad	-.03	.099	
Agg × Pop × Amer	-.09	.064	
Agg × Acad × Amer	**-.17**	.083	
Pop × Acad × Amer	-.01	.081	
Agg × Pop × Acad × Amer	-.04	.068	

Note. Agg = Aggression; Pop = Popularity;

Acad = Academic Competence; Amer = All-American.

traditional modeling approaches as being insensitive to the hypothesized complexity of developmental systems.

In an effort to address such criticisms, our second logistic regression model included all possible product interactions between the four ICS predictors, including 6 two-way interaction terms, 4 three-way interaction terms, and 1 four-way interaction term. The addition of these terms resulted in a modest improvement in fit relative to the model containing only main effects, $\mathcal{X}^2(11) = 27$, $p < .05$. As shown in Panel B of Table 11.1, for this model, statistically significant effects included both the two-way interaction between popularity and all-American and the three-way interaction between aggression, academics, and all-American. In the absence of any further analysis, these interactions are rather difficult to interpret, given the parsing of lower and higher order effects. Following standard practice, however, we computed 'simple slopes' in an effort

FIGURE 11.1
Results of the logistic regression model for popularity.

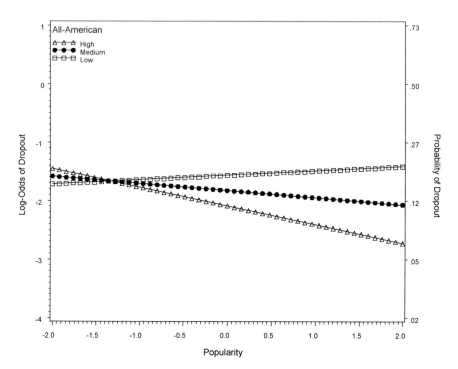

Note. The logg-odds and predicted probability of school dropout by the 11th grade as a function of 7th grade popularity at high, medium, and low levels of 7th grade all-American attributes.

to combine these estimates into a coherent picture of how the ICS variables interact to predict dropout.

We first consider the two-way interaction between popularity and all-American. Figure 11.1 plots simple slopes showing the effects of popularity on the log-odds and predicted probability of dropout at high, medium, and low levels of all-American (set at one standard deviation above the mean, the mean, and one standard deviation below the mean, respectively), holding aggression and academic competence at the mean. Figure 11.1 clarifies the assumptions of the model: First, that the log-odds of dropout are linearly related to popularity and, second, that the effect of popularity changes linearly with the level of all-American (i.e., that there is a bilinear interaction effect). The latter assumption is reflected in the symmetry of the regression lines for high and low all-American relative to the line plotted at the mean of all-American.

FIGURE 11.2
Results of the logistic regression model for aggression.

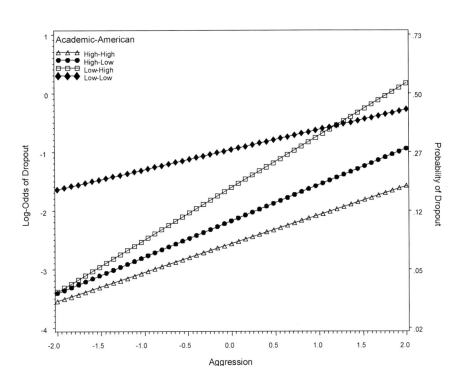

Note. The log-odds and predicted probability of school dropout by the 11th grade as a function of 7th grade aggression for specific combinations of high and low levels of 7th grade academic competence and all-American attributes.

To facilitate interpretation of these results, the scale on the right side of the figure translates the predicted log-odds into predicted probabilities of dropout via the nonlinear relation in Equation 2. As can be seen, the interaction indicates that popularity can reduce the risk of dropout, but only if paired with medium to high levels of all-American. That is, adolescents who are popular with peers and also good looking, confident, and athletic are less likely to drop out than those who are unpopular with peers. In contrast, for adolescents who do not possess these all-American attributes, popularity has little effect on the probability of dropout.

We now turn to the interpretation of the three-way interaction between aggression, academic and all-American. Figure 11.2 plots the effect of aggression on both the log-odds and predicted probability of dropout at high and low levels of academic and all-American, defined as one standard deviation above and below the mean, respectively, holding popularity constant at the mean. These values are plotted on the same scale as Figure 11.1, making immediately apparent the larger magnitude of the effects displayed in Figure 11.2. The strong main effect of aggression is clearly visible: higher levels of aggression are associated with higher levels of dropout, regardless of which values of academic and all-American are exhibited. Academic competence and all-American attributes serve as protective factors in this relationship: Youth who are aggressive but also high on these other two scales show a less pronounced probability of dropout than youth who are low in one or both of the academic and all-American scales. There is also an interesting crossover between the lines for low–low and low–high values of academics and all-American. For low to moderate levels of aggression, we see that being low in both academic competence and all-American attributes places an adolescent at greatest risk for dropout. However, for particularly aggressive youth, this trend reverses: For those who are low in academics, being high in all-American attributes actually *increases* the risk of dropping out.

Overall, Figures 11.1 and 11.2 indicate that all-American, which was not a significant main effect predictor in the first analysis, actually plays a complex interactive role with the other ICS variables in predicting dropout. Moreover, using a variable-centered model, we were able to consider how specific configurations of variables influenced the probability of dropout through the plotting of simple slopes for significant interactions. These results are consistent with the contention, prominent among methodologists, that variable-centered models can recover complex interactive patterns through the use of product terms. Furthermore, this approach has the advantage that the continuous nature of the data is preserved.

The results also provide support for the critics of the variable-centered approach, who maintain that the parsing of lower and higher order effects make holistic interpretations of the results difficult: Even with the plotting of simple slopes, each interaction must be considered separately. We now turn to a person-centered analysis of the same data as an alternative way to capture the relations between configurations of ICS variables and school dropout.

A PERSON-CENTERED APPROACH

As previously noted, the person-centered approach involves the identification of key configurations of values across a set of operating factors. In practice, these patterns are often identified through heuristic cluster analytic techniques, including partitioning algorithms like k-means and hierarchical or agglomerative clustering algorithms. Alternatively, finite mixture models like latent profile analysis and latent class analysis provide model-based approaches to pattern detection. Model-based clustering methods are distinguished from heuristic clustering algorithms in that they involve an explicit underlying statistical model. Due to the probabilistic basis of the models, a sample need not be partitioned into disjoint sets, but rather clusters may be overlapping and individuals can have non-zero probabilities of belonging to several clusters (i.e., cluster membership is 'fuzzy'). Given these important advantages of a model-based approach, we next conducted a latent profile analysis of the ICS data. As before, we begin with a general description of the model and then proceed to discuss the results obtained by conducting a LPA with the ICS data.

The Latent Profile Analysis Model

Latent profile analysis (LPA) was developed by Gibson (1959) as a continuous variable analog to traditional latent class analysis for binary variables. LPA can also be motivated from classical test theory. According to classical test theory, the observed scores for each individual are assumed to reflect both 'true scores' on the characteristics of interest as well as random error due to imperfections of measurement or momentary disturbances. Individuals are defined as representing a homogeneous cluster or *latent class* if they share a common set of true scores. The model for the observed scores can then be written as

$$x_i = \xi_k + \delta_i \tag{3}$$

where x_i is the vector of observed scores for individual i, ξ_k is the vector of latent true scores characterizing *all* individuals within latent class k, and δ_i is the vector of errors or disturbances. These random errors are assumed to be uncorrelated across both variables and persons, and to be normally distributed with expected values of zero. Under these assumptions, within each class, x_i is multivariate normally distributed with class mean vector equal to ξ_k and class covariance matrix equal to Δ_k, a diagonal matrix of within-class error variances for δ_i. The probability density function (PDF) for class k can then be designated $\phi_k(x_i; \xi_k, \Delta_k)$.

When individuals from many classes are mixed together in the population, then the aggregate density function for the population can be described as a weighted sum or mixture of the within-class PDFs:

$$f(x_i) = \sum_{k=1}^{K} \pi_k \phi_k(x_i; \xi_k, \Delta_k) \tag{4}$$

where K is the total number of classes in the model and π_k is probability that an individual case would be drawn at random from class k, also interpretable as the proportion of cases in the population belonging to class k.

Most methods of estimation for LPA, such as maximum likelihood, do not allow the number of classes K to be estimated directly from data.[4] In practice, the investigator instead fits a sequence of models with increasingly more classes until some stopping criterion is reached. The most common such criterion is to select the model with the minimum Bayesian Information Criterion (BIC), a measure that balances the ability of the model to reproduce the data against the parsimony of the model. Many other fit criteria exist, and the number of classes they suggest will not always be consistent with one another, given that they were developed with different rationales (McLachlan & Peel, 2000). Ideally, the choice of measure should be informed by studying its performance with simulated data of known structure and whether or not the measure was developed for a rationale that matches the investigator's goals. Other than model fit, the decision to adopt a given number of classes is often also based on theoretical considerations, such as whether or not a newly added class seems to contribute sufficiently unique information to warrant an increase in the complexity of the model.

An important additional consideration in estimating latent profile models, and other clustering models, is that the results can be sensitive to the initial values that are used to start the maximum likelihood fitting function. Many local optima may exist that represent inferior solutions and do not accurately recover the parameters that are being estimated. Using multiple sets of starting values is thus advisable to avoid accepting and interpreting such a solution (McLachlan & Peel, 2000). Fortunately, most software available for fitting these models (e.g., Latent Gold, M*plus*) now provide randomized start value routines. Convergence problems can also be encountered. Such problems most frequently arise when the variance-covariance matrices of the latent classes (Δ_k) are allowed to differ. If the within-class variances become very small, tending toward zero, this will produce a singularity in the likelihood surface (a spike to infinity) and the model will fail to converge. Setting the class covariance matrices to be equal (e.g. $\Delta_k = \Delta$) avoids this problem. Such constraints have the additional appeal of producing a more parsimonious model, yet they may not always be appropriate for the data. Finally, another common source of convergence problems is when one class collapses during the iteration process, that is, the class membership drops to zero. The use of alternative starting values may help to avoid this problem as well.

---

[4]Some Bayesian approaches to fitting LPA and mixture models do allow the number of classes to be estimated (e.g., Stutz & Cheeseman, 1996). However, these approaches are (at present) less common than maximum likelihood.

Once the number of classes is decided and estimates for the parameters of the model have been obtained, probabilities of class membership for the sample can be computed. Specifically, the probability that individual i belongs to latent class k given their observed scores $\mathbf{x}_i$ can be calculated as

$$p_{ik} = \frac{\hat{\pi}_k \phi_k(\mathbf{x}_j; \hat{\boldsymbol{\xi}}_k, \hat{\boldsymbol{\Delta}}_k)}{\sum_{k=1}^{k} \hat{\pi}_k \phi_k(\mathbf{x}_j; \hat{\boldsymbol{\xi}}_k, \hat{\boldsymbol{\Delta}}_k)} \tag{5}$$

Unlike clustering algorithms that assign cases to one and only one cluster, the *posterior probabilities* obtained from Equation 5 range between zero and one. For example, in a 2-class LPA, an individual might have a .8 probability of belonging to the first latent class and a .2 probability of belonging to the second latent class. These probabilities gauge uncertainty in assigning individuals to specific classes.

Let us now turn to the results of conducting LPA with the ICS data.

Results Obtained by Latent Profile Analysis

The LPA model we fit to the simulated ICS data actually differed slightly from the model described earlier in that the dichotomous dropout variable was also included (see L. K. Muthén & Muthén, 1998, Appendix 8, for analytic details).[5] Thus the resulting latent classes were defined by both mean differences on the ICS variables and different predicted probabilities of school dropout. This simultaneous analysis is preferable to first conducting the LPA exclusively on the ICS variables and then subsequently predicting dropout by class using a logistic regression model. Such a two-stage analysis would require that the class probabilities be taken into account to prevent classification errors from biasing the results. Modeling the probability of dropout directly in the LPA takes account of this uncertainty in class assignments.

Our first task was to select the precise LPA model to use with the data. We began by estimating models with one through six classes both with and without invariance constraints on the within-class variances. Each model was estimated from 100 random starts to help avoid suboptimal (local) solutions and convergence problems. A comparison of the BIC values obtained from these different models is provided in Table 11.2. The two bolded entries in Table 11.2 reflect the best fitting models, according to the BIC. Although the 4-class model with homogeneity of variance constraints had the minimum BIC,

---

[5]All LPA models were fit in Mplus 3.1 (L. K. Muthén & Muthén, 1998). The data and program files are available at Quant.KU.edu

TABLE 11.2
Bayes' Information Criterion (BIC) Values for LPA Models Fit to the ICS Data

	Structure Imposed on Within-Class Variances	
Classes	Homogeneous Δ_k	Heterogenous Δ_k
1	24723.32	24723.32
2	23919.74	23931.06
3	23372.54	23407.61
4	**23272.77**	23353.27
5	**23303.54**	23405.80
6	23340.36	23462.56

comparison of the class means between this and the next-best 5-class model with the same constraints suggested that the 5-class model was theoretically more interesting. The estimated class means for the ICS variables from the 5-class model are presented in the profile plot in Figure 11.3. In the 4-class model, the fourth and fifth classes were collapsed into a single group; however, the differentiation of the fourth and fifth class is substantively important. Although both of these classes show high levels of aggression, average popularity and average all-American, the fifth class is distinguished by very low levels of academic competence, whereas the fourth class is average academically. Given our interest in school drop out, we viewed this difference as sufficiently important to warrant selecting the five class model. Thus, we interpret only the results of the 5-class model from this point onward.

As can be seen, the most common configuration of values is represented by latent class C2, comprising 56% of the sample. Individuals with a high probability of belonging to this class are effectively at the average (grand mean) on all of the ICS variables and have a dropout rate of 12.0%. Latent class C1 is the next most common pattern, comprising 23% of the sample, and is characterized by below average aggression and high popularity, academic competence, and all-American ratings. As one might expect, C1 also has the lowest estimated rate of dropout of all the classes, at only 1.3%.

Classes C3, C4, and C5 are particularly interesting given that they all share high levels of aggression, one of the variables of key interest in the original study. They are the least frequent data patterns, at 6.6%, 9.2%, and 5.2%, of the sample, respectively, but they have the highest dropout rates. These rates are not uniform, however, suggesting that for aggressive youth other social competencies play an important role in moderating the likelihood of dropout. The actual pattern of findings is unexpected. Latent class C3 would appear to be most at risk, with high aggression, low popularity, and a low all-American score, but in fact the estimated dropout rate for this class is only 19.2%. In comparison, latent class C4, high in aggression but average on the other variables, has a dropout rate of 56.0%. Latent class C5, with high aggression and low academics, is the configuration with the highest dropout rate at 70.4%.

These results are substantively interesting and far simpler to interpret than the results obtained earlier from the logistic regression model. However, two key questions remain unsettled. First, do the configurations represented by the latent classes capture interactive relations between the ICS variables? The dropout rate of configurations with high aggression differs with their levels on other ICS variables like academics and all-American, but this might simply reflect the accumulation of independent main effects across these variables rather than a true interaction. Second, even if the latent classes do capture interactions between the ICS variables in the prediction of school dropout, at what cost is this achieved? Many methodologists would no doubt question whether rendering continuous variation on the ICS variables into a few discrete latent classes does more harm than good. Whereas the logistic regression model produced the smooth predicted probability curves in Figures 11.1 and 11.2 for various configurations of values on the ICS variables, on its surface, the LPA appears only to provide five predicted probabilities, one for each latent class, discarding much information on individual differences. Drawing on analytic developments made by Bauer (2005), however, we show that the results obtained from the LPA can be used to generate curves similar to those presented in Figures 11.1 and 11.2 and these curves will allow us to answer both of the two questions raised above. In addition, these new curves will permit us to compare more directly between the predictions of the logistic regression model and the latent profile analysis.

TRANSLATING THE RESULTS OF THE PERSON-CENTERED APPROACH

The most literal interpretation of LPA is that there are K classes of individuals mixed together in the population, within which individuals are identical with respect to their true scores, but that there is some error variation around those true scores. Due to this error variation, sampled individuals cannot be assigned with perfect precision to their respective classes, hence the need for probabilistic measures of class membership. The difficulty of this interpretation is that it assumes the presence of discrete groups and this assumption can be difficult to justify on the basis of the available evidence (see Bauer & Curran, 2003a, 2003b, 2004). In the absence of such groups, LPA may appear to represent a gross simplification of the data.

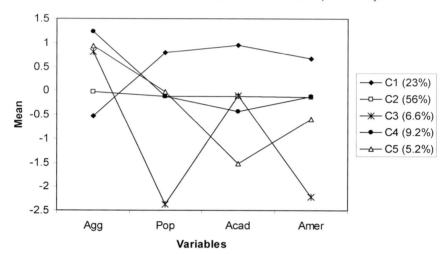

FIGURE 11.3

Plot of the means of the five classes identified in a latent profile analysis.

Note. (Agg = Aggression,Pop = Popularity,Acad = Academic Competence,Amer = All-American). The class labels and percent of the sample
predicted to belong to each class are indicated in the legend.

An alternative (and more easily defended) interpretation of LPA begins with
two key concessions. First, the distribution of true scores may not be discrete
(i.e., it may be continuous). Second, the latent classes may not directly represent true groups within the population (i.e., the population may consist of
individuals that differ only quantitatively and not qualitatively). Given these
caveats, it may seem puzzling why one would use a model involving discrete
latent classes at all. LPA can still be justified, however, by the argument that
the estimated latent classes represent discrete points on a potentially continuous but unknown multivariate distribution (an interpretation that even Gibson,
1959, considered; see also Nagin, 1999, Nagin & Land, 1993). We can then conceptualize these points as being similar to landmarks on a map from which we
can triangulate the position of any new location. In the LPA, this triangulation
is accomplished through consideration of the posterior probabilities of class
membership, which, to continue the analogy, can be thought of as distances
from the known landmarks. For instance, if a sampled individual had modest
posterior probabilities of belonging to both latent class C1 and latent class C2,
then we would guess that the individual's dropout probability would be midway
between the dropout probabilities estimated for C1 and C2 but would probably
not be close to the probabilities estimated for C3, C4, or C5.

More formally, extending analytic developments made in Bauer (2005), we can estimate the probability of an event given a particular set of values on the continuous predictors $\mathbf{x}_i$ to be

$$\tau_i = \sum_{k=1}^{K} p_{ik} \tau_k \qquad (6)$$

where τ_k is the probability of the event occurring for members of class k and p_{ik} is the posterior probability of class membership given $\mathbf{x}_i$ as defined in Equation 5. In other words, the probability of the event given $\mathbf{x}_i$ is simply a weighted sum of the probabilities of the event of the K classes, where the weights correspond to the posterior probabilities of class membership. Importantly, Equation 6 shows that continuous variation on $\mathbf{x}_i$ need not be discarded in a LPA — each individual can be assigned their own probability of experiencing the dichotomous outcome based on their particular set of observed scores for $\mathbf{x}_i$.[6] This observation may partially allay the concern of methodologists that this individualized information would be lost in the estimation of discrete latent classes.

Equally important is the fact that Equation 6 can also be used to translate the predicted probabilities estimated for the discrete latent classes into the same smooth curves previously presented in Figures 11.1 and 11.2, that is, to translate the person-centered results into a variable-centered framework. Specifically, rather than compute predicted values for every configuration of $\mathbf{x}_i$ observed in the sample, we can instead systematically select various configurations of values for $\mathbf{x}$ and use Equation 6 to calculate the model-implied probability of dropout for each selected configuration.[7] Here, we generate plots in this fashion for the primary purpose of comparing the complex interaction patterns implied by the logistic regression model to the LPA model. Such plots may, however, be of interest in their own right, as they reveal the underlying continuous relations that are implied by the latent profile model. Ideally, theory would suggest that two or three variables are particularly likely to interact and these variables may be used to generate the plots. In the absence of theory, the cluster profiles may suggest important combinations to consider. Additionally, variables whose

---

[6] In M*plus*, the posterior probabilities for the sample can be obtained using the command SAVEDATA: SAVE = CPROB.

[7] This can be done using a matrix-based programming language such as SAS PROC IML. Alternatively, one could "trick" M*plus* or other LPA model fitting software into computing these conditional probabilities by first generating an artificial data set with the desired levels of the predictors represented as individual cases and then fitting an identical LPA model to this data but with the parameter values fixed at the estimates from the model fit to the original sample. As with the original sample posterior probabilities, these new probability values can be saved into a new file for use with Equation 6.

FIGURE 11.4
Results of the latent profile analysis for popularity.

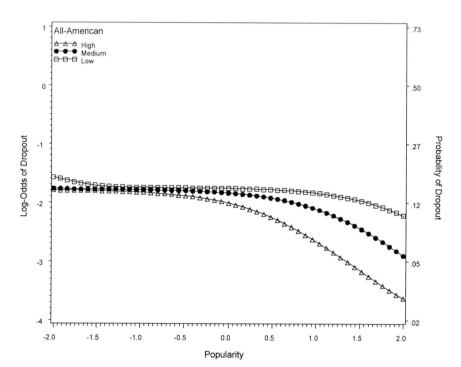

Note. The logg-odds and predicted probability of school dropout by the 11th grade as a function of 7th grade popularity at high, medium, and low levels of 7th grade all-American attributes.

means do not differ across classes should not be included in such plots, as they would be noninformative with regard to the outcomes of interest.

In the present case, to generate a graph like Figure 11.1 for the ICS data from the LPA, we calculated predicted probabilities via Equation 6 for fixed values of popularity varying between -2 and 2 at low, medium, and high values of all-American (-1, 0, and 1, respectively) while holding aggression and academic competence constant at their means (0). The obtained predicted probabilities were then translated into log-odds via the transformation shown on the left side of Equation 1. The results are presented in Figure 11.4 and can be directly compared to Figure 11.1. Similarly, to evaluate the aggression × academic × all-American interaction, the plots shown in Figure 11.5 were generated for comparison to those previously presented in Figure 11.2. These plots provide

FIGURE 11.5
Results of the latent profile analysis for aggression.

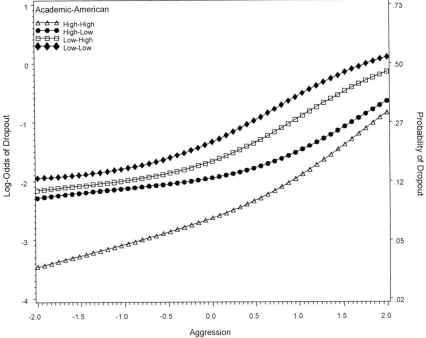

Note. The log-odds and predicted probability of school dropout by the 11th grade as a function of 7th grade aggression for specific combinations of high and low levels of 7th grade academic competence and all-American attributes.

a basis from which to directly compare the results provided by the logistic regression model and the LPA.

COMPARISON OF PERSON-CENTERED AND VARIABLE-CENTERED APPROACHES

We first note a particularly important feature of both Figure 11.4 and 11.5; the curves relating popularity and aggression to the log-odds of dropout are not parallel across the selected levels of other ICS variables. For instance, in Figure 11.4, the curve describing the relation of popularity to the log-odds of dropout when all-American is low is much flatter than the corresponding curve when all-American is high. Similarly, in Figure 11.5, the distances between the curves describing the relation of aggression to log-odds of dropout are not equal for all values of aggression. The lack of parallelism seen in both of these plots is the hallmark of an interaction (at least as interactions are conventionally defined in linear models). To our knowledge, these figures provide the first verification that interactions can be captured by person-centered methodology.

Given that both the person-centered and variable-centered approaches can capture interactive patterns, what are the differences between the two approaches? First, while the logistic regression model assumes that the log-odds of dropout are linearly related to the ICS variables, the LPA makes no such assumption. This difference is clearly seen by contrasting Figures 11.1 and 11.2 with Figures 11.4 and 11.5. In Figure 11.4, for instance, the effect of popularity on the log-odds of dropout is clearly nonlinear: If an adolescent is unpopular (below the mean), their level of unpopularity is relatively unimportant; but if an adolescent is popular (above the mean), the more popular the better (particularly if they also exhibit all-American attributes). Figure 11.2 leads to broadly the same conclusions, however, the assumption of linearity requires the log-odds of dropout to change (or not) at a constant rate across the entire range of popularity, suggesting that even differences among unpopular adolescents have small effects.

Comparison of Figures 11.2 and 11.5 is equally instructive. As before, the logistic regression model assumes that aggression is linearly related to the log-odds of dropout in Figure 11.2. In contrast, the curvature permitted by the LPA in Figure 11.5 suggests that differences in aggression above the mean are most predictive of the log-odds of dropout (with the exception that low aggression differentially benefits adolescents who are also high in academics and all-American).

Similarly, in the logistic regression model the interactions are also assumed to be linear in form. The assumption implies that the regression lines plotted in Figure 11.1 for popularity at high and low levels of all-American must be simple reflections of one another (i.e., reflections about the regression line plotted at the mean of all-American). In contrast, in Figure 11.4 the curve for high all-American diverges more sharply from the curve for average all-American than does the curve for low all-American. Higher order interactions, such as the three-way interaction between aggression, academics, and all-American plotted in Figure 11.2, are also assumed to be linear with respect to the log-odds in the logistic regression model. In the LPA, interactions are not constrained to have a specific form.

Thus a key advantage of the LPA is that it does not make any specific assumptions about the functional form (e.g., linear, bilinear, etc.) of the predictive relationships in the model. One could counter that if theory suggested the presence of nonlinear effects, then polynomial terms could be added to the logistic regression model (e.g., quadratic or cubic). The inclusion of product interactions involving polynomial terms would further relax the assumption that the interactions are linear in nature. Adding these terms would, however, increase the complexity of the model considerably, requiring the parsing of additional lower and higher order effects. Generating a coherent interpretation of the model estimates would become correspondingly more difficult. Issues of power also quickly come into play. In contrast, the LPA does not require that nonlinear effects be specified a priori — they emerge naturally through the estimation of the posterior probabilities in Equation 5. Furthermore, profile plots like Figure 11.3 are relatively easy to interpret.

A second key advantage of LPA is that one can consider only those combinations of values on the predictors that are most characteristic of the data patterns in the sample. Specifically, the configurations plotted in Figure 11.3 can be considered as prototypical of the actual data patterns within the sample. Attention can then be focused immediately on these prototypical patterns. In contrast, when using the method of plotting simple slopes with traditional linear models, one must select on an ad hoc basis which configurations of values to consider. Particularly when considering higher order interactions such as the one plotted in Figure 11.2, the particular configurations chosen may be quite uncommon in the sample. For instance, fewer than 2% of the cases in the simulated ICS data have aggression scores below -.5, academic scores below -.5, and all-American scores above .5. Similarly, less than 2% have aggression scores below -.5, academic scores above .5 and all-American scores below -.5. This sparseness is partly responsible for the lack of replication of the middle two lines of Figures 11.2 and 11.5 across the two methods: The predictions made for low levels of aggression are largely based on extrapolations from other regions of the data space and are inevitably closely bound to the different assumptions of the two models. The advantage of LPA is that attention naturally focuses on the configurations represented by the latent class means rather than ad hoc combinations of values that may characterize very few individuals.

THEORY AND METHODOLOGY

Let us now consider how these results inform the debate between theoreticians and methodologists that inspired this chapter. Overall, the results appear to support the intuition of the theoreticians. Analysis of the simulated data indicated that person-centered methodology could indeed recover nonlinear and/or interactive effects. In addition, for the LPA, we demonstrated how such interactions were recovered through the probabilistic basis of the clustering model. Use of a probabilistic clustering model like LPA overcomes one of the most serious concerns of methodologists, that person-centered methodology represents nothing more than a complex categorization scheme that discards infor-

mation on continuous individual differences. In fact, this individual variation
in the observed continuous variables can still be taken into account through
the probabilistic basis of the model, as we demonstrated with Equation 6. On
this point, however, we must also acknowledge that probabilistic clustering approaches have been applied relatively infrequently in person-centered analyses
(see Shanahan & Flaherty, 2001, for a rare exception). More commonly used
disjoint clustering algorithms, like k-means or Ward's method, would not have
this important advantage, and hence the concerns of methodologists with these
techniques are entirely justified.

Variable-centered models are also capable of capturing complex relationships, as was the case with the logistic regression model. Typically, nonlinear
or interactive effects are specified through the inclusion of polynomial or product terms. Such terms may or may not readily capture the complex nature of
the effects and, even when adequate, partition the effects of variables into lower
and higher order components that can make coherent holistic interpretations
difficult. The plotting of simple slopes at specific configurations of values for
moderator variables can aid in the interpretation of complex interactions. As
our example showed, however, there is no guarantee that the specific combinations of values chosen are actually representative of common configurations in
the sample or population. In part, this is due to the fact that these values are
typically chosen on the basis of univariate statistics computed for each variable
separately (e.g., standard deviations or quartiles), and these statistics may not
reveal relative sparseness at the multivariate level. The person-centered approach avoids each of these difficulties. The specific nature of complex effects
need not be specified a priori nor assumed to have a particular form. Furthermore, modal configurations within the data are identified at the outset. This
facilitates holistic interpretations by focusing attention on the relations between
these specific configurations and outcomes of interest, obviating the need to select ad hoc combinations of values that may or may not be representative of
the actual patterns in the data.

We have intentionally highlighted the advantages of the person-centered approach here in part to challenge methodologists to consider the potential of
these models more seriously. In the past, methodologists have often shown little interest in such models. For instance, when Gibson (1959) developed the
latent profile model, he hoped that it would be considered a viable alternative
to the continuous linear factor analysis model of Thurstone (1935). However,
subsequent comparisons of the two models have often been relatively dismis-
sive of latent profile analysis. For example, in their compendium on latent
variable modeling, Bartholomew and Knott (1999) introduced LPA with the
remark "The latent profile model can be thought of as a factor model with a
discrete (multivariate) prior distribution... For this reason we shall not give

an extended treatment to latent profile models," (p. 22). True to their words, Bartholomew and Knott dedicated only 4.5 pages to LPA, primarily to draw a comparison to traditional factor analysis (the subject of a 27 page chapter). Moreover, while empirical applications of factor analysis and other linear modeling approaches abound, there are comparatively few examples of latent profile analysis or other person-centered methodology in the substantive literature. We hope that the results presented here will encourage both methodologists and applied researchers to explore the possible advantages of latent profile analysis and related models for capturing complex relations between variables.

But there are drawbacks to person-centered approaches as well. For instance, while we have shown how probabilistic clustering models can recover complex nonlinear and/or interactive effects, we have not evaluated their performance for this purpose. Bauer (2005) presented results indicating that clustering models can provide unbiased and reasonably efficient estimates of continuous nonlinear bivariate relations, but it is unclear whether these results will carry over to more complex patterns involving multiple variables. In addition, direct comparisons between person-centered and variable-centered models will be of importance. For instance, variable-centered methods may outperform person-centered methods if the assumption of linearity (or bilinearity) is only modestly violated. Because variable-centered models often require fewer parameters, they may well produce more accurate and stable results with small samples than person-centered models, even when higher order effects are of primary interest. Much future research will be required to investigate and compare the finite sample performance of these models. To motivate these investigations, we would like now to discuss two areas of research where we believe the person-centered approach holds great promise, namely, the modeling of person-context interactions and developmental change.

CAPTURING PERSON-CONTEXT INTERACTIONS

There is a certain irony involved in the use of person-centered approaches for modeling interactionist theories of human development: In their focus on the person, context effects are often marginalized, despite the theoretical emphasis on interactions both within and between levels of developmental systems. This is clear even in the empirical example that we used in this chapter, where the variables were distinctly personal, in keeping with the majority of empirical applications we have seen. Several possible approaches to modeling context effects can, however, be considered.

One possibility is to define clusters or classes on the basis of both intrapersonal and contextual variables. The resulting configurations will then capture potential interactions between the two types of variables in the way shown here. For instance, in the Cairns, Cairns, and Neckerman (1989) study that motivated our empirical example, socioeconomic status (SES) was included among the measures that were clustered to identify the individual profiles. The obtained profiles then indicated how patterns of individual functioning within specific levels of SES predicted school dropout. Clearly, one could also include several finer grained contextual variables alongside variables measuring personal characteristics.

A second strategy is to separately cluster on intrapersonal variables and contextual variables and then to examine the associations between the two sets of clusters. For instance, Xie, Cairns, and Cairns (2001) conducted parallel cluster analyses of the ICS and other measures for both individuals and the peers with whom they affiliated. Individual and peer clusters were then crossed both to determine their correspondence (typically high) and to determine whether particular combinations of individual and peer cluster membership were related to teen parenthood. Xie, Cairns, and Cairns (2001) found that, for girls, peer cluster membership was the dominant factor predicting teen motherhood. In contrast, for boys, individual and peer cluster membership interacted such that boys in high risk clusters who affiliated with peers also occupying high risk clusters were the most likely to become teen fathers.

Last, one could analyze a single set of variables that are constructed to measure the individual's transactions with his/her environment. Very little attention has been devoted to measures that capture such transactions by simultaneously referring to aspects of both person and context. One simple possibility, however, is suggested by Shanahan and Flaherty's (2001) analysis of how much time teenagers spent engaged in several domains (e.g., in the workplace, school, with peers, parents). Such measures are behavioral, and yet begin to describe the social worlds that youth construct and participate in.

Further thought should be given to these and other ways of optimally modeling context effects from a developmental systems perspective.

DEVELOPMENT

A second apparent inconsistency in the use of person-centered approaches for modeling developmental systems is that there are relatively few options for modeling change over time. As noted by Bergman (1998), two general strategies have been considered. The first strategy is to classify individuals into categories based on their patterns of change on a specific variable of interest (e.g., aggression or alcohol use). Here, three approaches have been proposed. The first approach is to cluster analyze or conduct an LPA on the repeated measures across time for a single construct. The results can then be described as longitudinal profiles. An advantage of this approach is that the repeated measures need not be commensurate. For instance, when studying a construct that shows heterotypic continuity, the measurement of the construct might change from one age to the next. With commensurate measurement across time, the longitudinal profiles can be thought of as trajectories of change over time. One may then wish to impose a specific structure on these trajectories, such as a linear or quadratic trend. Imposing such a structure on an LPA model leads to the latent class growth model of Nagin (1999).

In Nagin (1999) approach, latent trajectory classes are defined similarly to the LPA. All individuals within a class are presumed to share a common class trajectory (true scores). The only difference is that the class trajectory (true scores) are assumed to follow a particular polynomial trend over time. If the assumption of homogeneity within classes is relaxed, then the growth mixture model of Verbeke and Lesaffre (1996) is obtained, a model that has recently been extended and popularized by B. Muthén and Shedden (1999). In the general growth mixture model, each individual is assumed to follow a unique trajectory, however, within each latent class, the individual trajectories are normally distributed around the class mean trajectory. That is, there is both between-class and within-class heterogeneity in change over time (fixed and random effects).

The increasing popularity of latent class growth models and growth mixture models, particularly in research on developmental psychopathology and substance use, attests to their appeal for examining heterogeneous patterns of change. The complexity of these models will, however, often preclude modeling change in more than one or two variables simultaneously. The strategy of forming longitudinal clusters is thus not really person-centered because it is not suited to modeling the possible interactions that may occur among a set of variables over time.

An alternative advocated by Bergman (1998) is to identify configurations of variables at each point in time and then to link configurations over time. The potential of this strategy to identify new patterns as they emerge developmentally is particularly appealing. However, linking configurations over time also has drawbacks. First, transition patterns are typically examined between successive waves of assessment, requiring relative age homogeneity within wave and ignoring potentially lagged trends between, say, Wave I and Wave III that are not mediated by Wave II. Furthermore, interpretation can become considerably more cumbersome as the number of waves increases, particularly if there are more than a few within-wave clusters.

A second limitation of this strategy concerns implementation. Typically, individuals are assigned to clusters at each point in time and then movement is examined from one cluster to another over time. In addition to introducing classification errors that may bias estimates of the frequencies of these transitions, if the individual probabilities of class membership are not retained then information on potentially important individual differences is likely to be obscured. A latent transition analysis is an alternative probabilistic clustering approach that would avoid these difficulties (Collins, Hyatt, & Graham, 2000; Lanza, Flaherty, & Collins, 2002).

CONCLUSIONS

Capturing emergent and changing person-context interactions is unequivocally one of the most significant methodological challenges that developmental researchers face. A key goal of this chapter was to suggest that the person-centered approach may well play an important role in addressing this challenge in the future. We demonstrated that some person-centered methods, namely probabilistic clustering models, appear to be particularly well-suited to capturing complex interaction patterns within time. We also suggested several possible ways that these models could be extended to examine interaction patterns over time. Our hope is that this initial demonstration of the promise of these models will help to spur research by other methodologists and applied researchers to further evaluate the usefulness of these models for studying person–context interactions in human development.

REFERENCES

Aiken, M. S., & West, S. G. (1991). *Multiple regression: testing and interpreting interactions.* Newbury Park, CA: Sage.

Bartholomew, D. J., & Knott, M. (1999). *Latent variable models and factor analysis* (2nd ed.). London: Arnold.

Bauer, D. J. (2005). A semiparametric approach to modeling nonlinear relations among latent variables. *Structural Equation Modeling: A Multidisciplinary Journal, 4*, 513-535.

Bauer, D. J., & Curran, P. J. (2003a). Distributional assumptions of growth mixture models: Implications for over-extraction of latent trajectory classes. *Psychological Methods, 8*, 338-363.

Bauer, D. J., & Curran, P. J. (2003b). Over-extracting latent trajectory classes: Much ado about nothing? reply to rindskopf (2003), muthén (2003), and cudeck and henly (2003). *Psychological Methods, 8*, 384-393.

Bauer, D. J., & Curran, P. J. (2004). The integration of continuous and discrete latent variable models: Potential problems and promising opportunities. *Psychological Methods, 9*, 3-29.

Bergman, L. R. (1998). A pattern-oriented approach to studying individual development: snapshots and processes. In R. B. Cairns, L. R. Bergman, & J. Kagan (Eds.), *Methods and models for studying the individual: Essays in honor of marina radke-yarrow* (pp. -). Thousand Oaks: Sage.

Bergman, L. R., & Magnusson, D. (1997). A person-oriented approach in research on developmental psychopathology. *Development and Psychopathology, 9*, 291-319.

Bergman, L. R., Magnusson, D., & El-Khouri, B. M. (2003). *Studying individual development in an interindividual context: A person-oriented approach (paths through life, volume 4)*. Mahwah, NJ: Lawrence Erlbaum Associates.

Bronfenbrenner, U., & Morris, P. A. (1998). The ecology of developmental processes. In W. Damon (Series Ed.) & R. M. Lerner (Vol Ed.) (Eds.), *Handbook of child psychology: Vol. 1. theoretical models of human development* (5th ed., 993-1028). New York: Wiley.

Cairns, R. B., Cairns, B. D., & Neckerman, H. J. (1989). Early school dropout: configurations and determinants. *Child Development, 60*, 1437-1452.

Cairns, R. B., & Rodkin, P. C. (1998). Phenomena regained: from configurations to pathways. In R. B. Cairns, L. R. Bergman, & J. Kagan (Eds.), *Methods and models for studying the individual: Essays in honor of marina radke-yarrow* (pp. 245-264). Thousand Oaks, CA: Sage.

Cohen, J. (1978). Partialled products are interactions; partialled powers are curve components. *Psychological Bulletin, 85*, 858-866.

Cohen, J. (1983). The cost of dichotomization. *Applied Psychological Measurement, 7*, 249-253.

Collins, L. M., Hyatt, S. L., & Graham, J. W. (2000). LTA as a way of testing models of stage-sequential change in longitudinal data. In T. D. Little, K. U. Schnabel, & J. Baumert (Eds.), *Modeling longitudinal and multiple-group data: Practical issues, applied approaches, and specific examples* (pp. 259-288). Hillsdale, NJ: Lawrence Erlbaum Associates.

Eccles, J. S., & Midgley, C. (1989). Stage-environment fit: Developmentally appropriate classrooms for early adolescents. In R. E. Ames & C. Ames (Eds.), *Research on motivation in education* (Vol. 3, pp. 139-186). New York: Academic Press.

Elder, G. H., Jr. (1998). The life course and human development. In W. Damon (Series Ed.) & R. M. Lerner (Vol Ed.) (Eds.), *Handbook of child psychology: Vol. 1. Theoretical models of human development* (5th ed., 939-991). New York: Wiley.

Gariépy, J.-L. (1995). The evolution of developmental science: Early determinism, modern interactionism, and a new systemic approach. In R. Vasta (Ed.), *Annals of child development,* Vol. 11 (pp. 167-222). London: Jessica Kingsley.

Gibson, W. A. (1959). Three multivariate models: Factor analysis, latent structure analysis, and latent profile analysis. *Psychometrika, 24*, 229-252.

Gottlieb, G., Wahlsten, D., & Lickliter, R. (1998). The significance of biology for human development: A developmental psychobiological systems view. In W. Damon (Series Ed.) & R. M. Lerner (Vol Ed.) (Eds.), *Handbook of child psychology: Vol. 1. Theoretical models of human development* (5th ed., pp. 233-273). New York: Wiley.

Humphreys, L. G. (1978). Research on individual differences requires correlational analysis, not ANOVA. *Intelligence*, *2*, 1-5.

Jaccard, J., Turrisi, R., & Wan, C. K. (1990). *Interaction effects in multiple regression.* Newbury Park, CA: Sage.

Lanza, S., Flaherty, B. P., & Collins, L. M. (2002). Latent class and latent transition analysis. In J. Schinka & W. Velicer (Eds.), *Research methods in psychology*, Vol. 2 (pp. 663-685). *Handbook of psychology.* New York: Wiley.

Lerner, R. M. (1998). Theories of human development: contemporary perspectives. In W. Damon (Series Ed.) & R. M. Lerner (Vol Ed.) (Eds.), *Handbook of child psychology: Vol. 1. Theoretical models of human development* (5th ed., pp. 1-24). New York: Wiley.

MacCallum, R. C., Zhang, S., Preacher, K. J., & Rucker, D. D. (2002). On the practice of dichotomization of quantitative variables. *Psychological Methods*, *7*, 19-40.

Magnusson, D. (1998). The logic and implications of a person-oriented approach. In R. B. Cairns, L. R. Bergman, & J. Kagan (Eds.), *Methods and models for studying the individual: Essays in honor of marina radke-yarrow* (pp. 33-63). Thousand Oaks, CA: Sage.

Magnusson, D., & Cairns, R. B. (1996). Developmental science: Toward a unified framework. In R. B. Cairns, G. H. Elder Jr, & E. J. Costello (Eds.), *Developmental science* (pp. 7-30). New York: Cambridge University Press.

Magnusson, D., & Stattin, H. (1998). Person-context interaction theories. In W. Damon (Series Ed.) & R. M. Lerner (Vol Ed.) (Eds.), *Handbook of child psychology: Vol. 1. Theoretical models of human development* (5th ed., pp. 685-759). New York: Wiley.

Maxwell, S. E., & Delaney, H. D. (1990). Bivariate median-splits and spurious statistical significance. *Psychological Bulletin*, *113*, 181-190.

McLachlan, G., & Peel, D. (2000). *Finite mixture models.* New York: Wiley.

Muthén, B., & Shedden, K. (1999). Finite mixture modeling with mixture outcomes using the em algorithm. *Biometrics*, *55*, 463-469.

Muthén, L. K., & Muthén, B. O. (1998). *Mplus user's guide* [Computer Manual, Version 2]. Los Angeles, CA: Muthen and Muthen.

Nagin, D. (1999). Analyzing developmental trajectories: A semi-parametric, group-based approach. *Psychological Methods*, *4*, 139-157.

Nagin, D., & Land, K. C. (1993). Age, criminal careers, and population heterogeneity: Specification and estimation of a nonparametric, mixed poisson model. *Criminology*, *31*, 327-362.

Richters, J. E. (1997). The hubble hypothesis and the developmentalist's dilemma. *Development and Psychopathology*, *9*, 193-229.

Sameroff, A. J. (1983). Developmental systems: contexts and evolution. In P. H. Mussen (Gen. Ed.) & W. Kessen (Vol Ed.) (Eds.), *Handbook of child psychology: Vol. 1. History, theory, and methods* (4th ed., pp. 237-294). New York: Wiley.

Shanahan, M. J., & Flaherty, B. P. (2001). Dynamic patterns of time use in adolescence. *Child Development*, *72*, 385-401.

Shanahan, M. J., & Hofer, S. M. (2005). The contextual moderation of genetic influences in theory and research. *Journal of Gerontology: Psychological and Social Sciences, 60B (Special Issue I)*, 65-76.

Shanahan, M. J., Valsiner, J., & Gottlieb, G. (1997). Developmental concepts across disciplines. In J. Tudge, M. J. Shanahan, & J. Valsiner (Eds.), *Comparisons in human development: Understanding time and context*. Cambridge, England: Cambridge University Press.

Stutz, J., & Cheeseman, P. (1996). Autoclass: A bayesian approach to classification. In J. Skilling & S. Sibisi (Eds.), *Maximum entropy and bayesian methods* (pp. 117-126). Dordrecht, The Netherlands: Kluwer.

Thurstone, L. L. (1935). *The vectors of the mind*. Chicago: University of Chicago Press.

Verbeke, G., & Lesaffre, E. (1996). A linear mixed-effects model with heterogeneity in the random-effects population. *Journal of the American Statistical Association, 91*, 217-221.

Xie, H., Cairns, B. D., & Cairns, R. B. (2001). Predicting teen motherhood and teen fatherhood: Individual characteristics and peer affiliations. *Social Development, 10*, 488-511.

CHAPTER TWELVE

Accounting for Statistical Dependency in Longitudinal Data on Dyads

Niall Bolger
Patrick E. Shrout
New York University

Although social and developmental psychology define dyadic processes as an important part of their subject matter, there is still considerable uncertainty in these fields about how to analyze dyadic data. The reason for this uncertainty is that conventional statistical methods are designed for studying independently sampled persons, whereas the most interesting feature of dyadic data is their lack of independence. Moreover, in recent years this problem has been compounded as researchers have increasingly adopted intensive repeated-measures designs to study dyads in natural settings (Bolger, Davis, & Rafaeli, 2003).When one collects repeated-measures data on dyads, one must not only contend with nonindependence of the members within the dyad but also nonindependence of the observations within a dyad member.

The goal of this chapter is to present a potential solution to this problem. We present a model for the covariance structure of dyadic diary data, a model that can account for where the dependencies in the data lie, and one that can be used as a baseline for explanatory work on the causal processes that produce the dependencies. As we show, the general model can be estimated using either of two equivalent statistical approaches, a structural equation model (SEM) approach, and a multilevel model approach.

Our general model is related to Kenny and Zautra's Trait-State-Error model (also known as the STARTS model; Kenny & Zautra, 1995, 2001), which used an SEM approach to decompose a person's measured level on some psychological characteristic at a particular time into a component reflecting their typical level, a component reflecting their true current state, and a component reflecting measurement error. Like Kenny and Zautra, we distinguish stable and time-varying sources of dependence, but we do so in the context of dyads and we do not make adjustments for measurement error.

More directly related to our approach is the Actor–Partner Interdependence Model, also developed by Kenny and his colleagues (e.g., Cook & Snyder, 2005; Kashy & Kenny, 2000; Kenny, 1996). In its application to longitudinal data on dyads, the model assesses the extent to which dyad members influence themselves and their partners over time. Actor effects reflect the extent to which a member's prior score on some variable affects his or her subsequent score on that variable. Partner effects are the extent to which a member's prior score on some variable affects his or her partner's subsequent score. It is important to note that actor effects are estimated controlling for partner effects and vice versa.

Our approach is less ambitious than the Actor–Partner Interdependence Model in the sense that we do not attempt to estimate actor and partner effects. Instead we estimate the covariances between dyad members' scores, covariances that can be the result of causal effects of members on one another or of common environmental events. Furthermore, we distinguish between covariance that is constant over time and covariance that is not (akin to Kenny and Zautra's State-Trait-Error Model). We see the causal modeling of interpersonal and environmental influences as a subsequent analytic step that can be accomplished by adding additional predictors and directed paths to our model.

A third related approach is the model presented by Gonzalez and Griffin (1997, 1999, 2002; Griffin & Gonzalez, 1995) in which they analyze associations between variables into their components at multiple levels of analysis. However, whereas Gonzalez and Griffin explicitly estimate dyad-level and individual-level associations, we give priority to the individual level, but we do so in a way that takes account of time-invariant and time-varying dependencies that in their approach would emerge at the dyad level.

Finally, our approach is related to Raudenbush, Barnett and Brennan's work on analyzing dyadic longitudinal data (Barnett, Marshall, Raudenbush, & Brennan, 1993; Raudenbush, Brennan, & Barnett, 1995) in the sense that we present a multilevel model modified to take account of dependencies that are specific to dyadic data. We will elaborate further on these links when we have described our approach in more detail.

The Dyadic Process Model

We first describe some basic features of a dyadic process using as an example reports of anger by each dyad member over time. Figure 12.1 illustrates the structure of these data. We expect that some persons will report more anger than others, and that anger on one day will tend to be followed by anger on another. Anger will have consequences in the dyad such that anger felt by one partner will often be met by anger in the other. These considerations lead us to ask the following questions: To what extent does the average tendency to be angry covary between partners in an intimate relationship? How strong is the association of anger on one day with anger on the next day within a given person? To what extent is anger in one partner related to anger in the other partner on the same day?

METHOD

Participants and design. The sample and design was described in detail by Bolger, Zuckerman, and Kessler (2000) and is only briefly described here. In the spring before they graduated, we recruited third year law students who were in romantic relationships with partners of the opposite sex for at least the previous 6 months, and who expected to be living with their partners in the weeks before the state bar examination. We excluded couples if both partners were preparing for the bar exam. Couples were paid $50 for completing the study. Ninety nine couples initially agreed to participate after recruitment material was left at law schools, and a final sample of 68 couples (69%) completed the majority of the study forms. For the current analyses we limited the sample to the 64 couples that had complete data on all relevant variables. Among these couples, the examinee was male in 65% of the dyads. Examinee mean age was 28.9 years (SD = 5.0), and partner mean age was 29.0 (SD = 6.1). Seventy one percent of the couples were married, and couples had been living together for an average of 3.1 years (SD = 3.1). The quality of their relationships was generally high. The mean value of the global Dyadic Adjustment Scale (Spanier, 1976) was 103.2 and the standard deviation was 14.4. More than 90% of the couples were white. All the examinees were law school graduates, and 85% of their mates were college graduates.

At the end of each day each partner rated 18 moods adapted from the Profile of Mood States (POMS; McNair, Lorr, & Droppleman 1992). We focus only on a four-item Anger scale composed of the average of items "annoyed," "peeved," "angry," and "resentful." This scale has been "shown to be reliable" measure of within-person change over time, with a generalizability coefficient of 0.75 (Cranford et al, 2005). To make our model easy to represent graphically, we focus on a 7 day period, days 4 to 10. Because we wished to focus on a period of relative stationarity, we omitted the first three diary days and chose a period that began 1 month in advance of the examination.   Although this cannot be

FIGURE 12.1
Study design: Diary reports from individuals in two roles nested within sixty five couples crossed with seven days.

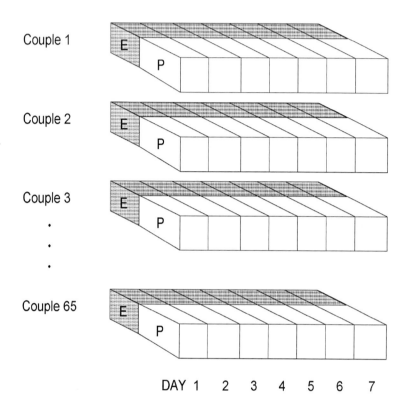

considered a low-stress period, it involved considerably less stress than weeks closer to the event.

Statistical Methods

As noted earlier, we used two approaches to the data analysis, one involving multilevel models and the other involving structural equation models. In the first approach, the relationships among data points displayed in Figure 12.1 was initially ignored in the organization of the data: Daily reports of anger were treated as the outcome and reports of examinees were not differentiated from those of partners, nor were earlier reports differentiated from later reports. We then applied the following model to the data, one that began to differentiate the source and timing of the reports. In the model, A_{icd} is the anger rating of person i ($i = 1$ or 2) in couple c ($c = 1$ to 64) on day $d(d = 1$ to 7).

$$A_{icd} = (I_{1cd})M_{1c} + (I_{2cd})M2c + r_{icd} \qquad \text{(1a)}$$

$$M_{1c} = \phi_1 + U_1 \qquad \text{(1b)}$$

$$M_{2c} = \phi_2 + U_{2c} \qquad \text{(1c)}$$

In equation 1a, I_{1cd} is dummy coded to be 1 for the examinee and 0 for the partner, regardless of the couple or day. Similarly, I_{2cd} is dummy coded to be 1 for the partner and 0 for the examinee for all couples and days. These indicator variables allow M_{1c} to be interpreted as the intercept (mean over days) for the examinee in couple c and M_{2c} to be the intercept (mean over days) for the partner in the same couple c. The term r_{icd} is that part of the Anger rating of person i in couple c on day d that is not explained by the average rating of person i in couple c. We say more about this term later.

In Equation 1b the intercepts for individual examinees are decomposed into a grand mean for all examinees (ϕ_x) plus a specific mean for the examinee in each couple c (U_{1c}). In multilevel model terminology, the latter is a random effect in a level 2 model. Similarly, equation 1c decomposes the intercepts for partners into a grand mean for all partners (ϕ_y) and a specific mean for partners in each couple c (U_{2c}). It is possible to specify that the random effects for an examinee and partner within the same couple are correlated. This is made explicit by specifying that the expected variance covariance matrix of (U_{1c}, U_{2c}) is a 2 by 2 symmetric matrix (G) with the following unique elements, $\text{Var}(U_{1c}) = G_{11}$, $\text{Var}(U_{2c}) = G_{22}$ and $\text{Cov}(U_{1c}, U_{2c}) = G_{12}$. An estimate of the latter value characterizes the degree to which (across couples) examinees whose mean anger ratings are high tend to be paired with partners whose mean anger ratings are also high.

Returning to the residual term, r_{icd}, we note that anger variations within a person can be correlated from day to day, and that the variation of the examinee can be related to that of the partner. If we were to assume a completely general pattern of such covariation this would result in large number of covariance parameters to estimate. In fact, with two persons per couple and 7 days, there would be 105 distinct elements to estimate in the resulting 14 by 14 symmetric matrix. We greatly simplify the estimation of these covariances by assuming that the examine– and partner variances are stable over time, that adjacent days are correlated by a lag-1 autoregressive process, and that the examinee-partner covariance is stable over time. These assumptions allow us to fit all 105 covariance elements with only four parameters: the variance of the examinee residuals, the variance of the partner residuals, the covariance of the examinee

FIGURE 12.2
SEM diagram for dyadic process model.

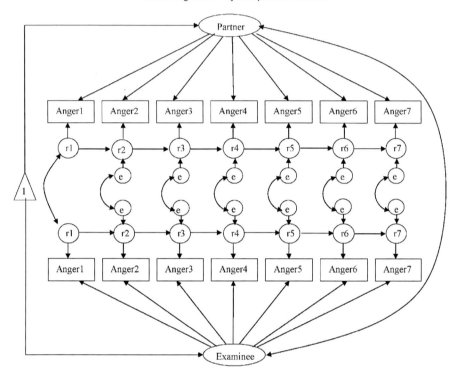

and partner residuals, and the autocorrelation of lag one residuals over examinee days and partner days.[1]

Unlike the multilevel approach, the SEM approach considers data that are organized by independent unit, in this case dyad. Figure 12.2 shows a graphical representation of this SEM. Each line of input data contains 14 values, seven for the examinee and seven for the partner. If one or more of these values are missing, special efforts are needed either to impute the values directly, or to estimate the sample covariance matrix using the EM algorithm. To simplify our discussion, we ignore these issues by working with complete data only, although this strategy can only be justified if the data are missing completely at random

---

[1] We are able to apply these simplifying assumptions to the residual covariance matrix using options in the MIXED procedure of the SAS system. There is a REPEATED section in the syntax that allows specification of correlated residuals, and one option is TYPE=UN@AR(1). This coding refers to a Kronecker Product (e.g. see Bock, 1975) of a 2 by 2 covariance matrix for persons within couple, and of a 7 by 7 correlation matrix with the lag 1 autoregression pattern.

(see Schafer & Graham, 2002, for more details on estimation in the presence of missing data).

Returning to Figure 12.2, there are two latent variables represented by ovals, one denoting individual differences (at the couple level) in mean anger for examinees and one denoting similar differences in mean anger for partners. Following Willet and Sayer (1994), these are defined by constraining the loadings of the latent variables to the daily anger reports to be equal to one. These couple-level random variables are assumed to be correlated, as indicated by the double headed arrow connecting the two. In addition to latent means, each anger report is determined by a daily fluctuation represented by the residual (r) effect in circles. The daily fluctuation for the examinee is assumed to be correlated with the daily fluctuation of the partner and the size of the fluctuation on one day is assumed to partly determine the size on the following day. On each day the fluctuations are also affected by a random variable (e) that is assumed to be uncorrelated with other variables in the system. These assumptions are virtually the same ones we made when considering the data from a multilevel perspective.[2]

We fit the data from the multilevel approach using the MIXED procedure of SAS because of the flexibility it affords in modeling the correlation structure of the residuals. To estimate the structural equation model we used EQS version 6.1 (Multivariate Software, 2004). The syntax used in each case is presented in the Appendix (see Quant.KU.edu).

Descriptive Results

Table 12.1 shows the means and standard deviations for the 7 days in our analysis. The ratings were on a 0 to 4 scale, and it is clear that most of the sample did not experience high levels of anger. Examinees had slightly lower levels of reported anger during this week than their partners, but this difference was not statistically significant.[3] Days 4 and 5 were weekend days, and the tendency for both partners to have slightly less anger on Sunday is apparent in

---

[2]The multilevel model fits the overall structure of the residual variance covariance matrix without decomposing the variance into autoregressive and random shock influences, in contrast to the SEM approach. Moreover, the multilevel model assumes that the autoregressive process on the residuals is stationary, which means that the variance of the residual is equal to the variance of the random shocks divided by $(1-\rho^2)$, where ρ^2 is the squared autocorrelation. This constraint cannot be readily imposed in EQS, but we approximated the restraint by iteratively estimating the autocorrelation and random shock variance and fixing the initial residual variances to these derived values.

[3]As the exam draws closer in time, examinees begin to report higher levels of anger than their partners.

TABLE 12.1
Correlations Among Seven Daily Reports of Examinee (E1, E2, ...,E7) and Partner Anger (P1, P2, ...,P7)

	Mean	SD	E1	E2	E3	E4	E5	E6	E7	P1	P2	P3	P4	P5	P6	P7
E1	.664	.813	1													
E2	.621	.914	.42	1												
E3	.520	.573	.23	.55	1											
E4	.570	.840	.04	.21	.40	1										
E5	.426	.580	.18	.27	.31	.54	1									
E6	.435	.556	.16	.01	.16	.43	.42	1								
E7	.488	.580	.11	.14	.20	.38	.27	.45	1							
P1	.727	.801	**.16**	.07	.06	-.12	-.08	-.01	-.06	1						
P2	.836	.944	.19	**.32**	.30	.04	.11	.09	.24	.37	1					
P3	.645	.905	-.05	.20	**.25**	.20	.14	-.07	-.13	.18	.15	1				
P4	.551	.894	.07	.13	.29	**.57**	.33	.23	.14	.05	.05	.45	1			
P5	.566	.980	.00	.16	.33	.37	**.38**	.30	.21	.20	.30	.20	.60	1		
P6	.465	.818	-.17	.02	.17	.35	.26	**.41**	.34	.06	.20	.08	.33	.66	1	
P7	.523	.711	-.07	.08	-.01	.21	.04	.09	**.22**	.18	.24	.11	.34	.49	.43	1

the means. In fact, the mean level of anger for examinees correlates 0.78 with that of partners over the 7 days.

Table 12.1 shows the between person correlations for each of the 14 days, 7 daily reports by the examinee and 7 daily reports by the partner. In the upper left hand quadrant of the matrix are the correlations among anger reports by the examinee. The largest correlations are for adjacent days, and the correlations tend to decline with increasing lag. The correlations for the largest lags are no longer significant, but all the correlations are positive. A similar pattern is observed in the lower right hand quadrant, which contains correlations among the daily reports by the partner. All the correlations are positive, but the largest are for lag 2 and lag 1 comparisons.

The lower left hand quadrant shows the correlations among the examinee and partner reports for the 7 days. Many of these correlations fluctuate around zero, some negative and some small and positive. However, the same day correlations tend to be larger, with the median correlation being 0.32. The only other moderate size correlations tend to be for lag 1 associations.

Modeling the Association Patterns

Table 12.2 shows the results of fitting the model in Figure 12.2 using multilevel and SEM approaches. The model provides a rough description of the patterns

TABLE 12.2
Parameter Estimates for Model Displayed in Figure 12.1

	Multilevel		SEM	
	Estimate	SE	Estimate	SE
Mean of Examinee Mean Anger	0.537	0.053	0.538	0.053
Mean of Partner Mean Anger	0.617	0.065	0.621	0.065
Variance of Examinee Mean Anger	0.080	0.035	0.088	0.034
Variance of Partner Mean Anger	0.116	0.053	0.118	0.051
Covariance of Examinee and Partner Mean Anger	0.045	0.031	0.050	0.030
Implied Correlation of Examinee and Partner Mean Anger	0.469		0.491	
Variance of Examinee Daily Anger Residuals	0.417	0.035	0.386	†
Variance of Partner Daily Anger Residuals	0.631	0.053	0.639	†
Covariance of Examinee and Partner Daily Anger Residuals	0.134	0.027	0.136	†
Implied Correlation of Examinee and Partner Daily Anger Residuals	0.262		0.274	
First-Order Autocorrelation of Daily Anger Residuals	0.316	0.046	0.296	0.047

Note. † Values in these cells were computed rather than estimated directly, hence standard errors are not available.

of association, even though the fit indices suggest that the nuances of the relations shown in Table 12.1 are not well represented (From EQS, NNFI = .73; RMSEA = .10). The two approaches provide very similar estimates and standard errors. For simplicity, we use the estimates from the multilevel approach to make substantive comments. The grand means for the examinees ($\phi_1 = 0.537$) and their partners ($\phi_2 = 0.617$) show that the majority of the participants report low levels of anger on average. The spread of the distribution of these random effects is indicated by the variance of the level 2 random effects. These are similar for examinees ($G_{11} = 0.08$) and partners ($G_{22} = 0.12$). Because these are not significantly different from each other, a reasonable estimate of the standard deviation of the random effects is the square root of the midpoint 0.10, which is 0.32.

The covariance of the random effects is $G_{12} = 0.045$, yielding a correlation estimate of 0.47. Although the point estimate is suggestive of a medium to large effect, this estimate is not significantly different from zero. The failure to be statistically significant is due to the imprecision of the estimate of this correlation, which is adjusted for measurement error, in the same way that correlations can be corrected for attenuation using classical test theory (Lord & Novick, 1968). When we calculated the sample averages for each respondent over the 7 days and correlated these directly, we obtained a correlation of 0.40, which was statistically significant with p < .001. As one would expect, this latter estimate is somewhat smaller than the correlation between the latent means because of measurement error.[4]

In addition to the association of the examinee and partner in their tendency to have high or low scores overall, Table 12.2 shows that there is an association among residual scores of examinees and partners on a given day (multilevel estimate = .134; SEM estimate = .136). This association could be due to events that the members of the dyad shared, such as arguments that lead to unusually high anger ratings, or shared pleasant events that lead to unusually low anger. In this case the covariance reflecting this association is statistically significant, although the implied correlation is modest (r = 0.26).

The final association reported in Table 12.2 is the autocorrelation of residuals on one day with residuals on the next for a given participant. This correlation is estimated to be 0.316 using the multilevel approach, and the small standard error implies that it is reliably different from zero. Part of this correlation could be due to a tendency for persons to be increasing or decreasing steadily in anger (Rogosa, 1988; Rogosa, Brandt, & Zimowski, 1982). We estimated a model that included linear growth effects for examinee and partner and found that neither random effect had reliable variance. When we included a fixed growth parameter only the autocorrelation was reduced from 0.32 to 0.30.

The parameters of the dyadic process model can be used to generate predicted correlations among the 14 daily anger measures, analogous to the actual correlations presented in Table 12.1. In Table 12.3 we summarize these predicted correlations. In general, these are reasonably similar to the actual correlations, but it can also be seen that these predicted correlations miss considerable variability within any given time lag. It is worth considering how much of a given examinee–partner correlation is attributable to influences at the between-person and within-person level. Although the correlation between the mean anger of examinees and partners is substantially greater than the day-level correlation (.469 vs. .262), because most of the variance in anger resides at the daily level vs. person level (e.g., .42 vs. .08 for examinees and .63 vs. .12

---

[4]It might seem unintuitive that an unbiased estimate of a correlation is less precise than biased estimate. However, these characteristics of estimators are completely distinct (see Welsh, 1996, for other examples). In our case, the adjustment of the correlation for measurement error depends on estimates of the error-free variances of the latent variables, and the uncertainty of these estimates leads to imprecision of the correlation estimate.

TABLE 12.3

Model-Predicted Correlations as a Function of Time-Lag Based on Parameter Values in Table 12.2

Day t with	Within examinee	Within Partner	Examinee-Partner
t	1.000	1.000	0.292
t-1	0.501	0.433	0.152
t-2	0.320	0.228	0.102
t-3	0.255	0.154	0.084
t-4	0.232	0.128	0.077
t-5	0.223	0.118	0.075
t-6	0.220	0.114	0.074

for partners), 75% of the predicted same-day correlation of .292 is due to shared variance at the daily level, whereas only 25% is due to shared variance at the person-level.

CONCLUSIONS

We have described a model of dyadic longitudinal data that we believe is a useful starting point for researchers whose principal focus is to understand within-rather than between-dyad processes. In this respect our model has more in common with the Kenny and colleagues models (Cook & Snyder, 2005; Kashy & Kenny, 2000; Kenny, 1996; Kenny & Zautra, 1995, 2001) and the Raudenbush et al. (1995) model than it has with the Gonzalez and Griffin model (Gonzalez & Griffin, 1997, 1999, 2002; Griffin & Gonzalez, 1995). In the Gonzalez and Griffin model, the covariance among measures obtained on multiple individuals in multiple dyads is partialed into within- and between-dyad components. Our model does not estimate dyad-level relationships directly; their influence can only be seen through the correlations between latent variables at the individual level (e.g., between the latent means for anger for examinees and partners.)

As discussed in the methods section, the multilevel model formulation of our model is similar to (and draws on) the work of Raudenbush and colleagues on dyadic data analysis. Their approach was more complex than ours in the sense that they formed replicate-measures subscales of their dependent variable to take account of measurement error. Our model is more complex than theirs, however, in the sense that our error structure handles autocorrelation over time within a person and between persons within a dyad.

Of the three alternative approaches, ours is most similar to a combination of the State-Trait-Error Model and the Actor-Partner-Interdependence Model. Like the State-Trait-Error Model, we show that the relation among variables over time can be decomposed into a stable component, the correlation among latent means, and a time-varying component, consisting of a model of temporal relationships within and between dyad members. Like the Actor–Partner Interdependence Model, we focus on dyadic relationship over time, but, as noted earlier, we limit ourselves to estimating dyadic covariances rather than directed effects that can be interpreted as within-dyad causal influences. We also note that the State-Trait-Error model was developed within an SEM framework, thereby allowing one to estimate and remove measurement error from the temporal data. This is as yet an infeasible option within the multilevel modeling framework.

We have shown that our model can be thought of as a place-holder for the influence of conceptually important factors on the covariance between examinee and partner anger. Thus, the same-day covariance between the anger scores of dyad members can be the result of shared daily experiences or of direct influence between the members. The covariance between the stable components of the anger scores, can, as Gonzalez and Griffin do, be thought of as a couple-level covariance. It might reflect a tendency for assortative mating based on tolerance–intolerance of anger or it could be the result of an environmental influence on both dyad members that is stable over time. An example of the latter might be high ambient noise levels that represent a chronic stressor on the dyad.

Our hope is that researchers interested in modeling dyadic processes can begin their analysis by estimating the covariance structure specified in our model and then by adding suitable predictors document the causal mechanisms that underlie that structure. Variations of our model could be developed that take account of the possibility that the autocorrelation process might be different on weekends than weekdays, or one partner's level of Y could have a lagged effect on the other partner's level at the next time point. In some applications, the model could be simplified. For example, if neither partner was facing an acute stressor it is conceivable that the partners might resemble exchangeable rather than distinguishable dyad members. Both approaches we have illustrated have some capacity to accommodate expanded models or constrained models. We hope relationship researchers will begin to use these methods to identify the processes underlying the substantial dependencies in longitudinal dyadic data.

ACKNOWLEDGMENTS

This research was supported by grant MH60366 from the National Institute of Mental Health.

REFERENCES

Barnett, R. C., Marshall, N. L., Raudenbush, S. W., & Brennan, R. T. (1993). Gender and the relationship between job experiences and psychological distress: A study of dual-earner couples. *Journal of Personality & Social Psychology, 64*, 794-806.

Bock, R. D. (1975). *Multivariate statistical methods in behavioral research.* New York: McGraw Hill.

Bolger, N., Davis, A., & Rafaeli, E. (2003). Diary methods: Capturing life as it is lived. *Annual Review of Psychology, 54*, 579-616.

Bolger, N., Zuckerman, A., & Kessler, R. C. (2000). Invisible support and adjustment to stress. *Journal of Personality & Social Psychology, 79*, 953-961.

Cook, W. L., & Snyder, D. K. (2005). Analyzing nonindependent outcomes in couple therapy using the actor-partner interdependence model. *Journal of Family Psychology, 19*, 133-141.

Cranford, J., Shrout, P. E., Rafaeli, E., Yip, T., Iida, M., & Bolger, N. (2005). *Ensuring sensitivity to process and change: The case of mood measures in diary studies.* New York University: Unpublished manuscript, Department of Psychology.

Gonzalez, R., & Griffin, D. (1997). On the statistics of interdependence: Treating dyadic data with respect. In S. Duck (Ed.), *Handbook of personal relationships: Theory, research and interventions* (2nd ed., pp. 271-302). New York: Wiley.

Gonzalez, R., & Griffin, D. (1999). The correlation analysis of dyad-level data in the distinguishable case. *Personal Relationships, 6*, 449-469.

Gonzalez, R., & Griffin, D. (2002). Modeling the personality of dyads and groups. *Journal of Personality, 70*, 901-924.

Griffin, D., & Gonzalez, R. (1995). Correlational analysis of dyad-level data in the exchangeable case. *Psychological Bulletin, 118*, 430-439.

Kashy, D. A., & Kenny, D. A. (2000). The analysis of data from dyads and groups. In H. T. Reis & C. M. Judd (Eds.), *Handbook of research methods in social and personality psychology* (pp. 451-477). New York: Cambridge University Press.

Kenny, D. A. (1996). Models of interdependence in dyadic research. *Journal of Social and Personal Relationships, 13*, 279-284.

Kenny, D. A., & Zautra, A. (1995). The trait-state-error model for multiwave data. *Journal of Consulting & Clinical Psychology, 63*, 52-59.

Kenny, D. A., & Zautra, A. (2001). Trait-state models for longitudinal data. In L. M. Collins & A. G. Sayer (Eds.), *New methods for the analysis of change* (pp. 243-263). Washington, DC: American Psychological Association.

Lord, F., & Novick, M. (1968). *Statistical theories of mental test scores.* Reading, MA: Addison-Wesley.

McNair, D. M., Lorr, M., & Droppleman, L. F. (1992). *Manual for the profile of mood states.* San Diego, CA: Educational & Industrial Testing Service.

Multivariate Software. (2004). *EQS Version 6.1.* Encino, CA: Author.

Raudenbush, S. W., Brennan, R. T., & Barnett, R. C. (1995). A multivariate hierarchical model for studying psychological change within married couples. *Journal of Family Psychology, 9*, 161-174.

Rogosa, D. (1988). Myths about longitudinal research. In K. W. Schaie & R. T. Campbell (Eds.), *Methodological issues in aging research* (pp. 171-209). New York: Springer.

Rogosa, D., Brandt, D., & Zimowski, M. (1982). A growth curve approach to the measurement of change. *Psychological Bulletin, 92*, 726-748.

Schafer, J. L., & Graham, J. W. (2002). Missing data: Our view of the state of the art. *Psychological Methods, 7*, 147-177.

Spanier, G. B. (1976). Measuring dyadic adjustment: New scales for assessing the quality of marriage and similar dyads. *Journal of Marriage and the Family, 38*, 15-28.

Welsh, A. H. (1996). *Aspects of statistical inference.* New York: Wiley.

Willett, J. B., & Sayer, A. G. (1994). Using covariance structure analysis to detect correlates and predictors of individual change over time. *Psychological Bulletin, 116*, 363-381.

CHAPTER THIRTEEN

Coupled Dynamics and Mutually Adaptive Context

Steven M. Boker

The University of Notre Dame

Jean-Philippe Laurenceau

University of Delaware

Humans are adaptable organisms. We change our behavior as a consequence of changes in our environment, but we also strive to make changes in our environment. One of the components of our daily environment is our own internal processes and we also make changes in our own behavior in response to our internal state. These behavioral changes may in turn change our internal state: In other words we self–regulate. Carver and Scheier (1998) define self–regulation as follows:

> ldots we argue that human behavior is a continual process of moving toward, and away from, various kinds of mental goal representations, and that this movement occurs by a process of feedback control. This view treats behavior as the consequence of an internal guidance system inherent in the way living beings are organized. ldots we refer to the guidance process as a system of *self–regulation* (p. 2).

Self–regulation by feedback control implies that self–perception is part of the process of self–regulation. That is to say, if the perceived internal state is somehow different than a desired equilibrium state (i.e., mental goal representation), then behavioral changes are enacted to initiate change in the internal state such that over time the internal state comes closer to the desired equilibrium.

In addition to being self-regulating organisms, humans are also social organisms. Thus the context to which we adapt may include the adaptive behavior of others in our environment. Not only may there be self–regulatory processes at work — simultaneously there may be many examples of mutual regulation in which individuals adapt to the perceived state of others. The desired equilibrium may include satisfying some internal goals or needs, satisfying the goals or needs of another individual, as well as potentially maintaining an overall balance to the process of mutual adaptation. As a case in point, successfully married couples manage to mutually regulate in such a way that their dyadic relationship remains acceptably close to the mutually desired equilibrium.

Dynamical systems analysis includes strategies for expressing mathematical models of these types of coupled mutually regulating systems. Such models can be expressed as simultaneous differential equations for self–regulation of each individual in a coupled system as well as the responsiveness of each individual to the others. This chapter will describe an instance of a coupled differential equations model for dyadic interaction and provide a practical example of the use of this type of model as fit to data from a daily–diary study of self–disclosure within married couples. We will begin by presenting a dynamical systems framework within which self–regulation and coupled regulation may be considered. We will then present a differential equations model for this system and discuss its implications, thereby providing a rationale for why this model was chosen. We will next discuss some of the considerations required for fitting this type of model to real data. Finally we will apply the model to an example data set and discuss the implications of the resulting estimated parameters.

EQUILIBRIA AND FLUCTUATIONS

Many psychological systems are likely to have some stable or slowly changing intraindividual *stable equilibrium* value (or alternatively, this is called a *set point* or a *point attractor*). By this we mean that the goal state for any moment in time can be represented by a single value for each variable making up the system. Thus if the system is far from the goal state, the system's state values are likely to change in such a way that they will become closer to the goal state over time. If such a system remains undisturbed for a sufficient interval of time, it will return to its stable equilibrium.

A chosen psychological system may be in one of many possible states. If these states can be ordered on a continuum and if repeated measurement of the states results in a frequency distribution of state values with an approximately Gaussian distribution, then in most cases dynamical systems models with point attractors will be good candidates for modeling the chosen psychological system. Frequently, repeated measurements of psychological variables result in relatively stable trait constructs whose residual variability has a roughly Gaussian distribution. When such systems may be theoretically considered within the framework of self–regulation, then dynamical systems with point attractors are likely candidates for expressing models of the intraindividual variability around these constructs.

However, short term fluctuations of a construct's value around a relatively stable trait value could be attributed to mechanisms other than self–regulation. For instance, it might be that the measured values are, to some degree, unreliable and so measurement error is contributing to the observed fluctuations in the value of the construct over time. Also, it may be that there are exogenous influences that are reliable but unmeasured that contribute to short–term fluctuations in a measured construct. A successful dynamical systems analysis ideally should be able to distinguish between these independent sources of variability in the chosen construct. In order to partition these sources of variability from one another, one tool that may be used is the time–scale of these three sources. Measurement error is by definition independent of the time scale of the measurement. Exogenous influences may be discrete events that are separated by intervals that have some distribution, frequently Poisson. Finally, self–regulation happens quickly enough that it may be considered as indistinguishable from a continuous process in comparison with the time scale at which psychological variables are likely to be measured.

ASSUMPTIONS OF CONTINUITY AND DIFFERENTIABILITY

A variable is continuous with respect to time if, for any selected times t and $t + \tau$ where the variable takes on the values $x(t)$ and $x(t + \tau)$, implies that the variable took on some value for every time between t and $t + \tau$ and that variable took on every value between $x(t)$ and $x(t + \tau)$ at some time between t and $t + \tau$ (see Boker, 2002, for an extended discussion of continuity). It may be easier to think about continuity in terms of when a variable does not meet the assumption of continuity. In Figure 1–a, the true function is continuous and thus has a value for every time between t and $t + \tau$ and takes on every value between $x(t)$ and $x(t + \tau)$ at some time in the interval t to $t + \tau$.

In Figure 1–b, the function is both discontinuous in time, that is to say some times it has no value at all, and is discontinuous in value, that is to say some values between $x(t)$ and $x(t+\tau)$ are not represented during the interval t to $t+\tau$. However, the values of the function at the 9 occasions of measurement in Figure 1–b are the same as in Figure 1–a. From the standpoint of discrete measurement such as occurs in psychology, these two functions are indistinguishable. No matter how often we measure, we can never prove continuity of psychological systems — continuity must remain an assumption.

FIGURE 13.1

Continuous and discontinuous functions. (a) The true function is continuous and is measured at 9 occasions between t and $t + \tau$. (b) The true function is discontinuous, but is indistinguishable from a continuous function if all that is known are the data from the 9 occasions of measurement.

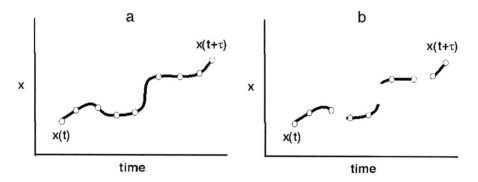

The assumption of continuity has proved to be very useful for modeling dynamical systems and comes at little cost. The advantages of continuous time modeling include the following:

1. Parameter values can be estimated so as to be independent of the sampling interval. The values of the parameters of discrete time models such as autoregressive and cross–lag models are a nonlinear function of the sampling interval.

2. Lagged and simultaneous effects can be estimated by the same parameter. The basis of continuous time modeling is that instantaneous relationships between the derivatives of a system lead to deterministic and measurable differences in the values of variables as a function of time. Simply by picking a particular desired time lag, the continuous time model can be used to make time–forward predictions about the future state of the system given the current state of the system.

3. Parameter estimates may have better substantive interpretation. When the model is expressed in terms of instantaneous change, the parameters frequently map directly onto concepts that are meaningful in the framework of self–regulation, growth, learning, aging and other areas of psychological theory.

FIGURE 13.2

Three plots visualizing a damped linear oscillator. (a) A trajectory plot of the displacement, x, of the oscillator from equilibrium versus time for a single initial condition. (b) A phase space plot of the displacement, x, and first derivative, $\dot{x}$, with respect to time for the same initial condition. (c) A vector field plot of the change in x and $\dot{x}$ during a short interval of time for a grid of initial conditions.

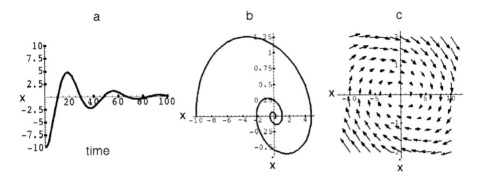

A SIMPLE CONTINUOUS SELF–REGULATING PROCESS

One of the simplest dynamical systems model with a point attractor and whose fluctuations lead to an approximately Gaussian distribution is a second order linear differential equation known as the damped linear oscillator. This system has a single point attractor: A stable equilibrium point. In the terms of self–regulation, the farther away from equilibrium this system is, the more it turns back toward equilibrium. Thus one might say that the system avoids being far from the equilibrium value: It self–regulates to return towards equilibrium. In addition, this system avoids rapid change: The faster it is changing, the more it attempts to decrease that rate of change. The damped linear oscillator may be written as

$$\ddot{x}(t) = \eta x(t) + \zeta \dot{x}(t) \tag{1}$$

where $x(t)$ is the displacement from equilibrium at time t, $\dot{x}(t)$ and $\ddot{x}(t)$ are the first and second derivative of x with respect to time at time t (Thompson & Stewart, 1986). The constant parameter η is a negative value that expresses how much proportional effect on the second derivative (i.e., the curvature of a trajectory) is due to the displacement from equilibrium. Similarly, the constant negative value ζ is the proportional effect on the second derivative of the first derivative (i.e., the slope of the trajectory).

Figure-2 diplays three views of the damped linear oscillator defined in Equation 1. Figure 2-a plots a single trajectory that is the predicted outcome over the interval $0 \le t \le 100$ for an individual who started with initial conditions of displacement $x = -10$ and slope $\dot{x} = 0$ at time $t = 0$. In Figure 2-a note that when the displacement from equilibrium is greatest (e.g., at $t = 20$ and $x = 5$) the curvature is greatest and the slope is zero. But when the displacement from equilibrium is zero (e.g., at $t = 10$ and $x = 0$), the slope is greatest and the curvature is near zero. The same trajectory is plotted as a *phase space* in Figure 2-b, that is the displacement is plotted against the first derivative. Again, note that when the displacement is greatest, the slope is zero and when the slope is greatest the displacement is near zero. Finally in Figure 2-c the outcomes of a grid of initial conditions for x and $\dot{x}$ are plotted where time is incremented only a small interval. Figure 2-c is called a *vector field plot* and allows one to visualize predicted outcome trajectories over a range of initial conditions.

CONTEXT AND SELF–REGULATING SYSTEMS

It seems evident that a self–regulating individual will interact with the environment. Thus, self–regulation may interact with the situational context in which the individual is embedded. One way this might happen is for the context to have an effect on the self–regulating system. A second expression of interaction between a self–regulating system and its context is that the system may have an effect on its context. Finally, we might consider a context that is itself a system with self–regulating dynamics. Let us consider in turn each of these three possibilities for context-system interactions. We present this thought exercise in hopes that it will spur the interested reader to explore how contextual interaction and self–regulation might be applied to her or his own theory and data.

For this discussion we will use a simple physical example of a self–regulating system: A pendulum with friction. The farther a pendulum is from its equilibrium point (i.e., hanging straight down), the more acceleration due to gravity is exerted on the pendulum. That is to say, there is an effect on the second derivative of the pendulum's position relative to equilibrium that is proportional to its position relative to equilibrium. If we also treat the proportional effect of friction as being proportional to the speed of the pendulum we will have a model for the dynamics of the pendulum that is exactly as is described in Equation 1.

Exogenous Effects on Self–Regulation

The first possible expression of a context-system interaction consists of the effect of some exogenous context on the pendulum. If there is no effect of context, then the pendulum will swing for a time, but will soon come to rest at equilibrium. Suppose now that there is a direct effect of the environment on the position of the pendulum. For instance, a person might grasp the pendulum, move it to an arbitrary position and then release it. Or, a person might give the pendulum a push. These would be direct effects on the displacement and velocity of the pendulum and could be modeled as a system of simultaneous regression equations,

$$\ddot{x}(t) = \eta x(t) + \zeta \dot{x}(t) + e_{\ddot{x}}(t) \tag{2}$$
$$\dot{x}(t) = b_1 z(t) + e_{\dot{x}}(t) \tag{3}$$
$$x(t) = b_2 z(t) + e_x(t), \tag{4}$$

where $\ddot{x}(t)$, $\dot{x}(t)$, and $x(t)$ are the acceleration, velocity and displacement of the pendulum at time t. The regression coefficients b_1 and b_2 represent the proportional effects on the velocity and displacement of the exogenous context variable $z(t)$ at time t. This system of equations could be fit using structural equations modeling software if sufficient data in the form of measurements of the exogenous variables and estimates of the displacement and derivatives of the system were available (Boker & Ghisletta, 1998; Boker, 2001, 2002).

There is another way that an exogenous context could have an effect on the pendulum. Rather than a direct effect, the exogenous context could have a moderating effect. That is to say, the context could have an effect that was like changing the length of the pendulum or the friction at its pivot. For instance, suppose the pendulum were in a room where the temperature was becoming warmer. As the pendulum became warmer the length of the pendulum would increase slightly and so the pendulum's cycle would become a little longer. Similarly, as the pivot became warmer it might result in less friction at the pivot. We could write a multilevel model for these types of moderating effects such that

$$\ddot{x}_i(t) = \eta_i x_i(t) + \zeta_i \dot{x}_i(t) + e_{\ddot{x}i}(t) \tag{5}$$
$$\eta_i = c_\eta + u_{\eta i} \tag{6}$$
$$\zeta_i = c_\zeta + u_{\zeta i}, \tag{7}$$

where $\ddot{x}_i(t)$, $\dot{x}_i(t)$, and $x_i(t)$ are the acceleration, velocity and displacement of the pendulum at time t for context i (Boker, 2001; Maxwell & Boker, in press). The regression coefficients η_i and ζ_i are themselves dependent on the context i such that they are functions of an overall constant, c_η and c_ζ as well as unique contributions from each context, $u_{\eta i}$ and $u_{\zeta i}$.

Effects of Self–Regulation on the Environment

The second possible expression of a context–system interaction involves the effect that the self–regulating system may have on the external environment. For instance, a pianist might be watching the pendulum and using it to help regulate her tempo as she plays a piece of music. The pianist may be attending to the position of the pendulum or may be attending to the velocity of the pendulum, or perhaps some linear combination of the two as in the following system of equations,

$$\ddot{x}(t) = \eta x(t) + \zeta \dot{x}(t) + e_{\ddot{x}}(t) \tag{8}$$
$$z(t) = b_1 x(t) + b_2 \dot{x}(t) + e_z(t), \tag{9}$$

where $\ddot{x}(t)$, $\dot{x}(t)$, and $x(t)$ are again the acceleration, velocity and displacement of the pendulum at time t. The regression coefficients b_1 and b_2 now represent the proportional effects of the velocity and displacement of the pendulum on the exogenous context variable $z(t)$ at time t. Note the striking similarity between the right hand sides of Equations 8 and 9. If the effect of the displacement and velocity of the pendulum were not on the value of the variable $z(t)$ but on its second derivative with respect to time $\ddot{z}(t)$,

$$\ddot{x}(t) = \eta x(t) + \zeta \dot{x}(t) + e_{\ddot{x}}(t) \tag{10}$$
$$\ddot{z}(t) = b_1 x(t) + b_2 \dot{x}(t) + e_{\ddot{z}}(t), \tag{11}$$

then the pendulum could be said to be regulating changes in the pianist's tempo in much the same way that the pendulum was self–regulating. This type of effect will result in the pianist's tempo matching the pendulum as long as the coefficients b_1 and b_2 are reasonably similar to the coefficients η and ζ. One way to express this "reasonable similarity" is to constrain the effect of the pendulum on the pianist to be a proportion of the pendulum's own self–regulation coefficients,

$$\ddot{x}(t) = \eta x(t) + \zeta \dot{x}(t) + e_{\ddot{x}}(t) \tag{12}$$
$$\ddot{z}(t) = \gamma(\eta x(t) + \zeta \dot{x}(t)) + e_{\ddot{z}}(t), \tag{13}$$

where γ now is the proportion of the pendulum's self–regulating mechanism that drives the tempo regulation of the pianist. But what of the pianist's self–regulation? Our development of this model should be expanded to include the possibility that the pianist has some internal mechanism that helps her regulate her own tempo. This possibility leads to a third type of system-context interaction.

Mutually Adaptive Context

The third expression of interaction of systems and context that will be discussed involves a situation where two self–regulating systems provide the context for each other (see Butner, Amazeen, & Mulvey, 2005; Chow, Ram, Boker, Fujita, & Clore, 2005, for other examples). Suppose now that two pianists, Xavier and Yolanda, are to play a duet. Let us assume that each of them self–regulates their own tempo as if they were a pendulum, but pays no attention to the other so that

$$\ddot{x}(t) \quad = \quad \eta_x x(t) + \zeta_x \dot{x}(t) + e_{\ddot{x}}(t) \tag{14}$$

$$\ddot{y}(t) \quad = \quad \eta_y y(t) + \zeta_y \dot{y}(t) + e_{\ddot{y}}(t), \tag{15}$$

where η_x may or may not be equal to η_y and ζ_x may or may not be equal to ζ_y. The only way that Xavier and Yolanda will be playing in sync with one another is if they start with the same initial conditions, $\{x(0) = y(0), \dot{x}(0) = \dot{y}(0)\}$, *and* if Xavier's and Yolanda's self–regulating frequency parameters are equal, $\eta_x = \eta_y$. Small differences in the pianist's self–regulation could lead to terrible sounding results on stage. Certainly, it would make sense if there were a mechanism for Yolanda and Xavier to listen to each other and adapt their own behavior to some combination of what they themselves are playing and what their partner is playing.

   A simple model that allows for mutually adaptive context is an extension of Equation 13 in which there is a one–way proportional effect. Suppose that Yolanda and Xavier have a mutual effect on one another. Further suppose that this mutual effect is such that the regulating effect that Yolanda has on Xavier is a proportion of the regulating effect she has on herself, and that the same situation holds for Xavier. We can then write a set of proportionally coupled equations as

$$\ddot{x}(t) \quad = \quad \eta_x x(t) + \zeta_x \dot{x}(t) + \gamma(\eta_y y(t) + \zeta_y \dot{y}(t)) + e_{\ddot{x}}(t) \tag{16}$$

$$\ddot{y}(t) \quad = \quad \eta_y y(t) + \zeta_y \dot{y}(t) + \gamma(\eta_x x(t) + \zeta_x \dot{x}(t)) + e_{\ddot{y}}(t), \tag{17}$$

where γ is the proportional effect that Yolanda and Xavier have on one another. This system is called a *symmetrically coupled* system because there is only one coupling constant γ, that is to say the proportional effect of Xavier on Yolanda is the same as the proportional effect of Yolanda on Xavier. The advantage of this coupling is that even if the internal frequency regulation parameters are similar but not equal, $\eta_x \approx \eta_y$, and the initial conditions are not equal, $\{x(0) \neq y(0), \dot{x}(0) \neq \dot{y}(0)\}$, given sufficient coupling strength, the two pianists will begin to play in synchrony after a short amount of time.

But, as everyone knows, Yolanda is a much better pianist than Xavier. So, it would make sense for Yolanda to only pay a little attention to what Xavier is doing, but Xavier should pay close attention to what Yolanda is doing. If so, Yolanda's superior self–regulation will improve the experience for Xavier and, as a result, improve the overall experience for the audience. We can write such an *asymmetrically coupled* system as

$$\ddot{x}(t) = \eta_x x(t) + \zeta_x \dot{x}(t) + \gamma_y(\eta_y y(t) + \zeta_y \dot{y}(t)) + e_{\ddot{x}}(t) \qquad (18)$$

$$\ddot{y}(t) = \eta_y y(t) + \zeta_y \dot{y}(t) + \gamma_x(\eta_x x(t) + \zeta_x \dot{x}(t)) + e_{\ddot{y}}(t), \qquad (19)$$

where $\gamma_y > \gamma_x$ if Xavier is affected more by Yolanda than she is by him.

In the example of the pianists Xavier and Yolanda we have ignored part of the behavior implied by the damped linear oscillator: The amplitude of the fluctuations decreases exponentially over time when $\zeta < 0$. Thus, Yolanda and Xavier would be performing a concert in which they were fading to silence as the musical piece progressed. We have also ignored exogenous effects on the pianists. In order to further develop the notion of mutually adaptive context, let us return to the example of the pendulum.

An asymmetrical proportionally coupled system of two damped linear oscillators as expressed in Equations 18 and 19 could also be visualized as a pair of pendulums as shown in Figure-3. The effect of pendulum X on pendulum Y is not the same as the effect of pendulum Y on pendulum X as represented by the imaginary unidirectional springs. But it should be evident that if one were to give a push to pendulum X, some part of that exogenous effect on X would be show up in the swing of pendulum Y. Similarly, this indirect effect of the exogenous variable would, having changed the swing of pendulum Y, again show up as an effect of Y on X. The momentary effect of the exogenous variable would *reverberate* through this system of two pendulums.

The trajectories described by two such coupled system of equations can be estimated using numerical methods such as Runge–Kutta integration (Butcher, 2003). Figure-4 presents the result of integrating the system of differential equations from Equations 18 and 19 when the starting values are of opposite sign, there is positive coupling, and the parameters are chosen so that the frequencies are relatively dissimilar and the damping parameters are of opposite sign. An example system for this might be a married couple, Xander and Yvette. Yvette tends to fluctuate on a day-to-day basis more rapidly than Xander. Xander tends to come quickly back to a stable state whereas Yvette tends to escalate into larger and larger fluctuations. As a couple, they are relatively stable, since they each have a positive proportional regulating effect on the other. Their fluctuations neither become too large or too small, but the

FIGURE 13.3

Two coupled pendulums x and y with different length and asymmetric coupling. The constant acceleration due to gravity G acts on each pendulum in a direction perpendicular to the rod resulting in an acceleration $\ddot{y}$ proportional the displacement from equilibrium y. Asymmetric coupling is represented by two diagrammatic "one–way" springs.

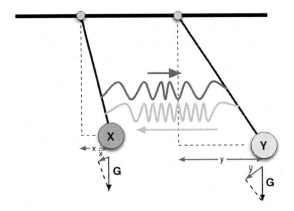

trajectories that they describe are relatively complex as can be seen in almost three months of simulated daily diary data in Figure-4. These data can also be plotted as trajectories in phase space as shown in Figure-4. By taking short samples from this phase space, we can reconstruct the type of data that is used to create the vector field in Figure-2 and thereby estimate parameters for the system of equations in Equations 18 and 19.

Let us consider one more model for mutually adaptive context by relaxing the proportional coupling constraint. Suppose that Xander and Yvette do not respond to one another in the same way as they regulate themselves. For instance, it might be that Xander's self–regulation results in moderate damping in response to his own change, but when he sees rapid change in Yvette, it results in high damping of his fluctuations. In contrast, Yvette's response to her own change is positive: Small changes lead to bigger ones. Thus, if Xander and Yvette are both fluctuating ($\eta_x < 0$, $\eta_y < 0$, and $\gamma_y \eta_y < 0$) the same damping parameter $\zeta_y > 0$ that accounts for Yvette's self–regulation cannot also account for the observed damping effect on Xander since this would imply that $\gamma_y > 0$ and $\zeta_y > 0$ and $\gamma_y \zeta_y < 0$. In order to fit this case, we must relax the assumption that a proportion of the same mechanism that regulates Yvette's fluctuations is the effect of Yvette on Xander. We can write this model as

$$\ddot{x}(t) \;=\; \eta_x x(t) + \zeta_x \dot{x}(t) + \eta_{yx} y(t) + \zeta_{yx} \dot{y}(t) + e_{\ddot{x}}(t) \qquad (20)$$

$$\ddot{y}(t) \;=\; \eta_y y(t) + \zeta_y \dot{y}(t) + \eta_{xy} x(t) + \zeta_{xy} \dot{x}(t) + e_{\ddot{y}}(t), \qquad (21)$$

FIGURE 13.4

One set of trajectories for two asymmetric proportionally coupled damped linear oscillators, X (dark gray) and Y (light gray). (a) Trajectory plot of the displacement X and Y over a range of time $0 \leq t \leq 80$. (b) Phase space plot of the displacement of X and Y against the first derivative of X and Y for the same trajectories as (a).

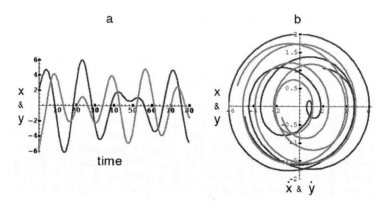

so that now η_y need not equal η_{yx}, ζ_y need not equal ζ_{yx} and so forth (Boker, Neale, & Rausch, 2004). This model is identified in practice as long as $\eta_x \neq \eta_y$ and $\zeta_x \neq \zeta_y$.

Suppose one were to perform an observational study on N couples, each of whom were measured on T occasions. It is reasonable to relax the assumptions of the model in Equations 20 and 21 in order to allow each dyad of oscillators to have its own parameters, conforming to the assumption that the parameters are normally distributed within the population and that the parameters are not changing during the study. One then could write a multilevel form of this coupled model as

$$\ddot{x}_i(t) = \eta_{ix}x_i(t) + \zeta_{ix}\dot{x}_i(t) + \eta_{iyx}y(t) + \zeta_{iyx}\dot{y}_i(t) + e_{i\ddot{x}}(t) \tag{22}$$

$$\ddot{y}_i(t) = \eta_{iy}y_i(t) + \zeta_{iy}\dot{y}_i(t) + \eta_{ixy}x(t) + \zeta_{ixy}\dot{x}_i(t) + e_{i\ddot{y}}(t) \tag{23}$$

$$\eta_{ix} = c_{\eta x} + u_{i\eta x} \tag{24}$$

$$\zeta_{ix} = c_{\zeta x} + u_{i\zeta x} \tag{25}$$

$$\eta_{iyx} = c_{\eta yx} + u_{i\eta yx} \tag{26}$$

$$\zeta_{iyx} = c_{\zeta yx} + u_{i\zeta yx} \tag{27}$$

$$\eta_{iy} = c_{\eta y} + u_{i\eta y} \tag{28}$$

$$\zeta_{iy} = c_{\zeta y} + u_{i\zeta y} \tag{29}$$

$$\eta_{ixy} = c_{\eta xy} + u_{i\eta xy} \tag{30}$$

$$\zeta_{ixy} = c_{\zeta xy} + u_{i\zeta xy}, \tag{31}$$

where a dyad i has parameters that are a combination of a constant c that is shared among all the dyads and a part u that is unique to the individual dyad.

We next present an example application of the use of dynamical systems models when mutually adaptive context is part of the theoretical construct: Self–disclosure within married couples. We will present two forms of the model, a univariate multilevel version that examines husbands' and wives' self–disclosure separately and a multivariate structural model version that examines husbands and wives as part of a mutually adaptive system. In order to help illuminate issues that can guide model choice, we will then discuss how the results of these models differ and how these differences might be interpreted.

SELF–DISCLOSURE WITHIN MARRIED COUPLES

One of the ways in which intimacy is maintained between married partners is a process of self–disclosure; one partner self–reveals and the other partner responds in turn with disclosures that convey understanding and validation (Laurenceau, Rivera, Schaffer, & Pietromonaco, 2004; Reis & Shaver, 1988). The level of self-revealing disclosure for each individual has an equilibrium range within which it fluctuates. Short term variation in this self–disclosure may be regulated both by the individual and their partner in such a way that marital intimacy is regulated within a desired range. Some (e.g., Prager & Roberts, 2004) have considered this regulation as a process in which the opposing needs of autonomy and intimacy are maintained, a theoretic perspective that focuses on what is far from equilibrium: Too much intimacy or too much autonomy. Others (e.g., Laurenceau, Feldman Barrett, & Rovine, 2005; Laurenceau & Kleinman, in press) have treated the same process as one of self–regulation around a desired goal state. Both of these theoretical perspectives can be considered to be views of the same class of dynamical systems model: A model with a point attractor.

A point attractor can be thought of as the lowest point in a hemispherical bowl; the farther one is away from the center of the bowl, the steeper the sides of the bowl. A marble dropped into the bowl will roll around and eventually come to rest in the center of the bowl, the point attractor. One may also describe the same bowl in terms of the rim of the bowl being a repellor, in other words the marble rolls around avoiding the edges until it comes to rest as far as it can from the rim of the bowl. In the same way, avoidance of excessive autonomy or intimacy on the one hand or attraction to a equilibrium goal state between autonomy and intimacy on the other hand can equally well be described by a point attractor dynamical systems model.

Married couples exhibit interdependent behaviors, that is the behaviors, emotional states and goal states of one partner are likely to influence that of the other partner (Kelley et al., 1983). This dyadic interdependence in close relationships typically translates into the emergence of both significant actor and partner effects (Kashy & Kenny, 2000), whereby an individuals outcomes are determined partly by some predictive characteristic of the individual (i.e., actor effect) and partly by the same characteristic of the partner (i.e., partner effect). Thus, we could expect that a dynamical systems model that described self– regulation for each partner would also need to include an aspect of coupled regulation in which the regulation of one partner influenced the regulation of the other (see Prager & Roberts, 2004, p. 55, for a discussion of dynamic adjustment). But, there is no a priori reason that the same mechanism that self– regulates one partner will be the regulation mechanism for the other partner's coupled regulation. For example, the degree to which a husband experiences discomfort in relation to being far from his own equilibrium may or may not be the same degree to which the wife experiences discomfort when her husband is far from his equilibrium.

For these reasons, we focus our attention on forms of the coupled differential equations models from Equations 20 and 21. We will explore the results of fitting a multilevel univariate form and multivariate form of this model to data from a six week long diary study of 96 married couples.

Procedure

Married heterosexual couples were recruited to participate in a "study on daily experiences in marital relationships." A research assistant was assigned to each couple and visited their home three times over the course of the study. Each spouses was instructed to complete independently a set of daily diary items during the evening on each of 42 consecutive days (6 weeks). Procedures were used to help insure response integrity on the diaries. The research assistant phoned couples the evening following the initial home visit and spoke to each spouse individually in order to answer any emerging questions about the diary procedure. Couples were also called on a weekly basis to help ensure compliance. A second visit was conducted at the end of the third week of diary recording where the research assistant collected each spouse's completed diaries for the first half of the recording period and scheduled a tentative final visit. Upon completion of the final week of diary recordings, the research assistant conducted a final home visit in order to collect the completed diaries from the second half of the recording period and to remunerate couples for their participation in the study. Additional details about study procedures can be found in Laurenceau, Feldman Barrett, and Rovine (2005).

Measures

The set of daily-diary items was constructed to assess the central variables theorized to underlie Reis and Shaver (1988)'s interpersonal process model of intimacy and was modeled after the diary form used by Laurenceau, Barrett, and Pietromonaco (1998). Responses to diary items were all rated using 5–point Likert scales (e.g., 1 = very little, 5 = a great deal). Being part of a larger diary form, only the disclosure-related diary variables are described here:

Disclosure

Spouses rated the amount that they disclosed facts and information (one item), the amount that they disclosed their thoughts (one item), and the amount that they disclosed their feelings (one item) across all the interactions that they had with their spouse during the day. Spouses also rated the amount they perceived that their partner disclosed facts and information (one item), the amount of perceived disclosure of their partner's thoughts (one item), and the amount of perceived disclosure of feelings (one item) across all the interactions that they had with their spouse during the day. A disclosure summary variable was created using the sum of these six items (for a discussion of the rationale for this sum see Boker & Laurenceau, 2005).

Descriptive Results

Daily diaries including the self–disclosure measures were completed by 96 couples for 42 consecutive days. Two couples, however, were excluded due to low response rates. Of the remaining 94 couples, the overall complete husband and wife response rate was 97%. Overall disclosure means and standard deviations for husbands ($M = 13.04$, $SD = 13.00$) and wives ($M = 12.85$, $SD = 15.60$) were similar, although the variability for wives was somewhat greater. The correlation between husbands' and wives' disclosure scores on the same day was positive, but relatively low (0.26). While this correlation is less than ideal, there are several reasons why a simulatneous (in our case, same–day) correlation may not be indicative of the magnitude of the effect between two time series. For instance, there may be lead and lag relationships between the two time series such that sometimes the husband's score predicts the wife's score on the next day, but other times the wife's score predicts the husband's score on the next day. Taking a simultaneous correlation between the time series can obscure the strength of this sort of mutual adaptation.

Figure-5 plots the husband and wife scores for disclosure from four selected couples. It is apparent that there is intraindividual variability in these disclosure

FIGURE 13.5
Four example time series of couples disclosure scores over 42 days.

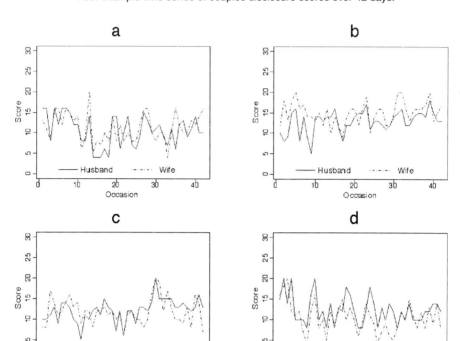

scores and that there may be a preferred equilibrium value or set point for each individual. Also note there appear to be *sychronization events* in which the husbands' and wives' scores seem to be displaced in the same direction from their own equilibrium within a day or two of each other. The plotted data were not inconsistent with our hypothesized dynamical systems model of coupled linear second order differential equations, i.e. coupled damped linear oscillators.

Multilevel Univariate Differential Equation Model

We first estimated models in which the husbands' and wives' regulation of disclosure were examined separately. In these models, we estimated the derivatives using local linear approximation (LLA) and a lag offset, τ, of 2 observations (for details on this method see Boker, 2001; Boker & Nesselroade, 2002). The lag offset was chosen to be 2 after analysis of the average R^2 of the models for a range of τ (Boker, Neale, & Rausch, 2004). In the following analyses, the second derivative of Disclosure was predicted as

$$\ddot{x}_{ij} = \eta_{ix}x_{ij} + \zeta_{ix}\dot{x}_{ij} + \eta_{iy}y_{ij} + \zeta_{iy}\dot{y}_{ij} + e_{ij} \tag{32}$$

$$\eta_{ix} = c_0 + u_{0i} \tag{33}$$

$$\zeta_{ix} = c_1 + u_{1i} \tag{34}$$

$$\eta_{iy} = c_2 + u_{2i} \tag{35}$$

$$\zeta_{iy} = c_3 + u_{3i} \tag{36}$$

where x_{ij} is the ith person's Disclosure score and y_{ij} is the Disclosure score of the ith person's spouse at the jth occasion. The estimated fixed effects, c_0, c_1, c_2, and c_3, are presented separately for husbands and wives in Tables 13.1 and 13.2 below. The rows in each table are labeled Husband's Disclosure, HD, first derivative of Husband's Disclosure, dHD, Wife's Disclosure, WD, and first derivative of Wife's Disclosure, dWD. Note that the first two rows in each table are the self–regulation parameters and the last two rows are the coupled regulation parameters.

The estimated cycle time for the husband and for the wife are approximately equal at 9 days. The only statistically significant coupling parameter is in the regulation of the husband's disclosure; WD, the displacement from equilibrium of the wife's disclosure has a small effect (about 4% the size of the self–regulation parameter). While these results are not unreasonable, one might suspect that fitting the husband and wife as separate models might be missing something about their mutually adaptive behavior.

In order to fit these two models as a simultaneous system, we used a technique known as Latent Differential Equations (Boker, Neale, & Rausch, 2004) which allows multivariate outcomes. Moreover, we used full information maximum likelihood so as to provide an estimate of fixed effects as in the model shown in Equations 22 through 31 (Chow, Ram, Boker, Fujita, & Clore, 2005).

TABLE 13.1

Regulation of Husband's Disclosure. Observations=3006, Groups=94, $\tau = 2$, Average R^2=0.6829, $\eta\tau^2$=-1.9332, $\lambda = 9.0$ day cycle, AIC = 7331, BIC = 7421, LogLikelihood = -3650

	Value	SE	DF	t	p
HD	-0.4833	0.00904	2909	-53.475	< 0.0001
dHD	-0.0100	0.01760	2909	-0.566	0.5713
WD	-0.0168	0.00581	2909	-2.894	0.0038
dWD	-0.0176	0.01572	2909	-1.121	0.2623

TABLE 13.2

Regulation of Wife's Disclosure. (Observations=3006, Groups=94, $\tau = 2$, Average R^2=0.7012, $\eta\tau^2$=-2.0592, $\lambda = 8.8$ day cycle, AIC = 8213, BIC = 8303, LogLikelihood = -4092).

	Value	SE	DF	t	p
WD	-0.5148	0.00984	2909	-52.3144	< 0.0001
dWD	-0.0113	0.01803	2909	-0.6288	0.5296
HD	-0.0112	0.00835	2909	-1.3372	0.1813
dHD	0.0016	0.02055	2909	0.0792	0.9368

Multivariate Latent Differential Equation Model

Latent Differential Equations (LDE) is a method for estimating regression co-efficients between the derivatives of a time series using only the covariances between latent variables constructed so as to estimate the needed derivatives. This method has roots in time–series filtering methods such as Savitzky–Golay filtering (Savitzky & Golay, 1964) as well as the substantial literature on latent growth models(e.g., Browne & Arminger, 1995; Duncan & Duncan, 1995; McArdle, 1986; McArdle & Anderson, 1990; McArdle & Epstein, 1987; Muthen & Curran, 1997; Willett & Sayer, 1994). The basic concept is to fit a latent growth model with constrained loadings equal to the appropriate indefinite integral series so that the latent variables are estimates of the displacement, first and second derivatives of the time series at a selected occasion within the time series. Thus, maximum likelihood estimates of the regression coefficients between these latent variables can be simultaneously estimated for multivariate coupled time series.

To start to unpack the previous paragraph, consider the path model shown in Figure-6. Husbands and wives have been measured on five occasions and a latent differential equation model of the displacement (H and W), the first derivative (dH and dW), and second derivative ($d2H$ and $d2W$) of the husbands' and wives' disclosure scores at occasion 3 has been constructed by constraining the loadings to the constants shown in Equation 37. The darker single–headed arrows are the regression coefficients estimating the effect of the latent displacement and latent first derivative on the latent second derivative for both the husbands and wives. These regression coefficients map onto the regression coefficients in Equations 20 and 21.

FIGURE 13.6

Coupled latent differential equations model with 5 occasions and assymetric linear coupling.

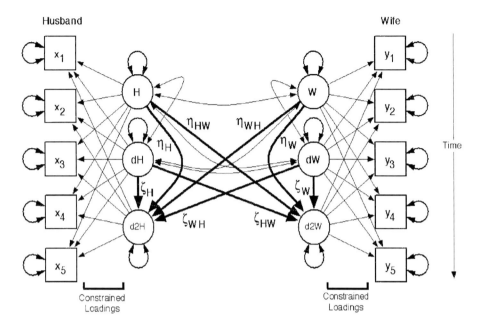

The constrained loadings in this model are constructed as follows

$$
\mathbf{L}_H \;=\; \begin{bmatrix} 1 & -2\tau & (-2\tau)^2/2 \\ 1 & -1\tau & (1\tau)^2/2 \\ 1 & 0 & 0 \\ 1 & 1\tau & (1\tau)^2/2 \\ 1 & 2\tau & (-2\tau)^2/2 \end{bmatrix}, \tag{37}
$$

where L_H are the constrained loadings for the husband and τ is the fixed interval of time between observations. Column 1 of L_H are the loadings from the latent displacement H to the observations $\{x_1, x_2, x_3, x_4, x_5\}$. The loadings in the second column are the indefinite integral of those in the first column centered at occasion 3 and so the latent first derivative is estimated and the latent displacement is estimated at occasion 3. Similarly, the third column is the indefinite integral of the second column and so the latent second derivative is estimated. Next, we set the constrained loading matrix for the wife to be the same as for the husband $\mathbf{L}_W = \mathbf{L}_H$ and augment these two into a block diagonal form so that

$$
\mathbf{L} \;=\; \begin{bmatrix} \mathbf{L}_H & 0 \\ 0 & \mathbf{L}_W \end{bmatrix}. \tag{38}
$$

We can now set up the structural part of the model following the RAM formulation (Boker, 2002; McArdle & McDonald, 1984) as

$$
\mathbf{A} =
\begin{bmatrix}
0 & 0 & 0 & 0 & 0 & 0 \\
0 & 0 & 0 & 0 & 0 & 0 \\
\eta_H & \zeta_H & 0 & \eta_{WH} & \zeta_{WH} & 0 \\
0 & 0 & 0 & 0 & 0 & 0 \\
0 & 0 & 0 & 0 & 0 & 0 \\
\eta_{HW} & \zeta_{HW} & 0 & \eta_W & \zeta_W & 0
\end{bmatrix},
\tag{39}
$$

and

$$
\mathbf{S} =
\begin{bmatrix}
V_H & & & & & \\
C_{HdH} & V_{dH} & & & & \\
0 & 0 & Ve_{d2H} & & & \\
C_{HW} & C_{dHW} & 0 & V_W & & \\
C_{HdW} & C_{dHdW} & 0 & C_{WdW} & V_{dW} & \\
0 & 0 & 0 & 0 & 0 & Ve_{d2W}
\end{bmatrix},
\tag{40}
$$

where the variances of the latent variables are represented by V_H, V_{dH}, V_W, and V_{dW}; similarly, the covariances between the latent variables are C_{HdH} etc.; and the residual variance of the second derivatives are Ve_{d2H} and Ve_{d2W}. Now, we can calculate the expected covariance matrix, $\hat{\mathbf{R}}$, of the observed timeseries as

$$
\hat{\mathbf{R}} = \mathbf{L}(\mathbf{I} - \mathbf{A})^{-1}\mathbf{S}(\mathbf{I} - \mathbf{A})^{-1'}\mathbf{L}' + \mathbf{U},
\tag{41}
$$

where $\mathbf{U}$ is a diagonal matrix of unique variances.

In order to set up our data to be fit with this model, we need to create a 10 column lagged data matrix, $\mathbf{Z}$ such that the first five columns are time–ordered disclosure scores from the husband and the last five columns are time–ordered disclosure scores from the wife. For each couple, i, we construct a lagged data matrix $\mathbf{Z}_i$

$$
\mathbf{Z}_i =
\begin{bmatrix}
x_1 & x_2 & x_3 & x_4 & x_5 & y_1 & y_2 & y_3 & y_4 & y_5 \\
x_2 & x_3 & x_4 & x_5 & x_6 & y_2 & y_3 & y_4 & y_5 & y_6 \\
x_3 & x_4 & x_5 & x_6 & x_7 & y_3 & y_4 & y_5 & y_6 & y_7 \\
\vdots & \vdots & \vdots & \vdots & \vdots & \vdots & \vdots & \vdots & \vdots & \vdots \\
x_{37} & x_{38} & x_{39} & x_{40} & x_{41} & y_{37} & y_{38} & y_{39} & y_{40} & y_{41} \\
x_{38} & x_{39} & x_{40} & x_{41} & x_{42} & y_{38} & y_{39} & y_{40} & y_{41} & y_{42}
\end{bmatrix},
\tag{42}
$$

$$
\tag{43}
$$

and then augment all 94 couples' $\mathbf{Z}_i$ matrices together as

$$
\mathbf{Z}_i =
\begin{bmatrix}
\mathbf{Z}_1 \\
\mathbf{Z}_2 \\
\mathbf{Z}_3 \\
\vdots \\
\mathbf{Z}_{93} \\
\mathbf{Z}_{94}
\end{bmatrix}.
\tag{44}
$$

TABLE 13.3

Fixed Effects Results of Coupled Second Order LDE Model Fitted to Husbands' and Wives'
Disclosure Scores. $(DOF = 1831, -2LL = 9081)$

Wives' Regulation	Value	Period
$W \rightarrow d2W$	-1.362	(5.4 days)
$dW \rightarrow d2W$	-.051	
$H \rightarrow d2W$	.423	
$dH \rightarrow d2W$	.127	

Husbands' Regulation	Value	Period
$H \rightarrow d2H$	-.928	(6.5 days)
$dH \rightarrow d2H$	-.134	
$W \rightarrow d2H$	.199	
$dW \rightarrow d2H$	.469	

We then fit the coupled LDE model to this lagged data matrix with full information maximum likelihood using the Mx structural equation modeling software
(Neale, Boker, Xie, & Maes, 1999). The results of this model are presented in
Table 13.3. The period of the wives' and husbands' oscillation was estimated as
5.4 and 6.5 days respectively. For the wives, a positive effect of the husband's
displacement from equilibrium was estimated with a strength of about 30% that
of their own displacement from equilibrium effect. For the husbands a positive
effect of the wife's first derivative was estimated with a strength of about 50%
that of their own displacement from equilibrium effect. Both of these strong
coupling effects were missed when the two husbands' and wives' systems were
estimated separately. Also, the cycle period was estimated to be longer when
using the LLA method. LLA is known to bias estimates of the period to be
somewhat larger than 4 times τ (Boker & Nesselroade, 2002), and in fact this
is what was estimated when using LLA in this case.

   In order to visualize the results of the coupled LDE model, we used Math-
ematica's Runge–Kutta integration routine to estimate a hypothetical couple's
trajectory who had the fixed effects coefficients and who started at time $t = 0$
with displacements of equal value, but opposite sign. Figure-7 graphs the results of this numerical integration as both trajectory plots and as phase space
plots. It is interesting to note that although the husband starts at $x(0) = -1$
and the wife starts at $x(0) = 1$, by the time that about 2 weeks have elapsed,
their trajectories are crossing the axis together, both with a positive slope.
This suggests that the coefficients estimated by this model lead to phase syn-
chronization between husband and wife within about 2 weeks in the absence of
exogenous influences.

FIGURE 13.7

Simulated outcomes using estimated fixed effects parameters of coupled dyadic system numerically integrated and plotted for husband and wife as trajectories over 20 days and as phase space plots. Initial values are $x(0) = -1$, $y(0) = 1$, $\dot{x}(0) = \dot{y}(0) = 0$, thus starting the simulated husband and wife to be $180°$ out of phase with one another.

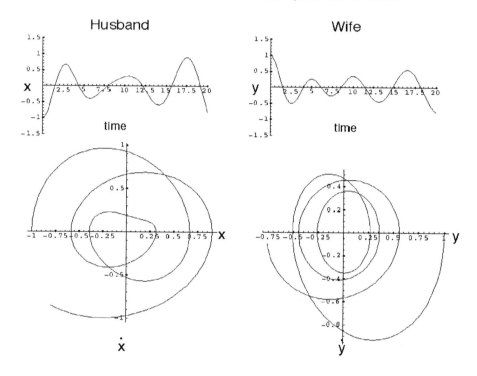

COUPLED LDE MODEL DISCUSSION

The results of fitting the coupled LDE model to the husbands' and wives' data provided a somewhat different picture of the mutual regulation of self–disclosure in marriage. The LDE–estimated period of the average fluctuation was shorter for both partners than the period estimated by LLA. In addition, wives' estimated average period was a full day shorter than the husbands' average period. This difference between the LLA and LDE results is likely due to the fact that LLA will tend to bias the estimation of η towards a period of 4τ (Boker & Nesselroade, 2002), in this case towards 8 days. This bias in the estimation of η will also tend to shrink the variance in the η coefficient, reducing any difference between husbands' and wives' estimated period of fluctuation.

The second main result from fitting the LDE model was that the estimated strength of coupling between the husbands and wives was much greater than in the LLA model. There was a positive coupling between the husbands' displacement from equilibrium and the wives' second derivative of disclosure. Thus, it appeared that wives were more affected by how different the husbands were from their equilibrium value than by how rapidly the husbands were changing.

In contrast, the husbands appeared to be more affected by how rapidly the wives were changing than they were by how far the wives' disclosure scores were from equilibrium. All LDE–estimated coupling parameters were considerably larger than the values estimated by LLA. One possibility to explain this difference is that the LDE model simultaneously estimated the two self–regulation parameters as well as the coupling parameters for both partners.

Finally, the estimated parameters from the LDE were used to project one possible set of hubands' and wives' trajectories for twenty days by numerical integration. The projected trajectories were not dissimilar to trajectories observed in the raw data. If a simulated husband and wife start 180 degrees out of phase, the model predicts it would take about 2 weeks for the couple to phase synchronize in the absence of external influences.

LIMITATIONS

There were several limitations to the current methods and data that should be kept in mind while considering the applicability of this methodological framework and estimation methods. The first consideration is a design consideration: We have found in simulations that the interval between samples must be short enough that there are an absolute minimum of 5 observations per cycle. At this minimum, it is difficult to distinguish between cyclic data and normally distributed random numbers. It is much better to sample at a rate such that there are 10 or more observations per cycle. The example data were weak in this respect, since there were only a little over 5 observations per cycle.

Another current limitation of the LDE method is that standard error estimates returned by default are smaller than they should be. This is due to the method of state space embedding used to construct the data matrix to which the model is fit. This is an active area of investigation and we expect that a solution can be found by a modified version of the bootstrap. In the mean time, we did not report standard errors for the LDE parameters.

Finally, we have run simulations that suggest that if the periods of the fluctuations of two coupled self–regulating systems are equal to one another, the coupled LDE method becomes empirically under–identified. In practice, this could mean that there may be no global minimum to the maximum likelihood function and thus coupling parameter estimates could grow without bound. Intuitively this situation is due to the two oscillations being synchronized and indistinguishable from one oscillation and is similar in a sense to a data matrix that is not of full rank. This behavior has been observed in fitting a coupled model to simulated data, but as yet we have not observed this problem in psychological data.

CONCLUSIONS

Dynamical systems analysis holds considerable promise for recasting statistical models into a form in which parameters map onto meaningful theoretical constructs. For instance, a damped linear oscillator's parameters are easily mapped onto notions from self–regulation: Avoidance of straying too far from equilibrium and avoidance of too rapid change. Coupled differential equations similarly hold promise in modeling theoretic notions of mutually adaptive context. This chapter has presented a small subset of possible dynamical systems models for self–regulation in context and has presented an example application of one of these models. It is our hope that these models will serve as a small step along the road to better congruence between theories of psychological processes and their implementation in statistical models.

REFERENCES

Boker, S. M. (2001). Differential structural modeling of intraindividual variability. In L. Collins & A. Sayer (Eds.), *New methods for the analysis of change (pp. 3-28).* Washington, DC: American Psychological Association.

Boker, S. M. (2002). Consequences of continuity: The hunt for intrinsic properties within parameters of dynamics in psychological processes. *Multivariate Behavioral Research, 37*(3), 405422.

Boker, S. M., & Ghisletta, P. (1998). A dynamical systems analysis of adolescent substance abuse. *Multivariate Behavioral Research, 33*(4), 479-507.

Boker, S. M., & Laurenceau, J. P. (2005). Dynamical systems modeling: An application to the regulation of intimacy and disclosure in marriage. In T. A. Walls & J. L. Schafer (Eds.), *Models for intensive longitudinal data* (p. 195-218). Oxford: Oxford University Press.

Boker, S. M., Neale, M. C., & Rausch, J. (2004). Latent differential equation modeling with multivariate multi-occasion indicators. In K. van Montfort, H. Oud, & A. Satorra (Eds.), *Recent developments on structural equation models: Theory andapplications* (pp. 151174). Dordrecht, Netherlands: Kluwer Academic Publishers.

Boker, S. M., & Nesselroade, J. R. (2002). A method for modeling the intrinsic dynamics of intraindividual variability: Recovering the parameters of simulated oscillators in multiwave panel data. *Multivariate Behavioral Research, 37*(1), 127160.

Browne, M., & Arminger, G. (1995). Specification and estimation of mean and covariancestructure models. In G. Arminger, C. C. Clogg, & M. E. Sobel (Eds.), *Handbook of statistical modeling for the social and behavioral sciences* (pp.311359). New York: Plenum Press.

Butcher, J. C. (2003). *Numerical methods for ordinary differential equations.* New York: Wiley.

Butner, J., Amazeen, P. G., & Mulvey, G. M. (2005). Multilevel modeling to two cyclical processes: Extending differential structural equation modeling to nonlinear coupled systems. *Psychological Methods, 10*(2), 159-177.

Carver, C. S., & Scheier, M. F. (1998). *On the self regulation of behavior.* New York: SpringerVerlag.

Chow, S. M., Ram, N., Boker, S. M., Fujita, F., & Clore, G. (2005). Capturing weekly fluctuation in emotion using a latent differential structural approach. *Emotion, 5*(2), 208-225.

Duncan, S. C., & Duncan, T. E. (1995). Modeling the processes of development via latent variable growth curve methodology. *Structural equation modeling, 2,* 187213.

Kashy, D. A., & Kenny, D. A. (2000). The analysis of data from dyads and groups. In H. Reis & C. M. Judd (Eds.), *Handbook of research methods in social psychology* (pp.451-477). New York: Cambridge University Press.

Kelley, H. H., Berscheid, E., Christensen, A., Harvey, J. H., Huston, T. L., & Levenger, G. (1983). *Close relationships.* New York: Freeman.

Laurenceau, J.-P., Barrett, L. F., & Pietromonaco, P. R. (1998). Intimacy as an interpersonal process: The importance of self-disclosure, and perceived partner responsiveness in interpersonal exchanges. *Journal of Personality and Social Psychology, 74,* 12381251.

Laurenceau, J.-P., Feldman Barrett, L., & Rovine, M. J. (2005). The interpersonal process model of intimacy in marriage: A dailydiary and multilevel modeling approach. *Journal of Family Psychology, 19,* 314-323.

Laurenceau, J.-P., & Kleinman, B. (in press). Intimacy in personal relationships. In D. Perlman & A. Vangelisti (Eds.), *Cambridge handbook of personal relationships.* New York: Cambridge University Press.

Laurenceau, J.-P., Rivera, L. M., Schaffer, A. R., & Pietromonaco, P. R. (2004). Intimacy as an interpersonal process: Current status and future directions. In D. J. Mashek & A. Aron (Eds.), *Handbook of closeness and intimacy* (pp. 61-78). Mahwah, NJ: Lawrence Erlbaum Associates.

Maxwell, S. E., & Boker, S. M. (in press). Multilevel models of dynamical systems. In S. M. Boker & M. J. Wenger (Eds.), *Data analytic techniques for dynamical systems in the social and behavioral sciences.* Mahwah, NJ: Lawrence Erlbaum Associates.

McArdle, J. J. (1986). Latent growth within behavior genetic models. *Behavior Genetics, 16,* 163-200.

McArdle, J. J., & Anderson, E. (1990). Latent variable growth models for research on aging. In J. E. Birren & K. W. Schaie (Eds.), *Handbook of the psychology of aging* (pp. 21-44). New York: Academic Press.

McArdle, J. J., & Epstein, D. (1987). Latent growth curves within developmental structural equation models. *Child Development, 58*, 110-133.

McArdle, J. J., & McDonald, R. P. (1984). Some algebraic properties of the reticular action model for moment structures. *British Journal of Mathematical and Statistical Psychology, 87*, 234-251.

Muthen, B., & Curran, P. (1997). General longitudinal modeling of individual differences in experimental designs: A latent variable framework for analysis and power estimation. *Psychological Methods, 2*, 371-402.

Neale, M. C., Boker, S. M., Xie, G., & Maes, H. H. (1999). *Mx: Statistical modeling.* Box 126 MCV, Richmond, VA 23298: Department of Psychiatry, 5th ed.

Prager, K. J., & Roberts, L. J. (2004). Deep intimate connection: Self and intimacy in couple relationships. In D. Mashek & A. Aron (Eds.), *Handbook of closeness and intimacy* (pp. 43-60). Mahwah, NJ: Lawrence Erlbaum Associates.

Reis, H. T., & Shaver, P. (1988). Intimacy as an interpersonal process. In S. Duck (Ed.), *Handbook of personal relationships* (pp. 367-389).

Savitzky, A., & Golay, M. J. E. (1964). Smoothing and differentiation of data by simplified least squares. *Analytical Chemistry, 53*, 1627-1639.

Thompson, J. M. T., & Stewart, H. B. (1986). *Nonlinear dynamics and chaos.* New York: Wiley.

Willett, J., & Sayer, A. (1994). Using covariance structure analysis to detect correlates and predictors of individual change over time. *Psychological Bulletin, 116*, 363-381.

CHAPTER FOURTEEN

Modeling Intraindividual and Intracontextual Change: Rendering Developmental Contextualism Operational

Nilam Ram
John R. Nesselroade
The University of Virginia

The quiet statisticians have changed our world; not by discovering new facts or technical developments, but by changing the ways that we reason, experiment, and form our opinions.....

—Ian Hacking

Statistical models exist at the confluence of theory and observation. In a sense, it is within these models that ideas collide with data. From these collisions we get indications of how well theories approximate reality. Statistical models, however, always construct a particular notion of reality. In using them we invoke a particular set of beliefs about the nature of the data and the types of relationships that exist in them. So, while the statistical models give us the freedom to make some inferences, at the same time they constrain our approximations of reality. In other words, each model invokes a particular construction of reality *a priori*. Thus, just as researchers take special care in adopting a theoretical position, special attention should also be paid to the selection of a statistical model with which to represent key aspects of one's data.

In this chapter we examine how individuals and their contexts might jointly be characterized within a framework of statistical models for studying "intra-entity" changes such as development. First, we examine how ecological context might be characterized within a basic empirical framework—the data–box (Cattell, 1952, 1966). Second, we briefly outline how aspects of developmental contextual theory might be instantiated via an elaborated data–box and "coupled" models of intraindividual and intracontextual variability and change. Finally, we illustrate with two examples how the dynamic interaction between individuals and their contexts has been examined within an intra–entity modeling framework.

THE DATA–BOX

We have found it useful to think about context using Cattell's (1952) data–box heuristic (Nesselroade & Ram, 2004). Typically, the data–box has been used to systematize the multiple ways that data can be organized and subsequently analyzed via covariation analysis. Data are located within a three-dimensional cube (persons × variables × occasions) as shown in Figure 14.1. Thus, each datum represents a specific person measured on a particular variable at a given occasion of measurement. Portions of various two-dimensional samples of the data–box serve as the raw data for most kinds of correlational analyses (Cattell, 1952, 1966). For example, in standard cross-sectional factor analysis (R–technique) a persons × variables data matrix for a single occasion of measurement is analyzed in order to identify patterns in the relationships among selected variables as they are defined across selected persons. Similarly, in longitudinal factor analysis (P–technique), the same statistical model is applied to an occasions × variables data matrix for a single person in order to identify the patterns in the relationships among variables as they are defined across occasions for that person (Cattell, Cattell, & Rhymer, 1947). Depending upon how the data–box is sampled and analyzed, different kinds of relationships are highlighted and examined.

Each application of a statistical model to a sample of data–box information invokes a particular set of rules regarding how the data are organized and assumptions about how persons, variables, and occasions are organized along their respective data–box axes. That is, each statistical model invokes a particular set of rules regarding, measurement, change, and individual differences. Questions to ask about our models include: What measurement model (organization of variables) is explicitly or implicitly implied by the statistical model?; How is change (organization with respect to occasions) incorporated or ignored by the statistical model?; When and in what manner can individuals differ from (or be related to) one another (organization with respect to persons)?

THE DATA–BOX AND CONTEXT

The data–box can also be used to characterize context. The organization of data within the box provides a mapping between our conceptual ideas regarding context and data. Elaborating the heuristic a bit, the three axes defining the

FIGURE 14.1

Cattell's three–dimensional data–box (persons × variables × occasions of measurement) as a heuristic for characterizing temporal, spatial, and interpersonal aspects of context.

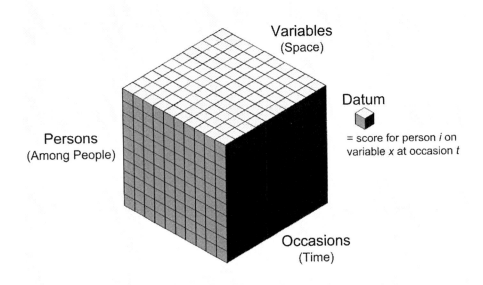

data–box can be regarded as three sets of features or characteristics that also define context. They include: The spaces in which the individual is embedded; the times in which the individual lives; and the persons with whom the individual interacts (proximally and distally). Thus, context can be conceptualized as the location of an individual vis–a–vis space (variables), time (occasions), and persons (persons).

Space (Variables)

Discussions of context emphasize the "space" in which an individual is embedded. In addition to proximal and distal significant others covered below under the persons dimension, key notions of context include objects, symbols, institutions, community, society, and culture (e.g., micro-, meso-, exo-, and macro-systems, or interpersonal and institutional networks; Bronfenbrenner, 1979; Lerner, 1991). For instance, variables such as socioeconomic status (SES), family and school characteristics, culture, and so forth, all characterize some aspect of the environment or space in which a person exists. Such "context"

FIGURE 14.2

A data–box split along the variables dimension to highlight the distinction between characteristics of the "person" (e.g., target behaviors) and characteristics of the "context" (e.g., environmental features).

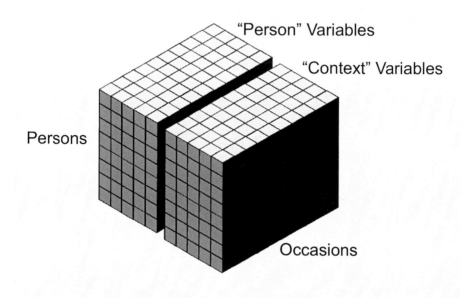

variables are often included alongside variables characterizing the "person" (target behaviors under study, e.g., cognitive performance, emotional state, and so on.). We illustrate the distinction between these two types of variables explicitly in Figure 14.2 by splitting the data-box into two parts, one section marked by "person" variables, and the other by "context" variables. Thus, along the variables dimension of the data–box there exists information about the individual and features of the environment or space in which he or she is embedded. Examinations of the interrelationships between these two sets of variables, either within or across persons, then, helps paint a picture of how contextual features are related to individual behavior. The organization of these two classes of variables over occasions of measurement serves to emphasize the possibilities of changes in both the person and the context, the mutual influences of both, and lagged, as well as concurrent relationships.

On a cautionary note, within a given study, the possible representations of the environment in which a person exists are, in a sense, limited to the variable space — those "context" variables that have been explicitly included in the model. Our understanding of the individual and the space in which he or she exists is limited to those portions of the micro-, meso-, exo-, and macro-system

(Bronfenbrenner, 1979) included in the model. Including other aspects of the individual or context into the model will affect analysis outcomes and their interpretations. Furthermore, the representations of the human ecology we invoke through our statistical models often make implicit assumptions about the "missing" unobserved variables–usually that they are equivalent (or relegated to error) across persons and/or occasions. That is, it is often implicitly assumed that the unmeasured aspects of context are the same for all individuals. Although such an assumption may be justified in some cases, it may not be in others.

Time (Occasions)

Representations of *time* are particularly prevalent in discussions of context. Individuals exist within a particular time (e.g., a historical epoch), change over time (e.g., develop, mature), and are affected by historical and social continuities, changes and transactions that also occur over time (e.g., Baltes, 1987; Bronfenbrenner, 1979; Elder, 1998; Lerner, 1986; Sameroff, 1983). The temporal context of an individual's life can be incorporated by elaborating the occasions dimension in conjunction with the variables dimension of the data–box. For example, measurements (on multiple variables) might be arranged according to the day and hour or year of measurement, the age of the individual, or in relation to the other occasions of measurement (e.g., Trial 3 of 12). These time indices provide key information about where the individual (or context) was located within time. Longitudinal studies, via systematic sampling on the occasions dimension, allow for the examination of how individuals change over time — weave their way through the constantly changing temporal context of life. Additionally, the simultaneous sampling of environmental features (i.e., "context" variables) allows us to examine the pattern of relationships (both lagged and concurrent) between environmental and individual characteristics that unfold over time. In sum, examining how the individual changed in relation to time (using an appropriate index) allows us to model and make inferences about the underlying processes of change (e.g., development, aging, maturation, learning, forgetting, socialization, and so forth.).

Even studies that measure only a single occasion or historical epoch invoke the occasions or time context dimension of the data–box. By treating the occasions dimension of the data–box as being only one occasion thick (R–data), an implicit assumption is made that all measurements occurred at a time that was identical, in some sense, for all entities. That is, where individuals exist within time is assumed to be the same for all individuals regardless of when they were actually measured (i.e., a "static" conception of time). Although this assumption may be justified in some cases it certainly appears not to be in others, as in the case of cross–sectional age comparisons. Whether cross-sectional or lon-gitudinal, the implicit or explicit ordering of measurements along the occasions dimension of the data–box provides valuable information about the temporal context of individuals' lives.

Among People (Persons)

Information concerning where a person exists in relation to other individuals can be indexed, in conjunction with the variables and occasions dimensions, along the persons dimensions of the data–box. Just as occasions can be or-ganized according to an index of time (e.g., day, year, age), persons can be indexed according to one or more of their features (variables). Individuals can be organized by group or category (e.g., gender) or ordered according to some continuous measure (e.g., one standard deviation above the mean). Each group-ing or ordering (i.e., interindividual differences) provides us with information about where an individual exists in relation to other persons. For instance, a subset of individuals with identical groupings or similar rank ordering might exist within time and space in much the same way. Likewise, differences in ordering or grouping might indicate that individuals exist within different time and space contexts.

   While providing information about where an individual exists among other persons along some scale, this interindividual difference notion of context pro-vides little, if any, information about the process by which individuals interact or "transact" (Sameroff & Chandler, 1975) with the other persons (e.g., signif-icant others) in their environment. Another possibility for understanding how an individual exists among others is to "couple" together two or more persons and to observe and examine the interactions between them in terms of variables and occasions information samples (see e.g., Ferrer & Nesselroade, 2003; Mitte-ness & Nesselroade, 1987). Thus, we see two main avenues of understanding where an individual exists among people. First, the qualitative and quantita-tive differences and similarities among persons can be located along the persons dimension of the data–box. Second, as we discuss in some detail subsequently, directly representing the interactions between two or more persons along the occasions and variables dimensions can inform us about how individuals behave within the context of other people.

   More generally, the three dimensions of the data–box provide a heuristic for organizing and analyzing data in order to capture key temporal, spatial, and personal aspects of context. By attending to how statistical models invoke the various dimensions of the data–box we can at the same time attend to how context can be represented and incorporated in the analysis. If the invocation jibes with the intended theory, then all is well.

If not, one might reconsider how well the statistical model, and the notion of reality it invokes, represents the theory and exploits the data.

MODELING DEVELOPMENTAL PROCESSES

Developmental research focuses on change and the study of processes leading to a specific outcome (Baltes, Reese, & Nesselroade, 1977). In developmental psychology a number of methods and models have emerged for studying and describing within–person change and process (Collins & Horn, 1991; Collins & Sayer, 2001). In particular, intraindividual variability and change methods have proven to be particularly useful operationalizations of process oriented theory (Browne & Nesselroade, 2005; Nesselroade, 1988, 1991). This class of models provides an avenue for describing the processes by which an individual changes (intraindividual change) from occasion–to–occasion, and possible reasons why individuals change in different (or similar) ways (interindividual differences in intraindividual change).

Intraindividual variability and change methods focus on how, when, and why the individual changes over time and is usually defined on P–data (variables × occasions) samples of the data–box (Nesselroade & Ram, 2004). The methods and models "capture" the patterns of changes that are defined over variables and organized over time (rather than the organization of variables defined over persons, as in traditional differential psychology). That is, this class of methods attempts to model process directly (Browne & Nesselroade, 2005) – how and why an individual changes from moment–to–moment–to–moment.

A Sample of P-data

For illustrative purposes, consider the single sample of P-data shown in Figure 14.3. This matrix consists of data from a single person measured on multiple variables on multiple occasions. Our primary objective is to explain or model how and when the observed characteristics of the individual change over time. In Figure 14.4 we exemplify a model of individual change — dynamic factor analysis — which is usually fit to one person's data. For contrast and comparison, we present in Figure 14.5 a latent difference score model which is usually fit to the data of several persons who have been measured on multiple occasions. Both models provide a "picture" of how a latent "process" variable changes from occasion to occasion. Details of the specific data requirements and how the models elucidate the change process can be found elsewhere (see especially

FIGURE 14.3
A slice of P-data representing data from a single person measured on multiple variables on multiple occasions.

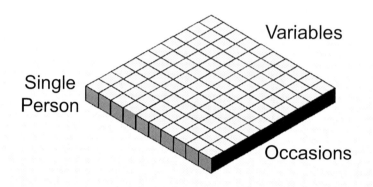

Browne & Nesselroade, 2005; McArdle & Hamagami, 2001). Our focus here is, instead, at a more general level. Each model, and the system of equations underlying it, describes the "form" (Pepper, 1942) of individual changes over time.

The dynamic factor model (McArdle, 1982; Molenaar, 1985), one specification of which is shown in Figure 14.4, models how, at any given point in time (t), the latent process (P_t), inferred via three observed or manifest variables ($y_{t,1}$, $y_{t,2}$, $y_{t,3}$) is determined by the state of the process at previous times ($\alpha_1 P_{t-1}$, $\alpha_2 P_{t-2}$) and some "shock" occurring at the present time (z_t). Together, the dynamic interaction among temporal contexts (lags), unobserved environmental influences (shocks), and prior and present individual states (unique factors) contributes to how the process (process factor) unfolds and is manifest in the observed behaviors. Thus, the model represents the dynamics or forces leading to change, for a single person or process (P), through explicit representation of the relationships within a slice of occasions × variables P-data (for further description and explanation see Browne & Nesselroade, 2005; Nesselroade, McArdle, Aggen, & Meyers, 2002; Wood & Brown, 1994).

The latent difference score model (McArdle & Hamagami, 2001) shown in Figure 14.5 also models change in a manifest variable explicitly. Individual changes are represented as latent differences (Δy_t) between latent true scores(i.e., y_t - y_{t-1}). Each of these changes, then, is represented as a function of constant individual growth (αy_s) and the true score at the previous occasion (βy_{t-1}). Thus at any, given time, a person's true score is an accumulation of their previous changes and their initial level (y_0). The dynamics, or forces leading to change (for a population of persons), are represented explicitly through the relationships between the latent changes and other variables in

FIGURE 14.4

Dynamic factor model (DNFS or Process Factor specification, e.g., McArdle, 1982). P_t represents a latent process inferred via three observed variables ($y_{t,1}$, $y_{t,2}$, $y_{t,3}$) and determined by the state of the process at previous times ($\alpha_1 P_{t-1}$, $\alpha_2 P_{t-2}$) and an unobserved "shock" occurring at the present time (z_t).

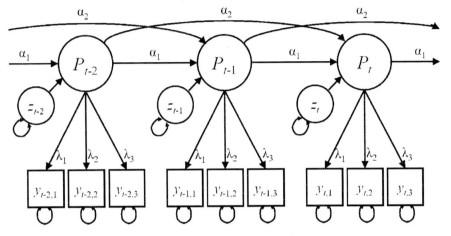

FIGURE 14.5

Latent difference score model. Individual changes are represented as latent differences (Δy_t) and are a function of constant individual growth (αy_s), the true score at the previous occasion (βy_{t-1}), and an initial score (y_0).

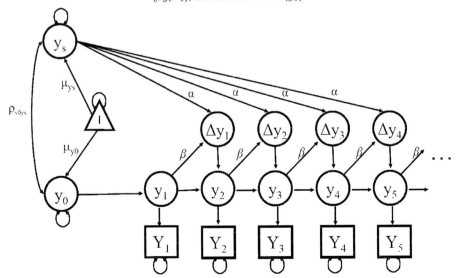

the model (e.g., α, β). The dynamic factor model has proven to be applicable for the modeling of short-term reversible (stochastic) processes, is usually fit to a lagged covariance matrix for a single person (e.g.,Nesselroade, McArdle, Aggen, & Meyers, 2002), and awaits further extension to more widely spaced measurements. The latent difference score approach (as illustrated here), meanwhile, appears to be more appropriate for longer term changes exhibiting "strong shapes" and is usually fit to data from multiple individuals (under the assumption that individuals are replicates of one another). However, there is flexibility in how each model can be parameterized and the types of data to which each can be applied. The main point is that these models provide a picture of the individual as a system of *changing* characteristics — something closer to the theoretical notions of an individual as a complex evolving organization of structures and processes– a "dynamic unit" or system (e.g., Ford & Lerner, 1992).

DEVELOPMENTAL CONTEXTUALISM

In addition to its focus on change and process, "developmental psychology recognizes that the individual is changing in a changing world, and that this changing context of development can affect the nature of individual change. Consequently, developmental psychology also deals with changes within and among biocultural ecologies and with the relationships of these changes to changes within and among individuals" (Baltes, Reese, & Nesselroade, 1977, p. 1). Developmental contextualists have long acknowledged that the individual *and* the environment in which he or she exists are constantly changing, often in mutually influential ways (Baltes, Reuter-Lorenz, & Rosler, 2006). Just as individuals develop, learn, mature, and so forth, contexts also transform and change shape and structure. Thus, from a theoretical viewpoint, we should place models of the changes occurring in the context—intracontextual change—alongside our models of intraindividual change. Furthermore, ecological and developmental systems theory suggest that there is a "dynamic interaction" between the individual and his or her context that occurs over time (e.g., Bronfenbrenner, 1979; Ford & Lerner, 1992; Lerner, 1991). In sum, the theoretical orientation underlying the study of development in ecological context is that individuals and contexts are changing while interacting with one another. As we will see, these notions dovetail rather well with the dynamical systems notion of *coupling*.

Multiple Samples of P–Data

In order for models to render theoretical notions of development in ecological context operational, three types of change processes should be considered:

FIGURE 14.6

Two slices of P-data, one consisting of measurements of the target person, and one consisting of measurements of his or her partner or context. "Coupling" between the two is represented by a lattice of bi-directional influences.

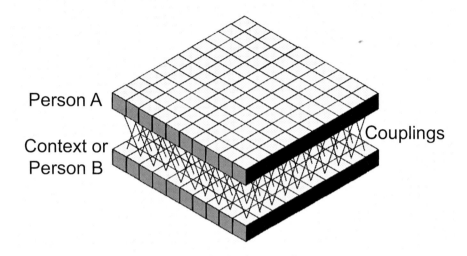

Intraindividual change, intracontextual change, and the interactions that occur between the two over time. Previously we discussed how change models could be applied to a single slice of P–data (variables × occasions for a single person) in order to model processes of intraindividual change. Suppose, for example, that within the data–box heuristic we could also locate the sample of P–data consisting of concurrent observations of an individual's partner. We might then produce another model of intraindividual change describing how the partner changed over the same span of time.

The dyad could be depicted using two concurrent models, one for the target individual and one for his or her partner. But, it would be a great failure to exploit the data if one stops there. These two individuals do not exist in isolation from one another. Indeed, the term dyad connotes more than just two individuals existing at the same time. Rather, it suggests mutual interactions and influences. By definition (or selection) the two members are "coupled" together. Each exists as part of the others' context (e.g., marriage network, social network, etc.; Lerner, 1991). Thus, there likely is a dynamic interaction occurring between them. By linking together the two "systems" (Ford & Lerner, 1992) over time (by aligning the two slices along their shared occasion dimension) we are able to represent and formally model such "couplings" or "transactions" (Sameroff & Chandler, 1975). Through an explicit representation of the bidirectional influences we can examine and test hypotheses about how the members of the dyad interact and influence one another. By aligning and coupling together two slices of P-data, as depicted in Figure 14.6 (and parameterized in the examples following as γ), we are able to model two individuals' intraindividual changes (development) within the dynamically interactive context of their relationship.

Another possibility for understanding how an individual exists within context is to couple him or her to other entities. For example, rather than constructing the initial data–box as a persons × variables × occasions cube, we expand the notion of persons to entities. In this manner both individuals and contexts are included along this dimension of the data–box. For example, one P-sample of data might consist of multiple measurements (characteristics) of an individual on multiple occasions (a sample from the "person" variables portion of Figure 14.2). Another sample of P-data might consist of multiple measurements (characteristics) of a contextual entity in which the person is embedded, such as a school or neighborhood, on multiple occasions (the corresponding slice from the "context" variables portion of Figure 14.2). From the first sample of data we could build a model of intraindividual change—how the characteristics of the individual change over time. From the second sample we could build a model of intracontextual change—how the characteristics of the context change over time. Finally, by aligning and "coupling" the two models together (perhaps with appropriate lags) we could represent the bidirectional influences between the individual and his or her context—the dynamic interaction. Thus, by expanding the variables dimension of the data–box to include both persons and contexts we can use some dynamic models of change to represent three theoretically important types of changes, intraindividual change (from a P-slice of individual data), intracontextual change (from a P-slice of individual or entity data), and the interaction between the individual and his or her context over time (coupling relationships).

EMPIRICAL EXAMPLES

Early in the development of intraindividual variability and change methods Cattell and Scheier (1961) presented a method they termed *stimulus-controlled* P-technique which involved analyzing the variation over time (e.g., daily) in contextual features and individuals' behavior in order to estimate the relationships between individuals' behaviors and contextual features over time. As discussed earlier, such an analysis can be framed as the simultaneous analysis of multiple P-data sets, one marking the variation in individual behavior, and

FIGURE 14.7

Coupled dynamic factor analysis model depicting interactions (γ_{pc} and γ_{cp}) between a person or process factor (P) and a second person, process, or context factor(C).

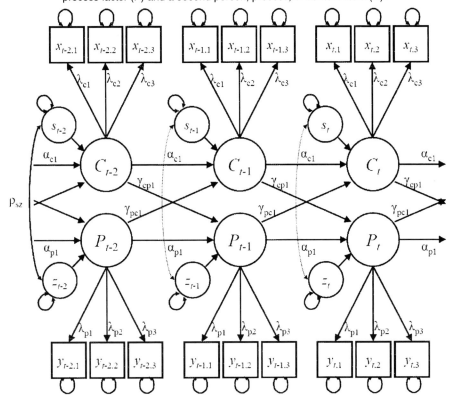

one (or several) marking the variation in contextual features. To illustrate such an analysis we review two recent studies that examined a "system" of person–context changes. The first (Ferrer & Nesselroade, 2003) examines two P-samples of "person" data obtained from a "marriage network." The second (Boker et al., 1998) examines the dynamic interaction between P-samples of "context" data containing environmental information and P-samples of "person" data obtained from multiple persons.

Ferrer and Nesselroade (2003) used an extension of "stimulus-controlled" P–technique, the dynamic factor model, to examine how a wife's and husband's emotions developed within the context of their interpersonal relationship. Using two such samples of P-data obtained concurrently, three kinds of patterns were examined; intraindividual changes in husband's mood, intraindividual changes in wife's mood, and the "dynamic interactions" (i.e., coupling) between the two. A general graphical representation of the coupled dynamic factor model is shown in Figure 14.7. One intraindividual process is represented using one set of factors (P_t). A second intraindividual (or intracontextual) process is represented using another set of factors (C_t). Dynamic interactions are represented by the arrows connecting one set of factors with the other (i.e., γ_{pc} and γ_{cp}). These coupling parameters depict how each individual (or entity) affects the other.

Ferrer and Nesselroade (2003) found that, within the social context of the marriage under study, the wife's current mood (e.g., P_t) was determined, in part, by her own mood on the previous day. The husband's current mood (e.g., C_t) was determined, in part, by his mood on the previous 2 days (i.e., his moods lingered longer). Additionally, the husband's current negative mood affected the wife's negative mood on the following day, but not vice versa. The wife's current mood did not affect the husband's future mood. The "coupled" model captures each partner's mood process and the interactive process by which one member of the social context affects the other. These lagged models greatly enrich the study of interactive processes compared to what can be determined by applying models that are strictly limited to concurrent relationships.

Boker and colleagues (1998) measured a series of daily weather variables as a context for changes in the moods of participants with bipolar affective disorder. As shown in Figure 14.8 two coupled oscillator models (see also Boker & Graham, 1998; Boker & Bisconti, 2006) were used to model three types of changes; oscillations in weather, oscillations in participants' mood, and the bidirectional influences of one system on the other (i.e., how weather affects mood, and how mood affects weather). In the "person" part of the model an individuals' location on a variable (y_p), their momentary rates of change (i.e., first derivative with respect to time, dy_p), and momentary rates of acceleration (i.e., second derivative with respect to time, d^2y_p) are specified using sets of factor loadings (similar in fashion to the changes specified in latent growth curve models; for details see Boker & Bisconti, 2006). Together with the relationships between these latent constructs (e.g., η_p, ζ_p) the loadings indicate the specifics of how individuals change (oscillate) over time. Changes in the context variables (x_t) are depicted in a similar manner (model of context). Finally the dynamic interactions between person and context changes (i.e., person–context couplings) are quantifications of how changes in one model or system affect the other (γ_{pc}, γ_{cp}).

In addition to extracting systematic oscillations in weather (model of context) and in the bipolar participants' affect (model of persons), Boker et al. (1998) found that their coupled systems indicated unidirectional influence of weather changes on mood changes. Specifically, changes in barometric pressure were a leading indicator of changes in mood (e.g., $\gamma_{cp} > 0$). As would be expected, changes in the participants' mood did not influence changes the   local

FIGURE 14.8

Model of two coupled oscillators, one modeling changes in person(s) variables and one modeling changes in context variables. Dynamic interactions between intraindividual and intracontextual change are represented by person-context couplings.

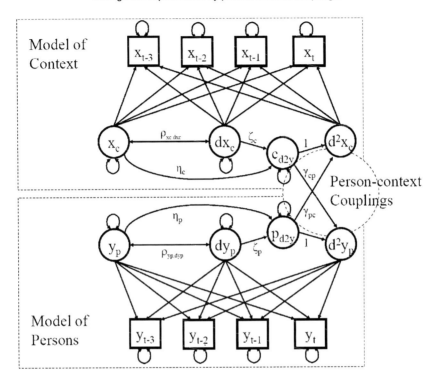

weather (e.g., $\gamma_{pc} = 0$). The coupled model used in this study illustrates how modeling multivariate multioccasion data from both persons and environmental contexts allows for the testing of specific hypotheses about the mutual influence of individuals and environments.

In both of these studies the intraindividual change processes were examined in relation to "naturalistic" contextual variation. Cattell and Scheier (1961) noted that the contextual elements might be introduced via "treatments" or experimentally introduced variation. With this in mind, experimental paradigms might also be reframed in terms of the person–context interactions. One might leverage known or predetermined changes in ecological context (experimental manipulations) to extricate more fully the processes by with individuals are affected by or affect their environments. Whether observing individuals in vivo or in the laboratory, restructuring and carving the data–box in a manner such that models that explicitly outline processes of intraindividual change, intracontextual changes,and the dynamic interactions between the two, appears to hold substantial promise in elucidating the nature of individual–context embedding.

CONCLUSIONS

We have illustrated and examined some key aspects of the relationships between selecting and organizing data and the theoretical notions of developmental contextualism. Using the data–box as an heuristic we examined how temporal, spatial, and interpersonal aspects of context can be located and studied. We have emphasized how one's chosen statistical model invokes a notion of reality and stressed that one needs to be concerned that, as much as possible, the model coincides with the theoretical notions of reality being tested. Depending on how variables, occasions, and persons are organized and when each dimension is introduced in the analysis has major implications for the interpretation of results and for which aspects of context are considered.

Developmental contextualist theory suggests three kinds of patterns to which the models discussed let us attend: Intraindividual change, intracontextual change, and the substantive interactions that occur between the two over time. We have outlined one approach for modeling and examining how individuals exist and change in context. Refining the data–box so as to place individuals and contexts side- by-side along one "entities" dimension allows the simultaneous analysis of individuals and their contexts using already established "intra–entity" methods. From the few studies that have done so, we find that dynamic models of intraindividual change, although still limited in some respects, can be used to provide more flexible and perhaps more meaningful representations of individuals and their contexts. Furthermore, although placing slices of data side–by–side and modeling person–person, person–context, or even context–context interactions can become rather complicated it promises further understanding of the specific processes through which we interact with, are changed by, and change our environments. In sum, structuring and modeling data in a manner that capitalizes on the interactions between and among intra–entity data slices we believe promises a greater understanding of human behavior in line with an ecological systems view of development and change (eg., Ford & Lerner, 1992).

REFERENCES

Baltes, P. B. (1987). Theoretical propositions of life-span developmental psychology: On the dynamics between growth and decline. *Developmental Psychology, 23*(5), 611626.

Baltes, P. B., Reese, H. W., & Nesselroade, J. R. (1977). *Lifespan developmental psychology: Introduction to research methods.* Monterey, CA: Brooks/Cole.

Baltes, P. B., Reuter-Lorenz, P., & Rosler, F. (2006). *Lifespan development in the brain: The perspective of biocultural co-constructivism.* New York: Cambridge University Press.

Boker, S. M., & Bisconti, T. L. (2006). Dynamical systems modeling in aging research. In C. S. Bergeman & S. M. Boker (Eds.), *Methodological issues in aging research* (pp. 185-229). Mahwah, NJ: Lawrence Erlbaum Associates.

Boker, S. M., & Graham, J. (1998). A dynamical systems analysis of adolescence substance abuse. *Multivariate Behavioral Research, 33,* 479507.

Boker, S. M., Postolache, T., Naim, S., & Lebenluft, E. (1998). Mood oscillations and coupling between mood and weather in patients with rapid cycling bipolar disorder. unpublished manuscript, department of psychology, university of notre dame.

Bronfenbrenner, U. (1979). *The ecology of human development: Experiments by nature and design.* Cambridge, MA: Harvard University Press.

Browne, M. W., & Nesselroade, J. R. (2005). Representing psychological processes with dynamic factor models: Some promising uses and extensions of arma time series models. In A. Maydeu-Olivares & J. J. McArdle (Eds.), *Contemporary psychometrics: A festschrift to roderick p. mcdonald* (pp. 415452). Mahwah, NJ: Lawrence Erlbaum Associates.

Cattell, R. B. (1952). The three basic factoranalytic research designs their interrelations and derivatives. *Psychological Bulletin, 49,* 499520.

Cattell, R. B. (1961). Theory of situational, instrument, second order, and refraction factors in personality structure research. *Psychological Bulletin, 49,* 160174.

Cattell, R. B. (1966). The data box: Its ordering of total resources in terms of possible relational systems. In R. B. Cattell (Ed.), *Handbook of multivariate experimental psychology* (1st ed., pp. 67128). Chicago, IL: Rand McNally.

Cattell, R. B., Cattell, A. K. S., & Rhymer, R. M. (1947). P-technique demonstrated indetermining psychophysical source traits in a normal individual. *Psychometrika, 12,* 267288.

Collins, L., & Horn, J. L. (1991). *Best methods for the analyis of change.* Washington, DC: American Psychological Association.

Collins, L., & Sayer, A. (2001). *New methods for the analysis of change.* Washington, DC: American Psychological Association.

Elder, G. H., Jr. (1998). The life course and human development. In W. Damon (Series Ed.) & R. M. Lerner (Vol Ed.) (Eds.), *Handbook of child psychology: Vol. 1. Theoretical models of human development* (5th ed., 939-991). New York: Wiley.

Ferrer, E., & Nesselroade, J. R. (2003). Modeling affective processes in dyadic relations via dynamic factor analysis. *Emotion, 3,* 344-360.

Ford, D. H., & Lerner, R. M. (1992). *Developmental systems theory: An integrative approach.* Newbury Park, CA: Sage.

Lerner, R. M. (1986). *Concepts and theories of human development* (2nd ed.). New York: Random House.

Lerner, R. M. (1991). Changing organism-context relations as the basic process of development: A developmental contextual perspective. *Developmental Psychology*, *27*, 2732.

McArdle, J. J. (1982). Structural equation modeling of an individual system: Preliminary results from a case study in episodic alcoholism.(unpublished manuscript, department of psychology, university of denver).

McArdle, J. J., & Hamagami, F. (2001). Latent difference score structural models for linear dynamic analysis with incomplete longitudinal data. In L. Collins & A. Sayer (Eds.), *New methods for the analysis of change* (pp. 139175). Washington, DC: American Psychological Association.

Mitteness, L. S., & Nesselroade, J. R. (1987). Attachment in adulthood: Longitudinal investigation of mother-daughter affective interdependencies by p-technique factor analysis. *The Southern Psychologist*, *3*, 3744.

Molenaar, P. C. M. (1985). A dynamic factor model for the analysis of multivariate time series. *Psychometrika*, *50*(2), 181-202.

Nesselroade, J. R. (1988). Some implications of the traitstate distinction for the study of development across the life span: The case of personality research. In P. B. Baltes, D. L. Featherman, & R. M. Lerner (Eds.), *Lifespan development and behavior* (Vol. 8, pp. 163189). Hillsdale, NJ.: Lawrence Erlbaum Associates.

Nesselroade, J. R. (1991). The warp and woof of the developmental fabric. In R. Downs, L. Liben, & D. Palermo (Eds.), *Visions of development, the environment, and aesthetics: The legacy of joachim f. wohlwill* (pp. 213240). Hillsdale, NJ.: Lawrence Erlbaum Associates.

Nesselroade, J. R., McArdle, J. J., Aggen, S. H., & Meyers, J. M. (2002). Alternative dynamic factor models for multivariate timeseries analyses. In D. M. Moskowitz & S. L. Hershberger (Eds.), *Modeling intraindividual variability with repeated measures data: Advances and techniques* (pp. 235-265). Mahwah, NJ.: Lawrence Erlbaum Associates.

Nesselroade, J. R., & Ram, N. (2004). Studying intraindividual variability: What we have learned that will help us understand lives in context. *Research in Human Development*, *1*, 929.

Pepper, S. C. (1942). *World hypotheses: A study of evidence.* Berkeley: University of California Press.

Sameroff, A. J. (1983). Developmental systems: Contexts and evolution. In W. Kessen (Ed.), *Handbook of child psychology: Vol. 1. History, theory, and methods* (4th ed., pp. 237-294). New York: Wiley.

Sameroff, A. J., & Chandler, M. J. (1975). Reproductive risk and the continuum of caretaking casualty. In F. D. Horowitz, E. M. Hetherington, S. Scarr-Salapatek, & G. M. Siegel (Eds.), *Review of child development research: Vol. 4* (pp. 187244). Chicago: University of Chicago Press.

Wood, P., & Brown, D. (1994). The study of intraindividual differences by means of dynamic factor models: Rationale, implementation, and interpretation. *Psychological Bulletin*, *116*(1), 166186.

CHAPTER FIFTEEN

The Shape of Things to Come: Diagnosing Social Contagion From Adolescent Smoking and Drinking Curves

Joseph Lee Rodgers
University of Oklahoma

Many developmental processes can be considered as the diffusion of one or more behaviors through a social network. Transition behaviors are ones that present adolescents with a decision-making dilemma to either start the behavior or not, and often are perceived (by adolescents, adults, and society-at-large) as indicative of transition to adulthood (see Rodgers & Rowe, 1993, for discussion and development). Many transition behaviors appear to spread through a social network as a result of social influence.

Cigarette smoking and drinking alcohol are examples. It would be hard to argue that there is a biological drive, or an otherwise natural tendency, for an adolescent to put a lighted "tobacco-stick" into their mouth and inhale deeply; the onset of smoking seems obviously to derive at least partly from social influence. Drinking alcohol also has obvious social origins. Even the expression "social drinking" suggests that there is an underlying social component to alcohol consumption, and to its onset. Although many other transition behaviors (both negative and positive) appear to spread at least in part through social influence, I focus in this chapter on smoking and drinking, two transition behaviors that are highly visible and that have substantial health implications related to their use.

Though it would be hard to argue against the potential for social influence on smoking and drinking in adolescence, there are different social explanations— different social influence process models—for how social influences actually affect the onset of smoking cigarettes or drinking. One model I consider suggests that many different general social influences, from peers, but also from the family, from media exposure, and others, all contribute to a general "smoking/drinking culture." This type of influence was referred to by Burt (1987) as a "structural equivalence" model. Another model I consider implies that one-to-one social influence, direct social contagion, is at the basis of the spread of cigarette smoking in adolescents. This type of process requires direct social contact and social influence. Burt referred to this type of influence as a "cohesion" process.

Furthermore, Burt (1987) specified the mechanism driving each model in relation to the social context in which the behavior spreads (his specific social network was the professional community of Medical Doctors). He referred to cohesion — direct social contagion — as the type of process illustrated by "conversations with colleagues" (p. 1287). On the other hand, structural equivalence — general diffusion — occurs when MDs behave according to "their perception of the action proper for an occupant of their position in the social structure of colleagues" (p. 1287). Translating this to adolescents, cohesion occurs when a direct, specific social influence (e.g., a conversation, verbal encouragement, immediate behavioral modeling, etc.) causes one adolescent to perform a behavior (e.g., smoking) because another adolescent actively influences them to do so. Structural equivalence occurs when an adolescent smokes for the first time because they believe that adolescents are supposed to experiment with cigarettes, with this belief emerging from the general adolescent culture (e.g., through media exposure, or through observing parents and other adolescents, but not through any specific one-to-one contact or any immediate and explicit peer influence).

Obviously, these two different conceptualizations for onset of adolescent smoking/drinking have substantially divergent implications for intervention programs to limit adolescent smoking/drinking. The cohesion perspective suggests the importance of face-to-face intervention, and posits that a peer is the direct, proximal prerequisite for the spread of smoking/drinking among adolescents. The physical locations for such direct person-to-person influence (the backyard, the playground, the neighborhood, the classroom) are the settings in which intervention matters. On the other hand, if the establishment of a general "smoking culture" is what leads adolescents to smoke, without direct peer influence, then interventions would work best in media settings or in general cultural settings (e.g., through legislation restricting smoking ads, by limiting smoking exposure by actors in television and movies, or by suggesting to parents that they hide or limit their smoking in front of their children). Or, perhaps both processes occur simultaneously, a possibility that is developed and actively measured using a revision of the Burt (1987) model.

In this chapter, I present a model that unites the two different theoretical perspectives developed by Burt (1987) into a single mathematical framework. The framework allows for either process to be diagnosed, but also allows for a mixture of the two processes to be identified as well. First, I develop the logic and mathematics defined by Burt and review the empirical application of his methods. Second, I review some past empirical work within the EMOSA framework (EMOSA = Epidemic Models of the Onset of Social Activities; Rodgers, 2000; 2003 ; Rowe, Rodgers, & Gilson, 2000) applied to adolescent smoking and drinking. Next, the EMOSA equations will be revised by adding a new parameter that accounts for the two processes defined by Burt. Then, the revised model will be fit to 2003 data collected from college students about their first smoking and drinking experience. I conclude with some summary statements and a strong note of caution about the limitations of such methods.

BURT'S (1987) TAXONOMY OF SOCIAL INFLUENCE PROCESSES

Burt (1987) developed a mathematical link between the developmental process involved in the spread of behaviors, and the social mechanism underlying that spread. The focus of this edited book, the role of contextual effects on developmental and longitudinal processes, was anticipated by Burt through his two equations. One equation implies that the context underlying the social influence process involves general cultural dynamics—Burt's social cohesion model. The other equation implies that the context underlying the social influence process is a direct, person-to-person, influence process—Burt's cohesion model.

Specifically, Burt (1987) suggested that the shape of the prevalence curve indicating onset of behaviors is diagnostic of the type of social process that influenced the behavior. His analytic method allows researchers to distinguish between social cohesion and structural equivalence. His method emerged from consideration of the basic mathematical forms by which epidemics spread through a social network. The process that Burt called "structural equivalence," I refer to as "general diffusion." The process that Burt called "cohesion," I refer to as "social contagion diffusion." (Alternatively, we have sometimes referred to the first process as "constant-rate diffusion," and the second process as "prevalence-driven diffusion." This terminology was developed in detail in Rowe, Rodgers, and Gilson, 2000).

The prevalence curve generated by a general diffusion process can be modeled through the following equation:

$$P_{t+1} = P_t + T(1 - P_t) \tag{1}$$

This equation is a monotonically-increasing negatively-accelerated exponential function (see the top graph in Figure 15.1). The statement of the model implied by this equation is that the prevalence of a behavior at time t + 1 (e.g., the proportion of smokers, P_{t+1}) is composed of two pieces – the proportion of those who had already engaged in the behavior at time t (i.e., those who had already smoked by the previous time interval, P_t) and the proportion of those who had not already engaged in the behavior at the previous time interval (1-P_t) multiplied by the transition probability T. T indicates the probability that those who haven't engaged in the behavior do so during the interval between t and t + 1. This is a very simple statement suggesting that some fraction of the at-risk population transitions to the new behavior during every time interval. The only structure of interest within this model is the proportion of the population that has not already engaged in the behavior.

On the other hand, social contagion diffusion adds an additional component to the model:

$$P_{t+1} = P_t + TP_t(1 - P_t) \qquad (2)$$

This equation generates a monotonically-increasing S-shaped curve (see the bottom graph in Figure 15.1). As noted by Burt (1987), "the most distinct evidence of social contagion is the initial period of slow diffusion among pioneer adopters" (p. 1304), the lower part of the S-shaped curve. The statement of the model implied by this equation is that the prevalence of a behavior at time t + 1 is still composed of two pieces, and the first is identical to that in Equation (1), the proportion who had already engaged in the behavior by time t. The second part also accounts for the proportion at risk, but in addition accounts for the proportion who have already engaged in the behavior. One interpretation of this equation (e.g., Rowe, Rodgers, & Meseck-Bushey, 1989) is that the population is paired into dyads through some process (either randomly or purposively), and those at risk who are paired with those who have already performed the behavior may be influenced to engage in the behavior with some transition probability T. Theoretically, T is a probability, and ranges from 0 to 1. In some practical situations, T can be estimated to be greater than 1. The epidemiological literature interprets this result in relation to the idea of "effective contacts." If someone who has performed the behavior can influence more than one person per time interval to make the transition into having performed the behavior, then the upper bound of T can be greater than 1.0. In other words, for T to be interpreted as a true probability, the model assumes that there is at most one effective contact per time interval. This assumption can either be imposed by defining bounds on the estimation routine, or can be evaluated by allowing T to be estimated without constraint.

These two equations are the beginning of a complex mathematical development used extensively in epidemiology (e.g., Anderson & May, 1991; May & Anderson, 1987). The epidemiological models are used to estimate parameters relevant to the spread of disease, including malaria, syphilis, AIDS, or the common cold. Our past use in modeling the spread of behaviors takes advantage of this mathematical development and the concept of contagion to apply these ideas in a behavioral context. We note that many contagious phenomena, both biological contagion and social contagion, are not necessarily negative in relation to health behavior. For example, playing in the school band may spread at least in part through social contagion, and many successful and valuable marketing innovations are driven through social contagion processes. In fact, the whole literature on "innovation diffusion" (e.g., Mahajan & Peterson, 1985) reflects this latter conceptualization. Further, the spread of biologically contagious processes can be a positive health benefit, as when immunity is created by mild exposure to health-threatening viruses (e.g., the natural immunity to polio discovered in low-SES environments in which children whose immune systems effectively fought the virus built a lifelong immunity to the disease).

FIGURE 15.1

Prevalence curves that are suggestive of general diffusion (top curve, connecting diamonds) and social contagion diffusion (bottom curve, connecting squares).

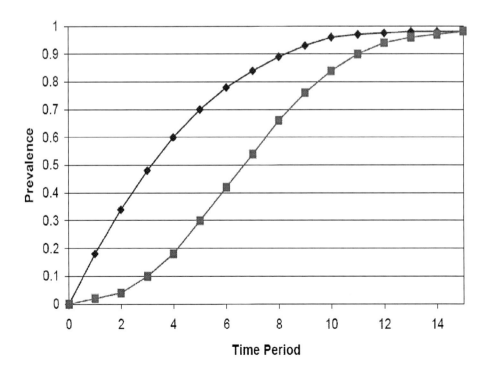

Burt's (1987) use of these equations was focused on distinguishing between general diffusion and social contagion diffusion. His particular focus was on the spread of the use of tetracycline as a new antibiotic drug through the medical community in the mid-1950s in several towns in Illinois. The original treatment of this spread was reported in Coleman, Katz, and Menzel (1966). After considering prevalence curves, Burt's conclusion was that most of the spread of the use of tetracycline occurred through the structural equivalence model, that is, physicians became aware of the drug through general channels like medical journals and general discussion at medical meetings (note that the term structural equivalence refers to a network of socially equal peers, such as the MDs within this particular medical community, who share information through general cultural mechanisms). Very little of the process was driven through direct social contagion, from close professional colleagues who suggested very directly "you should begin to use tetracycline." These conclusions were extracted from the shapes of the prevalence curves, as described earlier. The same type of analysis of onset curves for adolescent smoking and drinking is developed in this chapter.

EPIDEMIC MODELS OF THE ONSET OF SOCIAL ACTIVITIES (EMOSA MODELS)

EMOSA models combine a psychological theory of the spread of transition behaviors through an intact adolescent network with a set of mathematical models of that process (for elaboration see Rodgers & Rowe, 1993; Rodgers, Rowe, & Buster, 1998b). These models have relationships to those from epidemiology, innovation diffusion, nonlinear dynamic systems (e.g., Rodgers, Rowe, & Buster, 1998b) and hazards models (e.g. Stoolmiller, 1998). The EMOSA mathematical model is a straightforward mathematical extension of the conceptual model underlying the psychological theory. The process that is modeled suggests that a group of intact adolescents "pair up" with one another during the course of a time interval (e.g., a year). The model observes whether individuals enter a new status (e.g., ever having smoked a cigarette) during the course of the time interval, and keeps track of those in the total population who have ever engaged in the relevant behavior. For example, if a nonsmoker is paired with a smoker, there is potential for the smoker to influence the nonsmoker to try a cigarette for the first time. (Obviously, the basic form of the EMOSA model refers to social contagion diffusion.) The likelihood of this occurring is captured in a parameter of the model called a transition probability, which is a feature of Burt's (1987) model that is discussed earlier. In theory, two nonsmokers who are paired could make the transition to smoking status spontaneously. Although other EMOSA models have allowed this type of transition (e.g., Rowe, Chassin, Presson, Edwards, & Sherman, 1992), in this chapter we focus on the type of social influence that passes directly from those who have smoked/drank to those who have not (which is the type of social influence which Burt developed).

The basic EMOSA equations that capture this process are similar in form to – though often more complex than — Equations (1) and (2) . In many different senses, they expand and elaborate Burt's (1987) equations. In other words, EMOSA equations, like those from Burt, explicitly (through mathematics) refer to the social context underlying adolescent developmental processes.

The first EMOSA model described the spread of nonvirginity through a community of adolescent (Rowe, Rodgers, & Meseck-Bushey, 1989). This is a two-gender model, with filters that account for pubertal maturity (filters are described later in this section). A number of additional and more complex EMOSA sexuality models have been developed. Rodgers, Rowe, and Buster (1998b) modeled a combination of sexuality curves, pubertal development curves, and pregnancy curves with an EMOSA system. Furthermore, they wrote equations to model transition to onset of sexually transmitted disease (STDs), although prevalence curves for STDs during adolescence were not available to support empirical testing and model fitting. Rodgers (2003) developed a number of policy implications of past EMOSA sexuality models, including specific recommendations for implementation of intervention programs that emerge from the EMOSA perspective.

Two past substantive findings from EMOSA sexuality models are described, both of which were surprising and would not have been observable except in the context of a nonlinear model built to explicitly describe the processes being modeled (see Rodgers, Rowe, & Buster, 1998b, for further discussion of this point). Rowe and Rodgers (1991b) found a new interpretation for the often-noted difference in sexual behavior levels between White and Black adolescents; Blacks are empirically more sexually precocious than Whites at a given age. Past explanations have focused on social and cultural processes. Rowe and Rodgers found that including a female pubertal maturity filter — which accounted for slightly earlier pubertal maturity among Black females than White females — fully accounted for the race difference in the context of this nonlinear dynamic model (i.e., a small difference around age 10–12 in female pubertal maturity accounted for a relatively larger difference in rates of sexual behavior in older adolescence). Another finding of interest identified using EMOSA sexuality models emerged from a complex model that combined sexual behavior and pregnancy, investigated in Rodgers, Rowe, and Buster (1998b). Their best-fitting model defined an approximately constant probability of pregnancy across ages 12 to 18 (whereas they expected decreased probability with older ages as contraceptive efficacy improved). They speculated that two processes are approximately compensatory; as knowledge of and use of contraceptives improves, so does average coital frequency. These two processes may approximately compensate for one another across ages.

The first EMOSA model for smoking and drinking was presented in Rowe and Rodgers (1991a), applied to data from two countries. Several more complex EMOSA models of smoking were developed (e.g., Rowe, Chassin et al., 1992; Rowe, Chassin, Presson, & Sherman, 1996; Rowe, Rodgers, & Gilson, 2000). Finally, Rodgers and Johnson (2006) reported a data collection project (which generated the data that are used in the current study) assessing retrospective reports of the onset of smoking and drinking among college students. The purpose of the Rodgers and Johnson study was to empirically address some of the questions that emerge from EMOSA models. In this chapter, I use the simple form of the EMOSA system that is equivalent to equations (1) and (2).

Our development of EMOSA models has involved specifying the EMOSA equations to explicitly model a given behavioral phenomenon. For example, EMOSA sexuality models necessarily define separate equations for males and females, whereas EMOSA smoking models can potentially combine males and females into a single prevalence curve. Furthermore, filters play an important role in EMOSA models. These are equivalent conceptually and analytically to categorical covariates in linear models. They are also related to moderating variables and to time-invariant categorical covariates in hazards models. Filters condition the estimation routine in relation to certain subsets of the data, so that different estimates are obtained across subsets. For example, Rowe et al. (1996) found that EMOSA smoking models fit significantly better when transition probabilities were estimated separately for adolescents whose parents smoked compared to those whose parents didn't smoke. Rowe, Rodgers, and Meseck-Bushey (1989) and Rodgers and Rowe (1993) found that female pubertal development stages (but not male stages) were effective filters in EMOSA sexuality models. Although our use of EMOSA models has generally involved building the model to fit the behavior, EMOSA models have relationships to more standard analytic tools, and can be applied through those more traditional approaches as well. For example, Stoolmiller (1998) showed the mathematical relationship of certain EMOSA models to traditional hazards models, suggesting that at least some EMOSA systems could be estimated from hazards modeling software. In Rodgers, Rowe, and Buster (1998a), we acknowledged the value of recognizing such relationships, but also explain the importance of directly linking a particular model to the behavior that it describes.

The fitting of EMOSA models involves optimizing the relationship between predictions of the model and empirical values. Many different optimization criteria exist, including least-squares, chi-square, AIC, and maximum likelihood. Rodgers and Rowe (1993) discuss these, and compare results across different loss (gain) functions. Both the chi-square and maximum likelihood have a particular attraction, because they can be used to test statistically the difference between two different nested models. If the two models only differ in a specific parameter, then the comparison between the models is a statistical test of the importance of the parameter to the system. The AIC can be used even when models to be compared are not nested. In this chapter, I define a specific parameter that measures the role of the two different diffusion processes defined by Burt. Because my primary focus is on estimation (of this parameter, along with the transition probability) — rather than statistical comparison of models — I will use a basic loss function, the least-squares criterion.

To conclude this brief review of past EMOSA models, I note that there are many potential policy applications for the EMOSA perspective, and research applications for EMOSA models. Many adolescent behaviors, both transition behaviors, and broader behavioral domains that extend on both sides of adolescence, have social dynamics that underlie their development. In addition to smoking and drinking alcohol, many problem behaviors (some of which are also classified as transition behaviors) spread at least in part through the type of social influences captured in the two diffusion models discussed in this chapter. Examples include bullying, cheating on tests, delinquent and other antisocial behaviors, drug use, and driving illegally/unsafely. Many other behaviors emerge from underlying social influence as well, including some positive and healthy behaviors. Playing high school sports, playing in the school band, participating in school clubs, and developing good study skills and academic discipline are examples. It is important to note that the EMOSA modeling systems are developed explicitly to explain the *onset* of behaviors with a social influence component. However, EMOSA models can also account for continuing developmental processes by defining stagewise progressions through levels of behavioral involvement, and modeling the onset of behavioral development at each stage over time (e.g., see Rowe et al., 1992, for a four-stage smoking model and Rodgers and Rowe, 1993, for a five-stage sexuality model). Studying onset of other adolescent behaviors, and/or defining stagewise models of progression through levels of involvement, would support future EMOSA developments with both policy and research implications.

REVISION OF THE BURT (1987) EQUATIONS: AN INTEGRATIVE MODEL

Equations (1) and (2) can in fact be combined into a single equation. This equation can be used to measure the contribution of each of the two processes — general diffusion and social contagion diffusion. The integrative model involves adding a new parameter, to be estimated from the data, which allows us to combine the two models. The integrative model is the following:

$$P_{t+1} = P_t + TP_t{}^C(1 - P_t) \qquad (3)$$

Within this model, the exponent C supports both Equations (1) and (2) to be special cases of this general model. When C = 0, Equation (3) becomes Equation (1), and the model is one of general diffusion. When C = 1, Equation (3) becomes Equation (2), and the model is one of social-contagion (prevalence-driven) diffusion. The real value of this re-formulation, however, does not occur at the extremes. The model can now accommodate a mixture of these two processes — general diffusion and prevalence-driven diffusion — through the estimation of C. If C is estimated to be around .5, then by inference, both processes would be contributing approximately equally. If C is estimated to be lower than .50, the inference would be that general diffusion is the primary source, with a smaller amount of social contagion diffusion. Alternatively, if C is estimated to be close to unity, the inference would be that social contagion diffusion is the important process.

To illustrate this estimation process, I fit Equation (3) to the two curves shown in Figure 15.1. These curves were not generated from either model, but rather from visual inspection and trial-and-error, to illustrate a prototype negatively accelerated exponential curve and a prototype S-shaped curve. When Equation (3) was fit to the top curve — the one used to conceptually illustrate general diffusion in the discussion in the previous section — the optimal values of the parameters C and T were estimated to be C = .29, T = .30. This pattern suggests that the top curve in Figure 15.1 reflects primarily general diffusion (as expected), with some social contagion diffusion as well, and a transition probability of T = .30. When equation (3) was fit to the bottom curve in Figure 15.1, the optimal parameter estimates were C = .65, T = .38. This pattern suggests that social contagion diffusion is the primary process, with some general diffusion contributing at a lower level as well, and a transition probability of T = .38. It is interesting to note that the estimated transition probabilities — the Ts — were close to the same value. In other words, these two very different types of prevalence curves could be generated from very similar transition probabilities, acting on different types of diffusion.

As a second illustration, the model in Equation (3) was fit to the tetra-cycline curve from Burt (1987), the curve indicating the increasing prevalence over time of the use of tetracycline as an antibiotic among Illinois MDs. Burt concluded from the shape of this curve that this spread was primarily based on a general diffusion process, rather than social contagion. Fitting equation (3) to those data further supported this conclusion; the estimated values of the two parameters were T = .11 and C = .02. In other words, a general diffusion model was almost exclusively supported for these data, even when other social contagion processes were permissible within the model.

FITTING THE INTEGRATIVE MODEL TO SMOKING AND DRINKING DATA

The Survey

In April, 2003, data were collected from 306 undergraduate students at the University of Oklahoma using a survey instrument titled "The First Time I Smoked Cigarettes and Drank Alcohol." Respondents indicated their age of first cigarette/alcoholic drink, and then followed those responses (for those who indicated they had smoked or drank alcohol) with more detailed information about their first smoking/drinking experience (location, others who were there, etc). Next, the instrument requested two open-ended verbal descriptions of their first smoking/drinking experience, one short (in one sentence), the other more extensive ("write a short description of your first experience . . . . You may want to imagine that you are telling a story to someone as you describe this event"). For the current chapter, the more extensive open-ended responses were used. Details of the data patterns were presented in Rodgers & Johnson (2006).

The demographic characteristics of this sample were the following: Average age = 19.6, with low variability ($SD = 2.7$). There was an even distribution by gender (53% female, 47% male). The ethnicity distribution (77% Caucasian, 7% African American, 6% Native American, 4% Hispanic, and 6% Other) was approximately proportionate to that in the OU student population. Of the 306 respondents, 66% had ever smoked cigarettes and 91% had ever drunk alcohol. Of those who had ever smoked, 85% first did so in the presence of one or more friends, and 15% in the presence of one or more family members (and these family members were always siblings, virtually never parents). There was 8% overlap (i.e., 8% first smoked with both friends and family present). Of those who had ever drunk alcohol, 81% did so in the presence of one or more friends, and 32% in the presence of one or more family members. There was 17% overlap (i.e., 17% first drank alcohol with both friends and family present). These patterns are suggestive that both smoking and drinking occur in the social context of friends; drinking onset appears to have a stronger social context from within the family.

The open-ended responses were coded for whether the respondent explicitly described a process that appeared to be social contagion from friends/peers.

A conservative standard was used for coding for social contagion from friends; in other words, respondents had to very explicitly indicate that a friend had a direct influence on their initiation to smoking/drinking. Examples of statements that led to such a coding were the following:

"Everyone else talked me into it — I had never smoked before."

"My buddy just happened to have cigs and gave me one. He said I needed [one] after taking the big English test."

"I felt peer pressure to be cool."

"Everyone else [at the party] was doing it [drinking] and it seemed like fun."

"People wanted me to [drink]."

The Analysis

As in a number of previous publications demonstrating how to fit EMOSA models (e.g., Rodgers & Johnson, 2005; Rodgers & Rowe, 1993), prevalence curves were constructed from the responses to the "age at first cigarette use" and "age at first alcohol use" questions. The model in Equation (3) was programmed in PROC NLIN in SAS, which estimated parameters to maximize the fit (using a least squares loss function) between the model and the empirical prevalence curves.

Next, respondents were separated into two categories, those who indicated in the open-ended questionnaire that social influence from a peer was an important component of their first smoking/drinking experience, and those who did not so indicate. Prevalence curves were generated for each of these two categories, separately for smoking and drinking (i.e., four new prevalence curves, in addition to the original two).

Prevalence curves are plotted, and can be inspected in terms of whether there is the characteristic S-shaped curve associated with social contagion, or a negatively accelerated structure like that associated with general diffusion. Analysis results are presented in terms of the optimally estimated parameters. Every model, without exception, showed an excellent fit; most of the residual sums of squares were less than .001. The quality of these fits can be observed graphically by noting the smooth structure in plots of the empirical prevalence curves emerging from the survey data.

Results

Among the 199 respondents who described their first smoking experience, 38% explained that experience in a way that unambiguously referred to social contagion/social influence from peers. Among the 258 respondents who described their first drinking experience, 17% referred to social contagion/social influence as an important contributor. We note that many of the verbal descriptions were cryptic and relatively noninformative. In other words, we view these percentages as lower bound estimates of the role of social contagion; likely, these are substantial underestimates. Many of those who did not explicitly describe social influence may still have been influenced by their peers in connection with their smoking/drinking debut. In support of this position, it should be noted that whereas 38% explicitly referred to social contagion processes in describing their first smoking experience, 85% smoked for the first time in the presence of a friend, and similar patterns occurred for drinking as well.

For the purpose of evaluating the new integrative model in Equation (3), prevalence curves were developed for the onset of smoking/drinking. The first set of prevalence curves is presented in Figure 15.2, which is a slight reformulation of this same information presented in Rodgers and Johnson (2005). These are the smoking curve and the drinking curve, developed by using the responses to the "age at first smoking/drinking" reports from the OU survey. When these curves were fit (i.e., optimal T and C parameters were estimated from Equation 3) using PROC NLIN in SAS, the following results were obtained. For onset of smoking, $T = .25$, $C = .80$. This pattern is suggestive that the smoking process is primarily driven by social contagion, with a small component of general diffusion. For onset of drinking, $T = .49$ and $C = 1.0$, even more strongly suggestive of a social contagion process (with no component of general diffusion detected by the model). The difference between the T parameters reflects different transition probabilities for smoking and drinking; given a "contact" between an experienced adolescent drinker/smoker and one who has never drunk/smoked, the probability that the non-drinker becomes a drinker during a given time period is almost twice a high as that of a non-smoker becoming a smoker. This transition probability difference is capturing, at least in part, the higher prevalence at which the ever-drinking curve asymptotes compared to the smoking curve.

Next, I defined prevalence curves separately for those who were classified as "yes" or "no" for social contagion. There were several different methods by which these prevalence curves could be constructed. In Figures 15.3 (for first smoked a cigarette) and Figure 15.4 (for first drank alcohol), I assumed that there are separate processes occurring for those in each social contagion category, and that the asymptote estimates the total saturation of the particular

FIGURE 15.2

Smoking and drinking prevalence curves, 2003 OU survey, proportion ever drank alcohol (top
curve, connecting squares) and smoked a cigarette (bottom curve, connecting diamonds).

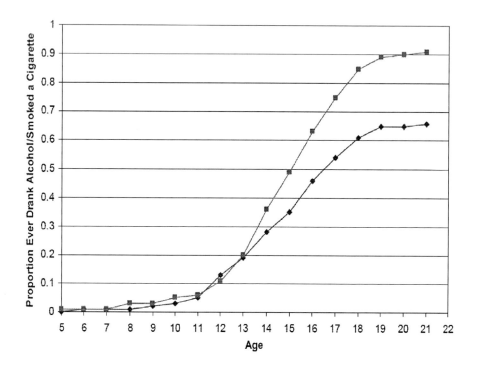

process within each population. In this case, for smoking the model estimated
T=.48 and C=.77 for those who did not report a component of social contagion,
suggestive that most of the process was socially contagious diffusion, with a
small component of general diffusion. For smoking for those who did report a
component of social contagion, T=.79 and C=.97, suggestive that virtually all
of the process was driven by social contagion. This is in the direction to support
that the two different curves do diagnose the difference between social contagion
and general diffusion. Further, the transition probability was notably higher
for the social contagion group. However, it is important to note that in both
categories, the spread of smoking was strongly supportive of social contagion
as the primary method by which social influence acts on the first smoking
experience.

For drinking, for those who did not report a component of social contagion,
$T = .58$ and $C = 1.0$; for those who did report a component of social contagion,
$T = .82$ and $C = 1.0$. In each case, the social contagion process was all that
was necessary to account for the shape of these drinking prevalence curves; no

FIGURE 15.3
Smoking prevalence curves, 2003 OU survey, separately for those whose open-ended responses
suggested that social contagion was a component of first smoking (curve connecting squares,
ends on top) and those whose open ended responses were not suggestive that social contagion
was relevant (curve connecting diamonds, ends on bottom).

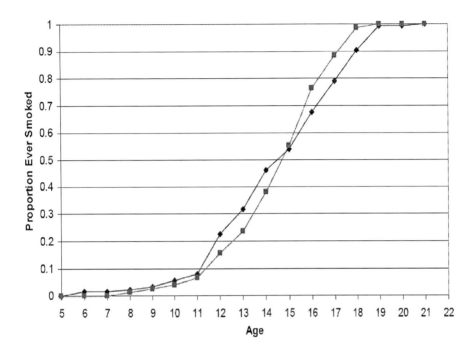

general diffusion component was necessary at all. The only difference between the two curves — which obviously have the same basic S-shaped geometric structure — was the transmission probability, captured by the T parameter.

The proportions used to construct the prevalence curves earlier were ones that were computed using in the denominator the total number who indicated in their open-ended responses that social contagion was occurring (for the curves connecting boxes in Figures 15.3 and 15.4), and the total number who did not indicate in their open-ended responses that social contagion was occurring (for the curves connecting diamonds in Figures 15.3 and 15.4). There are other reasonable ways to define these prevalence curves, however. I used two other approaches to construct proportions, one in which the denominator of the proportions was the total in the sample, and the other the estimated total in the sample in each contagion category. These patterns resulted in prevalence curves that had asymptotes at lower levels than those in Figures 15.3 and 15.4, and as a result, the estimated t and C parameters were both smaller. It is important

FIGURE 15.4

Drinking prevalence curves, 2003 OU survey, separately for those whose open-ended responses suggested that social contagion was a component of first drinking (bottom curve, connecting squares) and those whose open ended responses were not suggestive that social contagion was relevant (top curve, connecting diamonds).

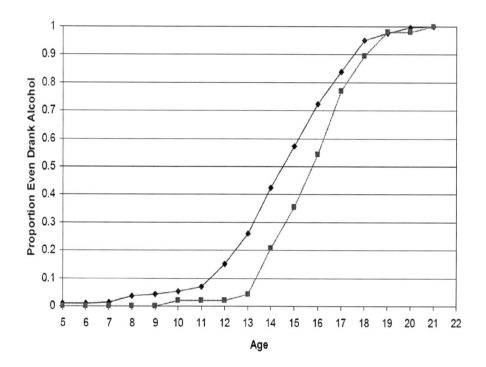

to note that the structure of these curves is like that in Figures 15.3 and 15.4, but the asymptote changes. The findings comparing those who reported social contagion and those who did not were approximately the same under each of these models; for all four categories — for smoking and drinking, crossed with those who reported social contagion as a component and those who didn't — the estimated C parameter was similar across the two social contagion categories, with either equivalent or slightly higher values for the category of those indicated social contagion was relevant. As noted by Burt (1987), social contagious diffusion is characterized by an "initial period of slow diffusion." In both curves in Figures 15.3 and 15.4 (as well as those for the other denominators), the slow diffusion is slightly more apparent for those in the social contagion category than for those who aren't — although both categories have a strong appearance of the S-shaped curve characteristic of socially contagious diffusion.

CONCLUSIONS

The goal of this chapter was to extend the work of Burt (1987) in relation to the EMOSA modeling approach. Burt suggested that prevalence curves are diagnostic of the type of diffusion process that generated them. The findings above are both supportive of this position, and also raise some challenges. There are, furthermore, challenges that emerge from deeper consideration of the mathematics involved.

If the simple diffusion model underlying the Burt (1987) framework is accepted as an accurate and relatively complete explanation of the processes that are at work in adolescent friendship networks, then several interesting findings emerge from these empirical analyses. Most importantly, smoking and drinking are both processes that spread through direct social influence, that is, through a social contagion process. Those who report that friends provided a direct and specific influence on their first smoking experience — that is, those who verbally account for contagious diffusion as a part of their own personal onset process — are so indicated at a slightly stronger level than those who do not (and the two processes for drinking are estimated to be identical). But it is important that even those who do not indicate that friends were an integral part of their first smoking/drinking experience have prevalence curves suggestive that social contagion is the primary type of diffusion that underlies the spread of smoking/drinking through an adolescent network.

One challenge to this interpretation emerges from the observation that the respondents in the OU Survey did not necessarily begin drinking/smoking as part of a common friendship network (as the EMOSA model assumes). That is, these students came from different parts of the state and the country, with potentially many different cultural influences on the timing and nature of their first smoking/drinking experience. A response to this challenge emerges from the EMOSA research presented in Rowe, Rodgers, and Meseck-Bushey (1989) and in Rowe and Rodgers (1991b). In those papers, EMOSA sexuality models were fit to both local prevalence curves from two cities on the east coast of the United States, and to national data from both the United States and Denmark. The estimates of the transition parameters were remarkably similar. Furthermore, those sources review sociological literature suggestive that many diffusion processes operate similarly between local and larger network settings. A recent popular/scholarly book (Watts, 2003) supported that diffusion processes often are not easily distinguished between local and larger levels within communication networks. The implication of this argument is to suggest that the social influence processes that impinge on adolescent smoking and drinking behavior are approximately the same across the whole U.S. culture (and, quite likely, also across other well-developed countries), so that fitting diffusion models to data from different settings presents approximately the same modeling challenges as using data from a single source that nearly matches the "intact adolescent network" assumption of the EMOSA modeling approach.

A larger challenge to the perspective developed in Burt (1987) and applied here to EMOSA modeling is the observation that the Burt model assumes a very simple process, one that is probably not realistic in capturing the complexity of the spread of behaviors through a social environment. Often, statistical tests are robust to simplifying assumptions (as described in the previous paragraph). In this case, however, we have evidence that this may not be the case. For example, using a slightly more complex EMOSA model than the one that emerges from the Burt model, Rodgers and Rowe (1993) generated prevalence curves *using an explicit social contagion model* that had the characteristic negatively accelerated structure of the general diffusion model. Specifically, one of the figures in the Rodgers and Rowe paper (Figure 7, p.498) show both positively and negatively accelerated prevalence curves, generated by a rather more complex diffusion model (specifically, a four-stage diffusion model defined separately for each gender that includes filters).

In other words, Burt's distinction between the shape of the two types of diffusion is only diagnostic of this distinction if the diffusion model operates according to the very simple process implied by Equations (1) and (2). A proper revision of this perspective would suggest that a negatively accelerated prevalence curve is suggestive that either general diffusion is occurring, or that a more complex form of contagious diffusion is occurring than the one captured in Equation (2). It is important to note, however, that the empirical smoking and drinking prevalence curves from the OU survey were *not* of this structure; rather, they had the S-shaped structure characteristic of Burt's social contagion diffusion process. It seems less likely that such curves could be easily generated by the equations used to generate a general diffusion process. As previously discussed, social contagion is characterized by a long period of slow building up, representing the bottom of the S-shaped function. However, whether general diffusion curves can be adapted to mimic social contagion diffusion curves — which can certainly occur in the reverse direction — will await further research, using either simulation or empirical model-fitting exercises. If the previous suggestion — that S-shaped functions remain strongly diagnostic of social contagion diffusion — are supported then the basic empirical finding of this paper remains intact: Many adolescents like those represented by those in the OU Survey are strongly influenced by their friends and peers — in an active version of social contagion that involves direct social influence — as they engaged in smoking and drinking for the first time.

REFERENCES

Anderson, R. M., & May, R. M. (1991). *Infectious diseases of humans.* New York: Oxford University Press.

Burt, R. S. (1987). Social contagion and innovation: Cohesion versus structural equivalence. *American Journal of Sociology, 92,* 1287-1335.

Coleman, J., Katz, E., & Menzel, H. (1966). *Medical innovations.* New York: Bobbs-Merrill.

Mahajan, V., & Peterson, R. A. (1985). *Models for innovation diffusion.* Beverly Hills, CA: Sage.

May, R. M., & Anderson, R. M. (1987). Transmission dynamics of HIV infection. *Nature, 326,* 137-142.

Rodgers, J. L. (2000). Social contagion and adolescent sexual behavior: Theoretical and policy implications. In J. Bancroft (Ed.), *The role of theory in sex research* (pp. 258-278). Bloomington, IN: Kinsey Institute.

Rodgers, J. L. (2003). Emosa sexuality models, memes, and the tipping point: Policy and program implications. In D. Romer (Ed.), *Reducing adolescent risk* (pp. 185-192). Thousand Oaks, CA: Sage.

Rodgers, J. L., & Johnson, A. (2006). Nonlinear dynamic models of nonlinear dynamic behaviors: Social contagion of adolescent smoking and drinking at aggregate and individual levels. In S. M. Boker & M. Wenger (Eds.), *Data analysis techniques for dynamic systems* (in press). Mahwah, NJ: Lawrence Erlbaum Associates.

Rodgers, J. L., & Rowe, D. C. (1993). Social contagion and adolescence sexual behavior: A developmental emosa model. *Psychology Review, 100,* 479-510.

Rodgers, J. L., Rowe, D. C., & Buster, M. (1998a). Nonlinear dynamic modeling and social contagion: Reply to stoolmiller (1998). *Developmental Psychology, 34,* 1117-1118.

Rodgers, J. L., Rowe, D. C., & Buster, M. (1998b). Social contagion, adolescent sexual behavior, and pregnancy: A nonlinear dynamic emosa model. *Developmental Psychology, 34,* 1096-1113.

Rowe, D. C., Chassin, L., Presson, C., & Sherman, S. J. (1996). Parental smoking and the epidemic spread of cigarette smoking. *Journal of Applied Social Psychology, 26,* 437-454.

Rowe, D. C., Chassin, L., Presson, C. C., Edwards, E., & Sherman, S. J. (1992). An 'epidemic' model of adolescent cigarette smoking. *Journal of Applied Social Psychology, 2,* 261-285.

Rowe, D. C., & Rodgers, J. L. (1991a). Adolescent smoking and drinking: Are they epidemics?. *Journal of Studies in Alcohol, 52,* 110-117.

Rowe, D. C., & Rodgers, J. L. (1991b). An 'epidemic' model of adolescent sexual inter-course prevalences: Applications to national survey data. *Journal of Biosocial Science, 23,* 211-219.

Rowe, D. C., Rodgers, J. L., & Gilson, M. (2000). Epidemics of smoking: Modeling tobacco use among adolescents. In J. S. Rose, L. Chassin, C. C. Presson, & S. J.

Sherman (Eds.), *Multivariate applications in substance use research*. Mahweh, NJ: Lawrence Erlbaum Associates.

Rowe, D. C., Rodgers, J. L., & Meseck-Bushey, S. (1989). An 'epidemic' model of sexual intercourse prevalences for black and white adolescents. *Social Biology, 36*, 27-145.

Stoolmiller, M. (1998). Comment on Social Contagion, Adolescent Sexual Behavior, and Pregnancy: A Nonlinear Dynamic EMOSA Model. *Developmental Psychology, 34*, 1114-1116.

Watts, D. J. (2003). *Six degrees: The science of a connected age*. New York: Norton.

CHAPTER SIXTEEN

A Dynamic Structural Analysis of the Impacts of Context on Shifts in Lifespan Cognitive Development

Kevin J.Grimm
University of Virginia

John J. McArdle
University of Southern California

One theme of this book is the study of contextual effects on psychological change. Any empirical study attending to these issues benefits from both (a) a formal representation of change and its measurement, and (b) explicit hypotheses regarding the components affecting change. In the study of behavioral development, theories of behavioral change often revolve around chronological age. In the research presented here we combine aspects of cognitive theory with a few well-known hypotheses about the impacts of stressful events in life. The new empirical results presented here are based on our use of new techniques in *dynamic structural equation modeling* (DSEM) applied to the seminal data from the *Institute of Human Development* (IHD) at the University of California, Berkeley (Eichorn, Clausen, Haan, Honzik, & Mussen, 1981).

Developmental Changes in Cognition

Lifespan theory involves studying individual development from birth to old age making the major assumption that development does not end at maturity, but extends from birth to death (Baltes, Staudinger, Lindenberger, 1999). Baltes and colleagues outlined four objectives to lifespan psychology: Organize the structure and sequence of development through the lifespan; identify relationships between earlier and later development; describe and separate the factors and mechanisms of lifespan development; and specify the biological/environmental opportunities and constraints which shape the lifespan.

It is well known that all animal species undergo rapid changes in many behavioral dimensions during the earliest phases of life. Not surprisingly, there are a wide variety of theoretical perspectives on cognitive development in infants, children, and adolescents. In contrast, there seem to be far fewer changes during the early phases of adulthood and older age, and correspondingly fewer theoretical representations. One of the most prominent theories of adult development comes from the early work of Cattell and Horn on the "theory of fluid and crystallized intelligence" (Gf-Gc; Cattell, 1943, 1963, 1967, 1971; Cattell & Horn, 1978; Horn & Cattell, 1966, 1967). The first proposition of Gf-Gc theory distinguished two broad cognitive functions: Fluid intelligence (Gf) indicated by tasks requiring reasoning or thinking in novel situations, and crystallized intelligence (Gc) indicated by tasks requiring the use of stores of acquired knowledge. The second proposition was that Gf and Gc had divergent lifespan developmental patterns. Gf is expected to have a substantial increase through childhood and adolescence before reaching a peak in early adulthood and showing a marked decline through older adulthood. In contrast, Gc is expected to follow a similar pattern through childhood, but during adolescence there is a slower deceleration in growth as Gc is not expected to peak until the mid-30s and is maintained into older adulthood. The third important aspect in a theory of change is to describe the variables that change is conditional upon. The components affecting change can be static, such as gender or changing themselves, such as social economic status and memory ability. In Cattell and Horn's Gf-Gc theory, there are several hypotheses regarding the events that influence change. These hypotheses range from variables predictive of the absolute level and rate of change of cognitive ability (i.e., SES) to variables that affect change, which are also changing, such as dynamic interplay between Gf and Gc in the "investment" hypothesis (Cattell, 1987). The investment hypothesis describes a set of developmentally lagged relationships between the growth of cognitive abilities such that fluid intelligence is the driving force and helps to produce changes in crystallized intelligence (for details, see Ferrer & McArdle, 2004; McArdle, Hamagami, Meredith, & Bradway, 2001; McArdle, Ferrer-Caja, Hamagami, Woodcock, 2002). In this research we presume lifespan changes in cognitive abilities reflect change that is more or less stable over time as opposed to change that is reversible over a short period of time (Nesselroade, 1991).

The Impacts of Bioecological Context

The variables that influence cognitive change remain an open question in most prior theories. These influences can be idiosyncratic, such as the individual experiences of the person. But they can also be broader, affecting large numbers of persons, such as impacts from living in a particular neighborhood, or being involved in military service. These broad influences on change are what some researchers call environmental or contextual effects. Elder's (1975, 1991, 1994, 1995, 1996, 1998a, 1998b, 2000; Elder & Caspi, 1988; Elder & Johnson, 2002; Elder & Rockwell, 1979) theoretical model of life course and human development defines a framework which guides research in terms of problem identification and formulation, variable selection, and strategies of design and data analysis for evaluating the interaction between development and social change. This interaction of social change and development can be seen as a specific example of context effects in the "bioecological" theory of Bronfenbrenner (1977, 1979, 2001) as well as in Baltes's "selective optimization with compensation" model of lifespan developmental theory (Baltes, 1979, 2003, Baltes, Lindenberger, & Staudinger, 1998; Baltes, Staudinger, & Lindenberger, 1999). Indeed, the fourth objective of lifespan psychology is the central idea of the life course theory of Elder and Bronfenbrenner.

Bronfenbrenner decomposes the biological and environmental opportunities and constraints in his bioecological theory of developmental processes (Bronfenbrenner, 1977, 1979, 2001). In the bioecological model, the "context" is comprised of four related components that shape human development and are the nested levels of ecology. These nested levels of ecology include microsystems, mesosystems, exosystems, and macrosystems. The microsystem comprises the immediate setting that the individual is behaving and the enduring reciprocal interactions between the individual and the immediate external environment are referred to as proximal processes (Bronfenbrenner, 2001). The set of microsystems is the mesosystem, which is the individual's place within a given period of development. Then there is the exosystem, which is slightly more removed from the developing individual and finally the macrosystem or the superordinate level of the ecology of human development. This upper level involves culture, governments, and public policies.

This upper level of influences forms the basis of Elder's "life course" model, and leads to questions about the generalizability of research. Life course theory is "based in large measure on sociocultural theories of age and social relations, the concept of life course refers to a sequence of socially defined, age-graded events and roles that the individual enacts over time" (Elder, 1998a, pp. 941). For example, consider the social transformations that occurred in 20th century (i.e., World War I, the roaring 20s, the Great Depression, World War II, the war on poverty in the 1960s), Elder suggested it would be difficult to generalize family research from the 1920s and early 1930s to the era of the second world war since the structure of the family changed for many Americans. Elder argued the meaning of childhood, adolescence, and young adulthood change depending on the era in which you experience each of these developmental periods. Elder's work encourages researchers to consider social meanings of age instead of the chronological meaning of age. In his theory, Elder describes events as occurring early, on-time, and late in an individual's life in relationship to expectations (social norms at the time) instead of considering the chronological age at which the event occurs.

There have been specific historical events that spurred psychologists to evaluate context effects. These events are wide-spread touching many lives across the country. Some of the historical events that had a major impact on many lives include the Great Depression, World War II, the War on Poverty in the 1960's, and most recently, the events surrounding 9-11 and Hurricane Katrina. Research on the effects of the Great Depression and World War II are discussed here since the participants in the studies presented in this project grew up in the face of the Depression and many served in WWII.

The Great Depression and World War II are events which brought about social change. These events changed the structure of the family and these changes can be linked to individual development. For example, many families experienced a substantial loss in economic status during the Depression as men were laid off and children and women were brought into the workforce. This economic loss would likely have different effects on children of different ages (Elder, 1974). Older children may have dropped out of school to earn money for their family, while younger children may have felt isolated without having their mother at home.

Longitudinal Design

The previous theoretical statements can be represented in a more formal mathematical and statistical basis. For example, Elder's life course theory is about the heterogeneity in the population with respect to societal change that is not considered in the analysis of data or the design of a study. This implies that the design of longitudinal studies needs to make some considerations based on life course theory. One way to examine the effects of contexts, including those of historical time, is to use the "accelerated longitudinal" approach of Bell (1953, 1954). In this design, the participants are heterogeneous in age at the first occasion of measurement and are then repeatedly assessed at defined time intervals. If there are no context effects, then the age curve from this approach represents the longitudinal changes that would be present in a single-sample longitudinal study in which the participants are homogeneous in age at the initial measurement occasion. The benefit of this design over a cross-sectional design is that the follow-up measurement occasion(s) allows the researcher to model the individual differences in change.

An extension of the basic accelerated longitudinal design that enables the separation of effects due to maturational, cohort, and historical period is the cohort-sequential design (Schaie, 1965, 1986, 1994; Schaie & Baltes, 1975). Maturational effects are those changes due to an increase in age, cohort effects are differences due to when the participants were born, and finally, period effects are differences due to a historical context. The cohort-sequential design begins as the accelerated longitudinal design with a sample of participants that are heterogeneous in terms of age. However, a new sample of participants, similar to the original study members, is brought into the study at the first retest occasion for the original study members. A new sample is incorporated into the study at each retest occasion. In this general developmental model, age, cohort, and time period are completely confounded such that knowing two of these pieces of information provide complete information regarding the third. Nesselroade and Baltes (1974) extended the general developmental model to include cross-sectional and longitudinal sequences that involve variation in age, cohort, and time period. These sequences consist of successive cross-sectional or longitudinal studies.

The Berkeley-Oakland Studies and Contexts

The data used in this study come from the Integenerational Studies of the Institute of Human Development. These data combine three longitudinal studies - the Oakland Growth Study (OGS), Berkeley Growth Study (BGS), and the Guidance Control Study (GCS). The children of the OGS were born between 1920 and 1922 and were 9 to 11 years old during the heart of the Great Depression. The children of the BGS and GCS were born between 1928 and 1930 and in the early stages of life during the Depression.

In his earlier work on this topic Elder (1979) found males in the BGS and GCS whose families experienced substantial economic loss were more likely to be judged low on self-adequacy, goal-orientation, and social competence compared to the nondeprived males of the BGS and GCS. Elder (1979) also found the BGS and GCS males from families who sustained economic loss during the Depression to be heavy drinkers, have low psychological health, and dispirited attitudes toward work. This was not the case in the OGS as males from deprived families were seen as more resilient and resourceful in adulthood than nondeprived counterparts. The females seemed to tell a different story as the BGS and GCS females from deprived families were more similar to the OGS males as they were resilient and resourceful in adulthood, the OGS females from deprived families experienced more negative outcomes.

Elder also addressed the different effects of WWII on the BGS, GCS, and OGS samples. Elder's work with the OGS showed early entry into military service was linked with less academic success and a large family, whereas early entry for the BGS and GCS was linked with an economically deprived family in the 1930's, academic trouble, and low self-esteem. Overall, the early entries entered adulthood with less education and did not fare well on occupational achievement by midlife. However, the early entrants had more personal success as they experienced more marital stability as their marriages tended to come later than those who entered the military later in life (Elder, 1986).

Our current research uses contemporary statistical methodology to reexamine these ideas. In this project we attempt to model different patterns of lifespan cognitive development for participants who experienced significant historical events at different developmental periods. Specifically, we use longitudinal structural equation models to evaluate cohort differences in the cognitive development of participants who were born in the early 1920s with the late 1920s and assess the attribution of differences due to the timing of the Great Depression and World War II in their lives. We expect the subjects born in the early 1920s to have lower levels of cognitive abilities in adulthood than subjects born in the late 1920s since the former group experienced the height of the Great Depression during adolescence and WWII during their pursuit of higher education. This research uses the longitudinal structural models to examine the group and individual changes in cognition related to these different contexts.

METHODS

Participants

The participants in this project come from the Intergenerational Study from the Institute of Human Development at the University of California, Berkeley. The members of the Oakland Growth Study (OGS; $N = 201$) were selected from students in five Oakland elementary schools who were planning to attend the same junior and senior high school where the majority of data collection was to take place. The Oakland Growth Study was initiated by Harold Jones in 1932 to study physical, physiological, and psychological growth and evaluate the interrelationships between development and behavioral potentials and tendencies (Jones, 1958; Jones, 1967). The participants of the OGS have been studied since age 11 through the most recent measurement occasion at the age of 61. The participants of the OGS were born in 1920 and 1921 and therefore experienced the Great Depression around age 10 and World War II at age 21. The participants were measured with a standardized cognitive test at the ages of 11 and 17 with a version of the Stanford-Binet and at ages 50 and 61 with the Wechsler Adult Intelligence Scale and the revised edition, respectively.

The participants of the Berkeley Growth Study (BGS; $N = 61$) were selected from infants born in hospitals near and around Berkeley, California and was initiated by Nancy Bayley in 1928 to trace the normal intellectual, motor, and physical development of children through the first year. Cognitive data collection with standardized intelligence tests began in 1934 when the children were 6 years of age. The sample continued taking intelligence tests every year until age sixteen. In adulthood, the sample took an intelligence test at ages 18, 21, 25, 36, 53, and most recently at age 70.

The participants of the Guidance Control Study (GCS; $N = 248$) were selected from the population of every third infant born in Berkeley between January 1928 and June 1929 and was initiated by Jean Macfarlane. Approximately half of the mothers were offered guidance by the principal investigator about general issues of childhood behavior and development (Jones & Meredith, 2000). The participants whose mother's received guidance were called the *Guidance Group* and the children whose mother's did not were called the *Control Group*. The participants from this study took standardized intelligence tests almost every year from age 6 (1934) to age 15 and then at ages 18, 40, and 53. The participants in the BGS and GCS were born just before the Great Depression and were therefore infants during the heart of the Depression. These children were in junior high and high school during at the beginning of WWII and some males entered military service at the end of WWII. The majority of the military service of the BGS and GCS was in the Korean War. Table 16.1 is an outline of the testing occasions for the OGS, BGS, and the GCS.

The two samples are expected to differ in terms of social class and years of education because of their place of residence in the San Francisco Bay Area (Oakland vs. Berkeley) and the different opportunities because of World War II. The children in the higher social class tended to have fathers with jobs as executives, business managers, and administrative personnel, while the lower class children had fathers with jobs as technicians, skilled laborers, machine operators, and unskilled laborers. Surprisingly, social class was fairly equally spread across both cohorts with approximately two-thirds of families in the higher class for each sample. The later cohort (M = 14.9, SD = 2.7) had slightly more years of education than the earlier cohort (M = 14.3, SD = 2.3), but this difference was not significant. However, this information was collected when the participants were at least 35 years of age and therefore does not represent the amount of continuous schooling.

Military service and notions of the military were very different for the 1921 and 1929 cohort. The 1921 cohort was of age before the United States entered World War II, while the 1929 cohort was of age toward the end of WWII and

TABLE 16.1
Outline of Measurement Occasions and Intelligence Tests Given to the Berkeley Growth Study
(BGS), Guidance Study (GS), and the Oakland Growth Study (OGS)

Intelligence Test	Year	Sample	N	Max Repeats
1916 Stanford-Binet	1934-1937	BGS	101	3
	1934-1937	GS	410	3
	1931	OGS	201	1
Stanford-Binet Form L	1937-1947	BGS	197	5
	1936-1944	GS	631	6
Stanford-Binet Form M	1939-1950	BGS	151	3
	1937-1943	GS	375	6
	1937	OGS	152	1
Wechsler-Bellevue I	1944-1953	BGS	141	4
	1946	GS	157	1
WAIS	1964	BGS	54	1
	1968	GS	118	1
	1968	OGS	78	1
WAIS-R	1983, 2000	BGS	74	2
	1982	GS	118	1
	1982	OGS	78	1
Woodcock-Johnson Revised	2000	BGS	33	1

for the Korean War. Most of the men (39/45) from the 1921 cohort served in
the military while approximately three fourths (60/83) of the men served in the
military from the 1929 cohort.

Cognitive Measures

Through the intergenerational studies (IGS) the principal investigators wanted
to use age-appropriate and current intelligence batteries. The tests admin-
istered to these participants have changed through the years to reflect this
desire. The participants in these three studies have taken the 1916 Stanford–
Binet (Terman, 1916), Stanford–Binet Form L & M (Terman & Merrill, 1937),
Wechsler–Bellevue Form I (Wechsler, 1946), Wechsler Adult Intelligence Scale
(WAIS; Wechsler, 1955), Wechsler Adult Intelligence Scale — Revised (WAIS–
R; Wechsler, 1981), and the Woodcock–Johnson Psycho-educational Battery
Revised (Woodcock & Johnson, 1989).

Bayley (1956) studied the cognitive development of the BGS participants
through infancy, childhood, and early adulthood by attempting to link the
scores on several different measures of intelligence (i.e., First-year Mental Scale,

Revised Stanford–Binet, Wechsler–Bellevue Form I) with the 16D scores. McArdle, Grimm, Hamagami, Bowles, and Meredith (2006)[1] extended Bayley's work by equating nine intelligence tests taken by the BGS, GCS, and the Bradway-McArdle Longitudinal Study (BMLS) in measures of verbal ability and short-term memory using the item responses and the Partial Credit Model (Masters, 1982). The verbal items included all of the vocabulary subtests of the intelligence tests, the information subtest of the Wechsler tests, and verbal items from the Stanford–Binet tests. The memory items included all short-term memory items such as digit span, memory for names, and memory for sentences. McArdle et al. modeled the ability estimates from the partial credit model to evaluate the development of verbal and memory abilities in the BGS, GCS, and the BMLS from the ages of 5-72 using latent growth curves

In this work (McArdle, Grimm, Hamagami, Bowles, & Meredith, 2006), the growth and decline of vocabulary and memory ability were evaluated using structured curves (Browne & du Toit, 1991; Browne, 1993) using well-known SAS programs (PROC MIXED and NLMIXED; Littell, Milliken, Stroup, & Wolfinger, 1996). The development of vocabulary matched the predicted growth of crystallized intelligence with a sharp increase through childhood and adolescence before decelerating in the 20s, reaching a peak in the late 30s, and showing a small amount of decline into the 70s. Memory ability showed a different development pattern from vocabulary, but closely matched previous work with short-term memory (McArdle, Ferrer-Caja, Hamagami, & Woodcock, 2002) and fluid intelligence. Short-term memory increased rapidly through adolescence, reaching its maxima in the early 20s before shoring a marked decrease

---

[1]The work by McArdle et al. to equate the vocabulary and memory scales of the various intelligence tests given to the *BGS*, *GCS*, and *BMLS* was done by person- and item-equating. McArdle and colleagues first attempted to equate the tests at the scale level (McArdle & Hamgami, 2004); however this data lacked overlap (covariance coverage) at this scale level and would have required several untestable equality assumptions (i.e. the Wechsler-Bellevue is the same as the Wechsler-Adult Intelligence Scale). The items of the intelligence scales were then evaluated for overlap (i.e. The WAIS vocabulary test is not the same as the WAIS-R test, but the WAIS-R contains 33 items in common with the WAIS). The items provided a way to equate the tests by person- (i.e. the participants of the *BMLS* took the WAIS and the SB-L at the same measurement occasion) and item-equating (i.e. the vocabulary test of the 1916 Stanford-Binet and the Stanford-Binet share 34 items). All of the vocabulary (and separately the memory) items were arranged into a single data matrix as if there was a single test (with 278 items) and each participant at each time point received some of the items. The participants were considered to be independent of themselves at a separate occasion of measurement. The Partial Credit Model was fit to this data matrix using the Winsteps program (Linacre, 2003), where McArdle et al. assessed the fit and output the person ability estimates which were then modeled against their age at testing. The ability estimates are independent of items administered and provide a common scale to evaluate changes in ability.

through middle and late adulthood. Similar verbal and memory ability estimates from an item response analysis are used in this project.

Longitudinal Latent Growth Models

In this project latent curve models are used to assess cohort differences and the
effects of gender, social economic status, and military service on the growth and
change of vocabulary and memory abilities. Assume we have measured n to N
people on a single variable, Y, at multiple occasions t to T, the latent growth
curve is of form

$$Y[t]_n = y_{0n} + y_{1n} \cdot A[t] + e[t]_n \tag{1}$$

where lowercase letters represent unobserved or latent variables and uppercase
letters represent the observed or manifest variables. In this model y_0 is the
latent intercept, y_1 is the latent slope, $A[t]$ is the basis of timing, and $e[t]$ is
a time dependent residual. Predictors of the latent intercept and slope can
be added to the growth curve in an attempt to explain the variation in these
latent variables. For example, the growth factors can be regressed on the cohort
(which can be dummy or effect coded) of the participants such that

$$y_{0n} = \beta_{00} + \beta_{10} \cdot cohort + e_0, \tag{2}$$

and

$$y_{1n} = \beta_{01} + \beta_{11} \cdot cohort + e_1. \tag{3}$$

In this second-level part of the growth curve model, β_{00} and β_{01} are the
intercepts (expected value when cohort equals zero) and β_{10} and β_{11} are the
coefficients representing the effect of cohort on the latent intercept (y_0) and
slope (y_1). The multilevel approach can be used whether or not the predictor
variable (i.e., cohort) is continuous or categorical (dichotomous, multicategory).
The growth curve can also be represented as a restricted common factor model
in which the loadings from the intercept are fixed to one and the basis of timing
($A[t]$) compose the loadings of the slope factor. Figure 16.1 is a path diagram
of a multilevel growth curve with an exogenous predictor (X) of the intercept
and slope.

Another way of evaluating group differences is with a multiple group model.
The benefit of the multiple group model is that any estimated parameter can be
free or constrained to be equal between the groups. This allows for evaluating
whether the variance components and the basis of timing are invariant between
groups as well as mean differences. In the multilevel approach, only mean

FIGURE 16.1

A path diagram of a latent growth curve (y_0, y_1) with an extension variable (X) predicting the growth factors.

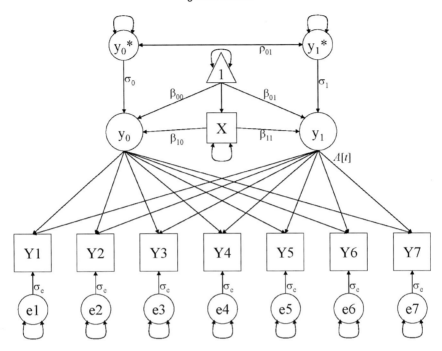

differences can be assessed. The multiple group model is appropriate when there is a discrete number of groups of interest (i.e., two cohorts).

A two group model of this form could be fit by writing

$$Y[t]_n^{(g)} = y_{0n}^{(g)} + y_{1n}^{(g)} \cdot A[t]^{(g)} + e[t]_n^{(g)}, \tag{4}$$

where (g) denotes a grouping variable. Therefore, in this approach each group can follow a distinct functional form with varying growth means and covariances. The differences between groups are evaluated by assessing the change in fit between the model with invariant parameters and the model with varying parameters between groups. The group models are fit in a systematic way to discern the parameters that are different between the two groups. The systematic fitting of models begins from complete invariance to less restrictive models and finally to models with no restrictions following the work in factorial invariance. Therefore, the first model is the invariance model and all of the parameters are constrained to be equivalent between groups. The next model allows the means of the growth factors to vary between groups. If this model is an improvement in fit then the two groups may differ in the mean of the level and/or slope. The third model also allows the random components (variances and covariances) to vary between groups and the final model allows the basis coefficients (slope loadings) to vary as well.

This strategy of multiple group model fitting is a top-down approach (starting with latent variable parameters and moving down to manifest parameters) as opposed to some of the recent literature in factorial invariance encouraging a bottom-up approach. The bottom-up approach initially assumes each group is different and evaluates where the groups are similar. This strategy begins with the parameters related to the observed variables such as the means and factor loadings before moving up to the latent parameters. In the top-down approach, we initially assume there is a single growth function for all of the groups and relax restrictions to determine the location of group differences. The relaxation of parameters is in the opposite direction as the bottom-up approach. However, in both cases the means are the first parameters relaxed or constrained. In growth modeling the means of the manifest variables are set to zero to push the means up to the latent level as opposed to estimating manifest means and have zero factor means. A researcher could employ the bottom-up approach in growth modeling by allowing all parameters to be free, constraining the slope loading (basis of timing) to be equivalent, and then move up to the variance/covariance parameters before constraining the means of the growth factors. It's important to note that these methods are equivalent and will arise at the same conclusion as long as the criteria for model comparison are the same.

The multilevel growth model used in this project is the bilinear multiphase growth model (Cudeck & Klebe, 2002; Hall et al., 2001) in order to evaluate the differences in early and later development. A structured nonlinear curve (i.e., exponential) would not allow for the examination of cognitive development through childhood and adulthood separately. The bilinear growth model is an extension of the spline regression model and follows the form

$$Y[t]_n = y_{0n} + y_{1n} \cdot age1 + y_{2n} \cdot age2 + e[t]_n, \tag{5}$$

where Age1 is equal to the participant's age minus the age at the knot point if the participant's age is less than the knot point and zero elsewhere. Age2 is equal to the participant's age minus the knot point if the participant's age is greater than or equal to the knot point and zero else. Conceptually, the knot point is a "turning point" in the growth curve. This set of equations recenters age to be at the knot point (turning point, age at which the two linear components connect) and therefore the mean of y_0 is the predicted level of ability at the age of the knot point in development.

The location of the optimal age for the knot point is found using a "profile likelihood" search technique (see Hall et al, 2001) in which the bilinear model is repeatedly fit with the knot point set to every whole age between 5 and 50. The misfit indices (based on -2 log-likelihood) of these models are compared to find the two lowest consecutive values. The search is then redefined to test every tenth of a year between the two consecutive lowest values. This search technique is similar to how this model would be fit with a nonlinear multilevel modeling program (i.e., SAS NLMIXED), but is computationally more efficient. The only advantage for fitting a multiphase model in a program such as NLMIXED is to allow for interindividual differences (variation) in the location of the knot point.

Once the optimal knot point is found, predictors of the level and two slopes are included to explain the variance in the growth factors. The predictors include cohort, years of education, gender, military service, and social class in 1929. Each of these predictors is effect coded, except for years of education, which is a continuous variable and re-centered at 12 years of education. Cohort is coded -0.5 for the Oakland Growth Study participants who were born in 1920 and 1921 and 0.5 for the Berkeley Growth Study and Guidance Study participants who were born in 1928 and 1929. The effects of these predictors are evaluated using the multilevel approach previously mentioned. For example, the multiphase growth curve in equation (5) includes predictors of the growth factors such as

$$y_{0n} = \beta_{00} + \beta_{10} \cdot cohort + e_0, \tag{6}$$

$$y_{1n} = \beta_{01} + \beta_{11} \cdot cohort + e_1,$$

$$y_{2n} = \beta_{02} + \beta_{12} \cdot cohort + e_2$$

A multiphase growth curve with an extension variable is contained in Figure 16.2.

Statistical Procedures

The first step is to locate the turning point for the development of short-term memory and verbal ability using the simultaneous search technique, previously mentioned. Once the optimal turning point is determined, the bilinear (spline) growth model is fit to the memory and verbal ability data for the sample as a whole. Predictors of the growth factors are then included beginning with cohort, gender and the interaction between the two. This model evaluates whether cohort and gender are predictive of the growth factors and whether the cohort differences are the same between genders. Elder noted cohort by gender interactions in several measures in his work and this model evaluates

FIGURE 16.2

A path diagram of a latent growth curve with multi-phase components (y_0, y_1, y_2) with an extension variable (X).

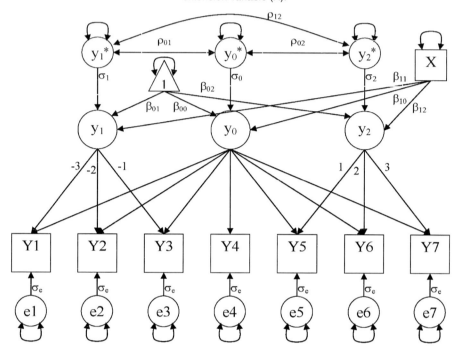

the same type of effects on cognitive development. The next model retains the significant effects from the previous model and adds the effects of educational background (years of education) and social class since these variables are known to affect the development of cognitive abilities. This model is used to determine whether the effects due to cohort and gender are still apparent when accounting for known predictors of cognitive development. Finally, the effects of military service are added as predictors of cognitive development. This model evaluates whether military service had differing effects on the growth of memory and verbal abilities for the males of the earlier and later cohorts.

RESULTS

The Basic Latent Growth Model

The multiphase growth models were fit to the vocabulary and memory data to find the optimal knot point. The misfit (-2LL) for the multiphase models with a knot point fixed at each whole year from age 5 to age 40 for memory and vocabulary are plotted against the fixed knot point in figure 16.3. The knot (turning) point for the bilinear model for verbal and short-term memory ability was estimated to be 15.4 and 13.6 years, respectively. The mean level for verbal ability was 4.9 and is the predicted score at 15.4 years of age and there is significant variation in the level. The linear slope before 15.4 years was 0.81 while the linear slope after 15.4 years was 0.02 and there are significant individual differences in both slope coefficients. The slope during childhood is much greater than the slope through adulthood, but the secondary slope is still positive showing verbal ability continues to increase through adulthood. The bilinear model fit to the memory data showed a similar relationship with age as verbal ability. The group results show a sharp increase in ability during childhood and the slope after 13.6 years is positive, but very small. There is also substantial variation in the level, first and second slope, and this is the starting point for investigating the individual differences in the development of memory.

Results of Cohort and Gender Comparisons

Cohort and gender effects were introduced into the model to evaluate whether the earlier cohort showed a different pattern of development than the later cohort and whether these patterns are the same for males and females. There are slight accurate differences between the two cohorts in the childhood (primary) slope and the level of ability in adolescence for short-term memory. The later (1928, BGS, GCS) cohort has a slower rate of change up to the knot point, but is not different to the earlier cohort of the development in adulthood. The greater slope for the earlier cohort (1920, OGS) translates into a slightly lower level of ability in early childhood than the later cohort; however, since the curves are not significantly different in adulthood the earlier cohort has caught up by adolescence (age 13.6). There was a significant interaction between cohort and gender in the level of ability at age 13.6. This interaction was in favor of the females from the later cohort and the males from the earlier cohort. For verbal ability, there are differences between the cohorts in each of the three aspects of the bilinear model as well as gender differences in the rate of change through adulthood. The 1928 (BGS, GCS) cohort has a shallower (0.4) initial slope (as in memory ability), lower level of ability (0.5) at the turning point (15.4 years), and a slightly more positive (0.02) secondary slope through adulthood. The older 1921 (OGS) cohort has a more pronounced earlier development possibly due to a lower ability in early childhood and a near zero secondary slope showing a lack of growth in adulthood. The gender differences in the adult-

FIGURE 16.3

The profile likelihood (-2 log likelihood) against the knot point in the search for the optimal knot point for (a) short-term memory and (b) verbal ability.

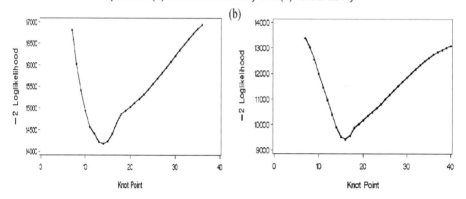

hood slope were small and favored the males. Figure 16.4 contains plots of the verbal and memory ability estimates by cohort with the mean predicted multiphase model.

Cognitive Development, Education, Social Class, Gender, and Cohort

The effect of social class on cognitive development was evaluated to determine if the cohort differences are due to differential social classes and educational background of the two cohorts. The growth factors (level and slopes) of the bilinear models for verbal and memory abilities were regressed on whether the family was in a higher class (+0.5) versus a lower class (-0.5) in 1929, the number of years of education (centered at 12 years), and the significant cohort and gender effects from the previous models.

In terms of memory, the participants in the higher social class and with more education had a greater ability at 13.6 years. The interaction between gender and cohort on the intercept was not accurate with the addition of social class and educational attainment, but the effect of cohort on the primary slope remained accurate. Again this effect entailed the later cohort having a shallower growth before 13.6 years of age and this difference may be linked to a greater level of ability in early childhood. The addition of social class and educational attainment on verbal development yielded several main effects, eliminated the need for the effect of gender on the adulthood rate of change, but did not affect the cohort effects previously found. Children who would attain more education had a greater verbal ability at the turning point, a greater slope through childhood, and a more negative slope through adulthood. The effect of the participants' 1929 social class was found in the intercept or level of ability

FIGURE 16.4

Trajectory plot with mean predicted bilinear model for (a) verbal ability for 1920 cohort, (b) verbal ability for 1928 cohort, (c) short-term memory for 1920 cohort, and (d) short-term memory for 1928 cohort.

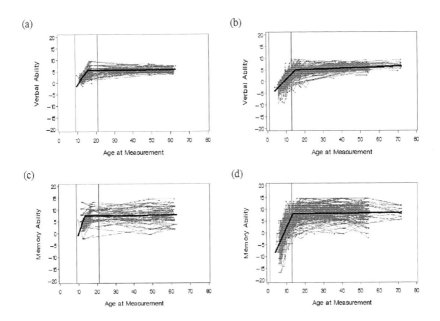

at 15.4 years with the children in the higher social class having a greater ability at this turning point in development. As previously mentioned, the cohort effects are still apparent in each of the three components of the growth curve with the older (1920) cohort having a greater ability at the turning point, a greater primary slope, and a more negative secondary slope.

The parameter estimates for these models are contained in Table 16.2. The order of the parameter estimates in the table begins with the mean of the level or the predicted level of ability at the knot point (grand mean when the number of years of education equals 12). The next series of parameter estimates are the coefficients representing the effects of the background variables (main effects and interactions) on the intercept. The mean of the primary slope (slope1) comes next in the table and this is the grand mean of the slope for a participant with a high school education. The mean is followed by the coefficients representing the effects of the background variables (cohort, class, education) on the primary slope. The final fixed (group) effects are the mean of the secondary slope and the coefficients for the effects of cohort, class, education, and gender on the secondary slope. The random effects are then presented and these coefficients represent the amount of individual differences in the three components of the growth model and the residual variation, which is the average amount of variation that is not predictable from the model.

Cognitive Development and Military Service

To investigate the effects of military service on cognitive development in the IGS the growth factors were regressed on their cohort, whether or not the participant served in the military, the interaction between the two, and the significant effects from the previous model in a single multilevel model. If the

TABLE 16.2
Parameter Estimates for Bilinear Multilevel Model for Memory and Verbal Abilities With Effects of Cohort, Gender, Education, and 1929 Social Class.

	Memory Ability	Verbal Ability
Fixed Effects		
Mean Level (μ_0)	7.15*	4.57*
Cohort (β_{01})	—	-0.79*
Class (β_{02})	0.99*	0.66*
Education (β_{03})	0.30*	0.31*
Gender*Cohort (β_{05})	-0.64	—
Mean Slope1 (μ_1)	2.11*	0.98*
Cohort*Slope1 (β_{11})	-0.81*	-0.49*
Class *Slope1 (β_{12})	0.002	0.01
Education*Slope1 (β_{13})	-0.010	0.02*
Mean Slope2 (μ_2)	0.004	0.02*
Cohort*Slope2 (β_{21})	—	0.02*
Class *Slope2 (β_{22})	-0.011	-0.007
Education*Slope2 (β_{23})	-0.000	-0.002
Gender*Slope2 (β_{24})	—	0.004
Random Effects		
Level Deviation (σ_0)	1.91*	1.20*
Slope1 Deviation (σ_1)	0.19	0.08*
Slope2 Deviation (σ_2)	0.03	0.02*
Level, Slope1 Correlation (ρ_{01})	-0.04	0.08*
Level, Slope2 Correlation (ρ_{02})	0.002	-0.02*
Slope1, Slope2 Correlation (ρ_{12})	0.002	-0.001*
Error Deviation (σ_e)	1.98*	0.90*

interaction between cohort and military service is significant, then the effect of military service, or the difference between males who joined the military and those who did not, depends on the cohort in which the individual was born.

In the development of verbal ability, military service was not an accurate predictor of any of the three components of the growth model (intercept, primary, and secondary slopes) nor was the interaction between military service and cohort. The results for short-term memory mirrored those of verbal ability with a series of null results for military service. Therefore, the males who entered the military in both of these cohorts were not different from the males who did not enter the military when the effects of cohort, social economic status, and education on cognitive development are included.

CONCLUSIONS

The development of verbal and memory abilities were investigated in the Intergenerational Studies with special attention for differences between the older and younger cohorts. A multiphase growth curve was fit to verbal and short-term memory estimates to evaluate child and adulthood development. There were small reliable differences in the development of verbal ability between the cohorts, but the cohorts did not differ much in the growth of short-term memory ability. The nature of these differences are in line with Gf-Gc theory as verbal ability is a crystallized ability that is dependent on acculturation, while the memory ability is more fluid and dependent on genetic influences. The participants of the Oakland Growth Study may have received less continuous education because of the Great Depression and World War II. The differences in the development of verbal ability between the cohorts were not due to differences in social class, educational attainment, or military service (in the men) as the cohort effects remained when these variables were added.

The effect of social class on the development of verbal ability showed mostly main effects with the children who were better off in terms of social class having an overall greater level of ability throughout the lifespan. The educational attainment of the participants was predictive of each component of the multiphase growth curve as the participants who would obtain more education had a greater rate of change in development though childhood and reach a greater level of ability in adolescence. However, these participants also showed a shallower growth in verbal ability through adulthood. When military service was evaluated there were no differences between the men who entered the military and those who did not after accounting for social class, education, and cohort.

The differences due to cohort, social class, education, and military service in the development of short-term memory were small relative to verbal ability.

Social class, education, gender, and cohort were evaluated together and yielded reliable differences due to social class and education on the overall ability level with the participants in a higher social class and with more education having greater memory through the lifespan. The cohort effect on the growth of short-term memory was through early childhood with the earlier cohort having a sharper rate of increase, possibly due to a lower level of ability in early childhood. The consistent difference between the older and younger cohorts is in the rate of change through early childhood into adolescence that is likely due to a lower level of ability for the 1921 cohort in early childhood. A greater level of ability for the 1929 cohort in early childhood was unexpected since they experienced the heart of the Great Depression (before age 2) while they were heavily dependent on the family that was changing in structure (Elder & Caspi, 1988).

Elder (1974) focused his work on developmental differences between children whose families did or did not experience severe economic change as a result of the Great Depression. These comparisons were not made in this series of analyses since the change in family economic status during the Great Depression was not in the archives of the Intergenerational Studies in the Institute of Human Development at the University of California, Berkeley. Therefore, we cannot comment on whether the children whose families experienced severe economic loss exhibited different patterns of cognitive development than children whose families did not have to adapt to such an economic loss.

Cognitive development over the lifespan is often viewed as a result of the interaction between the environment and the individual. The longitudinal structural models we used allowed us to consider this proposition in detail. In doing so, we found specific cognitive abilities (verbal) to be more greatly affected by these interactions and dependent on the social network in which the individual develops. Such cognitive abilities are believed to represent crystallized intelligence that has been previously shown to be dependent on acculturation and experience and these findings are in line with the predictions of Cattell and Horn's Gf/Gc theory. The benefits of the merger of lifespan theory with contemporary data analysis methods have been discussed many times before (e.g., Nesselroade & Baltes, 1974). We hope these analyses serve as an illustration of this merger.

REFERENCES

Baltes, P. B. (1979). Life-span developmental psychology: Some converging observations on history and theory. In P. B. Baltes & O. G. Jr, Brim (Eds.), *Life-span development and behavior* (Vol. 2, pp. 225-279). New York: Academic Press.

Baltes, P. B. (2003). On the incomplete architecture of human ontogeny: Selection, optimization, and compensation as foundation of developmental theory. In U. M. Staudinger & U. Lindenberger (Eds.), *Understanding human development: Dialogues with lifespan psychology* (pp. -). Boston, MA: Kluwer.

Baltes, P. B., Lindenberger, U., & Staudinger, U. M. (1998). Life-span theory in developmental psychology. In W. Damon & R. M. Lerner (Eds.), *Handbook of child psychology: Vol. 1. Theoretical models of human development* (5th ed.,pp. 1029-1144). New York: Wiley.

Baltes, P. B., Staudinger, U. M., & Lindenberger, U. (1999). Lifespan psychology: Theory and application to intellectual functioning. *Annual Review of Psychology, 50*, 471-507.

Bayley, N. (1956). Individual patterns of development. *Child Development, 27*, 45-74.

Bell, R. Q. (1953). Convergence: an accelerated longitudinal approach. *Child Development, 24*, 145-152.

Bell, R. Q. (1954). An experimental test of the accelerated longitudinal approach. *Child Development, 25*, 281-286.

Bronfenbrenner, U. (1977). Toward an experimental ecology of human development. *American Psychologist, 32*, 513-531.

Bronfenbrenner, U. (1979). *The ecology of human development: Experiments by nature and design.* Cambridge, MA: Harvard University Press.

Bronfenbrenner, U. (2001). Bioecological theory of human development. In N. J. Smelse & P. B. Baltes (Eds.), *International encyclopedia of the social & behavioral sciences* (pp. 6963-6970). Amsterdam, and New York: Elsevier.

Browne, M. W. (1993). Structured latent curve analysis. In C. M. Cuadras & C. R. Rao (Eds.), *Multivariate analysis: Future directions 2* (pp. 171-197). Amsterdam: Elsevier Science.

Browne, M. W., & Toit, S. du. (1991). Models for learning data. In L. M. Collins & J. L. Horn (Eds.), *Best methods for the analysis of change: Recent advances, unanswered questions, future directions* (pp. 47-68). Washington, DC: American Psychological Association.

Cattell, R. B. (1943). The measurement of adult intelligence. *Psychological Bulletin, 40*, 153-193.

Cattell, R. B. (1963). Theory of fluid and crystallized intelligence: A critical experiment. *Journal of Educational Psychology, 54*, 1-22.

Cattell, R. B. (1967). Theory of fluid and crystallized intelligence checked at the 5-6 year-old level. *British Journal of Educational Psychology, 37*, 209-224.

Cattell, R. B. (1971a). *Abilities: Their structure, growth, and action.* Oxford, England: Houghton Mifflin.

Cattell, R. B. (1971b). *Intelligence: Its structure, growth and action.* Amsterdam: North-Holland.

Cattell, R. B., & Horn, J. L. (1978). A check on the theory of fluid and crystallized intelligence with description of new subtest designs. *Journal of Educational Measurement, 15*, 139-164.

Cudeck, R., & Klebe, K. J. (2002). Multiphase mixed-effects models for repeated measures data. *Psychological Methods, 7*, 41-63.

Eichorn, D., Clausen, J. H., Hann, N., Honzik, M., & Mussen, P. (1981). *Present and past in middle life.* New York: Academic Press.

Elder, G. H., Jr. (1974). *Children of the great depression: Social change in life experience.* Chicago: University of Chicago Press.

Elder, G. H., Jr. (1975). *Age differentiation and the life course. in annual review of sociology* (Vol. 1). Palo Alto, CA: Annual Reviews.

Elder, G. H., Jr. (1979). Historical change in life patterns and personality. In P. B. Baltes & J. O. G. Brim (Eds.), *Life-span development and behavior* (Vol. 2, pp. -). New York: Academic Press.

Elder, G. H., Jr. (1986). Military time and turning points in men's lives. *Developmental Psychology, 22*, 233-245.

Elder, G. H., Jr. (1991). Family transitions, cycles, and social change. In P. A. Cowan & E. M. Hetherginton (Eds.), *Family transitions. advances in family research series* (pp. 31-57). Hillsdale, NJ: Lawrence Erlbaum Associates.

Elder, G. H., Jr. (1994). Time, human agency, and social change: Perspectives on the life course. *Social Psychology Quarterly, 57*, 4-15.

Elder, G. H., Jr. (1995). The life course paradigm: Social change and individual development. In P. Moen & G. H. Elder (Eds.), *Examining lives in context: Perspectives on the ecology of human development* (pp. 101-139). Washington, DC: American Psychological Association.

Elder, G. H., Jr. (1996). Human lives in changing societies: Life course and developmental insights. In R. B. Cairns, E. J. Costello, & G. H. Elder (Eds.), *Developmental science. cambridge studies in social and emotional development* (pp. 31-62). New York, NY: Cambridge University Press.

Elder, G. H., Jr. (1998a). The life course and human development. In W. Damon & R. M. Lerner (Eds.), *Handbook of child psychology: Vol. 1, theoretical models of human development* (5th ed., pp. 939-991). New York: Wiley.

Elder, G. H., Jr. (1998b). The life course as developmental theory. *Child Development, 69*, 1-12.

Elder, G. H., Jr. (2000). Life course theory. In A. E. Kazdin (Ed.), *Encyclopedia of psychology, vol. 5* (pp. 50-52). Washington, DC: American Psychological Association.

Elder, G. H., Jr, & Caspi, A. (1988). Human development and social change: An emerging perspective on the life course. In N. Bolger, C. Avshalom, G. Downey, & M. Moorehouse (Eds.), *Persons in context: Developmental processes. human development in cultural and historical contexts* (pp. 77-113). New York: Cambridge University Press.

Elder, G. H., Jr, & Johnson, M. K. (2002). Perspectives on human development in context. In C. von Hofsten & L. Backman (Eds.), *Psychology at the turn of the millennium, Vol. 2: Social, developmental, and clinical perspectives* (pp. 153-172). Florence, KY: Taylor & Frances/Routledge.

Elder, G. H., Jr, & Rockwell, R. C. (1979). The life-course and human development: An ecological perspective. *International Journal of Behavioral Development, 2*,

1-21.

Ferrer, E., & McArdle, J. J. (2004). An experimental analysis of dynamic hypotheses about cognitive abilities and achievement from childhood to early adulthood. *Developmental Psychology, 40,* 935-952.

Hall, C. B., Ying, J., Kuo, L., Sliwinski, M., Buschke, H., Katz, M., et al. (2001). Estimation of bivariate measurements having different change points, with application to cognitive ageing. *Statistics in Medicine, 20,* 3695-3714.

Horn, J. L., & Cattell, R. B. (1966). Refinement and test of the theory of fluid and crystallized general intelligences. *Journal of Educational Psychology, 57,* 253-270.

Horn, J. L., & Cattell, R. B. (1967). Age differences in fluid and crystallized intelligence. *Acta Psychologica, 26,* 107-129.

Jones, H. E. (1958). The oakland growth study - fourth decade. *Newsletter of the Gerontological Society, 5,* 3-10.

Jones, M. C. (1967). A report on three growth studies at the university of california. *Gerontologist, 7,* 49-54.

Jones, W., C. J.and Meredith. (2000). Developmental paths of psychological health from early adolescence to later adulthood. *Psychology & Aging, 15,* 351-360.

Linacre, J. M. (2003). *Winsteps (version 3) [computer software].* Chicago, IL: MESA Press.

Littell, R. C., Milliken, G. A., Stroup, W. W., & Wolfinger, R. D. (1996). *Sas system for mixed models.* Cary, NC: SAS Institute Inc.

Masters, G. N. (1982). A rasch model for partial credit scoring. *Psychometrika, 60,* 523-547.

McArdle, J. J., Ferrer-Caja, E., Hamagami, F., & Woodcock, R. W. (2002). Comparative longitudinal structural analyses of the growth and decline of multiple intellectual abilities over the life span. *Developmental Psychology, 38,* 115-142.

McArdle, J. J., Grimm, K. J., Hamagami, F., Bowles, R. P., & Meredith, W. (2006). Modeling lifespan growth curves of cognition using longitudinal data with changing scales of measurement. *Manuscript submitted for publication.*

McArdle, J. J., & Hamagami, F. (2004). Methods for dynamic change hypotheses. In K. van Montfort, J. Oud, & A. Satorra (Eds.), *Recent developments in structural equation models: Theory and applications* (pp. -). The Netherlands: Kluwer.

McArdle, J. J., Hamagami, F., Meredith, W., & Bradway, K. P. (2001). Modeling the dynamic hypotheses of gf-gc theory using longitudinal life-span data. *Learning and Individual Differences, 12,* 53-79.

Nesselroade, J. R. (1991). The warp and woof of the developmental fabric. In R. Downs, L. Liben, & D. Palermo (Eds.), *Visions of development, the environment, and aesthetics: The legacy of joachim f. wohlwill* (pp. 213-240). Hillsdale, NJ: Lawrence Erlbaum Associates.

Nesselroade, J. R., & Baltes, P. B. (1974). Adolescent personality development and historical change: 1970-1972.

Schaie, K. W. (1965). A general model for the study of developmental problems. *Psychological Bulletin, 64,* 92-107.

Schaie, K. W. (1986). Beyond calendar definitions of age, time, and cohort: The general developmental model revisited. *Developmental Review, 6*, 252-277.

Schaie, K. W. (1994). Developmental designs revisited. In S. H. Cohen & H. W. Reese (Eds.), *Life-span developmental psychology: Methodological contributions* (pp. 45-64). Hillsdale, NJ: Lawrence Erlbaum Associates.

Schaie, K. W., & Baltes, P. B. (1975). On sequential strategies in developmental research: Description or explanation. *Human Development, 18*, 384-390.

Terman, L. M. (1916). *The measurement of intelligence*. Boston, MA.

Terman, L. M., & Merrill, M. A. (1937). *Measuring intelligence*. Boston, MA.

Wechsler, D. (1946). *The wechsler-bellevue intelligence scale*. New York.

Wechsler, D. (1955). *Manual for the wechsler adult intelligence scale*. New York.

Wechsler, D. (1981). *Wais-r manual*. New York.

Woodcock, R. W., & Johnson, M. B. (1989). *Woodcock-johnson psycho-educational battery-revised*. Allen, TX.

CHAPTER SEVENTEEN

Intrauterine Environment Affects Infant and Child Intellectual Outcomes: Environment as Direct Effect

Keith F. Widaman

University of California, Davis

The developing child undergoes many varied and marvelous transitions and transformations that begin at conception and continue through gestation and birth, infancy, childhood, and adolescence. Attaining early adulthood, the developing person appears to change more slowly, but even during adulthood many new challenges arise and require adaptation or change. Finally, when transitioning into middle age, old age, and senescence, negative changes seem to dominate, yet even in old age positive changes can be found. Across the life span, change seems more the order of the day than does quiescence, stability, or lack of change.

This concentration on assessing and modeling change has become the commonly accepted and standard approach for developmental psychology, although this was not always the case. More than 30 years ago, Wohlwill (1970) called for a reorientation of research on psychological development, incorporating age into the definition of the outcome variable to be explained. In effect, Wohlwill called for a more concentrated focus on change as the construct to be examined. About a decade later, Baltes and Nesselroade (1979) laid down their five goals of longitudinal studies, which embrace (a) direct identification of intraindividual change, (b) direct identification of interindividual differences in intraindividual change, (c) analysis of relations among indices of intraindividual change, (d) analyzing causes or determinants of intraindividual change, and (e) analyzing causes or determinants of interindividual differences in intraindividual change.

Having these goals clearly laid out, an unprecedented surge of interest and developments in longitudinal modeling has ensued during the past quarter century.

With our focus as a field now placed directly on the modeling of change, questions naturally arise regarding the basic underlying factors responsible for or supporting change. The seemingly regimented behavioral progression exhibited by infants and children seems to argue for the strong influence of genetically programmed factors governing developmental advances. That genetic sources contribute to behavioral development is consistent with the typical findings from behavioral genetic research that genetic sources of variance explain substantial portions of individual difference variance on many psychological traits, such as intelligence (Plomin, DeFries, McClearn, & Rutter, 1997). However, genetic factors alone cannot produce a phenotype; environmental inputs must occur for the phenotype to be realized. Moreover, common sense and observation offer evidence that environmental or contextual influences may have strong main or interactive effects on behavioral development. Of course, common sense and observation may be wrong — what appears to the observer to be evidence of an environmental effect may, in fact, reflect only the unfolding of a genetically programmed sequence. Discriminating between genetic and environmental influences — and thereby adjudicating conclusions arrived at by common sense and observation regarding underlying mechanisms — is one major goal of developmental science. But, we have other goals that are more pressing, including the study of contextual influences on development.

The present chapter has three major goals. The first goal is to discuss briefly current conceptions of environmental contexts, including ways in which contexts can affect behavioral development, and to urge the extension of these models to be more fully inclusive of likely contextual effects. The second goal is to outline a series of seven general considerations in the modeling of the effects of contextual or environmental influences. The third and final goal is to describe some results from the Maternal Phenylketonuria (PKU) Collaborative Study, which sought to understand the influence of prenatal exposure to phenylalanine (PHE) on various behavioral outcomes of offspring. In a final section, I discuss the implications of the contributions of this chapter to the ways in which we should think about and model contextual effects on behavioral development.

CONCEPTIONS OF ENVIRONMENTAL CONTEXT

To consider the nature of environmental effects on behavioral development, one must first consider the nature of the environment and environmental contexts. Psychologists have done a good job of cataloging individual differences in behavioral domains such as mental abilities and personality, but have done a

FIGURE 17.1
Figural portrayals of environmental contexts: Panel A: Bronfenbrenner's social ecology model.
Panel B: Model for physical ecology. Panel C: Superordinate model showing combined effects of
social ecology, physical ecology, and the personal qualities or characteristics of the child.

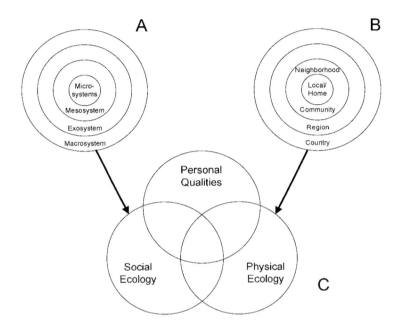

much less thorough job in characterizing environmental contexts. Only one major conception of environmental contexts has been formulated, by Bronfenbrenner (e.g., 1977, 1986a, 1986b, 1999), although the time seems ripe to expand this model by incorporating additional aspects of the ecology of the developing child.

Bronfenbrenner's Bioecological Model

Original Formulation. In his initial statement of his ecological model, Bronfenbrenner (1977) identified four systems, or levels, of environmental context that can influence development. The conception outlined by Bronfenbrenner was his attempt at understanding the environments within which children develop. In particular, Bronfenbrenner tried to capture important aspects of the developing child's ecology, considering the ways in which to differentiate environmental contexts for their relevance to, or effect on, the development of the child. In formulating these ideas, the goal was to provide a conception of the ecology of human development as a hierarchically organized set of environmental situations or contexts within which different levels or systems could interact to affect development. The four systems or levels were termed the levels of microsystems, mesosystems, exosystems, and macrosystems, shown as hierarchically nested circles in Panel A of Figure 17.1.

Microsystems consist of settings that afford face-to-face interactions among two or more persons. The nuclear family contains at least three dyads — mother-child, father–child, and mother–father — and perhaps additional dyads if the family has more than a single child. In addition, the family has at least one triad – the mother–father–child triad — and, again, additional triads if the family has multiple children. But, although the family context is a clear and important microsystem in which the person behaves and develops, other microsystems contain the person and therefore may affect or be affected by the developing person. These additional microsystems include neighborhood, school, peer (or friend), and work microsystems, among others. When considering any microsystem, a researcher should take note of the physical place, the features of the place, the amount of time, and the sets of activities in which persons were engaged, as well as the persons involved and the roles they played in the microsystem. Any of these features of the microsystem might relate to or interact with other features to enhance or constrain behavioral development within the microsystem.

The next higher level in the ecological system is the mesosystem, which consists of relations between microsystems. For children in elementary school, the mesosystem might include interrelations or interactions between the family, school, and peer microsystems. These three microsystems are perhaps the most common microsystems linked by mesosystem processes, but other microsystems, such as church and work, are also often linked. The key idea of the mesosystem is that the developing child engages in face-to-face interactions within microsystems, and the mesosystem represents the linkages between those microsystems in which the child is involved. The mesosystem contains no face-to-face interactions, but instead represents relations among settings containing persons in face-to-face interactions. Thus, the mesosystem relations can impinge directly on microsystems, altering the nature of the face-to-face interactions in which individuals are involved.

In a still broader set of interactions, linkages or relations between mesosystem entities are termed aspects of the exosystem. The exosystem consists of higher level social structures or societal institutions, such as the mass media, governmental agencies at all levels, economic systems, and so forth. Some exosystem elements are formal institutions; others are more informal in nature. These exosystem relations do not affect directly the personal relationships among persons within microsystem contexts, but can so affect mesosystem elements that the exosystem has an indirect influence on personal interactions within microsystems.

Finally, at the broadest level discussed by Bronfenbrenner (1977), the macrosystem consists of the overall patterns that characterize a culture, including the broad educational, political, economic, and social systems of the culture. As such, the macrosystem encompasses, and is instantiated through, the microsystems, mesosystems, and exosystems of the culture. The macrosystem reflects the basic values of the culture, providing the broadest and most encompassing set of contextual influences in the model. One of the more interesting aspects of the Bronfenbrenner model is that research can focus on any of the individuals in a family — father, mother, child, siblings — when attempting to understand developmental processes. In effect, this alters the traditional focus of developmental psychology on the development of the individual child to a focus on processes contributing to development of all persons involved in the family system.

Later Modifications. In later contributions, Bronfenbrenner (1986a, 1986b) reiterated the previous four levels of his ecological model, but added a fifth level — the chronosystem — which concerns the influence of time on ecological effects. Thus, the chronosystem consists of the ways in which the patterns of interactions within or between any of the levels of the ecological system change across time during the ontogenesis of an individual as well as how the ecological system changes over historical time. Effects associated with the chronosystem are not shown in Figure 17.1, as these effects would be difficult to represent in a two-dimensional figure. But, the ways in which the four levels of the ecological model change over time are likely to be of tremendous importance. Indeed, key public policy decisions, such as those surrounding Head Start, have clearly affected patterns of child development in positive ways in the past and, one trusts, will continue to do so in the future.

Need for More Inclusive Models of the Ecology of Human Development

The bioecological model proposed by Bronfenbrenner (1977, 1986a, 1986b, 1999) is a most important framework that can be easily adapted for conceptualizing different levels or aspects of social ecology. For example, Bradley (1999) used elements of the model to describe the home environment and its effects on child development; Brown (1999) adapted Bronfenbrennerian constructs to portray the ecology of peer relations and the effects that peers can have on the child; and Lawton (1999) used different terms than did Bronfenbrenner, but used similar ideas in describing the ecology of aging. Still others — Friedman and Amadeo (1999) on child care settings, Schooler (1999) on work environments, Talbert and McLaughlin (1999) on school environments, Vandell and Posner (1999) on after-school settings, Super and Harkness (1999) on environment as culture, and Stokols (1999) on effects of the internet — have found ways to utilize the ecological model proposed by Bronfenbrenner to understand different and largely nonoverlapping parts of human ecology.

But, the bioecological model developed by Bronfenbrenner and adapted by a host of others is almost solely a model of the social ecology of human development. Thus, the label for the model — bioecological — seems apt with regard to the ecological aspect of the label, but the "bio" (presumably for biological) part of the label is largely absent from writings on the model in its various adaptations. That is, the model focuses first on situations that afford face-to-face interactions or transactions between individuals as the most proximal, and perhaps the most important, environmental or contextual forces operating on the developing individual, moderating developmental advances based on qualities of the interactions that occur. These interactions are contained in, or comprise, the microsystems of which the child is a member. The higher levels of the Bronfenbrenner model then consist of contextual elements that are ever more remote from face-to-face interactions, even though these more remote elements can affect or moderate development. But, the ways in which physical or biological aspects of ecology affect child development are not often considered (but, see Evans, 1999).

Physical ecology. Although social ecology, which comprises social aspects of human ecology, is admittedly an extremely important — and arguably the most important — aspect of the developing child's environment, I contend that a more inclusive model should be developed. I am convinced that physical ecology may play as large a role or a larger role in child development than does social ecology, but evidence of this influence is just being accumulated. Recent work by Hubbs-Tait, Nation, Krebs, and Bellinger (2005) summarized what is known about effects of exposure to lead, mercury, cadmium, and manganese on child development. Although relatively much is known about teratogenic effects of lead and mercury poisoning, much less is known about other substances, but less knowledge cannot be used to justify a claim that these other substances are less dangerous. Furthermore, Dilworth-Bart and Moore (2006) argued that lead and pesticide exposure is correlated with many variables characterizing the person or the person's environment, including ethnic minority status and low income. Because of this, traditional findings of poorer developmental outcomes for children from ethnic minority or low income groups when contrasted with comparison group children may reflect more the teratogenic effects of their physical ecologies rather than presumed deficiencies of their social ecologies (e.g., low levels of maternal education or IQ). The development of an adequate conception of the physical ecology is beyond the scope of the current chapter, but I will offer some beginning ideas about how to think of such a model, given the potential importance of this issue.

As shown in Panel B in Figure 17.1, a model of the physical ecology could be developed to complement Bronfenbrenner's concentration on social ecology. In Figure 17.1, physical ecology is shown in the form of hierarchically nested circles, with levels that correspond to a proximal-to-distal gradient that parallels the gradient in Bronfenbrenner's social ecological model. The innermost circle, encompassing the most proximal aspects of the physical environment, is labeled *local, home* to denote the close-at-hand physical settings in which the developing child is found. The second circle is labeled *neighborhood, community*, representing a more extended, but still fairly proximal set of influences that may affect children growing up near one another. *Region* is contained in the third circle and refers to more inclusive general environments, such as Southern California, New England, or Big Sky Country (i.e., Montana). These regional environments may differ considerably in physical size, but generalizations regarding environmental effects within each region are likely to hold. The fourth, outermost circle is labeled *country*, but could include still larger divisions of the physical ecology. Finally, the physical ecology model must also contain a chronosystem. Aspects of physical ecology are likely to have very different effects on the person at different points in ontogenesis, perhaps having effects that substantially alter the life course if particular forces are encountered at an early stage of development, but having only minor, transitory, reversible effects if experienced after maturity has been attained. Complementing ontogenetic effects, our physical ecology appears to be undergoing profound and alarming historical changes, largely based on pollution that has increased exponentially since the dawn of the industrial age and on the increasingly large human population. Just how the degradation of our environment will influence individual ontogenesis and the ultimate survival of our species will play out over the next century or more, but the physical forces at work will likely have much larger effects than we have imagined.

Whether a model of the physical ecology of human development based on a series of nested circles that encompass ever broader physical divisions is the optimal way to build such a model should be left open for debate. The model shown in Panel B of Figure 17.1 is a simple and direct way to extend Bronfenbrenner's model of social ecology to the domain represented by physical ecology using a similar proximal-to-distal gradient, but simple and direct adaptations at times fail to capture the elements of a system in the most relevant fashion. Thus, the model shown in Panel B of Figure 17.1 is offered as an opening gambit, challenging others (and me) to figure out more adequate ways of thinking about physical ecology.

Let me say a word or two in favor of the proximal-to-distal gradient for physical ecology. The innermost circle represents the home and other very local environs. The home contains many non-social components that can have a major influence on behavioral development, components that can vary from home to home in a single neighborhood. One of the most obvious of these environmental variables is exposure to lead, which can occur if an infant ingests flecks of lead-based paint, but can occur in many other ways. The effects of lead poisoning are large on various forms of mental functioning, including intelligence test scores, memory performance, and reaction time. Furthermore, Chiodo, Jacobson, and Jacobson (2004) reported that many effects of lead exposure or poisoning appear at even very low levels of exposure, so no lower threshold, denoting "safe" levels of exposure, can be determined. In addition, at early stages of development, this innermost circle might encompass a very small and intimate space—the amniotic sac—that can have very important impacts on later developmental outcomes (cf. Wasserman et al., 2003; Hubb-Tait et al., 2005).

Widening the physical circle a bit to include the neighborhood or community, consider the effects of environmental pollutants found in Love Canal and other similar neighborhoods. Private companies routinely dump dangerous chemicals on company-owned property; at Love Canal, companies dumped dioxin and other chemicals on land abutting housing areas. The chemicals percolated down into the local water system and entered the drinking water for homes in the area. Exposure to dioxin can lead to disabilities in many domains, including physiological, social, and learning (Rahill, 1989). Furthermore, even if effects of the dioxin poisoning from Love Canal were not fully documented, the intense fears engendered by living near a toxic dump of its magnitude had important psychological effects on residents, who experienced extremely high levels of stress, leading to increased risk for anxiety and depression disorders (Gibbs, 1983).

Widening the circle still further, different regions of the United States are known for general features of their physical environments. For example, Southern California is regarded as the land of sunshine and warm temperatures, but is also known as the home of some of the worst particulate smog in the country. Recent publications reported results from a longitudinal study of more than 1,700 children and adolescents who were living in communities scattered across Southern California. Given their home locations, these children were exposed to varying levels of smog during development. Two studies by Gauderman and colleagues (Gauderman et al., 2002; Gauderman et al., 2004) reported that children in smog-impacted areas of Southern California had lowered respiratory function and much higher rates of breathing-related problems; and McConnell et al.(2002) found that exercising children in smog-impacted areas had much higher levels of asthma than did children in nonimpacted areas. Other studies have looked at the relation between air pollution and mortality in general and from certain specific causes (e.g., lung cancer) (Jerrett et al., 2005) or at the relation between particulate air pollution and cardiovascular mortality (Pope et al., 2004). Although these studies concentrated on lung function or mortality and not on psychological outcome variables, effects of exposure to pollution on psychological variables deserve study. Thus, children with severely reduced respiratory function due to their exposure to smog may have lower levels of physical self esteem or self concept or may be more tentative and overly cautious about sports and playing outside.

The final, largest circle in Panel B of Figure 17.1 encompasses the country or hemisphere in which the child lives. Here, it may be difficult to differentiate certain effects with regard to whether they belong in the social ecology or physical ecology models. When contrasting the United States with highly developed countries in Northern Europe, the United States clearly provides its citizens with, or exposes its citizens to, very different levels of access to health care, exposure to crime, and even access to high quality food, all of which may have sizeable impacts on psychological and behavioral development.

Personal Qualities. If a model of physical ecology can be developed to complement the components subsumed by Bronfenbrenner's model for social ecology, both of these should be nested within a superordinate model, such as the one shown in Panel C of Figure 17.1. There, three interlocking circles are shown: one for social ecology, a second for physical ecology, and the third labeled personal qualities. The first two of these have been discussed above: the social ecology circle reflects the model developed by Bronfenbrenner during his several-decades-long thinking about social influences on development, and the physical ecology represents aspects of the physical environment that I have already briefly introduced. The third circle, however, also must be discussed, again only briefly. By personal qualities, I refer to the personal characteristics that the developing child brings to his or her ecology. These personal qualities include individual differences in many domains of psychological functioning, including the domains of mental and cognitive functioning, personality, temperament, social skills, physical skills, and so forth, and including physical robustness or hardiness. Of course, Bronfenbrenner (1977, 1986a, 1986b) always argued that personal qualities of the individuals engaged in face-to-face interactions were most important constituents of the behavioral transactions in microsystems. But, with his focus on the nested layers of social ecology, personal qualities tend to take a back seat; the insertion here of a circle standing for these dimensions is designed to place them back at the forefront of consideration.

One key aspect of these personal characteristics is the degree to which these qualities of the individual child combine with the child's social and physical ecology to affect development. Certain personal qualities may enhance or retard the opportunities the child has to take part in or experience parts of the social or physical environment that can promote further development. For example, the more intelligent the child, the more likely the child will be able to benefit from courses of instruction that will lead to entrance to the best college or university. Or, an extroverted child is more likely to volunteer for social events in middle school that enhance that child's popularity and self-esteem, while the shy and introverted child hangs back and loses out on such possibilities. Another somewhat different take on the importance of personality qualities is manifested in the risk-and-resilience literature. Studies in this domain often search for personal qualities that lead a child to fall prey to negative environmental situations or to stand up against negative surroundings and achieve unusual success.

Similar ideas have been discussed in behavior genetic research in accounting for correlations between genotypes and environments (e.g., Plomin et al., 1997; Scarr, 1992). There, researchers have long noted at least three different mechanisms underlying genotype–environment correlation: passive, reactive (or evocative), and active. The passive mechanism is exemplified by family environments that are correlated with parental and child genotypes, so no actions by children are required to maintain the correlation. The reactive mechanism is reflected in the reactions by others to individuals based on their phenotypic characteristics, which are based at least partly on their genes, so genotypes of individuals indirectly evoke responses by others. The active mechanism is represented in actions by individuals to select environmental contexts, to modify or change their environments, or to modify their experiences all in ways that are related to their genotypes or genetic predispositions. But, I would prefer to broaden the issue of personal qualities beyond the discussion of genotype–environment correlation, because the latter retains the divisive orientation of attempting to determine which source—genes or environment—explains more variance in outcomes. Although this might be a legitimate question, the personal qualities in Figure 17.1C are phenotypic traits, and the personal phenotypic qualities of an individual are what may impact development regardless of the genetic or environmental contributions to these phenotypic characteristics. Thus, any final model that yields an acceptable understanding of behavioral development must consider social ecology, physical ecology, and the person's phenotypic characteristics as an interactive mix of ecological effects and personal responses and adaptations to those effects.

MODELING EFFECTS OF CONTEXT

When thinking about modeling the effects of context mathematically or statistically, researchers should consider at least seven aspects related to the effect of a contextual influence on one or more developmental outcomes. I refer to these seven aspects as the (a) timing of the application of the contextual influence, (b) patterning of the influence, (c) functional form of the effect, (d) numerical constants of the effect, (e) degree of specificity of the effect, (f) timing of the effect of the influence, and (g) directness of the effect. Each of these aspects is discussed in the following sections, with speculations regarding the likely nature of contextual influences on many developmental outcomes of interest.

Timing of Application of the Contextual Influence

The timing of application of an influence of context refers to the time during ontogenesis, from conception onward, when the contextual influence is applied to the organism and thus begins to have its developmental consequences. Issues involving timing of influences have often been discussed under the label *critical periods*, based on the presumption that the timing of notable effects of particular contextual influences was tightly circumscribed. But, continuing research tends to support the term *sensitive periods*, as the developing organism appears to be more susceptible to certain influences at particular ages, but the contextual influences may well have some, albeit reduced effect outside the bounds of the sensitive period. Because contextual variables are liable to exert their influences across considerable spans of development, the present concern for identifying when in an individual's life span a contextual variable is applied or encountered may seem somewhat arbitrary. But, the current concern for timing, when taken together with the idea of patterning of the influence, enables a researcher to begin thinking about both when and how contextual variables begin to influence development.

Before Birth. The developing human fetus typically spends about 9 months in the uterine environment, a time of rapid, fundamental, complexly patterned development. Contextual influences that occur during gestation can have profound influences on an individual's development, influences that can be revisited on succeeding generations. For example, Barker (1998) reviewed a broad range of effects of fetal malnutrition on subsequent health outcomes. The notion that prenatal, or in utero, influences can have many and varied behavioral sequelae is termed *fetal programming*. The hypothesis is that poor nutrition during gestation affects growth of various bodily systems at many levels, and these systems then function in altered fashion later in life. The levels at which fetal malnutrition can have effects are striking, from the level of organs (e.g., brain, thymus) to the level of neurotransmitters (e.g., corticosteroids).

In his review, Barker (1998) focused on the effects of malnutrition during fetal and early postnatal development on a range of health-related outcomes. For example, women who were themselves small for gestational age when they were born are more likely to have negative pregnancy outcomes, including a higher rate of perinatal infant mortality and a higher rate of offspring who are small for gestational age. Some might presume that these intergenerational influences are based on genetic factors passed from mothers to their daughters. However, numerous "experiments of nature," such as famines associated with wartime shortages, have been studied to understand the patterns of intergenerational transmission of environmental influences. Thus, babies who were born prior to the Dutch famine of 1944–1945 or who were conceived after the famine had comparable, normal birth statistics (e.g., birthweight, head circumference), and babies exposed to the famine during only the early part of their gestation also appeared to be unaffected. But, babies who were exposed to the famine during middle or later stages of gestation had substantially reduced birthweight, length, head circumference, and so forth. Later studies showed that these women who were themselves small for gestational age tended to have offspring who were small for gestational age. In rats, the offspring of undernourished rats were put on a normal diet, but it took three generations on normal diets for normal levels of growth and development of the offspring to be attained (see Barker, 1998).

Barker (1998) documented the negative effects of fetal malnutrition on many health outcomes, including coronary heart disease and diabetes. But, there is every reason to think that fetal malnutrition would also have effects on psychological outcomes as well. Furthermore, fetal malnutrition is not the only prenatal influence likely to influence behavioral development. Research on fetal alcohol syndrome has demonstrated the teratogenic effect of prenatal exposure to high levels of alcohol on offspring physical and mental development. For example, Streissguth, Bookstein, Barr, Sampson, O'Malley, and Young (2004) found that young adults who had fetal alcohol syndrome or the less severe fetal alcohol effects had much higher rates of disrupted schooling experiences, inappropriate sexual behavior, and involvement with law enforcement, among other outcomes, when compared with young adults without notable effects of prenatal exposure to alcohol. One additional instance of prenatal effects on later development, through prenatal exposure to high levels of PHE, is discussed later in this chapter.

During Infancy. Environmental or contextual variables can also be encountered during infancy, and their positive or negative consequences may also be pronounced. Moreover, the form or ultimate importance of contextual effects occurring during infancy may differ in fundamental ways based on the time point during infancy when the contextual variable is experienced. For example, rat pups that are poorly nourished between 3 and 6 weeks after birth have a marked stunting of their development during their period of malnutrition, and this poor nutrition sets them on a different track of physical development, resulting in permanently smaller adult size and weight, even after they are placed on a normal diet after 6 weeks of age. In contrast, rat pups that are poorly nourished between 9 and 12 weeks after birth exhibit an initial sharp drop in weight; but, after being placed on a normal diet after 12 weeks of age, these rat pups catch up to the normal growth trend and attain normal size and weight when reaching adulthood (Barker, 1998). These results indicate the importance of the timing of a contextual influence, even during the period of infancy, particularly with regard to whether rather temporary or more lasting effects are exhibited during later development.

In humans, infancy was historically regarded as a relatively unimportant period for the development of intelligence, at least with regard to determination of individual differences in intelligence, as scores on infant tests of intelligence (e.g., Bayley Scales of Infant Development) obtained within the first 2 years of life tend to correlate approximately zero with test scores obtained at maturity (e.g., at age 18; Bayley, 1949; Bloom, 1964). Based on these findings, researchers considered infant tests of intelligence to be good measures of current status, but of little use in predicting later status. Thus, whatever happens during infancy may be important in the short run with regard to the development of individual differences in intelligence, but in the longer term—extending to maturity—developments during infancy appeared to have little relevance to ultimate levels of higher cognitive function assessed by tests of intelligence during adolescence or adulthood. This view is consistent with the position that human infants are quite adaptable and resilient to environmental conditions. If environmental influences cause slower- than-expected development, infants can exhibit substantial catch-up development if the negative environmental conditions are corrected or alleviated. Thus, infants appear to follow closely some predetermined developmental trajectory, can be deflected from this trajectory by negative environmental conditions, but then catch up to the trajectory if conditions improve.

However, research during the past two decades has reversed this longstanding contention, showing that infant attention measures exhibit substantial correlations with intelligence later in childhood (Colombo & Frick, 1999; Fagan & Detterman, 1992) and adolescence, correlations that range between .40 and .60. Given correlations of this magnitude, consistent with a view that infant attentional abilities provide a foundation for later intelligence, future research should focus on conditions that facilitate or retard the development of infant attentional abilities. In another strand of research, children with phenylketonuria (PKU) exhibit a striking decline in intelligence during the first 2 years after birth if they are not on a phenylalanine-restricted diet. On a normal, unrestricted diet, infants with PKU appear normal at birth, but decline to the level of severe mental retardation, with a mean IQ of around 50, by age 2 years, and the resulting mental retardation is permanent. Thus, based on these two domains of research, it appears that certain influences during infancy can have long-term effects on adult intelligence.

During Childhood or Later. Contextual influences that occur during childhood or later are, of course, likely to exert effects on the developing child. Indeed, most theoretical accounts of development presume that developmental influences are a cascade, with experiences at one age having influences on outcomes at later ages that are close temporally. For example, experiences at age 7 years might be useful for understanding a child's behavior at age 10 years, but would be less useful for understanding the child's behavior at later points in time (e.g., age 15 years or age 20 years). Or, put another way, the usual presumption is that contextual influences during childhood are important for understanding development into adolescence, that experiences in adolescence may be important for understanding the transition to adulthood, and that experiences in each stage of adulthood are important for understanding and predicting outcomes at each succeeding stage.

Mathematically, this metatheory presumes that psychological development can be modeled by a first-order Markov or simplex process, with behavior at a given time t dependent on status at the preceding time $t - 1$, and not additionally on status at any prior times of measurement (e.g., times $t - 2$ or $t - 3$), once the influence of status at time $t - 1$ is estimated. This kind of model, with development unfolding as a function of status at the immediately preceding time of measurement plus perturbations that have occurred since the last time of measurement is a very useful model and one that may explain development in many domains. But, we must remain vigilant for potential influences that do not conform to this first-order autoregressive or simplex pattern.

Patterning of Contextual Influence

The hypothesized patterning of an effect of a contextual influence must play into the various aspects of the design of a study. Next, I discuss several options for patterns that contextual influences may take. In particular, I have identified three patterns termed (a) the big bang, (b) repetitious, smaller events, and (c) intermittent, but salient. These are but three patterns that might be present, and additional patterns should be identified to help structure the thinking of investigators as they design studies.

"Big Bang" Events. The "big bang" notion of a contextual influence is that of a single, major event that has a substantial influence on the developmental course of growth and development for an individual. The most probable form of a "big bang" influence is a nonnormative event that occurs at a particularly sensitive period of development, representing an acute stressor (Thompson, Mc-Cubbin, Thompson, & Elver, 1998). Numerous examples of big bang influences could be identified: the death of a parent at a sensitive time during early childhood, anoxia during birthing due to the umbilical cord being wrapped around the neck of a fetus, or an accident that leaves permanent physical or psychological scars. All such events share a common characteristic: each event is a single, unrepeated or unrepeatable event that alters the path of development, hence the term big bang denoting the lasting influence of a single event.

Because big bang events tend to be nonnormative, statistical modeling of their influences will be complicated. A given big bang event such as death of a parent is likely to have differential effects as a function of many variables, including the age of the child at the time of the event, the nature of the parent–child relation, the child's psychological make-up, and the nature of psychological supports for the child, among others. Moreover, the nonnormative status of the events means that the incidence of such events within a given period of time will be rather low. Although the impact of a big bang event is hypothesized to be strong, the low frequency of these events will often require either very large sample sizes or an extremely nuanced approach to analyses to capture the importance of the events within any statistical model.

Repetitious, Smaller Events. A second pattern of influence is the presence of numerous, smaller events that occur over a span of time and thus are repetitious in nature, but that cumulate to affect the course of development. Whereas big bang events represent acute stressors, repetitious events reflect chronic events that gain the power to deflect or moderate development through their steady, day-by-day influence. In the study of stress, researchers have long contrasted the effects of major life events with the effects of daily hassles on psychological stress. Although major life events, such as the death of a parent or spouse, have notable influences on stress, daily hassles—the many, repetitious, minor inconveniences of everyday life—appear also to have strong effects on felt stress. But, the category of chronic, repetitious influences need not be negative in tone. Most positive parenting behaviors take on this pattern, with parents offering explanations for how to behave, urging children to act in as mature fashion as possible, and so forth. As any parent well knows, inculcating mature forms of behavior in offspring is a time-consuming task, accomplished in a-thousand-and-one ways every day.

Repetitious, smaller events represent an easier task for the researcher modeling contextual effects on development. The high frequency of these influences leads to a greater ability to assess the general level of these events, and the average level of these stressors in a child's life-space may be the most appropriate measure of the events. Because most children will experience some level—whether high or low—of these repetitious events, assessing these events is not difficult. Indeed, parents and observers tend to show moderate levels of agreement when assessing certain parenting behaviors, such as marital quality and parent–child relationship quality (Ge, Conger, Lorenz, Elder, Montague, & Simons, 1992).

Intermittent, but Salient. The third pattern of influence considered here is that of intermittent, but salient events. Examples of this kind of influence can be generated according to many scenarios. For example, attachment to the mother or primary caregiver can be affected by many characteristics of the caregiver. But, unprovoked, explosive behavior by the caregiver constitutes experience that is potentially most damaging to the secure attachment of the child. Consider the child who approaches the caregiver, seeking the comfort that the caregiver should provide as the nurturing, secure base for the child. When the child seeks comfort, the caregiver may usually engage in warm and nurturing interactions with the child, but sometimes—without warning—react with anger, coldness, or harsh rejection. Such patterns of behavior by the parent are a classic forerunner of insecure attachment by the child to the caregiver (e.g., Isabella, 1993).

Due to the intermittent nature of these events, the likelihood that a sufficient number of events will occur when a parent is assessed or observed interacting with his or her child is relatively low. Hence, measurement may have to rely on participant reports of behavior. In such situations, assessing the behavior of an individual parent is optimal when multiple reporters or informants are employed, such as self-report, partner report, child report, and observer report. Combining information from multiple informants is likely to lead to the best estimate of an individual's levels of intermittent behaviors.

Functional Form of Effect

The functional form of an effect refers to the mathematical or statistical function relating an independent variable to a developmental outcome variable. To provide some context for this discussion, I refer in this section to Figure 17.2. Each of the panels in Figure 17.2 is drawn with intelligence as the outcome variable along the Y axis and an unnamed contextual variable as the independent, or predictor, variable along the X axis. Naturally, any developmental outcome could take the place of intelligence as the outcome variable; because the primary example used later in this chapter involves intelligence I have used

FIGURE 17.2

Relation between alimentary or teratogenic variables with developmental outcomes. panel a: linear relation. panel b: pure quadratic relation. panel c: mixed quadratic relation, diminishing returns. panel d: mixed quadratic relation, cumulative effects. (note: in all panels, ------- alimentary variable; - - - - - teratogenic variable).

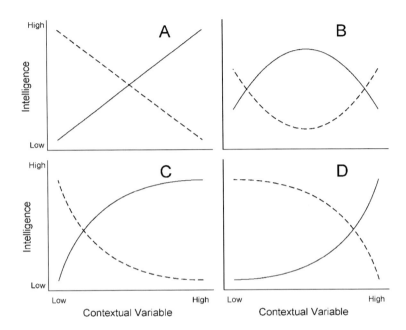

it in Figure 17.2. The nature of the contextual variable is kept deliberately implicit by referring to it simply as the contextual variable of interest, and readers are encouraged to consider their own dimensions of greatest interest in the place of the contextual variable.

One other convention embodied in Figure 17.2 is the use of solid and dashed lines. Because the outcome variable, intelligence, is one for which higher scores are generally deemed better, a solid line is used to represent the influence of an *alimentary*, or *beneficial*, context variable, because higher levels of the contextual variable tend to be associated with higher outcome variable scores. Conversely, a dashed line represents the effect of a *teratogenic*, or *unfavorable*, context variable, as higher levels of the context variable tend to be associated with lower scores on the outcome variable. Of course, if the developmental outcome were a variable on which higher scores reflected increasingly negative

FIGURE 17.2 (Continued)
panel e: cubic relation. panel f: threshold effect, low-end effect. panel g: threshold effect,
high-end effect. panel h: threshold effect, differential effect. (note: in all panels, ------- alimentary
variable; - - - - - teratogenic variable).

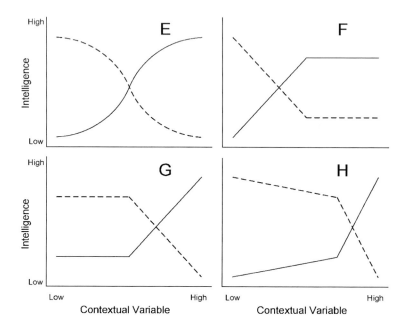

forms of behavior (e.g., externalizing behaviors), then the role of alimentary and teratogenic contextual variables would be reversed.

Linear Effect. Although many different functional forms of contextual effect can be considered, clearly the simplest to consider is a linear form. A linear form presumes that a straight line best represents the relation between the contextual variable and an outcome variable, as shown in Figure 17.2A. In the vast majority of developmental research studies, a linear effect is the only functional form considered. Bivariate correlation and standard forms of simple and multiple regression invoke explicitly or implicitly the presumption of a linear relation.

Despite the overwhelming use of linear models to estimate effects of beneficial or teratogenic contextual variables on developmental outcomes, a linear function is probably the least likely candidate for the true relation between a contextual variable and a developmental outcome. What is the basis for this contention? A linear function is usually a poor ultimate functional form because of the fundamental nature of the linear function: A linear function represents the contentions that "more is better" and "the same amount of more is equal to the same amount of better" throughout the entire range of the independent and dependent variables. Consider for a moment the influence of the number of books in a home and a child's reading achievement or intelligence. The number of books in the home is a common item in scales that assess the developing child's home environment, and researchers often find a positive relation between number of books in the home and child school achievement. But, a linear function represents the hypothesis that the difference between 0 books and 500 books in the home will lead to an increase in achievement equal to that occasioned by the difference between 5,500 and 6,000 books in the home. But, the former difference, between having 0 and 500 books in the home, is likely to have a much larger effect than the latter difference. If so, then a linear function is an unlikely a priori form, and a statistical model representing a decreasing marginal increase in the effect of the contextual variable as the value of that variable increases is in order.

If a linear function is an unlikely form of the true relation between a contextual variable and an outcome, why are linear functions so commonly used? Several answers might be given to this question. One reasonable response concerns the standard education in graduate programs on the use of linear models, such as multiple regression analysis. As a result of their training, most practicing scientists have ready knowledge of and familiarity with linear models, but have little experience or acquaintance with nonlinear models. Furthermore, most statistical programs have user-friendly programs for specifying linear regression models, with little information for models that posit nonlinear relations. Additionally, linear models may be "good enough" for our research purposes, as we often simply want to know whether any relation at all exists between two variables, rather than wishing to specify precisely the mathematical form of this relation. Finally, researchers often implicitly incorporate nonlinear functions into their measurements. For example, when assessing drug use, a researcher might use the following scale: 0 = no use, 1 = used 1 or 2 times, 2 = used 3–10 times, 3 = used 11–30 times, 4 = used 31–99 times, and 5 = used 100+ times. Thus, the answer options 0–5 are nonlinearly related to seriousness of drug use, as represented by the number of times a person used the particular drug. The scores on the manifest item that vary between 0 and 5 may be related linearly to important outcomes, even though these linear functions translate into nonlinear relations between "number of times the drug is used" and the outcome variables. Of course, an alternative strategy would be to assess the number of times a person used a given drug and then use statistical models to estimate the nonlinear relation between "number of times the drug is used" and the outcome variables, rather than imposing a specific, non-smooth, haphazard nonlinear function through the measurement process.

Quadratic Effect, Pure. If a linear relation is an unlikely candidate for the relation between a contextual variable and an outcome, what alternatives are available? As shown in Figure 17.2B, the relation between a contextual variable and a developmental outcome may be best described using a quadratic curve, which has a single arc of curvature. One candidate for quadratic effect is a U-shaped or inverted U-shaped curve. The quadratic curves shown in Figure 17.2B are *pure* quadratic curves because fitting a linear model to the data would lead to explained variance of zero, and all explained variance would be associated with the quadratic term. The identification of one of the curves in Figure 17.2B as reflecting an alimentary effect and the other as a teratogenic effect is somewhat arbitrary. For example, the solid curve representing an inverted U-shaped curve leads to higher predicted performance when the contextual variable is in the middle of its range, but worse performance for extreme high or low levels of the contextual variable. The predictions based on the dashed line lead to the opposite predicted pattern, with relatively high performance at either high or low values of the contextual variable and relatively low values for middling values of the contextual variable. If the population distribution of values on a contextual variable were unimodal and fairly symmetric, then most observations would fall relatively near the midpoint on the dimension, justifying the choice of the inverted-U function as an alimentary variable. However, if only very low or very high levels of the contextual variable are included for study, the roles of the alimentary and teratogenic variables might be reversed.

Quadratic Effect, Mixed. As a priori contenders, pure quadratic effects seem as unrealistic in most situations as do linear effects. Thus, what may be called mixed quadratic effects, depicted in Figures 17.2C and 17.2D, are more likely to occur. These curves are termed mixed quadratic effects because a linear function fit to the data would have a significant contribution, but the quadratic term adds significant explained variance and additional specificity to the relation between the contextual and outcome variables. Note that a very smooth shape of the relation between independent and dependent variables characterizes these curves.

The quadratic relations shown in Figure 17.2C might be termed relations depicting diminishing returns of the contextual variable or relations characterized by "low end" effects of the contextual variable. The alimentary curve shown in Figure 17.2C might well describe the relation between a dimension, such as number of books in the home, and the outcome variable of intelligence. The lowest level of books in the home is associated with low levels of intelligence. As the number of books increases, we see a corresponding increase in the predicted level of intelligence. However, the effect of any increase in number of books is greatest at the low end of the scale, and the predicted increase in intelligence for a one-unit increase in books in the home is smaller and smaller as one moves up the scale of number of books. The dashed line, representing the effect of a teratogenic variable, is still a "low end" relation, as the major negative effect of the contextual variable occurs at the low end of the scale, with more minimal negative effects at high levels of the contextual variable.

In contrast to curves depicting diminishing returns of a contextual variable, the quadratic relations shown in Figure 17.2D convey what may be termed cumulative effects of the context variable or relations characterized by "high end" effects of the contextual variable. In Figure 17.2D, the positive effect of the alimentary variable is rather meager when moving from a low level to a medium level, but past the medium level the positive effect is very strong. A similar characterization can be made of the teratogenic variable in Figure 17.2D, with little negative effect of the teratogenic variable until a rather high level of the variable is present.

Cubic Effect. The nonlinear pattern relating an independent variable to an outcome variable may have at least one additional point of curvature beyond that shown by a quadratic function; the name for a curve with two points of inflection is a cubic trend. Cubic relations between a contextual variable and the outcome variable are shown in Figure 17.2E. The curve for the alimentary variable is an S-shaped curve moving from the lower left to upper right corner of the graph. This shows that the relation between the contextual variable and the outcome variable is a strong and approximately linear one, but only in the range of middle values of the contextual variable; at either rather high levels or rather low levels of the contextual variable, little relation between predictor and outcome are in evidence. Another way to characterize the relation is to say that the curve has a lower asymptote at the lower left of the figure and an upper asymptote at the upper right, and the relation describes a nonlinear trend between these two asymptotes.

Threshold Effect. Rather than representing the relation between a contextual variable and an outcome variable as a linear function or smooth nonlinear function, some form of threshold effect could be posited as a reasonable representation of this relation between predictor and outcome variable. A threshold effect suggests that the relation between a contextual predictor variable and an outcome variable is characterized by a rather abrupt change, with one function up to a *knot* point and a rather different function after the knot point. Models of this sort are often termed *spline* models, and the trends on either side of the knot point can be linear or nonlinear. Here, we deal only with two-piece linear spline models. Two-piece linear spline relations for alimentary and teratogenic variables are shown in Figure 17.2F and 17.2G. The spline models shown in Figure 17.2F can be characterized by "low end" effects, much as shown in Figure 17.2C for quadratic curves, because the contextual variable has a strong effect on the outcome only at relatively low levels. Correspondingly, the spline models shown in Figure 17.2G reflect "high end" effects, with the contextual variable having an effect on the outcome variable only at rather high levels of the predictor variable, similar to relations depicted in Figure 17.2D for the smooth quadratic curves.

Due to the similarity of curves in Figures 17.2C and 17.2F, researchers might have a difficult time deciding which type of model – a quadratic model or a two-piece linear spline model—provides better fit to a set of data. Thus, if a two-piece linear spline model like that in Figure 17.2F were the true model underlying the relation between an alimentary contextual variable and intelligence, the spline model should fit the data well. But, good fit of a spline model would likely be difficult to differentiate from good fit of a quadratic model, given the similar functions described by the two models. In such cases, theory might well lead one to choose one model over the other, particularly in the absence of notable differences in fit of the two alternative models.

The final type of relation to be considered is a two-piece linear spline model that has non-zero effects at all points along the score continuum of the contextual variable; such relations are shown in Figure 17.2H. As shown there, the alimentary relation exhibits a relatively shallow, but positive relation between the contextual variable and intelligence from very low to moderately high values of the contextual variable, but then exhibits a very strong relation between the two variables at very high levels of the contextual variable. Clearly, the choice between two-piece linear models shown in Figures 17.2G and 17.2H would be based on the statistical significance of the slope coefficient at low levels of the contextual variable. If one fit a model like that in Figure 17.2H, but the first, low-end slope coefficient did not differ significantly from zero, then a model like that in Figure 17.2G would probably be a preferred representation of the relation.

Numerical Constants for Effects

Several numerical constants can be identified for the varied functional forms that contextual influences are likely to have on developmental progress. Certain of these numerical constants will be applicable for some functions, but not for others; few functional forms will contain all constants. Still, the theoretical models we develop should have implications for the nature of the statistical models we construct to represent these theoretical conjectures; and the numerical constants estimated should have implications for the theoretical questions we ask.

Intercept. In a linear regression model, the intercept is the predicted outcome variable score when all predictors are simultaneously zero. For example, consider the following general linear regression equation:

$$Y_i = B_0 + B_1 X_{i1} + B_2 X_{i2} + \ldots + B_p X_{ip} + E_i \tag{1}$$

where Y_i represents the score of individual i on the outcome or dependent variable Y, B_0 is the intercept, B_1 through B_p are the raw score regression coefficients for independent variables X_1 through X_p, respectively, E_i is the error score for individual i and represents failure of the weighted predictors to account perfectly for scores on Y, and the independent variables X_1 through X_p have i subscripts to denote the score of individual i on these variables. In Equation 1, the intercept term is B_0 and is the estimated score on Y when all predictors X_1 through X_p are simultaneously zero.

The intercept in a linear regression model is termed an additive constant that allows the appropriate vertical placement of the regression line. In addition, the intercept is frequently treated as an uninterpretable constant in the equation, because predictor variables often cannot take on values of zero. For example, if a scale consisted of 10 items and each item were answered on a 1-to-10 scale, the sum of the 10 items would have logical limits ranging from 10 to 100, and the average item score could range from 1 to 10. Under neither scaling—the sum of the 10 items or the average of the 10 item scores—would a score of zero be possible for a respondent. As a result, the intercept provides an estimate of the dependent variable score completely outside the possible range of the predictor variable, and the intercept has no obvious interpretation. However, appropriate transformations of scores on predictor variables can lead to an intercept term that has a direct and meaningful interpretation.

Slope. The slope constant is the predicted change in the outcome variable Y for a one-unit change in the given predictor variable. Referring back to Equation 1, coefficients B_1 through B_p are the raw score regression coefficients for independent variables X_1 through X_p, respectively. The magnitude of the B_1 coefficient is an estimate of the predicted change in Y for a one-unit change in X_1, and similar interpretations hold for the remaining regression weights. In a linear model such as Equation 1, the slope constant for a given predictor variable represents the constant predicted increase in Y for a one-unit increase in the associated predictor variable regardless of the value of the predictor variable. That is, the predicted increase in Y is the same at all points along the range of values that the predictor variable can take.

Maximum or Minimum. Certain relations, such as a linear relation between predictor and criterion, have no easily specified maximum or minimum. For other curves, however, one can determine a maximum or minimum of the curve. Consider the pure quadratic curves shown in Figure 17.2B. There, the alimentary variable attains a maximum near the middle of the range of the contextual variable. If such a relation held between two variables, a researcher would be justified in recommending that middling values on the contextual variable be utilized, as these are associated with the highest predicted level on the outcome variable.

Asymptote. An asymptote is a limiting value of a function, either at the low or high end of the predictor scale. If a curve has an asymptote, the asymptote is a valuable parameter estimate, as it represents the highest (or lowest) value the function is approaching as the predictor variable increases in value. The relations shown in Figures 17.2A and 17.2B have no asymptotes. In contrast, the relations in Figure 17.2C have asymptotes at the high end of the predictor variable; for the alimentary variable, the asymptote of the curve is the value approached as one moves to higher and higher values of the contextual variable. The relations in Figure 17.2D have asymptotes at the low end of the predictor variable, and the relations in Figure 17.2E have asymptotes at both low and high levels of the predictor variable.

Point of Inflection. The point of inflection of a curve is the point at which a function (a) changes from increasingly negative to increasingly positive (or vice versa) or (b) changes from one described (e.g., linear) function to another function. For example, the smooth alimentary relation shown in Figure 17.2E begins at a low level at the low end of the contextual variable. As the contextual variable increases, the alimentary relation becomes increasingly positive (i.e., has an increasingly positive tangent to the curve) until one reaches the middle value of the contextual variable, after which the curve is negatively accelerated and therefore its slope becomes more negative (or, at least, less and less positive). As another example, the relations shown in Figure 17.2F also have a clear point of inflection near the middle of the scale of the contextual variable, as the positive slope of the alimentary relation for low values of the contextual variable changes to a null slope after the point of inflection.

Strength or Magnitude of Effect. The final numerical estimate associated with a fitted function is an estimate associated with the strength or magnitude of the effect. One useful indicator of strength of effect is the regression weight (or slope) for a predictor, as this provides the predicted change in Y for a one-unit change in the particular predictor variable. Different predictor variables are usually on different metrics, so standardized regression coefficients are a second useful index of magnitude of effect. An equation with standardized regression coefficients enables the researcher to compare the relative predictive power of the multiple predictors in the same equation. But, rather than merely citing which coefficients are larger than others, one can test the difference between regression coefficients, using procedures such as those discussed by Cohen, Cohen, West, and Aiken (2003. pp. 640-642), as relative differences between predictor variables should be discussed only if the predictors differ significantly in their predictive power.

A third and final index of strength or magnitude of effect is some function of the squared multiple correlation. For example, one might report the squared semipartial correlation for each predictor, which is an estimate of the proportion of Y variance explained uniquely by a predictor. The sum of the squared semipartial correlations across all predictors in an equation should be less than or equal to the overall squared multiple correlation, unless suppression effects are present (Cohen et al., 2003). Alternatively, one could report the stepwise increase in the squared multiple correlation as each individual predictor variable is added to the equation. The latter approach is most reasonable if the researcher has provided an a priori rationale for the order of entry of every predictor, or every set of predictors, to be included in the equation. This approach has the added benefit that the sum of the hierarchically estimated changes in the squared multiple correlation will equal the overall squared multiple correlation.

Specificity of Effect

The degree of specificity of the effects of an environmental influence concerns how general or limited are its effects on behavior. At the least, researchers should investigate whether the influence of a contextual variable generalizes across populations of participants, across domains of outcome variables, and across the range of other variables.

Generality Across Populations. One form of generality is generality across populations. In developmental psychology, researchers often compare and contrast results for boys and girls. If similar patterns of influence are found across sex groups, then the influence of the contextual variable generalizes across groupings based on gender. Similar comparisons are often conducted across groups identified on the basis of race or ethnicity, level of socioeconomic status, and country of origin, among others. If a contextual variable has consistent and similar effects across populations, theories about the contextual variable are simplified. However, research on developmental processes often finds that key contextual variables have differing effects for different populations, requiring alterations to theory to explain the specificity of effects.

As one example of lack of generality of contextual variables across populations, Steinberg, Dornbusch, and Brown (1993) found that parenting practices, family values regarding education, and adolescents' views about the relation between school success and occupational rewards had different effects on academic achievement for students from different ethnic groups. On non-school-related outcome variables such as psychosocial development and psychological stress, adolescents from authoritative homes had more positive outcomes than those from nonauthoritative homes for all ethnic groups. In contrast,

on school-related outcome variables, authoritative parenting was positively related to achievement for White and Hispanic students, but not for African
American or Asian American students. Thus, the results for non-school-related
outcomes demonstrated generality across the four ethnic groups, whereas the
results for school-related variables exhibited lack of generality of effects across
certain groups.

Generality Across Domains of Behavior. A second form of generality concerns whether a contextual variable has effects on multiple domains of behavior
or has effects restricted to only one or a small number of behavioral domains.
Some contextual influences are likely to have effects on a fairly circumscribed set
of outcomes, but other influences have much broader causal influence. For example, Streissguth et al. (2004) found that children with fetal alcohol syndrome
(FAS) had problematic outcomes across many domains of behavior. Thus, children with fetal alcohol syndrome had deficits in the cognitive domain, with
deficits exhibited in attention, memory, and executive function. Furthermore,
these children also showed disruptions in social behavior, including higher rates
of delinquency and antisocial behaviors, and also showed impairments in school-
related behaviors. The social and school-related problems of children with FAS
may result from a primary deficit in intelligence or information processing.
Still, the reach of prenatal exposure to alcohol across multiple domains is as
impressive as it is discouraging.

Generality Across the Range of Other Variables. A third form of generality
is shown if the effect of a contextual variable is the same at all levels of other
variables. The issue here is the presence or absence of interactions of a contextual variable with other predictors. If the effect of a given predictor is the
same at all levels of other, theoretically relevant variables, then the effect of the
predictor need not be qualified by citing the level of the other contextual variables. For example, consistent with prior research (e.g., Steinberg et al., 1993),
assume that authoritative parenting is positively related to school achievement
for White adolescents. However, suppose that this relation was much stronger
for adolescents who had good relationships with their parents, whereas the
effect of authoritative parenting was essentially nil for adolescents with poor
relationships with their parents. If this pattern of relations held, then the "authoritative parenting affects school achievement" relation would not be general
across all levels of adolescent relationships with parents. Whether research in
developmental psychology tends to have sufficient power to detect interaction
effects, whether developmental theory is sufficiently advanced to identify which
interactions are worthy of consideration, and whether interactions uncovered
in one study are sufficiently large and robust to be found in other studies are
reasonable concerns. But, if contextual influences are moderated by other vari-

ables in important ways and these interactive effects are not uncovered because researchers fail to investigate them, then important information about contextual influences is lost.

Timing of the Effect

After a contextual variable is encountered, the immediacy of the effect of that variable on the developing child is of issue. At least three levels of timing are reasonable candidates: immediate, delayed, and varied.

Immediate. A contextual variable can have a virtually instantaneous effect on the developing child, as would occur with a big bang event like the death of a parent. Any major nonnormative event of this nature might lead to an immediate reaction by the child, who would muster personal resources to comprehend and react to the event. With a big bang event, the initial reaction would often be the most salient effect of the event, although efforts to cope with the event might take years. If this occurred, the continued coping with the event over many years would also take the form of delayed or varied timing, discussed next.

Something must be said about the meaning of the label *immediate.* Some contextual influences may lead to an effect on the child within minutes, hours, or days, and such effects clearly deserve the immediate label. Other influences may take longer to moderate the development of the child, on the order of 6 months or a year, and still deserve being identified as an immediate effect. Thus, in proposing the descriptor immediate, no definite time interval is implied. Whether the effect of a contextual variable is immediate or more delayed may depend more on the design of a study and the span of development encompassed than on any particular temporal denotation of the term immediate.

Delayed. If a contextual variable has an effect on a child outcome variable only after a considerable span of time has elapsed without having had an effect earlier, this pattern deserved its description as a delayed effect. The delayed effect could be termed a "sleeper effect," as no immediate change is observable, yet an effect at a much later time can be tied to the earlier experience. For example, if a child experiences an event at age 5 years, exhibits no effects within the next few years, but has a notable reaction at age 10 years, this would be consistent with a delayed effect. Whether many delayed effects occur during human ontogenesis is open to question. Because of the general first-order Markov metatheory discussed earlier, researchers are not attuned to looking for delayed effects of contextual variables. If more time were dedicated to searching for such relations, a larger number of delayed effects might be uncovered.

Varied. If delayed effects are rarely uncovered in developmental research, varied timing of effects are much more common. By varied I refer to effects of

FIGURE 17.3
Conceptual model for the relations among four sets of variables: Background, pregnancy-related,
birth-related, and offspring outcome measures.

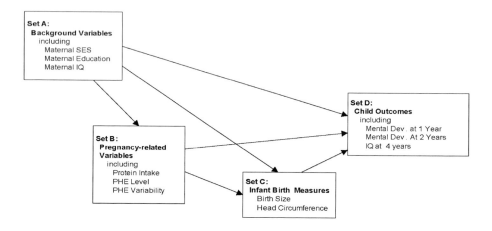

a contextual variable at different times or ages after the contextual variable
is encountered. Consider once again the developmental outcomes of children
with FAS (e.g., Streissguth et al., 2004). Immediately after birth, many children with FAS have facial anomalies; indeed, facial anomalies are one class of
variable that is useful in diagnosing FAS. Later, during elementary and middle
school, children with FAS have various types of problems in school, including
lower academic achievement and disruptive behavior. Still later, children with
FAS are at much higher risk for delinquency and other types of antisocial behavior. Thus, the timing of certain effects of prenatal exposure to alcohol is
almost immediate, whereas other effects occur much later in time.

Directness of Effect

By the directness of an effect, I refer to the place of a contextual variable in a
theoretical model and in any empirical statistical models that test the theoretical connections in a model. At least two types of effect can be distinguished,
direct and indirect. To instantiate the notion of direct and indirect effects, consider the relations shown in the conceptual path diagram shown in Figure 17.3.
In Figure 17.3, four sets of variables are shown that contain, respectively, maternal background variables, pregnancy-related variables, birth outcome measures,
and infant intelligence measures. I call the diagram in Figure 17.3 a conceptual
path diagram because there is no indication either of all variables that might
be included in each of the boxes or of all of the specific paths hypothesized

from one variable in one box to another variable in another box. Still, the path diagram is consistent with the general hypothesis that variables in Set A might affect variables in Sets B, C, and D, that variables in Set B might influence variables in Sets C and D, and that variables in Set C might effect variables in Set D. The variables listed in the various boxes in Figure 17.3 are indicative of those obtained in the Maternal PKU Collaborative Study, which is described in a later section. Here, I use the diagram in Figure 17.3 to explicate the notions of direct and indirect effects.

Direct Effect. A direct effect is simply that — the direct or unmediated effect of a predictor variable on an outcome variable. In a figural presentation such as that in Figure 17.3, a direct effect is represented as a single-headed arrow from one variable to another variable. If one represents one's theory in a graphical statistical model, a direct effect of a context variable is a direct, unidirectional arrow from a contextual variable to an outcome variable. The path coefficient associated with such a direct effect is an indictor of the magnitude or importance of the effect, as described above. When performing analyses with structural equation models, most researchers readily consider direct effects of multiple predictor variables on a given outcome variable. When more than a single direct effect is specified to an outcome variable, the resulting path coefficient is a partial coefficient, holding constant statistically the other variables affecting the outcome. The estimated path coefficient is then an estimate of the unique effect of the contextual variable on the outcome variable, over and above the effects of other predictors. For example, returning to Figure 17.3, if maternal IQ from Set A had an effect on infant mental development at 1 year of child age, this would be an example of a direct effect.

Indirect Effect. In contrast to a direct effect, an indirect effect is the effect of a contextual variable on an outcome variable through its influence on one or more other variables. In the context of the figural model in Figure 17.3, an indirect effect of maternal IQ on infant mental development at 1 year of age might take the form of a direct effect of maternal IQ on average maternal blood phenylalanine (PHE) level during pregnancy and a direct effect of average PHE level during pregnancy on infant mental development at 1 year of age. If, controlling for average PHE level during pregnancy, maternal IQ has no direct effect on infant mental development at 1 year, then maternal IQ has only an indirect effect on infant mental development at 1 year through its effect on average PHE level during pregnancy. Moreover, average PHE level during pregnancy is said to mediate the effect of maternal IQ on infant mental development at 1 year. Mediational analyses have been a topic of intense interest ever since Baron and Kenny (1986) highlighted the distinction between mediation and moderation, and any detailed presentation of issues and analytic choices in the investigation of mediation effects is far beyond the scope of the present chapter. Still, the presence of an indirect or mediated effect of a contextual variable on a developmental outcome is important to understand, even if the contextual variable has no direct effect on the outcome. The importance of studying any indirect effect of a contextual variable is this: the outcome variable may be influenced in an important way by the contextual variable, even if this effect is indirect, through the effect of the contextual variable on one or more mediator variables. For a state-of-the-art presentation of procedures for modeling mediation and moderation effects within structural equation models, consult Little, Card, Bovaird, Crandall, and Preacher (chap. 9, this volume).

Potential Artificiality of Distinction Between Indirect and Direct Effects. A word is in order, at this point, regarding the distinction between direct and indirect effects, a distinction that is potentially artificial. General writings on path analysis and structural modeling stress the need to consider carefully all paths specified in a model, including all direct and indirect effects among variables. The specification of paths required in a model is often termed the internal specification of the model. Experts on path analysis also stress that future research may well examine the processes underlying a given direct effect. For example, assume that a researcher finds that the contextual variable of maternal IQ has a direct effect on the outcome variable of infant mental development at 1 year over and above any indirect effects maternal IQ might have through mediator variables shown in Boxes B or C. Given the current state of theory and empirical investigation, the direct effect was all that could be specified and estimated. But, in later investigations, a researcher might postulate that additional variables not measured in current studies, variables such as authoritative parenting or the responsiveness of toys in the home environment, are potential mediators of the direct relation between maternal intelligence and infant mental development at 1 year. In later research, the investigator could then measure these proposed mediators as well as maternal IQ and infant mental development. If analyses revealed that the mediating variables fully mediated the effect of maternal IQ on infant mental development, then the influence of maternal IQ on intelligence would no longer be considered direct, but would be indirect through the effects of maternal IQ on the mediators of authoritative parenting or responsiveness of toys in the home.

Thus, if a researcher confirms a direct effect of a given contextual variable on an outcome variable, the directness of this effect is confirmed only for the current data set. This should set the stage for further research that postulates potential mediators of the effect of the predictor on the outcome variable; if successful, this research would move the contextual variable back in the chain of influence. Hence, a direct influence confirmed in one or more studies does not ensure that the direct influence of contextual variable on an outcome will remain always and forever a direct effect. Moreover, later research showing that the contextual variable has only an indirect effect on the outcome through specifiable mediator variables should not be interpreted as decreasing the importance of the contextual variable for the outcome variable. Instead, the later research would explicate the processes through which the contextual variable has its effects on the outcome, representing an interesting form of scientific advance.

Given the preceding considerations regarding the modeling of context effects on child development, I now turn to a consideration of an interesting form of context effects—provided by the prenatal environment—and demonstrate how the preceding concerns play out in the study of children of mothers with PKU.

ONE IMPORTANT SYSTEM FOR DISCUSSING CONTEXTUAL EFFECTS: CHILDREN OF MOTHERS WITH PKU

Phenylketonuria

The potentially devastating effects of phenylketonuria, or PKU, on ontogenetic development are well known. Identified in the late 1930s, PKU is the most common inborn error of metabolism. PKU involves an inability to metabolize phenylalanine (or PHE) into tyrosine. The build-up of PHE in the blood is then thought to be a teratogenic agent leading to severe brain damage, although lowered levels of tyrosine resulting from the lack of PHE metabolism might be an equally or more powerful culprit. Regardless, the disrupted metabolism of PHE into tyrosine damages the central nervous system in profound ways, even if these ways are yet to be understood fully (see Dyer, 1999). If an infant with PKU is on a normal diet during infancy, a precipitous decline in intellectual functioning occurs. Otherwise apparently normal at birth, the infant with PKU will exhibit a decided drop in functioning to the severe level of mental retardation (e.g., mean IQ of 50) by age 2 years, a decline that cannot be remediated. On the other hand, if an infant with PKU is placed on a special diet low in PHE within the first week of life and continues strictly on the diet during the developmental period (e.g., until age 20 years), the individual will show a normal or near-normal pattern of development.

Subsequent to the identification of the PKU syndrome in 1938, Bickel, Gerrard, and Hickmans (1953, 1954) developed a diet that was low in PHE and demonstrated the beneficial effects of this diet on a young child with PKU. Then, in 1962, Guthrie developed a cheap and accurate screening test that relied on a drop of blood collected on filter paper. Within the first week of life, an infant can have his/her heel punctured by a needle; blotting the heel on filter paper secures the blood sample. The blood sample is then transported to a laboratory, where the blood is assayed for high levels of phenylalanine, which is an indicator of PKU because the infant was unable to metabolize PHE in a normal fashion. The ease of collecting and transporting the blood sample, the accuracy of the test, and the inexpensiveness of the procedures involved led to the rapid adoption of the Guthrie test across all of the United States within one year of its development, and the Guthrie test is routinely used on all births in many nations of the world.

PKU is a recessive trait, so a person will exhibit symptoms of PKU only if the person receives the gene defect from both parents. Persons with PKU are homozygous for the PKU gene defect, meaning that they have the gene defect from both mother and father. If a person receives a gene defect from one parent but a nondefective gene from the other parent, the person is called heterozygous for the PKU gene defect, will show no signs or symptoms of PKU, but will be a carrier of the gene defect and may have children with PKU. Although much remains to be learned, a good deal has been uncovered about the genetic defects underlying PKU. PKU is caused by mutations on the phenylalanine hydroxylase (PAH) gene. The website for the Phenylalanine Hydroxylase Locus Knowledgebase is http://www.pahdb.mcgill.ca/ . At that site, one will see that more than 500 different mutations on the phenylalanine hydroxylase gene have been identified so far. Moreover, many of these mutations have been evaluated for their severity. To index severity of a mutation, persons with PKU are given a PHE-loading test, ingesting food that is high in PHE. After a specified time to allow food digestion, blood is drawn and evaluated for level of PHE in the blood. Persons with higher levels of PHE in their blood have metabolized less PHE and therefore must have a more severe mutation.

Classifications of the severity of PKU are often used when treating persons with PKU. One common classification is as follows: (a) classic PKU, indexed by PHE levels of 20 mg/dL or more; (b) moderate PKU, indexed by PHE levels between 15 and 20 mg/dL; (c) mild PKU, indexed by PHE levels between 10 and 15 mg/dL; (d) mild hyperphenylalaninemia, indexed by PHE levels between 3 and 10 mg/dL; and (e) normal, indexed by PHE levels below 3 mg/dL. Persons with more severe mutations on the PAH gene are more sensitive to PHE in their diet, so require greater monitoring to ensure that low levels of PHE are maintained. At first, experts advised parents that children with PKU should remain on a low-PHE diet for the first decade or so of life, but most experts now advise parents to keep children with PKU on a low-PHE diet at least throughout the developmental period (or into the early 20s). Once the central nervous system has completed its development, discontinuing the low-PHE diet is often accompanied by either no notable cognitive effects or minor cognitive problems or regressions that can be ameliorated by resuming a low-PHE diet.

Because such cognitive problems are possible, many physicians now advise patients with PKU to remain on a low-PHE diet throughout life.

In many ways, the story of PKU—including detection of the PKU syndrome, development of a proper diet, and development of an accurate and simple detection test—is a scientific success story. Until the early 1960s, biology was destiny, and the heritability of the PKU phenotype was very high. If a child were homozygous for the PKU mutation, diagnosis of the presence of PKU usually happened so late during development (even if during infancy or early childhood) that severe, lasting brain damage had occurred and could not be remedied. Then, after development of the Guthrie screening test, children could be placed early and continuously on a low-PHE diet, and brain damage could be largely or completely circumvented. Moreover, the heritability of the PKU syndrome fell to very low levels in a single generation, due to a key environmental manipulation—the use of a low-PHE diet.

Maternal PKU

The success of medical science in treating PKU is well known, but less widely known are the potentially devastating effects of maternal PKU. The first reports of negative birth outcomes for women with PKU surfaced in the late 1970s. In a seminal paper, Lenke and Levy (1980) reported results of more than 500 pregnancies of untreated women with PKU, or women who were not on a low-PHE diet during pregnancy. Infants born to mothers with PKU had a high rate of various birth defects even though these infants never would have exhibited symptoms of PKU because they were heterozygous for the PAH gene defect. Instead, the high level of PHE in the mother's blood passed the placental barrier and exposed the developing fetus to high levels of PHE in the prenatal environment. The extent of the birth defects was extreme. Lenke and Levy reported that more than 90% of infants born to mothers with classic PKU had mental retardation, and more than 70% had microcephaly. Of infants born to mothers with moderate PKU, more than 70% percent had mental retardation, and 68% had microcephaly. Infants born to mothers with mild PKU or mild hyperphenylalaninemia were less affected by prenatal exposure to PHE, presumably due to being exposed to lower levels of PHE in the prenatal environment; but, rates of mental retardation and microcephaly for these offspring still ranged between 20% and 35%, much higher than in a normal population.

The Maternal PKU Collaborative (MPKUC) Study was initiated in 1984 to monitor the pregnancies of women with PKU. The aims of the study were first to intervene and attempt to maintain the mothers on a low-PHE diet during their pregnancies and second to study the relation between levels of PHE in the mothers' blood during pregnancy and birth outcomes of the offspring.

Four coordinating centers across the United States monitored pregnancies in 78 clinics across the country, and one center in Canada and one in Germany followed pregnancies in those countries. The MPKUC Study enrolled pregnant women in the study through 1996, and the 413 offspring of the pregnancies were assessed at five points: birth, 1 year, 2 years, 4 years, and 7 years.

Timing of Exposure to PHE. All 413 offspring comprising the sample of child participants in the MPKUC Study were heterozygous for genetic defects on the PAH gene, having received a PAH gene defect only from their mothers and PAH genes without defects from their fathers. So, these children of mothers with PKU never would have exhibited any signs or symptoms of PKU at any point in their lives because they would have metabolized PHE normally. However, these children were exposed to varying levels of PHE exposure during gestation, as indexed by PHE in the mother's blood. Therefore, the exposure to PHE that is the apparent driving force behind any maladaptive developmental outcomes must have occurred prior to birth, during prenatal development.

Note, however, that the period of gestation is a prolonged one, having an average duration of 9 months. Exposure to high levels of PHE at early points in gestation might have rather different effects than exposure to high levels of PHE at later points in gestation, and these differential effects of differential timing of PHE exposure may vary across outcome variables. Matalon, Acosta, Azen, and Matalon (1999) found that exposure to high levels of PHE during the first 2 months of gestation led to an increased risk of congenital heart disease, particularly if accompanied by low levels of dietary protein intake. Presumably, exposure to PHE was particularly crucial for congenital heart problems if this exposure occurred during the first 2 months of gestation because that is the period during which the basic structure of the heart is developed. If brain structures that are crucial for intellectual abilities undergo major structural development or differentiation later in gestation, then PHE exposure at later points in gestation may be more crucial for predicting intellectual deficiencies. At present, these ideas regarding the importance of timing of PHE exposure during gestation for intellectual outcomes represent conjectures, which should be followed up in future research.

Patterning of Exposure to PHE. Several different ways of assessing or representing PHE exposure were computed based on the multiple measures of PHE obtained from maternal blood samples during pregnancy, and each of these measures reflected hypotheses concerning the pattern of exposure to PHE that had the strongest relation to offspring intellectual outcomes. The first measure, referred to in shorthand form as *average PHE during pregnancy*, was the simple average of all PHE readings obtained from blood samples taken during the pregnancy. This measure is consistent with the hypothesis that (a) consistent and chronic exposure to PHE is most likely to affect the fetus, and (b) the average of all PHE measurements throughout the entire pregnancy is the best index of this consistent and chronic exposure. A second measure was the standard deviation of all PHE measurements during pregnancy, under the hypothesis that occasional peaks in PHE exposure might be more damaging to the fetus than would chronic, lower levels of exposure. Two additional measures were scored as the week during pregnancy after which all subsequent PHE readings were below 6 mg/dL or below 10 mg/dL. Prior work on prenatal PHE exposure suggested that some value between 6 and 10 mg/dL might be an important threshold, with exposure below the threshold unlikely to lead to important negative outcomes. In addition, the earlier during pregnancy an expectant mother kept her PHE levels controlled below a critical level, the better the intrauterine environment for the developing fetus. Research on data from the MPKUC Study consistently found that average PHE during pregnancy was more strongly related to child outcomes at each of the times of measurement than were the other measures of PHE exposure, so I concentrate later on this indicator of prenatal exposure to PHE.

Functional Form Relating PHE Exposure to Intellectual Outcomes. Because average PHE during pregnancy was most strongly related to intellectual outcomes, several functional forms were entertained for the relation between PHE exposure and child outcomes. The two primary models were the standard linear regression model and a two-piece linear spline model. Results enabling the comparison of these models are shown in Table 17.1. In Table 17.1, the infant outcomes were the Mental Development Index (MDI) and the Psychomotor Development Index (PDI) from the Bayley Scales of Infant Development, which was used in the assessment battery at infant ages 1 year and 2 years. Then, at 4 years of age, the McCarthy Scales of Children's Abilities was used, yielding a General Cognitive Index (GCI) that is a full-scale score; at 7 years of child age, participants were administered the Wechsler Intelligence Scale for Children–Revised, that provided Verbal IQ (VIQ), Performance IQ (PIQ), and Full Scale IQ (FSIQ) scores. All three assessment instruments yield scores that fall on a typical IQ scale metric, with population mean and *SD* of 100 and 15, respectively, and all scores will be referred to here as IQ scores, although the lack of strong relation between infant intelligence scores and later adolescent IQ scores suggests large changes across ages in the constructs assessed using these instruments. Additional outcome measures were assessed at each of the four times of measurement, but the results shown in Table 17.1 are representative of findings.

When considering models, the first reasonable model was a simple linear model. Under this model, the intercept provides an estimate of offspring IQ if average PHE exposure were zero, and the slope estimates the change, here a decrease, in IQ for every one mg/dL increase in PHE exposure. However, researchers have long presumed that some form of threshold for PHE exposure might be reasonable, with no negative effects of exposure up to some critical level of mg/dL, after which a teratogenic effect would be expected. Therefore, I also fit a restricted form of two-piece linear spline model to the outcome variables. This spline model had three parameters: an intercept, a threshold or knot point, and a slope after the knot point. Many two-piece linear spline models have four parameters, allowing a slope between the intercept and knot point in addition to the three parameters listed above. But, such a model would not be in accord with the theory proposed by MPKUC Study researchers, who thought that PHE exposure would have no effect at all until the threshold or knot point. Therefore, in my restricted three-parameter model, the intercept provides an estimate of IQ for any level of PHE exposure between 0 mg/dL and the knot point, the knot point estimates the level of PHE exposure at which a teratogenic effect of exposure begins to occur, and the slope is an estimate of the change, or decrease, in IQ for every one mg/dL increase beyond the threshold or knot point.

As shown in Table 17.1, the linear regression model explained a large amount of variance for each of the eight outcome variables listed. However, with a single exception (i.e., the MDI at 2 years of age), the two-piece linear spline model explained more variance than did the linear regression model. This might be expected from a statistical point of view: the linear regression model was a two-parameter model, having intercept and slope parameters, whereas the two-piece linear model was a three-parameter model, with intercept, knot, and slope-after-knot estimates. Hence, that a three-parameter model explains data better than does a two-parameter model is not surprising, at least based on the consideration of the number of parameter estimates. But, as discussed in the next section, the mere better fit of one model over another is less important than the degree to which either model captures trends in the data.

Numerical Constants of the Function. One preliminary numerical outcome of model fitting is the variance explained by an equation. As shown in Table 17.1, the linear model accounted for about 35% of the variance of MDI scores in infancy and about 23% of variance in PDI scores. In comparison, the spline models explained about 36% of variance in MDI scores and 25% of variance in PDI scores, not a major increase in variance explained. However, a plot of MDI scores at 1 year of age including the predicted scores from the two-piece linear spline is shown in Figure 17.4, and this figure gives visual evidence that the spline model is a good representation of the data, with no apparent effect of average PHE exposure during pregnancy until some moderate level of exposure is attained. For MDI scores at 1 year of age, this threshold was estimated as 6.60 mg/dL (SE = 0.67). The resulting equation thus represents PHE exposure during pregnancy as having no effect on MDI scores until average PHE exposure

FIGURE 17.4

Two-piece linear spline model for predicting Bayley Mental Developmental Index scores at 1 years of age from average PHE level in the mother's blood during pregnancy.

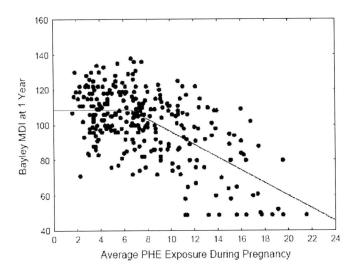

reaches 6.60 mg/dL, after which point every increase of one mg/dL of PHE exposure is associated with a 3.62 point predicted drop in MDI scores.

Continuing to consider variance explained values, note that both the linear regression and two-piece spline models explain even more variance in outcomes at later child ages, with linear models explaining between 41% and 47% of the variance of outcomes at 4 and 7 years of age, and spline models explaining 42% and 50% of the variance. This is a signal finding: As the length of time increases between exposure to PHE and assessed outcome, the relation between these variables increases in strength. This pattern contrasts with typical findings in developmental psychology, in which a contextual influence tends to have larger effects in the near term, but any effects of the influence are smaller and smaller as the length of time between exposure to the influence and the outcome increases. Thus, over time, the impact of the contextual influence decreases. In the present situation, the strength of the relation between the contextual influence—average PHE exposure during pregnancy—and the developmental outcome increases in strength.

Next, we should consider the parameter estimates associated with the linear and spline models. As seen in Table 17.1, the intercept estimate in each of the eight linear regression models fell between 112 and 121, which is the estimated

TABLE 17.1
Predicting Infancy and Childhood Cognitive Outcomes From Measures of Maternal Average PHE
Level During Pregnancy

Outcome Variable	Equation	Intercept SE	Slope SE	Knot SE	R_2	F	df	RMSE
Outcomes at 1 years of age								
MDI	Linear	121.43 (2.06)	-2.72 (0.23)		.331	136.47	1.276	16.17
	Spline	108.42 (1.44)	-3.62 (0.37)	6.60 (0.67)	.358	68.12	2,275	15.87
PDI	Linear	113.53 (2.06)	-1.98 (0.23)		.214	71.27	1,262	16.09
	Spline	104.71 (1.53)	-2.54 (0.35)	6.03 (0.98)	.238	40.31	2,261	15.87
Outcomes at 2 years of age								
MDI	Linear	121.34 (2.42)	-3.11 (0.28)		.359	126.55	1.266	18.16
	Spline	110.21 (2.40)	-3.26 (0.35)	3.39 (1.01)	.355	60.04	2,225	18.25
PDI	Linear	116.97 (2.47)	-2.45 (0.29)		.254	69.98	1.206	17.72
	Spline	106.51 (1.89)	-2.97 (0.44)	5.60 (1.05)	.261	36.20	2,205	17.67

(continued)

average IQ for any offspring exposed to an average PHE level of zero mg/dL during pregnancy. Given the nature of this sample of mothers with PKU, exposure to an average of zero mg/dL of PHE during pregnancy would be unlikely; from Figure 17.1, it appears that the lowest average PHE levels during pregnancy observed in this sample were approximately 2 mg/dL. Still, a predicted IQ score about one standard deviation above the mean or higher if average PHE levels were nil seems an unrealistic estimate. As for slope estimates, these ranged between about -2 and -3.5, indicating that IQ scores would decrease between 2 and 3.5 points for every additional 1 mg/dL of PHE exposure above zero mg/dL.

TABLE 17.1 (continued)

Outcome Variable	Equation	Intercept SE	Slope SE	Knot SE	R_2	F	df	RMSE
Outcomes at 4 years of age								
GCI	Linear	112.12 (2.17)	-3.23 (0.23)		.413	192.68	1,274	16.31
	Spline	99.51 (2.28)	-3.41 (0.28)	4.31 (0.85)	.419	55.09	2,273	16.25
Outcomes at 7 years of age								
VIQ	Linear	118.59 (2.08)	-3.35 (0.23)		.429	209.96	1,280	16.85
	Spline	103.78 (1.63)	-4.01 (0.33)	5.66 (0.63)	.451	46.97	2,279	16.54
PIQ	Linear	118.12 (2.02)	-3.29 (0.22)		.434	214.54	1,280	16.40
	Spline	101.99 (1.36)	-4.43 (0.36)	6.82 (0.55)	.474	54.97	2,279	15.84
FSIQ	Linear	120.17 (2.07)	-3.64 (0.23)		.471	249.41	1,280	16.79
	Spline	102.69 (1.64)	-4.73 (0.33)	6.56 (0.61)	.504	57.50	2,279	16.29

Note. For child outcome variables, MDI and PDI stand for the Mental Development Index and Psychomotor Development Index, respectively, from the Bayley Scales of Infant Development, GCI for the General Cognitive Index from the McCarthy Scales of Children's Intelligence, and VIQ, PIQ, and FSIQ for the Verbal IQ, Performance IQ, and Full Scale IQ scores, respectively, from the Wechsler Intelligence Scale for Children. Intercept is the additive constant in the regression model, Slope is the predicted change in IQ for each increment of 1 mg/dL of PHE exposure, and Knot is the point (in mg/dL) in spline models after which the effect of PHE exposure on child outcome begins to take place. R^2 is the squared multiple correlation for the regression analysis, F is the F ratio for the full equation, df provides the numerator and denominator degrees of freedom, and RMSE is the root mean square error, or residual SD of the outcome variable. All squared multiple correlations significant at $p < .001$.

Turning to the spline models, the intercept estimates are much more reasonable values than was the case for the linear models, ranging between 100 and 110, and at the more mature ages of 4 and 7 years the intercept values fell between 100 and 104, very close to the mean of the population. The threshold or knot point values varied somewhat across analyses, but they appear to average around 6 mg/dL, so that exposure below this level is not associated with a teratogenic effect. Finally, estimates of the slope after the knot point ranged between about -2.5 and -4.7. Probably the most relevant for predicting outcomes in maturity are results presented for the VIQ, PIQ, and FSIQ at 7 years of age. There, the intercepts fell very close to the population mean, varying between 102 and 104, the knot points averaged around 6.3 or 6.4 mg/dL, and the slopes after the knot point averaged near -4.4. These results suggest that low levels of PHE exposure during pregnancy are unlikely to have any teratogenic effect on intelligence, that the teratogenic effect on intelligence begins at about 6.4 mg/dL, and that the predicted decline in intelligence is about 4.4 points for every 1 mg/dL increase after the knot point of 6.4 mg/dL. Thus, the predicted mean IQ score for persons who experience an average PHE exposure during pregnancy of 10 mg/dL would be $[(10 - 6.4)$ X $-4.4] = -15.8$ points, or approximately one SD below the performance of persons experiencing less than 6.4 mg/dL PHE exposure.

Specificity of the Effects of PHE Exposure. Results presented in this chapter demonstrate that, across the outcomes considered here, effects of PHE exposure during pregnancy occur for all of the developmental outcomes evaluated, hence are not specific to one subdomain of functioning. That is, PHE exposure during pregnancy could have influenced only certain of the outcome measures, such as affecting only the PIQ rather than the VIQ from the WISC administered at age 7 years. However, all of the infant and child intelligence measures appear to be affected by exposure to high levels of PHE during pregnancy.

In research not reported in detail in this chapter, Matalon et al. (1999) found that high levels of PHE exposure during the first 2 months of pregnancy led to a much higher risk for congenital heart disease, particularly if these high levels of PHE exposure were accompanied by low levels of protein intake by the mother. Also, Rouse et al., (1997) reported that high levels of PHE exposure were associated with a range of craniofacial anomalies and malformations in offspring. Thus, the teratogenic effects of PHE exposure during pregnancy are not limited to the intelligence domain, but effects are seen in various forms of physical development. Given the limited range of psychological measures administered during the MPKUC Study, one cannot judge just how broad the effects of prenatal exposure to PHE may be. For example, high levels of PHE exposure might well affect personality, social functioning, and so forth. Given the effects on intelligence and on physical development, including heart problems and craniofacial anomalies, teratogenic effects of high levels of PHE exposure are likely to occur across a quite broad set of domains.

Timing of the Effect of PHE Exposure. Again, given results presented in this chapter, the effects of high levels of PHE exposure appear to be immediate, rather than delayed. As discussed in the next section, high levels of prenatal PHE exposure led to smaller infant size, indexed by lower weight and shorter length, and had an even stronger effect on head size. Thus, the effects of prenatal PHE exposure were evident at birth. Then, strong effects of prenatal PHE exposure were found at each of the four times of measurement—at child age 1, 2, 4, and 7 years. Not only were the effects of prenatal PHE exposure strongly evident at birth and at 1 year of child age, but, as discussed earlier, the effects only grew stronger at later times of measurement. Therefore, the timing of the effects of PHE exposure were immediate, but also varied—with stronger effects at later, more mature ages.

Directness of Effects of PHE Exposure. The final issue to be considered here is whether prenatal exposure to PHE has direct effects on infant and child intellectual outcomes and, if so, whether the direct effects of prenatal exposure to PHE trump those of more traditional predictors of infant and child intellectual outcomes, including maternal IQ, education, and socioeconomic status (SES). I note in passing that maternal IQ, education, and SES are often also considered to be contextual variables, with mothers having higher status on any or all of these three variables tending to provide more positive environments for their developing offspring. Therefore, researchers might concentrate on the traditional maternal background variables when identifying contextual variables or related processes that are likely to affect child intellectual outcomes. However, research on children of mothers with PKU suggests that the intrauterine environment may be far more powerful in determining later levels of child intelligence than are the traditional predictors, so I am concentrating on the intrauterine environment as encompassing the contextual processes that deserve the most dedicated interest here.

An initial specification of relations between maternal background variables and child outcomes would include paths from each of the maternal variables to each of the child outcomes. When this was done, but restricting attention here only to the infant outcomes at ages 1 and 2 years, many of the path coefficients were statistically significant, but others were nonsignificant. Deleting paths that were nonsignificant led to the model shown in Figure 17.5. As shown in Figure 17.5, all five maternal background variables had significant effects on infant MDI scores at 1 year, with the strongest effects associated with mother's SES ($\beta =$ .28), mother's IQ ($\beta = .21$), and the severity of the mutation on the mother's PAH gene ($\beta = -.21$). These results suggest that higher levels of maternal SES and IQ are associated with higher levels of infant mental development at 1 year,

FIGURE 17.5

Initial model of the relations between maternal background variables and offspring outcome variables.

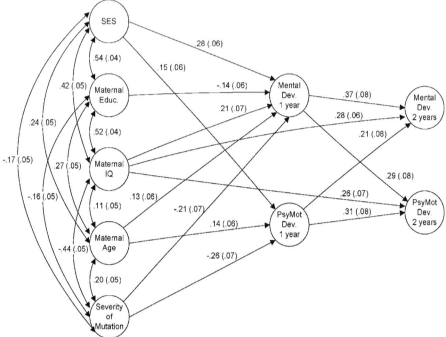

and that higher levels of severity of the mother's PAH mutation are associated with lower levels of infant mental development—all of these findings were in the expected directions.

In contrast, only three background variables had significant effects on psychomotor development scores at 1 year, and only one of these effects was greater than .20 in absolute magnitude—the effect of severity of the mother's PAH mutation (β = -.26). Again, this effect was in the expected direction, but psychomotor development was not as broadly affected by maternal background variables as was mental development.

Turning to mental development and psychomotor development outcomes at 2 years of age, we find moderate levels of stability in both mental development (β = .37) and psychomotor development (β = .31), as well as cross-lagged paths from earlier mental to later psychomotor development (β = .29) and from earlier psychomotor to later mental development (β = .21). Of even more interest is the need to specify direct paths from maternal IQ to both mental development (β = .28) and psychomotor development (β = .26) at age 2 years. Even though maternal IQ had indirect effects on both outcomes at 2 years through its effects

FIGURE 17.6

Final model of the relations between maternal background variables, pregnancy-related variables, birth outcome measures, and infant intelligence measures.

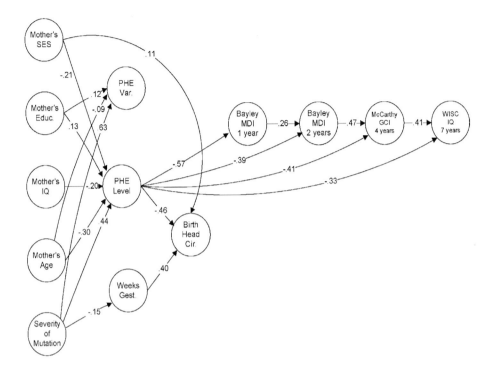

on those variables at 1 year, additional direct paths were required to explain the patterns in the data. Note that maternal IQ was the only one of the five background variables that needed direct paths to the outcomes at 2 years of child age, attesting to the importance of maternal IQ in understanding later levels of infant development.

When the pregnancy-related and birth outcome variables were added into the model, variables that comprised Sets B and C in Figure 17.3, a very different impression of the developmental outcomes is seen. The final model is shown in Figure 17.6. In Figure 17.6, we see that all five maternal background variables have effects on PHE level during pregnancy, the most important indicator for which was average PHE in the mother's blood. Of these effects, the strongest was for severity of mother's PAH gene mutation ($\beta = .44$), but maternal age also had a strong effect ($\beta = -.30$). Of the remaining three effects, two were above .20 in absolute magnitude, the effects of maternal IQ ($\beta = -.20$) and maternal SES ($\beta = -.21$). All four of these coefficients were in the predicted direction, with lower (i.e., better) levels of PHE in the mother's blood during pregnancy for mothers with less severe PAH gene mutations and with higher levels of age, IQ, and SES. But, note that the most important of these effects were for severity of the mother's PAH gene mutation and maternal age. The effect of severity of PAH gene mutation underscores the difficulty that mothers with more severe mutations have in keeping their PHE levels under control. In addition, it may be that older mothers had a better understanding of the need to stay more carefully on a prescribed diet to keep their PHE levels low, hence the relatively large path from maternal age to average PHE level. Once these two background variables were controlled statistically, the remaining background variables—including maternal IQ—were more weakly related to PHE level during pregnancy.

The model in Figure 17.6 shows that the maternal background variables had effects on other pregnancy-related variables, such as variability in PHE values during pregnancy and weeks gestation, but these results are of less interest because these other pregnancy-related variables were not directly related to later infant and child intellectual outcomes. Next, consider the birth outcome of head circumference. This outcome was strongly affected by average PHE level during pregnancy ($\beta = -.46$) and weeks gestation ($\beta = .40$). Both of these effects were in the expected direction: Higher levels of PHE during pregnancy were associated with smaller head circumference in offspring, suggesting that developing fetuses subjected to high prenatal levels of PHE were at much greater risk of microcephaly, a well-known predictor of later mental retardation. Additionally, fetuses with longer gestational periods had larger head circumferences, an expected effect. But, despite the prominence of microcephaly as a predictor of later lower levels of intelligence, the model in Figure 17.6 shows that birth head circumference was not a predictor of later intelligence if average PHE level during pregnancy was allowed to predict the later child outcomes.

The most impressive set of outcomes shown in Figure 17.6 involve the effects of average PHE level during pregnancy on later infant and child intellectual outcomes. As shown, PHE level had a strong effect on mental development at 1 year ($\beta = -.57$). Then, the infant and child mental outcomes had a semblance of first-order autoregressive effects, as mental development at 1 year had a moderate effect on mental development at 2 years ($\beta = .26$), mental development at 2 years had a strong effect on IQ at 4 years ($\beta = .47$), and IQ at 4 years had a fairly strong effect on IQ at 7 years ($\beta = .41$). However, PHE level during pregnancy had moderate-to-strong direct effects on mental development at 2 years ($\beta = -.39$), IQ at 4 years ($\beta = -.41$), and IQ at 7 years ($\beta = -.33$). These represent additional direct influences in addition to the indirect effects that PHE level during pregnancy had on these outcome through its effects on the infant and childhood outcomes that precede each of these outcomes.

The final notable aspect of the model in Figure 17.6 is the lack of any direct effects of maternal background variables, particularly maternal IQ, on any of the infant or child intellectual outcomes. Thus, the effects of maternal IQ on infant and child outcomes are mediated completely by average PHE level during pregnancy. As mentioned earlier, maternal IQ had an effect on average PHE level during pregnancy, whereby mothers with higher IQ had lower levels of PHE. But, once the effects of average PHE level on later infant and child intellectual outcomes were estimated, maternal IQ had no direct effect at all on these later outcomes. Instead, the environmental or contextual variable of average PHE level during pregnancy—which constituted a most important prenatal influence on the developing fetus—had strong and continuing direct effects on child intellectual outcomes at all ages between 1 year and 7 years.

CONCLUSIONS

The present chapter had three major goals. The first goal was a brief discussion of the types of models that have been proposed for environmental effects on ontogenetic development of human infants and children. The major models developed to date have stressed the social ecology of the child, which encompasses an extremely important, and perhaps *the* important, aspects of the environment *in general* in the lives of children. But, at least two attendant shortcomings accompany such a focus: By concentrating on aspects of the child's ecology that are important influences in general, one might fail to identify equally important nonsocial influences that operate in particular situations; and by ignoring or downplaying aspects of physical ecology, one might fail to include contextual influences that rival the effects of processes from social ecology.

The second major goal was presentation of a number of considerations that arise when attempting to specify the effect of a contextual variable on an outcome. The seven issues included: (a) timing of exposure to a contextual influence; (b) patterning of the contextual influence; (c) functional form of the relation between contextual influence and outcomes; (d) numerical constants describing the contextual influence—outcome relation; (e) specificity of effects of the contextual influence; (f) timing of effects of the contextual influence; and (g) directness of effects of the contextual influence on outcomes. In seminal work on the relations between attitudes and behavior, Ajzen and Fishbein (e.g., 1980) argued that great specificity was needed in identifying the behavioral action, the target of the action, the context within which the action would occur, and the time frame involved. Only if great care were taken to specify precisely these aspects of the behavioral referents of attitudes and behaviors could advances be made in understanding the relations between attitudes and behaviors.

The focus here on the seven characteristics of environmental effects is an impetus in the same direction. It is impossible to state "the" effect of a given contextual variable, because there is no single effect of a contextual variable. Instead, one must specify when in the child's life the contextual variable was experienced, what the pattern of application of that contextual variable was, what the functional form of the relation between contextual variable and outcome was, and so forth. Only if one characterizes the nature of the contextual variable and the nature of the relations between the contextual variable and specified outcomes at various child ages will an understanding be possible of the effects of contextual variables on child outcome variables or behaviors.

The third and final goal of the chapter was the presentation of research results from the MPKU Collaborative Study, a study of the development of children born to mothers with PKU. These results were presented to allow the opportunity to demonstrate how a salient contextual variable might have direct effects on important child outcome variables. These results demonstrated that (a) the developing organism was exposed to the contextual influence prior to birth, during gestation; (b) the patterning of the influence of average PHE level, based on the measure used, was chronic and repetitious and encompassed the entire gestational period; (c) the functional form of the relation between the contextual influence—exposure to PHE during gestation—and each intellectual outcome was nonlinear, specifically, a two-piece linear spline; (d) the numerical constants that described this spline relation, for intelligence assessed at child age 7 years, were an intercept of approximately 100, a knot point around 6.5 to 6.8 mg/dL, and a linear predicted decrease of 4.5 IQ points for every 1.0 mg/dL increase in PHE above the knot point; (e) the effects of exposure to high levels of PHE prenatally are not highly specific, as this contextual variable had important teratogenic effects on other outcomes such as heart disease and craniofacial anomalies; (f) the timing of the effect of the contextual influence appeared to be immediate, rather than delayed, with effects on birth outcomes as well as effects on outcomes at all ages in infancy and childhood at which assessments were conducted; and (g) the effect of PHE exposure during gestation on later infant and child intellectual outcomes appears to be direct, rather than mediated, even through middle childhood.

Proper modeling of the effects of contextual influences on development of individuals throughout the life span is a challenging, daunting task. Complicated processes are at work, affecting development through complex interactions and transactions. The principal goal of the practicing scientist has several prongs: thorough understanding of theory in the area, use of the best measures and study designs, and optimal selection or development of statistical methods that capture optimally the processes under study and their effects. The present chapter was concerned primarily with the last of these prongs, and I hope that the issues surveyed here will add some statistical tools or concepts that can aid others in pursuing these aims.

ACKNOWLEDGMENTS

This research was supported in part by Grant DA017902 from the National Institute on Drug Abuse and the National Institute on Alcohol Abuse and Alcoholism (Rand Conger, Principal Investigator). The helpful comments by Katherine Gibbs, Rand Conger, and the editors of this volume on many aspects of this chapter are gratefully acknowledged.

REFERENCES

Ajzen, I., & Fishbein, M. (1980). *Understanding attitudes and predicting social behaviors.* Englewood Cliffs, NJ: Prentice-Hall.

Baltes, P. B., & Nesselroade, J. R. (1979). History and rationale of longitudinal research. In J. R. Nesselroade & P. B. Baltes (Eds.), *Longitudinal research in the study of behavior and development* (pp. 1-40). New York: Academic Press.

Barker, D. J. P. (1998). *Mothers, babies, and health in later life* (2nd ed.). Edinburgh: Churchill Livingstone.

Bayley, N. (1949). Consistency and variability in the growth of intelligence from birth to eighteen years. *Journal of Genetic Psychology, 75,* 165-196.

Bickel, H., Gerrard, J., & Hickmans, E. M. (1953). Inuence of phenylalanine intake on phenylketonuria. *The Lancet, 262,* 812-813.

Bickel, H., Gerrard, J., & Hickmans, E. M. (1954). Influence of phenylalanine intake on the chemistry and behavior of a phenylketonuric child. *Acta Paediatrica, 43,* 64-77.

Bloom, B. S. (1964). *Stability and change in human characteristics.* New York: Wiley.

Bradley, R. H. (1999). The home environment. In S. L. Friedman & T. D. Wachs (Eds.), *Measuring environment across the life span: Emerging methods and concepts* (pp. 31-58). Washington, DC: American Psychological Association.

Bronfenbrenner, U. (1977). Toward an experimental ecology of human development. *American Psychologist, 32,* 513-531.

Bronfenbrenner, U. (1986a). Ecology of the family as a context for human development: Research perspectives. *Developmental Psychology, 22,* 723-742.

Bronfenbrenner, U. (1986b). Recent advances in research on the ecology of human development. In R. K. Silbereisen, K. Eyferth, & G. Rudinger (Eds.), *Development as action in context: Problem behavior and normal youth development* (pp. 287-309). Heidelberg: Springer-Verlag.

Bronfenbrenner, U. (1999). Environments in developmental perspective: Theoretical and operational models. In S. L. Friedman & T. D. Wachs (Eds.), *Measuring environment across the life span: Emerging methods and concepts* (pp. 3-28). Washington, DC: American Psychological Association.

Brown, B. B. (1999). Measuring the peer environment of american adolescents. In S. L. Friedman & T. D. Wachs (Eds.), *Measuring environment across the life span: Emerging methods and concepts* (pp. 59-90). Washington, DC: American Psychological Association.

Chiodo, L. M., Jacobson, S. W., & Jacobson, J. L. (2004). Neurodevelopmental effects of postnatal lead exposure at very low levels. *Neurotoxicology and Teratology, 26*, 359-371.

Cohen, J., Cohen, P., West, S. G., & Aiken, L. S. (2003). *Applied multiple regression/correlation analysis for the behavioral sciences* (3rd ed.). Mahwah, NJ: Lawrence Erlbaum Associates.

Colombo, J., & Frick, J. (1999). Recent advances and issues in the study of preverbal intelligence. In M. Anderson (Ed.), *The development of intelligence: Studies in developmental psychology* (pp. 43-71). Hove, England: Psychology Press/Taylor & Francis.

Dilworth-Bart, J. E., & Moore, C. F. (2006). Mercy mercy me: Social injustice and the prevention of environmental pollutant exposures among ethnic minority and poor children. *Child Development, 77*, 247-265.

Dyer, C. A. (1999). Pathophysiology of phenylketonuria. *Mental Retardation and Developmental Disabilities Research Reviews, 5*, 104-112.

Evans, G. W. (1999). Measurement of the physical environment as a stressor. In S. L. Friedman & T. D. Wachs (Eds.), *Measuring environment across the life span: Emerging methods and concepts* (pp. 249-277). Washington, DC: American Psychological Association.

Fagan, J. F., & Detterman, D. K. (1992). The Fagan Test of Infant Intelligence: A technical summary. *Journal of Applied Developmental Psychology, 13*, 173-193.

Friedman, S. L., & Amadeo, J.-A. (1999). The child-care environment: Conceptualizations, assessments, and issues. In S. L. Friedman & T. D. Wachs (Eds.), *Measuring environment across the life span: Emerging methods and concepts* (pp. 127-165). Washington, DC: American Psychological Association.

Friedman, S. L., & Wachs, T. D. (1999). *Measuring environment across the life span: Emerging methods and concepts.* Washington, DC: American Psychological Association.

Gauderman, W. J., Avol, E., Gilliland, F., Vora, H., Thomas, D., Berhane, K., et al. (2004). The effect of air pollution on lung development from 10 to 28 years of age. *New England Journal of Medicine, 351*, 1057-1067.

Gauderman, W. J., Gilliland, G. F., Vora, H., Avol, E., Stram, D., Mc-Connell, R., et al. (2002). Association between air pollution and lung function growth in southern california children: Results from a second cohort. *American Journal of Respiratory and Critical Care Medicine, 166*, 76-84.

Ge, X., Conger, R. D., Lorenz, F. O., Elder, G. H., Jr, Montague, R. B., & Simons, R. L. (1992). Linking family economic hardship to adolescent distress. *Journal of Research on Adolescence, 2*, 351-378.

Gibbs, L. M. (1983). Community response to an emergency situation: Psychological destruction and the Love Canal. *American Journal of Community Psychology,*

11, 116-125.

Hubbs-Tait, L., Nation, J. R., Krebs, N. F., & Bellinger, D. C. (2005). Neurotoxicants, micronutrients, and social environments: Individual and combined effects on children's development. *Psychological Science in the Public Interest, 6*, 57-121.

Isabella, R. A. (1993). Origins of attachment: Maternal interactive behavior across the first year. *Child Development, 64*, 605-621.

Jerrett, M., Burnett, R. T., Ma, R., Pope, C. A., III, Krewski, D., Newbold, K. B., et al. (2005). Spatial analysis of air pollution and mortality in los angeles. *Epidemiology, 16*, 727-736.

Lawton, M. P. (1999). Environmental taxonomy: Generalizations from research with older adults. In S. L. Friedman & T. D. Wachs (Eds.), *Measuring environment across the life span: Emerging methods and concepts* (pp. 91-124). Washington, DC: American Psychological Association.

Lenke, R. R., & Levy, H. L. (1980). Maternal phenylketonuria and hyper-phenylalaninemia: An international survey of the outcome of untreated and treated pregnancies. *New England Journal of Medicine, 303*, 1202-1208.

Matalon, K. M., Acosta, P., Azen, C., & Matalon, R. (1999). Congenital heart disease in maternal phenylketonuria: Effects of blood phenylalanine and nutrient intake. *Mental Retardation and Developmental Disabilities Research Reviews, 5*, 122-124.

McConnell, R., Berhane, K., Gilliland, F., London, S. J., Islam, T., Gauderman, W. J., et al. (2002). Asthma in exercising children exposed to ozone: A cohort study. *Lancet, 359*, 386-391.

Plomin, R., DeFries, J. C., McClearn, G. E., & Rutter, M. (1997). *Behavior genetics* (3rd ed.). San Francisco: W. H. Freeman.

Pope, C. A., III, Burnett, R. T., Thurston, G. D., Thun, M. J., Calle, E. E., Krewski, D., et al. (2004). Cardiovascular mortality and longterm exposure to particulate air pollution: Epidemiological evidence of general pathophysiological pathways of disease. *Circulation, 109*, 71-77.

Rahill, A. A. (1989). The effects of prenatal environmental toxin exposure (dioxin): A case study. In D. L. Peck (Ed.), *Psychosocial effects of hazardous toxic waste disposal on communities* (pp. 13-29). Springfield, IL: Charles C. Thomas.

Rouse, B., Azen, C., Koch, R., Matalon, R., Hanley, W., Cruz, F. de la, et al. (1997). Maternal Phenylketonuria Collaborative Study (MPKUCS) offspring: Facial anomalies, malformations, and early neurological sequelae. *American Journal of Medical Genetics, 69*, 89-95.

Scarr, S. (1992). Developmental theories for the 1990s: Development and individual differences. *Child Development, 63*, 1-19.

Schooler, C. (1999). The workplace environment: Measurement, psychological effects, and basic issues. In S. L. Friedman & T. D. Wachs (Eds.), *Measuring environment across the life span: Emerging methods and concepts* (pp. 229-246). Washington, DC: American Psychological Association.

Steinberg, L., Dornbusch, S. M., & Brown, B. B. (1992). Ethnic differences in adolescent achievement. *American Psychologist, 47*, 723-729.

Stokols, D. (1999). Human development in the age of the internet: Conceptual and methodological horizons. In S. L. Friedman & T. D. Wachs (Eds.), *Measuring environment across the life span: Emerging methods and concepts* (pp.327-356). Washington, DC: American Psychological Association.

Streissguth, A. P., Bookstein, F. L., Barr, H. M., Sampson, P. D., O'Malley, K., & Young, J. K. (2004). Risk factors for adverse life outcomes in fetal alcohol syndrome and fetal alcohol effects. *Journal of Developmental & Behavioral Pediatrics, 25,* 228-238.

Super, C. M., & Harkness, S. (1999). The environment as culture in developmental research. In S. L. Friedman & T. D. Wachs (Eds.), *Measuring environment across the life span: Emerging methods and concepts* (pp. 279-323). Washington, DC: American Psychological Association.

Talbert, J. E., & McLaughlin, M. W. (1999). Assessing the school environment: Embedded contexts and bottom-up research strategies. In S. L. Friedman & T. D. Wachs (Eds.), *Measuring environment across the life span: Emerging methods and concepts* (pp. 197-227). Washington, DC: American Psychological Association.

Thompson, E. A., McCubbin, H. I., Thompson, A. I., & Elver, K. M. (1998). Vulnerability and resiliency in native Hawaiian families under stress. In H. I. McCubbin, E. A. Thompson, A. I. Thompson, & J. E. Fromer (Eds.), *Resiliency in Native American and immigrant families* (pp. 115-131). Thousand Oaks, CA: Sage.

Vandell, D. L., & Posner, J. K. (1999). Conceptualization and measurement of children's after-school environments. In S. L. Friedman & T. D.Wachs (Eds.), *Measuring environment across the life span: Emerging methods and concepts* (pp. 167-196). Washington, DC: American Psychological Association.

Wachs, T. D. (1992). *The nature of nurture.* Newbury Park, CA: Sage.

Wachs, T. D. (1999). Celebrating the complexity: Conceptualization and assessment of the environment. In S. L. Friedman & T. D.Wachs (Eds.), *Measuring environment across the life span: Emerging methods and concepts* (pp. 357-392). Washington, DC: American Psychological Association.

Wachs, T. D. (2000). *Necessary but not sufficient: The respective roles of single and multiple inuences on individual development.* Washington, DC: American Psychological Association.

Wasserman, G. A., Factor-Litvak, P., Liu, X., Todd, A. C., Kline, J. K., Slavkovich, V., et al. (2003). The relationship between blood lead, bone lead and child intelligence. *Child Neuropsychology, 9,* 22-34.

Wohlwill, J. F. (1970). The age variable in psychological research. *Psychological Review, 77,* 49-64.

CHAPTER EIGHTEEN

Conceptualizing and Measuring the Context Within Person ⟸⟹ Context Models of Human Development: Implications for Theory, Research and Application

Helena Jelicic
Tufts University

Christina Theokas
Child Trends

Erin Phelps
Richard M. Lerner
Tufts University

What is the nature of human development and how may we study it? Answers to this question derive from the integrated use of the theoretical and methodological tools of the developmental scientist (e.g., Cairns & Cairns, 2006; Lerner, 2006; Magnusson & Stattin, 2006; Teti, 2005; Valsiner, 2006; Wohlwill, 1970).

Over the course of the past 30 years, the theoretical and metatheoretical bases of depictions of the course of human development have been discussed repeatedly (e.g., see Lerner, 2002; Overton, 2006). This literature has emphasized that choices of methodology are shaped by the metatheoretical (paradigmatic or world view) perspectives of developmental scientists and, in turn, by the theoretical models of ontogenetic change that derive from these philosophical presuppositions. Developmentalists infrequently recognize that views of human development derived from empirical work are shaped largely by methodological features that are not solely determined by theory (e.g., Dixon and Nesselroade, 1883; Lerner, Dowling, and Chaudury, 2005; Lerner, Skinner, and Sorell,

1980; Wohlwill, 1970). Simply, what we see in our data about the bases and course of human life are reflections of both our theoretical proscriptions and prescriptions and our window on the developmental landscape provided by the methodological tools of our science. However, the window on reality provided by the methods of science is, in actuality, many different windows, with each providing a somewhat different exposure to the empirical world. For instance, as Ram and Nesselroade (chap. 14, this volume) explain, the methods of developmental science constitute filters through which our observations of both individuals and settings must pass. These filters determine, first, what observations are regarded as "data" and what are seen as noise or error. Second, our methodological filters determine the substance, shape, and meaning of our data. Methodological choices determine whether our observations are, for instance: (a) treated as additive, interactive, or irrelevant to each other; (b) whether one observation is reducible to another, and therefore qualitatively continuous, or whether data involve noncommensurate variables or levels of organization; (c) whether the distribution of our observations across levels of independent variables are linear or curvilinear; (d) if the set of information we gather may be constituted as a unified phenomenon or if it can or should be partitioned into components, for instance, associated with individual, variable, and temporal sources of variance; (e) or whether our data reflect phenomena that are static and generalizable across time and place or, instead, are dynamic, plastic, and contingent on temporal conditions.

In past eras within developmental science, the theoretical models that framed decisions regarding the choice of methodological filters used to study ontogenetic change were associated with a set of options for research designs, measurement, and data analysis procedures that were quite similar to the methodologies employed in nondevelopmental areas of behavioral and social science. For instance, Bijou and Baer (1961, 1965) forwarded an approach to studying development that emphasized the precedence of experimental or quasi-experimental designs to understand the (environmental) bases of human development. In turn, Nunnally (1982) suggested that a between-within, mixed model analysis of variance design (with "time of measurement" being the within-subject, repeated measurement dimension) was the preferred analytic procedure for assessing longitudinal change.

Developmental scientists' approaches to methodology between the 1960s and 1980s reflected in large part a coupling of theoretical and methodological reductionism (Cairns & Cairns, 2006; Overton, 1998, 2003, 2006). For instance, the discipline of psychology focused on the conceptualization and measurement of the individual and of individual level contributions to the variance in outcomes of changes in developmental processes; however, relatively little attention was paid to the conceptualization and measurement of the changing ecology of human development as more than a context within which individual development unfolded and/or as composed of proximal influences that acted on the individual's behavior (e.g., as the stimulus source for respondent or operant behavior, for example, as in Bijou & Baer, 1961, or Gewirtz & Stingle, 1968). Apart from the enormous contributions of Urie Bronfenbrenner (1977, 1979, 2001, 2005; Bronfenbrenner & Morris, 2006) and Glen Elder (1974, 1980, 1998; Elder & Shanahan, 2006), few efforts were made to conceptualize, measure, and model the multilevel context of human development as levels of organization qualitatively distinct from but impacting the individual.   However, beginning by at least the 1980s, burgeoning in the 1990s, and — at this writing — existing as the predominant metatheoretical and theoretical approach to the study of both human and nonhuman development (see Gottlieb, Walsten, & Lickliter, 2006; Lerner, 2006; Thelen & Smith, 2006), a dynamic, developmental systems theoretical model has been coupled with developmental methodology to constitute a new, nonreductionist, integrative, and multidisciplinary approach to describing, explaining, and optimizing ontogenetic change. Overton (1998, 2006) terms such models *relational*, and notes that their defining feature is a postmodern rejection of Cartesian dualities that have mired developmental science across its history in counterproductive debates about counterfactual splits among the variables and processes involved in human development (e.g., splits involving nature and nurture, organism and environment, maturation and learning, continuity and discontinuity, or stability and instability).

The emergence of a relational and dynamic approach to developmental science has involved mutually influential changes in theory and method. As evidenced by the rich and varied contributions to the present volume, developmental systems theory has required methodologies that measure and analyze the effects of a developmental context that is distinct from but fused with individuals across the life spans. As we explain in greater detail shortly, this focus exists because such models emphasize that the basic unit of analysis within the integrated and dynamic developmental system involves a mutually influential relation between a developing person and a multilevel and changing ecological context (represented as a person ⇐⇒ context relation). Brandtstädter (1998, 2006) explains that these bidirectional relations constitute developmental regulation that, when mutually beneficial to both person and context, reflect adaptation and the basis for the continuation of healthy and positive individual and ecological changes.

As the measurement, modeling, and analysis of contexts has advanced in relation to these theoretical requirements, theoretical innovations have emerged to accommodate new insights about the impact of the context on the course of individual development. Examples of such theoretical innovations deriving from methodological advances fill the pages of the present volume (e.g., Boker &

Laurenceau, chap. 13, this volume, and Bolger & Shrout, chap.12, this volume, in regard to the social dynamics in dyads; Flora, Khoo, & Chassin, chap. 10, this volume, in regard to substance use; Grimm & McArdle, chap. 16, this volume, in regard to life-span changes in cognitive development; Rodgers, chap. 15, this volume, in regard to social development; and Widaman, chap. 17, this volume, in regard to intrauterine influences on intellectual development). In turn, theoretical innovations in understanding the course of person $\Leftarrow\Rightarrow$ context relations have derived from methodological innovations in other laboratories not represented in the present volume (e.g., Eccles, 2004, 2005) as well as in our own laboratory (e.g., Theokas & Lerner, 2006).

In essence, the present volume both reflects and extends significantly the mutually influential theoretical and methodological contributions being made in contemporary developmental science to advancing a dynamic view of the person $\Leftarrow\Rightarrow$ context relations that are the building blocks of the diverse life spans that comprise the landscape of human development. The important contributions of this volume to the description and explanation of human development and, through this work, to applications aimed at optimizing ontogenetic change for diverse groups, may best be discussed within a presentation of the developmental systems theoretical perspective that the scholarship in this book advances so significantly.

We present the conceptual features and foundations of developmental systems theories and point to how the features of such models provide a frame for the advances presented in this book about measures and methods useful for understanding the contributions of the context to the person $\Leftarrow\Rightarrow$ context relations comprising human development. We will note some of the general methodological requirements for research that are designed to test models of human development derived from developmental systems theories. Within this discussion, we indicate how the contributions presented here both reflect and extend these contributions and, through this discussion, we make recommendations for directions for future advances in relational methods and measures pertinent to the integrated and changing developmental system.

DEFINING FEATURES OF DEVELOPMENTAL SYSTEMS THEORIES

We have noted that the focus within the contemporary study of human development is on concepts and models associated with developmental systems theories (Cairns & Cairns, 2006; Gottlieb et al., 2006; Lerner, 2002, 2006; Overton, 2006). The roots of these theories may be linked to ideas in developmental science that were presented at least as early as the 1930s and 1940s (e.g., Maier & Schneirla, 1935; Novikoff, 1945a, 1945b; von Bertalanffy, 1933), if not even significantly earlier, for example, in the concepts used by late 19th century and early 20th century founders of the study of child development (see Cairns & Cairns, 2006). There are several defining features of developmental systems theories. These include the following.

A Relational Metatheory

Predicated on a postmodern philosophical perspective that transcends Cartesian dualism (which splits the world into discrete categories, such as "mind vs. body," or "nurture vs. nurture"; Overton, 1998, 2006), developmental systems theories are framed by a relational metatheory for human development. There is a rejection of all splits between components of the ecology of human development (e.g., between nature- and nurture-based variables), and between continuity and discontinuity and between stability and instability. Systemic syntheses or integrations replace dichotomizations or other reductionist partitions of the developmental system.

The Integration of Levels of Organization

Relational thinking and the rejection of Cartesian splits is associated with the idea that all levels of organization within the ecology of human development are integrated, or fused. These levels range from the biological and physiological through the cultural and historical.

Developmental Regulation Across Ontogeny Involves Mutually Influential Individual $\Longleftrightarrow$ Context Relations

As a consequence of the integration of levels, the regulation of development occurs through mutually influential connections among all levels of the developmental system, ranging from genes and cell physiology through individual mental and behavioral functioning to society, culture, the designed and natural ecology and, ultimately, history. These mutually influential relations may be represented generically as Level 1 $\Longleftrightarrow$ Level 2 (e.g., Family $\Longleftrightarrow$ Community) and, in the case of ontogeny may be represented as individual $\Longleftrightarrow$ context.

Integrated Actions, Individual $\Longleftrightarrow$ Context Relations, are the Basic Unit of Analysis Within Human Development

The character of developmental regulation means that the integration of actions — of the individual on the context and of the multiple levels of the context on the individual (individual $\Longleftrightarrow$ context) — constitutes the fundamental unit of analysis in the study of the basic process of human development.

Temporality and Plasticity in Human Development

As a consequence of the fusion of the historical level of analysis — and therefore temporality — within the levels of organization comprising the ecology of human development, the developmental system is characterized by the potential for systematic change, by plasticity. Observed trajectories of intraindividual change may vary across time and place as a consequence of such plasticity.

Relative Plasticity

Developmental regulation may both facilitate and constrain opportunities for change. Thus, change in individual $\Longleftrightarrow$ context relations is not limitless, and the magnitude of plasticity (the probability of change in a developmental trajectory occurring in relation to variation in contextual conditions) may vary across the life span and history. Nevertheless, the potential for plasticity at both individual and contextual levels constitutes a fundamental strength of all human's development.

Intraindividual Change, Interindividual Differences in Intraindividual Change, and the Fundamental Substantive Significance of Diversity

The combinations of variables across the integrated levels of organization within the developmental system that provide the basis of the developmental process will vary at least in part across individuals and groups. This diversity is systematic and lawfully produced by idiographic, group differential, and generic (nomothetic) phenomena. The range of interindividual differences in intraindividual change for a given functional or structural characteristic of human development that is observed at any point in time describes the potential plasticity (i.e., in this case the range of systematic between-person variation) for that characteristic. Focus on such variance gives the study of diversity fundamental substantive significance for the description, explanation, and optimization of human development.

Optimism, the Application of Developmental Science, and the Promotion of Positive Human Development

The potential for and instantiations of plasticity legitimate an optimistic and proactive search for characteristics of individuals and of their ecologies that, together, can be arrayed to promote positive human development across life. Through the application of developmental science in planned attempts (i.e., interventions) to enhance (e.g., through social policies or community-based programs) the character of humans' developmental trajectories, the promotion of positive human development may be achieved by aligning the strengths (operationized as the potentials for positive change) of individuals and contexts.

Multidisciplinarity and the Need for Change-Sensitive Methodologies

The integrated levels of organization comprising the developmental system require collaborative analyses by scholars from multiple disciplines. Multidisciplinary knowledge and, ideally, interdisciplinary knowledge is sought. The temporal embeddedness and resulting plasticity of the developmental system requires that research designs, methods of observation and measurement, and procedures for data analysis be change-sensitive and able to integrate trajectories of change at multiple levels of analysis.

Key Empirical Questions

What, then, becomes the key empirical question for developmental scientists interested in describing, explaining, and promoting positive human development by focusing on person $\Longleftrightarrow$ context relations, as the basic unit of analysis within developmental systems theories? The key question is actually five interrelated "what" questions:

1. What attributes?; of

2. What individuals?; in relation to

3. What contextual/ecological conditions?; at

4. What points in ontogenetic, family or generational, and cohort or historical, time?; may be integrated to promote

5. What instances of positive human development?

Therefore, to advance theory and method in an integrated manner, developmental scientists must be able to measure, model, and analyze changes in individuals and settings, with variables from each level of organization within the developmental system of concern in a given study potentially serving as both a product and a producer of changes in variables at the other levels of interest in the study. Most certainly, this is a complex and arduous scientific task. As illustrated throughout the present volume, developmental scientists must focus principally on both intraindividual *and* intracontextual change (e.g., Ram & Nesselroade, chap. 14, this volume) — in their measures, models, and analytic methods and, in fact, their dependent variables as well as their independent or predictor variables must be able to reflect change in both the individual and/or the ecology (e.g., Embretson, chap. 4, this volume).

Indeed, such sensitivity to change, and to the dynamics of the developmental system, necessitates a more plastic understanding of the status of variables that may play moderator or mediator roles at given points in ontogeny, for specific groups of people, studied in regard to specific variables within specific settings (e.g., Flora, et al., chap. 10, this volume; Little, Card, Bovaird, & Crandall, chap. 9, this volume). As well, developmental scientists must attend, often simultaneously, to the complex and dynamic interactions between individual and contextual levels involved in person $\Longleftrightarrow$ context relational models (e.g., Bauer & Shanahan, chap. 11, this volume; Curran, Edwards, Wirth, Hussong, & Chassin, chap. 5, this volume; Grimm & McArdle, chap. 16, this volume), and thus to devising and testing multilevel models of growth in the person $\Longleftrightarrow$ context system (e.g., Bovaird, chap. 7, this volume), often through the use of innovative procedures for partitioning the changing nature of covariance between individuals and settings (e.g., Hedeker & Mermelstein, chap. 8, this volume; Little, Card, Slegers, & Ledford, chap. 6, this volume; Preacher, Cai, & MacCallum, chap. 3, this volume). All this difficult and innovative change-, context-, and relationally-sensitive work must be accomplished within the context of longitudinal research designs that, while affording the repeated measures of individuals and contexts that enable change to be assessed, are fraught with statistical problems encountered when research participants present at one time of testing are not assessed (for a myriad of reasons) at a subsequent time or times (e.g., Hofer & Hoffman, chap. 2, this volume; Nesselroade & Baltes, 1974; Widaman, chap. 17, this volume).

How may such work be accomplished? This volume offers cutting-edge instances of theoretically predicated methodological scholarship exemplifying the possible answers to this question. It is useful to discuss some of the instances of change-, context-, and relationally sensitive methodological options presented both in the present volume and in other facets of the methodology literature of developmental science. By pointing to how these options enable key issues of development to be brought to the fore, we will be able to point to the not-too-distant horizon of a new, integrated theoretical and methodological frame for the study of human development.

REPRESENTATIVE INSTANCES OF CHANGE-, CONTEXT-, AND RELATIONALLY-SENSITIVE METHODOLOGIES: FRAMING THE RESEARCH AGENDA OF HUMAN DEVELOPMENT

Answering the abovenoted five-part question requires a nonreductionist approach to methodology. Neither biogenic, psychogenic, nor sociogenic approaches are adequate. Developmental science needs integrative and relational models, measures, and designs (Lerner, Dowling, & Chaudhuri, 2005).

Examples of the use of such methodology within developmental systems oriented research are the scholarship of Eccles and her colleagues on stage ⇐⇒ environment fit (e.g., Eccles, 2004; Eccles, Wigfield, & Byrnes, 2003); of Damon and his colleagues on the community-based youth charter (Damon, 1997, 2004; Damon & Gregory, 2003); of Theokas (2005; Theokas & Lerner, 2006) on the role of actual developmental assets associated with families, school, and neighborhoods on positive youth development; and of Leventhal and Brooks-Gunn (2004), and of Sampson, Raudenbush, and Earls (1997) on the role of neighborhood characteristics on adolescent development. In addition, the work of Bolger and Shrout (chap. 12, this volume), on the use of multilevel models and structural equation models (SEMs), in accounting for statistical dependency in longitudinal data about dyads, and of Boker and Laurenceau (chap. 13), on methods useful in the analysis of dynamic interdependencies between couples (i.e., treating dyadic data through either a focus on a single individual at a time or a focus on dyads as a single, mutually regulating system) extend the methodological innovations of other laboratories to the study of ongoing person ⇐⇒ person relationships in ontogeny.

The methodology employed in individual ⇐⇒ context integrative research must also include a triangulation among multiple reports and, ideally, both qualitative and quantitative approaches to understanding and synthesizing variables from the levels of organization within the developmental system. Such triangulation may usefully involve the "classic" approach offered by Campbell and Fiske (1959) regarding convergent and discriminant validation through multitrait-multimethod matrix methodology. Simply, triangulation across different observational systems is needed to establish convergent and divergent validation.

Of course, diversity-sensitive measures are needed within such approaches. That is, indices need to be designed to measure change and, at the same time, to possess equivalence across temporal levels of system (age, generation, history), across differential groups (sex, race, religion), and across different contexts (family, community, urban-rural, culture). Moreover, to reflect the basic, integrative nature of the developmental system, researchers should seek to use scores derived from relational measures (e.g., person-environment fit) as their core units of analysis. Accordingly, trait measures developed with the goal of excluding variance associated with time and context are clearly not optimal choices in such research. In other words, in order to reflect the richness and strengths of our diverse humanity, our repertoire of measures must be sensitive to the diversity of person variables, such as race, ethnicity, religion, sexual preferences, physical ability status, and developmental status, *and* to the diversity of contextual variables such as family type, neighborhood, community, culture, physical ecology, and historical moment. Bauer and Shanahan's work (chap. 11, this volume) on distinctions between modeling complex interactions within person-centered versus variable-centered approaches to data analysis constitutes an important analytic approach to capitalizing on data about the person-related variation in human development.

Diversity- and change-sensitive measures must of course be used within the context of change-sensitive designs. Options here include longitudinal or panel designs (Cairns & Cairns, 2006; Lerner et al., 2005; Magnusson & Stattin, 2006) and the various sequential designs proposed by Schaie (1965; Schaie & Strother, 1968). Ram and Nesselroade (chap. 14, this volume) note that it is critical that both intraindividual and intracontextual change be modeled appropriately within such designs.

It is particularly important that our change-sensitive designs and measures be sensitive as well to the different meanings of time. Divisions of the x-axis in both our designs — and in the analyses of our data — should be predicated on theoretical understanding or estimation of the nature of the changes prototypic of a given developmental process.

For example, are the changes continuous or abrupt? For instance, are their periods of "punctuated equilibria" (e.g., Gould & Eldridge, 1977) that are preceded or followed by rapid change in the slope of growth? Are changes linear or curvilinear? Since understanding of the developmental process is of paramount importance in such analyses, developmental scientists should consider inverting the x- and the y-axis, and make age the dependent variable in analyses of developmental process (Wohlwill, 1970). That is, if we believe that a process is linked systematically to age, we should be able to specify points along the x-axis that reflect different points in the process and these points should then be associated with distinct ages.

Widaman (chap. 17, this volume) points as well to the usefulness of Wohlwill's (1970) ideas, in the context of a discussion of the importance of the intrauterine environment in influencing infant and child intellectual development. As Widaman suggests, these ideas are consistent with the classic work of Schneirla (1957), which may be seen as presaging Widaman's developmental systems-oriented discussion of the role of intrauterine development for later-life developmental outcomes.

Wohlwill's (1970) work also provided an early foundation for developmental scientists to more creatively use representations of the form of the developmental process to understand the bases of ontogenetic change. Methodological innovations that are reflective of Wohlwill's pioneering work are found in the contributions of Embretson (chap. 4, this volume), on the impact of measurement scales in modeling developmental processes and ecological factors that are antecedents of dependent variables reflecting trends (changes over time); of Rodgers (chap. 15, this volume), on using developmental curves to "diagnose" (estimate) the types of social processes that generated the curves; and of Curran et al. (chap. 5, this volume), on the use of categorical measurement models in the analysis of individual growth.

Not unrelated here, of course, is the selection of participants in developmental research. Theory should decide what types of individuals are studied at what points in ontogenetic time. For instance, researchers should decide whether it is important theoretically to use age as the selection criterion for participants or whether different status along a developmental process should be used as the basis for the selection of individuals and for the partitioning of participant variance. Often, of course, several groups of participants are selected for study within a developmental design (e.g., groups that are differentiated by birth cohort, gender, race, etc.) and, in such situations, the work of Little, Card, Slegers, and Ledford (chap. 6, this volume), on representing contextual effects in multiple-group mean and covariance structures models for examining the effects of ecological/contextual influences on ontogenetic development, and of Hedeker and Mermelstein (chap. 8, this volume), on the use of mixed-effects regression models with heterogeneous variance in the analysis of ecological momentary assessment data, seem especially important.

Insightful formulations about the different meaning of time within the dynamic developmental system have been provided by Elder (1998; Elder & Shanahan, 2006), Baltes (Baltes, Lindenberger, & Staudinger, 2006), and Bronfenbrenner (2005; Bronfenbrenner & Morris, 2006). Our methods must appraise, then, age, family, and historical time and must be sensitive to the role of both normative and non-normative historical events in influencing developmental trajectories.

Choices of data analytic procedures should also be predicated on optimizing the ability to understand the form and course of changes involving multiple variables from two or more levels of organization. Accordingly, multivariate analyses of change, involving such procedures as structural equation modeling, hierarchical linear modeling, or growth curve analysis, should be undertaken. It is important to note here that, over the course of the last decade or so, there have been enormous advances in quantitative statistical approaches, arguably especially in regard to the longitudinal methods required to appraise the changing relations within the developmental system between the individual and the context (e.g., see Duncan, Magnuson, & Ludwig, 2004; Laub & Sampson, 2004; McArdle & Nesselroade, 2003; Molenaar, 2004; Nesselroade & Ram, 2004; Phelps, Furstenberg, & Colby, 2002; Singer & Willett, 2003; Skrondal & Rabe-Hesketh, 2004; von Eye, 1990; von Eye & Bergman, 2003; von Eye & Gutierrez Pena, 2004; Willett, 2004; Young , Savola, & Phelps, 1991). Additional contributions to this methodological scholarship about the analysis of person $\Longleftrightarrow$ context developmental data have been provided by Bovaird (chap. 7, this volume), Flora, et al. (chap. 10, this volume), Grimm and McArdle (chap. 16, this volume), Little, Card, Bovaird, and Crandall (chap. 9, this volume), and Preacher, et al. (chap. 3, this volume).

The importance of qualitative methods has been increasingly appreciated, both as valuable tools for the analysis of the life course and as a means for triangulating quantitative appraisals of human development. As such, there has been a growth in the use of traditional qualitative methods, along with the invention of new qualitative techniques (e.g., Mishler, 2004).

In addition, to enhance the ecological validity of developmental scholarship and to increase the likelihood that the knowledge gained from research will be used in communities and families to improve the lives of people, our research methods should be informed by colleagues from multiple disciplines with expertise in the scholarly study of human development. Our methods should be informed as well by the individuals and communities we study (Lerner, 2002, 2004a, 2004b, 2004c; Villarruel, Perkins, Borden, & Keith, 2003). They too are experts about development, a point our colleagues in cultural anthropology, sociology, and community youth development research and practice have been making for several years.

Most certainly, participants in our community-based research and applications are experts in regard to the character of development within their families and neighborhoods. Research that fails to capitalize on the wisdom of its participants runs the real danger of lacking authenticity, and of erecting unnecessary obstacles to the translation of the scholarship of knowledge generation into the scholarship of knowledge application (Jensen, Hoagwood, & Trickett, 1999).

In sum, the possibility of adaptive developmental relations between individuals and their contexts and the potential plasticity of human development (Baltes et al., 2006; Gottlieb et al., 2006; Thelen & Smith, 2006) stand as distinctive features of the developmental systems approach to human development and provide a rationale for making a set of methodological choices that differ in design, measures, sampling, and data analytic techniques from selections made by researchers using split or reductionist approaches to developmental science. Moreover, the emphasis on how the individual acts on the context to contribute to the plastic relations with the context that regulate adaptive development (Brandtstädter, 2006) fosters an interest in person-centered (as compared to variable-centered) approaches to the study of human development (Magnusson & Stattin, 2006; Overton, 2006; Rathunde & Csikszentmihalyi, 2006).

Furthermore, given that the array of individual and contextual variables involved in these relations constitute a virtually open set (e.g., there are more than 70 trillion potential human genotypes and each of them may be coupled across life with an even larger number of life course trajectories of social experiences; Hirsch, 2004), the diversity of development becomes a prime, substantive focus for developmental science (Lerner, 2004a; Spencer, 2006). The diverse person, conceptualized from a strength-based perspective (in that the potential plasticity of ontogenetic change constitutes a fundamental strength of all humans; Spencer, 2006), and approached with the expectation that positive changes can be promoted across all instances of this diversity as a consequence of health supportive alignments between people and setting (Benson, Scales, Hamilton, & Semsa, 2006), becomes the necessary subject of developmental science inquiry.

CONCLUSIONS

Contemporary developmental science — predicated on a relational metatheory and focused on the use of developmental systems theories to frame research on dynamic relations between diverse individual and contexts — constitutes an approach to understanding and promoting positive human development that is both complex and exciting. It offers a means to do good science, work informed by philosophically, conceptually, and methodologically useful information from the multiple disciples having knowledge bases pertinent to the integrated, individual ⇐⇒ context relations comprising the ecology of human development. Such science is admittedly more difficult to enact than the ill-framed methodological approaches to research that were involved in pursuing the split and reductionist paths taken often within the field during prior historical eras (Cairns & Cairns, 2006; Overton, 2006).

However, the richness of the science and the applications that derive from developmental systems perspectives (e.g., see the four volumes of the *Handbook of Applied Developmental Science*; Lerner, Jacobs, & Wertlieb, 2003), as well as the internal and ecological validity of this work, are reasons for the continuing and arguably still growing attractiveness of this approach to developmental science. This approach to developmental science underscores the diverse ways in which humans, in dynamic exchanges with their natural and designed ecologies, can create for themselves and others opportunities for health and positive development. As Bronfenbrenner (2005) eloquently puts it, it is these relations that are essential in "making human beings human (p. 1)." Accordingly, the relational, dynamic, and diversity-sensitive scholarship that now defines excellence within developmental science may both document and extend the power inherent in each person to be an active agent in his or her own successful and positive development (Brandtstädter, 2006; Lerner, 1982; Lerner & Busch-Rossnagel, 1981; Lerner, Theokas, & Jelicic, 2005; Magnusson & Stattin, 2006; Rathunde & Csikszentmihalyi, 2006).

A developmental systems perspective leads us to recognize that, if we are to have an adequate and sufficient science of human development, we must integratively study individual and contextual levels of organization in a relational and temporal manner (Bronfenbrenner, 1974; Zigler, 1998). Anything less will not constitute adequate science. And if we are to help develop successful policies and programs through our scholarly efforts, then we must accept nothing less than the integrative temporal and relational model of diverse and active individuals that is embodied in the developmental systems perspective. The present volume is a key, indeed an essential, tool in providing researchers with the methodological means to conduct "best-practice" research using a developmental system perspective.

ACKNOWLEDGMENTS

The preparation of this chapter was supported in part by grants from the National 4-H Council and by the John Templeton Foundation.

REFERENCES

Baltes, P. B., Lindenberger, U., & Staudinger, U. M. (2006). Life span theory in developmental psychology. In R. M. Lerner (Ed.), *Theoretical models of human development: Vol. 1. Handbook of child psychology* (6th ed., pp. 559-664). Editors-in-chief: W. Damon & R. M. Lerner. Hoboken, NJ: Wiley.

Benson, P. L., Scales, P. C., Hamilton, S. F., & Semsa, A., Jr. (2006). Positive youth development: Theory, research, and applications. In R. M. Lerner (Ed.), *Theoretical models of human development: Vol. 1. Handbook of child psychology* (6th ed., pp. 894-941). Editors-in-chief: W. Damon & R. M. Lerner. Hoboken, NJ: Wiley.

Bijou, S. W., & Baer, D. M. (1961). *Child development: A systematic and empirical theory.* New York: Appleton-Century-Crofts.

Bijou, S. W., & Baer, D. M. (1965). *Child development: Universal stage of infancy* (Vol. 2). Englewood Cliffs, NJ: Prentice-Hall.

Brandtstädter, J. (1998). Action perspectives on human development. In W. Damon & R. M. Lerner (Eds.), *Handbook of child psychology: Vol. 1. Theoretical models of human development* (5th ed., pp. 807-863). New York: Wiley.

Brandtstädter, J. (2006). Action perspectives on human development. In R. M. Lerner (Ed.), *Theoretical models of human development: Vol. 1. Handbook of child psychology* (6th ed., pp. 516-568). Editors-in-chief: W. Damon & R. M. Lerner. Hoboken, NJ: Wiley.

Bronfenbrenner, U. (1974). Developmental research, public policy, and the ecology of childhood. *Child Development, 45,* 1-5.

Bronfenbrenner, U. (1977). Toward an experimental ecology of human development. *American Psychologist, 32,* 513-531.

Bronfenbrenner, U. (1979). *The ecology of human development: Experiments by nature and design.* Cambridge, MA: Harvard University Press.

Bronfenbrenner, U. (2001). Human development: Bioecological theory of. In N. J. Smelser & P. B. Baltes (Eds.), *International encyclopedia of the social and behavioral science* (pp. 6963-6970). Oxford, England: Elsevier.

Bronfenbrenner, U. (2005). *Making human beings human: Bioecological perspectives on human development.* Thousand Oaks, CA: Sage.

Bronfenbrenner, U., & Morris, P. A. (2006). The bioecological model of human development. In R. M. Lerner (Ed.), *Theoretical models of human development: Vol. 1. Handbook of child psychology* (6th ed., pp. 793-828). Editors-in-chief: W. Damon & R. M. Lerner. Hoboken, NJ: Wiley.

Cairns, R. B., & Cairns, B. (2006). The making of developmental psychology. In R. M. Lerner (Ed.), *Theoretical models of human development: Vol. 1 Handbook of child psychology* (6th ed., pp. 89-165). Editors-in-chief: W. Damon & R. M. Lerner. Hoboken, NJ: Wiley.

Campbell, D. T., & Fiske, D. W. (1959). Convergent and discriminant validation by the multitrait-multimethod matrix. *Psychological Bulletin, 56*(2), 81-105.

Damon, W. (1997). *The youth charter: How communities can work together to raise standards for all our children.* New York: The Free Press.

Damon, W. (2004). What is positive youth development? *Annals of the American Academy of Political and Social Science, 591,* 13-24.

Damon, W., & Gregory, A. (2003). Bringing in a new era in the field of youth development. In R. M. Lerner, F. Jacobs, & D. Wertlieb (Eds.), *Handbook of applied developmental science: Promoting positive child, adolescent, and family development through research, policies, and programs: Vol. 1. Applying developmental science for youth and families: Historical and theoretical foundations.* (pp. 407-420). Thousand Oaks, CA: Sage.

Dixon, R. A., & Nesselroade, J. R. (1983). Pluralism and correlational analysis in developmental psychology: Historical commonalities. In R. M. Lerner (Ed.), *Developmental psychology: Historical and philosophical perspectives* (pp.113-145). Hillsdale, NJ: Lawrence Erlbaum Associates.

Duncan, G., Magnuson, K., & Ludwig, J. (2004). The endogeneity problem in devel-
    opmental studies. *Research in Human Development, 1(1-2)*, 59-80.
Eccles, J., Wigfield, A., & Byrnes, J. (2003). Cognitive development in adolescence. In
    R. M. Lerner, M. A. Easterbrooks, & J. Mistry (Eds.), *Handbook of psychology:
    Vol. 6. Developmental psychology.* (pp.325-350). Editor in chief: I. B. Weiner.
    New York: Wiley.
Eccles, J. S. (2004). Schools, academic motivation, and stage-environment fit. In
    R. M. Lerner & L. Steinberg (Eds.), *Handbook of adolescent psychology* (pp.
    125-153). New York: Wiley.
Eccles, J. S. (2005). The present and future of research on activity settings as devel-
    opmental contexts. In J. L. Mahoney, R. W. Larson, & J. S.Eccles (Eds.), *Or-
    ganized activities as contexts of development: Extracurricular activities, after-
    school and community programs* (pp. 353-372). Mahwah, NJ: Lawrence Erlbaum
    Associates.
Elder, G. H., Jr. (1974). *Children of the great depression: Social change in life
    experiences.* Chicago: University of Chicago Press.
Elder, G. H., Jr. (1980). Adolescence in historical perspective. In J. Adelson (Ed.),
    Handbooks of adolescent psychology (pp. 3-46). New York: Wiley.
Elder, G. H., Jr. (1998). The life course and human development. In R. M. Lerner
    (Vol Ed.) & W. Damon (Series Ed.) (Eds.), *Handbook of child psychology: Vol.
    1. Theoretical models of human development (5th ed., pp. 939-991).* New York:
    Wiley.
Elder, G. H., Jr, & Shanahan, M. J. (2006). The life course and human development. In
    R. M. Lerner (Ed.), *Theoretical models of human development: Vol. 1. Handbook
    of child psychology* (6th ed., pp. 665-715). Editors-in-chief: W. Damon & R. M.
    Lerner. Hoboken, NJ: Wiley.
Gerwitz, P. J., & Stingle, K. G. (1968). Learning of generalization imitation as the
    basis for identification. *Psychological Review, 75(5)*, 374-397.
Gottlieb, G., Wahlsten, D., & Lickliter, R. (2006). The significance of biology for
    human development: A developmental psychobiological systems view. In R. M.
    Lerner (Ed.), *Theoretical models of human development: Vol 1. Handbook of
    child psychology* (6th ed., pp. 210-257). Editors-in-chief: W. Damon & R. M.
    Lerner. Hoboken, NJ: Wiley.
Gould, S. J., & Eldridge, N. (1977). Punctuated equilibria: The tempo and mode of
    evolution reconsidered. *Paleobiology, 3*, 115-151.
Hirsch, J. (2004). Uniqueness, diversity, similarity, repeatability, and heritability.
    In C. G. Coll, E. Bearer, & R. M. Lerner (Eds.), *Nature and nurture: The
    complex interplay of genetic and environmental influences on human behavior
    and development* (pp. 127-138). Mahwah, NJ: Lawrence Erlbaum Associates.
Jensen, P., Hoagwood, K., & Trickett, E. (1999). Ivory towers or earthen trenches?:
    Community collaborations to foster "real world" research. *Applied Developmen-
    tal Science, 3*(4), 206-212.
Laub, J. H., & Sampson, R. J. (2004). Strategies for bridging the quantitative and
    qualitative divide: Studying crime over the life course. *Research in Human*

Development, 1(1 & 2), 81-99.

Lerner, R. M. (1982). Children and adolescents as producers of their own development. *Developmental Review, 2*(4), 342-370.

Lerner, R. M. (2002). *Concepts and theories of human development* (3rd ed.). Mahwah, NJ: Lawrence Erlbaum Associates.

Lerner, R. M. (2004a). *Liberty: Thriving and civic engagement among american youth.* Thousand Oaks, CA: Sage.

Lerner, R. M. (2004b). Genes and the promotion of positive human development: Hereditarian versus developmental systems perspectives. In C. G. Coll, E. Bearer, & R. M. Lerner (Eds.), *Nature and nurture: The complex interplay of genetic and environmental influences on human behavior and development* (pp. 1-33). Mahwah, NJ: Lawrence Erlbaum Associates.

Lerner, R. M. (2004c). Diversity in individual ⟵⟶ context relations as the basis for positive development across the life span: A developmental systems perspective for theory, research, and application. *Research in Human Development, 1*(4), 327-346.

Lerner, R. M. (2006). Developmental science, developmental systems, and contemporary theories of human development. In R. M. Lerner (Ed.), *Theoretical models of human development: Vol. 1. Handbook of child psychology* (6th ed., pp. 1-17). Editors-in-chief: W. Damon & R. M. Lerner. Hoboken, NJ: Wiley.

Lerner, R. M., & Busch-Rossnagel, N. A. (1981). *Individuals as producers of their development: A life-span perspective.* New York: Academic Press.

Lerner, R. M., Dowling, & Chaudhuri, E. J. (2005). Methods of contextual assessment and assessing contextual methods: A developmental contextual perspective. In D. Teti (Ed.), *Handbook of research methods in developmental science* (pp. 183-209). Cambridge, MA: Blackwell.

Lerner, R. M., Jacobs, F., & Wertlieb, D. (2003). *Handbook of applied developmental science: Promoting positive child, adolescent, and family development through research, policies, and programs.* Thousand Oaks, CA: Sage.

Lerner, R. M., Lerner, J. V., Almerigi, J., Theokas, C., Phelps, E., Gestsdottir, S., et al. (2005). Positive youth development, participation in community youth development programs, and community contributions of fifth grade adolescents: Findings from the first wave of the 4-h study of positive youth development. *Journal of Early Adolescence, 25*(1), 17-71.

Lerner, R. M., Skinner, E. A., & Sorell, G. T. (1980). Methodological implications of contextual/dialectic theories of development. *Human Development, 23,* 225-235.

Lerner, R. M., Theokas, C., & Jelicic, H. (2005). Youth as active agents in their own positive development: A developmental systems perspective. In W. Greve, K. Rothermund, & D. Wentura (Eds.), *The adaptive self: Personal continuity and intentional self-development* (pp. 31-47). Göttingen, Germany: Hogrefe & Huber Publishers.

Leventhal, T., & Brooks-Gunn, J. (2004). Diversity in developmental trajectories across adolescence: Neighborhood influences. In R. M. Lerner & L. Steinberg (Eds.), *Handbook of adolescent psychology* (pp. 451-486). New York: Wiley.

Magnusson, D., & Stattin, H. (2006). The person in context: A holistic interactionist approach. In R. M. Lerner (Ed.), *Theoretical models of human development: Vol. 1. Handbook of child psychology* (6th ed., pp. 400-464). Editors-in-chief: W. Damon & R. M. Lerner. Hoboken, NJ: Wiley.

Maier, N. R. F., & Schneirla, T. C. (1935). *Principles of animal behavior.* New York: McGrawHill.

McArdle, J. J., & Nesselroade, J. R. (2003). Growth curve analyses in contemporary psychological research. In J. Schinka & W. Velicer (Eds.), *Comprehensive handbook of psychology, vol two: Research methods in psychology* (pp. 447-480). New York: Pergamon Press.

Mishler, E. G. (2004). Historians of the self: Restorying lives, revising identities. *Research in Human Development, 1*(1&2), 101-121.

Molenaar, P. C. M. (2004). A manifesto on psychology as idiographic science: Bringing the person back into scientific psychology, this time forever. *Measurement, 2,* 201-218.

Nesselroade, J. R., & Baltes, P. B. (1974). Adolescent personality development and historical change: 1970-1972. *Monographs from the Society for Research in Child Development, 9*(154), 1-80.

Nesselroade, J. R., & Ram, N. (2004). Studying intraindividual variability: What we have learned that will help us understand lives in context. *Research in Human Development, 1*(1&2), 9-29.

Novikoff, A. B. (1945a). The concept of integrative levels and biology. *Science, 101,* 209-215.

Novikoff, A. B. (1945b). Continuity and discontinuity in evolution. *Science, 101,* 405-406.

Nunnally, J. (1982). The study of human change: Measurement, research strategies, and methods of analysis. In B. Wolman (Ed.), *Handbook of developmental psychology*(pp. 133-148). Prentice Hall: Englewood Cliffs.

Overton, W. F. (1998). Developmental psychology: Philosophy, concepts, and methodology. In R. M. Lerner (Vol Ed.) & W. Damon (Series Ed.) (Eds.), *Handbook of child psychology: Vol. 1. Theoretical models of human development* (5th ed., pp. 107-187). New York: Wiley.

Overton, W. F. (2003). Metatheoretical features of behavior genetics and development. *Human Development, 46,* 356-361.

Overton, W. F. (2006). Developmental psychology: Philosophy, concepts, methodology. In R. M. Lerner (Ed.), *Theoretical models of human development: Vol. 1 Handbook of child psychology* (6th ed., pp. 18-88). Editors-in-chief: W. Damon & R. M. Lerner. Hoboken, NJ: Wiley.

Phelps, E., Furstenberg, F. F., & Colby, A. (2002). *Looking at lives: American longitudinal studies of the twentieth century.* New York: Russell Sage Foundation.

Rathunde, K., & Csikszentmihalyi, M. (2006). The developing person: An experiential perspective. In R. M. Lerner (Ed.), *Theoretical models of human development: Vol. 1. Handbook of child psychology* (6th ed., pp. 465-515). Editors-in-chief: W. Damon & R. M. Lerner. Hoboken, NJ: Wiley.

Sampson, R., Raudenbush, S. W., & Earls, F. (1997). Neighborhoods and violent crime. a multilevel study of collective efficacy. *Science, 277*, 918-924.

Schaie, K. W. (1965). A general model for the study of developmental problems. *Psychological Bulletin, 64*, 92-107.

Schaie, K. W., & Strother, C. R. (1968). A cross-sequential study of age changes in cognitive behavior. *Psychological Bulletin, 70*, 671-680.

Schneirla, T. C. (1957). The concept of development in comparative psychology. In D. B. Harris (Ed.), *The concept of development* (pp. 78-108). Minneapolis: University of Minnesota.

Singer, D., & Willett, J. B. (2003). *Applied longitudinal data analysis: Modeling change and event occurrence.* New York: Oxford University Press.

Skrondal, A., & Rabe-Hesketh, S. (2004). *Generalized latent variable modeling. multilevel, longitudinal, and structural equation models.* Boca Raton: Chapman & Hall.

Spencer, M. B. (2006). Phenomenology and ecological systems theory: Development of diverse groups. In R. M. Lerner (Ed.), *Theoretical models of human development: Vol. 1 Handbook of child psychology* (6th ed., pp. 829-893). Editors-in-chief: W. Damon & R. M. Lerner. Hoboken, NJ: Wiley.

Teti, D. M. (2005). *Handbook of research methods in developmental science.* Cambridge, MA: Blackwell.

Thelen, E., & Smith, L. B. (2006). Dynamic systems theories. In R. M. Lerner (Ed.), *Theoretical models of human development: Vol. 1 Handbook of child psychology* (6th ed., pp. 258-312). Editors-in-chief: W. Damon & R. M. Lerner. Hoboken, NJ: Wiley.

Theokas, C. (2005, February). *Promoting positive development in adolescence: Measuring and modeling observed ecological assets.* Unpublished Doctoral Dissertation. Medford, MA: Tufts University.

Theokas, C., & Lerner, R. M. (2006). Observed ecological assets in families, schools, and neighborhoods: Conceptualization, measurement and relations with positive and negative developmental outcomes. *Applied Developmental Science, 10*(2), 61-74.

Valisner, J. (2006). Developmental epistemology and implications for methodology. In R. M. Lerner (Ed.), *Theoretical models of human development: Vol. 1 Handbook of child psychology* (6th ed., pp. 166-209). Editors-in-chief: W. Damon & R. M. Lerner. Hoboken, NJ: Wiley.

Villarruel, F. A., Perkins, D. F., Borden, L. M., & Keith, J. G. (2003). *Community youth development: Programs, policies, and practices.* Thousand Oak, CA: Sage.

von Bertalanffy, L. (1933). *Modern theories of development.* London, England: Oxford University Press.

Willett, J. B. (2004). Investigating individual change and development: The multilevel model for change and the method of latent growth modeling. *Research in Human Development, 1*(1&2), 31- 57.

Wohlwill, J. F. (1970). The age variable in psychological research. *Psychological*

Review, 77, 49-64.

Young, C. H., Savola, K. L., & Phelps, E. (1991). *Inventory of longitudinal studies in the social sciences.* Newbury Park, CA: Sage.

Zigler, E. (1998). A place of value for applied and policy studies. *Child Development, 69,* 532-542.

Author Index

Subject Index